Great Lives from History

Inventors & Inventions

Great Lives from History

Inventors & Inventions

Volume 1

ᶜAbbas ibn Firnas - Philip Emeagwali

Editor
Alvin K. Benson
Utah Valley University

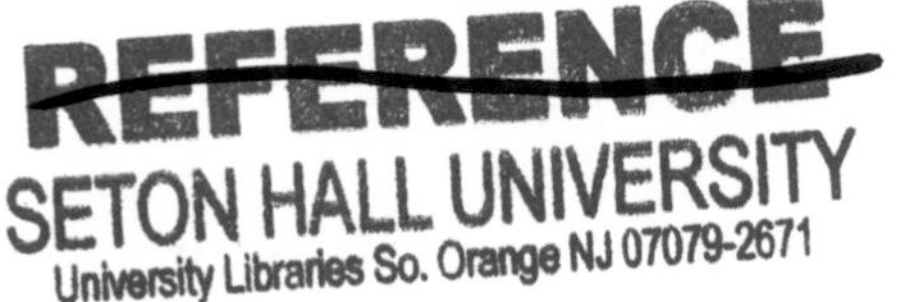

Salem Press
Pasadena, California Hackensack, New Jersey

Editor in Chief: Dawn P. Dawson
Editorial Director: Christina J. Moose
Development Editor: R. Kent Rasmussen
Manuscript Editor: Timothy M. Tiernan
Acquisitions Editor: Mark Rehn
Editorial Assistant: Brett Weisberg
Research Supervisor: Jeffry Jensen
Research Assistant: Keli Trousdale
Photo Editor: Cynthia Breslin Beres
Production Editor: Andrea E. Miller
Graphics and Design: James Hutson
Layout: Mary Overell

Cover photos (pictured clockwise, from top left): Madam C. J. Walker (The Granger Collection, New York); Model T (©Margojh/Dreamstime.com); Thomas Alva Edison (The Granger Collection, New York); Chinese paper (©iStockphoto.com); Leonardo da Vinci (The Granger Collection, New York); Vintage typewriter (©Michael Flippo/Dreamstime.com); Steve Jobs (Getty Images); Cristofori piano (The Granger Collection, New York); Nikola Tesla (The Granger Collection, New York)

∞ The paper used in these volumes conforms to the American National Standard for Permanence of Paper for Printed Library Materials, Z39.48-1992 (R1997).

Library of Congress Cataloging-in-Publication Data

Great lives from history. Inventors and inventions / editor, Alvin K. Benson.
p. cm. — (Great lives from history)
Includes bibliographical references and index.
ISBN 978-1-58765-522-7 (set : alk. paper) — ISBN 978-1-58765-523-4 (vol. 1 : alk. paper) — ISBN 978-1-58765-524-1 (vol. 2 : alk. paper) — ISBN 978-1-58765-525-8 (vol. 3 : alk. paper) — ISBN 978-1-58765-526-5 (vol. 4 : alk. paper)
1. Inventors—Biography. 2. Inventions—History. I. Benson, Alvin K. II. Title: Inventors and inventions.
T39.G75 2009
609.2'2—dc22

2009026443

PRINTED IN THE UNITED STATES OF AMERICA

Contents

Publisher's Note

Great Lives from History: Inventors and Inventions (4 vols.) joins the *Great Lives* series, which provides in-depth critical essays on important men and women in all areas of achievement, from around the world and throughout history. The series was initiated in 2004 with *The Ancient World, Prehistory-476 C.E.* (2 vols.) and followed in 2005 by *The Middle Ages, 477-1453* (2 vols.) and *The Renaissance and Early Modern Era, 1454-1600* (2 vols.); in 2006 by *The 17th Century, 1601-1700* (2 vols.) and *The 18th Century, 1701-1800* (2 vols.); in 2007 by *The 19th Century, 1801-1900* (4 vols.) and *Notorious Lives* (3 vols.); and in 2008 by *The 20th Century* (10 vols.). With this new installment, the entire series extends to 31 volumes, covering 4,885 lives.

Scope of Coverage

Great Lives from History: Inventors and Inventions features 409 essays covering 413 individual inventors (including 27 women) from all time, worldwide. All essays were written specifically for this new publication. The editors have included in this set those inventors recognized for shaping modern technology and the way we live today—coverage that is essential in any liberal arts curriculum. The editor's criteria for including these individuals in this publication took into account their fame as inventors, the significance of their inventions, the amount of time they spent inventing, their representation of world inventors, their relevance to class curricula, and their interest to high school, undergraduate, and general readers.

For purposes of this publication, the term "invention" was defined to include not only mechanical and other physical devices but also processes (e.g., the Bessemer process for making steel), software (such as Grace Hopper's invention of COBOL), and systems such as those applied to business management. Pure scientific theories (such as laws of physics) were excluded, although rare exceptions were made for such systems and tools that have had a comprehensive influence on our way of interacting with the world, such as Aristotle's invention of the first system of biological taxonomy, Newton's creation of the calculus, and Einstein's theories of relativity.

By category, the contents include persons whose inventions fall into one or more of the following areas: acoustical engineering (2), aeronautics and aerospace technology (32), agriculture (13), architecture (6), astronomy (15), automotive technology (16), biology (14), business management (12), cartography (1), chemistry (59), civil engineering (12), communications (31), computer science (36), electronics and electrical engineering (88), entertainment (3), fire science (1), food processing (6), genetics (6), geography (2), geology (2), horticulture (1), household products (21), industrial technology (3), manufacturing (40), maritime technology (3), mathematics (25), mechanical engineering (42), medicine and medical technology (34), military technology and weaponry (33), music (9), naval engineering (9), navigation (7), oceanography (1), optics (14), packaging (3), photography (9), physics (104), plumbing (1), printing (7), and railway engineering (8).

The inventors covered in these volumes are also identified with one or more of the following countries or regions: Australia (2), Austria (1), Belgium (4), Canada (11), China (3), Croatia (2), Czech Republic (1), Egypt (3), England (46), Estonia (1), France (20), Germany (39), Greece (2), Hungary (3), India (2), Iran (1), Ireland (3), Israel (1), Italy (9), Japan (4), Netherlands (9), Nigeria (1), Northern Ireland (2), Poland (2), Russia (8), Scotland (15), Sicily (1), Spain (1), Suriname (1), Sweden (5), Switzerland (5), Turkey (1), United Kingdom (63), United States (246), Uzbekistan (1), and Wales (1).

Essay Length and Format

Each essay is from 2,000 to 2,500 words in length (roughly 3 to 4 pages) and displays standard ready-reference top matter offering easy access to following biographical information:

- The essay title is the name of the individual as best known.
- The individual's nationality and occupation follow on the second line (e.g., Japanese physicist).
- A summary paragraph highlighting the individual's historical importance in relation to his or her inventions indicates why the person is studied today.
- The *Born* and *Died* lines list the most complete dates of birth and death available, followed by the most precise locations available, as well as an indication of when these are unknown, only probable, or only approximate; both contemporary and modern place-names (where different) are listed. A question mark (?) is appended to a

date or place if the information is considered likely to be the precise date or place but remains in question. A "c." denotes circa and indicates that historians have only enough information to place the date of birth or death near the year listed. When a range of dates is provided for birth or death, historians are relatively certain that the birth or death year could not have occurred outside the date range.

- *Also known as* lists other versions of the individual's name, including full names, given names, alternative spellings, pseudonyms, and nicknames.
- *Primary fields* lists all categories of invention, from Acoustical Engineering through Railway Engineering.
- *Primary inventions* lists the inventions for which the inventor is best known.

The body of each essay, which also includes a byline for the contributing writer-scholar, is divided into the following three parts:

- *Early Life* provides facts about the individual's upbringing and the environment in which he or she was reared, as well as the pronunciation of his or her name (if unfamiliar to English speakers). Where little is known about the person's early life, historical context is provided.
- *Life's Work*, the heart of the essay, consists of a straightforward, generally chronological, account of the period during which the individual's most significant achievements were accomplished.
- *Impact* is an overview of the individual's place in history, particularly as his or her inventions changed the way we live.

The end matter of each essay includes the following resources:

- *Further Reading*—annotated bibliography, a starting point for further research.
- *See also*—lists cross-references to essays in the set covering other inventors of interest.

SPECIAL FEATURES

Several features distinguish this series as a whole from other biographical reference works. The front matter includes the following aids:

- *Key to Pronunciation:* A key to in-text pronunciation of unfamiliar names appears in all volumes. Pronunciation guidelines for difficult-to-pronounce names are provided in the first paragraph of the essay's "Early Life" section.
- *Complete List of Contents:* This alphabetical list of contents appears in all four volumes.
- *List of Inventions:* This is an index of all the major inventions covered, showing the inventor in parentheses.
- *Sidebars:* A key feature of every essay in this publication is a sidebar on one of the inventor's most important inventions, which appears in a shaded box beside the biography.

The back matter to Volume 4 includes several appendixes and indexes:

- *History of U.S. Patent Law:* an essay discussing patent law in the United States
- *Chronological List of Entries:* inventors covered, arranged by birth year
- *Time Line*
- *Biographical Directory of Inventors:* an annotated listing of inventors that goes beyond the coverage in the essays
- *Electronic Resources*
- *Bibliography*

Finally, volume 4 ends with three useful indexes:

- *Category Index:* entries by area of achievement, from Acoustical Engineering through Railway Engineering
- *Geographical Index:* entries by country or region
- *Subject Index:* a comprehensive index including personages, inventions, concepts, technologies, terms, principles, and other topics of discussion, with full cross-references from alternative spellings and to the category and geographical indexes

CONTRIBUTORS

Salem Press would like to extend its appreciation to all involved in the development and production of this work. The essays have been written and signed by scholars of history, the sciences, and other disciplines related to the essays' topics.

Special thanks go to Alvin K. Benson, Professor of Physics at Utah Valley University, who developed the contents list and coverage notes for contributing writers to ensure the set's relevance to high school and undergraduate curricula. Professor Benson served as a Professor of Physics in the Indiana University system from 1972 to 1978; from 1978 to 1986 he worked in research and development for Conoco, Inc. and DuPont; and from 1986 to 2001 he was a Professor of Geophysics at Brigham Young University, retiring in September, 2001. He has authored or coauthored more than four hundred research articles, three books on geophysics, and a CD-ROM on geophysics, and he is the recipient of the Honorary Bausch and Lomb Award, Outstanding Young Man of America Award, Alcuin Teaching and Research Award, Distinguished Leadership Award, a Citation of Meritorious Achievement in geophysical research, Professor of the Year in the BYU College of Physical and Mathematical Sciences, Best Paper Award in the Physical Sciences from The Utah Academy of Sciences, Arts, and Letters (2005), and the Faculty Excellence Award in the UVSC School of Science and Health (2006).

Without all these expert contributions, a project of this nature would not be possible. A full list of the contributors' names and affiliations appears in the front matter of this volume.

EDITOR'S INTRODUCTION

Great Lives from History: Inventors and Inventions concentrates on inventors who centered much of their lives on the inventive process and whose inventions have raised the human standard of living. Emphasis is placed not only on the inventors' biographies but also on the stories behind their inventions: the forces and circumstances motivating them and the impact that their inventive genius and resulting inventions have had on humankind. Inventors were chosen based on whether their inventions have had an impact on the world in one or more of the following ways:

- by changing the way people work and play, contributing to the improvement of life
- by altering culture and society for the better
- by saving lives and extending longevity
- by helping to eliminate boring, hard work
- by teaching important principles and creativity
- by advancing science and technology
- by standing the test of time, being used by many people over generations.

Inventions range from tangible mechanical or other physical devices to mechanical and chemical processes. Each essay sheds light on the inventive process, the hard work, the numerous dead ends, and the successes that the inventors encountered.

Inventors and Inventions focuses on the lives of inventors who fostered an idea for something that did not exist until they made it happen, as contrasted to discoverers who found something inherent in nature that was always there just waiting to be brought to light, such as Alexander Fleming's discovery of penicillin in 1928. Nylon involved both a discovery and an invention. Using the discovery of the chemical structure of silk fibroin and cellulose, Wallace Hume Carothers invented synthetic nylon. Except for rare and very important instances, pure scientific theories and mathematical formulations are not included, and except for a few cases, innovators—those who moved an invention into a commercial mode—are likewise not included in this work. Most innovators have not been inventors. Some inventors have also been innovators, but most have not. For example, Theodore Harold Maiman not only invented the first operable laser but also established the scientific environment and business structure that led to its numerous applications and commercial success.

Inventors and their inventions provide a window on history that parallels the story of human progress and corresponds to the cultural revolutions that have impacted the world. Although inventions are not distributed evenly over time, they have for the most part developed systematically as dictated by human need or desire for improvement. Early inventions centered around the necessities of life, particularly farming, housing, and clothing. After the Middle Ages, the emphasis shifted to literacy and numerical skills. Johann Gutenberg's invention of the metal movable-type printing press was the foundation for the "learning revolution," as books became cheap and were made available to the general public. During the 1700's, the focus on inventions moved to devices and processes that increased the ease and efficiency with which human tasks could be accomplished. The invention of the steam engine fueled the Industrial Revolution. During the latter part of the nineteenth century, electricity was harnessed for practical usage. Invention of devices that could use electricity in the everyday world sparked the "communication revolution." In the twentieth century, more and more inventions were made using a systematic scientific approach in industrial research laboratories, research universities, and government laboratories. Inventions that include microelectronics, computers, telecommunications, robotics, and synthetic materials unleashed the "digital revolution" that led to the emergence of the World Wide Web, as inventors and their inventions concentrated increasingly on global connectedness. Included in *Great Lives from History: Inventors and Inventions* are the important inventors whose inventions span a diverse range of disciplines and who helped to spearhead and develop the learning, industrial, communication, and digital revolutions that dramatically changed and shaped the world.

Great Lives from History: Inventors and Inventions includes inventors from all time periods of human history, ancient to modern, and from all parts of the world, including many from thinly represented areas of the world. During ancient times, inventive prominence was centered in China, Egypt, and the Euphrates River Valley, then moved to Greece and Rome, then to the Islamic world, then to Europe, and finally to America. The oldest known wheel can be traced to Mesopotamia and is believed to date back more than 5,000 years ago. The invention of the papermaking process is attributed to Cai Lun in China around 105 C.E. Roger Bacon, an English medieval inventor, was one of the first Europeans to formulate the scientific method based on experimentation around 1250. Italian Leonardo da Vinci developed designs for the first flying machines in 1492. The first refracting telescope was assembled by Hans Lippershey in Holland in 1608.

The Industrial Revolution and the modern world emerged in large part as a result of post-Renaissance engineering, such as the invention of the first steam engine by Englishman Thomas Savery, around 1698. The development of steam power eventually revolutionized transportation, trade, and manufacturing, which in turn drove markets for other technologies. In 1793 Eli Whitney's cotton gin transformed the American South both economically and socially, making the United States the world's major supplier of cotton by the middle of the nineteenth century, which served to establish a growing foundation for slavery. A number of European and American inventors were involved with the invention and improvement of the sewing machine between 1790 and 1840. In 1857, Sir Henry Bessemer patented the process for making steel in England. The telephone was patented in 1876 in the United States by Alexander Graham Bell. As it is known today, the electric light was invented simultaneously in 1879 by Thomas Alva Edison in the United States and Joseph Wilson Swan in England.

One of the most impactful inventions of the past century and a half was the automobile. The automobile that was being produced by around 1900 evolved from a series of automotive inventions made by Nicolas-Joseph Cugnot and Étienne Lenoir in France, Nikolaus August Otto, Gottlieb Daimler, and Carl Benz in Germany, and Ransom Eli Olds, Henry Ford, and others in the United States. Like so many inventions before it, the automobile transformed the world not only economically but also socially. Home and work became geographically divided, teenagers took to the road and achieved a sometimes ill-advised independence, and Ford's assembly line transformed labor.

The great economic and social transformations of the twentieth century were grounded in the development of electricity in the nineteenth century. After innovators like Arthur James Arnot and Edison set the stage for the electric grid, night lighting extended productivity and telecommunications boomed. Well before Bell's invention of the telephone, English mathematician Charles Babbage laid the groundwork for the computer age by inventing the "difference machine" in the early nineteenth century, spending his life and fortune to develop this prototype of the digital computer. In 1946, the first fully electronic digital computer was invented by John Presper Eckert and John William Mauchly in the United States. With the invention of the World Wide Web protocol and language by Englishman Timothy Berners-Lee in 1990, the Internet emerged and eventually evolved into the dominant communications medium throughout the world.

In numerous instances, the names of the first inventors of many inventions are hard to find or have unfortunately been lost over time. The inventors of the first wheel, the first plow, the first compass, or the first smelting furnace, as well as the inventors of many other very important early inventions, remain unknown. Some inventions have involved the interaction and contributions of many people during their formulation, development, improvement, perfection, and implementation. Some have involved coinventors. In several such cases, the leading inventor is discussed in detail in this work, while the coinventor is discussed in the entry dealing with the main inventor. In some instances, there has been overlap of ideas and rival claims for the same invention. For example, Lenoir, Benz, Daimler, and Otto all have legitimate claims associated with the invention of the automobile that is powered by an internal combustion engine. Likewise, Ernst Alexanderson, Philo Farnsworth, and Vladimir Zworykin all have claims related to the invention of the television. These stories are captured and the claims sorted out in *Great Lives from History: Inventors and Inventions*.

Many of the inventors in these pages have been Nobel Prize winners. Several, including Alexander Graham Bell, George Washington Carver, Thomas Alva Edison, Nikola Tesla, and Alfred Nobel, have also been inducted into the National Inventors Hall of Fame, a nonprofit organization in the United States dedicated to recognizing, honoring, and encouraging invention and creativity. Special effort has been made to include female inventors, inventors from ethnic minority groups, and inventors who are often overlooked and almost never found in history books. Many of these inventors overcame great odds that were associated with discrimination and poverty to make important contributions through their remarkable creative abilities. Some inventors made useful inventions but otherwise left little trace in history. Thousands of inventors—too many to cover in depth within these four volumes—have made a broad range of useful and sometimes vital contributions to the progress of humankind. An appendix to this work, a "Biographical Directory of Inventors," is therefore included in volume 4. It offers not only a summation of the 413 individuals covered in the essays but 598 others as well.

Great Lives from History: Inventors and Inventions is written to engage high school students and to be wide-ranging, relevant, and interesting enough to appeal to undergraduates and to anyone interested in the history of technology. It is a tribute to human ingenuity and inventiveness that engenders an understanding of the conditions that can lead to useful inventions, as well as providing the necessary guidelines and role models to assist and inspire future inventors. A central theme included in every essay throughout this work is a concentration on the process of invention by means of a sidebar that highlights one of the inventor's most important inventions. This process involves the fermentation of ideas, attempts to implement the ideas, and the ultimate culmination of ideas that led to practical inventions and applications. It is hoped that the personal stories of the world's greatest inventors contained in this work, who have helped transform our homes, health care, work, environment, travel, and communication, will generate insights into the inventive process that will create curiosity and excitement within the reader. The vision, creativity, and persistence of the included inventors, who often faced great challenges in their lives, provides inspiration for anyone who is motivated to succeed in life and encourages future inventors to follow in their footsteps by producing devices and processes that will change and shape the world for the better. Annotated bibliographic entries for each essay in a "Further Reading" section, as well as cross-references to other inventors of interest, will help the interested readers to further their research interests and inventive pursuits.

Thanks are due to the many contributing authors for their diligence, expertise, literary skill, and cooperation in writing the essays for these four volumes. I also wish to express my deep, heartfelt thanks to my lovely, devoted wife, Connie Lynn, and to our loving family, whose encouragement and forbearance have been a constant influence throughout this project.

—Alvin K. Benson
Professor of Physics
Utah Valley University

Contributors

Bland Addison
Worcester Polytechnic Institute

Emily Alward
Henderson, Nevada, District Libraries

Rajkumar Ambrose
Monmouth College (Illinois)

Dale Anderson
Newton, Pennsylvania

Wladina Antoine
Fairleigh Dickinson University

Tel Asiado
Chatswood, New South Wales, Australia

Renzo Baldasso
The Walters Art Museum

Jane L. Ball
Wilberforce University

Raymond D. Benge, Jr.
Tarrant County College, Northeast

Harlan H. Bengtson
Southern Illinois University, Edwardsville

Alvin K. Benson
Utah Valley University

Milton Berman
University of Rochester

Cynthia A. Bily
Adrian College

Howard Bromberg
University of Michigan

Michael A. Buratovich
Spring Arbor University

Michael H. Burchett
Limestone College

Jennifer L. Campbell
Lycoming College

Byron Cannon
University of Utah

Avelina Carrera
Universidad de Valladolid

Michael J. Caulfield
Gannon University

Dennis W. Cheek
Pennsylvania State University Great Valley

Raymond D. Cooper
Eckerd College

Alejandro Coroleu
University of Nottingham

Robert L. Cullers
Kansas State University

Frank Day
Clemson University

Joseph Dewey
University of Pittsburgh, Johnstown

Charles A. Dranguet, Jr.
Southeastern Louisiana University

Thomas Drucker
University of Wisconsin—Whitewater

Val Dusek
University of New Hampshire

Robert P. Ellis
Worcester State College

Linda Eikmeier Endersby
Missouri State Museum

Thomas L. Erskine
Salisbury University

Thomas R. Feller
Nashville, Tennessee

Ronald J. Ferrara
Middle Tennessee State University

K. Thomas Finley
State University of New York, Brockport

Keith M. Finley
Southeastern Louisiana University

Dale L. Flesher
University of Mississippi

George J. Flynn
State University of New York, Plattsburgh

Alan S. Frazier
University of North Dakota

Maia Wellington Gahtan
University of Pennsylvania—Florence Program

Gayle Gaskill
College of St. Catherine

June Lundy Gastón
City University of New York

Sheldon Goldfarb
University of British Columbia

Nancy M. Gordon
Amherst, Massachusetts

Hans G. Graetzer
South Dakota State University

Johnpeter Horst Grill
Mississippi State University

Irwin Halfond
McKendree College

Paul B. Harvey, Jr.
Pennsylvania State University

C. Alton Hassell
Baylor University

Fran Hassencahl
Old Dominion University

Paul A. Heckert
Western Carolina University

Diane Andrews Henningfeld
Adrian College

Mark C. Herman
Edison College

Paul W. Hodge
University of Washington

Bruce E. Hodson
Baylor University

Samuel B. Hoff
Delaware State University

David B. Hollander
Iowa State University

John R. Holmes
Franciscan University of Steubenville

Gregory D. Horn
Southwest Virginia Community College

Tom A. Hull
Marshfield High School

Patrick Norman Hunt
Stanford University

Mary G. Hurd
East Tennessee State University

Raymond Pierre Hylton
Virginia Union University

Doresa A. Jennings
Shorter College

Bruce E. Johansen
University of Nebraska at Omaha

Edward Johnson
University of New Orleans

Karen N. Kähler
Pasadena, California

David Kasserman
Independent Scholar

George B. Kauffman
California State University, Fresno

Leigh Husband Kimmel
Indianapolis, Indiana

Grove Koger
Boise State University

Margaret A. Koger
Boise, Idaho

Narayanan Komerath
Georgia Institute of Technology

David B. Kopel
Independence Institute

Kathryn Kulpa
University of Rhode Island

Sally A. Lasko
University of Colorado

Steven Lehman
John Abbott College

Denyse Lemaire
Rowan University

Josué Njock Libii
Purdue University Fort Wayne

Victor Lindsey
East Central University

Eric v.d. Luft
SUNY, Upstate Medical University

R. C. Lutz
Madison Advisors

Roxanne McDonald
New London, New Hampshire

Thomas D. McGrath
Baylor University

Elizabeth A. Machunis-Masuoka
Midwestern State University

Marjorie C. Malley
Cary, North Carolina

Nancy Farm Mannikko
Centers for Disease Control & Prevention

Víctor M. Martínez
University of Illinois at Urbana-Champaign

Laurence W. Mazzeno
Alvernia College

Julia M. Meyers
Duquesne University

Leslie C. Miller
Mesa State College

Randall L. Milstein
Oregon State University

William V. Moore
College of Charleston

Edward T. Morman
National Federation of the Blind

Terry R. Morris
Shorter College

B. Keith Murphy
Fort Valley State University

Alice Myers
Bard College at Simon's Rock

John E. Myers
Bard College at Simon's Rock

John Nizalowski
Mesa State College

Robert J. Paradowski
Rochester Institute of Technology

Jim Pauff
Tarleton State University

David Peck
Laguna Beach, California

Barbara Bennett Peterson
California State University, San Bernardino

John R. Phillips
Purdue University Calumet

John Pichtel
Ball State University

Victoria Price
Lamar University

Maureen Puffer-Rothenberg
Valdosta State University

Steven J. Ramold
Eastern Michigan University

R. Kent Rasmussen
Thousand Oaks, California

John David Rausch, Jr.
West Texas A&M University

Kevin B. Reid
Henderson Community College

Rosemary M. Canfield Reisman
Charleston Southern University

Betty Richardson
Southern Illinois University, Edwardsville

Charles W. Rogers
Southwestern Oklahoma State University

Marc Rothenberg
National Science Foundation

Elizabeth D. Schafer
Loachapoka, Alabama

R. Baird Shuman
University of Illinois, Urbana-Champaign

Douglas D. Skinner
Texas State University, San Marcos

Billy R. Smith, Jr.
Anne Arundel Community College

Sonia Sorrell
Pepperdine University

Joseph L. Spradley
Wheaton College

Brian Stableford
Reading, United Kingdom

Polly D. Steenhagen
Delaware State University

Robert E. Stoffels
St. Petersburg, Florida

Theresa L. Stowell
Adrian College

Leslie A. Stricker
Park University

Donald D. Sullivan
University of New Mexico

Patricia E. Sweeney
Derby Neck Library

Nicholas C. Thomas
Auburn University at Montgomery

Jonathan Thorndike
Belmont University

Rebecca Tolley-Stokes
East Tennessee State University

Anh Tran
Wichita State University

Marcella Bush Trevino
Barry University

Sara Vidar
Los Angeles, California

Charles L. Vigue
University of New Haven

J. Francis Watson
New Jersey Synod, Evangelical Lutheran Church in America

Jane R. Watson
California State University, Sacramento

Shawncey Webb
Taylor University

Winifred Whelan
St. Bonaventure University

Thomas A. Wikle
Oklahoma State University

Bradley R. A. Wilson
University of Cincinnati

Richard L. Wilson
University of Tennessee, Chattanooga

Sheri P. Woodburn
Cupertino, California

Scott Wright
University of St. Thomas

Kristen L. Zacharias
Albright College

Key to Pronunciation

Many of the names of personages covered in *Great Lives from History: Inventors and Inventions* may be unfamiliar to students and general readers. For these unfamiliar names, guides to pronunciation have been provided upon first mention of the names in the text. These guidelines do not purport to achieve the subtleties of the languages in question but will offer readers a rough equivalent of how English speakers may approximate the proper pronunciation.

Vowel Sounds

Symbol	Spelled (Pronounced)
a	answer (AN-suhr), laugh (laf), sample (SAM-puhl), that (that)
ah	father (FAH-thur), hospital (HAHS-pih-tuhl)
aw	awful (AW-fuhl), caught (kawt)
ay	blaze (blayz), fade (fayd), waiter (WAYT-ur), weigh (way)
eh	bed (behd), head (hehd), said (sehd)
ee	believe (bee-LEEV), cedar (SEE-dur), leader (LEED-ur), liter (LEE-tur)
ew	boot (bewt), lose (lewz)
i	buy (bi), height (hit), lie (li), surprise (sur-PRIZ)
ih	bitter (BIH-tur), pill (pihl)
o	cotton (KO-tuhn), hot (hot)
oh	below (bee-LOH), coat (koht), note (noht), wholesome (HOHL-suhm)
oo	good (good), look (look)
ow	couch (kowch), how (how)
oy	boy (boy), coin (koyn)
uh	about (uh-BOWT), butter (BUH-tuhr), enough (ee-NUHF), other (UH-thur)

Consonant Sounds

Symbol	Spelled (Pronounced)
ch	beach (beech), chimp (chihmp)
g	beg (behg), disguise (dihs-GIZ), get (geht)
j	digit (DIH-juht), edge (ehj), jet (jeht)
k	cat (kat), kitten (KIH-tuhn), hex (hehks)
s	cellar (SEHL-ur), save (sayv), scent (sehnt)
sh	champagne (sham-PAYN), issue (IH-shew), shop (shop)
ur	birth (burth), disturb (dihs-TURB), earth (urth), letter (LEH-tur)
y	useful (YEWS-fuhl), young (yuhng)
z	business (BIHZ-nehs), zest (zehst)
zh	vision (VIH-zhuhn)

Complete List of Contents

Volume I

Volume 2

Volume 3

Volume 4

List of Inventions

Great Lives from History

Inventors & Inventions

ʿAbbas ibn Firnas

Spanish Arabic engineer

A Renaissance figure at the height of the Islamic golden age in Moorish Spain, ibn Firnas is most remembered for his revolutionary design of a glider, the first manually manipulated flying machine, and for executing the first recorded controlled flight.

Born: 810; Izn-Rand Onda, al-Andalus (now Ronda, Andalucia, Spain)
Died: 887; Córdoba, Spain
Also known as: ʿAbbas Qasim ibn Firnas (full name); Armen Firman
Primary fields: Aeronautics and aerospace technology; astronomy; mathematics
Primary invention: Glider

Early Life

That anything is known of ʿAbbas ibn Firnas (AH-bahs IHB-n FUR-nahz) is remarkable. Much in the archival records and libraries of the Islamic empire that evolved in the Iberian Peninsula across nearly seven centuries was systematically destroyed in the fifteenth century as part of the fierce religious wars that marked the closing century of the Muslim presence in Europe. Ibn Firnas was born in 810 in Izn-Rand Onda in al-Andalus, just over a century after nomadic Muslim invaders, specifically the Umayyad (modern-day Sunni Muslims), had begun to occupy what is contemporary Spain and Portugal after a fierce seven-year war. In the decades before ibn Firnas was born, tensions between East and West had largely severed the Muslim empire into two de facto independent cultural centers—one based far to the east around Baghdad, the other around the courts of Córdoba. With its military occupation under control by mid-century, the caliphate of Córdoba, under Abd al-Rahman II (who assumed the throne in 852), began an ambitious agenda that envisioned establishing the court as the leading cultural and scientific center of the civilized world, rivaling Baghdad, by attracting with huge sums of money the best Muslim minds and undertaking an ambitious program of public building and funding scientific and artistic endeavors.

It was to that court that ibn Firnas journeyed in his late thirties, most likely in his capacity as an accomplished musician and noted poet. It is conjecture, of course, but given the wide-ranging projects that ibn Firnas undertook upon arriving at the court and the scope of his scientific endeavors (he was proficient in chemistry, physics, astronomy, mathematics, and geology), his early education in the sciences must have been considerable or he was undoubtedly the most accomplished autodidact before Leonardo da Vinci.

Life's Work

Public records of ibn Firnas's achievements after establishing his presence at the court in Córdoba are far more reliable. In addition to his study of flight, ibn Firnas distinguished himself in the realms of astronomy and geology. In an era when clocks were used not to measure the hour so much as to measure astronomical movements and particularly the Sun's position, ibn Firnas designed a kind of grand water clock that drew on a steady stream of running water to create an accurate system of measuring the Sun's movement by relying on a waterwheel and chain drive.

Given the enormous geological riches of the Iberian Peninsula, specifically its crystal quartz reserves, the potential economic boom was frustrated because the Córdoba court had to rely on exporting the crystals, principally to Egypt, known at the time for its techniques of cutting crystals. Ibn Firnas devised a revolutionary system for cutting crystal that virtually eliminated the inconvenience and the expenses of exporting the rock. In addition, he experimented with ways to convert the abundant sand and stone of the region into crude optical glass.

Distracted by the often elaborate theorizing about the workings of the planets and the movement of the stars, ibn Firnas devised a precursor to the modern planetarium, an elaborate hanging system of interlocked rings that displayed (with the help of a hand-turned crank) planetary motions with remarkably accurate scale (this nearly seven centuries before Nicolaus Copernicus). That device gave theoretical astronomers the opportunity to test early hypotheses about the relationship between orbit and planet size and the effects of stars on heavy planet motion. Later, ibn Firnas devised a similar surrounding experimental environment that re-created with apparently mesmerizing effect the meteorological phenomena of clouds, thunder, and lightning (through cleverly concealed devices) and gave audiences breathtaking images of stars.

It was flight, however, that drew ibn Firnas in his later years. Ibn Firnas witnessed an attempt at flight in 852, when a court daredevil, using a gaudy winglike overcoat that worked less as a flying device than as a parachute, leaped amid a carnival-like atmosphere off a minaret tower in Córdoba. Ibn Firnas studied flight for nearly two decades before attempting his own flight in 875. Unlike that earlier flight, ibn Firnas envisioned controlling the flight and sustaining it beyond a slightly delayed fall. To that end, he designed a rudimentary one-person glider. Records of invited eyewitnesses indicate that ibn Firnas covered himself with a feather-suit and attached to himself a pair of winglike devices, wooden frames that mimicked the bone structure of wings and that were themselves strung with feathers. He launched himself from a considerable height, from the Mount of the Bride, a steep natural promontory outside Córdoba. Fortunately for ibn Firnas, or perhaps through his own calculations, his launch position was favorable to an extended flight: From the promontory, the hill sloped into a rather deep valley, thus providing sufficient updraft to keep the glider in air, which it did for nearly ten minutes. However, after navigating the device and actually returning to the point of his departure—thus accomplishing the first controlled flight—ibn Firnas had difficulty in the landing and essentially crashed, seriously injuring his back (he was in his mid-sixties at the time). Although he continued other scientific endeavors for nearly a decade after his storied flight, he never tried flight again. He died in 887 at the age of seventy-seven.

The Glider

Because experimental notes and laboratory logs that might detail ʿAbbas ibn Firnas's speculative process in designing his flight mechanism have never been recovered, contemporary aeronautic design engineers, interested in explicating how ibn Firnas achieved controlled flight for an extended period of time, begin with ibn Firnas's observation of a botched flight in 852. That flight device lacked any way for the pilot-rider to actually control the arc and trajectory of the flight and made inevitable a difficult and potentially life-threatening landing. Indeed, eyewitness accounts describe it as a breathtaking free fall rather than a flight. Ibn Firnas's glider, on the other hand, permitted him to change altitude and even bank and change the direction of his flight path.

Because eyewitness accounts describe ibn Firnas's device as "winglike," contemporary engineers assume that ibn Firnas studied the gliding flight of birds to design his glider. Given the extended period of his flight—nearly ten minutes—it is conjectured that his wing-style device, most likely strapped to his shoulders, must have been in the range of eight feet across, as wing length is crucial to achieving ascent. Generally, the wider the wing angle, the greater the lift. Ibn Firnas's device did not have a motor, nor did the wings flap. Thus, aeronautical engineers conclude that ibn Firnas essentially created not a flying machine but a glider. Some species of birds can glide for extended periods of time. That power comes not from the wings but from taking advantage of thermals—sharp, upward movements of air heated by the Sun as the day progresses. (Ibn Firnas took his flight late in the day.) Thermals rise off the Earth in layers that in turn save the birds tremendous amounts of energy and permit extended hovering. Birds actually float down on thermals. In this, ibn Firnas chose a high elevation and a valley slope to assist his gliding; such topography creates strong updrafts.

The problem came in ibn Firnas's landing. A glider must end its flight slowly. To land, a bird slows its wing beats and slowly lifts its wings at the shoulders even as gravity begins to pull it downward. It has to twist its tail to increase the surface area of the wing, which in turn generates more lift and slows down the landing like a brake, preventing the bird from dropping too fast. It is basically a controlled stall maneuver. Then the tail is spread open and lowered to execute a clean landing. A bird actually lands on its tail. Ibn Firnas's device had no tail apparatus, and thus his landing was quite difficult and indeed resulted in significant back injuries that prevented ibn Firnas from continuing his flight experiments. Accounts of his attempt, however, circulated throughout Europe centuries after his death, and his legendary experiment figured in later attempts at single-pilot glider flight conducted most prominently by Roger Bacon and Leonardo da Vinci.

Impact

Ibn Firnas is remembered as a Renaissance figure (more than five hundred years before the European Renaissance) for his contributions to several disciplines in the natural sciences. A scientist, ibn Firnas defined the pragmatic solution-driven side of the scientific enterprise, always seeing innovations and the application of insight as a way to address specific problems. Thus, he is a precursor to the industrial and technological revolutions that were at his time still several centuries off.

Although his work in geology and astronomy was groundbreaking (particularly his pioneering work in crystal cutting and artificial crystal manufacturing), he comes to contemporary audiences largely by virtue of his daring visionary certainty that controlled flight was scientifically feasible. As an aviation pioneer, ibn Firnas left a legacy that elevated the status of the individual scientist to that of a heroic figure flying—in this case, literally—in the face of conventional wisdom: Ibn Firnas executed his own designed flight against the popular assumption that flight was left for the gods, an experimental flight executed not as a stunt but rather as a laboratory test of a theory in the face of the threat of bodily harm, even death.

To a much larger degree, however, ibn Firnas has become a foundational figure in the assertion of the primacy and achievement of Islamic culture, how Islamic ingenuity and scientific acumen for seven hundred years in Moorish Spain predated Western advances in some cases by centuries, although the complete record of that achievement was deliberately destroyed. Thus, ibn Firnas, given the range of his work, the audacity of his experimentation, and the breadth of his vision, has been embraced by contemporary Islamic culture with the same enthusiasm and admiration that the Orville and Wilbur Wright or Leonardo da Vinci are held in Western culture. Indeed, he is one of the seminal figures used to demonstrate to contemporary audiences the importance of the caliphate era in Moorish Spain, as ibn Firnas's rise to prominence coincided with what has come to be regarded as continental Europe's greatest sustained era of culture—intellectual, artistic, scientific, and philosophical—after the collapse of Rome.

—Joseph Dewey

Further Reading

Fletcher, Richard. *Moorish Spain*. Berkeley: University of California Press, 2004. Engaging history of ibn Firnas's era, much neglected in standard readings of Western civilization, presents vivid anecdotal histories that draw from original sources. Includes an account of ibn Firnas's flight.

Gerli, E. Michael, ed. *Medieval Iberia*. New York: Routledge, 2003. Extensive encyclopedic survey of the reach and influence of the Moors at the time of ibn Firnas. Covers the scientific, cultural, and scientific context and particularly the place of the eclectic ibn Firnas and the importance of religious thought and religious tolerance as key to the widespread revolution in scientific development.

Grant, R. G. *Flight: One Hundred Years of Aviation*. New York: Dorling Kindersley, 2002. A broad and careful look at the history of flight that places ibn Firnas, a name frequently neglected in such histories, squarely in the development of the theory of controlled flight.

Hallion, Richard P. *Taking Flight: Inventing the Aerial Age, from Antiquity Through the First World War*. New York: Oxford University Press, 2003. Important history, as it includes an extensive look at what is termed "prehistory" attempts at flight, a survey of flight experiments (including ibn Firnas's) before the Renaissance.

Niccoli, Riccardo. *History of Flight: From the Flying Machine of Leonardo da Vinci to the Conquest of the Space*. Pittsburgh, Pa.: White Star Press, 2007. Places medieval experiments in flight in clear and graspable technological terms (and illustrations) and cites the critical importance of such attempts by linking their technology to flight experiments centuries later.

See also: Roger Bacon; George Cayley; Galileo; Louis-Sébastien Lenormand; Leonardo da Vinci; Joseph-Michel and Jacques-Étienne Montgolfier; Faust Vrančić; Wilbur and Orville Wright.

Edward Goodrich Acheson

American chemist

Acheson's research led to the discovery of carborundum, an important abrasive second only to the diamond in hardness. He also produced graphite in a very pure form, which resulted from heating carborundum to a high temperature.

Born: May 9, 1856; Washington, Pennsylvania
Died: July 6, 1931; New York, New York
Primary field: Chemistry
Primary inventions: Carborundum; graphite-making process

Early Life

Born and raised in southwestern Pennsylvania, Edward Goodrich Acheson was educated at home by his parents, William and Sarah Acheson. He briefly attended Bellefonte Academy in Bellefonte, Pennsylvania, but was largely self-taught. He excelled in mathematics and mechanics. In 1872, at the age of sixteen, he filed a patent caveat for a force auger for use in coal mining.

In the following year, his father died, and Acheson was forced to work full-time in order to provide for his mother and sisters. He worked at various railroad jobs

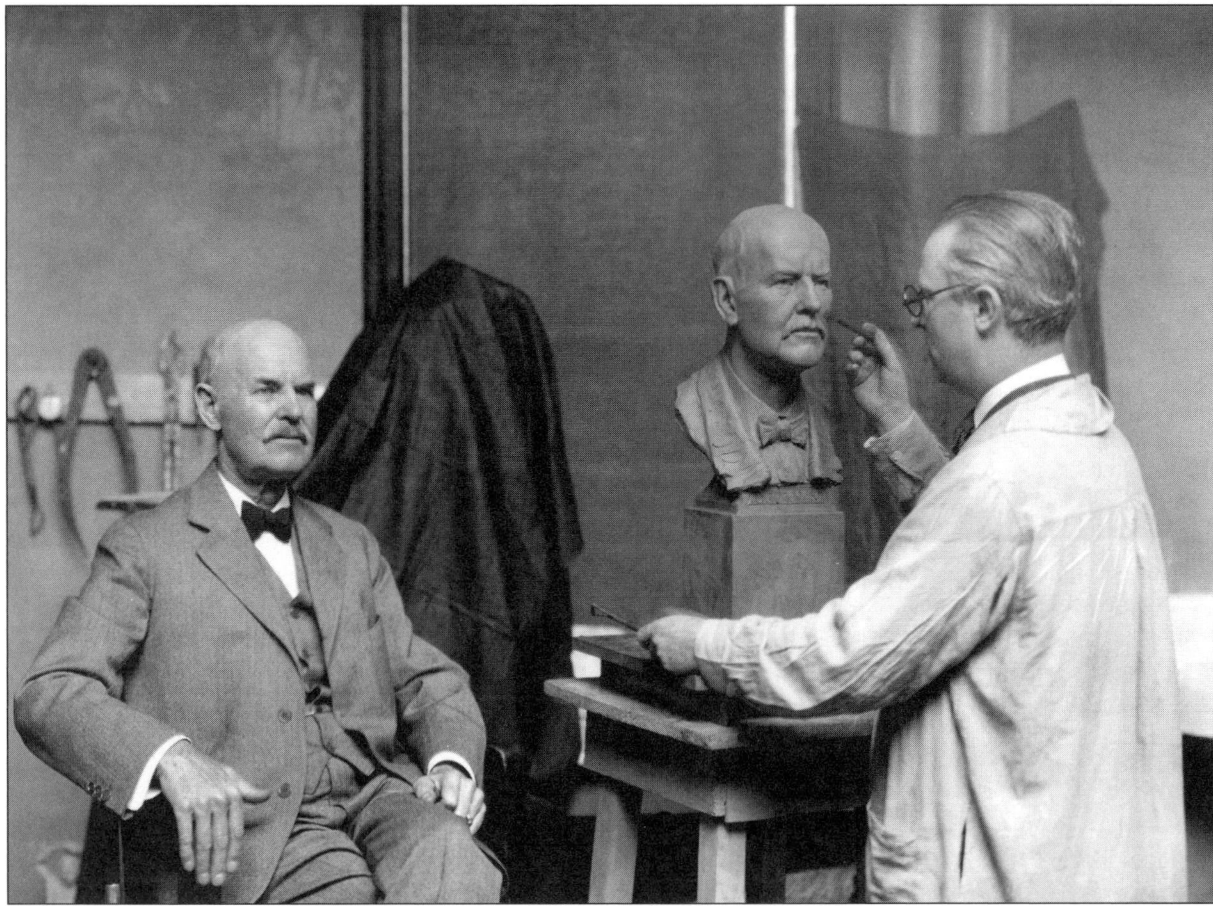

Edward Goodrich Acheson, who discovered carborundum (silicon carbide), an extremely hard synthetic abrasive useful for industrial applications, poses for a bust in this undated photo. (AP/Wide World Photos)

and surveyed tank capacities in the oil fields. Briefly, he even attempted mining iron ore in a partnership with his brother, William. Acheson continued to study and invent in the evenings, focusing mainly on electricity, and hoped to work for an employer manufacturing electrical equipment. He applied to Edward Weston, a manufacturer of electroplating dynamos, but was turned down. Working on his own, Acheson created an electric pile. He took the battery to Thomas Alva Edison, who saw promise in the young inventor and hired him on September 12, 1880, to work in his workshop in Menlo Park, New Jersey.

Life's Work

Working under John Kruesi, Acheson experimented with developing a conducting carbon for Edison's electric light bulb, and he was successful enough to be credited with contributing to Edison's invention. More important, Edison appreciated Acheson's inventiveness. About a year and a half after he started working for Edison, Acheson was sent to Europe as assistant chief engineer. During the next two and a half years, he installed electric generating plants and lamp factories in England, France, Italy, Belgium, and the Netherlands. Among the most notable public buildings in which he established successful electric lighting systems were the Hôtel de Ville in Antwerp, the Musée du Nord in Brussels, the Restaurant Krasnapolsky in Amsterdam, and the La Scala Theater in Milan.

In 1884, Acheson returned to the United States, stopped working for Edison, and became a competitor as the superintendent of a plant manufacturing electric lamps. He married Margaret Maher in the same year and started a family that eventually included four daughters and five sons.

Acheson's dream was to create artificial diamonds.

His experiments after 1884 were directed to that end, but the road to that goal was long and arduous. Along the way, he invented a number of other highly useful materials. He earned the first of his seventy patents in 1886 with his invention of a "conductor of electricity," which he sold to George Westinghouse. Subsequently, the Standard Underground Cable Company purchased the patent and developed it further in its electrical transmission business. Acheson continued his research into high-temperature electric furnaces, a necessary first step in the development of the abrasives for which he would become famous.

In 1891, he obtained the use of a powerful electric generating power plant in Port Huron, New York (at Edison's suggestion), where he worked to impregnate clay with carbon in an attempt to create artificial diamonds. The resulting mass contained some small, shiny specks, which turned out to be silicon carbide, which he called "carborundum"—a name based on his mistaken belief that he had combined carbon with alumina. On February 28, 1893, he patented a method for making silicon carbide. The silicon carbide he created was the hardest synthetic abrasive in the world, rivaling the diamond in hardness.

In 1894, Acheson started the Carborundum Company in Monongahela City, Pennsylvania, to produce a variety of grinding and abrasive tools and materials, including grinding wheels, knife sharpeners, whetstones, and abrasive powders. This plant quickly became too small to keep up with demand, so Acheson established a second, larger plant at Niagara Falls, New York, in 1895, when his factory became the second company to establish a long-term business arrangement with the Niagara Falls Power Company.

By 1896, Acheson had discovered that, if he heated carborundum to about 7,500° Fahrenheit (about 4,150° Celsius), the silicon would vaporize, leaving behind a very pure graphite (carbon). Later that year, he patented this process. Graphite was especially valuable at this time as an abrasive and, counterintuitively, as a lubricant. It was also used in the loop filaments in the incandescent lamps of the era.

In 1899, the Acheson Graphite Company was formed to manufacture the graphite, which was increasingly in demand for various uses. Acheson now was able to produce the graphite from calcine carbon and anthracite coal. This company merged with the National Carbon Company in 1928 and ultimately became Union Carbide.

Acheson also expanded the use of graphite as a lubricant. He suspended it in a variety of liquids such as oil and water, producing the commercial colloidal graphite products Oildag and Aquadag, which were manufactured by the Acheson Colloids Company (later Acheson Industries). Altogether, Acheson successfully established at least five major industrial corporations, including the International Acheson Graphite Company (1908) and the British Acheson Oildag Company (1911), in addition to those mentioned above.

Acheson was not a particularly effective manager. Many of his companies had to be reorganized or removed from his direct control by concerned investors, but this fact should not obscure the significance of his inventions. His accomplishments have been recognized by a number of honorary degrees and awards from a wide

Carborundum and Graphite

Edward Goodrich Acheson developed very high-temperature electric furnaces that he used in novel ways to create some very important industrial products, some of which were created by accident. In the 1880's, he was trying to create artificial diamonds by heating various carbon compounds to a very high temperature. In 1891, he discovered carborundum, mistakenly believing that he had created an alumina compound when in fact he had created silicon carbide. Silicon carbide occurs in nature as the extremely rare mineral moissanite (named for its discoverer, French chemist Henri Moissan). Silicon carbide is an extremely useful abrasive, and it is synthesized from inexpensive raw materials. Considered one of the most important inventions of the industrial age, the material is used in a variety of applications—from sandpapers to cutting tools to semiconductors—and has been used as a diamond simulant.

While heating carborundum to a temperature of 7,500° Fahrenheit (about 4,150° Celsius), Acheson created a nearly pure graphite, and the new process was duly patented. Graphite was an important material used in the carbon filaments in Thomas Alva Edison's incandescent light bulbs. This was Acheson's first claim to fame. Perhaps more important to world history was the fact that Acheson's graphite was also used as a neutron moderator in the nuclear fission experiments of Enrico Fermi, who created the world's first nuclear reactor in a secret laboratory at the University of Chicago in 1942. This was significant because the German nuclear program during World War II lacked access to high-quality graphite and instead used scarce heavy water as a moderator, delaying its development of nuclear fission and preventing the Germans from building an atomic bomb.

variety of chemical, industrial, technical, and manufacturing organizations. In 1997, he was inducted into the National Inventors Hall of Fame.

Impact

In 1926, the U.S. Patent Office rated Acheson's discovery of carborundum (silicon carbide) as one of the twenty-two most important patented inventions responsible for creating the industrial age. Carborundum has played a critical role in the manufacture of precision-ground interchangeable metal components. Without carborundum, mass production of these specialized parts would be impossible. Carborundum has also been used in the production of almost pure graphite.

Graphite has its own role to play as an abrasive and as a lubricant, but it has even played a significant role in the production of nuclear energy. Graphite is a valuable neutron moderator in nuclear reactors. Without a significant supply of graphite, the U.S.-British development of the atomic bomb in World War II might not have been possible, since the only known alternative to graphite was "heavy water" (an isotopic form of water), of which Germany possessed most of the world's supply.

Acheson was an active inventor, establishing five major industrial corporations that used electrothermal techniques. He patented seventy different abrasives, oxide reductions, refractories, and graphite products.

—*Richard L. Wilson*

Further Reading

Acheson, Edward Goodrich. *A Pathfinder: Discovery, Invention, and Industry*. New York: The Press Scrap Book, 1910. This autobiographic account is still available and provides Acheson's view of his wide-ranging development of several inventions.

Agassi, Joseph. *Science and Its History*. Boston: Springer, 2008. Provides a general history of science and technology, with insights into the role of inventions.

Cohen, H. Floris. *The Scientific Revolution: A Historiographical Inquiry*. Chicago: University of Chicago Press, 1994. A history of modern science and technology, including inventions.

Evans, Harold. *They Made America: From the Steam Engine to the Search Engine—Two Centuries of Innovators*. New York: Little, Brown, 2004. Provides a general history of innovations that includes useful material on many products dependent on carborundum and graphite.

Grissom, Fred, and David Pressman. *The Inventor's Notebook*. 5th ed. Berkeley, Calif.: Nolo Press, 2008. Offers a practical discussion of inventing, with some interesting insights into the process.

Langone, John. *How Things Work: Everyday Technology Explained*. Washington, D.C.: National Geographic Society, 2004. Provides clear explanations of how many major inventions work, including products made possible because of the discovery of carborundum and graphite.

Platt, Richard. *Eureka! Great Inventions and How They Happened*. Boston: Kingfisher, 2003. Examines the circumstances in which some of the world's best-known inventions were conceived and the genius of their inventors.

Schwartz, Evan I. *Juice: The Creative Fuel That Drives World-Class Inventors*. Boston: Harvard Business School Press, 2004. A theoretical look at the process of inventing that includes examples relevant to Acheson's work.

Smil, Vaclav. *Creating the Twentieth Century: Technical Innovations of 1867-1914 and Their Lasting Impact*. New York: Oxford University Press, 2005. Examines the period in which key inventions of the modern world were developed. Discusses Acheson.

See also: Walther Bothe; Enrico Fermi; H. Tracy Hall; Elijah McCoy; Nikola Tesla; Alessandro Volta.

George Biddell Airy

British astronomer

Airy's inventive genius was in the fields of optics, engineering, and computational methods. His most practical inventions included the optical method for correcting astigmatism in eyes and a method for compensating a compass on a metal ship.

Born: July 27, 1801; Alnwick, Northumberland, England
Died: January 2, 1892; Greenwich, England
Primary fields: Mechanical engineering; optics; physics
Primary inventions: Astigmatism-correcting lenses; compass compensation

Early Life

George Biddell Airy (EH-ree) was born into a family that could trace its origins back to the fourteenth century. His father, William, was a tax collector in Northumberland and his mother, Ann, was the daughter of a farmer in Suffolk. George was their first of four children. In 1802, William was appointed to Hereford, where his children attended elementary schools. George was a diffident child who was more popular with his teachers than with his peers, and he excelled at mathematics and writing. His father's transfer to Essex in 1810 made it possible for George to enter a more complete school at Sir Isaac's Walk, where he studied geography, orthography, and mathematics. George also read extensively among his father's books and committed to memory a prodigious amount of poetry. It was in reading his father's encyclopedia that he developed a fascination with technical matters, especially engineering, shipbuilding, astronomy, optics, and navigation.

Attending more advanced schools, Airy soon attained proficiency in Greek and Latin, as well as mathematics, chemistry, and physics. His uncle, George Biddell, recognized his potential and persuaded his father to send him to college. Airy was subsequently examined by scholars from Trinity College, Cambridge, and his performance easily paved the way to admission.

He entered Cambridge University in 1819 and graduated in 1823 after an exceptional academic career that included high distinction in his studies and several important early investigations and inventions, including designs for achromatic telescopes and experiments for the design of a mechanical computer. Upon graduation, he was appointed a fellow of Trinity College, a position of considerable responsibility involving teaching and research. While a fellow, he developed new mathematical methods for treating the motions of celestial bodies.

Life's Work

Airy's many publications and the quality of his lectures led to his promotion to the prestigious position of Lucasion Professor of Mathematics at the age of twenty-five. Continuing his rapid rise in academia, he was named Plumian Professor of Astronomy and Natural Philosophy and director of the Cambridge observatory in 1828, only two years later. The work that Airy did in expanding the observatory and its productivity brought him much favorable recognition. His fundamental investigations of planetary orbits, especially the rhythmic relationships of Earth's and Venus's orbits (called planetary inequalities), and his work in optical theory brought such honors as the Copley Medal and the Royal Astronomical Society's Gold Medal. As an inventor and innovator, his

George Biddell Airy. (The Granger Collection, New York)

Astigmatism-Correcting Lenses

Glasses to correct for eyes that focused incorrectly were well known in George Biddell Airy's time. Myopia, the condition in which the eye focuses short of the retina, leading to poor focus for distant objects, could be corrected by wearing concave lenses; hyperopia (far-sightedness), the opposite condition, was corrected by convex lenses. However, astigmatism, the condition in which the shape of the cornea is not symmetrical, causes the focus to be confused and irregular and cannot be corrected with a simple lens.

Airy's eyes were decidedly astigmatic, the left eye being especially so. In the 1820's, while he was exploring various properties of light, it occurred to him that he might be able to invent a way of correcting for astigmatism. In August, 1824, he carried out several experiments on his eyes that allowed him to deduce the shape of the cornea of each eye. With his knowledge of the behavior of light rays, he was then able to design a specially shaped lens (called a cylindrical lens) that would compensate for the nonsymmetrical shape of the cornea. When he ordered these lenses to be made, they were found to be effective, and he wore them from then on. He was said to carry several pairs of glasses in his pockets in case of emergency.

Unlike some of Airy's inventions, the discovery of astigmatism-correcting lenses was not one that he discussed much in his autobiography, which otherwise gives extensive and self-satisfied details about his many accomplishments. There are only two sentences about this discovery. He says, "On August 25th I made experiments on my left eye, with good measures, and on Aug. 26 ordered a cylindrical lens of Peters, a silversmith in the town, which I believe was never made. Subsequently, while at Playford, I ordered cylindrical lenses of an artist named Fuller, living at Ipswich, and these were completed in November, 1824."

Although he gave it little notice in his writings, the invention of astigmatism-correcting lenses was without doubt one of Airy's most important inventions. Basically the same design has been used for eyeglasses for millions of people and for nearly two hundred years.

work at Cambridge involved the design and building of an impressive observatory, one that was far more effective than the small facility he found when he took over as director.

In 1835, Airy began a new life as astronomer royal and director of the Royal Greenwich Observatory. Reluctantly giving up his Cambridge professorship, Airy moved his family to London and took up residence in the observatory. During Airy's remarkably long tenure at Greenwich, he accomplished a great deal, much of it related to astronomy, but also much concerned with the observatory's mandate of improving the means of accurate celestial navigation at sea. As was his habit, Airy approached all tasks with his penchant for precision and orderliness, as well as for mathematical representation of practical problems whenever it was possible. He was basically a theoretician, but he became an inventor or designer whenever it became necessary to achieve a particular goal.

An indication of Airy's range of interests and his inventive nature occurred in 1838, when he was asked to help solve the problem of the failure of magnetic compasses installed on iron ships, which were coming into use to replace wooden vessels. He investigated the problem theoretically and then experimented with a design of compensating magnets placed on the ship in appropriate places. The method was tested on the iron ship *Rainbow*, with Airy working on board the ship as it maneuvered in the Thames River near Deptford. The result was a perfect correction, allowing a subsequent voyage across the English Channel to Antwerp, with the compass performing excellently.

One of the major projects at Greenwich after Airy became the director was the design of a new kind of celestial position-measuring telescope, called the altazimuth telescope, which he designed in 1844. This new instrument permitted measurement of the position of the Moon precisely at any sky position. The determination of the Moon's position was needed for navigation, which was of great commercial and military importance to Great Britain. In the following year, he invented another type of telescope, called the reflex zenith tube, with which precise star positions could be determined at nearly any position in the sky.

Among the various nonastronomical projects that occupied Airy's inventive mind was a measurement of Earth's mean density, achieved in 1845 by measuring the pull of gravity at the surface and at the bottom of a mine using pendulums. Although the first experiments failed because of various disasters (including fires and floods), success was eventually achieved.

The year 1845 was also notable for what Airy did not do. The young Cambridge mathematician John Couch Adams had calculated a position for a hypothetical new planet beyond Uranus, having analyzed perturbations on the orbit of Uranus. Although various historians differ on the details of what happened next, it is probable that

Airy's curt dismissal of Adams's work when it was brought to him resulted in discouragement and inactivity. In the meantime, the French astronomer Urbain Le Verrier made similar calculations, transmitted them to Johann Galle in Germany, who immediately pointed his telescope in the indicated direction and discovered the new planet, eventually named Neptune. Airy's role in losing the distinction for Adams and for England resulted in something of a scandal. His autobiography states, "I was abused most savagely both by English and French."

Neptune was not the only mistake that Airy has become known for. In the early 1870's, he was asked by Thomas Bouch to evaluate the pressures that would be encountered by the Tay Bridge, a 2.25-mile-long railroad bridge that spanned the Firth of Tay near Dundee in Scotland. Airy used his new mathematical treatment of physical mechanics and concluded that the design should be able to withstand ten pounds per square inch. Bouch used that as a guide in the design, and the bridge was completed on September 26, 1877. During a violent winter storm on December 28, 1879, the bridge collapsed, taking a train and over seventy lives with it. Airy's contribution was only a small part of the reasons for the disaster, but his involvement nevertheless tended to tarnish his reputation, in spite of the many very positive achievements of his long life.

Impact

Few scientists have wielded as much power and influence for such a long period of time as Airy, who was astronomer royal of England for forty-six years. During his tenure, the Royal Greenwich Observatory became a major center for astronomical activity, especially with regard to stellar and planetary positions and issues of time. The world's prime meridian, from where all longitudes are reckoned, was established under Airy's directorship of the Royal Greenwich Observatory, and its exact position was established by the location of the Airy Transit Circle. The world's time, known as Greenwich mean time, was similarly established by that instrument, designed by Airy.

Airy was a brilliant mathematician, but he also had interests in other scientific fields, especially those in which his mathematical talents could be useful. His was an inventive mind, and he often turned his attention to practical matters, inventing new instruments and techniques and even doing such things as embarking on ships to test his ideas and his inventions. His colleagues would probably have said that his greatest impact was his insistence on the orderly and scientifically based approach to the solution of problems. He kept careful and complete notes about everything he did (which is why he could write an exhaustive autobiography), and his inventions and new designs were thoroughly documented through the stepwise approach he took to solving the problems that they were intended to solve.

—*Paul W. Hodge*

Further Reading

Airy, G. B. *Mathematical Tracts on Physical Astronomy*. Cambridge, England: J. Smith, 1826. Airy's first major book, which remained a standard text on the subject for many decades. It has been reprinted several times, and students can still gain some useful insight by reference to it.

Airy, George Biddell. *Autobiography of Sir George Biddell Airy*. Charleston, S.C.: Biblio Bazaar, 2006. This autobiography covers Airy's life from birth to 1871, with additions to the time of his death added by his son, Wilfrid Airy, who also wrote an excellent summary of the document. The text is a mix of descriptions of official documents and activities and a diary of more personal events in the author's life.

Gould, B. A. "George Biddell Airy." *Astronomical Journal* 11, no. 252 (1892): 96. A short announcement of Airy's death and a well-spoken account of his achievements written by the editor of the journal.

Jones, Harold Spencer. *The Royal Observatory, Greenwich*. London: Longmans, 1946. This brief account of the observatory was written by the tenth astronomer royal during his directorship.

National Maritime Museum. *A Guide to the Royal Observatory, Greenwich*. London: Author, 2000. This booklet offers an up-to-date description of the observatory, its activities, and its history, including the long directorship of Sir George Airy. A well-written work that includes excellent illustrations of the observatory and its instruments.

"Sir George Biddell Airy." In *Encyclopaedia Britannica*. Cambridge, England: Cambridge University Press, 1911. The famous 1911 edition of the *Britannica* includes a definitive article covering Airy's life and accomplishments.

See also: Hermann von Helmholtz; Elmer Ambrose Sperry; Rangaswamy Srinivasan.

GEORGE EDWARD ALCORN

American physicist

Alcorn designed innovative semiconductors and X-ray detection devices that were incorporated in numerous scientific, technological, and industrial applications. He also advanced aerospace, physics, and engineering technology through his roles as educator and administrator.

Born: March 22, 1940; possibly California
Also known as: George Edward Alcorn, Jr. (full name)
Primary fields: Aeronautics and aerospace technology; electronics and electrical engineering; physics
Primary inventions: Advanced semiconductors; imaging X-ray spectrometer

EARLY LIFE

George Edward Alcorn, Jr., was born on March 22, 1940, to George and Arletta Dixon Alcorn, both Kentucky natives. His parents aspired for him and his younger brother, Charles, to be well educated. Their father's technical abilities as an automobile mechanic may have inspired their interest in technology and science and their inventive curiosity. Both sons became physicists.

Alcorn's high school academic and sports achievements resulted in several honors, including the California Savings and Loan Outstanding Student Award and being selected a West Coast Fund fellow. Alcorn received a full college scholarship, funding four years of studies, and majored in physics when he enrolled at Occidental College, in Eagle Rock, California, in 1958. That college's student directory identified Alcorn's hometown as Los Angeles. In addition to excelling scholastically, Alcorn played football and baseball in college, lettering eight times in those sports.

In spring, 1962, Alcorn received a bachelor of science degree from Occidental, graduating with honors. Selected for a summer fellowship that year and the next, he conducted a computerized assessment of trajectory data associated with missile launches and their orbiting performance for North American Rockwell's Space Division. His work involved Saturn IV, Nova, and Titan 1 and 2 missiles. During the 1960's, Alcorn was among the few African American scientists and engineers affiliated with the National Aeronautics and Space Administration (NASA). Receiving a graduate fellowship, Alcorn continued studies at Howard University in Washington, D.C., specializing in nuclear physics to earn a master of science degree in 1963.

Alcorn pursued doctoral work at Howard in the fields of molecular and atomic physics, researching how negative ions form. He received a grant from NASA to fund his investigations and wrote his dissertation, "An Electron Impact Study of the Methylamine, Monoethylamine, Dimethylamine, and Trimethylamine." Alcorn graduated with a Ph.D. in 1967. During his studies, he qualified for Sigma Pi Sigma, the national physics honor society, and Sigma Xi, a science honor society. Alcorn married Marie Leatrice Davillier in Fallon, Nevada, on December 29, 1969, and their son was born in 1979.

LIFE'S WORK

For several years after receiving his doctorate, Alcorn held physics and engineering positions involving research, invention, and development in private industry, including Philco-Ford, Perkin-Elmer, and International Business Machines (IBM). He also joined the Electrochemical Society and the Institute of Electrical and Electronics Engineers (IEEE). In 1973, Howard University appointed Alcorn as IBM Visiting Professor for electrical engineering. He continued that professional affiliation throughout his career, eventually being promoted to adjunct full professor.

As an IBM inventor, Alcorn focused on semiconductor technology and secured U.S. and European patents that were assigned to IBM. In September, 1975, Alcorn and colleague James Downer Feeley filed for a U.S. patent for a plasma-etching method involving quartz surfaces: "Process for Controlling the Wall Inclination of a Plasma Etched Via Hole" (number 3,986,912; issued 1976). In December, 1977, Alcorn's "Process for Forming a Ledge-Free Aluminum-Copper-Silicon Conductor Structure," developed with Feeley and Julian Turner Lyman to eliminate electrical shorts present in other semiconductors, was approved as U.S. Patent number 4,062,720. Alcorn published abstracts describing his inventions in the *IBM Technical Disclosure Bulletin*.

In 1978, Alcorn resigned from IBM and accepted a position at NASA's Goddard Space Flight Center (GSFC), in Greenbelt, Maryland. Before he left IBM, he contributed to several U.S. patents, including a "Method for Forming Dense Dry Etched Multi-level Metallurgy with Non-overlapped Vias" (number 4,172,004; issued 1979) for etching circuit boards, and the "Hardened Photoresist

Master Image Mask Process" (number 4,201,800; issued 1980) for semiconductors.

At GSFC, Alcorn developed technology for space missions and to evaluate Earth's atmosphere. Some of his work, specifically defense-related projects, was classified. Alcorn designed his most notable invention, the imaging X-ray spectrometer, during his early years with NASA. He discussed this research at the 1982 International Electron Devices Meeting and published a report in that conference's proceedings. The 1984 patent for this spectrometer, which was created to image and analyze electromagnetic radiation X-ray sources more accurately than existing detectors, was assigned to NASA for use in such aerospace technology as telescopes. By June, 1985, Alcorn had filed a patent for a method of fabricating an improved spectrometer.

Alcorn encouraged minorities and women interested in engineering and science to achieve their goals in those fields. He assisted Dr. Freeman Hrabowski III, president of the University of Maryland, Baltimore County, in developing Meyerhoff Foundation programs, started in 1988, which helped African Americans earn doctoral degrees in mathematics, science, and engineering. Alcorn advised Meyerhoff scholarship recipients. He also created the Saturday Academy to provide inner-city children science and mathematics classes that were unavailable to them in their schools. Alcorn recruited minority engineers and scientists to work for NASA, which in 1984 presented him a medal recognizing his efforts to secure minority personnel and help minority-owned companies to develop effective research projects compatible with their technological needs and aspirations.

By 1990, Alcorn was GSFC's advanced programs manager, overseeing technology projects at that center. As deputy project manager of Space Station Advanced Development, his responsibilities included directing work to provide both immediate and long-term technology needs for the Space Station Freedom (now the International Space Station). In 1992, Alcorn became director of GSFC's Office of Commercial Programs. He promoted technology transfer, especially appropriation of aerospace devices and procedures created at GSFC laboratories by employees and contractors

The Imaging X-Ray Spectrometer

George Edward Alcorn applied his physics skills to develop instrumentation to analyze electromagnetic radiation X-ray sources for aerospace applications. With three colleagues, Alcorn initiated invention of an imaging X-ray spectrometer to aid researchers in acquiring data on the composition of distant planets and stars. His device functioned more consistently and accurately than existing imaging X-ray equipment, particularly electromagnetic radiation detectors. U.S. Patent number 4,472,728, "Imaging X-ray Spectrometer" (1984), cites information and prior patents that influenced his invention, including optical and electronics technical articles, a 1970 semiconductor radiation measurement device, a 1975 radiation image converter, a 1979 photosensitive matrix, and a 1980 semiconductor radiation detector.

Alcorn stated that the purpose of his spectrometer was for imaging X-ray sources, and he stressed that the device could be used for space research using X-ray telescopes. He described his spectrometer as consisting of a silicon semiconductor wafer containing an aluminum matrix inserted by thermomigration, a technique using heat to dope a semiconductor. X-ray detector cells, also called pixels, composed of silicon form a rectangular array. Aluminum electrodes in the cells deplete some silicon and electrical charges in the array, resulting in the X-ray energy present to start a photoelectric reaction with the remaining silicon and to create electrons that scientists secure for imaging purposes.

Alcorn emphasized that his invention could provide spatial and energy resolution of X-ray images more precisely than was possible with previous detectors, which often provided one type of resolution but not the other. He blamed insufficient silicon thickness, which he suggested should be approximately fifty mils, for limiting X-ray reactions, especially with high-energy X rays. Alcorn stated that his spectrometer could handle high-energy X-ray sources, performing capably in a wide band of energy measuring from one to 30 kiloelectronvolts. Inventors referred to Alcorn's spectrometer in patents for other spectrometers, detectors, and X-ray and imaging instruments from the 1980's into the early twenty-first century. Alcorn's imaging X-ray spectrometer was valuable for acquiring information about stellar and planetary phenomena inaccessible to space probes and manned spacecraft.

Recognizing structural and performance deficiencies in his spectrometer, such as current leakage, Alcorn utilized a laser-drilling technique he developed to construct an improved imaging instrument, which he described in a 1986 patent, "Method of Fabricating an Imaging X-ray Spectrometer" (number 4,618,380). He inserted phosphorous or other dopant materials, used to alter electrical charges, through laser-drilled holes in silicon semiconductors before thermomigration of aluminum electrodes in each cell occurred.

for industrial, business, educational, and governmental needs.

On a shuttle mission in September, 1994, Alcorn oversaw a Robot Operated Material Processing System (ROMPS) experiment, which evaluated possibilities for commercial manufacturing in microgravity. *Government Executive* magazine presented Alcorn a 1999 Government Technology Leadership Award to recognize his work establishing commercial applications for GSFC's Airborne Lidar Topographical Mapping System (ALTMS), for which he served as project manager. Alcorn stressed the benefits of this laser and digital technology with three-dimensional capabilities to map elevations effectively. In 2001, Donna M. Christian-Christensen, Democratic congresswoman from Vermont, commended Alcorn for helping businesses in the U.S. Virgin Islands through application of space technology. He served as GSFC Standards Review Board chairman in 2003.

In 2005, Alcorn was promoted to the position of assistant director for GSFC's Applied Engineering and Technology Directorate. In addition to NASA work, he continued teaching at Howard University and the University of the District of Columbia, which also designated him an adjunct full professor. Alcorn taught both undergraduate- and graduate-level physics and electrical engineering courses, including microelectronics and engineering mathematics, and discussed his insights regarding designing innovative semiconductors and other electronics devices. He received several campus awards recognizing this work.

Impact

Alcorn contributed to aerospace technology advancements as a physicist, teacher, and administrator. In the mid-twentieth century, scientists and engineers established basic semiconductor technology. Alcorn's experience in the 1960's working on molecular investigations and electronic procedures prepared him to envision and create innovative semiconductor devices and techniques that provided scientific and commercial benefits. Many of Alcorn's peers considered his development of plasma semiconductors as pioneering. Alcorn was one of the first scientists to use computer modeling to compare plasma etching with other etching procedures. His knowledge of particle physics, including competence with sputtering techniques and plasma, allowed him to improve on existing semiconductor designs. Since the late twentieth century, many semiconductor manufacturers produced Alcorn's designs and utilized processes, such as plasma-etching techniques, that he innovated.

In addition to offering practical applications, Alcorn's inventions, particularly the imaging X-ray spectrometer (for which he is best known) to analyze space materials, have advanced research possibilities. Scientists praised Alcorn for utilizing aluminum thermomigration, which they considered a novel approach, in that invention.

Alcorn received professional recognition for his inventions, including being named Inventor of the Year by NASA and the GSFC in 1984. In 1994, Howard University honored Alcorn in its Heritage of Greatness awards ceremony for scientific and technological accomplishments. He has also received financial awards recognizing his inventions. Through his example as teacher and inventor, Alcorn has inspired African Americans and other minorities to enter technological and scientific fields.

—*Elizabeth D. Schafer*

Further Reading

Alcorn, George E. "Determining Etch End Point in Plasma Etching of Via Holes." *IBM Technical Disclosure Bulletin* 19, no. 3 (August, 1976): 982-983. Text and illustration indicate how to perform this technique, specifying steps involving a silicon substrate, aluminum electrode, and quartz layer to achieve effective etching.

Dean, Joshua. "The IT Pioneers." *Government Executive* 31, no. 12 (December 1, 1999): 55. Discusses winners of Government Technology Leadership Awards, including Alcorn, and his achievements as ALTMS project manager. Provides quotations by Alcorn discussing this work, pursued in cooperation with scientists in Houston, Texas.

Dimitrijev, Sima. *Principles of Semiconductor Devices.* New York: Oxford University Press, 2006. Textbook explains basic semiconductor features, including atomic structures and materials used to make semiconductors. Although Alcorn is not mentioned, terminology for devices and processes to which his patents refer are incorporated in this text. Figures and illustrations clarify technical descriptions.

Plotkin, Henry H., and George E. Alcorn. "New Markets for Advanced Space Systems." *Aerospace America* 34 (November, 1996): 32-36. Alcorn and a senior research scientist at the University of Maryland, Baltimore County, identify technologies initially created at GSFC for aerospace purposes that also have commercial, medical, and military applications, including data systems, data compression, imaging, fiber-optic transceivers, radiation-tolerant components, and error-detection and error-correction processes and devices.

Sluby, Patricia Carter. *The Inventive Spirit of African Americans: Patented Ingenuity.* Westport, Conn.: Praeger, 2004. Patent agent notes Alcorn's affiliation with NASA and the legalities regarding patent rights and financial compensation associated with inventors who are U.S. federal government employees. Seven of Alcorn's patents are listed in an appendix.

See also: John Bardeen; Calvin Fuller; Dorothy Crowfoot Hodgkin; Nick Holonyak, Jr.; Sumio Iijima; Shuji Nakamura; Robert Norton Noyce; Stanford Ovshinsky; Heinrich Rohrer; Wilhelm Conrad Röntgen; William Shockley; Sir Alan Walsh; An Wang.

Ernst Alexanderson

Swedish American electrical engineer

Alexanderson developed a number of key innovations in broadcasting, in particular the Alexanderson alternator, the first reliable technology for voice radio broadcasting, and played a substantial role in the development of analog color television.

Born: January 25, 1878; Uppsala, Sweden
Died: May 14, 1975; Schenectady, New York
Also known as: Ernst Frederik Werner Alexanderson (full name)
Primary fields: Communications; electronics and electrical engineering
Primary invention: High-frequency alternator

Early Life

Ernst Frederik Werner Alexanderson grew up in a highly intellectual family. His father, Aron M. Alexanderson, was a professor of classical languages, first at the University of Uppsala and later at the University of Lund. His mother, Amelie (née von Heidenstam), belonged to the Swedish nobility and would have received a substantial education, although she appears to have held no professional responsibilities after her marriage, instead satisfying herself with the role of wife and mother. All the same, she instilled in her son a respect for education.

Alexanderson received a solid education, completing his secondary schooling at Lund High School and then attending the University of Lund for a year between 1896 and 1897. He then went to Stockholm to attend the Royal Institute of Technology, where he received a degree in mechanical and electrical engineering in 1900. Feeling that the relatively provincial institutes of higher learning in Sweden would limit his long-term career success, he decided to study abroad.

Alexanderson's next stop was Berlin, where he studied in the German Empire's Royal Technical Institute. One of his teachers there was Adolf K. H. Staby, who had developed a primitive sort of radio communication based on generating and detecting artificial bursts of static. It was more a proof-of-concept device than a working radio system, and when Italian inventor Guglielmo Marconi put himself forth as the inventor of radio, Staby made no protests.

By this point, Alexanderson had a good grasp of the potential of radio technology, but he was increasingly convinced that no European country would give him the opportunity to exercise his abilities to the fullest. Looking at the developments that were occurring in the United States at the time, he decided that the country would offer him the best opportunity for practical work.

Life's Work

Alexanderson arrived in New York in 1901 and soon made the acquaintance of Thomas Alva Edison, the folksy "elder statesman" of the electrical world. In 1904, Alexanderson passed General Electric's engineering examinations and was hired by the company. Thus, he was in a perfect position to make his reputation when radio pioneer Reginald Aubrey Fessenden was looking for someone to build an alternator that other engineers claimed was impossible. Alexanderson examined a prototype and made significant changes that permitted the device to reach the necessary speeds. However, he took no chances on its safety: The first time he started the alternator, he placed it in a sandbagged pit just in case it were to fly apart as others claimed it would.

After his success with the alternator, which subsequently bore his name in spite of Fessenden's rather vociferous complaints that he had originally conceived of the concept, Alexanderson developed an entire series of important radio inventions. He created the multiple-tuned antenna, which permitted a radio to broadcast or receive on several different frequencies. He also created a magnetic amplifier, then rendered it obsolete with an electronic modulator that used vacuum tubes to create the same effect more reliably and at even higher power levels.

During this time, Alexanderson also gained a reputation for eccentricity and for being something of an absentminded professor. During periods of frenetic activity on a project, he would forget to eat unless food was brought to him. He frequently greeted friends as though they were complete strangers if he met them on the street rather than in the laboratory or office, and he once gravely shook hands with his own daughter and addressed her as "miss."

However, such oddities of behavior were tolerated, if with a bit of wry humor, for the simple reason that Alexanderson was so prolific and his inventions so useful. After World War I, he became chief engineer for the newly created Radio Corporation of America (RCA). As RCA's executive director, David Sarnoff, moved the radio industry away from being a transmitter of wireless telegrams for individuals and companies to being a news and entertainment medium via voice radio broadcasting, Alexanderson concentrated increasingly on various devices that would help make the radio receiver into an appliance that would be usable by a person with no technical background.

His skills in radio technology development also had a personal benefit, when his son Vernor was kidnapped in 1923. A description of his son was transmitted over the air with a request that anyone with information about the crime contact the police. Although receivers were still relatively new at the time, a janitor heard the broadcast and recognized the boy as one he had seen in the upstate New York resort at which he worked. He passed the word to the police, who were able to capture the kidnappers and return the boy safely to his parents.

By 1924, Alexanderson was becoming increasingly interested in the developing technology of television and as a result quit his job at RCA in order to work full-time with General Electric. He concentrated almost entirely on mechanical methods of scanning. One of his earliest devices used individual wires to convey the information for each pixel of the image. Although this technique allowed him to score the coup of transmitting one of the first-ever television images, it was not a practical technology for broadcast use. He later began using various slotted disks and mirror drums to scan and reconstruct an image, although they were necessarily limited by the tolerances to which they could be machined and the fact that most of the light reflected off the object being televised would be lost.

The Alexanderson Alternator

One of the most difficult challenges faced by Reginald Aubrey Fessenden in realizing his dream of making radio waves carry the human voice was the problem of generating a continuous carrier wave. In 1901, neither the vacuum tube nor the transistor existed, so any device that would produce a carrier wave would have to be mechanical in nature. Fessenden, who recognized that radio waves were an electromagnetic phenomenon, conceptualized an alternator that would change phase far more frequently than the usual 60 cycles per second of American line voltage, perhaps as much as 100,000 cycles per second.

However, when this consummate theorist approached engineers to actually construct his alternator, they told him that it was impossible to build. Anything rotating as rapidly as he had described would tear itself to pieces the moment it was turned on. Frustrated, Fessenden fell back on a makeshift method of generating a carrier wave for his very first voice transmission. However, he did not cease his search for an engineer who could build his alternator and give him a real carrier wave.

Although Charles Proteus Steinmetz of General Electric, one of the era's foremost experts in electrical engineering, tried to build the device, he was only able to attain a speed of 4,000 cycles per second before the armature started shaking apart. Fessenden turned to Ernst Alexanderson, who had already established his reputation for both eccentricity and technical genius.

Alexanderson had to apply all his technical ingenuity, along with the construction resources of General Electric, to construct the device. Instead of just speeding up a normal alternator, he altered the structure of it so that the rotor became a flat disc that turned inside a stationary armature. The outside edge of the rotor turned at an amazing 700 miles per hour, but it was so perfectly balanced that it wobbled less than three hundredths of an inch.

Alexanderson's alternator would become the mainstay of voice radio transmission for more than a decade. However, it had several drawbacks, most importantly its huge size and difficulty of manufacture, which restricted the alternator to the largest of stations with the resources to acquire and operate one. Once Edwin H. Armstrong demonstrated that vacuum tubes could be used to generate and modulate a carrier wave, the Alexanderson alternator gave way to the new technology. Tubes would prove to have a surprising staying power, particularly for high-wattage stations, even after the transistor and the integrated circuit were introduced.

However, Alexanderson did provide some insights that were later used by Vladimir Zworykin in his work on the all-electronic television.

During World War II, Alexanderson worked on a number of projects for the U.S. military, including a direct-current generator that used a smaller current to control a much larger one. Although the generator was originally designed for use in steel mills, it later found application in the controls for antiaircraft guns. In 1948, Alexanderson retired from General Electric, although he continued to work as a consultant for the company and RCA. This arrangement allowed him to take only the projects that attracted his interest.

During the 1950's, Alexanderson made his last major contribution to broadcast technology. Peter Carl Goldmark of the Columbia Broadcasting System (CBS) had developed a hybrid mechanical-electronic system of color television and was touting it to the Federal Communications Commission (FCC) as a replacement for the National Television Standards Committee (NTSC) black-and-white television standard. The Goldmark system involved using a rotating disk with red, green, and blue lenses that would be passed over the electronic camera on the transmitter end, so that the image would be transmitted in sequential red, green, and blue frames that would be put together by a similar rotating disk over the picture tube. However, this system would have two major limitations. First, it would instantly render obsolete the existing NTSC televisions. Second, to attain a picture size much larger than a postage stamp would require a large disk. To create color televisions as big as sets already in existence would require disks as large as a house, and their outer edges would rotate at speeds of hundreds or even thousands of miles per hour, such that if they were to suffer mechanical failure, the fragments would become deadly shrapnel.

Sarnoff knew that the only workable solution was an all-electronic television. Alexanderson developed a system by which the camera would have three image tubes in parallel, one for each primary color, and the picture tube of the receiver would have three corresponding electron guns. In addition, Alexanderson's system separated the color information into a separate part of the signal for the brightness of each pixel, so that color signals could still be received on black-and-white sets. This compatible color scheme was quickly approved by the FCC and would remain the American color television standard until its replacement in the early part of the twenty-first century by digital television.

In his later years, Alexanderson was the recipient of many honors for his radio and television work. He also developed a strong fondness for sailing. He died at his home in Schenectady at the age of ninety-seven, having survived two wives.

Impact

Although most of Alexanderson's inventions have been superseded by more advanced technologies (the Alexanderson alternator with the triode vacuum tube and the NTSC compatible color system with digital television), his inventions enabled radio and television to become sufficiently commercially successful that continued innovation was profitable. On December 24, 1906, using Alexanderson's alternator, Fessenden broadcast the first transmission of voice over radio waves. Alexanderson also designed a color television receiver for RCA, establishing the color television standard that lasted for decades. Alexanderson earned more than three hundred patents during his lifetime.

—Leigh Husband Kimmel

Further Reading

Davis, L. J. *Fleet Fire: Thomas Edison and the Pioneers of the Electric Revolution.* New York: Arcade, 2003. A history of the early days of electricity, culminating in the invention of radio.

Leinwoll, Stanley. *From Spark to Satellite: A History of Radio Communication.* New York: Charles Scribner's Sons, 1979. An overview of the history of radio, placing Alexanderson's work in context.

Lewis, Tom. *Empire of the Air: The Men Who Made Radio.* New York: Edward Burlingame Books, 1991. Looks primarily at Alexanderson's contributions to the development of radio, in the context of the work of Lee De Forest and Edwin H. Armstrong.

Lyons, Eugene. *David Sarnoff.* New York: Harper & Row, 1966. A biography of the longtime head of RCA. Touches on Alexanderson's work with RCA.

Sobel, Robert. *RCA.* New York: Stein & Day, 1986. Corporate history of RCA from its beginnings to the mid-1980's, including Alexanderson's most productive years.

See also: Edwin H. Armstrong; Lee De Forest; Thomas Alva Edison; Philo T. Farnsworth; Reginald Aubrey Fessenden; Peter Carl Goldmark; Guglielmo Marconi; Vladimir Zworykin.

LUIS W. ÁLVAREZ
Spanish American physicist

Álvarez invented the microwave phased-array antenna and several radar systems that used it. He was coinventor of the exploding-bridgewire detonator for atomic bombs. He also developed the liquid-hydrogen bubble chamber, and with his son, an asteroid-impact extinction theory.

Born: June 13, 1911; San Francisco, California
Died: September 1, 1988; Berkeley, California
Also known as: Luis Walter Álvarez (full name)
Primary fields: Electronics and electrical engineering; military technology and weaponry; physics
Primary inventions: Phased-array antenna; exploding-bridgewire detonator; liquid-hydrogen bubble chamber

EARLY LIFE

Luis Walter Álvarez (AHL-vah-rehz) was born on June 13, 1911, in San Francisco, California. His mother was Harriet Smyth Álvarez, who grew up in China, where her Irish parents started a missionary school. His father was Walter C. Álvarez, a physician and medical researcher at the Universities of California and Minnesota (Mayo Foundation), who wrote a widely read syndicated medical column. His grandfather, Luis F. Álvarez, was born in Spain and educated in Cuba before medical studies at Stanford.

Luis Álvarez had two sisters, Gladys Álvarez Mead and Bernice Álvarez Brownson, and one brother, Robert Álvarez, all of whom lived in the San Francisco Bay Area. When Luis was eleven, he and his father built a crystal radio receiver, which could pick up the first music broadcast from San Francisco. Young Luis attended the Madison Elementary School for six years and the Polytechnic High School in San Francisco for two years. After his family moved to Minnesota in 1926, he graduated from Rochester High School in Rochester, Minnesota, where he attended for two years.

In 1928, Álvarez entered the University of Chicago, where he earned his bachelor of science degree in 1932, master's degree in 1934, and Ph.D. in 1936. While still an undergraduate, he published his first paper, "A Simplified Method for the Determination of the Wave Length of Light," using the grooves of a phonograph record as a reflection grating to form a spectrum. As a graduate student under Nobel Laureate Arthur H. Compton, he built a pair of Geiger counters, among the first in the United States, and used them to make the important discovery that most cosmic rays are positively charged. His Ph.D. thesis was published in 1936 as "The Diffraction Grating at Grazing Incidence." His first marriage was to Geraldine Smithwick in 1936, and a few years later his first two children were born, Walter and Jean.

LIFE'S WORK

Álvarez began his scientific career in 1936 as a research fellow at the University of California Radiation Laboratory, where he concentrated on nuclear physics and on the development of the cyclotron with its inventor, Ernest Orlando Lawrence, as his mentor. Using the 27-inch-diameter cyclotron, he studied neutron yields from deuteron (bound proton-neutron particle) reactions in 1938 and developed a method for producing beams of slow neutrons. With his student, Jake Wiens, he invented a mercury-vapor lamp by using neutron capture by the gold-197 isotope to transmute gold into mercury 198, which emitted a very pure form of green light that served as the accepted standard for many years. Soon after learning in early 1939 about the discovery of nuclear fission, he confirmed this by bombarding uranium with cyclotron-generated neutrons. During this period, he worked with Lawrence to design a new 60-inch-diameter cyclotron.

In November of 1940, as World War II spread across Europe, Álvarez was sent with other nuclear physicists to assist in the beginning of the Massachusetts Institute of Technology (MIT) Radiation Laboratory to develop radar (radio detecting and ranging) systems for military applications. Working with an airborne 3-centimeter microwave radar system for antisubmarine warfare, he invented the Vixen system, which "outfoxed" submarine listening sets by decreasing the strength of the radar signals during approach. In this way, U-boat crews would think they were undetected and remain on the surface long enough to be attacked.

This work with radar and his experience as a licensed pilot led Álvarez to invent the first ground-controlled approach (GCA) system for landing airplanes in conditions of low visibility. His idea required a very narrow fan-shaped beam so that a ground-based radar operator could guide a pilot in the blind landing of his airplane. Drawing on his experience with diffraction gratings, he invented the first phased-array antenna, consisting of a series of radiating elements from which the radiation is reinforced in one direction and suppressed in all other directions.

Later in 1941 as head of the Special Systems Division of the MIT Radiation Laboratory, Álvarez led the development of two more of his radar-system inventions using phased-array antennae. The microwave early warning (MEW) system could detect enemy aircraft in overcast skies early enough to defend against them. It was used to coordinate the D-day landing and to defend against German V-1 buzz bombs. The Eagle high-altitude bombing system could locate targets and aim bombs at night through overcast skies more accurately than visual bombsights during the day.

In the fall of 1943, Álvarez was asked to join the Manhattan Project to help develop the atomic bomb. For six months he worked with Nobel Laureate Enrico Fermi on continuing tests of the first nuclear reactor, which had been moved from the University of Chicago to the new Argonne National Laboratory in a Chicago suburb. Then, in the spring of 1944, he was invited to Los Alamos in New Mexico to assist with the implosion mechanism for triggering plutonium bombs. With his student Lawrence Johnston, Álvarez invented the exploding-bridgewire (EBW) detonator for spherical implosives in the Fat Man-type atomic bombs used in the first nuclear explosion at the Trinity Site near Alamogordo, New Mexico, and in the bomb dropped on Nagasaki, Japan. He flew as a scientific observer at both the Trinity and Hiroshima explosions.

After the war, Álvarez returned to particle-accelerator research at the University of California Radiation Laboratory and was named professor of physics. In 1947, he completed the design and construction of a 40-foot proton linear accelerator. He assisted in the development of one of the first proton synchrotrons, the 6-billion-electron-volt (6-GeV) Bevatron, a 36-meter-diameter cyclotron in which the magnetic and electric fields were increased synchronously with increasing proton energy and associated mass.

In 1954, Álvarez began developing the first liquid-hydrogen bubble chambers for detecting elementary particles from the trail of bubbles they produce in superheated liquid hydrogen. After demonstrating the technique with several smaller chambers, he led his group in the development of a 10-inch chamber in 1955 and a 72-inch chamber over the next four years for use in the Bevatron. During this time, he invented automatic tracking and recording methods and participated in the discovery of many new short-lived elementary particles. By the time he was awarded the Nobel Prize for this work in 1968, the 72-inch chamber was detecting 1.5 million events per year.

In the 1970's, inventions by Álvarez included a variable-focus thin lens used in the eye-care field, methods for stabilizing images in cameras and viewing devices, and a handheld color television system. In 1978, he was inducted into the National Inventors Hall of Fame. In the 1980's, he worked with his geologist son Walter Álvarez in inventing the asteroid-extinction hypothesis, which provided an explanation for the disappearance of the dinosaurs 65 million years ago. This was based on their discovery that a thin dark layer in the geological column at the Cretaceous-Tertiary boundary worldwide contained relatively large amounts of the rare element iridium. Since meteorites are rich in iridium, the scientists recognized that a large asteroid collision could have produced a global fallout of debris that would kill

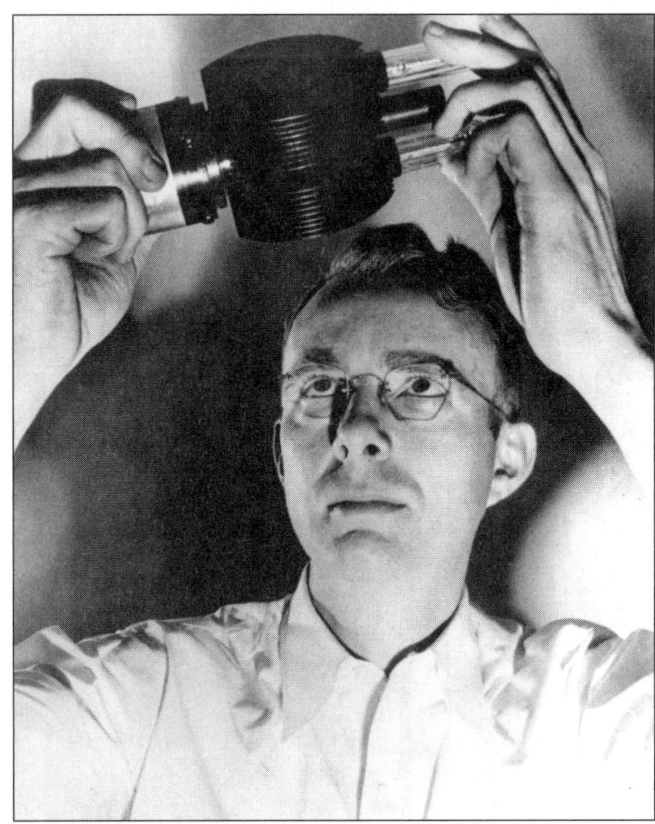

Luis W. Álvarez examines a radio transmitter used in his ground-controlled approach (GCA) system for landing airplanes in conditions of low visibility. (AP/Wide World Photos)

The Phased-Array Antenna

One of the lesser-known but most important inventions of Luis Álvarez was his microwave phased-array antenna. He needed a thin (3°) fan-shaped radar beam for the microwave early warning radar system, which would have required a rectangular reflector 8 × 75 feet when fed by a single radiating (dipole) element. He then realized that he could obtain better results from a series of many equally spaced radiating elements along a pipelike waveguide, which he found would require a length of only 24 feet for a 3° beam. Microwaves from the waveguide, radiating out from these elements, would overlap and reinforce each other in one direction and cancel in all other directions. This produced the desired fan-shaped beam perpendicular to the waveguide when the separation between the elements was one wavelength (or a phase difference of 360°).

When Álvarez used this new linear-array antenna concept in his Eagle bombing system, he realized that he could steer the beam by varying the width of the waveguide. This changed the wavelength of radiation in the waveguide and thus the phase of the radiating elements in such a way that radiation would be reinforced in differing directions. Later it was shown that rapid scanning of a phased-array antenna can also be achieved by varying the frequency of the generator or with electronic phase shifters between elements, which are often just slots along one side of the waveguide.

These phased-array techniques were developed after the war by Hughes Aircraft Company to produce a planar array with a pencil beam that could be rapidly scanned in any direction by changing the phase between elements in both dimensions. Since such antennae required no mechanical steering, they could be easily mounted in aircraft or built to nearly unlimited size for many military and civilian applications. They are used for missile guidance, as in the Patriot (phased array tracking radar to intercept of target) missile system, and for battle-control radar, such as the U.S. Navy Aegis combat system, which can simultaneously search and track more than one hundred targets. They are also used in very large ground-based radar antennae for over-the-horizon defense and in the MESSENGER spacecraft mission to Mercury for communicating back to Earth.

many species of life. On September 1, 1988, Álvarez died in Berkeley from cancer, perhaps due to years of radiation exposure, shortly before the discovery of a 200-kilometer-diameter crater near Chicxulub, Mexico, supporting the extinction theory.

Impact

Álvarez made many important contributions to both radar systems and high-energy physics, resulting in some forty patented inventions that helped win World War II and extended basic knowledge in physics. His invention of the phased-array antenna had important applications in World War II, and even more in the postwar period in both defensive and offensive radar systems. His antisubmarine Vixen system saved many lives and tons of allied shipping. His ground-controlled approach system for blind landing has saved many aircraft and their passengers in both military and civilian emergencies. The microwave early warning system and the Eagle bombing system played important roles in the safety and accuracy of allied missions. His work in the Manhattan Project helped to make the atomic bomb possible and to bring the war to an early end.

Both before and after World War II, Álvarez helped to make significant advances in high-energy physics. His work on the early development of cyclotrons, proton linear accelerators, and the synchrotron led to significant increases in the strength and energy of proton beams, helping to confirm nuclear fission and discover new elementary particles and their properties. His development of the liquid-hydrogen bubble chamber and invention of automatic tracking and measuring of high-energy particles led to many new discoveries and provided the experimental basis for the quark model of elementary particles. This and other work, ranging from optics to asteroid collisions, show an active and inventive mind.

—*Joseph L. Spradley*

Further Reading

Álvarez, Luis W. *Álvarez: Adventures of a Physicist*. New York: Basic Books, 1987. This autobiography covers all of the scientific activities and inventions of Álvarez and was published the year before he died. Contains eight pages of photos and a good index.

Oleksy, Walter. *Hispanic-American Scientists*. New York: Facts On File, 1998. Álvarez is the first of ten Latino American scientists described in brief biographical sketches with a few photos and a useful chronology.

Trower, Peter W., ed. *Discovering Álvarez: Selected Works of Luis W. Álvarez with Commentary by His Students and Colleagues*. Chicago: University of Chicago Press, 1987. The subtitle describes this book, which includes sixteen pages of photos, a short biography, and lists of publications and patents.

Veltman, Martinus. *Facts and Mysteries in Elementary Particle Physics*. River Edge, N.J.: World Scientific Publishing, 2003. This book for general readers describes elementary particle discoveries, theories, accelerators, and detectors. Includes a sidebar on Álvarez.

Visser, Hubregt. *Array and Phased Array Antenna Basics*. New York: Wiley, 2005. This 376-page introduction to phased-array antennae describes the operation and applications of phased-array antennae for nonspecialist readers with a minimum of mathematics. Includes two chapters on historical background.

See also: Hans Geiger; Donald A. Glaser; Ernest Orlando Lawrence; J. Robert Oppenheimer; Sir Robert Alexander Watson-Watt.

Marc Andreessen

American computer scientist and software engineer

While an undergraduate at the University of Illinois, Andreessen, along with Eric Bina, created Mosaic, the first Internet browser to allow graphics and text to be viewed at the same time. The browser's 1993 release led to the initial surge in the popularity of the World Wide Web. Andreessen followed the success of his first browser with his second, Netscape Navigator, which served as the general public's portal to the World Wide Web.

Born: July 9, 1971; Cedar Falls, Iowa
Primary field: Computer science
Primary inventions: Mosaic; Netscape Navigator

Early Life

Marc Andreessen grew up in New Lisbon, Wisconsin, a small, rural town with a population of 1,500. He lived ten miles outside of town and was raised by working parents. At the age of twelve, while he was recovering from surgery, Andreessen convinced his parents to purchase him a Radio Shack computer, and he quickly discovered a love for programming.

Andreessen attended a small high school, where he was a top scholar. He also politely challenged authority, questioning, among other issues, the relevancy of classroom practices. After graduation, he attended the University of Illinois at Urbana-Champaign, where he majored in computer science. He also landed a programming position with the National Center for Supercomputing Applications (NCSA), where he learned of Tim Berners-Lee's work with open standards for the World Wide Web.

Andreessen was originally hired to write software for three-dimensional scientific visualization. However, his enthusiasm for the early form of the Internet led him to begin working on writing the code for what he hoped would be an effective means of navigating the Internet. Andreessen and full-time University of Illinois employee Eric Bina collaborated on the creation of a Web browser (software that displays the files retrieved from the Internet) that would be both user-friendly and would allow graphics to be displayed as an integrated component of a Web page. (Earlier browsers could only show text and graphics files as separate pages.) The pair also wanted their browser to run on a wide range of computing platforms, from UNIX to Windows.

The result of their programming effort was a browser that they named NCSA Mosaic. Version 1.0 was released for UNIX's X Window System on April 22, 1993.

Life's Work

Andreessen never expected the Internet, nor Mosaic for that matter, to become wildly popular. His goal was to create a browser that would make the Internet easier to use through the graphical point-and-click interface. At first, it seemed that Andreessen's vision of the Internet as a small network community used by only a handful of scientists and researchers might hold true: In February, 1993, only twelve people were using the early versions of Mosaic. However, after the April release of version 1.0 and the late spring release of the PC and Macintosh versions, ten thousand users were using Mosaic. The one millionth Mosaic browser was downloaded and installed in early 1994, and the fuse had been lit for the Internet explosion.

Andreessen graduated from the University of Illinois in December of 1993 and headed to Palo Alto, California, to work at Enterprise Integration Technologies, where he connected with Jim Clark, the founder of Silicon Graphics. Clark and Andreessen decided to create a new start-up company whose goal was to become the "Microsoft of the Internet" by creating a browser that was more robust than Mosaic. They named the new company Mosaic Communications Corporation, and Andreessen put together an engineering team that included many of his old friends from NCSA. Their business plan was to create a commercially viable browser that would allow them to build their fortunes around it.

However, because the original Mosaic was the property of the University of Illinois, which objected to Andreessen and Clark's use of the Mosaic brand name, the company was renamed Netscape Communications Corporation. In December, 1994, the first full 1.0 version of the Netscape Navigator browser was released. The browser was freeware—that is, it was free for individuals to download for noncommercial purposes. Commercial interests could purchase licensed copies of the browser.

As the general public began to make use of the Internet in the mid-1990's, Netscape Navigator became the browser of choice, especially for PC systems. This growth was promulgated by the ever-increasing library of hypertext markup language (HTML) tags that Netscape Navigator made available to Web page designers. These tags were commands that gave Web designers increased flexibility in their designs and offered them the opportunity to produce dynamic pages with improved visual impact and greater levels of interactivity. Designers quickly utilized the new tags to make their pages more exciting, adding to their pages buttons that read, "Optimized for Netscape Navigator." The buttons were usually linked to a Web site where users could download the latest version of the Navigator browser for free.

On August 9, 1995, Andreessen became one of the early dot-com millionaires, as Netscape's initial public offering marked the beginning of the dot-com boom in the American stock market. At the age of twenty-four, he had become worth $58 million in just one day. He had also become one of the first popular icons among the Internet glitterati, as his face became a familiar sight on computing, finance, and news magazines of the day.

By 1996, two-thirds of all browsers in use were Netscape products. That success drew the attention of software giant Microsoft, which decided to enter the fray with a browser of its own. Microsoft's Internet Explorer, which began as a reworked version of Mosaic, would eventually eclipse Navigator. Microsoft accomplished this primarily through the practice of bundling the Internet Explorer browser with every Windows operating system and by producing a browser that was the technological equal of Netscape's product. Netscape was purchased by America Online (AOL) in 1998. Andreessen briefly served as AOL's chief technology officer before leaving in September of 1999.

MOSAIC AND NAVIGATOR

A Web browser is a software program that displays Web pages on a user's computer and allows him or her to "surf" the World Wide Web. Marc Andreessen and Eric Bina brought together all the potential that Tim Berners-Lee's World Wide Web technology had to offer, making their browser accessible and the Web easy to navigate. Earlier browsers such as Cello, Erwise, and ViolaWWW failed to deliver on either the integration of features or ease of use.

As a browser, Mosaic allowed seasoned users to continue to have access to older Internet technologies such as gopher (an early search protocol), file transfer protocol (FTP), and Usenet (discussion groups). Mosaic broke new ground in a number of areas. The browser was the first to include an image tag, allowing images to be displayed as an embedded component on a page. This marked the Web's first step toward becoming a multimedia communication medium.

Mosaic was also designed in a manner that made it intuitive, even for new users. The move away from a command-line interface made the browser user-friendly and helped drive its popularity. Mosaic's popularity was also boosted by the fact that it was designed to run on almost all of the available platforms of the day, including UNIX and Windows. The fact that the browser was available for free for noncommercial use was also an enormous factor in its popularity.

After Mosaic was released, the Web began to grow exponentially. Andreessen took his programming skills to Silicon Valley and, with Jim Clark, developed the next generation of browser by 1994, Netscape Navigator. In 1995, Microsoft, after observing the success of Navigator, licensed the Mosaic source code and built Internet Explorer, which was designed to directly challenge Netscape's market supremacy. The battle for users waged by the two companies, both in the marketplace and in the courtroom, has become known as the "browser wars."

IMPACT

NCSA Mosaic and Netscape Navigator were essential components in moving the World Wide Web from a supercomputer-based service that was utilized by a handful of academics, scientists, and engineers to its role as the communication medium of choice for a growing segment of the world's population.

Mosaic's impact lies in its technological innovation

and ease of use. The inclusion of the graphics tag, which allows images to appear as a component on a page, was groundbreaking. Mosaic also utilized graphical interfaces that used "clickable" buttons, allowing users to move easily through Web pages. Mosaic's visual style and graphical interface set the standard for browser technology and for many other Internet applications for the foreseeable future.

Andreessen and Bina also made the hyperlink a great deal more user-friendly. Hyperlinks are links (usually indicated by underlined text) in a document that allow users to quickly "jump" to a related document elsewhere on the Web. In earlier browsers, hyperlinks were indicated by reference numbers, similar to footnotes, that the user had to type into the navigation bar to retrieve the document. Mosaic streamlined the process, allowing a user to merely click on an underlined link to retrieve a document.

Perhaps the greatest impact of Mosaic came from the fact that Andreessen and Bina quickly developed versions for personal-computer users. Mosaic was not the first PC browser (that honor goes to Cello), but what set it apart was the fact that the browser was so simple to download and install that even novice users had little trouble getting the software up and running. Because of this ease of adoption, the easy-to-understand graphical interface, the browser's availability for PC platforms, and the fact that the browser was free for noncommercial use, Mosaic's popularity, and with it, the popularity of the World Wide Web, skyrocketed. Most scholars mark the 1993 release of Mosaic as the moment that the Internet and World Wide Web became available to the general public. It also marked the beginning of the Internet's boom in popularity.

—B. Keith Murphy

Further Reading

Berners-Lee, Tim. *Weaving the Web: The Original Design and the Ultimate Destiny of the World Wide Web*. New York: HarperCollins, 2000. In Berners-Lee's "biography" of the World Wide Web, Andreessen's Mosaic and Netscape Navigator are accurately placed in their historical context. Berners-Lee explains their importance to the Web's rapid ascension from scientists' tool to hugely popular forum and marketplace.

Clark, Jim. *Netscape Time: The Making of the Billion-Dollar Start-Up That Took on Microsoft*. New York: St. Martin's Press, 1999. Provides an incisive examination of Andreessen's role in developing Mosaic into Netscape Navigator and examines how Andreessen and Clark turned Netscape Navigator into the first must-have browser. Traces the role of Andreessen's browser in the development of the Web and the inevitable clash with Microsoft that would come to be known as the "browser wars."

Ehrenraft, Daniel. *Marc Andreessen: Web Warrior*. New York: 17th Street Productions, 2001. A comprehensive biography of Andreessen aimed at young adults. Addresses both Andreessen's life and his role in the history and growth of the World Wide Web.

Payment, Simone. *Marc Andreessen and Jim Clark: The Founders of Netscape*. New York: Rosen, 2007. Payment provides a biographical overview of Andreessen and Clark, although the bulk of this work focuses on their time together as they developed Netscape Communications Corporation into an international Internet megacorporation.

See also: Tim Berners-Lee; Robert Cailliau; Vinton Gray Cerf; Philip Emeagwali; Bill Gates; Bob Kahn; Robert Metcalfe; Larry Page.

ARCHIMEDES

Greek physicist, mathematician, astronomer, and engineer

Ancient Greek mathematicians were primarily interested in elegant conjectural theorems and proofs. Archimedes of Syracuse, exceptionally, if not uniquely, pursued not only abstract mathematical problems but also how solutions to those problems could be applied to create mechanical realities, including defensive weapons.

Born: c. 287 B.C.E.; Syracuse, Sicily (now in Italy)
Died: 212 B.C.E.; Syracuse, Sicily (now in Italy)
Also known as: Archimedes of Syracuse
Primary fields: Astronomy; civil engineering; mathematics; military technology and weaponry; physics
Primary inventions: Archimedes' principle; Archimedes' screw; claw of Archimedes

EARLY LIFE

Archimedes (ahr-kih-MEE-deez) was born c. 287 B.C.E. into a notable family in Syracuse, the wealthy and populous Greek city on the southeast coast of Sicily. His family had scientific credentials (Archimedes stated that his father, Phidias, was an astronomer, but all that is known of him is that he estimated the ratio of the diameters of the Sun and the Moon) and was manifestly wealthy: Archimedes received an elite education and corresponded with contemporary Greek intellectuals, including the mathematician and astronomer Konon of Samos (c. 245 B.C.E.) and the polymath Eratosthenes of Cyrene (c. 275-194 B.C.E.), sometime head of the Library of Alexandria (Egypt) to whom Archimedes dedicated two of his treatises. No information has survived as to whether Archimedes was married or had any children. He may have studied at Alexandria, but proof is lacking. He had no recorded employment and was said to be a kinsman of the long-term king of Syracuse, Hieron II (c. 305-215 B.C.E.).

LIFE'S WORK

The earliest firmly datable event in Archimedes' career came late in his life. Ancient literary authorities described Archimedes' applications of physical principles to mechanical inventions for the defense of his city. Archimedes reportedly constructed several (not entirely plausible) weapons to defend Syracuse, an ally of the Carthaginians in the Second Punic War, during a siege of the city by the Roman commander Marcus Claudius Marcellus in 213-211 B.C.E. Those reported weapons included gigantic metallic parabolic mirrors to focus the Sun's rays on the sails of Roman ships in Syracuse's harbor. More plausible are reports that he demonstrated the power of the compound pulley and block and tackle by constructing a track with cables to move very heavy ships into the water from dry land. That knowledge of applying the principle of leverage to the power of the compound pulley enabled the lifting of heavy objects. Thus, Archimedes constructed cranes to drop heavy weights (stones and lead) on attacking ships. Other cranes had an iron hook called "the claw" (attached to ropes), capable of lifting the prows of enemy ships out of the water and pulling up scaling ladders. These cranes were effective because Roman vessels attacking Syracuse had to sail close to the walls behind which the cranes operated.

Another ancient report also illustrates Archimedes' ability to find practical applications for physical principles. Archimedes stepped into a small bath, observed that his weight displaced water, then leapt from the bath shouting (so ancient sources say) "Eureka!" (actually,

Archimedes famously remarked about the lever, "Give me a place to stand and I shall move the Earth." (*Mechanics Magazine*, 1824)

Heureka, "I found [it]"). What Archimedes found was a solution to a problem posed by King Hieron II: What was the proportion of gold to silver in a wreath said to be of gold? Archimedes' bath suggested that the volume of an irregularly shaped object (a wreath or body) could be measured by the water displaced and that the specific gravity of different metals would displace different volumes of water—that is, a body immersed in water displaces a quantity of water equal to its own volume. By dividing the weight of the body immersed by the quantity of water displaced, the density of the object could be calculated. In this instance, the more water displaced by the wreath, the greater the gold content of the wreath. Archimedes himself set out the basic principle, now known in hydrostatics (the study of the pressures liquids exert or transmit) as "Archimedes' principle," in his treatise "On Floating Bodies," but he did not describe his bathing experience. The "Eureka" story is typical: Tradition reported Archimedes' more popularly understandable discoveries in the form of a concise quotation. "I found it" may be compared to his statement "Give me a place to stand and I shall move the Earth," thereby concisely expressing the power of a lever.

An Ancient Mechanical Engineer

One of Archimedes' most useful and influential inventions was the water screw (*kochlias*). King Hieron II of Syracuse commissioned the construction of a gigantic ship, named the *Syracusia*. This wooden ship was so large that leakage was a problem. Archimedes invented a device designed to remove bilge water from the hull of this and other large ships. "Archimedes' screw" consisted of a revolving metal screw blade placed within a cylinder. A fresco from ancient Pompeii shows how the screw was powered: continual treading on spokes attached to the cylinder of the screw. A machine that efficiently raised water from one level to another, this device could be (and, in many rural areas of the world today, still is) employed to lift water from a lake, stream, or river to an irrigation canal. In the ancient Mediterranean world, the screw was used for irrigation in Egypt and to drain water from mines in Spain.

Another practical invention, utilizing the principle of leverage, was the large-scale crane. In addition to their use in defense at Syracuse to drop weights on attacking ships and to lift the prows of the ships, these large wooden structures could be used for more peaceful purposes. Wooden cranes of the type Archimedes invented, employing pulleys and ropes, and operated, in several known instances, by men on a treadmill, were adopted by the Romans for constructing tall buildings and loading and unloading ships.

Archimedes' discovery of the principle of water displacement led to another invention: a more efficient water organ, in which air compressed above water in a chamber was channeled to the organ's pipes of differing length, thus producing different tones. Among Archimedes' lost treatises was the book *On Sphere-Making*. That book seems to have dealt with the construction of the invention of which Archimedes was most proud: a spherical planetarium demonstrating in one revolution how the independent motions of the Sun, Moon, and planets moved relative to the fixed stars as they do in one day. In addition, the planetarium enabled observation of the phases and eclipses of the Moon. Archimedes' planetarium is frequently mentioned by ancient authors, for some of whom it was the physical proof of Archimedes' genius.

Other mechanical inventions illustrating Archimedes' skills at applying abstract mathematical and geometrical principles to mechanical inventions include a screw for raising water (*kochlias*), and spheres (*sphairai*) on which the movements of stars and planets were modeled. One of these spheres apparently illustrated various constellations; the other one seems to have been a genuine planetarium showing the orbits of the five known planets, the Sun, and the Moon. These two spheres were reportedly seized as booty by Marcellus and taken to Rome: one was dedicated to the goddess Virtue, the other Marcellus kept for himself. One of Archimedes' more interesting inventions was an odometer. That device seems to have consisted of a cart with gears (attached to a wheel) that dropped a ball into a container after a specific distance had been traveled. Archimedes was also said to have improved, in some way not specified, the hurling capacity of the catapult.

During his life before the siege of Syracuse, Archimedes composed a body of treatises (more than twenty-seven, complete or partial, have survived) exploring problems of geometry and mathematics. His writings indicate particular interests in calculating the area and volume of geometric figures (the area under the arc of a parabola, for example) and the behavior of irregularly shaped geometric bodies (a trapezoid, for example) in liquids. Among his more stimulating and complex treatises is "The Sand Reckoner," in which he not only describes a new and effective method of calculating the diameter of the Sun but also hypothesizes how many grains of sand would be necessary to fill the known cosmos. As several commentators have observed, the apparent absurdity of Archimedes' goal is, fundamentally, little different from modern scientists' attempts to estimate the total mass of the universe. In many respects, Archimedes' most interesting treatise is "The Method," wherein he sets out his understanding of theoretical mathematical and geometrical reasoning and its practical applications.

Archimedes was executed in 212 B.C.E., reportedly because his preoccupation with his studies—he was working out geometrical problems by drawing in the sand, the ancient equivalent of a blackboard—did not permit him to obey a Roman soldier's command. His grave marker, a sphere within a cylinder, illustrated one of his proudest accomplishments—calculating the ratio of 3:2 between a cylinder and sphere. That tomb was rediscovered, in a forgotten thicket at Syracuse, by the Roman orator and politician Cicero in 75 B.C.E.

Impact

Archimedes reputedly sent copies of his theoretical studies to the library in Alexandria, Egypt, but no master edition of his works was, it seems, compiled and available for distribution. Thus, Archimedes' treatises do not appear to have been widely known or studied until the late fifth century C.E. Isidore of Miletus then collected and studied several of Archimedes' treatises, especially those bearing on his own interests as an architect. (He was the master builder of the emperor Justinian's great church of Hagia Sophia in Constantinople.) Commentaries on some of Archimedes' treatises were composed by the Byzantine Greek scholar Eutocius about 510 C.E. A number of Archimedes' works were preserved in Arabic by the translations of the Islamic scholar Thābit ibn Qurra (836-901), to return to European consciousness by about 1180 through medieval Latin translations. All of the known works of Archimedes were published, in Greek with a Latin translation, at Basel in 1544 by Thomas Gechauff. Four decades later, Galileo invented a method for weighing metals in water and air.

—*Paul B. Harvey, Jr.*

Further Reading

Clagett, Marshall, ed. *Archimedes in the Middle Ages*. Madison: University of Wisconsin Press, 1964-1984. The first volume of this five-volume work contains an introduction to, history of, and translations of the texts of Archimedes that survived in Arabic.

Dijksterhuis, E. J. *Archimedes*. Princeton, N.J.: Princeton University Press, 1987. This classic work contains translations of Archimedes' surviving treatises, with readily understandable line drawings and mathematical formulas. Dijksterhuis provides one of the best critical summaries of his works. Wilbur R. Knorr's valuable essay provides an excellent guide to the more recent literature on Archimedes.

King, J. E. *Cicero: Tusculan Disputations*. Cambridge, Mass.: Harvard University Press, 1960. In these philosophical dialogues (written in 45 B.C.E.), the Roman orator and politician Cicero includes a description of Archimedes' planetarium and a dramatic report of his own discovery of Archimedes' tomb.

Landels, John Gray. *Engineering in the Ancient World*. Rev. ed. Berkeley: University of California Press, 2000. Chapter 8 provides an expert discussion of Archimedes' place in the development of Greek theoretical and practical mathematical and mechanical knowledge.

Plutarch. *Makers of Rome*. Translated by Ian Scott-Kilvert. Baltimore: Penguin Books, 1965. This translation of a selection from the Greek biographer Plutarch's *Bioi paralleloi* (c. 105-115; *Parallel Lives*, 1579) includes a full discussion of the Roman general Marcus Claudius Marcellus's role in the siege of Syracuse and Plutarch's somewhat credulous report of Archimedes' role in the defense of that city.

Toomer, G. J. "Archimedes." In *Oxford Classical Dictionary*, edited by Simon Hornblower and Antony Spawforth. 3d rev. ed. New York: Oxford University Press, 2003. A concise essay on Archimedes' life and contributions to mathematics and mechanics. This dictionary also supplies reliable entries for all of the other ancient personalities mentioned in the present essay. Excellent bibliographies and index.

Wescoat, Bonna Daix, ed. *Syracuse, the Fairest Greek City*. Rome: De Luca, 1989. This lavishly illustrated exhibition catalog includes a stimulating discussion by Jonathan Spingarn on "Archimedes' Imagination." Fine bibliographies for further exploration of the material culture and personalities of this ancient Greek city.

See also: Giovanni Branca; Ctesibius of Alexandria; Galileo; Al-Jazarī; Al-Khwārizmī; Joseph-Michel and Jacques-Étienne Montgolfier; Evangelista Torricelli.

Aristotle

Greek philosopher

Aristotle, history's first empirical scientist, introduced the scientific method, the foundations for scientific taxonomy, formal categorical logic, the first scientifically grounded monotheism, and many other metaphysical beliefs still undergirding modern thought in the twenty-first century.

Born: 384 B.C.E.; Stagirus, Chalcidice, Greece
Died: 322 B.C.E.; Chalcis, Euboea, Greece
Primary field: Biology
Primary inventions: Biological taxonomy; scientific method

Early Life

Little is known about the early life of Aristotle (EHR-ihs-taw-tuhl). The only sources available, other than a few mentions in ancient fragments, are a page of text from Dionysius of Halicarnassus, written presumably two hundred years after Aristotle's death, and Diogenes Laërtius's entry on him in his *Philosophoi biol* (lives of the philosophers), written in the third century C.E. It is reasonable to suppose that, given this dearth of biographical information, he was not considered an important person during his lifetime, but only came to be recognized as such long after his death.

In 384 B.C.E., Aristotle was born in the northern Hellenic polis of Stagirus, a colony of the polis of Chalcis. His mother, Phaestis, was a wealthy descendant of one of the original colonizers, and this gave the family excellent social standing. His father, Nicomachus, was the friend and physician of Amyntas II, king of Macedonia, father of Philip, and grandfather of Alexander the Great. This link to Macedonia would be a problem for Aristotle later in life.

His early education would have been in accordance with standard upper-class Hellenic practices, but probably also included training in medicine, because of his father's profession. This training did not last long, as his father died when Aristotle was still young, leaving him to be raised by his uncle Proxenus. In 367, at the age of seventeen, Aristotle left Stagirus and went to Athens to study with Plato at his Academy. Plato's "school" was a gathering place for the intellectually minded, regardless of their particular interests. Plato encouraged the study of the sciences, especially mathematics and astronomy. Aristotle remained at the Academy, studying, learning, and eventually lecturing, for twenty years, until Plato's death in 347.

Life's Work

Plato's Academy was the first real institution of higher education in history, although it did not much resemble the university as it is known today. It is important to understand that at this time there was really only one discipline: philosophy. People were doing mathematics and studying poetry, of course, but the very concept of a discipline had not developed yet. The disciplines as they are now known are all offshoots from philosophy, most of which would not separate from philosophy until after the Renaissance, around 1400 C.E. Because there were no other schools, the Academy was a beacon for all the greatest minds of the time, gathering all manner of intellectually curious and adept thinkers.

Aristotle's time at the Academy would have thus been spent studying and teaching not only what are now considered the traditional philosophical subjects of reasoning, metaphysics, epistemology, aesthetics, ethics, and political theory but also many subjects that are no longer considered to be philosophy: mathematics, rhetoric, poetics, and what passed for natural science at the time. Indeed, it was in rhetoric that Aristotle first distinguished himself, writing in about 360 B.C.E. a dialogue titled *Gryllus*, in which he attacked the views of a contemporary rhetorician, Isocrates. Curiously, a famous response to this work criticized Aristotle for the time he wasted in collecting proverbs—evidence that by this time he was already hard at work collecting things for analysis and categorization. The work known today as Aristotle's *Rhetoric*, *Technē rhetorikē*, was begun at this time, and he continued to refine those ideas for most of his life.

Upon Plato's death in 347, Aristotle left Athens. He traveled around the eastern Aegean and began collecting and studying zoological specimens in earnest. It is not known why he left Athens, but as Plato's star pupil, he would probably have expected to become head of the Academy. He did not. There are stories that tell of him leaving in bitterness and disgrace because of this. However, there are also stories relating a rising anti-Macedonian sentiment in the Athenians at this time, due to the encroachment of Macedonia into Greek territory. Not being an Athenian citizen—then or ever—Aristotle may have felt uncertain about his safety.

The work he did during this Aegean period was to be his most far-reaching, for this was the work that would form the foundations of the empirical natural sciences. For unknown reasons, Aristotle returned to his home in

Stagirus after a few years and remained there until 343, when Philip of Macedonia summoned him to Mieza to tutor his son Alexander. In 340, for perhaps political reasons again, Aristotle left Alexander and returned to Stagirus to continue his scientific and philosophic work. In 335, in a supposed bid to take over as head of the Academy, Aristotle returned to Athens. Unsuccessful in his attempt to head the Academy, he founded his own philosophic school: the Lyceum. He would remain in Athens until a year before his death in 322, when, again, renewed anti-Macedonian sentiment drove him to his family's home in Chalcis.

The work done in his last Athenian period was probably the most extensive of his life. At this time, he would have done his most important philosophical and systematic thinking, bringing new insights to his earlier scientific work and blending that with his developing logic. The results would shake the world and form the basis of all thought for more than a thousand years. No other thinker has had as much influence on Western civilization and thought as Aristotle. Aristotle is the only person in history to have founded two new sciences from the cauldron of philosophy: logic and biology. In addition, in order to make biology a viable science, he had to develop the idea of what a science should be. Without Aristotle, the natural sciences would not have the form they do now.

Aristotle's works deserve a note here. What is now considered to be Aristotle's corpus is only a fraction of his actual output. Most of his work has been lost, and all of his writings designed for the consumption of others is gone. What remains are simply notes developed for his lecturing at the Lyceum. It cannot be said when the ideas in these notes were first formed, when the lecture notes were written, or how extensively or often (if at all) they were revised. The works that remain are now believed to have been originally published in about 60 B.C.E. by Andronicus of Rhodes, the last head of the Lyceum. The selection, ordering, and editing were certainly at his own hand, and not that of the long-dead Aristotle.

Aristotle. (Library of Congress)

Impact

It is not an exaggeration to say that there has never been an individual as influential on human civilization as Aristotle. To detail the impact of his thought would be to detail the history of European thought since his time. By the Renaissance, Aristotle's ideas had been considered received truth for some time; in Europe, there was no other authority, other than the Church, that received such unquestioning acceptance. The ideas and terminology used by him and his students at the Lyceum would become the framework for all further philosophic and scientific work.

The very idea of a scientific method is thoroughly Aristotelian. Before his work, science as it is known today did not exist. No one was collecting empirical data and reasoning about it. He introduced the idea that data is primary and theory must come afterward and developed the framework for theorizing and categorizing data. The biological work he did in the fourth century B.C.E. was to remain precisely how biology was conceived up until the nineteenth century C.E.

Aristotle's Biological Taxonomy

Aristotle devised and began to develop the first biological taxonomy during a tour of the eastern Aegean in 347 B.C.E. While taxonomies of other things were quite common at the time, no one had yet attempted to classify living things in any systematic way. Aristotle's taxonomy was not merely a means of organizing knowledge of the animal kingdom but was actually the attempt to describe the universe as it really is; in other words, his taxonomy was a description of the "natural" places of everything in the universe.

The biological level of this taxonomy was divided into two parts: animals and plants. Of these two parts, Aristotle focused only on animals. The current botanical taxonomy actually originated in the work of Theophrastus, Aristotle's best student and successor, who worked, of course, from Aristotle's example and within his metaphysical system.

Aristotle's divisions of genera and species were based on both his metaphysical schema of the universe and observation. Grouping animals based on their habitats and bodily structures, Aristotle concluded there were two basic types of animal: those with (red) blood, and those without. These classifications line up fairly well with current categories of vertebrates and invertebrates. Of the blooded animals, there were five kinds: land mammals, birds, reptiles/amphibians, fish, and cetaceans (dolphins, porpoises, whales). Those that had no blood were divided as such: arthropods (insects and spiders), crustaceans, shellfish, soft animals such as octopuses and squid, and then plantlike animals such as corals and jellyfish.

Aristotle's biological taxonomy was fairly quickly adopted by everybody with any interest, partly because it was the only one in existence and partly because it was so detailed. Using habitat and body structure to classify these animals also meant that he had gathered much information on their habits, anatomy, reproduction, life cycles, sustenance gathering and feeding, rearing of young, and so on. With Thomas Aquinas in the thirteenth century C.E. bringing Aristotle's metaphysical hierarchy into the Roman Catholic Church, Aristotle's science became the official worldview of the Church, and thus of Western culture. Because of this adoption by the Church, Aristotle's taxonomy was immune to rejection or revision for hundreds of years—until the Church's power was weakened enough for science as it is now known to develop.

After the Renaissance was made possible by the decline in the Church's power, numerous biologists began expanding on Aristotle's taxonomy, but it was not until Carolus Linnaeus (1707-1778) began to distinguish plants by their sexual parts that the taxonomic system used today began to take its more familiar shape. The age of exploration brought knowledge of previously unknown organisms that had to be classified. With this influx of data and the freedom to study it, biological taxonomy finally came into its own, but one can still see the influence of these men in the present taxonomic use of Aristotle's Greek and Linnaeus's Latin.

Philosophically, Aristotle was even more influential. His development of categorical logic as a tool for scientific reasoning and a method of scientific taxonomy worked so well that it was thought complete until the nineteenth century C.E. He introduced the very ideas of genus and species, matter and form, essence and accident, energy and potentiality, final causes, virtue ethics, and the first scientifically justified monotheism. Without these ideas, the Church would not have developed as it did, nor would have science or philosophy or Western culture.

—*Leslie C. Miller*

Further Reading

Aristotle. *The Complete Works of Aristotle: The Revised Oxford Translation*. Edited by Jonathan Barnes. Princeton, N.J.: Princeton University Press, 1984. Revised edition of the standard Oxford translation published between the years 1912 and 1954. Scholarship since the publication of the original translations has been taken into account in some new editorial work. Additionally, this edition contains several new translations as well as more fragments than the original Oxford edition.

Barnes, Jonathan. *Aristotle: A Very Short Introduction*. New York: Oxford University Press, 2000. A pleasant, concise, and surprisingly complete biography of the elusive Aristotle. The author is perhaps the most notable Aristotelian scholar of the twenty-first century and has a justifiable reputation as a fine writer as well, as evidenced by the prose in this volume.

_______, ed. *The Cambridge Companion to Aristotle*. New York: Cambridge University Press, 1995. Cambridge Companions are notoriously good, and this one is no exception. Leading Aristotle scholars contribute chapters on his logic, science, philosophy of science, ethics, metaphysics, psychology, political philosophy, rhetoric, and poetics. Also contains an extensive and relevant bibliography of the important secondary works on Aristotle.

Ross, W. D. *Aristotle*. 6th ed. New York: Routledge, 1995. One of the seminal works on Aristotle. Very comprehensive, including chapters on his life, logic, metaphysics, physics, rhetoric, political thought, ethics, his work in biology and psychology, as well as a bibliography that gets updated with each new edition.

Yu, Jiyuan. *The Structure of Being in Aristotle's Metaphysics*. New York: Springer, 2003. One of the most detailed examinations of Being in Aristotle to date. This work looks closely at a number of troublesome concepts in Aristotle's thought: essence, teleology, substance, matter and form, actuality and potentiality, as well as the Prime Mover (the concept in his thought that would become the Christian God of the Catholic Church).

See also: Roger Bacon; Giovanni Branca; Ctesibius of Alexandria; Galileo; Otto von Guericke; Zacharias Janssen; Antoni van Leeuwenhoek; Sir Isaac Newton; Ptolemy.

Sir Richard Arkwright

British manufacturer

Arkwright played a crucial role in the Industrial Revolution by devising, manufacturing, and exploiting a device that mechanized one of the oldest traditional crafts, spinning yarn.

Born: December 23, 1732; Preston, Lancashire, England
Died: August 3, 1792; Cromford, Derbyshire, England
Primary field: Manufacturing
Primary invention: Spinning frame

Early Life

Richard Arkwright was the sixth of seven surviving children of Thomas Arkwright (1691-1753) and Ellen Hodgkinson (1693-1778). The family was poor and Arkwright received little formal education, but two of his elder sisters attended Blue Coat School and passed on what they learned to their younger siblings. In his early teens, he was apprenticed to a barber in the nearby town of Kirkham, but moved to Bolton-le-Moors in 1750, initially to work for the wig maker Edward Pollit, and then, briefly for Pollit's widow. By 1755, he had set up a barber's stall in a passage leading to an inn, shaving chins for a penny. On March 31 of that year, he married Patience Holt, the daughter of a schoolmaster, and promptly borrowed £60 from her father to expand his business. The couple's only child, also named Richard, was born on December 19, but when Patience died on October 6 in the following year she was buried with her mother under her maiden name.

On March 21, 1761, Arkwright married Margaret Biggins of Pennington, and repaid the debt he owed his first wife's father with the bulk of an inheritance she had received; he invested the rest in an inn, the Black Boy, whose publican he became. The business soon failed, and he returned to wig making, also dabbling—as most nineteenth century barbers did—in bleeding and tooth extraction. He began buying hair on a large scale, ostensibly making use of a secret dyeing technique in making his wigs. Margaret bore him three children, one of which—Susanna, born December 20, 1761—survived into adulthood.

Life's Work

Arkwright's invention of the spinning frame was understandably shrouded in secrecy and inevitably embroiled in controversy. The search for a means of mechanizing the process had been urgent for some time, but an earlier machine patented by Lewis Paul and John Wyatt in 1738 had proved impracticable. Thomas Highs of Leigh subsequently claimed to have devised the innovations that he carelessly confided to Arkwright in conversation, but what is certain is that in 1767 Arkwright formed an association with a clockmaker named John Kay, who made him a model of a spinning machine, which the two of them began to hawk around.

After failing to find backers in Manchester and Preston, Arkwright and Kay took two of their relatives—the former publican John Smalley and the merchant David Thornley—into their partnership in order to build and exploit a full-scale machine in Nottingham. They petitioned for a patent on June 8, 1878, but it was not granted until July 3, 1769, perhaps because they had trouble scraping together the money to pay the fee. Thornley had to sell part of his share to Smalley when his own capital ran out, and a new fifth share in the association was taken by Samuel Need and Jedediah Strutt, who provided the finances necessary to construct a horse-drawn mill, to be managed by Arkwright and Thornley.

The Nottingham mill did not start production until Christmas, 1772, by which time the partners had already commissioned the construction of a new mill at Cromford in Derbyshire, driven by waterpower. The original intention had been to spin yarn for stockings—Strutt was already involved in that trade—but the yarn produced by Arkwright's machine was both thin enough and strong enough to serve as the warp on a loom, so the Cromford mill began to produce calico with an efficiency that astonished its owners and their rivals. Arkwright set up his headquarters there and began to expand his operation. Strutt joined forces with other entrepreneurs to lobby Parliament to reduce excise duties on British cotton goods; when they were successful, the Cromford mill's profits increased considerably, and the partners set out to dominate the trade, applying for further patents that would establish a virtual monopoly. The result of these moves was an intense competition, which was also reflected within the partnership as Arkwright attempted to squeeze out his associates.

Arkwright's legal wrangles came to a head in July, 1781, when he sued nine other manufacturers for breaching his patents. It was during this period that Highs came forward to lay charges of theft against Arkwright—charges that were never substantiated but probably contributed to the eventual result of the conflict, which was the cancellation of Arkwright's patents in 1785. By that time, however, most of Arkwright's original partners were dead and he was exceedingly rich, owing to the huge profits he had made during the previous decade. The cancellation of the patents initiated a free-for-all that brought about a boom in the cotton industry throughout the north of England.

Arkwright appears to have been just as desperate to make social progress as economic progress, although he labored under the handicap of a personality that did not allow him to make friends easily and often alienated those he had. Jedediah Strutt introduced him to Erasmus Darwin, enabling him briefly to associate himself with Darwin's prestigious Lunar Society—James Watt, another prominent member of the group and the inventor of the steam engine, was also a tireless lobbyist for the protection of patents—but Arkwright soon quarreled violently with Darwin, as he seemed to have done with many of his new acquaintances. He was, of course, deeply resented by the landed gentry of Derbyshire, who mocked him relentlessly as an upstart. He bought Willersley Manor, near Cromford, in 1782, and bought the manor of Cromford itself in 1789.

Arkwright also bought a town house in London in 1789 but actually lived for most of his later life in Rock House, situated on a hill overlooking his Cromford mills, while he commissioned and supervised the construction of a grandiose stately home he named Willersley Castle. He did not live long enough to make much use of it, dying in the year of its completion, 1792, but it accommodated his son and, in their turn, his further descendants, until 1925. In the meantime, he was knighted in 1786 and became high sheriff of Derbyshire in 1787. In 1790, he introduced the first steam engine into his works at Nottingham, thus completing the foundations of the revolution in textile production that changed the face of England in the early nineteenth century.

The Spinning Frame

The earlier spinning machine credited to Lewis Paul and John Wyatt substituted two mechanically rotated rollers for the wheel and distaff that had been used in spinning since time immemorial—to the extent that a famous English traditional rhyme begins "When Adam delved and Eve span." The Paul-Wyatt machine did not work very well, because the machine could not compensate, as a hand spinner instinctively did with skillful gestures, for two problems that inevitably arose as the process went on: the increasing diameter of the accumulated thread on the "distaff roller" and the tendency of the thread to become twisted in the drawing space.

Sir Richard Arkwright's machine solved both these problems, the first by moving the distaff roller so that the surface of the accumulating thread maintained a constant distance from the "wheel roller," and the second by weighting the upper roller so as to prevent the instabilities that caused twisting. These were minor adjustments, involving no particular technical complexities, but they were crucial to the success of the machine, in the sense that it could work for long periods without having to be stopped to correct problems. The quality of the yarn it produced was remarkably consistent—more consistent, in fact, than the thread produced by all but the most expert hand spinners—and that made it ideal for use as warp on a loom, enabling mechanized looms to produce not only cloth at a far greater speed than hand looms could produce but also cloth of a more even texture and quality. Such efficiency and consistency of manufacture was the essence of competent mass production, and Arkwright's contribution to that evolution was highly significant in historical terms.

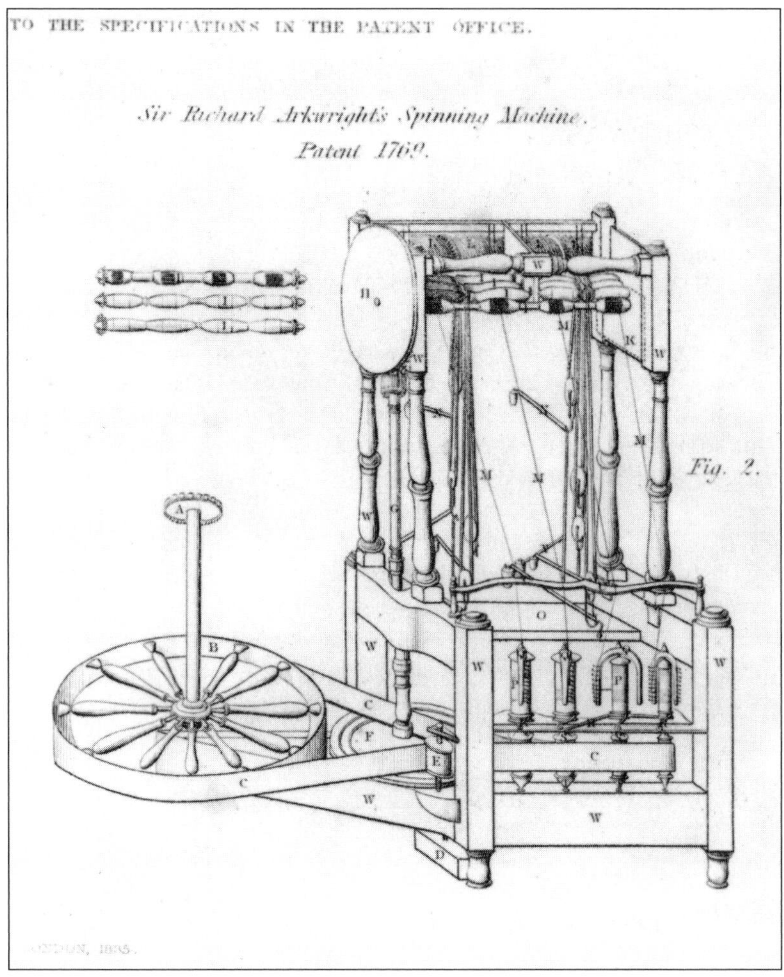

Sir Richard Arkwright's spinning frame. (Library of Congress)

Impact

Arkwright was the archetypal "self-made man" and became an important exemplar to future inventors and businessmen for that reason. Although he suffered all through his life from asthma, he insisted on working from 5:00 A.M. to 9:00 P.M. every day, and his taciturnity became as legendary as his industry. A devotee of retrospective psychology might be tempted to diagnose him as a victim of Asperger's syndrome, but the Victorian writers who appointed him a pioneering hero of the Industrial Revolution approved wholeheartedly of his dour determination and obsessive ruthlessness, and would have considered his combination of vaulting social ambition and churlish unsociability quite normal.

If Arkwright became a hero to the industrialists who followed him, he also became a villain in the eyes of subscribers to the "rage against the machine" carried forward by active Luddites and the Romantic writers who tended to equate industrialization with spoliation. One of his mills was said to have been demolished by rioters, while police and military forces looked on sympathetically, although the reports might have been exaggerated.

Arkwright's spinning frame, often known as a water frame because of its particular application at Cromford, was not the only one to be invented at the time—James Hargreaves's so-called spinning jenny was virtually contemporary. If Highs can be believed, Arkwright might not actually have originated the idea of his own machine, but he was the determined opportunist who carried that machine all the way through the developmental process to full-scale industrial production, joining forces with Jedediah Strutt along the way to change the political-economical environment so as to allow that production to flourish.

Arkwright was, in essence, the man who successfully reinvented the wheel—spinning being, for most of its history, as significant an application of the wheel as wheeled transport, whose utility was limited until roads improved sufficiently to accommodate such vehicles.

—*Brian Stableford*

Further Reading

Bell, David. *Derbyshire Heroes*. Newbury, Berkshire, England: Countryside Books, 2004. Arkwright is here considered in the company of other highly influential figures in the history of his adopted county; the text is part of a notable series of local-interest books.

Fitton, R. S. *The Arkwrights: Spinners of Fortune*. Manchester, England: Manchester University Press, 1990. A careful account of the contribution made by the first Richard Arkwright and his descendants to the textile revolution, focusing primarily on the economic aspects of their enterprise.

Hills, Richard Leslie. *Richard Arkwright and Cotton Spinning*. Broomall, Pa.: Main Line, 1980. A succinct account of Arkwright's technical achievement and its historical significance, skillfully tailored for the edification and instruction of general readers.

Witzel, Morgan. *Fifty Key Figures in Management*. New York: Taylor & Francis, 2003. A collection of exemplary accounts of ingenious entrepreneurialism, juxtaposing Arkwright and other makers of the Industrial Revolution with modern businessmen and making an interesting study in comparison and contrast.

See also: Edmund Cartwright; James Hargreaves; John Kay; Sakichi Toyoda.

Edwin H. Armstrong

American electrical engineer

Armstrong developed a number of key inventions in radio broadcasting, including the superheterodyne circuit, the regenerative circuit, and frequency modulation.

Born: December 18, 1890; New York, New York
Died: January 31, 1954; New York, New York
Also known as: Edwin Howard Armstrong (full name)
Primary fields: Communications; electronics and electrical engineering
Primary inventions: Frequency modulation (FM); regenerative circuit; superheterodyne circuit

Early Life

Edwin Howard Armstrong (AHRM-strahng) was a New York City boy born and bred. His father, John Armstrong, was one of the senior executives of the American branch of Oxford University Press. This position required an annual visit to London to confer with his superiors in the home office, and he would take the opportunity to acquire books that simply were not available in the United States at the time. As a result, young Edwin was exposed to a wide variety of books, including *The Boy's Book of Inventions* (1899), which sparked his fascination with gadgetry.

At the age of seven, Armstrong was stricken with Sydenham chorea (St. Vitus's dance), a movement disorder associated with rheumatic fever in which the person's muscles twitch and jerk uncontrollably. At the time, doctors believed that the disorder was psychological in origin, a nervous response to a sudden fright or other disturbance of the emotional equilibrium. The treatment was to keep the child quiet and avoid exposure to excitement or stimulation, which resulted in his being kept at home and tutored in his studies by a maternal great-aunt for two years. During this time, the family relocated to the suburbs in hopes of finding a more healthful environment for the boy.

Suburbia also proved an environment in which Armstrong could indulge his fascination with exploration more widely than was possible in the city. He developed a fondness for heights, climbing the steep escarpments of the Palisades. As a teenager, he would take his toolbox to a nearby road and wait for an automobile to break down so he could have the challenge of fixing it. He also became increasingly fascinated with radio, and after acquiring the necessary equipment he began making amateur transmissions to a number of friends in the area. He formed a friendship with inventor Charles Underhill and regularly visited to pick the man's brain.

In 1909, Armstrong entered Columbia University's electrical engineering program, commuting from home each day on a bright red motorcycle, a high school graduation present. This arrangement permitted him to indulge his growing fascination with speed and to continue his experiments in his home radio laboratory. His mastery of the subject of radio quickly surpassed that of many of the instructors, and he once severely annoyed a visiting professor from Cornell University by publicly challenging misinformation in a lecture.

Life's Work

In 1912, while still a student at Columbia, Armstrong was studying some of the peculiarities of the Audion, or triode vacuum tube, invented by Lee De Forest. At the time, its use as an amplifier was still so tricky that many wireless telegraph operators used a crystal detector (a sort of crude point-contact transistor) to pick up and amplify radio waves. When Armstrong realized that the Audion was oscillating in a steady rhythm, he had the insight that a person might be able to feed the current from the plate back through the grid, further amplifying it with each iteration. However, the exact method of doing this eluded him for some time, until he was vacationing in the Green Mountains of Vermont and had the key insight. He hurried home and set to work in his laboratory. On September 22, he made a workable regenerative circuit.

The principle of regeneration transformed the triode from a rather iffy competitor to a reliable powerhouse. Regeneration rapidly became a mainstay of every electronic circuit that required amplification, from radios to long-distance telephone lines to stereos and radar. Even after the transistor dislodged the vacuum tube from pride of place, the regenerative circuit continued to hold its own as a key element of electronic devices and was one of the earliest to be laid out as an integrated circuit, or microchip.

Although Armstrong's first invention would easily have secured his fame, his restless mind would not be satisfied with past achievements. He relentlessly explored all the features of the regenerative circuit and discovered that if one tuned it a particular way, it could become not only a receiver and detector of radio waves but also a transmitter. Moreover, it could produce a continuous carrier wave suitable for voice transmissions, a feat that previously had required a large alternator that rotated at extremely high speeds.

However, because Armstrong was still a student at the time, his father saw no reason to spend the $150 to register a patent on his ideas. In his father's eyes, the patent could wait until his son had finished his education. This parsimony would be the root of a lifetime of grief for Armstrong because it deprived him of the priority claim on his invention that would have spared him dozens of lawsuits against De Forest and others in the radio industry. When Armstrong graduated and applied for his patent, he further compounded the error of delay by having the patent written in a restrictive form rather than covering as many applications of his ideas as possible, leaving ample room for others to encroach upon his work without actually infringing, and thus being able to profit without needing to pay license fees to him.

Edwin H. Armstrong. (Smithsonian Institution)

When the United States entered World War I in 1917, Armstrong joined the U.S. Army Signal Corps, in which he tested the early radios used in airplanes. Because Germany was rumored to be using very high-frequency radio transmissions to evade detection by Allied signal intelligence, Armstrong worked on a technique to detect and decode these signals by using a second frequency to create a third frequency within the range of human hearing. This superheterodyne circuit would subsequently become the basis of precision radio tuning. While early radios had to be tuned by a specialist, a superheterodyne radio needed only three knobs, making it possible for ordinary people to operate them and thus making way for the golden age of radio.

Armstrong's next great breakthrough would come in the 1930's, when he developed a workable system of frequency modulation, or FM. However, when he presented the technique to the Radio Corporation of America (RCA), the company did nothing. In fact, RCA executive director David Sarnoff was planning to use the technique for the sound channel of television, which was in development at the time, but he did not want to make instantly obsolete the entire user base of amplitude modulation (AM) radios. Frustrated, Armstrong then created his own experimental FM station, and then an entire network of FM stations, the Yankee Network.

During World War II, Armstrong worked on various projects for the military, in particular techniques for allowing radars to distinguish between friendly and enemy aircraft based on their echo return patterns. After the war was concluded, he decided to take to task several companies, including RCA, for their use of his FM patents without paying royalties. RCA in particular battled him relentlessly, since it was under Sarnoff that the company bought patents outright rather than pay royalties on them.

As Armstrong's financial resources dwindled, his nerves frayed and finally gave way altogether. On January 31, 1954, he penned a letter to his wife, put on his coat and hat, and opened the window of his thirteenth-floor New York apartment and stepped out to his death. Although Sarnoff would always claim that he meant his old

Frequency Modulation

It was the desire to get rid of the annoying crackle of radio static that led Edwin H. Armstrong to invent frequency modulation, commonly abbreviated as FM. Armstrong's work began when David Sarnoff of Radio Corporation of America (RCA) expressed a desire for a device that would eliminate the static that plagued radio broadcasts. This static came from random electrical discharges in nature, mostly lightning but to a lesser degree sunspots and other solar phenomena.

Sarnoff had apparently imagined a sort of filter, but Armstrong envisioned a completely new approach to radio broadcasting. Ever since Reginald Aubrey Fessenden made his first voice broadcast in 1901, radiotelephony had imposed the information of the signal onto the amplitude of the carrier wave. However, Armstrong realized that if he could find a way to impose the information on the frequency of the waves, he could create a signal that would not be affected by this constant random electrical noise.

Creating a workable system of FM radio was not easy. Mathematician John R. Carson had claimed that radio theory proved it impossible to successfully impose information on the frequency of a carrier wave. However, Armstrong recalled that John Ambrose Fleming, technical adviser to Guglielmo Marconi, had claimed that the only way to operate a radio was by generating blasts of static to represent the dots and dashes of Morse code. The supposed impossibility of FM only served to spur Armstrong's efforts, until he realized that the key to a workable FM system lay in increasing the bandwidth of the signal far beyond that occupied by an AM station, thus giving the signal space to be imposed upon the frequency.

On December 26, 1933, Armstrong registered a patent on FM written in the broadest possible language. The following year, he approached Sarnoff with a finished device, but Sarnoff chose not to adopt it at the time. Although the obvious reason for his reluctance was that he wished to avoid instantly rendering obsolete an entire user base of amplitude modulation (AM) radios, Sarnoff in fact planned to use FM for the audio track for television then in development.

During Armstrong's lifetime, FM saw minimal commercial development. His own Yankee Network met with continual bureaucratic roadblocks from the Federal Communications Commission (FCC), the final one being a shift in the portion of the radio spectrum allotted to FM radio broadcasts. However, in the decades that followed, FM would become of increasing importance as high-fidelity radio receivers led to a demand for clear transmission of complex musical forms. By the late 1970's, almost all consumer radios had both AM and FM band capability, and by the end of the 1980's music stations were increasingly moving to FM, leaving AM entirely for news and talk stations. One of the last holdouts was WLS of Chicago, which in 1989 played its last rock record and became entirely a talk station.

friend no ill will, there was evidence that he felt somewhat uneasy about his own contribution to Armstrong's state of mind. Armstrong's widow subsequently won all the patent infringement suits, including the one with RCA, on behalf of her husband's estate.

Impact

By making the radio receiver into an appliance that anyone could use, Edwin Armstrong transformed radio into an entertainment medium. However, the lawsuits he launched first against Lee De Forest and then against David Sarnoff's company left a cloud of acrimony over his legacy.

—Leigh Husband Kimmel

Further Reading

Davis, L. J. *Fleet Fire: Thomas Edison and the Pioneers of the Electric Revolution*. New York: Arcade, 2003. A history of the early days of electricity, culminating in the invention of radio.

Leinwoll, Stanley. *From Spark to Satellite: A History of Radio Communication*. New York: Charles Scribner's Sons, 1979. An overview of the history of radio, placing Armstrong's work in context.

Lewis, Tom. *Empire of the Air: The Men Who Made Radio*. New York: Edward Burlingame Books, 1991. Focuses on the lives and battles of both Armstrong and Lee De Forest.

Lyons, Eugene. *David Sarnoff*. New York: Harper & Row, 1966. A biography of the longtime head of RCA, although it does somewhat whitewash Sarnoff's role in the battle over FM that led to Armstrong's suicide.

Sobel, Robert. *RCA*. New York: Stein & Day, 1986. Corporate history of RCA from its beginnings to the mid-1980's, including the period of Armstrong's key discoveries.

See also: Ernst Alexanderson; Karl Ferdinand Braun; Lee De Forest; Reginald Aubrey Fessenden; Guglielmo Marconi.

ARTHUR JAMES ARNOT

Australian electrical engineer

Arnot is credited with the invention of the electric drill. His invention was quickly modified by others, who built both large industrial machines and small hand tools for the average handyperson.

Born: August 26, 1865; Hamilton, Scotland
Died: October 15, 1946; Castle Hill, New South Wales, Australia
Primary fields: Electronics and electrical engineering; mechanical engineering
Primary invention: Electric drill

EARLY LIFE

Arthur James Arnot was born in Hamilton, Scotland, on August 26, 1865. His mother was Elizabeth Helen Macdonald Arnot, and his father was William Arnot, a commercial agent. Arthur attended Hutchisontown Grammar School and Haldane Academy in Glasgow, and in 1881 he began studies at the West of Scotland Technical College in Glasgow. He moved to London to continue his studies part-time while working for an electrical engineering company. In 1885, he became an assistant engineer at the Grosvenor Gallery power station, a privately owned generating station established by Sir Coutts Lindsay to provide electricity to light an art exhibit. The station was run by the engineer Sebastian Ziani de Ferranti, himself only twenty-three years old at the time Arnot was hired. Ferranti, a prolific inventor, made great improvements to the station's ability to transmit high-voltage power. By 1886, he had made the station the largest and most efficient supplier of public electricity in England. Working with Ferranti on an expanding project gave Arnot an unparalleled chance to experiment and innovate, and to learn the new business of producing and supplying electricity.

Arnot left the United Kingdom for Australia in 1889, under a two-year contract to build a large alternating-current-generating plant for the newly formed Union Electric Company in Melbourne, a city in the state of Victoria. He spent nearly the rest of his career and life in Australia.

LIFE'S WORK

Arnot designed and oversaw the building and management of Melbourne's Spencer Street Power Station, a coal-fired station that provided power for the city and sold surplus power to other municipal distributors. In March, 1891, the city council named Arnot Melbourne's first electrical engineer. He held the post until 1901, making occasional extended trips to England and the United States to keep up with new innovations in electrical engineering. In August, 1891, Arnot married Cornelia Ann, the daughter of one of the city councilors. At this time, the main use of municipal electricity was for lighting (electrical appliances and machines had not yet been developed). In 1891-1892, Arnot installed an array of electric streetlights in the city, replacing the gaslights that had been installed in the 1850's. He modeled his "series arc and incandescent system" on the system already in use in London and the United States. Soon, the central business district of Melbourne was illuminated with electric lights from a central source—a first in Australia.

Electricity generation at the end of the nineteenth century was a dangerous and largely unregulated enterprise, and many entrepreneurs, with varying degrees of expertise, set up their own generating stations and sold power to their neighbors. In 1896, Arnot drafted an Electric Light and Power Act that was passed by the parliament of the state of Victoria. Under the terms of this act, people could generate power for their own use but could not supply to others without a license.

Arnot had a long and distinguished career as an engineer in Melbourne, but his most lasting achievement as an inventor came during his first year in Australia. While he was engaged in the construction of the Union Electric Company's electrical plant, he sought a better way to dig coal and to drill foundation holes in rock. On August 20, 1889, he along with mining engineer William Blanch Brain and Frank Baker patented the world's first electric drill, which they called "an improved electrical rock-drill, coal-digger, or earth-cutter." Although the patent clearly names all three men (in fact, Brain's name appears first), Arnot is usually given sole credit for the invention. Arnot also worked on refinements to the electric motor that powered his drill, and in 1891 he was granted a patent for an improved alternating-current (AC) motor. Unlike the small hand drills common in the twenty-first century, Arnot's drill was a large industrial machine.

Known as a hardworking and creative man, Arnot was profiled as one of several "Coming Men" in a series of articles in the Australian science journal *Table Talk* in 1893. In 1899, he was elected a member of the Institution of Electrical Engineers in London and to the presidency of both the Victorian Institute of Electrical Engineers and the Electrical Association of New South Wales. During his time as Melbourne's electrical engineer, it seemed that direct current (DC) was superior to alternating current, and Arnot oversaw a substantial expansion of the DC grid during his tenure. With the later development of improved AC motors, however, it became apparent that alternating current was preferable, and a large amount of money and resources were spent in rewiring. In 1899, Arnot traveled to England and the United States to gather more opinions in the contentious battle between DC and AC.

In 1901, Arnot left Melbourne for Sydney to take the position of Australasian manager for Babcock and Wilcox, a large American firm that designed, engineered, built, and managed large steam-powered electrical generating stations. Babcock and Wilcox had provided some of the boilers for the Spencer Street Power Station. In this position, Arnot helped smaller cities and private power companies throughout Australasia build and manage electrical power plants using Babcock and Wilcox designs and equipment.

On September 29, 1904, Arnot's son Frederick Latham was born. Frederick went on to become a university lecturer in natural philosophy and later physics. Arnot joined the city council while in Sydney, and he was implicated in a corruption scandal involving the council's contract for a steam-raising plant. It was charged that he had paid a bribe to have his company's boilers chosen for the project. He was formally censured by Judge John Musgrave Harvey in 1928. Arnot retired from Babcock and Wilcox the next year.

During his years in Sydney, Arnot also participated in the military. He was commissioned a lieutenant in the Submarine Mining Company, Victorian Engineers, in 1894, when he was twenty-nine. The Victorian Engineers was part of a volunteer force defending the colony of Victoria. (The Commonwealth of Australia would not be established until 1901.) The Submarine Mining Company set explosives on the ocean floor and triggered them from shore. In 1915, near the beginning of World War I, Arnot joined the Australian Engineers, Australian Military Forces. At age fifty, he was unable to join his countrymen fighting with the Allies at the western front, but he could lend his expertise as an engineer. In 1916, he took command of the Sydney field companies and reinforcement camps. He retired from the military in 1925 with the rank of major.

Arnot lived quietly after his retirement from Babcock and Wilcox. He moved to Castle Hill in New South Wales, where he died on October 15, 1946.

The Electric Drill

Following the development of practical electric motors in the 1870's and 1880's, inventors and engineers rushed to find ways to put the motors to use. Electricity promised to make cumbersome tasks easier, and by the end of the nineteenth century electric motors were powering fans, carpet sweepers, vehicles, and industrial machinery. Because an electric motor converts electrical energy to mechanical energy, it could perform repetitive, laborious work such as drilling into rock.

Drills have been used by humans for thousands of years, dating back to the ancient Egyptian and Harappan civilizations (in present-day India and Pakistan). The earliest drills were bow drills, consisting of two sticks and a length of cord. By making a simple bow from one stick and the cord, and wrapping that cord around the other stick, the operator could rotate the second stick back and forth quickly. This tool could be used to make holes in soft materials or to ignite fires. Centuries of development led to larger machines and harder bits, but drilling—especially in rock—still took a great deal of time and labor. In the middle of the nineteenth century, drilling underground was done by hitting a steel rod with a sledgehammer. Simon Ingersoll invented a percussion drill that both pounded and rotated the steel rod, making it move forward quickly, and in 1870 he invented the steam-powered drill. The new drill was a great advancement, but the steam made it dangerous to operate. When Arthur James Arnot married the drill and the electric motor in 1889, he solved one of the great challenges facing an industrial world hungry for coal to power new machines.

The potential uses for the electric drill were immediately apparent, and other engineers rushed to make improvements. In 1895, six years after Arnot's drill was patented, brothers Wilhelm and Carl Fein of Stuttgart, Germany, took out a patent on a drill that could be held in the hand. They continued to work on ways to make the drill more portable, eventually making some components from aluminum to reduce the weight. In 1917, a young American company called Black and Decker patented a pistol grip and trigger switch for a handheld electric drill, and the success of its drill enabled the company to grow into a large international conglomerate. In 1929, Black and Decker opened a subsidiary in Sydney, and by 1946, the year of Arnot's death, the company was one of the largest industrial firms in Australia, producing power tools for home and industrial uses. There is no record of how Arnot responded to the tremendous success of the electric drill he had invented.

Impact

As an engineer, Arnot played an important role in the electrification of Australia. It is one thing to power a light bulb in a laboratory, and quite another to light an entire city. Arnot's design for the Spencer Street Power Station put Melbourne on the electrical map, and Arnot successfully managed the plant for more than a decade in which understanding of electricity and of electrical engineering grew at a rapid pace. The story of the early years of the power station includes controversies over the new field of electrification: the uses of AC and DC power, the struggles between municipal and private companies, the movement toward the standardization of amperes transmitted, and the rush to obtain coal for steam generation.

Arnot left his mark as an inventor. His need for a large and steady supply of coal for his Spencer Street Power Station led him and his colleagues Brain and Baker to use one of the new electric motors to power a drill to dig through rock more quickly than other methods. They could not have foreseen that this large industrial machine would become a common tool within forty years. From the tiny drills used in dentistry, to small handheld drills in the toolboxes of carpenters and homeowners, to large electric rock drills used in mining, the electric drill has played an important role in making work easier in the age of technology.

—*Cynthia A. Bily*

Further Reading

Creswell, Toby, and Samantha Trenoweth. *One Thousand One Australians You Should Know*. North Melbourne: Pluto Press Australia, 2006. Brief illustrated biographies of important Australians, including Arnot—in "Science, Invention, and Ideas."

Nagyszalanczy, Sandor. *Power Tools: An Electrifying Celebration and Grounded Guide*. Newtown, Conn.: Taunton Press, 2001. This illustrated guide is intended for consumers. Its section on "Drills and Drivers" includes a brief history, an exploded diagram showing how the modern electric hand drill works, and an analysis of different drills and their uses.

Smil, Vaclav. *Creating the Twentieth Century: Technical Innovations of 1867-1914 and Their Lasting Impact*. New York: Oxford University Press, 2005. An interdisciplinary history of innovation, including the generation and distribution of electricity.

See also: Thomas Alva Edison; William Sturgeon.

John Vincent Atanasoff

American mathematician and physicist

Atanasoff played a key role in the development of the electronic computer. He contributed to the computer revolution by proving that electronic computation was feasible and by incorporating some of the features basic to modern computers.

Born: October 4, 1903; Hamilton, New York
Died: June 15, 1995; Monrovia, Maryland
Also known as: Dzhon Vinsent Atanasov (birth name)
Primary fields: Computer science; mathematics; physics
Primary invention: Atanasoff-Berry Computer

Early Life

John Vincent Atanasoff (uh-ta-NUH-sahf) was born in Hamilton, New York, in 1903, to Iva Purdy and Ivan Atanasov, an electrical engineer. When his father had immigrated to the United States from Bulgaria, immigration officials changed his name to John Atanasoff. The family moved to central Florida when John Vincent was eight. He was the oldest of nine children.

Both John's father and mother encouraged him when his mathematical talents appeared. His father gave him a slide rule when he was about nine years old and showed him how to use it. Between the instruction book for the slide rule and a college algebra textbook, Atanasoff learned how to use the slide rule to perform complicated mathematics, including logarithms. His mother gave him a book that discussed number systems in different bases.

By the time Atanasoff reached high school, he knew that he wanted to be a theoretical physicist. However, the University of Florida did not offer a degree in that field, so he majored in electrical engineering. He graduated in 1925 and went on to earn a master's degree from Iowa State College (now Iowa State University) in 1926. The University of Wisconsin awarded him a Ph.D. in theoretical physics in 1930. Atanasoff returned to Iowa State with a faculty appointment in the Mathematics and later the Physics departments.

Life's Work

As a theoretical physicist, Atanasoff had to find solutions to large and complex sets of equations by hand. The main problem that Atanasoff was trying to solve was a system of linear equations. He estimated that it would take a human 125 hours to solve twenty equations in twenty unknowns. He decided to try calculators to speed up the process. His goal was a machine that could solve a system of thirty equations in thirty unknowns. He tried modifying an IBM tabulator or connecting several calculators together. However, mechanical machines proved cumbersome and limited the complexity of the problems they could solve. As the complexity of the machine grew, so did its size and the heat it produced. In addition, mechanical parts moving rapidly against one another caused wear and tear and required lots of maintenance.

One day in the winter of 1937, a frustrated Atanasoff went for a drive that would prove historic. A lover of whiskey and fast cars, he drove two hundred miles to cross the Illinois border (Iowa was still constrained by Prohibition), where he found a tavern and had a few drinks. He realized that he could design a device to store the coefficients of his equations. In addition, electronic components could more easily and accurately handle digital rather than analog data. Binary numbers were a natural "on-off" (charged-discharged) system for an electronic computer. By the time he left, he had written notes on the back of a napkin that outlined principles for an electronic computer. It included the use of base-2 (binary) numbers rather than the traditional base-10 (decimal), direct 0-1 logic rather than enumeration, and a separate memory with capacitors that would be "refreshed" to prevent the loss of data.

Back at Iowa State, Atanasoff decided to use logic circuits rather than simply mimicking the action of mechanical calculators. His machine would be the first to calculate with vacuum tubes and do arithmetic electronically. In 1939, with a grant from Iowa State, he hired graduate student Clifford Berry to assist him. Berry's skill in electronics complemented Atanasoff's skills in math and physics. By the fall of 1939, the team had built a crude, small prototype that could add and subtract.

In 1940, Atanasoff attended a lecture on computing by John William Mauchly. Atanasoff approached him, and they began to correspond. Mauchly visited Iowa in June, 1941. Atanasoff showed Mauchly the various parts of the machine that he and Berry were constructing and explained their functions. Atanasoff also showed Mauchly a proposal he had written, which was essentially a systematic blueprint for the construction of an electronic computer. It included details on the use of binary numbers, 0-1 logic, vacuum tubes, and capacitors for memory. Atanasoff's work influenced Mauchly's ideas when he and John Presper Eckert built the Electronic Numerical Integrator and Computer (ENIAC), the first general-purpose electronic computer.

John Vincent Atanasoff. (AP/Wide World Photos)

Atanasoff's proposal had been a grant request to the Iowa State College Research Corporation. In 1941, the corporation awarded the grant, and the college appointed a lawyer to patent the machine. Atanasoff negotiated a 50/50 split on any royalties. He also agreed that part of his half was to go to Berry, an unusual acknowledgment of a graduate student's contribution. While Atanasoff was responsible for the concept and ideas, Berry was responsible for most of the detailed design and construction. However, the attorney and the college never applied for the patent.

In 1942, Atanasoff and Berry had produced a working electronic special-purpose computer. What later became known as the Atanasoff-Berry Computer (ABC) employed various new techniques that Atanasoff had invented, including novel uses of logic circuitry and regenerative memory. However, the part of the machine that was to record intermediate results on paper did not fully work for large systems of equations, only small ones up to five equations and five unknowns.

The United States' entry into World War II ended Atanasoff and Berry's work, as they both left Iowa for jobs in the defense industry. Atanasoff went to work for the Naval Ordnance Laboratory in Maryland and focused on acoustics and seismology. The Atanasoff-Berry Computer remained in the basement of the physics building where they had built it. Atanasoff thought he would return to the work after the war; however, he declined Iowa State's offer to return and head the Physics Department. A new chair of the department needed the space in the basement and disassembled the ABC in 1948.

The U.S. Navy awarded Atanasoff the Distinguished Service Award in 1945 for his work with the Naval Ordnance Laboratory during World War II. Atanasoff worked for the Ordnance Lab through 1952, when he founded the Ordnance Engineering Corporation. He also served as president of Cybernetics, Inc., from 1961 to 1980. Although Atanasoff never received a patent for the ABC, he did hold patents for thirty-two other inventions.

In 1973, a federal court decision named John Vincent Atanasoff as the inventor of the first electronic computer. Sperry Rand had acquired rights to the ENIAC patents, and some computer manufacturers still paid royalties to Sperry Rand for some of the principles derived from the ENIAC. Honeywell no longer wanted to pay the royalties and challenged Sperry Rand based on Atanasoff's work. The case went to court in 1971. Judge Earl R. Larson of the Minneapolis Federal Court ruled that "the subject matter of one or more claims of the ENIAC was derived from Atanasoff, and the invention claimed in the ENIAC was derived from Atanasoff."

Atanasoff's work influenced developments during the next decade and the rapid development of electronic computers. His ABC was the first in a chain of machines that far outstripped their predecessors. He retired to his farm near Monrovia, Maryland, where he died on June 15, 1995, of a stroke.

THE ATANASOFF-BERRY COMPUTER

The Atanasoff-Berry Computer (ABC) was the size of a large desk or chest freezer and probably weighed almost seven hundred pounds. All the parts were mounted on a metal frame. There was an operator's control console on top with numerous switches, buttons, meters, and lights. Underneath the console was the arithmetic unit (performed addition and subtraction), which contained more than two hundred vacuum tubes. Beside it was a card reader and puncher for input and output. Two rotating drums served as the memory and sat behind the card equipment. Each drum had sixteen hundred capacitors set into its skin in thirty-two rows. Each drum stored thirty fifty-bit numbers (fifteen-place decimal numbers).

In the binary (base-2) system, there are only 1's and 0's (unlike the decimal system that has 0's, 1's, 2's, 3's, 4's, 5's, 6's, 7's, 8's, and 9's). Capacitors would represent a digit by being charged positively (1) or negatively (0). Since the capacitors drained their charge about the time a drum made one complete revolution, John Vincent Atanasoff designed a circuit to regenerate the charge on each rotation. While crude, this is the basis of the modern dynamic RAM in every computer.

Atanasoff designed the ABC to solve systems of linear equations. For example, a system of two equations and two unknowns could be: $2a + 11b = 30$; $4a + 6b = 28$. (The answer can be worked out by hand to $a = 4$ and $b = 2$.) Atanasoff wanted to be able to solve up to thirty equations and thirty unknowns.

The part of the machine that prevented it from working for large systems was the card puncher. Solving systems of linear equations required saving intermediate results. If the machine saved these by mechanically punching cards and then reading them back in, the process would take far too long. Atanasoff devised a way to create the holes electrically rather than mechanically. It was faster, but it failed once every 100,000 times. While this may seem like a minor problem, large systems of equations required hundreds of thousands of operations. Thus, the error would occur and produce incorrect results.

IMPACT

Atanasoff played a key and controversial role in the development of the electronic computer. His machine only worked for small systems of linear equations because error crept in with larger systems. However, his work influenced John William Mauchly, one of the designers of the first general-purpose electronic computer, the ENIAC. The ENIAC led to stored-program computers like the Electronic Discrete Variable Automatic Computer (EDVAC).

Particular components of the ABC were innovative and became basic elements in computers. The machine pioneered a regenerative memory. It used regenerative pulses to stop the charges in the capacitors from "leaking" away. This technique is still the basis of modern dynamic random access memory (RAM). Other innovations included the use of vacuum tubes, the use of binary numbers, and the use of electronic logic rather than simple enumerations.

A surprising number of things have not changed since the invention of the ABC. Supercomputers were optimized for matrix factoring and matrix multiplication—essentially the same problem as solving systems of linear equations. An Intel press release on its parallel processor (which had demonstrated over a trillion operations per second) indicated that the problem the processor solved was a linear system of 125,000 equations in 125,000 unknowns.

—Linda Eikmeier Endersby

Further Reading

Burks, Alice R., and Arthur W. Burks. *The First Electronic Computer: The Atanasoff Story*. Ann Arbor: University of Michigan Press, 1988. Technically oriented first chapter and appendix. Majority of the book focuses on the influence of Atanasoff's work on the ENIAC and the legal battle over the invention of the computer. Illustrations, references, index, appendixes.

Hally, Mike. *Electronic Brains: Stories from the Dawn of the Computer Age*. Washington, D.C.: J. Henry Press, 2005. Readable book with details of various machines and personalities significant in the development of the modern computer. Includes one chapter with information on Atanasoff's work. Useful appendixes explain technical terms, binary mathematics, and parts of the modern computer. Illustrations, references, index.

Mollenhoff, Clark R. *Atanasoff: Forgotten Father of the Computer*. Ames: Iowa State University Press, 1988. Readable work detailing Atanasoff's work on the computer. Focuses extensively on the later legal battles over the invention of the computer and the fight for recognition of Atanasoff's work. Illustrations, references, index.

Rojas, Raul, and Ulf Hashagen, eds. *The First Computers: History and Architectures*. Cambridge, Mass.: MIT Press, 2000. This technically detailed book includes a chapter about the reconstruction of the Atanasoff-Berry Computer in 1997 and provides some information about the workings of the computer that cannot be found elsewhere. Illustrations, sources, index.

Swedin, Eric C., and David L. Ferro. *Computers: The Life Story of a Technology*. Westport, Conn.: Greenwood Press, 2005. Provides a succinct and readable overview, from early calculators to modern computers. Includes a section with a short overview of Atanasoff's work. Illustrations, bibliography, index.

Williams, Michael R. *A History of Computing Technology*. 2d ed. Los Alamitos, Calif.: IEEE Computer Society Press, 1997. Contains chapters describing the various technologies and machines that contributed to the development of the modern computer. One section provides a succinct discussion of Atanasoff's work. Illustrations, further reading lists, index.

See also: Clifford Berry; Seymour Cray; John William Mauchly.

Hertha Marks Ayrton

English engineer and mathematician

Ayrton made improvements to the electric arc, an important illumination source in the nineteenth century. She also invented a drafting tool and a manually operated fan.

Born: April 28, 1854; Portsea, England
Died: August 26, 1923; North Lancing, Sussex, England
Also known as: Phoebe Sarah Marks (birth name)
Primary field: Electronics and electrical engineering
Primary inventions: Carbon electric arc; Ayrton fan

Early Life

Phoebe Sarah Marks was the third of eight children of Levi and Alice Theresa (Moss) Marks. Anti-Semitism had induced Levi to emigrate from his native Poland. He struggled to support his large family as a clockmaker and jeweler. In 1861, Levi died, leaving his family with debts. Alice, who was known for her civic and charitable activities, supported her children by selling needlework.

Sarah gained both mechanical talent and a compassionate concern for others from her parents. When she was nine years old, Sarah went to live with her maternal aunt in London, where she received her early education. Her cousin, a graduate of Cambridge University, taught mathematics to Sarah and introduced her to writers and other intellectuals. As a teenager, Sarah decided to leave the Jewish religion, though she remained proud of her heritage. The young agnostic took the name Hertha, the name of a Germanic earth goddess featured in a popular poem by Algernon Charles Swinburne.

Hertha Marks tutored students and sold embroidery to earn money, much of which she sent to her family. One of the founders of Girton College at Cambridge University, Barbara Leigh Smith Bodichon, offered to subsidize Marks's education. Marks passed entrance examinations in mathematics and English with honors and entered the college in 1876. While she was a student, Marks invented an instrument for recording pulse beats, but after learning that others had preceded her, she did not continue working on it. She completed the Cambridge Tripos examinations in 1881. Since Cambridge did not grant degrees to women, Marks was not eligible.

After inventing a drafting tool that was well received, Marks realized that she might be able to pursue a scientific career. With financial support from Madame Bodichon, she began studying in 1884 at Finsbury Technical College in London under William Ayrton, professor of physics and prominent electrical engineer. Marks and Ayrton married the next year. They had one daughter, Barbara.

Life's Work

Hertha Ayrton's first invention was a device for dividing a line into equal parts. Her design was based on the principle that corresponding sides in similar triangles are proportional, and was somewhat related to the drawing compass. Marks patented this invention in 1884 and engaged a British manufacturer.

After marrying Professor Ayrton in 1885, she became involved with his investigations of the electric arc. At that time, arc lamps were an important source of illumination for streets, factories, stores, and other public places. Their intense, harsh light made them best suited for commercial purposes. The electric arc was also used for searchlights. Unfortunately, arc lamps were also noisy, producing unpleasant hissing, humming, and sputtering, and they rotated spontaneously, which changed the color and intensity of light. Arc lamps were temperamental and required many adjustments to keep them operating. During use, the arc's high temperatures vaporized the carbon electrodes and melted most insulation materials. As the electrodes deteriorated, the distance between them changed, making corrections to the circuit and to positions of searchlight mirrors necessary.

The basic arc lamp consisted of two electrodes housed in a receptacle. When a high-voltage source was connected to the electrodes, molecules of the ambient air would break down into charged particles, or ions. A surge of current (discharge) resulted as the ions suddenly moved to the electrodes. The energy transmitted by these rapidly moving particles would heat the electrodes to incandescence. The electrodes were usually made of carbon, although other materials could be substituted.

The relationship of variables in the arc circuit were not well understood at that time, and Hertha Ayrton realized that this relationship was key to improving the arc. While experimenting with the arc circuit, she found that, for a constant current, the power required was directly proportional to the length of the arc. The current and electric potential were inversely proportional. Ayrton then turned to the question of the electrodes themselves. During the arc's operation, depressions (craters) developed in the tips of the electrodes as the carbon dissipated. She found that variations in these craters affected the potential needed to maintain the arc discharge.

Next, Ayrton attacked the vexing problem of the hissing arc. Besides being annoying, hissing arcs were not stable. Ayrton found that when a carbon electrode oxidized instead of vaporizing, the crater would spread from the tip to the sides. This change in shape left a path for air to rush in, turn the electrode, and make the unwanted hissing sound. Ayrton realized that manufacturers were creating the conditions required for a hissing arc by placing grooves along the sides of the electrodes. She also recognized that electrodes with flat ends would better resist degradation than the tapered carbons being marketed.

Ayrton's analysis and solution for the hissing arc quickly brought professional recognition. This achievement transformed Ayrton's public image from helpmate to established independent researcher. The Institution of Electrical Engineers broke tradition and permitted Ayrton to read her own paper in 1899 rather than requiring a man to present it. The institution awarded her a prize of £10 and made her its first female member.

After this feat, Ayrton was invited to participate in other meetings and conferences. She compiled her researches into a book on the electric arc that was published in 1902. The British Admiralty consulted with Ayrton on methods to improve carbons in searchlights. She also designed improvements for movie projectors. Ayrton patented many of her inventions.

In 1901, Ayrton noticed sand ripple patterns formed by ocean waves at the beach. Her curiosity led her to investigate water vortices and waves, resulting in several publications. She devised a pressure-difference gauge to confirm her analysis. In 1906, the Royal Society of London awarded Ayrton the prestigious Hughes Medal for her work on the electric arc and on sand ripples. Unlike the Institution of Electrical Engineers, the Royal Society did not grant her membership, deciding instead that a married woman was not eligible.

During World War I, dismayed by the deaths and suffering unleashed by poisonous gas warfare, Ayrton transferred her knowledge of sand ripples and hydrodynamics to the behavior of air. Soon she had invented a fan to move toxic gases out of the trenches, which she offered free of charge and hoped would save many lives. A frustrating combination of indifference and bureaucratic bungling prevented the fan's timely deployment, a source of deep pain to Ayrton. In 1917, she devised a mechanical version of her fan but apparently did not pursue this. Ayrton died in North Lancing, Sussex, on August 26, 1923.

The Ayrton Fan

The hand-operated fan Hertha Marks Ayrton developed for the British army was made of waterproof canvas and cane, with a wooden handle. Its fifteen-inch square blade had a firm center with side and end flaps. These loose flaps prevented fumes from rushing into the area behind the fan, ensuring they would be dispelled. Made to be portable, it was three and a half feet long, weighed less than one pound, and could be folded.

The fan worked by creating disturbances in the air that traveled toward the fumes. As the fan beat in a regular rhythm, this wave pattern could be reinforced, creating standing waves that caused the air to rise higher and higher. The up-and-down motion of the fan also produced a vortex in the air. Ayrton designed her fan so that the air vortices moved only in the forward direction. Successive beats of the fan created a series of vortices that combined their energy into a huge vortex that carried away the poisonous gases.

The Ayrton fan produced a partial vacuum in the region behind it that drew fresh air toward the fan at the same time as the rotational motion of the air in front of the fan moved air away from the device. With a small experimental model, Ayrton could clear a large smoke cloud in a few seconds, moving the air out to ten feet. The army fan could clear a much larger volume of fumes. British forces used the Ayrton fan during World War I for moving noxious gases from exploding shells out of trenches, mine craters, and other depressions.

Impact

Ayrton's work was part of an engineering tradition that attacked concrete physical problems without using abstract models or theories. Her work on the electric arc was significant for the electric lighting industry. Though electric arcs became less important for lighting after the invention of the incandescent lamp, they continued to be used in searchlights, in projectors, and for welding. Because arcs produce high temperatures, they were used in furnaces to make steel.

The electric arc was especially interesting for physical theory, as scientists recognized that the arc discharge took place in a special state of matter, an assemblage of ions. Investigations of electrical discharges in ionized gases occupied many physicists during the late nineteenth century. Now called plasma physics, the study of ionized gases has applications in physics, astrophysics, and meteorology.

Ayrton's line divider was patented and marketed for engineers, architects, artists, and other professionals, and her fan for removing toxic gases from trenches proved useful during World War I. However, Ayrton may be best remembered for her personal achievement in rising beyond her economically straitened origins and excelling in a field dominated by men. Ayrton struggled against economic, social, and cultural barriers to pursue her career. Her life is both an inspiration for young people and a case study for exceptional women. As with many women of her era, Ayrton's path was smoothed by an influential man. Like most successful scientists and engineers of either gender, she had supportive mentors and gained the necessary financial means to pursue her goals. Ayrton was also aided by her enthusiasm, charm, and sociability. She was a trailblazer, making way for other women to pursue careers in engineering and science.

—*Marjorie C. Malley*

Further Reading

Blühm, Andreas, and Louise Lippincott. *Light! The Industrial Age, 1750-1900*. New York: Thames and Hudson, 2000. Original, attractive book that places technological developments in their social and historical settings. The authors, curators from the Van Gogh Museum in Amsterdam and the Carnegie Museum of Art in Pittsburgh, emphasize implications of lighting for art. Illustrations, bibliographical references, index.

Bowers, Brian. *Lengthening the Day: A History of Lighting Technology*. New York: Oxford University Press, 1998. Informative book by the science curator of London's Science Museum that traces lighting from antiquity to modern times. Includes a chapter on the electric arc. Illustrations, bibliographical references, index.

Malley, Marjorie. "Hertha Marks Ayrton." In *Women in Chemistry and Physics*, edited by Louise S. Grinstein, Rose K. Rose, and Miriam H. Rafailovich. Westport, Conn.: Greenwood Press, 1993. Based on original publications, this essay relates and interprets major aspects of Ayrton's life and work. Part of a collection featuring many lesser-known scientists. Notes, bibliography.

Mason, Joan. "Hertha Ayrton (1854-1923)." In *Out of the Shadows: Contributions of Twentieth Century Women to Physics*, edited by Nina Byers and Gary Williams. New York: Cambridge University Press, 2006. Engaging sketch of Ayrton that includes several of her extrascientific activities, as well as an overview of her scientific work. Notes, portrait, bibliography.

Sharp, Evelyn. *Hertha Ayrton, 1854-1923*. London: Edward Arnold, 1926. Written by a friend, the only full length biography of Ayrton paints a portrait of a warm, spirited, resourceful woman of broad interests and endeavors. Illustrations.

See also: Meredith C. Gourdine; Peter Cooper Hewitt.

Charles Babbage

English mathematician and mechanical engineer

Babbage was the originator and cocreator (with his close friend Ada Lovelace) of the programmable computer. His primary invention, the difference engine, could calculate polynomials far faster and more accurately than previously possible.

Born: December 26, 1791; in or near London, England
Died: October 18, 1871; London, England
Primary fields: Computer science; mathematics
Primary invention: Difference engine

Early Life

Charles Babbage was one of four children born to Benjamin Babbage, a banker, and Betsy Plumleigh Teape. His birthplace is uncertain, but a memorial plaque at the intersection of Walworth Road and Larcom Street states that he was most likely born in the house at 44 Crosby Row, Walworth Road, in London, England. In 1808, Babbage's father moved the family to East Teignmouth, where he accepted a position as a warden of St. Michael's Church. Finding himself sufficiently supplied with money to pay for his son's private-school education, Benjamin sent Charles to a school in Alphington. Since he had recently recovered from fever, the boy was told not to study too hard. Later, Charles enrolled at King Edward VI Grammar School in Totnes, but, again, his health prevented him from making significant progress in his studies. Holmwood Academy, a school founded by the Reverend Stephen Freeman, was the real beginning of Babbage's education. Its library, well stocked with mathematical treatises, was inspiring. Babbage was accepted into Cambridge University in 1810.

When Babbage arrived at Trinity College, Cambridge, in October of that year, he had had significant exposure to such luminaries as Gottfried Wilhelm Leibniz, Joseph-Louis Lagrange, and Sylvestre François Lacroix. Consequently, he found that his chosen school had little else to teach him in the field of mathematics. With some of his college friends, Babbage created an Analytical Society in 1812 composed of a handful of Cambridge undergraduates: Babbage, George Peacock, John Herschel, Michael Faraday, Isambard Kingdom Brunel (a future railway pioneer and mentor for Charles's son Benjamin Herschel Babbage), and Edward Ryan. Ryan and Babbage married, respectively, Louisa and Georgiana Whitmore, the sisters of Wolryche Whitmore, a founder of South Australia and the member of Parliament who helped repeal the infamous Corn Laws. In hopes of finding a better education, Babbage transferred to Peterhouse, Cambridge, in 1812. Although he became Peterhouse's highest-ranked mathematician, he failed to graduate. In 1814, he received an honorary master's degree without examination and became a professor of mathematics.

Life's Work

Babbage and his beloved Georgiana were married on July 25, 1814, at St. Michael's Church and settled down to life at 5 Devonshire Street in London. Babbage's primary occupation at the time was studying the calculus of functions. In 1816, his mathematical prowess earned him a fellowship in the Royal Society and encouraged him to found the Astronomical Society (later the Royal Astronomical Society). By 1820, however, he had become fascinated by the idea of a mechanical calculator and began working on a machine that could calculate mathematical tables quickly and accurately. At the time, all calculations were performed by human "computers," whose function was to compute the value of numbers. Babbage disliked the inac-

Charles Babbage. (Library of Congress)

curacy of human computers and was inspired to study logarithmic tables and to refine earlier calculating machines invented by Blaise Pascal and Leibniz. In 1822, having hit upon what he felt was a workable design, Babbage wrote Sir Humphry Davy, the president of the Royal Society, a letter outlining his proposed mechanism and requesting funding. Finding approval from the Chancellor of the Exchequer, Babbage was able to start constructing the "difference engine" in 1823. Created specifically to compute the values of polynomial functions, the difference engine eliminated the need for multiplication and division in the fields of accounting and mathematics. Further, the automatic nature of the difference engine meant that a user did not need to be mathematically gifted to operate it.

The Difference Engine

The difference engine, a mechanical calculator based on Sir Isaac Newton's method of divided differences and designed to tabulate polynomial functions, consisted of columns (1 to n) that each stored one decimal number. A crank on the side of the engine caused the gears to move and add the value of column n + 1 to column n to produce the new value of column n. Further, column n could store only a constant, while column 1 displayed the value of the calculation. Despite this limited ability, both logarithmic and trigonometric functions could be calculated through the use of polynomials and, consequently, added more functions to even the limited nature of the original difference engine. Before its execution, the mechanism had to be programmed, with initial values set to the columns.

When Charles Babbage wrote a paper for the Royal Astronomical Society proposing the design and construction of a calculating machine, the government was impressed enough with the idea to award him limited funding in 1823. The failure of the original project, however, caused the withdrawal of support even though Babbage greatly improved the design of the original engine in his plans for his analytical engine and its successive versions. Babbage requested funding several times, but the lack of observable progress made his patron leery of investing in his designs. It was only the intense curiosity of curators at London's Science Museum and Babbage scholars that led to the construction and testing of Babbage's designs for the difference engine and the analytical engine. Although Babbage did not live to see the vindication of his theories, his faith in the promise of his calculators inspired many generations of later mathematicians to perfect his mechanisms.

Because Babbage was unable to secure sufficient funding for his devices, none of his inventions were ever completely constructed. The first version of the difference engine, weighing fifteen tons and composed of more than twenty-five thousand individual moving parts, was a monstrosity that defied completion. Eventually, in 1991, a fully working model of Babbage's machine was made based on his original blueprints, but throughout the inventor's life he only managed to build sections of his machines.

Despondent, but not defeated, Babbage continued his refinement of the calculator. The next incarnation of the difference engine, called the analytical engine, was more complex and even included a printer that could record its calculations on paper. Further, Babbage's friend, Ada Lovelace, designed a program for the analytical engine on a series of punch cards to control its functions, including looping, branching, and sequential control—functions present in modern computers. Additional designs for Babbage's difference engine, limited to theoretical sketches and mechanical designs, further modified the original functions of the difference engine. When it was finally constructed in 1991, the mechanical calculator was found to be able to calculate accurately to thirty-one digits.

Sadly, Georgiana passed away at the age of thirty-five on September 1, 1827, the same year that Babbage's father died. Additionally, of the couples' eight children, only two sons (Benjamin Herschel and Henry Prevost) and one daughter (Georgiana) survived childhood. The failure to finish building his engine, and the death of his father, wife, and one son in the same year, caused Babbage such grief that he delayed construction of the device.

Fortunately, Babbage was able to rely on the support of Ada Lovelace, whom he met in 1833. An impressive mathematician in her own right and considered by many later scholars as the "mother of programming," Lovelace had gone into the field of mathematics with the intent of obscuring the notoriety of her father, the poet Lord Byron. The program she devised for the analytical engine would have calculated Bernoulli numbers had it ever been run on the finished engine.

Babbage died of unspecified causes on October 18, 1871, at the age of seventy-nine, having never seen the completion of a single project. He was buried in London's Kensal Green Cemetery. His son Henry assembled part of Babbage's difference engine from recovered parts but also found the engine to be too daunting a task. Babbage's various engines, unwieldy and erratic, nevertheless share a structure with the modern computer.

Impact

It is difficult to judge the impact of Babbage's engines because not a single machine was ever completely constructed. Further, the few trials of the first incomplete difference engine were riddled with errors. The theoretical designs inspired the development of computers and computer programming, but scholars continue to debate whether Babbage's machines would have worked had he finished them while he was still alive. The Science Museum in London attempted to answer the debate by constructing two full-scale replicas between 1989 and 1991. Both are on display, one at the Science Museum and the other, owned by Nathan Myhrvold, on exhibit at the Computer History Museum in Mountain View, California. Interestingly, both replicas work astoundingly well, given the failure of their ancestors. The replica of Babbage's Difference Engine No. 2 (produced between 1847 and 1849) could hold seven numbers of thirty-one decimal digits each and thus could accurately calculate seventh-degree polynomials, more than many modern calculators.

Perhaps Babbage's greatest impact was his desire to replace human computers with accurate machines. Computing work, even with the aid of an abacus, was a hard and unrewarding job for the people assigned to add and subtract numbers. Accounting, consequently, tended to be drudgery, and a high rate of error was common. The modern era's reliance on accurate data is a direct result of Babbage's insistence on mechanical calculation.

—Julia M. Meyers

Further Reading

Babbage, Charles. *Passages from the Life of a Philosopher.* Silver Springs, Md.: Merchant Books, 2008. A reprint of a memoir by Babbage that relates many details of his life unrelated to his inventions. Very rare unabridged and digitally enlarged printing of Babbage's autobiography.

Dubbey, J. M. *The Mathematical Work of Charles Babbage.* Cambridge, England: Cambridge University Press, 2004. Primarily a discussion of the original difference engine, Dubbey's book goes into minute detail about the evolution of Babbage's invention. Highly informative concerning Babbage's career as an inventor.

Halacy, Dan. *Charles Babbage: Father of the Computer.* New York: Macmillan, 1970. A biographical account of Babbage and his invention of the difference engine that touches on the evolving nature of Babbage's computational theory. Discusses the implications of the difference engines for the development of the modern computer.

Hyman, Anthony. *Memoir of the Life and Labours of the Late Charles Babbage, Esq., F.R.S.* Cambridge, Mass.: MIT Press, 1988. Unpublished during Babbage's lifetime, this memoir by a contemporary is very useful for information about Babbage's personal habits and dedication to his work.

Swade, Doron. *The Difference Engine.* New York: Viking Press, 2001. As the leader of the team that built a replica of Babbage's difference engine on the occasion of the two hundredth anniversary of Babbage's birth, Swade is highly qualified to discuss Babbage's inventions. His book, describing Babbage's work in Kensington, is a fascinating tribute to the "father of computing."

See also: John Vincent Atanasoff; Clifford Berry; William Seward Burroughs; Seymour Cray; Sir Humphry Davy; John Presper Eckert; Ted Hoff; Herman Hollerith; Jack St. Clair Kilby; Gottfried Wilhelm Leibniz; John William Mauchly; John Napier; Sir Isaac Newton; Blaise Pascal; Alan Mathison Turing; Konrad Zuse.

Roger Bacon

English scientist

Bacon was one of the first Europeans to formulate the scientific method. Based on experiment, not accepted authority, his work depended upon observation. His work with optics was seminal, and he anticipated modern science by integrating logic and quantitative reasoning.

Born: c. 1220; Ilchester, Somerset, England
Died: c. 1292; Probably Oxford, England
Also known as: Doctor Mirabilis
Primary fields: Chemistry; mathematics; optics; physics
Primary inventions: Empiricism; experimentation with lenses and prisms

Early Life

Roger Bacon was born to wealthy parents in a family that valued education. One of several children, at least one of his older brothers also received an early education by a Latin tutor just as Roger did. His landowner parents, who were probably titled nobility, expected Roger to enter the Church and follow the normal route for a younger son who would not inherit the title or a majority of land as the eldest son would. This medieval system was known as primogeniture, from the Latin for "eldest-born [son]," and is still followed today to some extent in European titled families. Whether he attended some form of grammar school or was privately taught, he would have first studied Latin and basic arithmetic or computation.

While there is some debate about his exact year of birth (also possibly later in 1222), at the age of thirteen Roger Bacon entered Oxford University, where instruction was almost entirely in Latin and which at the time compressed secondary or high school and college together. At Oxford, Bacon would have built upon his early schooling with grammar, logic, and rhetoric in Latin and followed this with music, astronomy, arithmetic, and geometry. Bacon first earned his bachelor of arts degree by his late adolescence and his master of arts degree by his early twenties. It was at Oxford where Bacon was exposed to two subjects that would become lifetime influences, Aristotle and logic, and where his love of thinking honed through his studies would have naturally led him to methodical scientific observation and to reject any knowledge or philosophy based only on authority and not on what could be tested by experimental reasoning.

Life's Work

Bacon taught Aristotle at Oxford for at least a decade until around 1241. Study of Aristotle had fallen out of favor with the Church for a long time because he was considered a pagan philosopher, but Aristotle had been reinstated as worthy of study during and shortly after Bacon's time at Oxford and Paris. In 1241, Bacon moved to Paris and taught Aristotle at the University of Paris. This was the period when he began a visibly serious interest in science, possibly influenced by several contemporary medieval philosopher-scientists like the French scholar Petrus Peregrinus de Maricourt (mostly in the thirteenth century) and Robert Grosseteste of Lincoln (1175-1253).

Depiction of Roger Bacon patterned on a print by Flemish painter Aegidius Sadeler. (Library of Congress)

Petrus Peregrinus studied mathematics and magnetism and also described the principles and construction of an astrolabe. Robert Grosseteste wrote on astronomy, light, and tides and also made commentaries on Aristotle. It is likely that Bacon began studying Grosseteste while in his first Oxford period.

This is also the time when Bacon began his linguistic forays into other languages and cultures, as Paris and the Continent had far more manuscripts available to him than Oxford. Part of this manuscript access to oriental thought was due to the earlier Carolingian Renaissance of Charlemagne, but more so to the worldly influence of the Crusades, where new exposure was coupled with the intellectual legacy of individual kings like Frederick II (1194-1250), who was also leader of the Holy Roman Empire in Germany and welcomed Arab and Jewish scholars, as well as proximity of the Moors in nearby Spain.

Bacon heavily criticized the Scholastic biblical studies of his own day, noting their reliance on bad translations and faulty commentaries that showed ignorance of the original texts. He emphasized that the Scriptures were more important than the commentaries derived from them. In this sense, he anticipated the Reformation.

During his Paris years, regretting his own reliance on Latin translation, Bacon studied earlier scientists, notably the Arabic mathematicians and scientists such as Ibn al-Haytham (c. 965-1039), also known as Alhazen, and the much earlier polymath al-Kindī (c. 801-873), also known in Latin as Alkindus. Al-Haytham is often called the "father of optics" for his work on prisms, lens making, mirrors, reflection, magnifying glasses, and other visual phenomena described in his *Kitāb al-manāzir* (wr. 1011-1021; book of optics). Al-Kindi had been one of the pioneers in introducing numerals from India that formed the basis of Arabic numerals that ultimately liberated numeracy in the West from the cumbersome Latin number system. Al-Kindi also theorized on cryptography and frequency analysis, applying logic to codes. This was a revolutionary period in Bacon's life. After six years in Paris, Bacon may have returned to Oxford and in 1247 begun experiments that would be the hallmark of his life from then on, possibly performing hundreds of experiments in optics and applying geometry to optics.

It was thus that Bacon became the "father of empiricism." Understanding that he could only believe scientifically what could be verified repeatedly through experiment and the senses, Bacon's experiments carefully assembled the empirical method of science, starting with hypothesis, testable by experiment and laying out the influencing variables and permutations before arriving at any conclusions. Based on his own experiments with optics and lens making, he may have been one of the inventors of the telescope. In his own words he wrote:

> For we can so shape transparent bodies, and arrange them in such a way with respect to our sight and objects of vision, that the rays will be reflected and bent in any direction we desire, and under any angle we wish, we may see the object near or at a distance. . . . So we might also cause the Sun, Moon and stars in appearance to descend here below. . . .

The ability to draw the celestial bodies closer in—"Sun, Moon and Stars in appearance to descend here below"—seems impossible to achieve without the magnification power of a series of separate lenses of a telescope. Bacon also believed that Earth was a sphere, a deduction derivable by geometric principles, and that enough water existed in oceans to circumnavigate the planet. Also using geometry, he deduced the nearest stars were over 130 million miles distant, greatly in error considering the Earth-Sun distance is around 93 million miles, but nonetheless a huge sum for his day.

Bacon also wrote on prisms, correctly described the visible spectrum he could observe in light passing through water, and appears to have been the first in the West to have correctly experimentally determined the maximum reflective altitude of a rainbow as comprising 42° of arc at its greatest intensity. Using simple astronomy, he also proposed to the Church a logical overhaul of the Julian calendar, a proposal that was basically ignored for centuries. In his writing on chemistry, Bacon was the first to describe the making of gunpowder and firecrackers using saltpeter and sulfur, several decades before Marco Polo returned from China around 1299. Bacon's most important intellectual credo can be found in his own words, "Mathematics is the gate and key to the sciences."

At some point, Bacon had become a Franciscan friar, possibly to finance his experiments and writing because this order often harbored many thinkers and possibly because his once-wealthy family was now in poverty, penalized for having supported the wrong side in an English civil war. Because of his monastic vows, Bacon was also intermittently under intense scrutiny and possible persecution—or at least censure—for his beliefs and scientific thought when it clashed with perceived theology and doctrine. Although many early scientists often under the aegis of the Church practiced what was under-

Foresight with Lenses

Roger Bacon has been often credited with several inventions, including the telescope and working spectacles, although these are much debated. He was, however, one of the first Europeans to theorize about both of these inventions—certainly as early as 1234 in regard to telescopic lenses and 1268 in regard to corrective lenses—long before Galileo, who is also often credited considerably later with the telescope. It is most likely that the glassmaker ʿAbbas ibn Firnas in the ninth century and the polymath Ibn al-Haytham in the eleventh century should be credited with inventing early versions of corrective lenses, and in Italy Salvino d'Armate produced one of the earliest wearable spectacles around 1280, along with alternate credit also given to Fra Alessandro da Spina of Pisa about the same time, both not long after Bacon, who may have influenced them. Bacon's own words in *De iride* (on the rainbow) around 1235 suggest that lenses enable one "to correctly read the tiniest letters at very great distances." This does seem an ambiguous possible precedent for both spectacles and telescopes. Working telescopes seem to appear only after 1608 in northern European workshops of Hans Lippershey, Zacharias Janssen, and Jacob Metius almost simultaneously. Nonetheless, as a pioneer in optics, Bacon did make and use optical lenses. He was also probably the first European to fairly correctly theorize and describe the visible light spectrum as it is known today, which is a considerable achievement in itself.

By experimental observation, Bacon correctly observed the breaking up and separation of sunlight through water and the prism derived from it. Refraction of sunlight was not well known in Europe, described by Arab opticians like the eleventh century Ibn al-Haytham, whose *Kitāb al-manāzir* (wr. 1011-1021; book of optics) Bacon read carefully. However, Bacon described the range of colored light as progressing from red hues through orange, yellow and green to blue and violet hues, what we now understand as the visible infrared to ultraviolet range (650-350 nanometers in reverse order). In addition, Bacon also correctly measured the maximum altitude of the angle of intensity as around 42°, which could only have been understood by direct observation and empirical experimentation over multiple, repeated events. Thus, Bacon long anticipated Sir Isaac Newton's (1642-1727) prism experiments and the phenomenon Newton named the spectrum.

stood as alchemy, it is difficult to verify that Bacon did anything more than experiment with metals and minerals.

Bacon's major writing appears around 1267 in the *Opus majus* (major work), an 800-page proposal for an encyclopedic book on the sciences, where most of his seminal ideas on science appear. This work was mostly at the request of an apparently enlightened pope, Clement IV, whom Bacon had known for decades first as Cardinal Gui Foulques and under whose protection he served and wrote after Foulques became pope in 1265. Bacon also wrote an *Opus minor* (minor work) and an *Opus tertium* (third work). Unfortunately, although the pope received Bacon's treatise, he died soon thereafter in 1268, and Bacon was subject to less enlightened minds in the Church. Having returned to Oxford to the Franciscan friary around 1278, over the next years between 1280 and 1286 Bacon also possibly wrote his *Communia naturalium* (general principles of natural philosophy) and the *Communia mathematica* (general principles of mathematical science), although some of these writings were possibly suppressed because his theology was not in accord with the Church.

Bacon died around 1292 in Oxford as a member of the Franciscan priory. Shortly thereafter, he became known as Doctor Mirabilis (wonderful teacher) by those who followed him.

Impact

Scientists following Bacon gradually began to understand his enormous range of interests and the value of empirical experiment over perceived authority. Rationalism and empiricism did not find common intellectual acceptance until the Renaissance and afterward, so in some sense Bacon was ahead of his time.

Bacon's work in optics and on light anticipated Galileo (1564-1642) and Sir Isaac Newton (1642-1727) by about four centuries; his work on reversing lenses and a probable telescope invention likewise are in advance of instrumentation of the microscope in the inventions of Zacharias Janssen (c. 1580-1638), Robert Hooke (1635-1703), and Antoni van Leeuwenhoek (1632-1723). Bacon's study of gunpowder and incendiaries became important in European warfare and reduced the role of castles and like defenses, helping to make feudalism obsolete. His insistence on linguistic accuracy and original biblical texts possibly even influenced John Wyclif (c. 1328-1384) in biblical studies in anticipation of the Reformation, where authority of text was more important than authority of tradition. Overall, Bacon has to be one of the greatest minds in the history of science.

—Patrick Norman Hunt

Further Reading

Clegg, Brian. *The First Scientist: A Life of Roger Bacon.* New York: Carroll & Graf, 2003. A good biography about how Bacon's life in the medieval monastic setting was in tension with the scientific pursuit of experimentation even in a potentially scholarly environment. A lively and plausible explanation of Bacon's life and his methods of empirical research in physics and mathematics as well as who and what influenced him.

Goldstone, Lawrence, and Nancy Goldstone. *The Friar and the Cipher: Roger Bacon and the Unsolved Mystery of the Most Unusual Manuscript in the World.* New York: Doubleday, 2005. Excellent for showing the schisms between the Church and science as well as an alchemical manuscript (Voynich manuscript), often attributed to Bacon, important for demonstrating Bacon's interests in the logic of cryptography.

Hackett, Jeremiah M. "Adelard of Bath and Roger Bacon: Early English Natural Philosophers and Scientists" *Endeavor* 26, no. 2 (2002): 70-74. Shows Bacon not as "a medieval philosopher with scientific interests" but as a pioneer of scientific empiricism who had assimilated the best of Arabic mathematicians and physicists of optics.

Lindbergh, David, ed. *Roger Bacon's Philosophy of Nature: A Critical Edition.* South Bend, Ind.: St. Augustine's Press, 1997. Best for its excellent translations of selected Bacon texts of his *Opus Majus* and Lindbergh's modern explanations of what Bacon wrote about. The best critical readings of Bacon's thought as he actually wrote.

See also: ʿAbbas ibn Firnas; Aristotle; Galileo; Zacharias Janssen; Hans Lippershey; Sir Isaac Newton.

Leo Hendrik Baekeland

Belgian chemist

Baekeland's invention of Bakelite, the first thermosetting plastic, was critical to the industrial design of the Jazz Age by making it possible to produce large quantities of tough, durable plastic goods.

Born: November 14, 1863; Ghent, Belguim
Died: February 23, 1944; Beacon, New York
Primary field: Chemistry
Primary invention: Bakelite plastic

Early Life

Leo Hendrik Baekeland (BAYK-land) was born on November 14, 1863, in Ghent, Belgium. His father, an illiterate cobbler, wanted him to follow him into the shoemaker's trade and saw no purpose in formal education. By contrast, Leo's mother believed strongly in the value of education and saw that he received a solid foundation in the basics. When his father forced him to leave school and apprentice in the shoemaking trade, his mother encouraged him to take night courses. In spite of the difficulties of studying after having putting in a full day's work, he did well enough that he gained a scholarship that enabled him to attend the Ghent University, majoring in chemistry. In 1884, he completed his doctorate and subsequently became a research chemist and teacher.

Although he was a top student throughout his studies, he also had an irrepressible humorous streak that often

Leo Hendrik Baekeland, best known as the inventor of Bakelite, a popular plastic. (Getty Images)

came out in the form of practical jokes. One joke, in which he painted a classmate's face with silver nitrate, came to the attention of school authorities when the frightened classmate went to a doctor who applied hydrochloric acid in an effort to remove the marks and instead burned his patient badly. When summoned before the board, Baekeland demonstrated the harmlessness of his prank by marking his own face with silver nitrate and then erasing it with a harmless chemical from a vial he had in his pocket. School officials were sufficiently mollified that Baekeland received only a mild reprimand, but as word got around about his classmate's injury, the physician's reputation was permanently damaged.

In 1889, Baekeland and his new wife, Celine, left for the United States, officially on leave from his university position. However, he soon found a position with Richard A. Anthony, Eastman Kodak's principal rival in the photographic business, and never looked back at academic life or Europe. His first assignment was to find a better way to make photographic paper for the growing amateur photographic market, which had grown explosively since George Eastman's introduction of the American film, a roll of paper negatives that could be loaded into a point-and-shoot camera. Baekeland was so successful that he was soon given steadily greater responsibility.

He subsequently formed his own company to produce a new kind of film, and he became independently wealthy when it was bought out by Eastman Kodak. He was then able to pursue his own chemical interests without having to worry about their marketability. As he grew bored with the chemistry of photography, he began to search out other aspects of chemistry to explore. Since his own financial situation was secure, he did not have any pressure to focus only on things that could be turned into marketable products quickly, and could risk going into blind alleys.

Life's Work

Baekeland became interested in the chemistry of phenol (a coal-tar derivative) and formaldehyde (a wood alcohol derivative). Coal tars were originally a noxious waste product of the industrial burning of coal as an energy source, and particularly of the great coking furnaces that turned coal into coke for steelmaking. These tars tended to accumulate in the smokestacks and had to be periodically cleaned out to prevent disastrous fires. In 1856, William Henry Perkin was attempting to create synthetic quinine, an antimalarial drug, out of coal tar and in the process discovered mauvine, the first of the synthetic organic dyes. The brilliant, colorfast purple rivaled the tyrean purple that had been made from the shells of small marine invertebrates in ancient times. However, while tyrean purple had been so rare and expensive as to be reserved for monarchs, mauvine was well within the reach of the burgeoning industrial middle class, whose hunger to ape the wealthy through the use of cheap industrial substitutes for previous luxury goods led to mauvine becoming so popular that the 1890's was known as the Mauve Decade.

In the half century that had followed, numerous uses had been developed for coal-tar derivatives, including various salves and ointments. However, the promise of phenol in the production of plastic substances had been continually frustrated. Although celluloid showed the value of a substance that could be produced and molded in industrial quantities, its dangerous flammability limited its popularity. Furthermore, the success of the electrical industry in the 1890's was rapidly making shellac, the only viable electrical insulator at the time, unaffordable.

Baekeland knew that German chemist Adolf von Baeyer had produced an impervious substance as a result of an explosive reaction between phenol and formaldehyde. The resulting substance was an unworkable lump, which led von Baeyer to dismiss it as useless. However, Baekeland wondered if there was some way to control the reaction. If it could be made to progress more slowly and evenly, it might produce something useful. In order to gain that control, he used a pressure vessel, which allowed him to cook the mixture at a far higher temperature and far longer than had been possible at atmospheric pressure.

Throughout the summer of 1907, Baekeland worked to perfect his new substance, certain he was on the brink of a major discovery. It started as a pourable resin but soon hardened into a translucent amber solid impervious to heat and solvents. Baekeland had succeeded in inventing the first thermosetting plastic. Unlike thermoplastics such as celluloid, which can be melted down and reformed, thermosetting plastics form permanent molecular bonds as they cure.

Baekeland presented his new substance to the world under the trade name of Bakelite. Unlike earlier plastics, which often had proved to be commercial disappointments, Bakelite proved to be just the sort of artificial insulator the electrical industry needed so desperately. Furthermore, its hardness and elasticity approached that of ivory, making it the long sought-after ideal artificial billiard ball. Elephants would no longer need to be slaughtered to provide gentlemen with their pastime.

Bakelite

Throughout the nineteenth century, chemists and industrialists had searched for a cheap artificial substitute for a number of natural substances that were becoming increasingly rare. In particular, the rise of the middle class had led to a sharp increase in interest in the game of billiards and to a voracious demand for ivory to produce the balls. Because only a small portion of an elephant's tusk was suitable for making billiard balls, and because there was no way to determine if a given tusk had any suitable sections while still on the animal, entire herds of elephants were slaughtered to gain a few usable tusks. There was a very real concern that both African and Asian elephants might be driven extinct because of this relentless persecution.

As a result, there was strong pressure to produce an artificial substitute for ivory, and prizes were offered for the inventor who could produce a suitable substance. However, early work with various forms of nitrocellulose soaked in camphor produced only marginal results. In particular, such early plastics as collodion and celluloid retained the explosive characteristics of nitrocellulose, which had been originally developed as a smokeless substitute for gunpowder. One saloon owner who had been sent a sample of artificial billiard balls made of wood coated in celluloid complained that his patrons had a woeful tendency to draw their weapons when the balls struck together, since they produced a gunshot-like report rather than a soft click.

In addition, both collodion and celluloid were apt to lose their shape or even melt altogether if heated below their ignition point. Many owners of celluloid objects were quite disappointed to find a sticky mess under a sunlit window. The development of modern electrification created even further demand for a cheap substitute for natural substances, since shellac, the only good insulator for wiring, was in increasingly short supply.

When Leo Hendrik Baekeland discovered that a combination of phenol and formaldehyde, cooked at both high temperature and high pressure, would produce a resinous substance that cured into a hard, resilient solid impervious to both heat and solvents, his work was hailed as a miracle substance. It could be molded into just about any shape, although smooth curves with a slight angle, or draft, slid out of their molds more successfully than straight sides and sharp angles. It also readily took just about any color, which meant that it could be made to simulate the appearance of a variety of natural substances that were becoming difficult to obtain, including ivory, tortoiseshell, and rare tropical woods. Equally it could be made in forms that reveled in their artificial nature, including primary colors far too pure for any natural material.

The infant discipline of industrial design quickly embraced the possibility of Bakelite in creating new products for the new era. As domestic electrification moved from the very wealthy to a broad base of urban Americans in the 1920's, a whole range of appliances were created that frequently used Bakelite. The substance could be used to insulate against both heat and electricity or as an aesthetically pleasing case for a rat's nest of components. Because the molding process was most favorable to gently curved lines and because the Jazz Age had connected streamlining with not only speed but also modernity, many appliances such as radios were given sleek styling that would later be called the Art Deco look.

Industry quickly found thousands of uses for Bakelite, creating the first plastic age. The Bell System molded telephone cases from Bakelite, creating the characteristic desk sets of the early twentieth century. The developing radio receiver industry of the Jazz Age also found Bakelite an excellent substance for injection molding to produce inexpensive cases that could even be made to look like the wood used in more expensive models, or could be allowed to revel in their "syntheticness" for a futuristic look. The flexibility of Bakelite, along with the era's fascination with speed and streamlining, was a major factor in the development of the Art Deco style. By the late 1920's, forty-three industries had found a use for Baekeland's wonder substance.

Baekeland himself made the cover of *Time* magazine on September 22, 1924. In the 1930's, he became involved in the public debate over what should be the generic name for the family of substances to which Bakelite belonged. He quickly vetoed such outré terms as "synthoid," which he derided as having no meaning, although his own preferred term "resinoid" fared no better. The court of public opinion would ultimately settle upon "plastic" for the entire family of moldable substances and would identify individual types by their formulations: phenolic plastics, polyvinyl chloride (PVC), and so forth.

In 1939, Baekeland sold his company to Union Carbide. By this time, he had been in semiretirement for a number of years and had been spending most of his time in Coconut Grove, Florida, where he owned the former estate of William Jennings Bryan. He shared Bryan's pacifist leanings, and up to the attack on Pearl Harbor he strove to keep the United States out of World War II. He died on February 23, 1944, disappointed to see the world engulfed yet again in destructive war, but before the horrors of the Holocaust were revealed.

Impact

The inventor of the first thermosetting plastic, Leo Hendrik Baekeland was in a very real sense the "father of the plastic age." Although Bakelite has since been superseded by other plastics such as PVC, nylon, and polystyrene, its success was an important foundation for the wealth of inexpensive consumer goods that poured into the market during the Jazz Age. For the first time, products could be formed quickly and easily in enormous quantities from materials that had previously been regarded as industrial waste.

—*Leigh Husband Kimmel*

Further Reading

Fenichell, Stephen. *Plastic: The Making of a Synthetic Century*. New York: HarperBusiness, 1996. A historical overview of the development of plastics, includes a biographical chapter on Baekeland.

Galas, Judith C. *Plastics: Molding the Past, Shaping the Future*. San Diego, Calif.: Lucent Books, 1995. Includes a good chapter on the role of Bakelite in the Jazz Age.

Meikle, Jeffrey L. *American Plastic: A Cultural History*. New Brunswick, N.J.: Rutgers University Press, 1995. Places Baekeland and Bakelite into the context of the role of plastics in shaping America's culture of abundance.

See also: George Eastman; Earl S. Tupper.

Alexander Bain

Scottish engineer

Bain pioneered various applications of electricity in clockmaking and made significant contributions to the development of telegraphy, including a copying machine that is now recognized as the ancestor of the modern fax machine.

Born: October 10, 1810; Watten, Caithness, Scotland
Died: January 2, 1877; Kirkintilloch, near Glasgow, Scotland
Primary fields: Communications; electronics and electrical engineering
Primary inventions: Facsimile machine; chemical telegraph

Early Life

Alexander Bain was the fifth of the eleven children of John Bain, a crofter, and Isobel Waiter, who lived in a cottage at Leanmore, between the towns of Thurso and Wick in Caithness in the far north of Scotland. He was one of a pair of non-identical twins, the other being his sister Margaret. He received his elementary education at Blacklass village school before being apprenticed to a watchmaker, John Sellars, in Wick.

In 1837, Bain went to London and worked as a journeyman clockmaker in Clerkenwell. His employer was probably John Barwise, the "chronomoter maker" who was Bain's coapplicant for his first patent in 1841. It is not known whether Bain's employer was the same Clerkenwell clockmaker that William Fothergill Cooke had hired in April, 1836, to make a model of his first telegraph apparatus, but it is not unlikely. Bain took advantage of the opportunities London offered to attend lectures, exhibitions, and demonstrations of electrical phenomena and technology and became fascinated by the possibility of making use of electricity in clocks. He began applying for patents for such applications, the first of which was granted on January 11, 1841, to him and Barwise for a clock whose pendulum was moved by electromagnetic impulses.

Charles Wheatstone had demonstrated a clock to the Royal Society in December, 1840, similar to the one that Bain and Barwise patented, and Bain put about the story that he had visited Wheatstone on the recommendation of a magazine editor and that Wheatstone had stolen his design after advising him not to bother taking the idea further. Wheatstone claimed to have been working on his electric clock long before meeting Bain, and it is entirely likely that the two men came up with the idea independently.

Life's Work

The ten years following 1841 were an extraordinarily fertile period for Bain. In December of that year, he and Lieutenant Thomas Wright—also a Clerkenwell resident—took out a patent for a series of applications of electric technology to railway locomotives and signaling. Bain then introduced a crucial modification to telegraph transmission and reception, "inverting" the existing method of signaling, which used a needle pivoting under the influence of an electromagnet by suspending a movable coil between the poles of a magnet. On May 27, 1843, Bain patented a transmitting and receiving apparatus that could scan drawings and documents, which is now recognized as the ancestor of the fax machine.

Although the image-transmitting device attracted some publicity and contributed to Bain's being described in *The Times* as "a most imaginative and meritorious inventor" in April, 1844, it was ahead of its time and did not give rise to any immediate practical applications. Italian physicist Giovanni Caselli subsequently built a giant version with an eight-foot pendulum that he called the pantelegraph, which sent a message from Paris to Amiens in 1856 and was used in a Paris-Lyon line between 1865 and 1870. An invention of greater practical potential in the mid-nineteenth century was the chemical telegraph that Bain patented on December 12, 1846, which recorded signals at a telegraph receiving station by recording impulses on paper impregnated with an electromagnetically sensitive solution, on the same principle as the 1843 image transmitter.

On May 15, 1844, Bain married a widow named Matilda Bowe, née Davis; they had two sons and two daughters before she died in 1856. The family had apparently moved to Edinburgh by the end of 1846; the chemical telegraph patent was filed from there. When the Electric Telegraph Company was set up in 1846 by William Fothergill Cooke and John Lewis Ricardo, Bain complained that its devices infringed one of his earlier patents, and he gave evidence in support of his claim to select committees of both houses of Parliament. The company's sponsors were ordered to award him a payment of £7,500, which was a large sum by his own standards, although it was very much smaller than the payments the sponsors made to Cooke and Wheatstone, the other holders of the key patents in the field.

The payment Bain received from the Electric Telegraph Company enabled him to open a showroom and manufactory at 43 Old Bond Street in the heart of London's West End. In the Great Exhibition of 1851, he was awarded an exhibition medal for his clocks, and in May, 1852, his family was living at Beevor Lodge in Hammersmith. He probably overstretched his resources in funding this change of lifestyle; at any rate, his fortunes soon took a turn for the worse. He did not patent any further inventions of note after 1852, perhaps because he had decided to direct his energies to the exploitation of the chemical telegraph system.

Bain developed an automatic transmitting system using punched tape that enabled messages to be sent at the much higher speeds that the chemical receiver made possible, and his entire system transmitted and received information much more rapidly than the mechanical systems then in use. His system was first adopted for development in the United States by Henry O'Reilly and was subsequently taken up by others, but Samuel F. B. Morse and his associates immediately set out to kill it off, lest it supersede their own, much slower apparatus. Morse claimed patent infringement on the slender grounds that

The Fax Machine

In 1843, Alexander Bain received a British patent for his fax machine, titled "improvements in producing and regulating electric currents and improvements in timepieces and in electric printing and signal telegraphs." Bain's device—he did not, of course, use the term "fax machine," which is a conspicuously modern invention—employed a pair of carefully synchronized pendulums, one of which scanned a page containing text or a drawing, translating the presence of ink at a particular point on the page into an electrical impulse that could be reproduced at a remote location by causing paper impregnated with an electrochemically sensitive solution (a mixture of ammonium nitrate and potassium ferrocyanide) to darken at the equivalent point. Bain's fax machine did not catch on; nevertheless, Giovanni Caselli's pantelegraph was based on Bain's invention. Caselli's device became the first commercial fax machine, operating between Paris and Lyon from 1865 to 1870.

Bain applied for a new patent of an improved version of his copier in 1850 but could not obtain one because Frederick Bakewell had already obtained a patent for his own image telegraph in 1848; whether the latter should have been granted, in view of Bain's 1843 patent, is arguable, but as neither inventor managed to produce a marketable machine at the time, the question is probably irrelevant. The modern fax machine, however, uses the same principle, and its reinventors have been happy to give due credit to Bain for his remarkable anticipation. Indeed, Bain's fax machine was surely ahead of its time: It was not until the 1980's, about 140 years after Bain's patent was granted, that the fax machine saw widespread use.

the paper tape used in the automatic transmitter was his design, and that the alphabet used in signaling was also his intellectual property, although he had not invented it. The attempt to defend the case presumably drained Bain's resources and left him in dire straits, but there is no record of his activities in the late 1850's and throughout the 1860's, probably because he was not in Great Britain for much of that time. An automatic transmitting system designed by Wheatstone was, however, integrated with conventional receiving devices in the Electric Telegraph Company's system; Bain again felt that he had been robbed, but he could obtain no recompense this time.

Bain's other inventions included an electronic log to record the progress of ships at sea, translating signals from vanes rotating under the surface, and an electrical sounding apparatus for use at sea. Some of his electric signaling devices for use on the railways and for communication between railway carriages were adopted for use, but he does not appear to have made any money from them. He worked on dedicated telegraph systems for the use of fire and police services, but he was unable to get them adopted. He also invented a device enabling musical instruments to be played at a distance (a device of a sort pioneered by Wheatstone), a spill-proof inkwell, and a propelling pencil. He attempted some improvements to repeating firearms.

By 1872, Bain was back in Scotland repairing clocks for a living. He did some work for Lord Kelvin (William Thomson), an ingenious inventor who understood the import of Bain's innovations, having employed a variant of Bain's "inverted needle" system in his own siphon recorder. Kelvin took up his cause and managed to procure Bain a pension of £80 per year, beginning in 1873, and a grant of £150 from the Royal Society. Bain was in poor health by then, however, and when he lost the use of his legs Kelvin had to recommend him for admission to the Broomhill Home for Incurables at Kirkintilloch. After dying there, Bain was buried in the nearby Old Aisle Cemetery. His two sons survived him, but neither was living in Britain in the 1870's. One had emigrated to the United States, and the other was apparently resident somewhere in continental Europe.

Impact

In an era when so many inventors made money from their inventions, Bain suffered more than his fair share of misfortune—a circumstance probably connected to the fact that he was a highland Scotsman of humble origin and was thus regarded with a degree of contempt in England. Had he and the users of his chemical telegraph system been able to defend it successfully against the more aggressive and worldly wise Samuel Morse and his richer associates, that technology might have been standardized alongside systems translating received messages into sound, but the battle was fought on foreign soil against opponents who far outweighed him in terms of their resources. His copying systems—which were, in hindsight, much more interesting and potentially valuable than they seemed at the time—never won him the credit or the reward they warranted while he was alive. For these reasons, the direct impact of Bain's life and works was much less than it might have been, and it was left to historians of technology to provide respectful testimony to his awesome ingenuity.

—*Brian Stableford*

Further Reading

Burns, R. W. "Alexander Bain." *Engineering Science and Education Journal* 2, no. 2 (April, 1993): 85-93. A succinct account of Bain's technological achievements, with particular reference to their relevance to the development of telegraphy.

_______. "Alexander Bain." In the *Oxford Dictionary of National Biography*, edited by H. C. G. Matthew and Brian Harrison. New York: Oxford University Press, 2004. A summary of the (relatively few) recorded facts of Bain's life, without Munro's elaborations, which only lacks a few further details unearthed by local historians in Caithness.

Gunn, R. P. *Alexander Bain of Watten*. Thurso, England: Caithness Field Club, 1976. A pamphlet celebrating Bain's life and work, produced as an exercise in local history, which includes a few trivial details of Bain's early life not included in Munro or Burns.

Hackmann, W. D., ed. *Alexander Bain's Short History of the Electric Clock (1852)*. London: Turner and Devereux, 1973. A facsimile of Bain's first pamphlet—very few copies of which survive—with a brief account of its author and a commentary on the essay's significance as a historical document. Bain is credited with a second work, *A Treatise on Numerous Applications of Electrical Science to the Useful Arts* (1870), which is even rarer.

Munro, John. *Heroes of the Telegraph*. Whitefish, Mont.: Kessinger, 2004. A new edition of a work first published in 1883, whose ready availability in electronic form has resulted in its brief biographical note on Bain being reproduced and copied in many Internet sources, in spite of the fact that it compensates for a lack of hard information with dubious and colorfully expressed conjecture.

See also: Alexander Graham Bell; William Fothergill Cooke; Thomas Alva Edison; Elisha Gray; Lord Kelvin; Samuel F. B. Morse; Charles Wheatstone.

Benjamin Banneker

American mathematician and astronomer

Banneker was a largely self-educated African American astronomer. The series of almanacs he produced between 1792 and 1797 served to bring him international attention, both for their scientific content and for the role they played in the struggle against slavery.

Born: November 9, 1731; Baltimore County, Maryland
Died: October 9, 1806; Baltimore County, Maryland
Primary fields: Astronomy; mathematics
Primary inventions: Wooden striking clock; Banneker's almanac

Early Life

Benjamin Banneker (BAN-eh-kur) was born in Baltimore County, Maryland, on November 9, 1731. His grandmother was an English indentured servant named Molly Welsh who arrived in Maryland in the early 1680's and later married a former slave known as Bannka, Bannaka, or Banneka. Their oldest child, Mary (Benjamin's mother), in turn also married a former slave who, since he had no last name of his own, took his wife's name, which eventually became Banneker.

Benjamin grew up on his parents' farm, which was located close by the farm where his grandmother still resided. His grandmother, in fact, stands out as one of the important influences of his early years, instructing him in reading, writing, and religion and taking early note of his intellectual promise. She also arranged for him to attend a local Quaker school, where his intellectual gifts were further nurtured. He eventually demonstrated a particular ability in mathematics and practical mechanics and in his early twenties borrowed a watch that he studied in detail and used as a model for a clock of his own design and construction that became a source of local amazement. The clock, the inner workings of which were fashioned almost entirely of wood, struck the hours and continued to operate for more than fifty years until it was lost in a fire that destroyed Banneker's house at the time of his death in 1806. Following his own father's death in 1759, Benjamin took over the responsibility of running the family farm and had less time at his disposal to pursue his scientific and mechanical interests. He continued to read and educate himself as time permitted, and he also cultivated what was to become a lifelong interest in music, becoming a competent player of both the flute and the violin. For the most part, however, during the dozen or so years that followed he lived a quiet rural existence.

Life's Work

A major change occurred in Banneker's life in the early 1770's, when members of the Ellicott family—initially two brothers, John and Andrew—arrived in the area from Pennsylvania and began to construct a gristmill along the Patapsco River, just a short distance from the Banneker farm. This undertaking and the community that grew up in connection with it, known as Ellicott's Lower Mills, quickly captured Banneker's attention, while the workings of the mill itself served to expose him to the technological developments of the early stages of the Industrial Revolution. The Quaker background of the Ellicotts also offered a more enlightened racial outlook than that held by other whites in the area, some of whom seemed to have harassed Banneker at various times during his life.

Over the course of the years that followed, Banneker developed friendships with several members of the Ellicott family, drawing intellectual stimulation from the knowledge of science and technology that they brought into the area. With a third Ellicott brother, Joseph, who also settled in the community, Banneker shared a common interest in clockmaking, as this individual had also designed and built a clock that soon gained considerable local attention. Joseph Ellicott's clock, which was close to eight feet tall and was kept in the main hallway of his home, had four sides—the first showing the movements of the planets around the Sun, the second displaying time, the third listing and marking the names of twenty-four songs that played at each of the day's passing hours, and the fourth containing a glass window through which one could view the clock's inner workings. In many ways, these two local clocks, Banneker's wooden clock and Joseph Ellicott's far more complex technical achievement, serve to highlight the new level of scientific and technological sophistication that the arrival of the Ellicotts brought into Banneker's life.

Of all the Ellicotts, it was Andrew Ellicott's son George, a skilled land surveyor, mathematician, and astronomer, with whom Banneker developed the closest long-term relationship. Although separated by nearly thirty years in age—Banneker was forty-seven and George eighteen when they met—their shared interests provided an intellectual stimulus for both and would lead Banneker into what was to be his most important and productive period as a scientist. As time permitted after their initial meeting in 1778, Banneker and George Ellicott met and discussed their mutual areas of interest. In 1788, given his busy work schedule and lack of opportunity for pursuing his own scientific projects, Ellicott offered Banneker the use of some of his books on astronomy as well as some of the scientific instruments he had collected. Suspecting that Banneker would soon be making his own nighttime observations, Ellicott also provided him with a small wooden table and a tin candleholder to assist him with the recording of data.

Benjamin Banneker, 1980 commemorative U.S. postage stamp. (Arkent Archive)

Within a short period of time, Banneker was indeed using his nights to do astronomical observations and was soon undertaking the mathematical calculations of eclipses. This in turn led to an interest in producing an ephemeris, a compendium of astronomical facts and predictions, for one of the many almanacs that were being published in America at this time. Following several years of struggle and numerous setbacks for Banneker, his first almanac, entitled *Benjamin Banneker's Pennsylvania, Delaware, Maryland, and Virginia Almanack and Ephemeris, for the Year of Our Lord, 1792*, was published by the firm of Goddard and Angell in Baltimore in December, 1791. By that time, his work had come to the attention of then secretary of state Thomas Jefferson as well as several individuals prominent in the antislavery movement for the example it provided of the achievement potential of his race. The 1792 almanac was followed by similar annual publications in 1793-1797.

The year prior to the publication of his first almanac, and once again as a result of his connections with the Ellicott family, Banneker also participated in the land survey of the newly established District of Columbia. Following the passage of legislation in 1790 to create the District, Major Andrew Ellicott, the son of one of the original founders of the gristmill and community located near Banneker's farm, was chosen to undertake a survey of the new territory. Seeking individuals skilled in the use of scientific instruments and good at keeping accurate records, Ellicott first approached his cousin George to serve with him as an assistant. When George proved too busy with other work, he in turn suggested Banneker. Now close to sixty years old and seldom having ventured beyond the confines of his farm, Banneker nevertheless agreed to participate in the project. The survey, which began in February of 1791, proved to be a difficult undertaking. Living in a tent, engaging at night in the astronomical observations required by the project and then being unable to get sufficient rest during the day due to Andrew Ellicott's rigid dawn-to-dark, seven-day-a-week schedule, Banneker remained on the project until the latter part of April. Then, with the arrival of Andrew's younger brother Benjamin who was able to take over his role in the project, Banneker returned home to continue his own observations and study.

By the mid-1790's, Banneker's work had earned him both national and international attention. His almanacs were well known both in the United States and England, particularly among those engaged in the fight against slavery. The second edition of his almanac included a famous exchange of letters between Banneker and Thomas Jefferson on the subject of race as well as an essay against war by the prominent physician and writer Benjamin Rush. Subsequent issues of his almanac also included material dealing with the abolition cause and racial equality.

Following the publication of his last almanac in 1797, Banneker's life returned in large part to its earlier pattern of rural simplicity. Banneker's health gradually declined as he entered his final years. He continued to live alone, having never married, and to take care of himself. He kept a journal that included his thoughts and observations on nature and other subjects. He died peacefully at home following a morning walk on October 9, 1806.

BANNEKER'S WOODEN STRIKING CLOCK

While not an inventor per se (being best known for his astronomical calculations and almanacs), Benjamin Banneker is nevertheless remembered for the amazing wooden striking clock that he designed and built while still in his early twenties. Living an isolated existence as a free black in rural Maryland in the mid-eighteenth century, Banneker had little initial exposure to the scientific and technological discoveries of his day. Intrigued by a pocket watch that he saw one day and subsequently borrowed, he studied the instrument in great detail and determined to build a working clock of his own. Envisioning the problem of his clock's design as a kind of mathematical puzzle, he first calculated and diagrammed its inner works, then carefully and meticulously carved the individual parts out of hard wood, spending many hours modifying each part during the process of assembly.

The completed work was thus constructed almost entirely of wood. It had a hand-inscribed dial plate and carved wooden hands, and it accurately struck the hours of the day. The clock continued to operate for more than fifty years until it was destroyed in a fire at the time of his death in 1806. Sadly, the clock's destruction in the fire eliminated the possibility of knowing its precise design. Its existence, however, has been fully documented by Banneker's principal biographer, Silvio Bedini—an important point since so much of Banneker's life has entered the realm of legend. Throughout Banneker's lifetime, the clock remained a source of amazement to local citizens as well as to travelers to the area. While clearly not as significant as his other scientific work, Banneker's wooden striking clock nonetheless serves to highlight the amazing genius of this eighteenth century African American astronomer and scientist.

IMPACT

Banneker was a man of significant natural gifts. With almost no formal education, and living a quiet rural existence as a free black man in a state that still practiced slavery, he gained international recognition as an astronomer and mathematician. The series of almanacs that he published between 1792 and 1797 and the astronomical facts and calculations they contained were the chief source of his fame, but of close to equal importance was the social significance given to these works. Viewed and considered by individuals as prominent as Jefferson, the works helped to challenge the existing racial stereotypes of the age. Banneker's relationship with members of the Ellicott family, whose presence in his home region played an important part in his success, also offers an interesting example of enlightened race relations during the period as well as providing evidence of the manner in which scientific knowledge was disseminated and exchanged in eighteenth century America. Finally, his daily notes and journals provide valuable insights into the manner in which he worked as well as the way his methods evolved over time, information not widely available for other astronomers and ephemeris-producers of the period.

—Scott Wright

FURTHER READING

Bedini, Silvio A. *The Life of Benjamin Banneker: The First African-American Man of Science*. Rev. ed. Baltimore: Maryland Historical Society, 1999. The most complete biography of Banneker, exhaustively researched. Sorts out the facts and fictions surrounding his life and provides excellent historical background and context. Illustrations, bibliography, index.

Cerami, Charles. *Benjamin Banneker: Surveyor, Astronomer, Publisher, Patriot*. New York: John Wiley & Sons, 2002. A popular and readable biography of Banneker, but less well documented than Bedini's work. The author accepts, for example, material taken from Shirley Graham's largely fictionalized 1949 biography of Banneker on very tenuous grounds as well as exaggerating Banneker's abilities in relation to those of other prominent scientists and thinkers of the period. Bibliography, index.

Eglash, Ron. "The African Heritage of Benjamin Banneker." *Social Studies of Science* 27, no. 2 (April, 1997): 307-315. Offers a strong case for the influence of Banneker's African cultural background in his mathematical work, especially influences deriving from his father and grandfather. Illustrations.

See also: George Washington Carver; Thomas Jefferson.

John Bardeen

American physicist and electrical engineer

Bardeen's collaborative work led to the discovery of the transistor effect and to the development of a notable theory of superconductivity that resulted in his becoming the first person in history to win two Nobel Prizes in the same field—physics—one in 1956 and another in 1972.

Born: May 23, 1908; Madison, Wisconsin
Died: January 30, 1991; Boston, Massachusetts
Primary fields: Electronics and electrical engineering; physics
Primary inventions: Transistor; superconductivity theory

Early Life

John Bardeen was the son of Charles R. and Althea Harmer Bardeen. His father, a physician and professor of anatomy, was the founding dean of the University of Wisconsin Medical School in Madison, where John was raised. His mother was a teacher who was once associated with the Dewey Laboratory School at the University of Chicago.

Althea was instrumental in teaching John how to solve problems: break them down into their component parts, then work on solving each of these manageable parts. In his later life, this is precisely the way Bardeen approached the baffling problems on which he was working in physics. He also was exposed to progressive problem-solving techniques as a student at the University High School of the University of Wisconsin, which John entered after completing the third grade of elementary school. He completed high school when he was thirteen, but he took two more years of instruction at Madison Central High School (1921-1923) because Charles felt his son was too young and undeveloped socially to enter college.

When John was ten, his mother was diagnosed with cancer. Her children were shielded from the seriousness of her illness, but she was often away in Chicago for radiation and other treatments. Her children were stunned by her death in 1920. John's schoolwork suffered a temporary decline as he dealt with losing his mother.

The young man entered the University of Wisconsin in 1923 to study electrical engineering. As a student there, Bardeen encountered many impressive scientists and mathematicians. He took a tutorial with Warren Weaver, who encouraged Bardeen's mathematical development and who later became head of the Rockefeller Foundation's science program. Bardeen also studied with John Van Vleck, who introduced modern quantum mechanics to the midwestern campus and with whom Bardeen later was associated as a postdoctoral fellow at Harvard University, where Van Vleck was then teaching.

Bardeen postponed his college graduation for a year by taking extra courses and working for the Western Electric Company. Upon graduation in 1928, he had completed much of the course work for a master's degree, so he stayed on, receiving a master's degree in electrical engineering in 1929. He was recruited by the American Telephone and Telegraph Company (AT&T) to work on the diffraction of radio-length electromagnetic waves and antenna design, but before he could begin, a hiring freeze was imposed, so Bardeen went to work instead as a geophysicist for Gulf Oil.

Life's Work

When his interests veered more toward theoretical than applied physics, Bardeen decided to leave his secure job with Gulf Oil and enter the doctoral program in mathematics at Princeton University, to which many eminent German-Jewish mathematicians and physicists, including Albert Einstein, had flocked in an effort to escape Nazi Germany. He completed his doctorate in mathematical physics there in 1936, doing much of his research under his major professor, E. P. Wigner, who supervised the work of many students who later became some of the world's most celebrated figures in solid-state physics.

The night before he left for Princeton, Bardeen met Jane Maxwell, who taught at the Carnegie Institute of Technology and was a graduate student at the University of Pittsburgh. He visited her in Pittsburgh as often as he could. From 1935 until 1938, he was a junior fellow of the Society of Fellows at Harvard University, and in 1938, shortly after accepting a position as assistant professor of physics at the University of Minnesota, he married Jane. The couple subsequently had three children.

Bardeen was a self-effacing man with so soft a voice that some people referred to him as "the whisperer." He always preferred to work collaboratively with people in his field rather than pursue his research alone. After World War II, during which Bardeen was the principal physicist for the U.S. Naval Ordnance Laboratory in Washington, D.C., he was brought to Bell Telephone Laboratories in 1946 by William Shockley, whom Bardeen knew from their Harvard days. At Bardeen's urging, Shockley also brought Walter H. Brattain, a classmate of Bardeen in graduate school, to Bell Labs. The three collaborated on semiconduction, which led to their discovery of the transistor effect in 1947, for which the three shared the 1956 Nobel Prize in Physics.

The importance of the development of transistors cannot be overstated. Transistors are electronic devices made from semiconductor material capable of amplifying electrical signals, thereby bringing about many advances in technology. Bardeen's years in the Naval Ordnance Laboratory, where he worked on underwater ordnance and minesweeping, led inevitably to the work he did at Bell Labs. The transistor effect has broad implications for computers, radios, television broadcasting, satellite technology, industrial control systems, and navigation. Bardeen's work in this field also led directly to his subsequent work on the theory of superconductivity, for which he shared the 1972 Nobel Prize in Physics with Leon N. Cooper and John Robert Schrieffer.

Superconductivity has to do with the electrical reactions in metals and alloys whose temperature is reduced drastically, causing them to lose their resistance. Because of this lack of resistance in a superconducting circuit, when the temperature of the metal involved reaches absolute zero (–273.13° Celsius), the electrical current flows continuously. The implications of this for the generation of electrical power are immeasurable and are of sufficient importance that a great deal of subsequent research in the field has focused on achieving superconductivity at temperatures higher than absolute zero.

Bardeen left Bell Labs in 1951 to join the University

The Transistor

The understanding of the transistor effect stems from the observation that when an atom of phosphorus is forced upon an atom of silicon (replaced by germanium in later experiments), it contributes a negative electron to the silicon. On the other hand, when an atom of boron is forced upon an atom of silicon or germanium, it contributes a positive charge to the silicon or germanium and leaves a hole in the atomic structure that can migrate in semiconductors, thereby acting as a carrier of a positive charge.

On December 16, 1947, John Bardeen and Walter H. Brattain inserted two electrodes into a half-inch-long shred of germanium. They found that the electrical charge the germanium emitted was over one hundred times stronger than the charge that went in. This marked the beginning of transistors and of the information age. Bardeen and his colleagues initially were seeking to understand how to control rectifiers by adding an extra electrode. When they injected a positive probe close to a negative electrode, however, they discovered the transistor action that led to their understanding of the transistor effect. This theoretical understanding, in turn, eventually led, on an applied level, to the invention of transistors.

Transistors revolutionized the entire world of electronics on which modern society is so dependent. Whereas the vacuum tubes that were generally used as sources of power in their earliest electronic applications were large and cumbersome, transistors weigh little and are tiny. They can be mass-produced quickly and inexpensively. They are ideal for battery-powered uses because of the low voltages at which they can be operated.

Unlike vacuum tubes, transistors require no warm-up time but spring into action the moment the power source is engaged. They use power sparingly, so are notably power-efficient. They are generally rugged physically, although they can be subjected to interference from some electrical and magnetic fields. Transistors generally have a long life. Some have been in constant use since the late 1970's and are still operating. They can also control currents of several hundred amperes, which gives them a wide range of powerful uses.

Of considerable importance to such applications as the launching of spacecraft is the transistor's insensitivity to mechanical shock and heavy vibration. Transistors have made the exploration of space feasible because of their ability to withstand the vibrations involved in the launching of spacecraft.

The invention of the transistor has been called the most significant development of the twentieth century, and such a claim is not exaggerated. In an electronic age, the transistor affects the lives of everyone.

of Illinois at Urbana-Champaign as a professor of electrical engineering and physics. Working there in collaboration with Cooper and Schrieffer, he agonized over the theoretical aspects of superconductivity. Working mostly with little more than paper and pencils and examining closely all of the most significant theories of superconductivity, he and his colleagues unlocked the secret of the phenomenon, which is generally referred to as the BCS (Bardeen-Cooper-Schrieffer) theory. The method Bardeen, Cooper, and Schrieffer employed in dealing with the theoretical problems posed by their investigations provided a method for dealing with other physical problems. Their collaboration applied directly, for example, to understanding elementary particle theory.

From 1959 until his retirement in 1975, Bardeen taught at the Center for Advanced Study at the University of Illinois. He died of heart failure in Boston on January 30, 1991.

Impact

Were it not for the pioneering work of Bardeen, Shockley, and Brattain, the world would be much different today. There were computer systems as early as the 1940's, but they were powered by vacuum tubes that were large, cumbersome, and undependable. Physicist Miles Klein told an interviewer that the invention of the transistor and everything that grew out of it began an industrial revolution that was as equally as important as the first.

A machine called the Electronic Numerical Integrator and Computer (ENIAC) was developed by John Presper Eckert and John William Mauchly between 1943 and 1945 and was built at the Moore School of Electrical Engineering of the University of Pennsylvania. After the pair left the university, they set up their own company and produced the Universal Automatic Computer (UNIVAC), selling the first one to the U.S. Census Bureau in 1951. This computer could perform 1,905 operations per second, but it required 35.5 square meters of floor space and consumed power at a daunting rate. It originally cost $159,000, but the cost quickly rose to close to $1.5 million per unit, making it unobtainable for most colleges and universities as well as for industry.

Once the transistor was perfected, computers had a greatly increased capacity to carry out operations. Such computers were miniaturized to the point that they could sit on users' desks or even be held in the hand. The operations performed by the original UNIVAC soon were exceeded enormously by the relatively light personal computers (PCs) upon which many people currently depend.

Without transistors, it would have been impossible to engage in the sort of space exploration that has resulted in putting humans on the Moon and in establishing the International Space Station, which is in low Earth orbit at 17,210 miles per hour between 217 and 286 statute miles above Earth. Transistors have also made possible sophisticated medical hardware and complicated television sets, including high definition.

Bardeen's research has paved the way to finding methods of achieving superconductivity at temperatures well above absolute zero. The practical outcomes of doing so are incalculable. When superconductivity is

From left: John Bardeen, William Shockley, and Walter H. Brattain working at Bell Labs in Murray Hill, New Jersey, in 1956. The three men shared that year's Nobel Prize in Physics for their discovery of the transistor effect in 1947. (AP/Wide World Photos)

achieved at higher temperatures, many of the energy problems facing the world today should be greatly diminished.

—*R. Baird Shuman*

Further Reading

Ginzburg, V. L. *The Physics of a Lifetime: Reflections on the Problems and Personalities of Twentieth Century Physics*. New York: Springer, 2001. Ginzburg devotes a lucid six-page segment to Bardeen and superconductivity. A valuable brief overview.

Hoddeson, Lillian, and Vicki Daitch. *True Genius: The Life and Science of John Bardeen, the Only Winner of Two Nobel Prizes in Physics*. Washington, D.C.: J. Henry Press, 2002. This full-length study of Bardeen is detailed and readable, written by two people with close ties to the University of Illinois and to Bardeen. Indispensable for those interested in Bardeen's accomplishments and contributions.

Kursunoglu, Behram, and Arnold Perlmutter, eds. *Impact of Basic Research on Technology*. New York: Plenum Press, 1973. Bardeen's forty-two-page contribution to this volume, "History of Superconductivity Research," is a clear and comprehensive overview of all that led up to his own involvement in solving the mystery of superconductivity. This chapter, although sometimes quite technical, is generally understandable.

Riordan, Michael, and Lillian Hoddeson. *Crystal Fire: The Birth of the Information Age*. New York: W. W. Norton, 1997. The best, most lucid book in print on transistors and on Bardeen's contributions to the field.

Schrieffer, John Robert. *The Theory of Superconductivity*. Reading, Mass.: Benjamin-Cummings, 1988. This presentation of the theory of superconductivity by one of the three winners of the Nobel Prize for articulating the theory is at times quite technical, but it is a valuable resource. Schrieffer reproduces the Nobel addresses of the 1972 Nobel laureates.

Seiler, David G., et al., eds. *Characterization and Metrology for ULSI Technology*. Melville, N.Y.: American Institute of Physics, 2001. The thirty-page chapter entitled "John Bardeen and Transistor Physics" is particularly relevant. It is clear and detailed.

See also: Walter H. Brattain; John Presper Eckert; Nick Holonyak, Jr.; Jack St. Clair Kilby; John William Mauchly; Karl Alexander Müller; Stanford Ovshinsky; Gerald Pearson; Claude Elwood Shannon; William Shockley.

Patricia Bath

American opthalmologist

A lifelong advocate for the blind, Bath introduced a safe and accurate laser surgery device and method for the removal of cataracts.

Born: November 4, 1942; Harlem, New York
Also known as: Patricia Era Bath (full name)
Primary field: Medicine and medical technology
Primary invention: Laserphaco probe

Early Life

Patricia Era Bath was born to Rupert and Gladys Bath in Harlem, New York. Rupert Bath was an immigrant from Trinidad, British West Indies, and her American mother was the descendant of African slaves and Cherokee Native Americans. Her father worked in a variety of jobs; he served as a motorman for the New York City subway, a merchant seaman, and a newspaper columnist. Her mother was a housewife who also worked as a domestic, one of the few positions open for African American women in the 1940's, in order to save money for her children's education.

Bath was interested in problem solving from childhood. This interest was encouraged at Charles Evans Hughes High School in New York, where she took biology courses that first sparked her interest in the sciences. She excelled in school and earned numerous awards. She applied for a National Science Foundation Scholarship and was chosen in 1959 to work in a summer program for high school students at Yeshiva University. She was also able to work with the university and Harlem Hospital on cancer research. During this time, she worked with Rabbi Moses D. Tendler and Dr. Robert O. Bernard; it was her job to collect and analyze information in an effort to forecast the progression of cancer cells. She coauthored a research report presented at the Fifth Annual International Congress on Nutrition in Washington, D.C., on September 2, 1960. That same year, she won a Merit Award from *Mademoiselle* magazine. Bath completed high school in just two and a half years.

Bath's higher education began at Hunter College in New York, where she graduated with a bachelor's degree

The Laserphaco Probe

Dr. Patricia Bath began work on an invention for laser cataract surgery in 1981. Unable to find the appropriate lasers in the United States, she traveled to Berlin, Germany, where she studied the latest laser technology as she designed her "apparatus for ablating and removing cataract lenses," later called the laserphaco probe. Once the invention was complete, she successfully tested it on human cadavers. Her device was first used on live human subjects seven years after she began experiments, and she was awarded a patent for her laserphaco probe in 1988.

Bath's procedure uses a laser to destroy and remove the cataract coating of the eye. A flexible line (less than one millimeter in diameter) is inserted through an incision in the lens until it is next to the cataract. Low amounts of coherent radiation then blast the cataract by an optical fiber in the line. The line also contains a tube for irrigating the eye and a tube for removing the ablated pieces of the cataract during the procedure. A new lens is then inserted into the eye to replace the lens that held the cataract.

Bath's laser probe method was revolutionary in its ability to remove cataracts safely. It replaced traditional methods, the most common of which used a drill-like device to grind the cataract. This outdated technique was sometimes inexact and potentially harmful.

in chemistry in 1964. She continued her graduate education at Howard University Medical School, graduating with a medical degree in 1968. This was followed by an internship at Harlem Hospital (1968-1969), a fellowship at Columbia University (1969-1970), and a residency at New York University (1970-1973).

Life's Work

In 1967, while at Howard, Bath traveled to Yugoslavia to study children's health issues. A year later, she joined the Poor People's Campaign as they marched in Washington, D.C., for economic rights. After graduating from Howard, she studied ophthalmology at Columbia and became an assistant of surgery at hospitals throughout New York. During the following years, she traveled to Africa to serve as chief of ophthalmology at Mercy Hospital in Nigeria. She also worked with the White House Counsel for a National and International Blindness Prevention Program for two years.

Bath became interested in working with the visually impaired while she was at Columbia University. While serving at the Eye Clinic in Harlem, she observed a large number of African Americans suffering from vision problems. In a well-received report, she concluded that African Americans were twice as likely as the general population to suffer from blindness. Moreover, the study showed that African Americans were eight times more likely than whites to suffer from glaucoma-related blindness. Her work prompted her to create the practice of community ophthalmology, in which volunteers visit underserved communities to screen for vision problems.

In 1973, Bath completed her residency in ophthalmology at New York University. That year, she moved to California to join the faculty at the University of California, Los Angeles (UCLA), and Charles R. Drew University. In 1976, she cofounded the American Institute for the Prevention of Blindness. In 1983, she cofounded and chaired the Ophthalmology Residency Training Program at UCLA-Drew.

One of Bath's main areas of interest was cataract disease. A cataract is a clouding of the lens of the eye that can impair vision and sometimes cause blindness. Bath began researching laser surgery as a treatment for vision problems, and her research took her to Germany to study the latest technology. By 1986, she had designed a laser instrument for removing cataracts and successfully tested it. Bath's laser surgery method was faster, safer, and more accurate than traditional methods of cataract surgery.

Bath was granted U.S. Patent number 4,744,360 on May 17, 1988, for her laserphaco probe, becoming the first African American woman to be awarded a patent for a medical invention. The laserphaco probe works with a concentrated beam of light that breaks up and destroys the cataract. In the following years, she improved the invention and received three more patents: a method for breaking down and removing cataracts (number 5,843,071), in 1998; another laser product used for surgery on cataract lenses (number 5,919,186), in 1999; and an ultrasound method for the breaking and removing of cataracts (number 6,083,192), in 2000. She has also received patents in Europe, Japan, and Canada.

Dr. Bath is a professor emeritus and was nominated to the National Inventors Hall of Fame by the American Intellectual Property Law Association. After retiring from UCLA in 1993, she continued to promote vision care outreach, especially for the underprivileged.

Impact

As the first African American woman to receive a patent for a medical device, Bath is a role model for African

Americans, women, and other minorities. Her laser cataract surgery method has been used throughout the world, including India, Italy, and Germany. Bath's advocacy work with organizations such as the American Institute for the Prevention of Blindness was groundbreaking. Even after retirement, she has maintained a busy schedule, giving speeches to young people, promoting community ophthalmology, and traveling around the world doing surgery. It is her deepest wish to be able to eventually eliminate blindness. She has also promoted telemedicine, the use of electronic communications to deliver medical services to remote regions where medical care is limited or unavailable.

—*Theresa L. Stowell*

Further Reading

Apple, David J. *Intraocular Lenses: Evolution, Designs, Complications, and Pathology*. Baltimore: Williams and Wilkins, 1989. A technical discussion of the intraocular lens. Important as it relates to Bath's life work and inventions.

Henderson, Susan K. *African-American Inventors III: Patricia Bath, Philip Emeagwali, Henry Sampson, Valerie Thomas, Peter Tolliver*. Mankato, Minn.: Capstone Press, 1998. A set of short biographies written for a juvenile audience. Contains photographs, illustrations of the inventions, and copious references.

Pursell, Carroll W., ed. *A Hammer in Their Hands: A Documentary History of Technology and the African-American Experience*. Cambridge, Mass.: MIT Press, 2005. A collection of essays about African American achievements from colonial times to the twenty-first century. Though the book does not specifically address Bath, it is an invaluable source.

Sullivan, Otha Richard, and James Haskins. *African American Women Scientists and Inventors*. New York: Wiley, 2002. A simple, straightforward presentation of African American women who have influenced science and technology. Contains a chapter on Patricia Bath. Written for a juvenile audience.

Young, Jeff C. *Inspiring African American Inventors: Nine Extraordinary Lives*. Berkeley Heights, N.J.: Enslow, 2008. A juvenile book about African American scientists and mathematicians.

See also: Louis Braille; Charles Richard Drew; Rangaswamy Srinivasan.

Andrew Jackson Beard

American engineer

Beard's major invention was the automatic railroad car coupler, which dramatically improved the speed and safety for joining railroad cars. He also patented a rotary steam engine and an improved plow.

Born: March 29, 1849; Woodland, near Mount Pinson, Jefferson County, Alabama
Died: May 10, 1921; Birmingham, Alabama
Primary fields: Agriculture; railway engineering
Primary inventions: Jenny coupler; rotary steam engine

Early Life

Andrew Jackson Beard was born in 1849 as a slave on a plantation in Woodland, Alabama. His parents, a slave couple, chose the Beard surname from the owner of the plantation. Andrew had no formal education during childhood or at any other time during his life. Consequently, he could neither read nor write. Learning took place through interaction with others. By the time the fifteen-year-old Andrew became a free man, he had already developed skills in agriculture, carpentry, and blacksmithing. He chose to remain on the Beard farm until 1868, eking out a living as a sharecropper. He was able to accumulate enough assets to purchase an eighty-acre farm near Center Point, Alabama. There Andrew and his wife, Edie, raised three sons. He also raised the three sons and daughter of Hattie Horton, one of his sharecropper tenants, and gave them his surname.

Although Beard was proud of owning his own farm, farming became less and less appealing to him. His epiphany came in 1872, after an arduous three-week trip by oxcart to Montgomery. After that trip, Beard built a flour mill and a church (which also served as a school) on his land for his tenant farmers. Although Beard was illiterate, he had a great respect for education.

Beard's flour mill, located in Hardwicks, Alabama, ran smoothly and generated capital, but his mind began to drift to other projects. He began experimenting with designs for an improved plow, and he registered a patent for it in 1881. Another improved plow was patented in 1887. Selling his rights to the patents for nearly $10,000, Beard invested the money into a real estate business. Within a few years, his capital accumulation was $30,000. Once again, Beard's creative energies were channeled in other directions.

Life's Work

During the early 1890's, Beard became an employee of the Alabama and Chattanooga Railroad (which grew to become the Georgia Pacific and Southern Railway system). He became obsessed with designing a rotary steam engine that would be safer, more efficient, and more economical than the conventional steam engines of his time. Exploding steam engines were a common cause of injury or death, but Beard's rotary engine was not subject to explosion because of its more even distribution of internal pressure. His venture was closely supported by Melville Drennen, who served two terms as mayor of Birmingham. In July, 1892, Beard was granted a patent for the rotary engine by the U.S. Patent Office. Few would have predicted that a former slave, lacking basic literary skills and any sort of structured education, and operating in a deeply racist society, could have achieved so much. He was not only a financial success in several different careers but also a creative genius as an inventor. Although by the age of forty-three Beard had achieved much, his greatest invention was yet to come.

While working on his rotary steam engine, Beard also became intrigued with the problem of joining railroad cars together. Often, railroad yard workers were mutilated or killed while attempting the dangerous operation of dropping a pin at exactly the right moment into a receiver hole of a railroad car in motion. If the worker did not move away from the cars fast enough, he could be crushed. It was Beard's dream to remove the human element from the process and design a system based on the automatic coupling of cars. Beard worked at home tinkering on a safe and efficient means of coupling cars. He was not trained in either engineering or metalworking, so the venture must have seemed overly ambitious to observers. What he designed by 1897 was a system in which horizontal jaws placed at each end of a railroad car engage each other merely by bumping. On November 23, 1897, he received a patent for an automatic coupler. His application was signed with the characteristic *X*, witnessed by two observers.

To attract investors, Beard built a wooden model of the "Jenny coupler," which was displayed at a convention of the Master Car Builders' Association in Atlantic City, New Jersey. Based on the potential of his invention, Beard was made an honorary member of that association. This was a great honor for an uneducated former slave. The distinction also made it possible to attract several Birmingham investors and market his invention. He founded the Beard Automatic Coupler Company and registered four additional patents for improvements to the coupler between 1899 and 1904. Ultimately,

The Jenny Coupler

While much railroad technology advanced during the nineteenth century, some remained primitive, including the link-and-pin method used to link freight cars and passenger cars together. To accomplish linkage between cars, a switchman had to stand between the cars as they came together and drop a coupling link into a slot. To achieve this, the brakeman had to signal the engineer to back up into exactly the right position. Timing errors of even a few seconds could be fatal. As the number of railroad cars attached to a train became longer, visual contact in the operation became more difficult to maintain. The result was an ever-increasing loss of limbs and lives. Moreover, coupling pins suffered metal fatigue or were uneven in size and frequently broke. In fact, there was no standard design for a coupling pin, and train crews wasted valuable time trying to match pins and links. Also wasted were money and lives, since coupling-pin failure was a common cause of railroad accidents.

The knuckle coupler was invented by Eli H. Janney in 1873 and provided some relief for link-and-pin coupling problems. However, it was only used after 1888 in freight cars carrying heavy loads and had several drawbacks, including the all-too-frequent need to manually align cars after linkage failures. Hundreds of other coupling devices were patented after Janney's, but none proved efficient or appealing.

Andrew Jackson Beard's "Jenny coupler," patented on November 23, 1897, eliminated the need for workers to be used in the coupler process by having two horizontal jaws attached to the cars that locked together automatically. Because of its reliability and reasonable cost, Beard's invention gained rapid acceptance. In 1893, Congress passed the Railroad Safety Appliance Act, which took effect in 1900, making it unlawful to operate railroad cars that did not have automatic couplers. During the last year that link-and-pin coupling was legal in the United States, three hundred railroad worker deaths due to coupling accidents were recorded.

he sold the rights to the coupler to a New York company for $50,000. Further royalties made Beard the first African American millionaire in Jefferson County.

Beard's new fortune was heavily invested in real estate. For the African American residents of Birmingham, Beard's accomplishments were a source of pride. Often the mustached, bespectacled, well-dressed inventor could be seen with his fine horse and shiny buggy riding down the streets of Birmingham. However, while Beard's investments were at first successful, the issue of his illiteracy and business mismanagement caused many business failures and near bankruptcy. He continued with his inventions as much as declining health allowed but registered no new patents. In his later years, suffering from arteriosclerosis and virtually paralyzed, he lived with his foster daughter, Mamie, in Woodlawn. He was admitted to the Jefferson County Alms House soon before he died. His funeral was held at Jackson Street Baptist Church, and his remains lie in an unmarked grave in Woodlawn Cemetery.

Impact

Beard's well-designed rotary steam engine produced little impact in U.S. locomotive design. Ultimately, only a few rotary engines were constructed by European concerns and were used for limited purposes. His Jenny coupler, however, transformed railroad efficiency and safety for rail yard workers. In 1892 alone, there were 11,000 recorded accidents in the United States involving the coupling of railroad cars. In an age before workers' compensation and other types of worker insurance, crippling or deadly accidents such as those produced by being crushed between two railroad cars were tragedies both for the individual involved and for the family who relied on the worker's income.

In 2006, Beard was inducted into the National Inventors Hall of Fame for his contributions to rail transport coupler design. He is credited with inventing the first automatic railroad car coupler, which dramatically reduced serious injuries to railroad workers. Beard's invention, patented in 1897 and improved in 1899, was identified as a forerunner of automatic couplers used today. Automatic couplers also made possible the use of power air brakes, which had not been successfully used with link-and-pin couplers because of excessive slack in the coupling.

The fact that it has taken over a century for Andrew Jackson Beard to gain national recognition as a major American inventor is a situation that has an impact all its own, indicating that African Americans have made a larger contribution to the development of technology in the United States than has been officially recognized.

—Irwin Halfond

Further Reading

Daniels, Rudolph. *Trains Across the Continent: North American Railroad History*. Bloomington: Indiana University Press, 2000. An excellent study on the development of railroads in the United States. The chapter "Glory Years Technology" is particularly relevant to problems related to the development of coupling instruments. Contains index, notes, bibliography.

McKinley, Burt. *African-American Inventors*. Portland, Oreg.: National Book Company, 2000. Short studies on black inventors, including Andrew Beard. Includes bibliographic references.

Sullivan, Richard Otha. *African American Inventors*. New York: John Wiley & Sons, 1998. Written for a juvenile audience, this work contains a short biography of Beard.

See also: Peter Cooper; Elijah McCoy; George Mortimer Pullman; George Stephenson; George Westinghouse; Granville T. Woods.

J. GEORG BEDNORZ

German physicist

Bednorz, with Karl Alexander Müller, discovered high-temperature superconductivity in a new class of ceramic materials. Although this discovery did not lead immediately to technological applications, it galvanized scientists around the world to search for new and better superconductors.

Born: May 16, 1950; Neuenkirchen, North-Rhine Westphalia, West Germany (now in Germany)
Also known as: Johannes Georg Bednorz (full name)
Primary field: Physics
Primary invention: High-temperature superconductors

EARLY LIFE

Johannes Georg Bednorz (yoh-HAH-nuhs GEY-awrk BEHD-nawrts) was born in Neuenkirchen, a small town in the West German region of North-Rhine Westphalia. His parents, Anton and Elisabeth Bednorz, came from Silesia. During the convulsions of World War II, his parents along with his sister and two older brothers became separated, and the family was not reunited until 1949, with Georg being born in 1950. Anton got a job as a primary school teacher, and Elisabeth taught piano. His mother tried to interest her youngest son in classical music, but he rebelled, preferring to help his brothers in working on their motorcycle and automobile. After Georg began attending elementary school, a charismatic teacher inspired him to see how music and the arts could foster creativity and community spirit, and at thirteen he studied the violin and later the trumpet, which he played in the school orchestra.

As an adolescent, Georg became so interested in chemistry that he set up a laboratory in the basement of his home, where he conducted experiments. During his high school years, he was more fascinated with chemistry than physics, because his physics teacher stressed theories while his chemistry teacher encouraged him to devise his own experiments. In 1969, he entered the University of Münster, intending to major in chemistry, but he found the introductory chemistry classes large and impersonal, and he eventually discovered a group of crystallographers that functioned more as a family. Since he also enjoyed creating complex crystals and investigating their physical and chemical properties, he switched his major to crystallography.

During the summer of 1972, while still an undergraduate, he spent three months at the IBM Research Laboratory in Rüschlikon, Switzerland, a suburb of Zurich. Here he met such distinguished physicists as Karl Alexander Müller, expanded his knowledge of solid-state chemistry, and deepened his understanding of how to grow crystals. In 1973, he was able to spend six months at this laboratory, when he became interested in perovskites, natural minerals named for the Russian count and scientist L. A. Perovski. The perovskites had a fascinating crystal structure, a central feature of which is a metal atom surrounded by six oxygen atoms in an octahedral array. While at Münster, Bednorz met Mechthild Wennemer, a fellow student who became a close friend.

After graduating from Münster in 1976, Bednorz remained for a year to do research, before he joined the laboratory of solid-state physics at the Swiss Federal Institute of Technology (whose acronym, ETH, derives from its German name) in Zurich. He started work on his doctoral thesis under the joint supervision of Heini Gränicher and Müller. While engaged in his doctoral research, he grew close to Müller because of their mutual interest in perovskites. Wennemer came to ETH to pursue her own doctorate, and in 1978 she and Bednorz were married. After he completed his dissertation on the crystal growth of certain perovskites and an analysis of their electric and magnetic properties, he received his Ph.D. in 1982.

LIFE'S WORK

Once he and his wife settled in Switzerland, Bednorz continued to center his work on the perovskites, especially strontium titanium trioxide and lanthanum aluminum trioxide. When Müller asked him if he would like to investigate whether such oxides conducted electricity with no resistance at temperatures close to absolute zero (this phenomenon is called superconductivity), Bednorz agreed. Unfortunately, Bednorz encountered a series of failures when he made oxides with the metals nickel and copper and tested them for superconductivity.

His luck changed in 1986, when he made and tested a ceramic compound of lanthanum, barium, copper, and oxygen. Within a short time, he was able to show that this perovskite-type oxide superconducted at a temperature as high as 35 kelvins, twelve kelvins higher than the previous record. Because research in this area had become littered with damaged and ruined reputations when claims to have found high-temperature superconductors turned out to be false, Müller and Bednorz were cautious when they submitted their paper to *Zeitschrift für Physik* in April, titling it "Possible High T_c Superconductivity in the Barium-Lanthanum-Copper-Oxygen System." When their paper was published in September, it initially garnered a cautious response. Bednorz has recalled that in his early talks, audiences of scientists were skeptical. It was not until later in 1986 and early in 1987, when magnetic studies of their superconductor verified their claim, that excitement increased and quickly became contagious. Within a very short time, their paper, published without fanfare in a modest journal, gathered over a thousand citations, while scientists all over the world raced to discover more and better high-temperature superconductors.

Although Alfred Nobel had wanted his foundation to recognize recent pivotal discoveries, this had rarely been done, but in the case of Bednorz and Müller it was. In 1987, Müller and Bednorz received the Nobel Prize in Physics for their discovery of high-temperature superconductivity in a new class of materials. Some controversy followed this award, because not one of the scientists who had discovered better high-temperature superconductors than the one of Bednorz and Müller was a corecipient. Members of the Swedish Academy defended their choice by pointing out that the discovery of Bednorz and Müller had led to all the others.

Bednorz continued to do research in this new field that he had helped create, but none of his later discoveries proved to be as significant as his Nobel Prize-winning work. Throughout the remaining years of the twentieth and into the twenty-first century, he received many honors and awards from scientific societies and academic institutions in Europe, America, and Asia, including an honorary doctorate from the University of Silesia, which was especially meaningful to him because of his family's origins. At the IBM Research Laboratory, he studied how the ceramic oxides could be modified to make their use in microelectronic devices effective. For example, he found ways of manipulating certain ceramic oxides so that they might be used as computer memory elements. Unlike his work on the first high-temperature supercon-

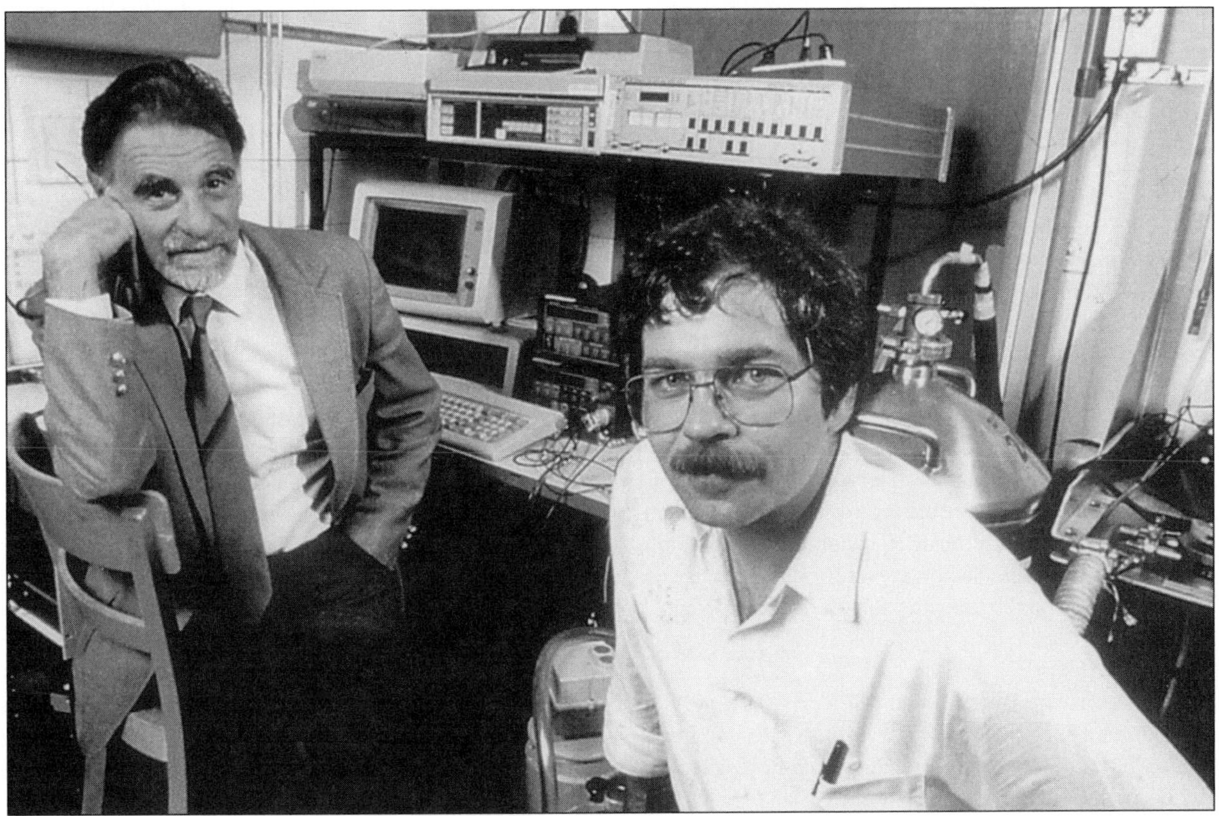

J. Georg Bednorz, right, and Karl Alexander Müller won the 1987 Nobel Prize in Physics for synthesizing a new ceramic substance capable of superconductivity at 35 kelvins. (IBM Corporation, AIP Emilio Segrè Visual Archives)

The First High-Temperature Superconductor

A revolutionary discovery often represents a dramatic transition from a previous state to a radically new one. In the field of superconductivity, not much had changed from 1911, when Dutch physicist Heike Kamerlingh Onnes discovered that mercury completely lost its resistance to electric current when cooled to 4 kelvins. By 1986, despite seventy-five years of research, scientists, using various metals and alloys, had only been able to increase superconductive temperatures to 23 kelvins. The revolutionary discovery of a new class of materials that superconducted at much higher temperatures was due to a confluence of causes. Karl Alexander Müller, after working in the United States, returned to Switzerland convinced that a high-temperature superconductor would have to be an oxide, and he put J. Georg Bednorz to work on such compounds as lanthanum nickel trioxide, a perovskite, but the results were unpromising. Bednorz and Müller moved on to copper-containing compounds, but these, too, gave disappointing results. A turning point occurred in 1985, when Bednorz read about a ceramic compound prepared by French chemists who were only interested in its catalytic properties. Bednorz, on the other hand, thought that this barium-doped lanthanum cuprate with a perovskite structure was a candidate for superconductivity.

Bednorz prepared a sample of the ceramic compounds of lanthanum, barium, copper, and oxygen in a low-temperature oven (had he used elevated temperatures, the resulting sample would have failed to superconduct). In January, 1986, he subjected this material to an electrical test, finding that its resistivity sharply dropped at temperatures as high as 35 kelvins. Preliminary evidence indicated that Bednorz and Müller had found a new superconductor with an unexpectedly high transition point. In April, 1986, they submitted their results for publication, and their paper appeared in September. Later in 1986, magnetic measurements in their own laboratory (with a new magnetometer) and in Tokyo confirmed their discovery, precipitating an avalanche of discoveries of many new superconductors with higher and higher transition temperatures. The importance of their work was recognized by a Nobel Prize in Physics and many other awards. They also had the pleasure of witnessing the explosion of interest and many applications of high-temperature superconductivity that their original discovery had started.

ductor, he was now not alone in searching for practical applications based on his discovery. He has become one participant among many seeking ways to develop technologies that will, by making insightful use of high-temperature superconductors, revolutionize all those devices that rely on the transmission of electric current.

Impact

The discovery by Bednorz and Müller of the first high-temperature superconductor was remarkable in part because it was totally unexpected, even by those scientists working in the field. Once this discovery had been verified, its impact was revolutionary. It galvanized physicists and chemists all over the world to search for new and better superconductors. With so many researchers engaged in this quest, successes followed, and other ceramic materials with higher and higher transition temperatures began to be discovered. Significantly, Maw-Kuen Wu and his associates showed that a yttrium-barium-copper-oxygen ceramic material manifested zero resistance at temperatures above 90 kelvins (it was called the 1-2-3 superconductor from the relative atomic proportions of its first three elements). Dr. Wu flew from Alabama to Houston, Texas, to perform tests on his new material using the sophisticated instruments of his former dissertation adviser, Paul Chu, thereby confirming his discovery; Chu subsequently became involved in the "race for new superconductors." With his colleagues, Chu created other compounds with increasingly higher transition temperatures, and in 2004 they prepared a compound of mercury, barium, calcium, copper, and oxygen that had a transition temperature to superconductivity in excess of 150 kelvins. The goal of many scientists now is to discover a material that will superconduct at room temperature.

High-temperature superconductors also challenged traditional theories that were satisfactory for low-temperature superconductors. However, despite the efforts of some of the world's best theoreticians, a satisfactory explanation for these new superconductors has yet to gain wide acceptance. Nevertheless, this has not prevented others from trying to discover applications for high-temperature superconductors. Researchers have generally categorized such applications by scale—that is, large and small. In large-scale applications, large currents are involved in such devices as generators, transmission lines, and transformers. In small-scale applications, small currents are involved, such as for analog and digital processing. Hoped-for future applications include high-temperature superconducting maglev trains that will run very efficiently by magnetic levitation. Some predict that improved superconductors will mean better, faster, and less expensive computers. The euphoria that characterized the early history of these superconductors has largely dissipated, replaced by a realization of the difficulties in creating such practical devices as wires from brittle ceramic materials. On the other hand, commercial products with ceramic superconductors are already on the market, and particle accelerators are making use of these superconductors. Judging by the new journals that have appeared, new discoveries continue to be made and new patents applied for and granted. Bednorz, for one, has predicted a bright future for these superconductors in the twenty-first century.

—*Robert J. Paradowski*

Further Reading

Dahl, Per Fridtjof. *Superconductivity: Its Historical Roots and Development from Mercury to the Ceramic Oxides*. New York: American Institute of Physics, 1992. Dahl, a physicist, surveys a century of developments in superconductors, culminating in the pivotal discovery of high-temperature superconductivity in 1986. Forty-seven pages of notes, an extensive bibliography, and a name as well as a subject index.

Ford, P. J., and G. A. Saunders. *The Rise of Superconductors*. Boca Raton, Fla.: CRC Press, 2005. The authors discover interesting parallels between Heike Kamerlingh Onnes's discovery of superconductivity early in the twentieth century and the discovery of high-temperature superconductors by Bednorz and Müller in the late 1980's. Notes, index of names, and subject index.

Hazen, Robert M. *Breakthrough: The Race for the Superconductor*. New York: Summit Books, 1988. Hazen, who was a member of Paul Chu's team that created some important high-temperature superconductors, tells the story of the basic discoveries that helped to create this new field. Written for general readers. Index.

Matricon, Jean. *The Cold Wars: A History of Superconductivity*. Translated by Georges Waysand. New Brunswick, N.J.: Rutgers University Press, 2003. Analyzes the evolution of the field, with an emphasis on its relationship to the rest of physics. Notes and index.

Schechter, Bruce. *The Path of No Resistance: The Story of the Revolution in Superconductivity*. New York: Simon & Schuster, 1989. Schechter, a physicist turned science journalist, interviewed many of the important researchers who helped create this revolution. His work, written for a wide audience, also deals with conflicting commercial interests that developed alongside and after the discovery. Source notes and index.

Tinkham, Michael. *Introduction to Superconductivity*. 2d ed. New York: Dover, 2004. This reprint of a "classic" text originally published in 1996 makes widely available to graduate students and others with advanced mathematical expertise a thorough description and analysis of the physical principles involved in superconductivity, including high-temperature materials. Bibliographical references and index.

See also: Heike Kamerlingh Onnes; Karl Alexander Müller.

Semi Joseph Begun

German American engineer

Begun made important contributions in the field of magnetic recording with his development of tape recorders. He was also one of the early researchers in telecommunications and underwater acoustics.

Born: December 2, 1905; Danzig, Germany (now Gdańsk, Poland)

Died: January 5, 1995; Cleveland Heights, Ohio

Primary fields: Electronics and electrical engineering; military technology and weaponry

Primary invention: Mail-a-Voice recorder

Early Life

Semi Joseph Begun (SEH-mee JOH-sehf BEH-guhn) was born in Danzig, Germany (now Gdańsk, Poland), on December 2, 1905. He studied at the Berlin Institute of Technology and graduated in 1929 with a master of science degree in communications engineering. He did his graduate work at the Berlin Technical Institute in Charlottenburg. There he developed an interest in magnetic recording and wrote a doctoral thesis titled "Magnetic Recording." Later, he also published a book with the same title. After graduating in 1933 with a doctorate in electrical engineering, Begun secured a position with the European division of International Telephone and Telegraph, which operated in Germany as Lorenz AG. He was soon promoted to the position of chief engineer. While working for Lorenz, Begun built the first tape recorder—a dictating machine that used wire for magnetic recording. This tape recorder enjoyed considerable popularity in Europe during the 1930's. Begun also developed the first steel tape recorder for mobile radio broadcasting, the Stahlton-Bandmaschine, which was used by the German Broadcasting System.

Life's Work

In 1935, Begun emigrated to the United States, where he found that broadcasting companies lacked any interest in his magnetic recording. While continuing to work with magnetic recording on his own, he accepted a position with Guided Radio Corporation. There he developed communication systems for ships. These systems were used to direct passengers to lifeboats in cases of fire or other disasters. Begun's system worked so well that it was adopted by the U.S. Navy. In 1937, Begun left Guided Radio and founded Acoustic Consultants. While involved in this consulting firm, he invented the Sound Mirror, the first tape recorder sold commercially to the public in the United States.

Begun's inventions attracted the attention of the Brush Development Company, located in Cleveland, Ohio. In 1938, he accepted a position in the company's research and development department. When the United States entered World War II in 1941, Begun contributed to the war effort by producing improved magnetic recorders for use in military aircraft. He also invented underwater acoustic sensors with piezoelectric crystals, as well as torpedoes equipped with sonar homing devices.

As a member of the National Defense Research Committee (NDRC), Begun worked to promote research in magnetic recording. During the war, there was a shortage of facilities producing the diamond dies needed to pull ferromagnetic steel into wire, which was used in wire recorders. The NDRC gave Begun a contract to research and develop a substitute for the steel wire used in the military recorders. Begun received a Presidential Certificate of Merit for his work as a member of the NDRC. The award was presented to him by President Harry S. Truman.

The Mail-a-Voice Recorder

While working for the Brush Development Company, Semi Joseph Begun developed an innovative concept in sound recording, resulting in his Mail-a-Voice recorder. The Brush Development Company manufactured and marketed Begun's invention. The recorder resembled a record player but was equipped with special features and used a special recording medium instead of the wire or tape normally used. The machine was equipped with a record/reproduce selector switch, an erase button for eliminating unwanted parts of a recording, and a pickup arm with special features, in addition to the standard power switch, volume control, and toggle switch for controlling the operation of the turntable. It also had a foot pedal control used to start and stop the turntable and a crystal transducer that functioned as a microphone or receiver in accord with the setting of the record/reproduce selector switch. The pickup arm had a magnetic record/reproduce head and an index and a tuner. The index positioned the magnetic head at any desired point on the recording. The tuner was used to accurately align the magnetic head with the sound track of the recording blank.

The Mail-a-Voice recorder used powder-coated paper disks for recording. Both sides of these disks could be used for recording. The disks were flat and 9 inches in diameter. The sound track was a spiral that ran from an inner five-inch diameter to the outer edge of the disk. The recording track, with a width of 0.014 inch, was closely spaced; the spiral's pitch was 0.025 inch. Yet the recording possessed good clarity with no appreciable cross talk. A tracking disk made the magnetic record/reproduce head in the pickup arm move in a spiral motion outward across the recording blank, magnetizing a track on it. The disk could be folded and mailed in a standard envelope just like a letter.

Designed to execute all of its functions with a minimum of tubes, the Mail-a-Voice recorder used only two double triode tubes. The machine used alternating-current biasing to make recordings but used direct-current saturation of the recording medium to erase previously recorded disks. The erasing was accomplished by holding a permanent magnet on the disk during several revolutions of the turntable.

At the time of its production, the Mail-a-Voice recorder had the simplest and most inexpensive mechanical and electrical design of any commercially produced magnetic recorder. The Brush Development Company manufactured two models of the Mail-a-Voice recorder. One model was principally suited for dictation, the other was meant for use in correspondence. Unlike the latter device, the dictation model was equipped with a solenoid that enabled the user to stop the turntable almost immediately with the foot pedal.

The Mail-a-Voice recorder provided a rapid, easy, and efficient means of sending voice messages. By using a powder-coated paper disk as a recording medium, Begun pioneered the way for the eventual development of the floppy disk.

In 1943, the Brush Development Company appointed Begun vice president of research. He continued his work in recording media and magnetic recording. He developed and demonstrated the first video recording head. He also invented the Mail-a-Voice recorder, composed of a recording/playback machine and powder-coated disks, which were forerunners of the floppy disk. Recording could be done on both sides of the disk. In his position, Begun was instrumental in the negotiation of a sourcing agreement for magnetic tape with the Minnesota Mining and Manufacturing Company (3M). This agreement resulted in a product line that earned $1 billion for 3M. In 1949, Begun wrote the first textbook on the subject of magnetic recording.

In 1952, the Brush Development Company merged with the Cleveland Graphite Bronze Company and became the Clevite Corporation. Begun served as a member of the new company's board of directors. In 1968, Clevite merged with Gould-National Battery to form the Gould Corporation. Begun was the main negotiator for Clevite in the merger. He became vice president of technology for Gould and served on the company's board of directors. In 1969, while working for Gould, he founded Science Management, Inc. (SMI), which provided investment groups and other clients with evaluations of high-technology products and appraisals of management ability of the new companies making the products. In 1971, Begun retired from Gould and founded yet another company, Auctor Associates. This company also provided consultation on high-technology products. The company enjoyed immediate success and served clients in Pittsburgh and Chicago as well as Cleveland.

Begun received numerous honors and awards for his research and development in the electroacoustics field. He received fifty patents during his career. In 1956, he was awarded the Emil Berliner Award by the Audio Engineering Society. In 1960, the society gave him the John H. Potts Medal. In 1993, he was inducted into the Ohio Science, Technology and Industry Hall of Fame. He was also a fellow of the Institute of Electrical and Electronics Engineers (IEEE) and a member of the Audio Engineering Society (AES).

In addition to being an inquisitive and competent researcher, Begun was involved with social concerns. He was particularly alarmed by the ever-increasing violence in American society. In an effort to effect change, he and his wife founded the Society for the Prevention of Violence and Aggression in Children. They also created the Begun Institute for Studies of Violence and Aggression at John Carroll University in Cleveland. Begun died at his home in Cleveland Heights on January 5, 1995. His collected papers are housed at the Smithsonian Institution in the National Museum of American History.

Impact

Begun was one of the most productive pioneers in research in the areas of magnetic recording, underwater acoustics, and telecommunications. While working in Germany, he developed the Dailygraph, and then the Stahlton-Bandmaschine. The latter was a major advance in mobile radio broadcasting. After emigrating to the United States, he developed a communication system for use on ships. His system contributed to the saving of innumerable lives in disasters at sea, as the system enabled ship crew members to direct passengers to safety.

With the invention of his Sound Mirror, Begun introduced the tape recorder to the American public. He was instrumental in the development of the sound recording industry in the United States. During World War II, Begun was instrumental in developing technology for the military. As a result of his research, military aircraft were equipped with magnetic recorders, and the Navy was supplied with underwater acoustic sensors and torpedoes equipped with sonar homing devices.

—*Shawncey Webb*

Further Reading

Begun, S. Joseph. *Magnetic Recording*. New York: Rhinehart, 1949. Written as a textbook on magnetic recording, Begun's work includes the best description of his magnetic recorders available. Well illustrated.

_______. *Magnetic Recording: The Ups and Downs of a Pioneer—The Memoirs of Semi Joseph Begun*. New York: Audio Engineering Society, 2000. An insightful look into Begun's life as a researcher, his successes, and the difficulties encountered.

Daniel, Eric D., C. Denis Mee, and Mark H. Clark, eds. *Magnetic Recording: The First One Hundred Years*. Piscataway, N.J.: IEEE Press, 1999. Discusses the development of magnetic recording in Germany. Excellent presentation of the role of Begun and the Brush Development Company in the field of magnetic recording.

Morton, David. *Off the Record: The Technology and Culture of Sound Recording in America*. New Brunswick, N.J.: Rutgers University Press, 2000. Contains some information on Begun. A good overview of the industry that Begun helped to develop in the United States.

_______. *Sound Recording: The Life Story of a Technology*. Baltimore: The Johns Hopkins University Press, 2006. Organized chronologically, the text traces the history of sound recording, discussing the technology itself as well as the economic and cultural effects on the technology. Treats both Europe and the United States. Contains good references to more technical books on the subject.

See also: Emile Berliner; Marvin Camras.

GEORG VON BÉKÉSY

Hungarian American biophysicist

Békésy won the 1961 Nobel Prize in Physiology or Medicine for his discoveries about the mechanics and physiology of hearing, which were seen as a benefit to the deaf.

Born: June 3, 1899; Budapest, Hungary
Died: June 13, 1972; Honolulu, Hawaii
Also known as: George Bekesy; György Malmö
Primary fields: Biology; medicine and medical technology; physics
Primary inventions: Modeling of middle and inner ear; audiometer

EARLY LIFE

Georg von Békésy (GAY-ohrg fon BAY-kay-shee) was the son of Alexander von Békésy, a diplomat in the service of the Austro-Hungarian Empire, and his wife, Paula, née Mazaly. His father's career meant that the family moved frequently and traveled much throughout central and eastern Europe. Besides Budapest, the young Békésy lived in Munich, Germany; Constantinople (now Istanbul), Turkey; and Zurich, Switzerland.

He studied the piano, not only becoming an accomplished player but also developing early the fine acoustic sense that would later be important in his research. Yet he preferred the contemplation of sculpture and other three-dimensional art forms. By the time he was in his mid-teens, he had already become a serious collector of art and would eventually become a self-taught expert in art history.

Georg von Békésy. (©The Nobel Foundation)

Békésy completed his secondary education in Zurich in 1916 and passed the Swiss *Maturitäsprüfung* (qualifying examination for higher education). With the defeat and dissolution of Austria-Hungary, the family fortune was at a low ebb at the end of World War I. Despite having to serve in the Hungarian army from 1918 to 1920, Békésy attended the University of Bern, Switzerland, from 1916 to 1920, receiving his bachelor of science degree in chemistry. He studied physics under Károly Tangl at the University of Budapest (now Semmelweis University) from 1920 to 1923, earning his Ph.D. with a dissertation on fluid dynamics and molecular weight.

LIFE'S WORK

In 1923, the national government hired Békésy in Budapest as a researcher for the Hungarian Postal, Telephone, and Telegraph System. Assigned to investigate why the quality of telephone sound was so poor, he learned that most of this distortion was caused by inadequate earpieces on the receivers. Accordingly, he then began studying the mechanics of the human ear in order to find ways in which these receivers might be improved by making them more compatible with natural processes.

Békésy's basic research led to his creation of working models of various parts of the ear and his invention of several pieces of equipment. He did much of the actual physical labor on these devices himself, using not only common tools such as saws, drills, and files, but also many of his own design. With the assistance of the University of Budapest Faculty of Medicine, he also used cadaver heads and skulls in his research. He would glue mirrors to eardrums to investigate tympanic response to different vibrations and would drill holes in skulls to test cranial resonance. With the freedom to conduct his research however he saw fit, he spent much time in autopsy rooms, morgues, metalworking shops, electrical shops, and hospital wards, as well as his own laboratory.

Except for supplementary employment as a laboratory consultant for the Siemens and Halske Company in Berlin (1926-1927), as a lecturer in physics at the University of Budapest (1932-1934), and as a professor of experimental physics (1939-1946), Békésy stayed with the postal, telephone, and telegraph service until 1946. He and his work were relatively undisturbed during World War II, but with the advent of the communist regime, he felt that he had to emigrate. Because he had neither wife nor children, leaving Hungary was not the problem for him that it sometimes was for those with families. From 1946 to 1947, he worked in Stockholm, Sweden, as a visiting researcher at the Karolinska Institute. While in Sweden, he invented a pure-tone audiometer that patients themselves could control to measure the sensitivity of their own hearing.

In 1947, Békésy came to the United States to accept an appointment in the Psycho-Acoustic Laboratory of Harvard University, which in 1949 promoted him to senior research fellow in psychophysics. At Harvard, he concentrated on improving his mechanical models of the inner and middle ears. His model cochlea in particular became an important instrument for his further research. While at Harvard, he became a naturalized U.S. citizen.

Békésy stayed at Harvard until 1966, when, soon to face Harvard's mandatory retirement age, he moved to the University of Hawaii, which, with funding from the Hawaiian Telephone Company, had promised to build and equip a special laboratory to his specifications. As

Modeling the Inner and Middle Ear

Before Georg von Békésy began his research into the mechanics of hearing, the prevailing view of this process was that of Hermann von Helmholtz, who in the 1860's had determined the interrelated functions of the tympanic membrane and the three bones of the middle ear. Helmholtz also discovered the importance of the basilar membrane in the inner ear for hearing, but contemporary techniques did not allow him or other late nineteenth century researchers, such as Italian anatomist Alfonso Corti, to work out the further details of the hearing process. In the 1920's, the purpose of the inner ear remained poorly understood. Part of the problem was the delicacy of the cochlea, which prevented both dissection and close study.

By 1928, Békésy had succeeded in dissecting the ear so that its auditory functions could be studied. He used a low-power microscope on a fresh cadaver under water. With very small mirrors and scissors of his own design, and by performing this complicated postmortem surgery very quickly, he was able to observe wave motion in the cochlea before the inevitable deterioration or damage to the organ made this study impossible. He made the sound waves visible to his microscope by sprinkling silver dust or some other reflective particles on the basilar membrane, then observing the vibrating membrane under an intense stroboscopic light.

The basilar membrane divides the median and tympanic canals within the cochlea. Békésy's new techniques allowed him to discover that as this membrane vibrates it stimulates the hair cells of the adjacent organ of Corti, whose motion is detected by the spiral ganglion of the eighth cranial nerve, the acoustic nerve, which then transmits these impulses to the brain so that hearing can occur. He was also able to correlate various types, amplitudes, and locations of waves along the basilar membrane with the transmission of various aspects of sound, such as pitch, volume, and tone. For example, the basilar waves of high frequencies peak near the entrance to the cochlea, while those of low frequencies peak deeper inside.

Békésy's results from these dissections gave him the knowledge to build functional models of the cochlea that would aid in his further study without the need for studying more cadavers. The most useful of these models, constructed while he was at Harvard University, consisted of a sealed, thirty-centimeter plastic tube filled with water. He would lay his bare forearm along the length of the tube, then introduce sounds at one end of it. Because he could feel the vibrations from each of these sounds each at a different place on his forearm, the nerves in his forearm thus became a substitute for the basilar membrane.

professor of sensory sciences, he investigated all five senses and their interrelations. He remained active in this laboratory until his death. The Békésy Laboratory of Neurobiology remains a major component of the Pacific Biosciences Research Center of the University of Hawaii at Manoa.

Throughout his life, Békésy chose the solitary enjoyment of libraries, museums, and laboratories rather than outdoor or social pursuits. Although he was never gregarious, he was not a typical intellectual recluse. He was friendly, charming, generous, and well-liked wherever he went. He donated his extensive art collection to the Nobel Foundation, his personal and scientific papers, photographs, movies, sound recordings, and other memorabilia from 1928 to 1972 to the Library of Congress, and his art books to the University of Hawaii.

Impact

The lifelong center of Békésy's research was the human cochlea, the portion of the inner ear where vibrations are transformed into impulses that the brain can interpret as sound. His Nobel Prize in 1961 was awarded "for his discoveries of the physical mechanism of stimulation within the cochlea," but that was not the extent of his scientific achievement. No problem concerned with hearing was uninteresting to him. Carl Gustaf Bernhard's presentation speech for Békésy's Nobel Prize cited a paper in which Békésy determined the properties of the ear that enable foghorns to be heard far out to sea, but not close by.

Even though he was not a medical professional, and indeed distrusted medicine, his discoveries in physics, physiology, and biomechanics had profound effects on surgery and the clinical sciences of audiology, otolaryngology, neurology, and hearing aid design. Throughout his career, his research involved all aspects of ear physiology and, especially while at Harvard and Hawaii, the physiology of all the senses. Building models and refining instrumentation and techniques was always an integral part of his quest to understand sensory processes.

Besides the Nobel Prize, he also won the 1931 Denker Prize in Otology, the 1937 Leibniz Medal of the German Academy of Sciences, Groningen University's 1939 Guyot Prize for Speech and Otology, the 1950 Shambaugh Prize in Otology, the 1955 Howard Crosby Warren Medal of the Society of Experimental Psychologists, the 1957 American Otological Society Gold Medal, the 1961 Acoustical Society of America Gold Medal, and many other awards. In 1984, the Acoustical Society of America established the Georg von Békésy Medal for excellence in psychological or physiological acoustics. The Hungarian Ministry of Education offers the Békésy György Postdoctoral Research Fellowship.

—*Eric v.d. Luft*

Further Reading

Békésy, Georg von. *Experiments in Hearing*. New York: McGraw-Hill, 1960. His magnum opus, presenting historical as well as physiological and psychological explanations of progress in auditory science.

_______. *Sensory Inhibition*. Princeton, N.J.: Princeton University Press, 1967. A series of Békésy's lectures.

_______. "Some Biophysical Experiments from Fifty Years Ago." *Annual Review of Physiology* 31 (1974): 1-16. Autobiographical account of the beginning of Békésy's scientific career.

Kovács, László. "Georg von Békésy, Nobel Laureate in Physiology, Experimental Physicist and Art Collector Was Born 100 Years Ago." *Science and Education* 10, nos. 1-2 (January, 2001): 149-152. Sympathetic overview of all facets of Békésy's life, as theoretical scientist, practical biophysical engineer, music lover, art connoisseur, and humanitarian.

Mook, Douglas G. *Classic Experiments in Psychology*. Westport, Conn.: Greenwood Press, 2004. Chapter 49, "Georg von Békésy: The Mechanics of Hearing," is an accessible explanation of Békésy's life's work.

Nagy, Ferenc. *The Nobel Foundation and Georg von Békésy: Biographical Documents*. Budapest, Hungary: Better, 1999. Basic information about Békésy and his work.

Ratliff, Floyd. "Georg von Békésy: June 3, 1899-June 13, 1972." *Biographical Memoirs of the National Academy of Sciences* 48, no. 2 (1976): 25-49. Detailed and authoritative obituary with a portrait and a comprehensive bibliography.

Wirgin, Jan, et al. *The Georg von Békésy Collection: Selected Objects from the Collection of Georg von Békésy Bequeathed to the Nobel Foundation*. Malmö, Sweden: Allhem, 1974. Description and appreciation of Békésy's contributions to art history and curatorship.

See also: Alexander Graham Bell; Hermann von Helmholtz; Miller Reese Hutchison.

Alexander Graham Bell

Scottish scientist and engineer

Bell was a prolific inventor and renowned teacher of the deaf, but he is best known for his invention of the telephone. What began as a crude prototype quickly became a useful tool that revolutionized communications.

Born: March 3, 1847; Edinburgh, Scotland
Died: August 2, 1922; Baddeck, Nova Scotia, Canada
Primary fields: Communications; electronics and electrical engineering
Primary invention: Telephone

Early Life

Alexander Graham Bell was born to Alexander Melville and Eliza Grace Bell in Edinburgh, Scotland, in 1847. His father, grandfather, and uncle were elocutionists. Bell's father had invented Visible Speech, a system that uses written symbols to teach the deaf how to articulate words. Bell demonstrated his inventiveness at the age of twelve, when he built a wheat-dehusking device for his neighbor, who used it for a number of years. Together with his brother, Bell built an automaton head that could "speak" a few words. Bell attended Edinburgh's Royal High School for two years and left at the age of fifteen. At sixteen, he secured a job as a pupil-teacher of elocution and music. He studied at Edinburgh University in 1864 and later at University College in London.

After his two brothers died from tuberculosis, Bell moved with his family to London and then to Brantford, Ontario, Canada, in 1870. At the Six Nations Reserve, he learned the Mohawk language and translated its vocabulary into Visible Speech symbols. For his work, he was awarded the title of honorary chief. In 1871, Bell provided an in-service program for instructors of the deaf at the Boston School for Deaf Mutes (now the Horace Mann School for the Deaf and Hard of Hearing) in Boston, Massachusetts. The program was repeated at the American Asylum for Deaf-Mutes in Hartford and the Clarke School for the Deaf in Northampton.

The next year, Bell opened a school for deaf pupils (among them Helen Keller) in Boston. Named the Vocal Physiology and Mechanics of Speech, the first class had thirty students. He became a professor of vocal physiology and elocution at the Boston University School of Oratory in 1873.

Though he was busy during the day, Bell stayed up late every night doing research in sound, attempting to find a way to transmit musical notes and articulate speech. (In his late teens, he had begun work on the transmission of sound using tuning forks. He was greatly influenced by the German physicist Hermann von Helmholtz, who had conveyed vowel sounds using a tuning fork.) The device Bell worked on was called a harmonic (or musical) telegraph, and he tried to build one that could send several messages at once through a single wire. He thought he could send multiple messages by varying their musical pitch. When his experiments led nowhere, he decided to concentrate on research and spend less time on his private practice. He had been suffering from severe headaches, and his health deterio-

Alexander Graham Bell speaking into his prototype telephone in 1876. (The Granger Collection, New York)

The Prototype Telephone

The first telephone that Thomas A. Watson built for Alexander Graham Bell used a transmitter with an acid-water mixture. The telephone consisted of a funnel, a diaphragm, a cup, and a receiver. A wire attached to the diaphragm floated in the liquid in the cup. Another wire attached the cup to the receiver. Speaking into the funnel caused the diaphragm at the bottom to move, which in turn moved the wire in the liquid. When the wire moved, it changed the resistance within the liquid. The varying current sent to the receiver caused the diaphragm to vibrate and produce sound.

Although this crude prototype proved that speech could be transmitted electrically, the device was not practical, and Bell did not use it in his public demonstrations. Instead, he used a prototype that used an electromagnet instead of liquid. The design consisted of a transmitter, receiver, and magnet. Attached to the transmitter and receiver was a metal diaphragm. Speaking into the transmitter caused the diaphragm to move and the phone line to transfer this motion to the receiver. When the diaphragm of the receiver vibrated, sound was produced. The drawback to this design was that it used a single microphone: The user spoke into it and then put it to the ear to listen. There was also a time lapse in the transmission. Thomas Alva Edison later improved the telephone by dividing it into two pieces: a movable earpiece and a stationary speaking tube. Another drawback to this prototype telephone was that it was voice-powered: The user had to shout into the transmitter to be heard as well as to overcome noise and distortions. Other inventors, notably Francis Blake, Jr., contributed to improving the telephone. Blake, like Edison, invented a transmitter that improved the sound clarity of the device.

rated. He retained only two students—George Sanders, deaf from birth, and Mabel Hubbard, who had lost her hearing because of scarlet fever at age five. Sanders's father provided Bell with free room and board and made arrangements for his son to live near Bell's boarding house. Ten years younger than Bell, Hubbard became the object of his affection.

Life's Work

During the summer of 1874, Bell made experiments on a teaching aid for the deaf called the phonoautograph, which was made from a dead man's ear. Speaking into this device caused the ear membrane to vibrate and move a lever, which wrote a wavelike pattern of speech on smoked glass. Bell thought it might be possible to use a membrane to vary an electric current in intensity with the spoken word. He also thought that multiple metal reeds (or springs) tuned to different frequencies could be used to convert the electric current back into sound. When Bell revealed his secret work on his harmonic telegraph to his two students' parents—Gardiner Greene Hubbard, a lawyer and the president of the Clarke School for the Deaf, and Thomas Sanders, a prosperous businessman—both showed interest in funding his research. In February, 1875, Hubbard, Sanders, and Bell signed an agreement that supported Bell financially in return for equal shares from any patent he developed. Anthony Pollok, Hubbard's patent attorney, would handle patent matters. Bell hired Thomas A. Watson, an experienced electrical designer and mechanic, as his assistant. In the following month, Bell met with Joseph Henry, who had pioneered electromagnetism and helped Samuel F. B. Morse with the telegraph. The scientist advised Bell to get the necessary electrical knowledge, drop the work on his harmonic telegraph, and concentrate on transmission of speech by electricity.

In June, 1875, Bell and Watson were working on the harmonic telegraph when he heard a sound come through the receiver. Watson had accidentally plucked one of the reeds. Also, one of the contact screws had been set too tightly, allowing current to run continuously. Bell realized that only one reed, not multiple ones, was needed, and that continuous current was essential for transmission of sound. Watson built the first telephone the next day. Called a "gallows" telephone because of its frame, it had a diaphragm substituted for the reed. It was able to transmit a few odd sounds, but not clear speech. Bell was very much disappointed, and his experimenting slowed through the rest of the year. He spent some time writing a patent application to protect his ideas even though he had not built a working model for his telephone. Fortunately, the U.S. Patent Office at that time did not require that a working model accompany a patent application.

On February 14, 1876, while Bell was in Boston, his patent application was filed by Pollok with the Patent Office. On the same day, Elisha Gray filed his caveat for a telephone using a water transmitter. A professional inventor, Gray, together with Thomas Alva Edison, had been contracted by Western Union to find a way to send multiple messages using only a single line on the telegraph. Who filed first is still a debate, and what happened that day is still a mystery. Bell's patent was eventually challenged by some six hundred lawsuits, five of which went to the Supreme Court. Even the U.S. government wanted to annul Bell's patent based on the grounds of fraud and misrepresentation. Gray's challenge to the patent was based on the rumor that Pollok had access to his caveat and copied the principle of variable resistance and the description of the liquid transmitter onto Bell's application. However, Bell won every case. The Patent Office issued to Bell U.S. Patent number 174,465 on March 7, 1876, for his electric speaking phone. In late 1877, Gray applied for a patent for the same invention, but the Patent Office determined that "his failure to take any action amounting to completion until others had demonstrated the utility of the invention deprives him of the right to have it considered."

Three days after his patent was issued, Bell was experimenting with a transmitter when he succeeded in getting his telephone to work. The liquid that Bell used for the transmitter was a mixture of acid and water. According to legend, when he accidentally spilled some of the liquid on his clothes, he called his assistant for help. Watson heard Bell's words clearly in the next room.

In August, 1876, Bell demonstrated that his telephone could work over long distances. His first message was sent from the telegraph office in Mount Pleasant to Brantford five miles away. Bell introduced his invention to the scientific community and the general public and also at the 1876 Centenary Exhibition in Philadelphia. Pedro II of Brazil ordered one hundred telephones for his country. Bell, Hubbard, and Sanders wanted to sell the patent to Western Union for $100,000, but the company's president declined the offer. (Afterward, he regretted his decision, saying that paying $25 million for the patent would have been a bargain.) In 1877, the Bell Telephone Company was established, and a few days later Bell married Mabel Hubbard. They had four children: two girls, and two boys who died in infancy.

In 1880, the French Academy, representing the French government, presented Bell the Volta Prize of 50,000 francs ($10,000) for his invention. With this money, Bell established the Volta Laboratory in Washington, D.C. Other honors included the Albert Medal from the Royal Society of Arts in London, an honorary Ph.D. from the University of Würzburg (Germany), the Edison Medal from the American Institute of Electrical Engineers, and induction into the Legion of Honor. Named after Bell, the decibel (dB), equal to 0.1 bel (B), is a unit for measuring sound intensity. Also named for him is the IEEE Alexander Graham Bell Medal, established in 1976 to award contributors in the fields of telecommunications.

Bell was issued fourteen patents for the telephone and the telegraph and four patents for the photophone, which transmits speech by light rays. He shared twelve other patents with his collaborators for the phonograph, aerial vehicles, hydroairplanes, and selenium cells. Other inventions included the audiometer, which measures acuity in hearing, and the induction balance, used to locate metal objects in human bodies.

Bell became a naturalized U.S. citizen in 1882. He alternated between two homes—Washington, D.C., and his private estate Beinn Bhreagh ("beautiful mountain" in Gaelic) in Baddeck, Nova Scotia. Bell has been claimed as a "native son" by the United States and Canada. Canada maintains the Alexander Graham Bell National Historic Site in Nova Scotia, the historic Bell Homestead, and the world's first telephone company building. Collections of Bell's documents reside at the U.S. Library of Congress, Manuscript Division, and at the Alexander Graham Bell Institute at Cape Breton University in Nova Scotia.

Bell died of pernicious anemia at his private estate on August 2, 1922, survived by his wife and two daughters.

Impact

Improvements to the prototype telephone helped develop it into a successful product. The use of the telephone spread quickly after the first commercial switchboard was set up in New Haven, Connecticut, in 1878. Four years later, 60,000 people owned telephones; the number jumped to 150,000 in 1886. Thanks to Thomas Alva Edison's invention of the carbon microphone, the telephone became a practical long-distance tool. In 1884, the first long-distance line was built, connecting Boston and New York. With the perfection of insulation, 11,000 miles of underground wires were used in New York City by 1889. By the turn of the century, the telephone had become a necessity, connecting people and paving the way for an interconnected world market and future developments in information technology. With 14,000 miles of copper wire strung across the country, the first transcontinental call was made in 1915.

—*Anh Tran*

Further Reading

Brown, Travis. *Popular Patents: America's First Inventions, from the Airplane to the Zipper*. Lanham, Md.: Scarecrow Press, 2000. The telephone is one of eight inventions presented. Each narrative includes a profile of the inventor and a discussion of how the invention has found its way into American culture.

Grosvenor, Edwin S., and Morgan Wesson. *Alexander*

Graham Bell: The Life and Times of the Man Who Invented the Telephone*. New York: Harry N. Abrams, 1997. Chronicles Bell's most famous invention, from its roots in deaf education to the growth of AT&T. Covers experiments later in his career and includes historical and family anecdotes.

Pasachoff, Naomi. *Alexander Graham Bell: Making Connections*. New York: Oxford University Press, 1996. Concentrates more on his work as an educator and inventor than on his personal life. Illustrations.

Shulman, Seth. *The Telephone Gambit: Chasing Alexander Graham Bell's Secret*. New York: W. W. Norton, 2008. Examines the race to build the first telephone and uncovers potential bombshells. Provides evidence of Bell's stealing Elisha Gray's research.

See also: Alexander Bain; Georg von Békésy; Emile Berliner; Martin Cooper; Glenn H. Curtiss; Thomas Alva Edison; Elisha Gray; Hermann von Helmholtz; Joseph Henry; Heinrich Hertz; Peter Cooper Hewitt; David Edward Hughes; Miller Reese Hutchison; Bob Kahn; Lewis Howard Latimer; Guglielmo Marconi; Samuel F. B. Morse; John Augustus Roebling; Frank J. Sprague; Alessandro Volta; Eli Whitney.

Carl Benz

German mechanical engineer and machinist

Benz designed and built the world's first practical horseless carriage, and he was the first to produce the first mass-produced automobile. The Mercedes-Benz automobile is one of his best-known legacies.

Born: November 25, 1844; Karlsruhe, Baden (now in Germany)
Died: April 4, 1929; Ladenburg, Germany
Also known as: Carl Friedrich Benz (full name); Karl Benz
Primary fields: Automotive technology; manufacturing; mechanical engineering
Primary invention: Gasoline-powered automobile

Early Life

Carl Friedrich Benz (behnts) was born on November 25, 1844, in Karlsruhe, Baden (now in Germany), to Josephine Vaillant and Johann George Benz, an engine driver on the Karlsruhe railway. Carl was two years old when his father was killed in a railway accident. The railway authorities awarded Josephine a small monthly pension. To supplement the meager pension, she took menial jobs.

Despite being impoverished, his mother strove to give her son a good education, and he attended the local grammar school. At the age of nine, after easily passing the entrance exam, Benz started at Karlsruhe Lyceum, a school renowned for its high standard of teaching in the natural sciences. Physics became a passion for him. His mother saved money to provide a small home laboratory for his studies and took in lodgers. Benz repaired clocks and watches in his spare time. He later attended Karlsruhe Polytechnical University under the instruction of Ferdinand Redtenbacher. There, Benz studied locksmithing, eventually focusing on locomotive engineering. In 1860, at the age of fifteen, he matriculated at the University of Karlsruhe, and he graduated in 1864. It was during his time at the university that Benz imagined the vehicle that would become the horseless carriage.

After graduation, Benz began his professional training in Karlsruhe, working at various mechanical engineering jobs for two years before moving to Mannheim to work as a draftsman and designer in a scales factory. In 1868, he began working for Gebrüder Benckiser Eisenwerke und Maschinenfabrik, a bridge-building company in Pforzheim, before going to Vienna to work at an iron construction company.

Life's Work

In 1871, at age twenty-seven, Benz founded his first company in Mannheim, an iron foundry and mechanical workshop. It was a joint venture with August Ritter, a partnership that proved disastrous within the first year. In 1872, Benz married Bertha Ringer, with whom he had five children: Eugen, Richard, Clara, Thilde, and Ellen.

By 1878, Benz was developing new engines and earning patents. That year, he created a reliable two-stroke engine, and he was issued a patent for this engine in 1879. He also registered a number of other inventions, including the speed regulation system, the carburetor, the clutch, the spark plug, and the water radiator.

Because of his factory's high production costs, the Mannheim banks demanded that Benz's factory be incorporated, and in 1882 it became Gasmotoren-Fabrik Mannheim. In 1883, he left the company, disgruntled that he was barely consulted for technical decisions. That year, he established Benz and Company, producing industrial machines with Max Rose and Friedrich Wilhelm Esslinger, owners of a bicycle repair shop in Mannheim. Benz turned to designing a vehicle with an internal combustion engine. By 1885, he had created the first practical gasoline-powered automobile, the Benz Patent Motorwagen, and was granted a patent in 1886.

By 1890, Benz and Company had grown to fifty employees and expanded to a larger facility. In 1893, Benz designed the Victoria, a two-passenger automobile with double-pivot steering. The following year, the Velo model was improved, and in 1895 Benz created the first truck in history. In 1896, he was granted a patent for the horizontally opposed piston engine.

By the early twentieth century, competition with Daimler-Motoren-Gesellschaft (DMG), which produced Mercedes cars, had become inevitable. It is not certain whether Benz and Gottlieb Daimler knew of each other's accomplishments, as Daimler died in March, 1900. In 1903, Benz retired from his company out of protest when French engineers at the Mannheim plant were hired. These engineers were supposed to help restore the competitiveness of Benz's company.

Benz moved his family first to Darmstadt, then to Ladenburg. In 1906, he founded C. Benz Söhne with his son Eugen. They produced automobiles and gas engines but, with the slump in gas engines sales, focused on automobiles. In 1908, Richard, Benz's second son, joined the company. In 1912, Benz liquidated his shares in C. Benz Söhne, leaving his family-held company in Ladenburg to his two sons, but he remained as a director of Benz and Company. On his seventieth birthday, he was awarded an honorary doctorate by his alma mater, the University of Karlsruhe, in his hometown celebration.

After World War I, with the slump in the German economy, both Benz and Company and DMG had sales difficulties. To survive the situation, in 1919 Benz and Company representative Karl Jahn proposed a merger with DMG, but the proposal was rejected in December. The economic situation worsened. In 1924, a mutual agreement was signed for both companies to market their automobiles jointly but to keep their respective brands. On June 28, 1926, Daimler-Benz was formed, and all its automobiles bore the brand name Mercedes-Benz. The new company created its logo: Daimler's three-pointed star, which represented the automaker's ambition to produce engines for land, air, and water, surrounded by the laurels from the Benz logo.

Carl Benz died of bronchial inflammation on April 4, 1929, at his home in Ladenburg. Bertha Benz continued to reside in their home until her death on May 5, 1944. Family members resided there for thirty more years. The Benz home has been designated as the historic headquarters of the Gottlieb Daimler and Karl Benz Foundation.

Impact

A pioneer in the automobile industry, Benz built the world's first commercial automobile powered by an internal combustion engine. In 1885, Benz fitted a scaled-

Carl Benz's two-seater tricycle, the first gasoline-powered automobile, invented in 1885. (Getty Images)

down engine to a two-seater tricycle, producing the first gasoline-powered automobile. His vehicle included electric ignition, mechanically operated engine valves, a water-cooled engine, and differential gears—all features found in today's automobiles. After success with his early two-stroke engine, Benz built a four-stroke that achieved great success when installed in a four-wheel vehicle.

In 1893, Benz's Velo model became the world's first mass-produced automobile. His lightweight, self-driven automobiles built to a standardized pattern set the standard for other automakers. With his genius, supported by the business acumen, pure devotion, and persistent optimism of his wife, Bertha, Benz had become the biggest maker of cars in the world by 1900. In 1926, Benz and Daimler merged to produce the famous Mercedes-Benz, a car that continues to stand for quality and excellence to this day.

—Tel Asiado

The Gasoline-Powered Automobile

Carl Benz, the "father of the automobile," designed his gasoline-powered two-stroke piston engine in 1878 and focused on developing a motorized vehicle while working as a designer and manufacturer of stationary engines. In 1885, Benz designed and built the first commercial automobile in history, the Benz Patent Motorwagen. It was awarded a German patent on July 3, 1886.

Benz's motorcar was the first automobile designed to generate its own power. It was a three-wheeled vehicle with a rear-mounted engine, and power transmitted by means of two roller chains to the rear axle. The first successful tests of the motorcar were carried out in the early summer of 1886. His Model 3 had two horsepower; its maximum speed was approximately ten miles per hour.

A Parisian bicycle manufacturer and engineer by the name of Emile Roger purchased an 1888 Benz and decided to add the automobiles to the line he carried in Paris. Roger became a key sales partner for Benz. The early 1888 version of the motorcar had to be pushed when driving up a steep hill, but this limitation was rectified after Bertha Benz made her famous trip driving one of the prototypes. She suggested to her husband the addition of a low gear for hills.

On August 5, 1888, Bertha began the first long-distance automobile trip to demonstrate the reliability of her husband's motorcar. Bringing along her teenage sons Eugen and Richard, she drove from Mannheim through Heidelberg, Wiesloch, and Durlach, to Pforzheim, where she sent a telegram to her husband notifying him of their arrival. The trip covered 180 kilometers (112 miles).

About twenty-five motorcars were built between 1886 and 1893. By the end of 1892, almost a dozen had been sold, and more were on order. At the turn of the twentieth century, Benz produced more than two thousand motorcars.

Further Reading

Adler, Dennis. *Daimler and Benz: The Complete History—The Birth and Evolution of the Mercedes-Benz*. New York: HarperCollins, 2006. A rich history of Daimler-Benz. Photographs.

_______. *Mercedes-Benz: 110 Years of Excellence*. Osceola, Wis.: Motorbooks International, 1995. An enthusiast's series of Mercedes-Benz full-color photographs. History and evolution, specifications, technical notes, and index.

Balchin, Jon. *Quantum Leaps: One Hundred Scientists Who Changed the World*. London: Arcturus, 2003. Examines the great ideas that have shaped the world. Alphabetical list of scientists.

Fanning, Leonard M. *Carl Benz: Father of the Automobile Industry*. New York: Mercer, 1955. A narrative on the birth of the automobile industry.

Nye, Doug. *Pioneers of Science and Discovery: Carl Benz and the Motor Car*. London: Priory Press, 1973. This biography of Benz includes more than thirty photographs, most from the Mercedes-Benz collection. Charts, glossary, index.

Stein, Ralph. *The Automobile Book*. London: Hamlyn, 1967. Discusses German engineers, including Étienne Lenoir and Gottlieb Daimler. Illustrated.

Williams, Brian. *Karl Benz*. New York: Bookwright, 1991. A good biography of Benz. Illustrated chronology, bibliography, glossary, index.

See also: Nicolas-Joseph Cugnot; Gottlieb Daimler; Rudolf Diesel; John Boyd Dunlop; Henry Ford; Charles F. Kettering; Étienne Lenoir; Hiram Percy Maxim; André and Édouard Michelin; Ransom Eli Olds; Stanford Ovshinsky; Sylvester Roper; Ignaz Schwinn; Felix Wankel; Alexander Winton.

Friedrich Bergius

German chemist

Bergius developed a method of converting coal to liquid fuel by high-pressure hydrogenation. He invented a procedure for converting wood into edible carbohydrates, and he perfected a process for manufacturing pure hydrogen gas from water and iron. Synthetic fuels made by the Bergius process were vital to the German war effort in the 1940's.

Born: October 11, 1884; Goldschmieden, near Breslau, Germany (now Wrocław, Poland)
Died: March 30, 1949; Buenos Aires, Argentina
Also known as: Friedrich Karl Rudolf Bergius (full name)
Primary field: Chemistry
Primary invention: Bergius process

Early Life

Friedrich Bergius (FREE-drihk BEHR-gee-uhs) was born in Goldschmieden, near Breslau, Germany (now Wrocław, Poland), where his father owned a chemical factory. Friedrich became familiar with chemical work at the factory and later worked in a larger plant in Mülheim. At the university, first at Breslau and later at Leipzig, he studied organic chemistry. At the latter institution, he worked under the direction of Arthur Hantzsch (1857-1935).

Having earned his doctorate in 1907 with a thesis on the use of 100 percent sulfuric acid as a solvent, Bergius went to Berlin to do postdoctoral work with Walther Nernst (1864-1941; Nobel Prize, 1920). With Nernst, Bergius did research on hydrogen-nitrogen-ammonia equilibrium, as had Fritz Haber (1868-1934; Nobel Prize, 1918). In Nernst's laboratory, Bergius had his first opportunity to conduct high-pressure reactions. Haber had moved on to Karlsruhe, and Bergius joined him there for a few months to continue his work with high pressures.

In 1909, Bergius joined the Hannover Institute of Technology, where the physical chemistry department was headed by Max Bodenstein (1871-1942). At the institute and in his own private laboratory, Bergius studied the equilibrium of calcium oxide, oxygen gas, and calcium peroxide, and he solved many fundamental problems with high-pressure valves and fittings and stirred reaction vessels. He abandoned work involving high-pressure oxygen after experiencing a serious explosion, but later he was able to patent a method for reacting sodium hydroxide with chlorobenzene to form phenol. This process became an important industrial source of phenol. During this period, Bergius became interested in the geochemical formation of coal and its duplication in the laboratory. This interest led him to the study of coal hydrogenation, leading to a process for making synthetic gasoline and oils, probably his most lasting achievement.

Life's Work

Petroleum is fractionally distilled in refineries to obtain useful products. The products in greatest demand tend to be those with the lowest boiling points (such as gasoline and kerosene) in which the hydrocarbon chains are fairly short. "Cracking" (a chemical process by which large molecules are broken down into smaller ones) of long-chain hydrocarbons produces more of the desirable products. Bergius studied cracking and found that high-pressure hydrogen in combination with high temperature gave better results than heating alone. Close temperature

Friedrich Bergius. (©The Nobel Foundation)

control minimized coke formation, a major drawback of thermal cracking. An apparatus was designed to permit removal of volatile products as hydrogenation occurred. Bergius hydrogenated and cracked many different specimens of heavy oil, obtaining lower-boiling liquids and gases. Plentiful supplies of hydrogen were needed for this research, and Bergius investigated methods for its production.

Carbon (usually coke is used) reacts with steam at high temperature—about 900° Celsius (1,652° Fahrenheit)—to give a mixture (water gas) of carbon monoxide and hydrogen. Modifying this reaction, Bergius tried reacting peat with water at high temperature and high pressure. He obtained carbon dioxide, hydrogen, and a solid residue resembling coal. This "artificial coal" reacted with high-pressure hydrogen to give a mixture of products soluble in organic solvents (such as benzene). Hydrogenation of natural coal gave similar results. A patent was filed in 1913 for the coal hydrogenation process. Artificial coal also resulted from the reaction of high-pressure water and steam on wood. Bergius theorized that coal might have originated in wood from primeval forests being buried and suffering the effects of heat and pressure under the earth.

Bergius engaged in a prolonged period of work to increase the output of his coal hydrogenation process, and he was soon forced to seek additional funds from a group of financiers. World War I had now begun, and Bergius needed to obtain a deferment from military service. His next step was an alliance with the firm Theodore Goldschmidt AG.

In 1915, Bergius began the construction of a new facility at Mannheim-Rheinau, where coal hydrogenation could be done on a larger scale. Because of the war and postwar collapse of the German economy, it took until 1924 to get the plant running, and expenses mounted. Financial problems led Bergius to sell interests in his plant to other interested firms: Shell Oil, Imperial Chemical Industries (ICI) in Britain, and eventually Badische Anilin- und Soda-Fabrik (BASF). The remaining development of coal hydrogenation fell to Carl Bosch at the Leuna plant of Interessen Gemeinschaft Farben (I. G. Farben, a chemical cartel), twenty miles west of Leipzig near Merseburg.

After about 1925, Bergius entered a new phase of work in which he became interested in making food from wood. Cellulose, the major structural material in wood and plants, is composed of long chains of glucose units linked by shared oxygen atoms. Some animals, such as deer, can digest cellulose, breaking the oxygen links and obtaining nourishment from the glucose. Humans cannot digest cellulose, but in a chemical reactor, cellulose can be broken down by strong acids to form sugars. Organic chemist Richard Willstätter (1872-1942) discovered that cellulose could be successfully broken down into sugars by the use of 40 percent hydrochloric acid at room temperature. Others had used sulfuric acid at higher temperatures. Bergius applied the hydrochloric acid method to the solubilization of the cellulose in wood waste, an abundant raw material. The cellulose was broken down in two stages: first to form sugars such as glucose, mannose, xylose, galactose, and fructose in tetrameric form, then after dilution and further heating, to form the monomeric sugars. The glucose, galactose, and mannose were fermentable by yeast to produce ethanol. One metric ton of dried wood yielded 320-338 liters of 95 percent ethanol. The lignin content of the wood precipitated out during the acid treatment and was recovered for use as fuel.

Bergius designed and operated a plant at Mannheim-Rheinau for the implementation of his cellulose process. The economical operation of the process required recovery of the acid by distillation. The hydrochloric acid presented serious corrosion problems in that it attacked most of the common materials of construction; therefore, ceramic parts were used in the still, which operated under vacuum at slightly above room temperature. It was also possible to recover acetic acid as a by-product.

In 1931, Bergius and Carl Bosch shared the Nobel Prize in Chemistry for their achievements in high-pressure chemistry. Bergius was the recipient of many other honors, including an honorary D.Phil. from the University of Heidelberg. After World War II, Bergius lived in Austria and Spain before settling in Argentina, where he served as a technical research adviser to the government from 1946 to 1949. He died in Buenos Aires on March 30, 1949.

Impact

Bergius took his coal hydrogenation process to pilot-plant scale at his Mannheim-Rheinau installation. He had demonstrated the process and shown that it could be an important source of synthetic fuels if implemented on a large scale. Further development was done by others at BASF and I. G. Farben, resulting in the opening of a large installation at Leuna in 1927. Improvements were made to the Bergius process at Leuna. Bergius's original single-step process was separated into a liquid-phase hydrogenation step catalyzed by metal sulfides or oxides, and a vapor-phase hydrocracking step. This resulted in better-

Production of Liquid Fuels by Hydrogenation of Coal

Germany has plentiful deposits of coal, particularly brown coal, or lignite, but very little petroleum. Friedrich Bergius sought to improve on the discoveries of Marcellin Berthelot (1827-1907), who in 1869 reported coal hydrogenation experiments using higher pressures of hydrogen, envisioning an industrial-sized operation. Since different types of coal vary in their suitability for hydrogenation, Bergius tested a multitude of coal samples and determined that soft coal and lignite rather than hard, or anthracite, coal work best for hydrogenation.

The reactions released heat, which needed to be dissipated since excessive temperature produced coke, which resisted hydrogenation. Powdered coal was made into a paste with oil and subjected to hydrogen gas. The oil helped to make the heating more uniform. The reaction produced various hydrocarbons as the hydrogen broke down the complex carbon-atom network in the coal. Bergius designed both rotating and stationary autoclaves to facilitate mixing and temperature control, and he was able to handle batches of four hundred liters. The inefficiency of the batch process led Bergius to develop a continuous process on a larger scale. The paste of powdered coal and oil was preheated and forced into a reactor by a ram, while products were continuously removed. The reactor consisted of a steel cylinder eight meters long and one meter in diameter mounted horizontally. Temperature control was important, and Bergius developed a heat-exchange method involving bathing the reactor in a stream of inert gas at the proper temperature.

The hydrogen needed for the process was available from the action of steam on hot coke (water gas reaction) but needed to be freed of carbon monoxide. Previous workers had done this by cooling the gas mixture enough to liquefy the carbon monoxide. Bergius was able to conduct the water gas reaction at a lower temperature by working at high pressure with a thallium chloride catalyst. Under these conditions, the carbon monoxide was converted to the dioxide, which could be removed by reaction with alkali. Serendipitously, Bergius discovered that the high-temperature water was reacting with the iron parts of the reactor, producing hydrogen gas. This reaction he developed into a method for making large quantities of pure hydrogen-reacting water with iron filings at high temperature and pressure. The by-product iron oxide could be reduced back to iron and reused.

quality fuels. By 1931, Leuna was producing synthetic fuels at the rate of 2.5 million barrels per year. By 1944, Germany had twelve plants and was producing at the rate of 25 million barrels per year, including almost all of the aviation fuel for the Luftwaffe.

Coal hydrogenation was developed in England by the British government and by ICI using Bergius's methods. By 1935, England had a plant that produced gasoline at the rate of 100,000 barrels per year. Synthetic fuels have tended to be more expensive than those derived from petroleum, and interest in them becomes greater when petroleum is expensive or scarce. Coal gasification followed by catalytic reaction of carbon monoxide and hydrogen (Fischer-Tropsch reaction) is an alternative to the Bergius process for liquid fuels. In the early twenty-first century, synthesis of liquid fuels from coal is practiced in many countries, including the United States, South Africa, and the United Kingdom.

The conversion of cellulose to ethanol is a promising renewable source of fuel, and it is a subject of active research in the twenty-first century. Interest, however, centers most on enzymatic processes rather than the acid hydrolysis favored by Bergius.

—*John R. Phillips*

Further Reading

Bergius, Friedrich. "Chemical Reactions Under High Pressure." In *Nobel Lectures, Chemistry, 1922-1941*. Amsterdam: Elsevier, 1966. Bergius's Nobel lecture traces his research on coal and oil hydrogenation, hydrogen production, and artificial coal. No mention of wood hydrolysis. Many pictures of industrial apparatuses.

_______. "Conversion of Wood to Carbohydrates" *Industrial and Engineering Chemistry* 29 (1937): 247-253. A discussion of the use of hydrochloric acid to convert wood to sugars. Many pictures of the Mannheim-Rheinau plant.

Cornwell, John. *Hitler's Scientists: Science, War, and the Devil's Pact.* New York: Viking Press, 2003. Broad study of science and scientists in the Third Reich. Covers poison gas, atomic weapons, synthetic fuels, ballistic missiles, and other topics.

Jahn, E. C., and Roger W. Strauss. "Industrial Chemistry of Wood." In *Riegel's Handbook of Industrial Chemistry*, edited by James A. Kent. New York: Van Nostrand Reinhold, 1974. General discussion of the chemical nature of wood and its conversion to products such as sugars, paper, cellophane, and rayon. Bergius's process is covered.

Lesch, John E., ed. *The German Chemical Industry in the Twentieth Century*. Dordrecht, Netherlands: Kluwer, 2000. Separately authored chapters treat the social, political and scientific aspects of the German chemical industry. Good chapter on synthetic fuels.

Stranges, Anthony N. "Friedrich Bergius and the Rise of the German Synthetic Fuel Industry." *Isis* 75, no. 279 (1984): 643-667. A complete history of Bergius's work on synthetic fuels, with many references to his patents and journal articles.

See also: Carl Bosch; Fritz Haber.

Emile Berliner

German American engineer

German immigrant Berliner's fascination with science and audio technology led to improvements in the telephone, the invention of the flat-disc gramophone, and a prototype helicopter.

Born: May 20, 1851; Hanover (now in Germany)
Died: August 3, 1929; Washington, D.C.
Primary fields: Acoustical engineering; aeronautics and aerospace technology; communications; music
Primary inventions: Gramophone; record disc; helicopter prototype

Early Life

Emile Berliner (EH-meel BUHR-lih-nuhr), one of thirteen children, was born in 1851 in Hanover (now in Germany) to Jewish parents. His father, Samuel, was a merchant and scholar, and his mother, Sarah Fridman, was a musician. Berliner's appreciation for music prompted him to take lessons on piano and violin. At age fourteen, Berliner had already graduated from the Samsonschule in Wolfenbüttel, a reputable school of languages and science. In order to lend financial support to the family, he ended his schooling and worked as a printer, then as a clerk in a fabric store. His first invention was an improved loom for weaving cloth.

Berliner immigrated to the United States in 1870, when he accepted a position in a dry goods store in Washington, D.C. After three years, he moved to New York City, working various day jobs as a traveling salesman and dry goods clerk while studying at the Cooper Institute (now known as the Cooper Union, a prestigious fine arts and engineering college in Manhattan) at night.

In 1875, Berliner worked in Constantine Fahlberg's research laboratory, which sparked his interests in inventing and science. A year later, Berliner returned to his position as a clerk in Washington, D.C. During the Centennial Exposition of 1876, Alexander Graham Bell's telephone discovery occupied center stage. Berliner was fascinated with the new invention and decided to pursue the development of his own telephone. He spent long hours at the Cooper Institute library studying electricity and physics. By 1876, Berliner had invented a new telephone transmitter, essentially a carbon microphone, which was patented a year later.

Emile Berliner stands with his flat-disc gramophone, the first of its kind. (Library of Congress)

Life's Work

The year 1877 was pivotal for Berliner. His transmitter was purchased

The Record Disc

Emile Berliner patented the flat record disc, his production methods, and the gramophone in 1887. Numerous improvements followed in subsequent years. The patent protected Berliner's design of etched grooves of a uniform depth, cut laterally, resulting in clearer sound production, durability, and increased volume compared to Thomas Alva Edison's cylinder recordings.

The gramophones of 1887-1888 recorded on a polished glass plate, later on zinc. The plates were covered with a thin coating of beeswax diluted by benzene. The recording grooves formed tracks that guided the sound box's movement across the record. The sound box holds the gramophone needle in place at about a 60-degree angle with a thumbscrew. The grooves' rigid walls reduce the side-to-side movement of the needle, diminishing wear.

The plate is mounted on a centered, vertical spindle within an etching trough. Both the spindle and the plate revolve together. The stylus (needle), diaphragm, and the mouth tube are attached to a carriage that gravitates toward the center of the plate. A friction wheel on a horizontal shaft on the side of and underneath the plate forces the rotation of the plate. The wheel is attached to a hand crank that extends outside the case. By cranking the handle, the wheel turns the plate.

As the plate revolves, the mouth tube receives the sound, which in turn causes the diaphragm to vibrate. With the continuous revolutions of the plate, the parallel moving needle and connected parts gravitate toward the plate's center in a spiral line, etching into the wax film. When the recording is finished, the needle is removed and acid flows into the etched trough from a bottle located just behind the crank. Once etched from the acid, the trough is removed and the acid returns to the bottle. The wax film is dissolved and the plate is then moved to a reproducer.

On the reproducer, the plate is again mounted on a vertical spindle and revolves. The diaphragm in this machine has a needle that follows the spiral grooves, initiating diaphragm vibrations. The diaphragm and reproducing needle are in close proximity to the small end of a conical horn. The needle exerts little pressure on the disc, allowing maximum sound production through the horn. To play the gramophone, the crank is wound clockwise and the brake is released by a lever. The needle is placed on the disc and the gramophone is in operation.

Edison's phonograph and Bell's graphophone, which both used cylinders, were already commercially viable when Berliner patented his gramophone, but the gramophone had a distinct advantage over the rival machines: The discs could be easily mass-produced from molds. Berliner also concocted a revolutionary and original marketing scheme. He employed popular musical artists of the day, Enrico Caruso and Dame Nellie Melba among them, to record for him. The "Red Seal" recordings proved to be legendary and financially successful. Berliner also capitalized on Nipper, who listened to "His Master's Voice," a visual trademark recognized throughout the world since 1900.

by the American Bell Telephone Company, and he was hired as a research assistant. First in New York, then in Boston, Berliner spent the next seven years devoted to the development of the telephone with Bell Telephone and as an entrepreneur. In 1881, Berliner became an American citizen, married Cora Adler, and resigned from Bell Telephone. The couple moved to a small house in Washington, D.C., where he established himself in the private sector. He continued to tinker with the telephone and transmitter, surrendering the rights to his patents to the Bell Company.

The invention of the gramophone in 1886 proved to be a major contribution to the music recording industry. Thomas Alva Edison had already invented the cylinder phonograph in 1877 but then directed his attention to incandescent lighting. Berliner's gramophone represented a newer, more practical way of recording and reproducing sound—discs. His house on Columbia Road also served as center of operations for his gramophone business.

Berliner patented the gramophone in 1887, at the same time Edison returned to his work on the cylinder phonograph. Alexander Graham Bell's Volta Laboratory had also introduced the graphophone, similar to Edison's cylinder phonograph. Berliner's disc sound system employed a needle that vibrated from side to side within grooves. His first disc recording was also produced that year. In 1890, *Scientific American* published a descriptive article, complete with illustrations of the new machine, that further promoted the commercial success of the Berliner Gramophone Company.

Berliner returned to Europe twice, in 1881 and 1888, to present lectures and publicize his gramophone. The Hanover Institute of Technology celebrated Berliner's lecture and invention at the Electrotechnical Society of Berlin, firmly establishing the virtues of the gramophone. In 1900, a painting by Francis Barraud of a dog listening to a gramophone became the symbol for the Berliner Gramophone Company. Nipper the dog eventually became the trademark of the Victor Talking Machine Company, founded by colleague Eldridge R. Johnson.

Berliner's love of music surfaced again later in life when he turned to composing. He had always deeply appreciated the opportunities afforded to him as an American citizen. He composed a patriotic song, "Columbia Anthem," written for the 1897 national council of the Daughters of the American Revolution. The song was so well received that it was programmed by the U.S. Marine Band, performed at the White House, and served as a daily anthem sung by schoolchildren in Washington, D.C., and New York.

Berliner continued his experiments with musical instruments and acoustics. He developed a violin with the strings attached directly to the body of the instrument as a way to allow more unrestricted vibrations of the strings. For twenty years, he studied concert hall acoustics and invented acoustic tiles, acoustic cement, and parquet carpet to enhance sound production. The tiles could be applied to wall surfaces and were used in many buildings, including the Stanley Theater in Jersey City and the Leicester Theatre in London.

Berliner's efforts to repay American society included health industry reforms. When Berliner's daughter Alice became gravely ill because of a gastrointestinal condition, he concluded that the 30 percent mortality rate of infants was due to the use of raw milk. As a result of his extensive crusade for scalding milk and pasteurization, the federal government established specific milk standards.

He also championed women's rights. Contrary to the beliefs of many male scientists of his era, Berliner held that women, given the proper opportunities, would excel in science as much as men. In honor of his mother, he established the Sarah Berliner Research Fellowship for physics, biology, and chemistry in 1908. From 1909 to 1926, awards were presented to women in those disciplines, extending to psychology, geology, and other fields.

Toward the end of his life, Berliner was preoccupied with his fascination with flight. As early as 1906, he pondered the possibilities of aircraft, constructing a helicopter prototype by 1907 and developing the first radial aircraft motor. By 1926, he had constructed three helicopters that had trial flights. He also continued experimenting with rotary motors, designing one version after another. In 1920, along with his son Henry, Berliner successfully launched a helicopter that lifted straight up and proceeded in a forward direction. In 1923, an advanced version hovered in the air for fifteen minutes. The era of the helicopter had arrived, and Emile Berliner and son Henry were celebrated as creators.

In a letter to Cora in 1928, Berliner noted his wishes for a simple, inexpensive funeral, with piano music performed by his daughter Alice. On August 3, 1929, Emile Berliner died from a heart attack. He was buried in Rock Creek Cemetery, Washington, D.C.

Impact

The life of Berliner exemplifies the best of the human spirit. He immigrated to America with hopes of pursuing his dreams. With great resolve and patience, he conducted scientific investigations and experiments, forging new paths in communications, entertainment, acoustics, and aeronautical engineering. Berliner invented the flat-disc gramophone, the helicopter, the carbon microphone, acoustical tiles, and acoustic flooring. In 1913, the Franklin Institute awarded Berliner the Elliott Cresson Medal in recognition of his pioneering achievements in telephony and acoustics. The National Air and Space Museum in Washington, D.C., houses two of Berliner's helicopters in tribute to his accomplishments in aerospace technology, a 1924 Berliner Helicopter No. 5 and a Berliner 1932 monocoupe that was featured in air shows.

Although proud to be an American citizen, Berliner revered his roots. Devoted to religion and philosophy, he authored many articles on Zionism in support of Israel and vigorously supported the Hebrew University of Jerusalem. His convictions that one should not squander the blessings of American citizenship motivated him to thank America by advocating health industry reform and promoting women's rights. Hundreds of thousands of children's lives were spared because of Berliner's effective crusade to better inform the public about the perils of substandard health practices.

—Douglas D. Skinner

Further Reading

Baumbach, Robert W. *Look for the Dog*. Los Angeles: Mulholland Press, 1981. Comprehensive guide to all Victor machines of Berliner's designs. Catalog pictures and maintenance guides are included.

Brooks, Peter W. *Cierva Autogiros: The Development of Rotary-Wing Flight*. Washington, D.C.: Smithsonian Institution Press, 1988. An account of Spanish aeronautical engineer Juan de la Cierva, who invented the autogiro, predecessor of the helicopter.

Goldmann, Philipp. *The Origin and History of the Family and Branches of the Berliners of Hannover, 1720-1997*. Miami, Fla.: Author, 1997. The grandson of Berliner's youngest sister, Goldmann privately published this historical look at the Berliner family. A copy resides in the Emile Berliner room at the Smithsonian Institution and is available from the author.

Marco, Guy A. *Encyclopedia of Recorded Sound in the United States*. New York: Garland, 1993. Pre-World War II comprehensive examination of recorded sound and the recording industry in the United States.

Wile, Frederic William. *Emile Berliner, Maker of the Microphone*. New York: Arno Press, 1974. Berliner's involvement in the development of the gramophone, microphone, and flat discs is described. Includes information on Berliner's views of public health and poetry.

See also: Alexander Graham Bell; Thomas Alva Edison; Peter Carl Goldmark; Elisha Gray; David Edward Hughes; Eldridge R. Johnson; James Russell; Granville T. Woods.

Tim Berners-Lee

British computer scientist

Berners-Lee's development of the World Wide Web began in March of 1989, when he found a means of bringing together the idea of hypertext and the young Internet. This combination paved the way for the rapid snowballing of ideas, software, and technology that grew into the contemporary World Wide Web.

Born: June 8, 1955; London, England
Also known as: Timothy John Berners-Lee (full name)
Primary field: Computer science
Primary inventions: World Wide Web; HTML

Early Life

Timothy John Berners-Lee was born in London on June 8, 1955. His parents were both mathematicians and were both a part of the team that built the first computer produced for commercial sale, the Ferranti Manchester Mark I. Berners-Lee grew up playing with discarded five-hole punch tape for computers and building his own "computers" out of cardboard boxes. He was also constantly taught mathematics by his parents.

The training served him well, as he sailed through coursework at both Sheen Mount Primary School and Emmanuel School in Wandsworth. At Queens College, Oxford University, Berners-Lee studied physics, which he saw as a compromise between mathematics and engineering. While at Oxford, he was caught hacking into the university computer system using a computer he had cobbled together with a soldering iron, an old television, some TTL gates, and an M6800 processor. After that incident, he was banned from the university's computer system.

Berners-Lee received his physics degree in 1976 and took a job with Plessey Telecommunications, where he worked on distributed transaction systems and message relays. In 1978, Berners-Lee left Plessey for D. G. Nash, where he wrote typesetting software. He left Nash in 1980 to work at the European Organization for Nuclear Research, known as CERN, in Geneva, Switzerland, where he would lay the groundwork for a creation that would literally change the way most people see the world.

Life's Work

CERN hired Berners-Lee as a consultant/software engineer. While he was there, he decided he needed to write a database program for his personal use that would allow him to store and retrieve information through the use of hyperlinks. Hyperlinks are connections from one document, or any type of data, to another, which allow that data to be dynamically organized. An example of this is the familiar hyperlink on Web sites that, when clicked upon, takes the user to another Web page. Berners-Lee wanted his program to use hyperlinks to help him keep track of the vast array of researchers employed at CERN and their individual research projects.

Berners-Lee named this database program Enquire, for an 1856 how-to book on domestic life titled *Enquire Within upon Everything*—a title that he saw as a near-perfect analogy for the information portal he was envisioning. While Enquire was never made public, it served as the seed idea for what would become the World Wide Web.

Berners-Lee left CERN in 1981, taking a technical design position at John Poole's Image Computer Systems, where he worked with communications software and firmware. During this hiatus, he never stopped thinking about developing broader applications for hypertext. In 1984, he returned to CERN, but it would be another five years before he could begin weaving his Web.

CERN still presented Berners-Lee with the same logistical nightmare he faced that led to the creation of Enquire. By 1989, however, his vision had expanded to include a global information space where computers were linked together and researchers from anywhere in the world could "surf" from one data collection to another. He envisioned a system in which data could be shared in a matter of days or hours. This new system would be a true democracy in that it would work on all computer platforms, in nearly all languages, across all geographic borders, and without bureaucratic delays or dictatorial censorship. In 1989, Berners-Lee submitted a proposal to CERN for just such a system.

After nearly a year had passed, Berners-Lee was given the go-ahead, and his "global hypertext" project, based on the Enquire program, got underway in October of 1990. He named the program "WorldWideWeb"; the Web browser was distributed within CERN in December and posted on the Internet by the summer of 1991. Berners-Lee also posted Web server software and began a word-of-mouth campaign for the project by posting on newsgroups. The number of servers, Web sites, and users continued to grow at astonishing rates. Cyberspace, once an environment inhabited primarily by physicists and other researchers in the hard sciences, was suddenly becoming a popular destination for college students, government agencies, businesses, and, as better Web browsers and faster network speeds became available, the general public.

Specifications and protocols for hyperlinks and the other critical bits of hypertext markup language (HTML) were initially specified by Berners-Lee and then refined after discussions by user groups. In October of 1994, Berners-Lee established the World Wide Web Consortium (W3C) at the Laboratory for Computer Sciences at Massachusetts Institute of Technology. The role of W3C is to coordinate the development of the Web by maintaining the standard protocols for HTML.

As the cultural importance of the Web became evident, Berners-Lee became a celebrity. In 1997, he was awarded an Order of the British Empire for his work establishing the Web. He won a MacArthur Fellowship "genius grant" in 1998. In 1999, *Time* magazine named Berners-Lee one of the 100 Greatest Minds of the Century, and he was named the inaugural holder of the 3Com Founders Chair at MIT, where he was allowed to continue his Web work as a senior research scientist. In July, 2004, he was knighted by Queen Elizabeth II and became chair of the Computer Science Department at the University of Southampton. In June, 2007, Berners-Lee joined the elite Order of Merit, a gift bestowed by the Queen.

Impact

The World Wide Web has changed the world in a number of ways; namely, it has democratized information. The Web makes uncensored news reports, blogs, and alternative or marginalized points of view readily available to most of the world. Individuals who may have never had access to the corporate or governmental news media have found such access available on the Web. The very nature of the medium is such that a hypertext document produced by a poor villager in Laos can theoretically reach as many readers as a document produced by such established newspapers as *The New York Times*.

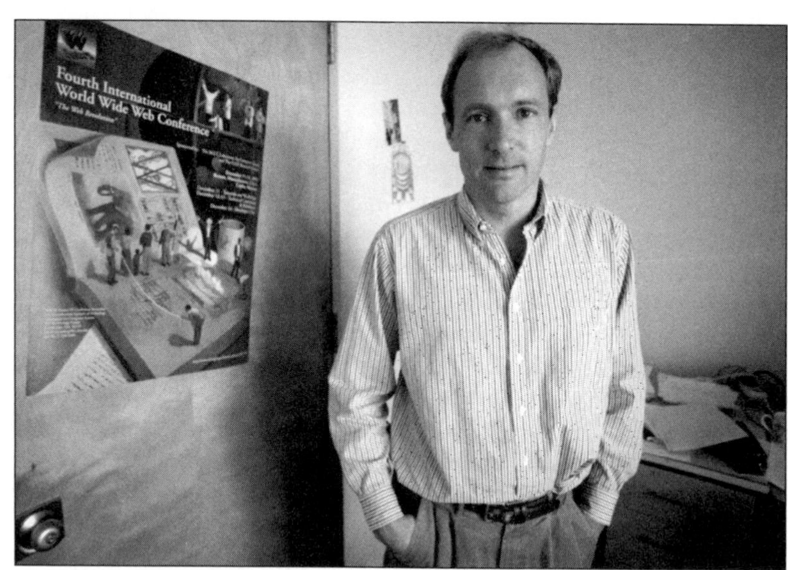

Tim Berners-Lee, inventor of the World Wide Web. (AP/Wide World Photos)

The Web has also changed the way information currency and relevancy is viewed. Thanks to the instantaneous nature of the Web, live Web cams and blogs can bring users to both sides of the front lines of war zones in real time. Such instantaneous and global access to data makes it difficult for information to be suppressed. The Web user's ability to tailor the flow of information to fit only his or her interests means that the relevance of a particular story is no longer determined by an editor

UDIs, Hypertext, WWW, HTML, and a Linked World

Tim Berners-Lee's dream was to create a common information space in which people engage in communication through the sharing of information via hypertext links. Hypertext is, simply put, a text command on one computer that will lead a user to a related piece of information that resides in another computer. That notion of linking is the very basis of the Web.

Berners-Lee made this possible by creating a number of smaller components that were necessary to make the hypertext linking appear seamless to the user. The first component was to create a means of giving each piece of data available on the Web its own unique identity so that hyperlinks could be built to link to a specific piece of data. He did this by creating a protocol called the universal document identifier (UDI; now called the uniform resource locator, or URL), perhaps best known as a "Web address." Berners-Lee also needed a language with which to write hypertext code and, later, page layout and formatting specifications. This Web-specific language was known as hypertext markup language (HTML). Next, Berners-Lee needed to construct a protocol governing the retrieval and presentation of data over the Web, which he named hypertext transfer protocol (HTTP).

Next, Berners-Lee constructed the first hypertext editor so that documents could be prepared for presentation on his fledgling Web. In 1990, he completed the editor, which he named "WorldWideWeb." There was also the question of how those hypertext documents would be made available, so Berners-Lee also wrote the first Web server software, called "httpd," for "hypertext transfer protocol daemon."

The first Web site went online at the European Organization for Nuclear Research (CERN) on August 6, 1991. The initial site had pages explaining the Web and how to obtain a browser and set up a server. With all the groundwork in place, Berners-Lee began circulating the software, first among the physicists at CERN, then by posting the software on the Internet and talking about it via posts in newsgroups.

As new Web browsers were developed and made available—Erwise, Viola, Cello, and Lynx being among the first—the number of users grew. When a student at the University of Illinois, Marc Andreessen, developed the user-friendly Mosaic (released in 1993), the first browser to incorporate inline graphics, Web usage skyrocketed. Andreessen went on to develop the Netscape Navigator Web browser, released in 1994.

From an idea designed to create an information utopia, the World Wide Web has become, in a short period, a commercial backbone, a critical component of the U.S. government and military, a tool for continual education, information gathering, and entertainment, and one enormous social network. The future Web promises even more, with bigger bandwidth, more content, and metadata that will allow searching and indexing to become even more precise.

serving a broad community but rather by the needs and desires of the end user. These changes have altered the way news and information is covered and packaged for the end user, resulting in a wider variety of information for the user.

With the advent of the Web, new businesses cropped up and continued to do so as entrepreneurs explored the possibilities of the new medium. The Web changed the way businesses were run, as most corporate outlets and even small-town stores established their own Web presence. Sites like Amazon.com proved that using the Web to change the extant business model for bookstores was a multimillion-dollar idea. As a result of peer-to-peer file sharing cutting deeply into music industry profits, the industry became more Web-driven.

The Web also holds the promise of creating a society in which more people have the freedom to work or be educated from home rather than having to travel to a job or campus. Perhaps the most important impact of the World Wide Web is that it is allowing "netizens" to share information, research, news, entertainment, old books, photos, music, and conversation in a way that can unite people worldwide. This remains a critical part of Berners-Lee's dream for the Web.

—*B. Keith Murphy*

Further Reading

Berners-Lee, Tim. *Weaving the Web: The Original Design and Ultimate Destiny of the World Wide Web.* New York: HarperCollins, 2000. Although lacking in technical depth, the book explains how and why the World Wide Web came into being. Berners-Lee shares the glory of creating the WWW revolution and holds that the Web can be a means of creating more harmony within world society.

_______, et al., eds. *Spinning the Semantic Web: Bringing the World Wide Web to Its Full Potential.* Cambridge, Mass.: MIT Press, 2005. A rather technical look at the future of the World Wide Web, the book focuses on the tagging of data for more reliable and faster indexing. This work is of most interest for Berners-Lee's foreword.

Hafner, Katie, and Matthew Lyon. *Where Wizards Stay Up Late: The Origins of the Internet*. New York: Simon & Schuster, 1996. Tells the tale of the birth of the modern Internet. Ranging from the launch of Sputnik and the Defense Department's Defense Advanced Research Projects Agency (DARPA) network projects to the Web, Hafner's book puts Berners-Lee's contribution into its context within this fascinating and arcane history.

See also: Marc Andreessen; Robert Cailliau; Vinton Gray Cerf; Philip Emeagwali; Bill Gates; Bob Kahn; Robert Metcalfe; Larry Page.

Clifford Berry

American electrical engineer

While John Vincent Atanasoff developed the concept for the Atanasoff-Berry Computer (ABC), Berry deserves equal credit for the detailed design and construction. Berry's work on the ABC showed that an electronic computer could be built for digital calculation. This influenced future development of the computer.

Born: April 19, 1918; Gladbrook, Iowa
Died: October 30, 1963; Plainview, New York
Also known as: Clifford Edward Berry (full name)
Primary field: Computer science
Primary invention: Atanasoff-Berry Computer

Early Life

Clifford Edward Berry was born in Gladbrook, Iowa, in 1918. He was the first of four children born to Fred and Grace Strohm Berry. Fred, a self-taught engineer, had an electrical appliance and repair store in Gladbrook and worked on electrical projects, including building the small town's first radio. Clifford, also known as Cliff, showed early interest in engineering and electronics when he, with his father's oversight, built his own radio.

The Berry family moved to Marengo, Iowa, when Cliff was eleven. Tragedy struck the family when Fred, a manager at the Iowa Power Company, was shot and killed by an employee who had been fired from his job. Before his death, Fred had decided that Cliff would attend Iowa State College (now Iowa State University) because its college of engineering had a national reputation. When Cliff was ready for college, the family moved to Ames, Iowa, and he studied electrical engineering at Iowa State. There he excelled, graduating in 1939. One of Berry's professors recommended him to John Vincent Atanasoff when the latter was looking for an electrical engineering graduate student to assist in his computer project.

Life's Work

In the spring of 1939, Berry began to work on Atanasoff's project to build a prototype of an electronic digital computer. For Atanasoff's research, he had to find solutions to large and complex sets of equations. Doing this by hand was extremely tedious. It could take a human 125 hours to solve twenty equations and twenty unknowns. Atanasoff designed a fully electronic computer that could solve a system of thirty equations and thirty unknowns.

Berry's skill in electronics complemented Atanasoff's skills in math and physics. Berry took Atanasoff's rough sketches of some parts of the machine and worked out the details. Eventually, Berry worked independently on the machine without detailed instructions from Atanasoff and suggested his own improvements. They worked in the basement of the physics building next to a student workshop, where they could carefully build each component and test it before moving on.

Berry found that vacuum tubes were expensive, used a lot of space, emitted much heat, and broke often. After testing, he chose a kind that consumed the least power and worked well with the condensers. The tubes provided enough voltage to recharge the condensers, and the condensers provided enough voltage to actuate the tubes.

By the end of 1939, Berry and Atanasoff had a working prototype, which they demonstrated to Iowa State officials. The prototype was a breadboard-size device with the electrical components mounted crudely on its surface. While small, the machine had all the important parts to show that they could make the design work. They received a grant to build a full-scale machine, and the college decided to apply for a patent.

Atanasoff, with Berry's assistance, wrote a thirty-five-page manuscript entitled "Computing Machines for the Solution of Large Systems of Linear Algebraic Equations," with drawings of the machine. The manuscript was sent to a college-appointed lawyer to proceed with the patent application. While Iowa State College officials refused to grant a portion of income from a patent to a graduate student, they agreed not to interfere if Atanasoff chose to give Berry a portion of his 50 percent. Atanasoff wanted to acknowledge the importance of Berry's contribution. In the end, however, the attorney and the college never applied for the patent.

Berry received his master of science in physics in 1941. On May 30, 1942, he married Martha Jean Reed, Atanasoff's secretary. They had two children, Carol and David. Also that year, Atanasoff and Berry produced a working electronic special-purpose computer, known as the Atanasoff-Berry Computer (ABC). This computer employed various new techniques, including novel uses of logic circuitry and regenerative memory. However, the part of the machine designed to record intermediate results on paper worked for small systems of equations, not for large ones.

The U.S. entry into World War II ended Berry and Atanasoff's work and may have prevented their innovations from being published, patented, and given proper credit. They both left Iowa for jobs in the defense industry. Atanasoff went to work for the Naval Ordnance Laboratory in Maryland. Berry moved to Pasadena, California, where he took a position with Consolidated Engineering Corporation (CEC) for defense-related work. The Atanasoff-Berry Computer remained in the basement of the physics building, where Atanasoff and Berry had built it. When neither returned to Iowa after the war, the chair of the Physics Department needed the space in the basement and disassembled the ABC in 1948.

While employed at CEC, Berry arranged with Iowa State to complete the requirements for a Ph.D. in physics, which he received in 1948 with his dissertation "The Effects of Initial Energies on Mass Spectra." CEC's market strength was in mass spectrometers, which produced large amounts of data. To analyze the data, one had to solve a set of simultaneous linear equations similar to the work Atanasoff had done. Berry (with Sibyl Rock) developed and patented an analog computer to accomplish this in 1945.

In 1949, Berry became chief physicist at CEC, and he was promoted to assistant director of research in 1952. In 1959, he became director of engineering of the Analytical and Control Division and also served as technical director. Berry received nineteen patents in the area of mass spectrometry and eleven in the areas of electronics and vacuum tubes.

The Atanasoff-Berry Computer (ABC)

The ABC was the size of a large desk or chest freezer and weighed about seven hundred pounds. All the parts were mounted on a metal frame. There was an operator's control console on top with numerous switches, buttons, meters, and lights. Underneath the console was the arithmetic unit (to perform addition and subtraction), which contained over two hundred vacuum tubes. Beside it was the equipment for input and output. Two rotating drums served as the memory. Each drum had sixteen hundred capacitors set into its skin in thirty-two rows. The capacitors represented a digit by being charged positively (1) or negatively (0). Each drum stored thirty fifty-bit numbers (fifteen-place decimal numbers). Since the capacitors drained their charge about the time a drum made one complete revolution, Clifford Berry and John Vincent Atanasoff designed a circuit to regenerate the charge on each rotation. While crude, this became the basis of the modern dynamic random access memory (RAM) in computers.

Because the machine's memory could not hold enough of the intermediate results required in the calculation, these results needed to be stored and reloaded later. Berry and Atanasoff used high-voltage arcs to burn holes in paper. A hole signified a 1 and no hole a 0. In the binary, or base-2, system that they used, there are only 1's and 0's (unlike the decimal system that has the numerals 0 through 9). After the intermediate results were burned in, the paper was read when it was passed between electrodes at a lower voltage than was used to create the holes. The arc would form in the reader if there was a hole in the card, but not if the paper remained intact.

Berry's master's thesis, "Design of Electrical Data Recording and Reading Mechanism," presented the best means for recording and reading of intermediate results. He found the correct voltage to write (3,000 volts) and to read (2,000 volts), which allowed the ABC to record the entire contents of one memory drum in one second; the correct thickness of paper; and the correct spacing of electrodes to write and read.

For small systems of equations, the ABC was much faster and more reliable than hand calculation. ABC's calculating speed far outstripped its ability to handle input and output. The calculations had errors only once every 100,000 times, so the machine was successful for these small systems of equations. However, while this small error made no difference for small systems of equations, large systems required hundreds of thousands of operations. Thus, the error would occur and produce incorrect results.

In 1963, Berry left CEC for a position at the Vacuum-Electronics Corporation in Plainview, New York. Before his family could join him, he died suddenly on October 30. His death was listed as a "possible suicide" from suffocation.

Impact

Berry played a key role in the development of the electronic computer. Berry and Atanasoff's work communicated the ideas of fully electronic digital logic and dynamic regenerative capacitor storage to other early computer designers and played an important role in the eventual development of a fully programmable electronic general-purpose computer.

Particular components of the ABC were innovative and became basic elements in computers. The machine pioneered a regenerative memory. It used regenerative pulses to stop the charges in the capacitors from "leaking" away. This technique is still the basis of modern dynamic random access memory (RAM). Other innovations included the use of vacuum tubes, the use of binary numbers, and the use of electronic logic.

In the 1960's, when the legal battles over who invented the first electronic computer began, Atanasoff began to refer to the machine as the "Atanasoff-Berry Computer," or "ABC," to give Berry appropriate credit. Atanasoff said that the assembly procedure for the logic circuit that Berry had designed had made the circuits perfect. The ABC would not have been built and would not have worked without Berry's contribution.

—Linda Eikmeier Endersby

Further Reading

Burks, Alice R., and Arthur W. Burks. *The First Electronic Computer: The Atanasoff Story*. Ann Arbor: University of Michigan Press, 1988. A technically oriented book, the majority of which focuses on the influence of Atanasoff's work on the Electronic Numerical Integrator and Computer (ENIAC) and the legal battle over the invention of the computer. Illustrations, references, index, appendixes.

Gustafson, John. "Reconstruction of the Atanasoff-Berry Computer." In *The First Computers—History and Architectures*, edited by Raúl Rojas and Ulf Hashagen. Cambridge, Mass.: MIT Press, 2000. Technically detailed chapter detailing the reconstruction of the Atanasoff-Berry Computer in 1997. Provides some information about the working of the computer that cannot be found elsewhere. Illustrations, sources, index.

Hally, Mike. *Electronic Brains: Stories from the Dawn of the Computer Age*. Washington, D.C.: J. Henry Press, 2005. Readable book with details of various machines and personalities significant in the development of the modern computer. Includes one chapter with information on Berry and Atanasoff's work. Includes useful appendixes explaining technical terms, binary mathematics, and parts of the modern computer. Illustrations, references, index.

Mollenhoff, Clark R. *Atanasoff: Forgotten Father of the Computer*. Ames: Iowa State University Press, 1988. Very readable work that provides many details on Berry's life and work in the first half of the book. Second half of book has little on Berry. Illustrations, references, index.

See also: John Vincent Atanasoff; John Presper Eckert; John William Mauchly; Konrad Zuse.

Sir Henry Bessemer

British engineer

Bessemer developed a relatively inexpensive process for the mass production of steel, which was previously a scarce and expensive commodity. His Bessemer converter helped launch a revolution in manufacturing commonly termed the Second Industrial Revolution.

Born: January 19, 1813; Charlton, Hertfordshire, England
Died: March 15, 1898; London, England
Primary field: Manufacturing
Primary invention: Bessemer process

Early Life

A grade school dropout, Henry Bessemer nevertheless went on to become one of England's most prolific inventors, registering 110 patents and becoming fantastically wealthy in the process. His informal education stemmed almost exclusively from his father's influence. Anthony Bessemer was a successful typefounder and inventor who made his fortune developing a process and dyes for making gold chains. Bessemer learned metallurgy in his father's type foundry, built in the grounds of the family house at Charlton. When only seventeen years old, he founded his own business for producing art metals and fusible alloys. By age twenty, he was an exhibitor at the Royal Academy and had invented a process for making dated embossed stamps used on title deeds and other government documents. Formerly, stamps were taken off old deeds to save the buyer the £5 government fee. With the new embossed stamp dyes, which were capable of producing thousands of dated facsimile impressions, the British government made a handsome profit in fees. Married at twenty-one, Bessemer had a home built at Northampton Square. As his wealth grew, he had larger London-based homes built at St. Pancras, Highgate, and Denmark Hill. He built a foundry at his residence (called Baxter House) in the London suburb of St. Pancras.

Bessemer earned considerable money developing a process for compressing powdered graphite dust to form lead pencils and for embossing velvet wallpaper by using a succession of steamrollers. He also developed a steam-driven fan for ventilating mines, an improved method for producing sheet glass, and a compact-sized press using a screw extruder for efficiently extracting over 600 gallons of juice per hour from sugarcane, for which he received the Royal Society of Arts Albert Medal. However, his main fortune was made in 1843, when he developed a complex yet cheap process for turning bronze into a dust, oxidizing the dust to produce a brilliant gold color, and using it to make gold paint. The process involved a series of six steam-powered machines. It took thirty-five years for others to duplicate the process. Meanwhile, Bessemer became wealthy producing the stylish color used extensively in the time period termed the Gilded Age. While a brilliant inventor, Bessemer was also an astute businessman. For this combination of abilities he became known as "the ingenious Mr. Bessemer."

Life's Work

In 1853, as Bessemer turned forty, the Crimean War began. Anglo-French forces stood against Russia, which had by far the largest army in Europe. At the start of the war, Bessemer produced experimental conical shells that were far heavier than cannon balls and with spiral grooves cut into the sides. Escaping gases would make the shell spin and deliver its payload with considerable accuracy. In November, 1854, he patented the artillery shell but found no interest in it by the British War Department. The French emperor Napoleon III seemed intrigued, but wrought iron cannon barrels proved too weak to handle the heavy gas pressure emitted by the shell. Attempts to line the barrel with steel, a rare commodity at the time, proved insufficient. Bessemer left France obsessed with thoughts about how to produce stronger cast iron. Within a year, he found the answer—blowing air through the bottom of a vat of molten iron. His first experiment sent in too much air at once, producing a volcanic-type reaction that nearly destroyed his Baxter House foundry in St. Pancras.

Sir Henry Bessemer. (Library of Congress)

In 1855, Bessemer successfully produced a low-grade steel from molten pig iron in a side-blown fixed converter without any external source of heat. The Bessemer converter was an egg-shaped vat that held molten iron. Cold air was blown into tiny perforations in the bottom, removing carbon and other impurities in the iron. The blast of air also superheated the iron, allowing it to be easily poured. Workers needed no special skills. The end result was high-quality steel produced cheaply. He patented the process, and on August 24, 1856, he described the process in a paper "The Manufacture of Iron Without Fuel," presented at a meeting of the British Association in Cheltenham. The presentation was important enough to be published in its entirety in the London *Times*. Immediately, five firms eager to save money in time, labor, and fuel applied to produce under Bessemer's patents.

The wrought iron producers who tried the Bessemer

process failed to produce quality steel. The cause was soon found. British pig iron was phosphorus-rich, which led to brittleness in forging. No immediate solution to the problem could be found. In his own experiments, Bessemer was fortunate to use iron from the one place in England that did not contain phosphorus.

Bessemer proceeded to establish steelworks in Sheffield in 1858, using phosphorus-free ore mainly imported from Sweden. It was in Sheffield where the bottom-blown tilting converter was introduced in 1860. Soon, the Sheffield plant could undersell all competitors since crucible steel cost twice as much as Bessemer steel. In the United States, the Bessemer process was patented in 1857, but Bessemer's priority was challenged by William Kelly. As the prospect of a long legal battle threatened, a settlement was reached in which the two rival companies consolidated. In 1865, the first U.S. plant using the Bessemer process began operation in Troy, New York, to be soon followed by one in Harrisburg, Pennsylvania. In the United States, thirteen cities would be named Bessemer.

In spite of its initial drawbacks, the process made Bessemer a multimillionaire. His methods were ten times faster than any previous methods, used no fuel once the pig iron melted, and could make thirty tons of steel at once rather than the fifty pounds using other methods. By 1879, Sydney Gilchrist showed that phosphorus could be removed by using basic instead of acidic furnace linings and fluxes. The open-hearth steelmaking process was developed, which became established in England. However, the rest of Europe and the United States continued to use the standard Bessemer process. One American who made a fortune from it was Andrew Carnegie. It was not until 1907 that the open-hearth method surpassed the Bessemer method in the production of steel.

Old age did not slow up Henry Bessemer. He invented a solar furnace and designed and built an astronomical telescope, as well as machines to efficiently polish diamonds. His last ventures were in the construction of steamships designed to ease seasickness on the rocky trip across the English Channel. He invented a system to keep the cabin stable by mounting it on gimbals. Thus, the cabin would remain horizontal as the ship pitched in the waves. A prototype was built by Maudslay, Sons and Field in 1875. It had two sets of paddle wheels and was extremely difficult to steer. It twice crashed into the pier at Calais and was abandoned after its maiden voyage.

In 1879, Bessemer was knighted and made a fellow of the Royal Society. His final years were spent designing numerous improvements to his own home and those of his children. He died at his Denmark Hill estate in 1898.

The Bessemer Process

The Bessemer process was used to manufacture steel from molten pig iron. The principle involved is that of oxidation of the impurities in the iron by the oxygen of air that is blown through the molten iron. The heat of oxidation raises the temperature of the mass, keeping it molten during operation. The process is carried on in a large, egg-shaped container called the Bessemer converter, which is made of steel and has a lining of silica and clay or of dolomite. The capacity ranges from eight to thirty tons of molten iron; the usual charge is fifteen or eighteen tons. At its narrow, upper end, it has an opening through which the iron to be treated is introduced and the finished product is poured out. The wide, bottom end has a number of perforations through which the air is forced upward into the converter during operation. The container is set on pivots so that it can be tilted to receive the charge, turned upright during the "blow," and inclined for pouring the molten steel after the operation is complete. As the air passes upward through the molten pig iron, impurities such as silicon, manganese, and carbon unite with the oxygen in the air to form oxides; the carbon monoxide burns off while the other impurities form slag. Dolomite is used as the converter lining when the phosphorus content is high; the process is then called basic Bessemer. The silica and clay lining is used in the acid Bessemer, in which phosphorus is not removed. In order to provide the elements necessary to give the steel the desired properties, another substance (often spiegeleisen, an iron-carbon-manganese alloy) is usually added to the molten metal after the oxidation is completed. The converter is then emptied into ladles, from which the steel is poured into molds; the slag is left behind. The whole process is completed in fifteen to twenty minutes. The Kelham Island Museum at Sheffield maintains an early example of a Bessemer converter.

Impact

Prior to the Bessemer process, steel was expensive and difficult to produce. It was used largely for specialized cutting tools and fine swords. Henry Bessemer pioneered the steel industry. He made steel plentiful and relatively cheap to produce. Lighter, stronger, and more flexible than either cast iron or wrought iron, steel became a driving force behind the Second Industrial Revolution. It would be used for skyscrapers, bridges, weapons, machines, tools, and transportation. Steel became the basic component of the physical structure in modern urban industrial society. Although Bessemer's process would be supplanted by other steel-producing processes in the twentieth century, especially the oxygenization process of the 1950's, it nevertheless began the rapidly accelerating process of worldwide steel usage on a large scale.

As an individual, Bessemer stands out as not only an innovative genius and capable businessman but also one of the most important inventors of the nineteenth century.

—*Irwin Halfond*

Further Reading

Bessemer, Henry. *Sir Henry Bessemer, F.R.S: An Autobiography*. Brookfield, Vt.: Institute of Metals, 1989. This comprehensive autobiography is loaded with details and many illustrations and photos. The concluding chapter was written by his son.

Bodsworth, C., ed. *Sir Henry Bessemer: Father of the Steel Industry*. London: IOM Communications, 1998. A collection of nine essays covering a variety of topics related to Bessemer's life and the operation of the Bessemer process.

Stearns, Peter N. *The Industrial Revolution in World History*. 3d ed. New York: Westview Press, 2007. A comprehensive study, from an international and human perspective, and by a leading historian of the growth of the Industrial Revolution and its revolutionary transformation of life.

See also: Abraham Darby; Robert Stirling.

Edwin Binney

American chemist

Binney's first major invention was dustless chalk, and he developed several manufacturing processes for black carbon, but he is best remembered for his 1903 invention, along with his cousin C. Harold Smith, of Crayola brand crayons, which were marketed as a children's toy.

Born: 1866; Shrub Oak, New York
Died: December 18, 1934; Greenwich, Connecticut
Primary field: Chemistry
Primary inventions: Crayola crayons; dustless chalk

Early Life

Edwin Binney's father, Joseph W. Binney, came to upstate New York from England in 1860. He started the Peekskill Chemical Works in Peekskill, New York, in 1864, two years before Edwin's birth. The chemical company initially produced a hardwood charcoal and a black pigment called lampblack. The company moved to New York City in 1880, and Edwin joined the company, as did his cousin C. Harold Smith. Smith was born in London in 1860. Upon reaching adulthood, Smith immigrated to New Zealand, where he fell in love with a Maori woman and narrowly escaped death at the hands of her tribe. He decided the United States would be safer and moved to New York to join his extended family.

Joseph Binney retired from the business in 1885, and the two cousins changed the name of the company to Binney & Smith—a partnership that was eventually incorporated in 1902. The product line was expanded to include black shoe polish, ink, and chalk. Red paint, used to paint barns, was another early product. With the discovery of oil in Pennsylvania came a new type of petroleum-based black pigment, and the cousins took an active role in production and development of carbon black from natural gas wells. They even bought into some of the companies that produced the carbon black. This new pigment soon became the main ingredient in many of the company's products. One of the products affected by the black pigment was the tire manufactured by B. F. Goodrich. Goodrich produced white rubber tires. (The color was caused by zinc oxide in the rubber compound.) When Goodrich used Binney & Smith pigment to expand its product line to include black tires, the company discovered that the black pigment not only changed the color of the product but also made it five times more durable. Soon after, white tires disappeared from America's roadways. The growth of the tire business led Binney & Smith to other inventions, including a formula for putting black carbon into pellets to eliminate dust from the production process.

Binney and Smith made great partners. Binney was product- and finance-oriented, while Smith was a master salesman. Soon Smith had expanded the company's customer base for black pigment worldwide, and the company prospered. The company's headquarters were moved to Easton, Pennsylvania, in 1902 when the company incorporated. In 1900, the company had bought an old water-powered mill on Bushkill Creek near Easton and used it to grind up old slate from the region's many slate quarries. The resulting product was a pencil of superior quality. This product led Binney & Smith into the education market—a market that was to make them famous. Meetings with school teachers convinced Binney of the need for a better quality of chalk and lower-priced crayons. This led to the invention of An-Du-Septic, a dustless chalk that was sturdier than traditional chalk. In 1904, Binney's invention won a gold medal at the St. Louis World's Fair.

Life's Work

At about the same time that experiments were being conducted on dustless chalk, there was similar work being done on crayons. The first invention was a black wax crayon called Staonal ("stay on all"), named so because it would work on any type of surface; Staonal was designed as a marker for writing on boxes and barrels. The overnight success of Staonal led to experiments with other types of pigments to create colored wax crayons for use by schoolchildren. Artists already had access to imported crayons, but the cost of these tools was prohibitive for other than professional use. From the beginning, the concept was to use nontoxic pigments, since the end consumer was to be small children. Binney's wife, Alice, was a former schoolteacher, and she took a special interest in the product. In fact, she is credited with creating the name "Crayola." Teachers were already familiar with the company's quality pencils and chalk, so the introduction of Crayola crayons was an overnight success.

By 1911, the company had become quite profitable and allowed Binney and his family to spend much time in St. Lucie County, Florida, where he owned over one thousand acres of citrus groves. The community was known then as Fort Pierce Farms. Binney was an avid sportsman and fisherman. He was also a community activist and contributed much to his adopted Florida home. In 1919, Binney advocated having Fort Pierce become a

In 2008, Crayola celebrated the fiftieth anniversary of its sixty-four-count box with a limited-edition set that included eight new colors chosen by children. (AP/Wide World Photos)

Crayola Crayons

The first boxes of eight Crayola crayons were produced by Edwin Binney, along with his cousin C. Harold Smith, in 1903. The factory was in Easton, Pennsylvania. The price for a box of eight crayons was five cents. Binney's London-born wife, Alice Stead Binney, created the name "Crayola" from the French word *craie* (chalk) and "ola" (oleaginous, oily), since the crayons were produced from a petroleum-based wax. The eight original colors were black, brown, blue, red, purple, orange, yellow, and green. Today, there are more than 120 colors produced by Crayola, including some that sparkle, glow in the dark, and wash off of walls. Actually, Binney did not invent the crayon, he merely invented an improved crayon. Crayons had been invented earlier in Europe and were basically a mixture of charcoal and oil. Binney's contribution was to produce a better quality crayon that was nontoxic and affordable and to market it as a toy for children.

By 1920, Crayola products had expanded to include special crayons for art students and fine art crayons that could be sharpened. In 1948, the company began providing in-school training for art teachers across the nation. In 1958, the first box of sixty-four crayons was marketed. The box even had a built-in sharpener. In 1978, the company's product line expanded to include Crayola markers, and in 1987 washable markers were introduced. In 1990, eight crayon colors were retired into the Crayola Hall of Fame; these were maize, raw umber, lemon yellow, blue gray, orange yellow, orange red, green blue, and violet blue. However, a year later, those retired colors were offered in a special collectors' edition. The company's ninetieth birthday celebration in 1993 included the introduction of the company's largest crayon box ever, ninety-six colors. The 100 billionth Crayola crayon was produced in 1996, and this number continues to increase by more than 13.5 million every day. The company's best seller is the box of twenty-four crayons—a quantity that provides adequate variety, but at a reasonable price.

Binney & Smith changed its name to Crayola in 2007. The Crayola brand name has 99 percent name recognition among American consumers. The scent of crayons, according to studies, is one of the most recognizable scents to the American people. Crayolas are sold in over eighty countries and are packaged in boxes written in twelve languages. The invention of Edwin Binney has transformed the way the world looks at art and has made it economically possible for every child to be a budding artist. Many of the world's great artists of the past century likely started their career with a box of wax crayons from Binney & Smith. For example, American Gothic artist Grant Wood began his career with a Crayola contest. Wood later stated that by winning the Crayola contest, he was given the confidence and encouragement to pursue a career in the art world.

port city with an inlet to the Atlantic Ocean that would accommodate oceangoing vessels. Through his support, this was accomplished in 1922. In 1928, he contributed the funds to restore a bridge that linked the city with the nearby beach. When the Great Depression began in 1929, Binney put up his own money to keep the doors open at the St. Lucie County Bank. He also helped establish the local troop of Sea Scouts (a division of the Boy Scouts of America) and donated land that eventually became the Fort Pierce Coast Guard Station and the Pelican Yacht Club. Binney had four children: Edwin, Jr., Dorothy, Helen, and Mary. Although his son died at a young age, his namesake grandson, Edwin III, became a noted philanthropist in his own right.

Although Binney seemed happy in his life and career, such may not have been the case for his partner, Smith. In 1929, because he despised his fortune, Smith sponsored a contest, with a $1,000 prize, for the best idea as to how he could use his $10 million fortune for the good of humanity. The winning idea, submitted by a Columbia University psychology professor, was the creation of a C. Harold Smith Institute of Mental Hygiene. The institute never materialized. Smith died in 1931—three years before Binney. Both Binney and Smith were inducted into the Toy Industry Hall of Fame in 2006.

The Smithsonian National Museum of American History Archives Center houses the Binney & Smith archival materials dealing with technology, inventions, and innovations. These archives include advertising materials, financial and sales records, and various research and development records. The company itself has been a subsidiary of privately owned Hallmark Cards, Inc., since 1984. In 2007, the company had over 2,600 employees.

Impact

The Crayola brand name of Binney & Smith has become one of the most recognizable and most respected brands in the world. The green-and-yellow box equates to fun in the minds of children everywhere. The company has always been known for colors—from red barns to black automobile tires—but the more than 120 different crayon colors has been the lasting legacy of Binney. One study claimed that the average child uses 730 crayons by his or her tenth birthday—thus making crayons one of the most often used products in the world. All of this has been accomplished with very little advertising; the product has sold itself. To this day, Crayola company executives will still sign official correspondence with a crayon. After all, crayons are the company's franchise.

—Dale L. Flesher

Further Reading

Gillis, Jennifer Blizin. *Edwin Binney: The Founder of Crayola Crayons*. Chicago: Heinemann, 2005. This is a thirty-two-page children's book, but it is the only real biography on Binney that has been published.

Kitchel, Helen Binney. *Memories*. Greenwich, Conn.: n.p., 1978. This memoir by Binney's daughter tells of her years growing up in Connecticut, which was near the New York office of her father's company. Although the book does not deal with inventions, it gives background on Binney's life.

_______. *More Memories*. Greenwich, Conn.: n.p., 1979. This memoir by Binney's daughter expands her life story, including some travels with her father.

Mehegan, Sean. "Brand Builders: The Color of Money." *Brandweek*, September 15, 1997, 22. Discusses the Crayola advertising, or the lack thereof, over the years. Much of the article deals with new videos and video games that the company was planning to introduce.

Petroski, Henry. *The Pencil: A History of Design and Circumstance*. New York: Alfred A. Knopf, 1993. Although mostly about the history of pencils, this volume includes a section on the history of crayons. Includes bibliographical references and index.

See also: Joshua Lionel Cowen; Beulah Louise Henry.

Gerd Binnig

German physicist

Binnig made significant contributions to the field of physics with his invention of the scanning tunneling microscope and the atomic force microscope. These two microscopes were key to the emergence of nanotechnology and opened new fields of scientific research.

Born: July 20, 1947; Frankfurt am Main, West Germany (now in Germany)
Also known as: Gerd Karl Binnig (full name)
Primary field: Physics
Primary inventions: Scanning tunneling microscope; atomic force microscope

Early Life

Gerd Karl Binnig (gehrt kahrl BIH-nihk) was born in Frankfurt am Main, West Germany, on July 20, 1947. His mother, Ruth Bracke Binnig, was a drafter and his father, Karl Franz Binnig, worked as a machine engineer. Binnig and his younger brother spent their childhood playing among the ruins left by World War II, an experience that had a significant influence on his life. He attended both elementary and secondary school in Frankfurt and Offenbach, as his family lived in both cities at various times during this period. Although he did not really understand what a career in physics entailed, by the age of ten Binnig had decided that he wanted to be a physicist.

Once he started studying physics, Binnig began to question his choice. It was theoretical physics in particular that caused him to doubt whether he had chosen the right career. He found the discipline lacking any philosophical or imaginative elements. For a while, he became very interested in music and devoted more time to playing and writing music than to studying physics. Having grown up in a family that appreciated classical music, he learned to play the violin at fifteen and played in the school orchestra. Then, because of his brother's influence, he developed an appreciation for music by groups such as the Beatles and the Rolling Stones. Eventually, he was playing in rock bands and writing songs himself.

Physics was, however, still a part of Binnig's life and gained new importance when he began studying at Johann Wolfgang Goethe University in Frankfurt. He was placed in a program directed by Dr. W. Martiessen and worked under the supervision of Dr. E. Hoenig. During his study with these professors, Binnig had the opportunity to perform experiments. This emphasis on doing rather than reading about the discipline restored his interest in physics. He received his bachelor's degree in 1973 and a doctorate in physics in 1978. His dissertation dealt with superconductivity, the phenomenon of zero-resistance conduction at extremely low temperatures (near absolute zero) in metals and ceramics.

While attending the university, he met Lore Wagler, a psychology student. In 1969, they married, and she was instrumental in convincing him to take a position at the International Business Machines (IBM) Research Laboratory in Rüschlikon, Switzerland, immediately upon completing his Ph.D. The couple had two children, a daughter and a son.

Life's Work

Accepting the position at the IBM lab provided an excellent career choice for Binnig. There he joined a research team that included Christoph Gerber, Edmund Weibel, and Heinrich Rohrer. Both Rohrer and Binnig had been doing research in the field of superconductivity. Rohrer did much to renew Binnig's enthusiasm for physics by his attitude toward scientific investigation, which combined humor with serious devotion to research. In 1981, the team designed a system for studying the tunneling effect of electrons. In 1984, Binnig became the group leader.

The team's work earned them recognition in the physics community and several awards, including the German Physics Prize, the Otto Klung Prize, the Hewlett Packard Europhysics Prize, and the King Faisal Prize. From this research, Binnig and Rohrer developed the scanning tunneling microscope (STM), which allows scientists to view surfaces at the atomic level. Binnig and Rohrer earned the 1986 Nobel Prize in Physics for this invention. They received the award at a time when the microscope's full spectrum of uses was yet to be discovered; it had been only five years since the microscope was first tested. However, the prize committee expressed confidence in the STM as an instrument that would expand the study of the structure of matter and create new fields of research. Binnig and Rohrer shared the prize with the German scientist Ernst Ruska.

From 1985 to 1986, Binnig was sent to the IBM Almaden Research Center in San Jose, California. Continuing to work with Gerber and also working with Calvin F. Quate, a professor at Stanford University, Binnig invented the atomic force microscope (AFM). This microscope charts surface atomic structure; it accomplishes this by measuring the force acting on the tip of its probe. The tip is made of either ceramic or semiconductor material and is one atom wide. The AFM is able to image, measure, and manipulate matter at the nanoscale. In 1987, Binnig was appointed an IBM fellow and became

Gerd Binnig. (©The Nobel Foundation)

head of the IBM physics group at the University of Munich. From 1987 to 1988, he was a visiting professor at Stanford University.

While devoting his time primarily to scientific research in the field of physics, Binnig continued to value imagination and philosophy. In 1989, he published *Aus dem Nichts* (out of nothing), in which he explored the relationship of human creativity and chaos. He proposed that human creativity results from disordered thoughts. In 1990, he began to pursue an interest in politics and became a member of the board of the Daimler-Benz holding company.

In 1994, Binnig founded his own company, Delphi Creative Technologies, in Munich to develop knowledge-based systems. He held the positions of chief researcher and scientific coordinator and led his research team to design a technology that closely replicates human thought patterns, called Cognition Network. The company was renamed Definiens Cognition Network Technology and eventually became a subsidiary of Definiens AG. In 1995, Binnig resigned as head of the IBM physics group in Munich.

Binnig continued to work at the IBM research laboratory in the early twenty-first century. Much of his research has been involved with his theory of "fractal Darwinism," used to describe complex systems. In 2003, he presented the plenary lecture at the Electrochemical Society meeting in Paris. In his lecture, he discussed the IBM project Millepede, which is concerned with increasing the density of data storage capacity.

The Scanning Tunneling Microscope

The scanning tunneling microscope (STM) was invented in 1981 by Gerd Binnig and Heinrich Rohrer at the International Business Machines (IBM) Research Laboratory in Rüschlikon, Switzerland. Both Binnig and Rohrer had been engaged in research on superconductivity. Starting from this common interest, they began to study and explore the surfaces of materials.

At first, they used spectroscopy, which measures the interaction of radiant energy with matter. This technique proved inadequate for revealing the complex characteristics of a surface. While doing research on superconductivity as a graduate student, Binnig had examined tunneling, a phenomenon of quantum mechanics. Tunneling occurs when electrons, because of their wavelike makeup, escape from the surface of a solid and create an electron cloud around the solid. Binnig and Rohrer knew that electrons are capable of tunneling through clouds, which touch and overlap between surfaces. (Ivar Giaever had proven this in 1960.)

Binnig and Rohrer proceeded to cause electrons from a solid surface to tunnel through a vacuum to a sharp probe resembling a needle. In their experiment, they brought the tip of the probe to within one-billionth of a meter (one nanometer) of the solid surface, causing the electron clouds of the probe and the surface to touch and a tunneling current to begin to flow. In order to create a three-dimensional map of the surface, atom by atom, it was essential that the probe follow the tunneling current at a constant height above the atoms of the surface. To maintain this height, the probe had to be isolated from vibration and noise, both of which caused serious problems. To solve these issues, Binnig and Rohrer devised a number of technical innovations, including a probe tip that was one atom wide.

As Binnig and Rohrer used the scanning tunneling microscope to explore many different surface structures, including that of deoxyribonucleic acid (DNA), and to observe the interaction of chemicals, the value and importance of the microscope became more and more apparent. Using the STM, Binnig himself actually saw a virus escape from a cell; it was the first time anyone had witnessed this happen. The STM was the first microscope capable of imaging individual atoms. In 1990, a team of researchers at the IBM research laboratory succeeded in moving and rearranging individual atoms. The scanning tunneling microscope is readily applicable in a number of fields. The work of chemists, physicists, bioengineers, and medical researchers has been enormously enhanced by the STM.

Impact

With the invention of the scanning tunneling microscope in collaboration with Heinrich Rohrer and the invention of the atomic force microscope in collaboration with Christoph Gerber and Calvin Quate, Binnig made a significant impact on the world of scientific research. These microscopes played a key role in the emergence of nanoscience and significantly expanded research possibilities in a wide variety of fields, including chemistry, physics, medicine, bioengineering, and microelectronics. With the STM and the AFM, researchers can image materials that are electrically conductive or nonconductive and can see individual atoms. Binnig's work in complex knowledge-based systems and nanomechanical systems of data storage have opened up new possibilities for creating tools and systems capable of addressing the needs of a social system based on a global information network.

—*Shawncey Webb*

Further Reading

Chen, C. Julian. *Introduction to Scanning Tunneling Microscopy*. 2d ed. New York: Oxford University Press, 2007. Discusses both the scanning tunneling microscope and the atomic force microscope. Clear explanations of how these microscopes work, their uses, and later developments.

Flegler, Stanley L., John W. Heckman, and Karen L. Klomparens. *Scanning and Transmission Electron Microscope: An Introduction*. New York: W. H. Freeman, 1993. Discusses the microscope technology from which the STM developed. Excellent for understanding the electron microscope from both a practical and a theoretical standpoint. Clear explanations accompanied by elucidating diagrams.

Ratner, Mark A., and Daniel Ratner. *Nanotechnology: A Gentle Introduction to the Next Big Idea*. Upper Saddle River, N.J.: Prentice Hall, 2003. Good presentation of the technology made possible by Binnig and Rohrer's scanning tunneling microscope. Gives detailed information on uses in medicine, optoelectronics, communications, and consumer products. Treats business, technology, and ethical issues.

Shorte, Spencer L., and Friedrich Frischknecht, eds. *Imaging Cellular and Molecular Biological Functions*. New York: Springer, 2007. Good selection of essays on imaging, and its development and application. Discusses the Definiens Cognition Network and Binnig's work.

See also: Sumio Iijima; Heinrich Rohrer; Ernst Ruska.

Clarence Birdseye

American industrialist and naturalist

Birdseye is best remembered for his contributions to food preservation and processing. Although his name is usually associated with the freezing of food, he also perfected means of dehydrating food and preserving it in other ways.

Born: December 9, 1886; Brooklyn, New York
Died: October 7, 1956; New York, New York
Also known as: Clarence Frank Birdseye II (full name)
Primary fields: Food processing; packaging
Primary invention: Quick freezing

Early Life

From childhood, Clarence Frank Birdseye II was fascinated by nature. At age five, he preserved the skin of a mouse, proudly presenting it to his mother as a gift. Born in Brooklyn, New York, to Clarence and Ada Underwood Birdseye, Clarence had two consuming passions: natural history and food.

Before Birdseye was a teenager, his family moved to Montclair, New Jersey. Here, part of Birdseye's destiny unfolded when he enrolled in a cooking class at the local high school. He had already become such a proficient taxidermist that he ran advertisements in a sporting magazine announcing his availability for teaching the art of animal preservation, showing early signs of the business astuteness that was to mark his later life. He named his company the American School of Taxidermy.

Following high school, Birdseye enrolled in Amherst College as a biology major. Financial pressure forced him to work in order to earn money to finance his education. He worked and continued as a full-time student for two years, partly by raising and selling to the Bronx Zoo frogs that would be used to feed many of the zoo's snakes. He trapped and sold over one hundred specimens of black rats to a Columbia University professor for use in breeding experiments the professor was conducting. These enterprises earned him the nickname of "Bugs" among his friends and classmates.

Clarence Birdseye. (Getty Images)

Despite his efforts to sustain himself and continue his schooling, Birdseye finally realized that his attendance was irregular because of the pressure to earn money and that his college career was being severely compromised by his need to support himself and struggle to pay his tuition. On completing his sophomore year, he withdrew from Amherst.

After working in New York City for a while, Birdseye was hired by the U.S. Department of Agriculture in 1910 as a field naturalist, a position that led to the publication of his monograph, *Some Common Mammals of Western Montana in Relation to Agriculture and Spotted Fever*, which appeared in 1912. In his job as a field naturalist, Birdseye traveled through much of the American Southwest. He began a fur-trading business that he quickly turned into a moneymaking enterprise.

The success of this venture caused him to go to Labrador in 1912 with the medical missionary Sir Wilfred Grenfell to engage more fully in the fur trade. He remained in Labrador for the next five years, but his time there ended with the entry of the United States into World War I in 1917.

Life's Work

During a holiday in the United States in 1915, Birdseye married Eleanor Gannett. He returned to Labrador alone because his wife was pregnant, but after the birth of the child, Eleanor and the infant went to Labrador with Birdseye. The couple would have three more children. Now with family responsibilities, Birdseye needed to provide for his family in Labrador's harsh and inhospitable climate. In particular, he had to be sure that they had enough to eat.

The beginning of Birdseye's experiments in freezing food came about when he observed that the Labrador natives, when they pulled fish from the water and laid it on the ice, ended up with solidly frozen fish that, if kept frozen, could be thawed and cooked weeks or even months later. Fish preserved in this way tasted as good as they would have on the day they were caught as long as they were solidly frozen until they were cooked.

Birdseye also observed that fish caught in the height of the winter, when temperatures approached –50° Fahrenheit, tasted better when they were finally cooked than similar fish that had been caught in the autumn and frozen more slowly when temperatures, although still well below freezing, were higher. He concluded that the secret to keeping frozen food as fresh as possible depended upon what he termed "quick freeze."

Experimenting with various methods of freezing food, Birdseye was able to preserve not only fish, seafood, and meat but also vegetables that grew profusely in Labrador's sunlit summer and that could be frozen when the temperatures sank. He was able to feed his family well with the food he froze.

Although he may not have understood fully the theoretical aspects of what he was doing, Birdseye's method of quick freezing preserved the freshness of food because it did not allow large ice crystals to form in it. Had these crystals formed, they would have altered drastically the cellular structure of the food being preserved, thereby reducing its flavor and texture as well as its vitamin content.

Birdseye spent two years, 1917 to 1919, as a purchasing agent for the United States Housing Corporation. He then became assistant to the president of the United States Fisheries Association, serving from 1920 until 1922. His interest in freezing food grew. In 1923, he set up shop in the periphery of an ice house in New Jersey and, with capital of seven dollars, continued his experiments. These experiments led him to the discovery that fish packed in boxes could be frozen rock-solid and preserved effectively.

He found that perishables could be quick-frozen by pressing them between belts that permitted a heat exchange between the belts—later replaced by refrigerated metal plates—and the food to be frozen. The only problem was that once the food was frozen, it had to be preserved in freezers, so the notion of selling frozen food in typical markets seemed impossible.

Not to be daunted, Birdseye, who by now had established the General Seafood Corporation with the aid of some affluent partners, demonstrated his exceptional acumen as a businessman. He persuaded executives at the American Radiator Corporation to manufacture display units that would preserve frozen foods at temperatures low enough to keep them solidly frozen. He then prevailed on this company to lease these display units to grocery stores for eight dollars per month.

Once this accord was reached, the mass sale of frozen foods was just a matter of time. The first sale of frozen foods on a retail basis occurred on March 6, 1930, in Springfield, Massachusetts. During the next fifteen years, frozen food ceased to be a novelty and became a necessity for many people who now could buy the ingredients for entire meals in frozen form and prepare them for use in a short time, a definite boon to the working women much in evidence during World War II.

In 1944, Birdseye expanded his business by leasing insulated railway cars that could transport his goods anywhere in the nation. The following year, airlines began to stock frozen dinners to serve to passengers, and by 1954, the so-called TV dinner appeared in stores.

On August 12, 1930, Birdseye received a patent for his "double-plate" method of freezing food, one of over three hundred patents he was granted during his life. This method involved placing food in cartons that were then frozen between two flat, refrigerated surfaces under pressure.

In 1929, the Postum Company, skilled at marketing food products, and the Goldman Sachs Trading Corporation bought Birdseye out for just under $25 million, an almost unimaginable amount at that time. Ever ambitious, the newly minted millionaire continued to work on food preservation and developed a method of dehydration known as the anhydrous method. He also invented and patented an infrared heat lamp and a recoilless harpoon gun.

In 1953, at age sixty-seven, Birdseye embarked on a two-year venture in Peru, where he worked on developing a process using the waste product of sugarcane, bagasse, to make paper stock. Peru's high altitude affected him adversely and possibly contributed to the heart problems that took his life on October 7, 1956.

Quick Freezing

When Clarence Birdseye perfected his method of quick freezing, the frozen food industry was on the road to becoming the behemoth it has grown into. Earlier experiments with freezing foods involved slow freezing, in which a significant loss in flavor occurs and in which vitamins and minerals are diminished. Quick freezing overcomes these difficulties.

The most common form of quick freezing is the air-blast method, in which food is subjected to a steady blast of air chilled to about –50° Fahrenheit. This air is forced into an insulated tunnel through which food passes on a conveyor belt. Generally the food has already been packaged, although sometimes fruits and vegetables are frozen before packaging. This method of freezing is in common use because it is relatively inexpensive and produces dependable results.

Also in common use is the indirect-contact method, in which packaged foods are placed between metal plates that have been chilled to about –28° Fahrenheit. As these sheets absorb heat from the food packages, the contents of the packages are frozen solid.

A more dramatic result is achieved through nitrogen freezing, which uses liquid nitrogen under pressure. At –280° Fahrenheit, liquid nitrogen is vaporized. The vapor is then forced into a chamber where it freezes food almost instantly. Although this method of quick freezing is highly effective, its use is limited because it is considerably more expensive than the two methods discussed above.

Even more expensive than nitrogen freezing is dry-ice freezing that uses powdered dry ice rather than nitrogen. The dry ice vaporizes very quickly and immediately freezes the food that is exposed to it. Despite the effectiveness of this method, it is seldom used because of the cost.

A final method, liquid-CFC freezing, involves spraying or dipping into liquid chlorofluorocarbons (carbons that contain carbon, chlorine, and fluorine) food that is to be frozen. Because CFCs are environmentally harmful, their production in the United States has been banned since 1956, forcing food processors to rely on one of the four alternate methods for quick freezing.

Impact

It is difficult to conceive of a modern food event with the far-reaching consequences of the frozen food industry, which as early as 1976 had turned into an enterprise that brought over $17 billion into the U.S. economy annually. Almost every home in the United States has a refrigerator with a frozen food compartment with a constant temperature around zero. Many homes have deep freezes as well for storing large quantities of food for long periods of time.

The Food and Drug Administration has acknowledged that quick freezing preserves the vitamin and mineral content of foods. It is possible to ship frozen foods anywhere to feed people who might otherwise have diets deficient in the beneficial elements found in fresh food. In the contemporary United States, where both parents in typical families work, frozen food has become a necessity because of its variety and ease in preparation.

In 2005, the National Inventors Hall of Fame posthumously elected Birdseye to membership for the impact his work has had on American society. This prestigious organization recognizes people whose work has altered society and enhanced the lives of Americans.

—R. Baird Shuman

Further Reading

Brown, Travis. *Historical First Patents: The First United States Patents for Many Everyday Things*. Metuchen, N.J.: Scarecrow Press, 1994. A brief but highly readable assessment of Birdseye's contributions to food processing in the section titled "Frozen Food."

Carlisle, Rodney. *Inventions and Discoveries*. Hoboken, N.J.: John Wiley & Sons, 2004. Carlisle packs many specifics into the two pages he allots to Birdseye.

Harper, Charise Mericle. *Imaginative Inventions*. Boston: Little, Brown, 2001. The brief section on Birdseye is useful and readable.

Rondeau, Amanda. *Vegetables Are Vital*. Edina, Minn.: Abdo, 2003. An appreciative assessment of the impact that Birdseye's inventions relating to food preservation have had on society generally.

See also: George Washington Carver; John Harvey Kellogg; Henri Nestlé.

Katharine Burr Blodgett

American physicist and chemist

Working with thin films of fatty acids deposited on glass, Blodgett was able to build up more than two hundred successive layers. In a series of studies, she developed important applications for these films.

Born: January 10, 1898; Schenectady, New York
Died: October 12, 1979; Schenectady, New York
Primary fields: Chemistry; physics
Primary inventions: Langmuir-Blodgett films; nonreflecting glass

Early Life

Katharine Burr Blodgett was born in Schenectady, New York, on January 10, 1898. Her attorney father, George Bedington Blodgett, was head of the patent department at the world-class research laboratories of the General Electric Company (GE). Since Mr. Blodgett had died a few weeks before Katharine's birth, she was raised by her mother, Katharine Buchanan Blodgett, née Burr. The family, including her older brother, moved to New York City and later to Europe, where the children became bilingual and were exposed to French culture. The Blodgetts returned to New York briefly, and Katharine studied for a short time at an American school in Saranac Lake. Following further European travels, chiefly in Germany, Katharine completed her early education at the Rayson School in New York City.

At the age of eighteen, Blodgett earned a scholarship to Bryn Mawr College. She excelled in physics under James Barnes and mathematics under Charlotte Agnes Scott. In interviews later in life, Blodgett recognized these two teachers as making important contributions to the atmosphere that challenged her mind. In 1917, she received her bachelor's degree and went to the University of Chicago, where she studied the adsorption of gases on charcoal. After World War I, this work was published jointly with her mentor Harvey B. Lemon.

Prior to her studies at Chicago, Blodgett visited the General Electric laboratories at Schenectady and was guided around by Irving Langmuir, her father's colleague and the future Nobel laureate in chemistry. He recognized her talent and perhaps suggested that she might become his assistant after acquiring more scientific background. After completing her master's degree at Chicago, she joined Langmuir as the first female scientist at GE. There followed six years of productive collaboration.

Katharine Burr Blodgett. (Library of Congress)

Langmuir appreciated what a talented associate he had found in Blodgett, and she realized that her career would be severely limited without a doctorate. With his help, she was accepted at Cambridge University in the laboratory of Sir Ernest Rutherford (Nobel laureate in chemistry, 1908). The essential new knowledge contained in her thesis appeared under her own name in the *Philosophical Magazine* in 1926. These studies dealt with the flow of electrons in mercury vapor. In the same year, she became the first woman to be awarded a doctoral degree in physics by Cambridge University.

Langmuir-Blodgett Films

In 1934, Katharine Burr Blodgett published a brief "communication" in the *Journal of the American Chemical Society* in which she described a technique for depositing a single layer of fatty acid molecules on glass. The study of these molecular size layers, now known as Langmuir-Blodgett films, constitutes her greatest scientific accomplishment and led directly to several practical inventions. Such molecules possess both a polar, hydrophilic region and a nonpolar, hydrophobic region. The attraction between such pairs of opposite polarity in a single molecule allows the buildup of successive layers on a surface. In addition to glass, she was able to build her films on a variety of metal surfaces.

Using this new technique, Blodgett was able, over the next year, to build up more than two hundred successive layers, and she found that each succeeding layer produced a distinctive interference color. These changes in color allowed her to construct a sensitive instrument for measuring the thickness of each layer of very thin arrays. The utility of her thickness gauge was shown to be between 1 and 100 nanometers, or in the ten millionths of an inch range. Her original gauge, being quite fragile, limited its widespread application. It was converted into a more robust instrument that was quickly marketed by General Electric. What had long been a tedious process of measurement became a simple comparison for determining a film's thickness.

Further research led Blodgett to her most celebrated invention—nonreflecting glass. The popular press universally insisted on calling it invisible glass, and it did transmit 99 percent of light that struck the glass. The technique involved controlling both the thickness and the refractive index of the film layers. She used a mixture of a fatty acid and its barium salt. When the layers formed, they were washed with benzene, and the fatty acid was dissolved, leaving a skeleton film of the salt and air. This approach allowed her to control the refractive index with great precision.

Blodgett continued to make other significant applications of her basic studies. For example, by building up three thousand layers of a mixture of barium and copper salts of stearic acid, she created the first controlled-thickness X-ray "grating." By oxidizing hydrocarbon molecules, she invented an "indicator oil." The invisible film of this product allowed her to add an oil that did not otherwise spread and to control its precise thickness. The material and the technique of using it allows one to detect the edge of invisible films and to demonstrate their optical properties. The scientific importance of Blodgett's research is reflected by her authorship of six U.S. patents.

Life's Work

When Dr. Blodgett returned to Schenectady, Langmuir, her mentor-collaborator, had begun a series of studies that were to win him the Nobel Prize in Chemistry in 1932. The work concerned the behavior of thin films involving a single molecule in thickness. His studies of the forces of adsorption led to a great improvement in the understanding of the molecular attractions between the phases. For the next six years, she would collaborate with Langmuir, and together they published a series of significant articles in the *Journal of the American Chemical Society* (*JACS*) and the *Physical Review*. Some of these early studies dealt with gases and the properties of tungsten and are clearly related to Langmuir's general interests and his efforts to improve the efficiency of electric light bulbs. In addition to their joint publications in scientific journals, they successfully applied for several patents.

In 1933, when Langmuir returned from Sweden after receiving the Nobel Prize, he asked Blodgett to begin working with him on the behavior of thin films; especially those having a thickness of a single molecule. They were able to develop techniques for the study of solids, liquids, and gases. In time, their work even included the large and complicated proteins. In 1935, they published a paper dealing with "new methods for research with monomolecular films" in the German journal *Kolloid-Zeitschrift*. In 1937, an article appeared in *Physical Review*.

Langmuir had never treated Blodgett as an assistant, and she rewarded his confidence with a scientific life of her own. While making significant contributions to their joint research, she was also striking out on her own. In 1934, she published a work under her own name in the *Journal of the American Chemical Society*. Its title, "Monomolecular Films of Fatty Acids on Glass," foreshadowed much of her future scientific career. In the same year, she reported on interference colors in oil films on water in the *Journal of the Optical Society of America*. In 1935, the same year as her joint study with Langmuir, she returned to the *JACS* with a very long article (sixteen pages) describing her technique in great detail.

For twenty years, until her retirement in 1963, Blodgett continued to perfect her techniques and to devise practical applications for them. Her most celebrated accomplishment was the discovery in 1938 of a nearly nonreflecting glass. An avalanche of popular articles appeared reporting on the woman who invented "invisible glass." It is instructive to observe just how close the competition is in exciting areas of science: Just two days after Blodgett's publication, two physicists at the Massachusetts Institute of Technology (MIT) announced that they had produced nonreflecting glass by a completely different process. While neither the GE nor the MIT product was stable enough for most practical applications, it was a short time before others solved the problem by building on Blodgett's insights. Today, people take for granted the presence of nonreflecting glass in all kinds of optical instruments as well as windshields, picture frames, and eyeglasses.

In World War II, GE contributed to the war effort, and Blodgett worked with Langmuir to develop an improved generator for military smoke screens. The apparatus was a great success and undoubtedly saved many lives in the invasions during the war. Blodgett was among the earliest users of a huge analog computer built by GE. Her calculation of the trajectories of cloud droplets was important in dealing with the critical problem of icing on aircraft wings.

A number of schools awarded Blodgett honorary degrees, including Elmira College and Brown University. The American Association of University Women presented her with its Annual Achievement Award in 1945. In 1951, she received the Garvan Medal from the American Chemical Society. She died in her Schenectady home when she was eighty-one.

IMPACT

The most striking characteristic of Blodgett's career must be her absolute dedication to science. Rather than seeking professional acclaim and financial advantage, she spent her entire life probing nature's secrets. As the protégé, and later colleague, of an internationally celebrated scientist, she displayed an independence that was remarkable for her time and is still rare. As a scientist, her career exemplifies discipline, and she truly inspired those with whom she worked. Her ability to turn the highest quality research in pure science into practical products is admirable. Equally remarkable is the rapidity with which her devices became tools that opened exciting new opportunities in pure science.

A little-noticed aspect of Blodgett's contribution is found in her practical work during both world wars. In the waning years of "the war to end wars," her research for her master's degree centered on the adsorption of gases on charcoal. These studies, which sought to lessen the terror of chemical warfare, were not published until after the war. In the 1940's, Blodgett worked with Langmuir on developing a highly successful smoke generator that served in the invasions of Africa, Sicily, and Normandy. In those same years, she worked on the problems associated with deicing the wings of aircraft.

—*K. Thomas Finley*

FURTHER READING

Davis, Kathleen A. "Katharine Blodgett and Thin Films." *Journal of Chemical Education* 61 (1984): 437-439. Certainly the best treatment of Blodgett's life and work, with emphasis on scientific aspects. Excellent drawings of her apparatus and of the relationship of molecules in thin films. Some technical detail, but understandable to the high school chemistry student.

Finley, K. Thomas, and Patricia J. Siegel. "Katharine Burr Blodgett (1898-1979)." In *Women in Chemistry and Physics. A Biobibliographic Sourcebook*, edited by Louise S. Grinstein, Rose K. Rose, and Miriam H. Rafailovich. Westport, Conn.: Greenwood Press, 1993. A somewhat longer than usual biographical sketch that treats her life and scientific career in equal depth. A fairly detailed list of her scientific publications and the numerous articles about her and the public's reaction to her discoveries.

Jacoby, Mitch. "Just Surface Deep, But Not Shallow." *Chemical and Engineering News* 81 (2003): 37. In celebrating the 125th year of the *Journal of the American Chemical Society*, brief articles describing the most often cited articles published in this distinguished journal were presented. A photograph of Blodgett in her laboratory is accompanied by an excellent description of her work and its importance. Her professional relationship with Irving Langmuir is described.

Rudavsky, Shari. "Katharine Burr Blodgett: 1898-1979." In *Notable Twentieth-Century Scientists*, edited by Emily J. McMurray. New York: Gale Research, 1995.

A brief biographical sketch with a photograph and a short list of writings by and about Blodgett.

Schaefer, Vincent J., and George L. Gaines, Jr. "Obituary: Katharine Burr Blodgett, 1898-1979." *Journal of Colloid and Interface Science* 76 (1980): 269-271. This brief article provides important insight to her work, life, and personality only possible from authors who were her colleagues. Schaefer worked closely with Blodgett.

Wise, George. "Blodgett, Katharine Burr." In *American National Biography*, edited by John A. Garraty and Mark C. Carnes. New York: Oxford University Press, 1999. The most up-to-date brief biography. Well written and covering all aspects of her life and work. Annotated biographical notes.

See also: Irving Langmuir; Isaac Merrit Singer.

Marie Anne Victoire Boivin

French midwife

Boivin was one of the leading midwives and female medical researchers in nineteenth century France. She wrote extensively on gynecological diseases and invented the Boivin bivalve vaginal speculum.

Born: April 9, 1773; Montreuil, near Versailles, France
Died: May 16, 1841; Paris, France
Also known as: Marie Anne Victoire Gillain (birth name)
Primary field: Medicine and medical technology
Primary invention: Bivalve vaginal speculum

Early Life

Marie Anne Victoire Boivin (mah-ree ahn veek-twahr bwah-van), née Gillain (zhee-lan), was born in 1773 in Montreuil, an eastern suburb of Paris. She received her early education in the arts and sciences from the nuns of the Visitation of Marie Leszczyńska. After the French Revolution broke out in 1789, the sixteen-year-old lived with and studied under an order of nursing nuns in Étampes, roughly thirty miles southwest of Paris. Through a hospital surgeon, Gillain learned about midwifery and anatomy. She lived and worked in Étampes for eight years, gaining much valuable medical knowledge.

In 1797, the twenty-four-year-old Gillain returned to her family's home in Montreuil. Later that year, she married Louis Boivin, who worked as an assistant in the Bureau of National Domains. Their marriage was to be brief: By the end of 1798, she was left a widow with an infant daughter.

Putting her medical education to work, Boivin sought a position at the Hospice de la Maternité in Paris. This free, government-sponsored maternity facility, recently established in a former abbey, was a teaching hospital that provided care to poor and unwed mothers. The Maternité took Boivin on as a student midwife. There she became an assistant to the midwife in chief and head of practical teaching, Marie-Louise Dugès LaChapelle (today regarded as the mother of modern obstetrics). The Maternité awarded Boivin a diploma in midwifery in 1800.

Life's Work

After graduating, Boivin worked for a short time as a midwife in Versailles. When her young daughter died in an accident, Boivin ended her independent practice and returned to Paris and the Maternité, where she became supervisor in chief.

Over the next decade, Boivin's talents grew and flourished at the Maternité. She worked alongside LaChapelle, who was also widowed and supporting herself, and whose obstetrical knowledge was vast. (LaChapelle had assisted her midwife mother as a child, been married to and learned from a surgeon, and studied in Germany, which was renowned for the quality of training afforded its female physicians and midwives.) The Maternité appears to have been a comparatively positive environment for female physicians. The prominent obstetrician heading the Maternité, Jean Louis August Baudelocque, was committed to providing midwives with a quality education, and he was not above respecting or acknowledging the abilities of female colleagues. That said, he ignored LaChapelle's and Boivin's opinions regarding the contagion hazard posed by having large groups of onlookers present during births and his liberal use of forceps and other instruments to extract the baby from the birth canal.

In 1812, at the urging of Maternité physician in chief François Chaussier, Boivin published *Mémorial de l'art des accouchemens*, a reference book for midwives, which included more than a hundred of her careful illustrations

THE VAGINAL SPECULUM

The vaginal speculum is an instrument that is inserted into the vagina to facilitate visual inspection or medical treatment. By the nineteenth century, the vaginal speculum was hardly new—Greek and Roman writings mention the instrument, and bivalve, trivalve, and quadrivalve models were excavated at Pompeii. (It is unclear whether these were intended as examination and diagnostic tools or a means to hasten labor.)

Centuries later, specula fell into disfavor. The propriety of their use was debated, and—in the case of turnscrew models that required two people to operate them—their awkwardness of operation was daunting for doctor and patient alike. In 1801, French physician and professor of medicine Joseph Récamier repopularized the speculum among medical professionals, using a simple tin tube for vaginal examinations. Marie Anne Victoire Boivin initially used such a speculum.

The instrument that Boivin created in 1825 returned to the old bivalve model, but with improvements. The blades were small and, when closed, formed a slim cone. The overall design was intended to cause as little discomfort as possible. Boivin abandoned the difficult turnscrew mechanism for opening the blades, instead equipping her speculum with rounded, scissorlike handles that spread the blades when squeezed. A screw could be used to widen the handle end of the speculum farther.

Récamier independently developed a similar speculum at about the same time, and both he and Boivin are generally credited with inventing the modern bivalve vaginal speculum. Boivin later improved on her design, devising a speculum in 1836 that had a fenestrated blade to allow inspection of the vaginal wall. A sliding shaft was used to open and close the opening.

Boivin's speculum, coupled with her extensive research and writings, allowed medical practitioners to treat gynecological diseases more effectively. No longer limited to treatments determined by diagnoses based on external symptoms, physicians were able to diagnose with greater accuracy and treat accordingly. Visual examination also helped doctors and midwives develop a better understanding of the female reproductive organs and their pathologies. While Victorian prudery kept use of the speculum from becoming universal in the nineteenth century, it has since been integrated into routine medical monitoring for adult female patients. The speculum used today during regular pelvic examinations and Pap smears is descended from Boivin's invention.

of the fetus in the uterus. The book was in great demand in France and abroad; by 1824, it was in its third edition. However, Boivin's position at the Maternité was terminated around the time of the book's initial publication. Historians have suggested that she and the Maternité parted ways because LaChapelle or male colleagues were jealous of her success.

Boivin went on to become codirector of the general hospital at Seine-et-Oise in 1814. That year, her work was recognized by King Frederick William III of Prussia, who awarded her the Order of Civic Merit. In 1815, she assumed the directorship of a temporary military medical hospital. She later headed the maternity hospital in Bordeaux and the Maison Royale de Santé. In 1818, she translated two important English works on uterine hemorrhage and wrote a comprehensive review of the literature on the subject. Her own book on hemorrhages of the uterus, *Memoire sur les hemorrhagies internes de l'uterus*, won an open competition in 1819 held by the Medical Society of Paris. (The society selected her book as the winner under the mistaken assumption that the author was male.)

In 1827, she published *Nouvelles Recherches sur l'origine, la nature et le traitement de la môle vésiculaire ou grossesse hydatique*, her original research into the hydatidiform mole, a sometime malignant condition in which an abnormal fertilized egg or placental overgrowth mimics pregnancy. Also in that year, the University of Marburg in Prussia conferred upon her the honorary degree of doctor of medicine. The following year, she received a commendation from the Royal Society of Medicine in Bordeaux for her research into miscarriage.

In 1833, she published her most important work, *Traité pratique des maladies de l'uterus et des annexes*. This two-volume treatise on diseases of the uterus listed as its coauthor Antoine Dugès, LaChapelle's nephew and a professor of medicine at Montpellier. The book included the first recorded observation of urethral cancer in a woman. Modern for its time, the treatise was widely used as a textbook in France and beyond. It was translated into English the year after its first printing in France.

Boivin introduced several innovations to the practice of gynecology and obstetrics. After René-Théophile-Hyacinthe Laënnec invented the stethoscope in 1816, Boivin was one of the first to employ it to monitor the fetal heartbeat. She used the vaginal speculum (at the time, a long-neglected instrument experiencing a resurgence) not for obstetrics but for checking the health of the cer-

vix. She also designed gynecological instruments, notably a bivalve vaginal speculum (1825) that was a forerunner of the ones used today, a fenestrated speculum (1836), and an "intropelvimeter" (1828), her improvement on the device commonly used for measuring the diameter of the pelvis. She was one of the first surgeons to excise a cancerous cervix.

During her career, Boivin turned down prestigious offers—including one from Catherine the Great of Russia—instead choosing to continue her work with indigent women. When she retired, she received an exceedingly small pension, reflecting a lifetime of low wages. She died in poverty in 1841 at the age of sixty-eight.

Impact

Boivin was one of many women of her time who gained a foothold in the traditionally male world of medicine through the traditionally female practice of midwifery. She was held in high esteem not only by other midwives but also by male colleagues. Guillaume Dupuytren, a well-known surgeon who asked Boivin to deliver his grandchild before her retirement, famously remarked that she worked as if she had eyes at the tips of her fingers. While some all-male professional organizations barred her from their ranks, she was a member of several other medical societies.

Unable to gain admission to mainstream French medical schools, Boivin nonetheless made and publicized important, original medical discoveries. Her use of a stethoscope in obstetric monitoring has become commonplace, as has the employment of a bivalve speculum for vaginal examinations. Hygienic practices she and LaChapelle advocated have also become routine in modern medicine.

Boivin advanced the fields of gynecology and obstetrics, improving the lives and health of women and their babies. Thanks to her many publications, Boivin had an impact on the midwives of her generation and the next, in her own country and beyond. Her influence even reached the New World: Marie Durocher, midwife to the imperial family of Brazil, relied heavily on Boivin's texts.

—*Karen N. Kähler*

Further Reading

Burton, June K. *Napoleon and the Woman Question: Discourses of the Other Sex in French Education, Medicine, and Medical Law, 1799-1815.* Fashioning the Eighteenth Century series. Lubbock: Texas Tech University Press, 2007. Chapter 4, "The First National System of Midwifery Education," discusses the Hospice de la Maternité, and a section is devoted to Boivin and her mentor LaChapelle. Illustrations include a portrait of Boivin and a drawing from her classic treatise on uterine disorders. Notes, glossary, chronology of primary sources, index.

Gould, Vivian. *Daughters of Time: 2000 Notable Women—Antiquity to 1800.* North Charleston, S.C.: BookSurge, 2005. The profile of Boivin includes a chronological listing of her publications and medical achievements. An index helps set Boivin in the context of her relationships with other notable women of her day.

Hellerstein, Erna Olafson, Leslie Parker Hume, and Karen M. Offen. *Victorian Women: A Documentary Account of Women's Lives in Nineteenth Century England, France, and the United States.* Stanford, Calif.: Stanford University Press, 1981. In chapter 45, two brief but enlightening passages translated from Boivin's *Mémorial de l'art des accouchemens* provide insight into Boivin's attitudes regarding the suffering of her patients and the excessive use of instruments in the birth process.

Shearer, Benjamin F., and Barbara Smith Shearer, eds. *Notable Women in the Life Sciences: A Biographical Dictionary.* Westport, Conn.: Greenwood Press, 1996. A thorough biography of Boivin includes her accomplishments as a medical professional, commentary from her contemporaries, and a list of her life's milestones. Notes, bibliography, index.

Wilbur, C. Keith. *Antique Medical Instruments.* Atglen, Pa.: Schiffer, 2008. A hand-illustrated historical guide depicts vaginal specula designed by Boivin and others. Evolution of the instrument from its earliest known use is discussed in detail. Illustrations, index.

See also: Helen M. Free; René-Théophile-Hyacinthe Laënnec.

H. CECIL BOOTH

English engineer

Booth invented the first suction vacuum cleaner, a machine that cleaned carpets and upholstery efficiently and without simply blowing dirt, dust, and other debris from one spot to another. The fundamental principles of Booth's invention are still seen in modern vacuum cleaners.

Born: July 4, 1871; Gloucester, Gloucestershire, England
Died: January 18, 1955; Purley, Surrey, England
Also known as: Hubert Cecil Booth (full name)
Primary fields: Household products; manufacturing
Primary invention: Vacuum cleaner

EARLY LIFE

Hubert Cecil Booth was born in Gloucester, England, in 1871. One of six sons of a lumber merchant, Booth excelled at all things mechanical. His early schooling was under the direction of the Reverend H. Lloyd Breerton at Gloucester County School and Gloucester College. In 1889, Booth moved to London, where he enrolled at Central Technical College at the City and Guilds College. W. C. Unwin directed his three-year course in civil and mechanical engineering. Booth graduated as the second highest scoring student, obtaining his diploma of associateship. He then enrolled at the Institution of Civil Engineers. Booth became acquainted with Francis Tring Pearce, the director of Priday, Metford & Company, and married one of Pearce's daughters.

In December, 1882, Booth began working for Maudslay, Sons and Field as a drafter. The company was well known in England for its manufacture of engines. Booth initially worked on the design of two Royal Navy battleships, and his talent for designing machinery soon attracted attention; he left Maudslay to join a company that developed the huge wheels of the kind invented by the American G. W. G. Ferris in the 1890's. Steam-operated Ferris wheels were already creating a sensation in Great Britain.

LIFE'S WORK

In 1901, at the age of thirty, Booth created his own engineering consulting firm and wanted to manufacture large industrial equipment; he certainly had no thought of creating a small machine that picked up dirt. That machine, the modern vacuum cleaner, was invented almost on a whim. As the story goes, Booth had been invited by a friend to the Empire Music Hall to see a demonstration of an American-made cleaning machine called a mechanical aspirator. The machine, invented by a St. Louis, Missouri, railway worker to clean railway cars, blew compressed air into the carpet from two directions in an attempt to deflect the loosened dirt into a box, creating a

VACUUM CLEANERS

The idea of mechanical carpet- and upholstery-cleaning machinery dates from the nineteenth century. In 1869, a dirt-removing machine was created to blow dirt from carpets, but it operated by hand: one person to pump the bellows and the other person to point the nozzle at the floor. Most significant, the debris was blown in the air and thus was not removed completely. Gradually, human power was replaced by either coal or petroleum-powered machines, but they, too, operated by blowing air through and around dirty carpets.

H. Cecil Booth's cleaner used a machine to create a vacuum that sucked dirt and dust out from carpet and upholstery, conveying the debris through a flexible tube into a chamber closed off by a filtering device. This is the essence of Booth's invention, and the basic principle is still used in today's vacuum cleaners. The machine creating the vacuum was powered by a gasoline engine and was so large that it had to be transported on a horse-drawn cart.

As electricity became more readily available in homes, Booth invented an electric motor to create the vacuum. This motor was much smaller and more efficient, making the product even more cost efficient. By 1926, Booth was able to market this machine under the product label Goblin. Other inventors soon introduced the use of rollers with bristles attached to the machine to loosen the dirt. The same motor that created the vacuum turned the roller by means of a belt.

In the United States, inventors using Booth's design made a number of variations familiar to homemakers and cleaning services. The Hoover Company developed the idea of mounting the bag for the debris on a stick or handle and added wheels that made it possible to wheel the vacuum cleaner around a room. The Electrolux Corporation chose to mount a canister for the dirt on sled-like skids, which could be dragged behind the operator who vacuumed up the dirt with a nozzle attached to a hose. All used Booth's basic idea of a motor to create the vacuum, a filter to capture the dirt, and a container for the debris.

large cloud of dust, most of which settled back into the carpet. Booth wondered if suction could be used instead. He pondered the problem for several days and devised experiments.

Booth was convinced that suction would work. One of his experiments involved placing a wet handkerchief over an upholstered chair at home and sucking on it to draw a large amount of dust into the cloth. He later demonstrated a similar method for his friend in a restaurant (and even choked on the dust he sucked up). He then built a large machine, which he called a Puffing Billy, which was powered by a gasoline engine and pulled on a horse-drawn cart. A suction pump was attached to a hollow tube connected by a flexible hose at one end and a filter at the other. Booth patented his device on August 30, 1901.

A British woman uses a vacuum cleaner of 1910. (Popperfoto/Getty Images)

Before attempting to sell his new invention, Booth demonstrated its operation before audiences. In one case, he persuaded a restaurant owner to clean a dining room in front of a crowd. The demonstration was successful and word spread rapidly; the device eventually came to the attention of the British royal family. Booth was invited to clean the large blue carpets used at Westminster Abbey for the coronation of King Edward VII in 1902. Later that year, King Edward arranged for a demonstration for himself and the queen. One of the machines was purchased for use at Windsor Castle. Booth also demonstrated his machine for the French president, the German kaiser, and the Russian czar. Booth also gave a demonstration at the Royal Mint.

In 1903, Booth created the Vacuum Cleaner Company Limited, a cleaning service that later merged with his engineering consulting firm. The vacuum itself, however, was center stage at the homes of wealthy families, who invited friends to their homes to see the machine in operation. Booth operated the cleaning service for the first few years, charging his clients the equivalent of the annual salary of a chambermaid. His profits were reduced, though, after he had to pay fines for a range of infractions, including blocking traffic and frightening the horses of taxi operators with the horse-drawn cleaning machine. Finally, in 1907, he developed a portable machine small enough to be sold to individuals. In 1926, he began marketing all his machines under the trade name Goblin, a name derived from a chance comment by the wife of an associate, who said the vacuum was "'goblin' up the dirt."

Booth was forced to defend his patent against a number of claimants but won all suits for patent infringement; he even was paid for his legal defense. Later in life he wrote an article on his invention, "The Origin of the Vacuum Cleaner" (1934-1935), which was published in *Transactions of the Newcomen Society*.

Impact

By today's standards, it is difficult to understand why those who created carpet and upholstery cleaning equipment did not think of using suction to eliminate dust and dirt instead of attempting to blow it away. Booth's invention, patented in 1901, now seems so simple.

Decades later, Booth's machine was made smaller and was eventually powered by electricity (although the usefulness of an electric carpet-cleaning machine depended on the widespread use of electricity). Eventually, the machine included a roller bar with a brush, which loosened the dirt and dust, making it easier for the machine to suck up the debris. Booth did not invent these later devices, but his basic concept for a vacuum set this entire industry in motion.

—*Richard L. Wilson*

Further Reading

Evans, Harold. *They Made America: From the Steam Engine to the Search Engine—Two Centuries of Innovators.* New York: Little, Brown, 2004. General history of innovations that helped define America. Includes useful discussion of the vacuum cleaner and its further development following Booth's invention.

Furnival, Jane. *Suck, Don't Blow! The Gripping Story of the Vacuum Cleaner and Other Labour Saving Machines Around the House.* London: Michael O'Mara, 1998. History of the invention of the vacuum cleaner and its impact on modern living.

Lancome, John. *How Things Work: Everyday Technology Explained.* Washington, D.C.: National Geographic, 2004. This book provides very clear explanations of how many major inventions work. Includes a section on vacuum cleaners.

Nye, Mary Jo, ed. *The Cambridge History of Science.* New York: Cambridge University Press, 2003. Volume 5 of this multivolume set discusses Booth's invention. The Cambridge series is an international standard in the history of science.

Platt, Richard. *Eureka! Great Inventions and How They Happened.* Boston: Kingfisher, 2003. Platt examines the circumstances in which some of the world's best-known inventions were conceived and discusses the genius of their inventors. Includes references to the invention of the vacuum cleaner.

Smil, Vaclav. *Creating the Twentieth Century: Technical Innovations of 1867-1914 and Their Lasting Impact.* New York: Oxford University Press, 2005. Examines the period with the most concentrated development of the key inventions of the modern world. Includes discussion of the vacuum cleaner.

See also: James Murray Spangler.

Carl Bosch

German chemist and engineer

Bosch led the group of scientists and engineers who took the ammonia synthesis invented by Fritz Haber (1868-1934) and Robert Le Rossignol (1884-1976) and developed it from laboratory-scale to industrial-scale production during the years 1909-1913. New techniques for high-pressure chemical reactions were invented, and the ammonia production revolutionized agriculture.

Born: August 27, 1874; Cologne, Germany
Died: April 26, 1940; Heidelberg, Germany
Also known as: Karl Bosch
Primary fields: Agriculture; chemistry
Primary inventions: Haber process; gasoline synthesis

Early Life

Carl Bosch (BOSH) was born in Cologne, Germany, the eldest son of Paula and Karl Bosch. Young Carl's father had come to Cologne from the south of Germany near Ulm and operated a successful plumbing business. Carl's uncle Robert (his father's brother) established a company (still in existence) that manufactures automobile parts and tools. As a youth, Carl developed a wide interest in science, collecting mineral specimens as well as plants and insects. He worked in his father's shop, developing skill with tools, and did chemical experiments in a small home lab. Upon graduation from the *Oberrealschule* (German equivalent of high school), Bosch became an apprentice in a foundry called Marienhütte in the town of Kotzenau. Here he became familiar with metallurgy and metalworking equipment.

Entering the Technische Hochschule in Berlin-Charlottenburg, he studied chemistry and engineering for two years, after which he moved to the University of Leipzig, where he was awarded the Ph.D. degree, summa cum laude, in 1898, and stayed on for a time as assistant to Johannes Wislicenus (1835-1902), who had directed his doctoral research.

Bosch's doctoral thesis was in the field of organic chemistry and concerned a study of a reaction of acetonedicarboxylic acid and diethyl ester. In 1899, Bosch went to work for the chemical firm Badische Anilin- und Soda-Fabrik (BASF). His initial assignment was in connection with the production of synthetic indigo, under the direction of Rudolf Knietsch (1854-1906).

Life's Work

Bosch began his industrial career in Ludwigshafen, where he improved the process for making phthalic anhydride (a chemical precursor for the alkyd resins used in paint). Later, he reinvestigated some work done by Wilhelm Ostwald (1853-1932) on catalysis of the ammonia equilibrium. In this investigation, he found that Ostwald's results were in error.

Continuing research on nitrogen fixation, Bosch studied the formation of cyanides and cyanamides from reactions of carbides with nitrogen. Calcium cyanamide is able to react with steam to form ammonia, and this process was used for manufacturing ammonia.

Carl Bosch. (© The Nobel Foundation)

Beginning in 1909, Bosch worked on scaling up Fritz Haber's ammonia synthesis. The result was that after a remarkably short time of four years, BASF had developed and brought onstream a synthetic ammonia plant at Oppau (near Ludwigshafen) in 1913. In 1917, a second, larger plant was opened at Leuna (near Leipzig). These plants supplemented the ammonia produced from the cyanamide process and helped to reduce Germany's dependence on imported nitrates from South America. After the start of World War I, the ammonia became a vital raw material for the production of nitric acid, and hence the explosives like TNT (trinitrotoluene) and cordite, for which nitric acid is needed.

Bosch was promoted to managing director at BASF in 1919, and when Interessen Gemeinschaft Farben (I. G. Farben) was founded in 1925, he became a director there. I. G. Farben was organized as a chemical cartel to market and control prices of chemical products, mainly dyes. (The German word *färben* means "dye.") At the end of World War I, the victorious Allies, particularly France, were concerned that a resurgent Germany would become warlike again. The Versailles treaty imposed monetary reparations on Germany, and attempts were made to obtain the technical details of Bosch's ammonia and nitric-acid processes and to accomplish the destruction of the Oppau plant. Bosch was a delegate to the treaty negotiations and was able to head off the French plans to destroy the Oppau works. Ironically, the plant vanished in a gigantic accidental explosion in 1921 that destroyed the town and resulted in six hundred fatalities. Bosch organized the rebuilding of the facilities, which was accomplished in three months with the aid of ten thousand workers.

In addition to ammonia and nitric acid, Bosch was involved in taking the coal hydrogenation process of Friedrich Bergius (1884-1949) from pilot plant to large-scale production. In 1925, Bergius sold the rights of the method to BASF. The process at that stage had a number of shortcomings that were corrected by Bosch and his associates. Bergius had accomplished coal hydrogenation in one step, combining crushed coal with heavy oil or pitch and subjecting the mass to high-pressure hydrogen

The Haber Process

Fritz Haber demonstrated the ammonia synthesis in Karlsruhe in the presence of Carl Bosch and Alwin Mittasch on July 2, 1909. Haber's apparatus produced 100 milliliters of liquid ammonia that day, operated at a pressure of 200 atmospheres and a temperature of 500°-600° Celsius, and involved a 0.75-meter-tall reactor.

Bosch and his coworkers at Badische Anilin- und Soda-Fabrik (BASF), having acquired the rights to develop the process, immediately tried to scale up to an industrial-sized apparatus. They needed to solve at least three problems: First, they needed a supply of pure hydrogen (nitrogen was readily available from liquid air); second, they had to find a suitable catalyst; third, they needed a technique for handling hydrogen-nitrogen mixtures at high temperatures and pressures. In the succeeding three years, these difficulties were overcome, in part, through inventions by Bosch.

The hydrogen needed was initially obtained by electrolysis, but later it proved less expensive to use the water-gas reaction. Steam reacted with red-hot coke, giving a mixture ("water gas") of carbon monoxide and hydrogen. A catalyzed "shift reaction" allowed the carbon monoxide to react with more steam to form additional hydrogen and carbon dioxide. To purify the hydrogen, the carbon dioxide and residual carbon monoxide were removed by scrubbing with water and copper formate solution.

The catalysts used by Haber for ammonia synthesis were rare metals (osmium and uranium) too costly to use on an industrial scale. The BASF chemists, led by Mittasch, conducted thousands of experiments to discover a cheap, effective catalyst. Their eventual choice was an iron catalyst containing small amounts of iron oxide and other metal oxides.

The early attempts to scale up the ammonia synthesis resulted in catastrophic failure of the steel reactors after about eighty hours of operation. Metallographic examination showed cracking of the metal caused by exposure to high-pressure hydrogen. The carbon steel used in the reactor was vulnerable because of its carbon content. The carbon in the metal could slowly react with high-pressure hydrogen, forming hydrocarbon gases that forced the metal apart, creating cracks. Pure iron was unaffected.

Bosch solved the hydrogen embrittlement problem by an ingenious invention. By lining the inside of the reactor with soft iron, it was possible to circulate the high-pressure gases over the catalyst in such a manner as to prevent them from contacting the carbon steel containment vessel. Cool gas was circulated between the walls and the inner liner.

Bosch also supervised the design of pressure-, flow-, and temperature-recording instruments that enabled close control of the reaction conditions. These instruments are the ancestors of those used in all modern high-pressure industrial processes.

The reactor size was steadily increased over the period 1909-1915. The largest reactor was 12 meters long, 1.08 meters in diameter, and weighed 75 tons. The ammonia plant at Oppau began production late in 1913, and soon was fixing 20 tons of nitrogen per day. Ammonia became a major source of profits for BASF. Converted to ammonium sulfate fertilizer, ammonia relieved Germany from dependence on imported nitrates. Oxidation of ammonia (Ostwald process) afforded a route to nitric acid needed for making explosives.

in a long horizontal reaction vessel. After the reaction, products were separated from residual ash and fractionated. Bergius had not had the facilities to explore possible catalysts for the reaction, nor had he conducted the reaction in two stages, which the I. G. Farben chemists now found beneficial, separating the hydrogenation and cracking aspects and conducting the latter in the vapor phase. These improvements enabled I. G. Farben to manufacture synthetic gasoline at its plant in Leuna in ever-increasing amounts. As Bosch moved into administration, he had less engineering work to do but was active in negotiations with Bergius and in persuading the other directors to persist with the very expensive coal hydrogenation program. In 1935, Bosch became chairman of the board of directors at I. G. Farben. In this position, he traveled to foreign countries, including the United States, to negotiate commercial agreements for oil and coal hydrogenation.

Beginning in 1933, the rise of Adolf Hitler and the Nazis to political power in Germany began to have an impact on all aspects of life. Bosch opposed the anti-Semitism of the regime and tried to help some of the non-Aryans who had lost their positions and wanted to leave Germany. For example, he tried to obtain an exit visa for the physicist Lise Meitner (1878-1968), who wanted to immigrate to Denmark. Such an undertaking on his part was not without personal risk, because of the extreme suspicion of the Gestapo.

In 1937, Bosch succeeded Max Planck as the president of the Kaiser-Wilhelm Institute, Germany's most important scientific society, and left I. G. Farben. Over the next three years, culminating in his death in 1940,

Bosch became increasingly pessimistic about the future of Germany and increasingly a user of drugs and alcohol.

Impact

In 1931, Bosch and Bergius shared the Nobel Prize in Chemistry for their achievements in developing high-pressure methods. The synthetic ammonia industry pioneered by Bosch and Haber made nitrogen fertilizer available in hitherto unimaginable quantities and made possible the harvests of wheat and other grains to feed the world.

Within a few years, the Haber-Bosch process was implemented around the world, and today ammonia is produced in eighty countries in amounts that approach 140 million metric tons annually. High-pressure techniques, as perfected by Bosch and others, are used routinely in the modern chemical process industries. On a more somber note, it is likely that Germany in 1914-1918 could not have waged war as long as it did without the explosives made possible by the ammonia and nitric-acid syntheses, and conventional modern warfare is equally dependent on the manufacture of these chemicals.

—John R. Phillips

Further Reading

Borkin, Joseph. *The Crime and Punishment of I. G. Farben*. New York: Free Press, 1978. Carl Bosch was chief executive of I. G. Farben, the giant chemical monopoly. Many photographs, and an account of Bosch's activities at the Versailles peace conference. Tells of the war crime trials of I. G. Farben executives in 1947-1948 after Bosch's death.

Bosch, Carl. "The Development of the Chemical High Pressure Method During the Establishment of the New Ammonia Industry." In *Nobel Lectures, Chemistry, 1922-1941*. Amsterdam: Elsevier, 1966. Bosch's Nobel Prize lecture describing the work that led to the first large-scale ammonia synthesis. Many diagrams of equipment.

Cornwell, John. *Hitler's Scientists: Science, War, and the Devil's Pact*. New York: Viking Press, 2003. Wide-ranging study of science, medicine, and engineering under the Nazis.

Hayes, Peter. *Industry and Ideology: I. G. Farben in the Nazi Era*. 2d ed. New York: Cambridge University Press, 2001. A study of the corporate culture at I. G. Farben. According to Hayes, the executives were gradually seduced into cooperating with Nazi ideology by being allowed to make large profits. Several members of the management were imprisoned at the end of World War II for condoning slave labor.

Leigh, G. J. *The World's Greatest Fix: A History of Nitrogen and Agriculture*. New York: Oxford University Press, 2004. Good diagrams of Bosch's reactors, compared with modern ones. Discussion of natural fixation of nitrogen and the environmental impact of nitrogen fertilizers. Well illustrated.

Smil, Vaclav. *Enriching the Earth: Fritz Haber, Carl Bosch and the Transformation of World Food Production*. Cambridge, Mass.: MIT Press, 2001. A history of nitrogen in agriculture. Describes the growth and importance of the synthetic ammonia industry during the twentieth century and its impact on world hunger and the environment.

Travis, Tony. "The Haber-Bosch Process: Exemplar of Twentieth Century Chemical Industry." *Chemistry and Industry* 15 (August, 1993): 581-585. Traces the various attempts to synthesize ammonia and gives an account of the life and work of Haber, as well as some of the contributions of Bosch.

See also: Friedrich Bergius; Fritz Haber.

Walther Bothe

German physicist

Bothe developed the device and method that made possible the coincidence method of particle detection, a crucial step in the development of nuclear physics. He also helped build Germany's first cyclotron, one of the world's first particle accelerators for conducting nuclear research.

Born: January 8, 1891; Oranienberg, Germany
Died: February 8, 1957; Heidelberg, West Germany (now in Germany)
Also known as: Walther Wilhelm Georg Bothe (full name)
Primary fields: Military technology and weaponry; physics
Primary invention: Coincidence method of particle detection

Walther Bothe. (©The Nobel Foundation)

Early Life

Walther Wilhelm Georg Bothe (VAHL-tuh VIHL-hehlm gay-OHRG BOH-tuh) was born in Oranienberg, a town near Berlin in the eastern part of Germany. After completing his early education in Oranienberg, he entered Frederick William University (later the University of Berlin), where he studied chemistry, mathematics, and physics. His work in physics was most notable, and he became a pupil—and later teaching assistant—to the world-famous physicist Max Planck. After studying there from 1908 to 1912, he joined the Physikalisch-Technische Reichsanstalt (PTR), or Reich Physical and Technical Institute, where he became an assistant to Hans Geiger, the director. In 1914, Bothe completed his doctorate in physics under the direction of Planck; his thesis centered on the molecular theory of refraction, reflection, scattering, and absorption of light rays.

In May, 1914, Bothe joined the German cavalry. When World War I broke out, he served on the eastern front and was captured by the Russians in 1915. He was held prisoner for five years but managed to continue studying and working on theoretical physics. He also learned the Russian language and met a Russian woman, Barbara Below, whom he married before returning to Germany.

Life's Work

In 1920, Bothe returned to Germany, where he began teaching physics at the University of Berlin. He also accepted an invitation from Geiger to return to PTR, where he served on Geiger's staff until 1927, when he succeeded Geiger as the director of the Laboratory of Radioactivity at PTR after Geiger moved to a new position at the University of Kiel. While Bothe and Geiger worked together, Bothe began work on the coincidence method of particle detection. In 1924, he published on the coincidence method of particle detection and continued his research, applying this method to the study of nuclear reactions, the Compton effect, and the wave-particle duality of light.

In 1925, while still at the PTR, he also completed his habilitation (on gaining tenure at the university) and became a *Privatdozent* (lower-level professor). In 1929, he became an *ausserordentlicher Professor* (mid-level professor), and a year later an *ordentlicher Professor* (full professor) at the University of Giessen. In 1932, he succeeded the Nobel laureate Philipp Lenard as the director of the Physical and Radiological Institute at the University of Heidelberg.

Bothe's rapid rise in the various university ranks suffered a setback in the wake of Adolf Hitler's ascension to power as German chancellor in January, 1933. With Hitler's rise, the anti-Semitic and anti-theoretical physics concept of *Deutsche Physik* (German physics), proposed by Lenard in a book of the same name, gained prominence. The *Deutsche Physik* movement adamantly opposed the "Jewish physics" of Albert Einstein. Since a number of prominent theoretical physicists were Jewish (Bothe was not), all theoretical physicists were persecuted based on guilt by association. Although retired, Lenard had enough power to have Bothe removed as the director of the Physical and Radiological Institute. Bothe threatened to leave Germany altogether as other theoretical physicists had done, but he was persuaded to stay when he was appointed director of the Institute of Physics at the Kaiser Wilhelm Institute for Medical Research in 1934, a position he held until his death in 1957.

Despite this political turmoil, Bothe continued to conduct significant research in nuclear physics. In the late 1920's, he had begun studying the effects of alpha-particle bombardment in the transmutation of light elements. In 1928, he conducted joint research correlating the reaction products of nuclear interactions to nuclear energy levels. By 1929, Bothe had begun work with cosmic radiation, research he continued for the rest of his life. In 1938, he published a paper on the energy dependence of the nuclear photoeffect, and he used a Wilson cloud chamber to begin the work that resulted in the publication of the *Atlas of Typical Cloud Chamber Images* (1940). This book became the widely recognized scientific reference for identifying scattered particles.

Because of their success with the cloud chamber, as well as building a Van de Graaf generator, Bothe and his colleagues began making plans to build a cyclotron, a particle accelerator. Bothe initially encountered difficulties in raising the money but eventually obtained funding once the German military considered a nuclear energy project. Eventually, the government decided that an atomic bomb was not a realistic near-term possibility in World War II and transferred the research back into nonmilitary hands. Nevertheless, the government continued to fund the research.

After Germany conquered France in 1940, the Germans gained control of a cyclotron that the French physicist Frédéric Joliot-Curie was building. Bothe and his colleagues were sent to examine it, and they gained a great deal of knowledge from the French developments. In 1941, Bothe received the necessary funding to build Germany's first cyclotron; in March, 1943, the critical magnet was delivered. By December, the first deuteron

The Coincidence Method of Particle Detection

Since nuclear energy knowledge is pervasive today, it may be difficult to realize that it has been only little over a century since Albert Einstein's first publication of the theory of relativity. Einstein had theorized but not experimentally demonstrated that mass could be converted to energy. To do this required methods for measuring extremely small subatomic particles. Nuclear physicist Walther Bothe was intimately associated with providing the necessary proof. One of Bothe's early teachers, Hans Geiger, created the basic device to measure radioactivity—the Geiger counter—but additional steps were needed to detect and measure particles and the rate of their emission.

More specifically, Bothe sought to show that, when a single portion of an atom passes though two or more Geiger counters, the rate of passage is almost "coincident" in time. The rate of passage, or pulses, is then sent through a coincidence circuit to show that they are coincident in time. Banks of Geiger counters can be used to show small angular variations in the rate of passage of cosmic rays. Bothe applied his method to the study of the Compton effect, for example, whereby high-energy electromagnetic radiation increases in wavelength when it collides with electrons. His demonstration of the small angular scattering of light rays provided strong support for the corpuscular theory of light.

Classical physics held that the energy of incoming X rays ought to equal the combined momentum and energy of the electrons and the scattered X rays after collision. Bothe sought to validate the theories of Einstein and other theoretical physicists that held that the result of the collision was not equal in momentum and energy. To do this, Bothe combined two (or more) Geiger counters with a single amplifier that registered pulses only when particles triggered counters simultaneously. This process, called the coincidence method of particle detection, allowed Bothe to find small-scale variations, a crucial early step in the development of nuclear physics and nuclear energy. For this discovery and other discoveries that followed, Bothe and Max Born shared the 1954 Nobel Prize in Physics.

(a deuterium nucleus) had been emitted. After Germany surrendered in May, 1945, the Allies seized the cyclotron, and Bothe returned to teaching in Heidelberg. The Allies later returned the cyclotron to Bothe, and he continued his research until his death.

During the war, Bothe conducted significant research into the best material to use as a moderator, a substance used for slowing neutrons in a nuclear reactor in order to induce fission. Such research was a necessary step in the creation of an atomic bomb. Bothe's research convinced him that the best moderator would be heavy water—a rare, isotopic form of water that contains deuterium. As a result, the Germans rejected continued research into graphite—a relatively plentiful mineral—as a possible moderator. Unbeknownst to the Germans, Italian American physicist Enrico Fermi, working for the Allied nuclear effort, reached the opposite conclusion and successfully created the first self-sustaining nuclear reactor at the University of Chicago in December, 1942. Fermi's successful research resulted in the first atomic bomb being developed in 1945, while Bothe's conclusion led the Germans on a wild-goose chase. With heavy water as a moderator, the bomb would be twice as difficult to build since two rare substances (heavy water and uranium 235) were needed for a nuclear weapon.

Regarding his work in attempting to develop nuclear energy (and potentially the atomic bomb) for Germany during World War II, Bothe was a patriotic German who did not apologize for his research. However, his dissatisfaction with National Socialist policies led to his being suspected of disloyalty and investigated by the Gestapo.

Impact

Bothe's research in the 1920's was an absolutely essential early step toward the development of nuclear energy and the atomic bomb, although the British and Americans were able to exploit this development, while the Germans were not. Bothe, along with the German-born British scientist Max Born, received the 1954 Nobel Prize in Physics as a result of their research. Bothe was close to the center of nuclear physics research for most of his professional life. His single biggest professional misjudgment—favoring heavy water over graphite as a nuclear reactor moderator—was a critical factor in Germany's failure to develop the atomic bomb during World War II, a fact for which many in the world are grateful.

—Richard L. Wilson

Further Reading

Bernstein, Jeremy. *Hitler's Uranium Club: The Secret Recordings at Farm Hill.* Woodbury, N.Y.: AIP Press, 1996. Contains the annotated transcripts of the secret recordings of the top German nuclear scientists captured and incarcerated in Britain in 1945 and includes discussions of Bothe's role.

Dahl, Per F. *Heavy Water and the Wartime Race for Nuclear Energy.* Philadelphia: Institute of Physics, 1999. Provides a comprehensive history of Nazi Germany's attempts to use heavy water as a moderator for nuclear fission experiments to build a nuclear reactor.

Groves, Leslie R. *Now It Can Be Told: The Story of the Manhattan Project.* New York: Da Capo Press, 1962. Groves, the highest-ranking U.S. military officer in charge of developing the atomic bomb during World War II, provides his account of the bomb's development, including his understanding of Bothe's role as a part of the German effort.

Mehra, Jagdish. *The Golden Age of Theoretical Physics.* River Edge, N.J.: World Scientific, 2001. A broad history of the development of quantum mechanics and nuclear physics that examines Bothe's work in the context of the twentieth century development of nuclear energy and modern physics.

Nye, Mary Jo, ed. *The Cambridge History of Science: Volume 5—The Modern Physical and Mathematical Sciences.* New York: Cambridge University Press, 2002. The Cambridge history of science series is regarded as one of the best available. Addresses the history of nuclear research.

Platt, Richard. *Eureka! Great Inventions and How They Happened.* Boston: Kingfisher, 2003. Platt examines the circumstances in which some of the world's best-known inventions were conceived and the genius of their inventors. Discusses Bothe.

Powers, Thomas. *Heisenberg's War: The Secret History of the German Bomb.* New York: Alfred A. Knopf, 1993. Bothe was a close associate of Werner Heisenberg, and their joint efforts are discussed in some detail in this popular history, which has gone through a number of editions.

Schwartz, Evan I. *Juice: The Creative Fuel That Drives World-Class Inventors.* Boston: Harvard Business School Press, 2004. A theoretical look at the process of inventing that includes examples relevant to Bothe's coincidence method of particle detection.

See also: Enrico Fermi; Hans Geiger; Ernest Orlando Lawrence; M. Stanley Livingston; J. Robert Oppenheimer.

Herbert Wayne Boyer

American biochemist

Boyer, along with Stanley Norman Cohen, developed the basic techniques used in genetic engineering. Boyer and Cohen were the first to use restriction endonucleases to cut DNAs from two different sources, splice them together to make a recombinant DNA molecule, and express the recombinant DNA molecule after insertion into E. coli *cells.*

Born: July 10, 1936; Derry, Pennsylvania
Primary fields: Biology; genetics
Primary inventions: First recombinant DNA organism; human insulin

Early Life

Herbert Wayne Boyer was born in 1936 in the western Pennsylvania town of Derry. After graduating from Derry High School, where he played football, Boyer commuted to St. Vincent College in Latrobe, Pennsylvania, where he majored in premed biology, receiving a B.S. in biology and chemistry in 1958. He then attended graduate school at the University of Pittsburgh. In 1959, he married Marigrace Hensler. Boyer completed his Ph.D. work in 1963, after which he did three years of postgraduate work focusing on biochemistry at Yale University in the laboratories of Edward Adelberg and Bruce Carlton. While conducting postdoctoral research, Boyer was active in the Civil Rights movement.

Life's Work

In 1966, Boyer accepted an assistant professorship of biochemistry and biophysics at the University of California, San Francisco (UCSF). His research focused on the isolation and characterization of *Eco*R1, a restriction endonuclease enzyme from *Escherichia coli* (*E. coli*) that cuts molecules of deoxyribonucleic acid (DNA) at very specific nucleotide sequences. Boyer discovered that *Eco*R1 creates DNA molecules with short (four-nucleotide), single-stranded, complementary, "sticky" overhang ends.

In 1972, Boyer teamed up with Stanley Norman Cohen, a professor, research scientist, and physician at Stanford University who had been studying the insertion of small, circular, nonchromosomal DNA molecules called plasmids, which reside and replicate in a variety of bacteria, into *E. coli*. Cohen had realized that two DNAs cut with Boyer's *Eco*R1 restriction endonuclease could easily be spliced together because of the complementary overhangs. In 1973, Boyer, Cohen, Annie Chang, and Robert Helling cut, combined, and ligated two different plasmids and inserted them into *E. coli*, marking the construction of the first recombinant DNA using restriction endonucleases as well as the beginning of the era of genetic engineering, also known as gene cloning. Now scientists could recombine DNAs at will and insert them into other organisms. In 1974, Boyer and Cohen, along with Chang, Helling, John Morrow, and Howard Goodman, succeeded in constructing a recombinant DNA molecule from the DNA of a plasmid and the ribosomal RNA-coding DNA of *Xenopus laevis*, the African clawed frog. After insertion of the recombinant plasmid/*Xenopus* DNA into *E. coli*, the recombinant DNA was transcribed into *Xenopus laevis* ribosomal ribonucleic acid (rRNA). This was the first demonstration of a eukaryotic DNA molecule (the rRNA gene from *Xenopus laevis*) being expressed in a foreign organism, *E. coli*. Boyer and Cohen next patented their gene-splicing technique.

In 1976, Boyer was promoted to professor of biochemistry and biophysics at UCSF, a position he would hold until his retirement in 1991. In April, 1976, Boyer and Robert Swanson, a financier and venture capitalist who studied chemistry and management at the Massachusetts Institute of Technology (MIT), incorporated Genentech (Genetic Engineering Technology), a company whose first focus was to synthesize the human insulin gene, recombine it with a plasmid, and insert it into *E. coli* with the hope that the *E. coli* would synthesize human insulin. Swanson conceived of the project because the incidence of diabetes in the United States was increasing while the availability of bovine and porcine insulin was decreasing. Swanson and Boyer joined forces with Arthur Riggs, a geneticist at the City of Hope, a clinical research hospital in Duarte, California. By 1978, the Genentech/City of Hope team had successfully cloned and expressed the human insulin gene in *E. coli*. Genentech licensed the production and marketing of human insulin to Eli Lilly. Genentech, one of the leading biotechnology companies in the world, became a publicly traded company in 1980. In 1985, it became the first biotechnology company to produce and market its own medicinal product, human growth hormone (hGH), marketed under the name Protropin.

Boyer was vice president of Genentech until 1990, when he became a member of the board of directors. In 1994, he became a member of the board of directors of Allergan, Inc., a company that focuses on the discovery and development of innovative pharmaceuticals. He served as chairman from 1998 to 2001 and was elected vice chairman in 2001.

Boyer is the recipient of numerous awards, including the Albert Lasker Award for Basic Medical Research (1980), the National Medal of Science (1990), the Lemelson-MIT Prize for Invention and Innovation with Stanley Cohen (1996), the Albany Medical Prize (2004), and the Shaw Prize in Life Sciences and Medicine (2004). He was elected to the American Academy of Sciences in 1979 and to the National Academy of Sciences in 1985. In 1991, after a substantial gift by Boyer and his family, Yale University dedicated the Boyer Center for Molecular Medicine. In 2007, St. Vincent College renamed the School of Natural Science, Mathematics, and Computing the Herbert W. Boyer School. After retiring, Boyer became professor emeritus of biochemistry and biophysics at UCSF.

Impact

Boyer and Cohen's collaboration that led to the development of gene-splicing and genetic-engineering techniques had a profound impact on biology by revolutionizing the study of genetics and molecular biology. Their development of these techniques allowed for the construction, insertion, cloning, and expression of recombinant DNA molecules in foreign hosts and spawned the development of the biotechnology and biopharmaceutical industries.

Although the polymerase chain reaction (PCR) eventually replaced cloning as a method to amplify specific DNA molecules, the cloning of recombinant DNA molecules gave scientists a method to amplify and isolate specific DNA molecules to provide enough copies for DNA sequencing and analysis of gene structure and function. These analyses provided scientists with basic knowledge of the structure of the gene, the nature of mutations, and the control of gene expression.

The expression of recombinant DNA molecules in foreign hosts provided a mechanism for the production by foreign hosts of a variety of human proteins and enzymes to treat human disease. The first medicinally valuable protein that became commercially available was

Production of Human Insulin

Although Herbert Wayne Boyer, Stanley Norman Cohen, and their colleagues developed the basic techniques of gene splicing and genetic engineering, it was Boyer who orchestrated the development of these techniques into ones that could be exploited in the production of medicinally important proteins and enzymes, leading to the birth of the biotechnology and biopharmaceutical industries.

Financier Robert Swanson thought that the techniques could be used to produce human insulin, a protein that would be needed in the near future since the number of diabetics in the United States was increasing while the supply of bovine and porcine pancreases from which diabetics received their insulin was decreasing. Boyer and Swanson founded Genentech to produce human insulin. The Swanson-Boyer Genentech team elicited the assistance of Arthur Riggs and his colleagues at the City of Hope clinical research hospital in Duarte, California, in the project. Since the use of human DNA in recombinant DNA experimentation was not permitted by the National Institutes of Health guidelines involving recombinant DNA research, the Genentech-City of Hope team thought that the best approach was to synthesize the human insulin "gene" rather than to isolate it. Under a loophole in the guidelines, the use of a synthetic human gene in constructing recombinant DNA molecules would not be banned. The strategy was to synthesize, clone, and express in *Escherichia coli* (*E. coli*) bacteria cells a human gene that would code for human insulin. Riggs suggested that he and his colleagues Keiichi Itakura, Herb Heyneker, and John Shine first synthesize, clone, and express the human somatostatin gene since somatostatin was considerably smaller—fourteen amino acids compared to insulin's fifty-one amino acids. This project was completed in August, 1977, and published in December, 1977.

Soon after the somatostatin project was completed, the Genentech-City of Hope team, with the assistance of Itakura, David Goeddel, Dennis Kleid, and Roberto Crea, began the human insulin project. Since insulin is composed of two polypeptide chains, the strategy was to synthesize, clone, and express separately in *E. coli* a gene coding for each chain. The chains would then be isolated, mixed, joined, and folded into a functioning insulin molecule. On September 6, 1978, Genentech and City of Hope announced that they had successfully cloned and expressed the human insulin gene in *E. coli*. Twelve days earlier on August 25, Genentech licensed the production of human insulin to Eli Lilly. In 1980, a small-scale clinical trial involving fourteen patients was begun in England, followed by a much larger clinical trial in the United States in 1982. Human insulin became the first human protein of medicinal value to be produced by genetic-engineering techniques and approved for use by the U.S. Food and Drug Administration (FDA). The FDA approved the use of human insulin, marketed under the name Humulin, on October 29, 1982.

human insulin, in 1982. Insulin was quickly followed by the production of other recombinant human proteins, including hGH, interferon, tissue plasminogen activator (t-PA), and factor VIII clotting factor.

The Boyer-Cohen techniques also led to the development of a variety of transgenic strains of animals and plants. Today, animals such as goats, sheep, pigs, and cows are engineered to produce a variety of human proteins and enzymes of medicinal value, including t-PA, lactoferrin, factor VIII, factor IX, and alpha 1-antitrypsin. Plants are engineered to be insect-resistant, virus-resistant, and pesticide-resistant, allowing for increased yield and a reduction in the use of pesticides. Plants are also engineered to increase nutritional value. Rice, for example, has been engineered to produce beta-carotene, the precursor of vitamin A.

—*Charles L. Vigue*

Further Reading

Drlica, Karl. *Understanding DNA and Gene Cloning: A Guide for the Curious*. 4th ed. New York: John Wiley & Sons, 2004. Addresses all aspects of gene cloning, beginning with the structure and expression of DNA and ending with the construction of recombinant DNA and its subsequent cloning and expression.

Hall, Stephen S. *Invisible Frontiers: The Race to Synthesize a Human Gene*. New York: Atlantic Monthly Press, 1987. An well-referenced account of Genentech's success in synthesizing the human insulin gene and its subsequent expression in *E. coli.*

Martineau, Belinda. *First Fruit: The Creation of the Flavr Savr Tomato and the Birth of Biotech Food*. New York: McGraw-Hill, 2001. An authoritative account of the development and subsequent marketing and demise of Calgene's Flavr Savr tomato, the first genetically engineered food to come to market. The author was an employee of Calgene and intimately involved with the development of the tomato. Excellent references.

See also: Stanley Norman Cohen; Robert Charles Gallo; Mary-Claire King.

Otis Boykin

American electrical engineer

Boykin designed and produced electronic resistors and devices that were appropriated for various communication, military, and medical technologies. His inventions enabled faster and cheaper manufacturing of those basic electrical components that enhanced computer and other equipment performance.

Born: August 29, 1920; Dallas, Texas
Died: March, 1982; Chicago, Illinois
Also known as: Otis Frank Boykin (full name)
Primary field: Electronics and electrical engineering
Primary invention: Resistor

Early Life

Otis Frank Boykin was born on August 29, 1920, in Dallas, Texas, to Walter and Sarah Cox Boykin, both Texas natives. Walter identified his profession as a farmer in his World War I draft registration in September, 1918. At some point before the census of 1930, he became a Primitive Baptist minister.

Otis did not record details about his childhood or any educational, employment, or other experiences that might have shaped his inventiveness when he was a youth. According to census and primary records, he had four older brothers and a younger brother and sister. His family owned a house on Kynard Street in Dallas and had a radio that might have sparked Boykin's interest in electronics.

In 1938, Boykin completed high school and moved to Nashville, Tennessee, to begin studies at Fisk University, an African American college. He married Pearlie Mae Kimble on September 30, 1940. After meeting graduation requirements in three years, Boykin received an A.B. degree in 1941. He secured employment with the Majestic Radio and TV Corporation in Chicago and moved into a Maryland Avenue home. In that business's laboratory, Boykin evaluated automatic control systems used in airplanes and achieved promotions, eventually becoming foreman.

Scientific and industrial activity in Chicago and some local inventors and entrepreneurs probably encouraged Boykin's electronic endeavors. Sources do not indicate whether Boykin encountered any racial discrimination associated with his technological aspirations. He credited the Chicago Economic Development Corporation for providing African Americans, including himself, money to develop and market inventions. At some point,

The Resistor

Otis Boykin improved the design of resistors, electronic components that restrict current in electrical appliances and machines. Concerned about costs and complicated procedures to produce resistors, Boykin sought to design resistors that could be made quickly and inexpensively in addition to minimizing their inductance and enhancing sealing and mounting processes. He considered his experiences with resistors in radios and other equipment at home, work, and school. He consulted patent records, technical journals, and electrical engineer Frederick Emmons Terman's *Radio Engineers' Handbook* (1943) to evaluate technical aspects of resistors.

With colleague Dr. Hal Fruth, Boykin devised his first resistor, and they received a patent for the device in 1953. Boykin constructed this resistor by shaping wire into a coil around an insulator, folding the sides toward the coil's center to lower inductance, and placing and sealing the coil in a tube-shaped structure. Boykin attached wire ends in the tube to terminals that emerged from the tube. Grooves on the tube aided the use of hardware to mount the resistor in appliances. The resistor could be set to specific resistance levels.

Boykin continued to improve his resistor design while working for the Chicago Telephone Supply Company (CTS). For his second patent, "Wire Type Precision Resistor" (number 2,891,227), issued in 1959, Boykin wrapped wire in several separate areas around a flat insulator, which he referred to as a tape, with each section's wires being wrapped in alternating directions. He folded the tape so that the wire sections touched. A plastic covering or similar material contained the folded tape.

For his third patent, "Electrical Resistor" (number 2,972,726), approved in 1961, Boykin addressed problems associated with resistor wires, wrapped around spools or bobbins, that stretched during reverse winding in production and how the size of those resistors hindered their use. He stated that his flat design, shaped to achieve maximum transfer of heat, did not involve reverse winding and had better terminals. His other resistor improvements incorporated glass, refractory materials, and metal oxides, as well as various mixing, shaping, and heating processes to strengthen resistor structures and conductivity.

Electronics inventors recognized the value of Boykin's resistors soon after his patents were approved. Patents that reference Boykin's various resistor patents include resistor designs using high resistance or thick films, such as the "Composite Film Resistors and Method of Making the Same" (number 6,480,093), issued in 2002. Boykin's wire-type precision resistor patent retained industrial significance, being referenced by inventor Kenneth M. Hays in his patent "Heating Elements with Reduced Stray Magnetic Field Emissions" (number 6,734,404), assigned to the Boeing Company in 2004.

Boykin joined such professional organizations as the American Association for the Advancement of Science (AAAS), the Physics Club of Chicago, and the International Society for Hybrid Microelectronics.

Life's Work

In 1944, Boykin accepted a position with P. J. Nilsen Research Labs in Oak Park, Illinois, performing engineering tasks. Sources do not indicate whether Boykin's work was associated with World War II programs or whether he served in any military capacity. He experimented with electrical materials to fashion unique devices and that year began designing a resistor, a device that limits the flow of an electrical current. Between 1947 and 1949, Boykin took classes at the Illinois Institute of Technology. He read technical books and periodicals on electronics and spoke with peers who had secured patents for various inventions.

Shortly after he left P. J. Nilsen Research Labs in 1949, Boykin established Boykin-Fruth, Inc., with physicist Dr. Hal Fruth and served as that corporation's president. Fruth, a telephone and radio electronics expert who had several patents, recognized Boykin's inventive potential. In addition to managing his business, Boykin earned income from other sources. The 1950 AAAS member directory listed his professional position as a research engineer for Lytle and Canon Engineering Laboratory.

On June 23, 1952, Boykin and Fruth filed with the U.S. Patent Office for a resistor with low inductive and reactive capacity that was inexpensive and easy to manufacture. In that year, they closed their company, and Boykin accepted a position at Radio Industries in Chicago, heading ceramics and plastics chemistry work. Boykin and Fruth were awarded a patent for the resistor on April 7, 1953 (U.S. Patent number 2,634,352). The following year, Boykin filed a patent for a wire-type precision resistor, which used precise currents for specific applications.

Boykin remained employed with Radio Industries through 1955. On February 27, 1956, he filed as the sole inventor for another electrical resistor, which had wires resilient to extreme temperatures and physical stresses, including acceleration and vibrations associated with rocketry, and which could be efficiently and economically manufactured. In 1957, Boykin began working for the Chicago Telephone Supply Company (CTS) in Elkhart, Indiana, as a senior project engineer. On June 16, 1959, the patent for his wire-type precision resistor (number 2,891,227) was assigned to CTS. His 1961 electrical resistor patent (number 2,972,726) was also assigned to his employer. During the early 1960's, Boykin applied for patents for his improved resistor designs, thin-film electrical capacitors, and electrical resistance capacitors. Some devices were designed in collaboration with CTS colleagues. Those patent rights were also assigned to CTS. After he retired from CTS in 1964, Boykin worked as an electronics consultant for businesses in the United States and Paris.

Boykin's inventions attracted the attention of the National Aeronautics and Space Administration (NASA). Aerospace engineers working in the Apollo program recognized the value of Boykin's resistors for essential control functions in spacecraft guidance systems. His devices were also used in guided missiles. Many sources incorrectly attribute the invention of the pacemaker to Boykin. Although he did not invent that cardiac device, his electrical components improved pacemaker technology.

In summer, 1975, Boykin sued CTS for $5 million in a New York district court, accusing the company of denying him profits generated by his resistor inventions. Boykin apparently had not received compensation beyond his salary, and he had been unable to sue before 1975 because of legal expenses. A letter from CTS claiming that Boykin had stolen materials from that corporation provoked him to pursue litigation. In October, 1977, Boykin filed a patent for a composite glass resistor he had designed with CTS colleagues and was awarded the patent (number 4,267,074) four years later.

On March 16, 1982, the *Chicago Tribune* printed a brief notice announcing Boykin's death but failed to indicate the exact death date or death place. Most sources state that Boykin suffered a heart attack and died in Chicago, but Cook County vital records do not have a death certificate for Boykin. Two of Boykin's patent applications for electrical resistors were approved posthumously, in 1983 and 1985.

Impact

Boykin made improvements to electrical components, particularly resistors, which have been used in a number of devices ranging from computers to pacemakers. One of Boykin's improved resistors could withstand extreme temperatures and shock, making it ideal for use in aerospace technology, particularly guided missiles. Concerned with manufacturing expenses, Boykin strove to design high-quality electronic components and efficient production methods, which appealed to manufacturers. As a result, Boykin's resistors were widely incorporated in domestic, business, and military electrical equipment. Starting in the 1960's, most radios and televisions and many appliances were built with Boykin's resistors.

Engineers relied on Boykin's resistors for use in computers—first in laboratories and government facilities, then in home computers starting in the 1980's. Though Boykin died before computer use became ubiquitous, his resistors greatly benefited the industry. One of Boykin's resistors was used in the pacemaker, a device that uses electrical pulses to regulate the heart rate, thus enhancing the health and life spans of millions of heart patients.

Although Boykin's inventions have played a fundamental role in advancing modern electronics technology, he received minimal recognition for his accomplishments. In Chicago, the Old Pros Unlimited Club presented Boykin its Cultural Science Achievement Award to recognize his inventiveness. Boykin never received national or international honors.

—*Elizabeth D. Schafer*

Further Reading

Carmody, Sherri, and Stephen J. Mraz. "Seventy-five Years of Innovators." *Machine Design* 76, no. 1 (January 8, 2004): 62-66, 68, 70, 72. Cover story commemorating this journal's seventy-fifth anniversary features Boykin among such notable inventors as Philo T. Farnsworth, Henry Ford, and Robert Norton Noyce.

Greatbatch, Wilson. *The Making of the Pacemaker: Celebrating a Lifesaving Invention.* Foreword by Seymour Furman. Amherst, N.Y.: Prometheus Books, 2000. Author describes his work related to pacemaker technology, referring to people who improved that device, but does not acknowledge Boykin's contributions to the technology. Explains technical details of pacemakers. Illustrations, glossary, endnotes, and appendixes.

Shnay, Jerry. "Chicagoan Aids Effort in Space." *Chicago Tribune*, October 27, 1968, p. NA3. Discusses Boykin's technological contributions to NASA and pacemaker advances. Provides quotations in which Boykin discusses financial support he received from Chicago African Americans for his work and patents. Notes local recognition of Boykin's achievements.

Taborn, Tyrone D. "Separating Race from Technology: Finding Tomorrow's IT Progress in the Past." In *Learning Race and Ethnicity: Youth and Digital Media*, edited by Anna Everett. Cambridge, Mass.: MIT Press, 2008. Historical analysis emphasizes that Boykin's electronics inventions were essential for the expansion of computer technology in the late twentieth century and aided the development of digitized processes.

See also: Wilson Greatbatch; Jack St. Clair Kilby; Gerald Pearson.

Willard S. Boyle

Canadian physicist

In addition to the first continuously operating ruby laser, Boyle's principal contribution was the invention of the charge-coupled device (CCD) with George E. Smith. The device is ubiquitous in modern imaging hardware, including digital cameras, camcorders, and telescopes.

Born: August 19, 1924; Amherst, Nova Scotia, Canada
Primary fields: Electronics and electrical engineering; physics
Primary inventions: Charge-coupled device; continuously operating ruby laser

Early Life

Willard S. Boyle was born in Amherst, Nova Scotia, Canada, in 1924 to Ernest Boyle and Bernice Dewar. When Willard was three years old, the family relocated to Chaudière in northern Quebec, where, because of the remote location, Boyle was home-schooled by his mother until the age of fourteen. He then moved to Montreal, where he attended Lower Canada College. Boyle excelled at school and was expected to progress to university; however, his matriculation was delayed when at the age of nineteen, during the latter stages of World War II, he joined the Fleet Air Arm of the Royal Canadian Navy. Although he became a qualified Spitfire pilot, he was not involved in serious confrontations, and the war ended soon after he enlisted.

After the war, Boyle returned to Montreal to pursue an academic career at McGill University, where he earned bachelor's and master's degrees in science (1947, 1948) and a Ph.D. (1950) in physics. After receiving his doctorate, he spent another year at McGill University as a postdoctoral researcher and then two years as an assistant professor teaching physics at the Royal Military College of Canada. In 1953, he moved to New Jersey to take a position at Bell Labs, where he began research into lasers and semiconducting materials.

Life's Work

While at the Royal Military College of Canada, Boyle collaborated with David C. Baird in an investigation of variations in the thermal and electrical conductivity of copper at liquid helium temperatures. These experiments necessitated the invention of an apparatus that allowed for the accurate regulation of temperature within a liquid helium bath, detailed in a 1954 publication. In 1953, while working for Bell Labs, Boyle continued his investigations into the electrical properties of materials, publishing work in 1955 and 1956 that showed the differing characteristics of short arcs generated between palladium and tungsten electrodes, the latter at high vacuum, dependent upon the voltage applied. Short-arc lamps are used today in a wide range of applications, including medical, military guidance, and fiber-optic illumination.

In the mid-1800's, a unique class of materials was identified whose ability to conduct electricity could be varied depending on the given conditions; these materials were dubbed "semiconductors." The importance of electricity and what was to become the electronic industry grew over the following decades, significantly with the advent of electrical lighting and radio communications. The latter was only possible through the invention of a semiconductor device known as a rectifying diode, which allowed electrical current to flow in only one direction through the radio transmitter. At Bell Laboratories, Russell Ohl had discovered that semiconductors could be "doped" with other elements to tailor their properties even further. This led to the invention of the silicon-based solar cell in 1941 and laid the groundwork for further exciting developments at Bell Labs.

The field of semiconductors continued to see significant advances in the later part of the twentieth century, including contributions from Boyle. Boyle's early studies on semiconductors at Bell Labs focused on their interaction with infrared radiation. His investigations dealt with the quantum mechanical aspects of the materials—

that is, the discrete energy levels allowed for the individual particles therein. In 1958, he published the first measurements of the energy levels of particles in cyclotrons, as deduced from infrared spectroscopic studies. Many of his studies involved the element bismuth, and in 1963 he published a comprehensive review of the properties of the element with other members of Bell Labs, including George E. Smith, with whom he was to have other fruitful collaborations.

In 1960, Theodore Harold Maiman shone an intense pulsing lamp onto a sample of ruby coated in silver and found that an intense beam of coherent visible light was emitted in pulses from the ruby; he called the device a laser. The intense lamp used in the experiment excited atoms in the ruby sample, causing it to emit light of a very specific wavelength. Excitation of the sample is known as "pumping" the laser, and a number of methods and devices exist for doing this. In the months following Maiman's report, a similar laser using a mixture of helium and neon gases instead of ruby was reported by Ali Javan, William Bennett, and Donald Herriott at Bell Labs. The light was continuously emitted rather than appearing in pulses as in Maiman's machine. These happenings significantly influenced the work of Boyle, who in collaboration with Donald Nelson developed the first continuously pumped ruby laser at Bell Labs in 1962. Their invention relied on an arc lamp (of which Boyle had experience from his 1956 studies) that shone continuously rather than the flash lamp used by Maiman. In 1962, Boyle (with David Thomas) filed for the first patent proposing a semiconductor injection laser. Lasers produced with a semiconducting material are significantly easier to fabricate than those that use more traditional materials such as ruby or gases. As a result, they are used in numerous everyday applications such as bar-code scanners, compact disc players, and laser pointers.

In 1962, Boyle worked briefly for Bellcomm, a subsidiary of Bell Labs, as the director of Space Science and Exploratory Studies; however, he returned to Bell Labs in 1964 as executive director of Device Development to continue his study of the physics and application of semiconductors. This appointment led to his invention in 1969 of the charge-coupled device (CCD) with George E. Smith. Concurrently, a separate group at Bell Labs

The Charge-Coupled Device

Willard S. Boyle and George E. Smith originally envisioned the charge-coupled device (CCD) to be used for memory storage. The device in its simplest form can be seen as a row of discrete capacitor units made from semiconducting materials. As the name suggests, capacitors are vessels capable of storing electrical charge, and so either the presence or lack of charge in a series of units can be interpreted as a series of ones and zeros, hence the possibility of a binary memory system. By carefully applying a varying voltage to a row of capacitor units in a CCD, stored electrical charge can be passed along from each unit to its neighbor, rather like a line of people holding buckets, the contents of which are poured from one bucket to the next in line. The content of each bucket (the charge) is assessed when it reaches the end of the line, where it can be recorded as a series of ones and zeros. The name "charge-coupled device" comes from the fact that neighboring capacitor units are in effect coupled, and electrical charge is transferred between them.

The area in which the CCD has had the biggest impact is undoubtedly the electronic-imaging industry. A simple imaging CCD is a row of capacitors covered with a photosensitive layer of silicon. When the device is exposed to light (an image, usually through a focusing lens), the charge accumulated in each of the capacitors is proportional to the energy of the light rays incident upon the silicon. When the packets of charge are passed along the CCD and read off, the differing amounts can be reconstructed into an image. This type of one-dimensional CCD is used in fax machines to scan documents; successive 1-D images of the document are taken as it moves through the machine, and these are combined to give an overall picture in digital format. Rather than taking individual strip images, a two-dimensional CCD array can be constructed to provide an instant 2-D image, as used in modern digital cameras, camcorders, and cell phones.

The digital information gathered by CCDs can be easily manipulated with modern computers. Another great benefit of the CCD imaging system is that the device is solid state and is therefore both robust and easily fabricated. Today, CCDs can be manufactured with several billion capacitor units packed into a tiny area. Each tiny unit has the ability to detect individual photons incident upon it, making these devices incredibly sensitive. Since the 1980's, astronomers have been harnessing this sensitivity, building telescopes that can study extraplanetary objects far fainter than previously imagined and mapping the surface of Earth with exceptional detail using satellite imaging. The famous Hubble Space Telescope uses a number of highly specialized CCDs to produce stunning X-ray, ultraviolet, infrared, and visible-wavelength images of the cosmos. These pictures have helped to further our basic understanding of the universe.

was investigating the manipulation of bubbles of magnetism on the surface of metals. Boyle and Smith extended these ideas to packets of charge that could theoretically be manipulated on a semiconductor surface. The initial brainstorming session took less than an hour, and the working model of a charge-coupled device was assembled in the following few weeks. The CCD was originally conceived for the purpose of memory storage; however, its potential as an imaging device was realized soon after its invention. By 1975, a CCD had been incorporated into a television camera.

Boyle was named director of research in Bell Labs' Communications Sciences Division in 1975 and remained active in research until his retirement in 1979. He has received a number of awards in recognition of his role in the invention of the CCD and is a member of many professional organizations. He and his family reside in Nova Scotia.

Impact

Boyle worked at Bell Labs during a very exciting period of discovery in the fields of laser and semiconductor research. He was responsible for fundamental innovations in both fields that have become commonplace in modern-day technology. Part of this success is due to the collaborative nature of research at Bell Labs and its supportive environment.

Boyle's contributions to laser technology came at a time just after the first laser device had been fabricated. Following his invention of the continuously pumped ruby laser, devices using this technology were used extensively until the late twentieth century, when more efficient lasing materials were discovered. Semiconductor lasers are used in a wide range of applications today, and Boyle is credited with expanding this field.

Boyle will be best remembered for his coinvention of the charge-coupled device, which was first fully described as a memory device in the *Bell Systems Technical Journal* in 1970. However, its most important applications have been in imaging technologies. The imaging CCD is an array of many millions of light-sensitive semiconductor-based units. When the array is illuminated, as when a photograph is taken, an image can be built up based on the interactions of each semiconductor unit with different quantities of incident light. The sensitivity of the CCD, and hence the sharpness of the image, is restricted only by the number of semiconductor units. Fabrication of CCDs is relatively easy, and since they are solid-state devices, they are both durable and practical. CCDs have become ubiquitous in all modern digital cameras, camcorders, and even powerful telescopes. Moreover, their use is not restricted to visible light: Modern innovations have led to devices that interact with X-ray, ultraviolet, and infrared radiation. CCDs were used to map the background microwave radiation left over from the big bang event.

—Bruce E. Hodson

Further Reading

Amelio, G. F. "Charge-Coupled Devices." *Scientific American* 230, no. 2 (1974): 22-31. A review of the burgeoning subject of charge-coupled devices and their relation to existing semiconductor technology. Published four years after the original paper by Boyle and Smith, this article contains a simple pictorial description of how the CCD works.

Boyle, W. S., and G. E. Smith. "Charge-Coupled Semiconductor Devices." *Bell Systems Technical Journal* 49 (1970): 587-593. The first publication detailing the CCD invention.

Janesick, James R. *Scientific Charge-Coupled Devices*. Bellingham, Wash.: SPIE Press, 2001. Gives an excellent and comprehensive account of the history, design, and workings of the CCD. Numerous diagrams and pictures are presented, including copies of the original notebook entries made by Boyle and Smith after their famous brainstorming session that resulted in the invention of the CCD.

Shell, Barry. *Sensational Scientists: The Journeys and Discoveries of Twenty-four Men and Women of Science*. Vancouver: Raincoast Books, 2005. One chapter of this book deals with Willard S. Boyle. Includes a brief résumé with a portrait photograph, in addition to anecdotes about the events surrounding the invention of the charge-coupled device. Boyle's early life is discussed in a separate section. Quotes from and photographs of the inventor in later life are included, as well as a pictorial explanation of a CCD unit.

See also: Ali Javan; Theodore Harold Maiman.

Louis Braille

French teacher

As a blind teenager, Braille invented the Braille code, a system of raised dots that allows blind people to read with their fingers and to write using special tools.

Born: January 4, 1809; Coupvray, France
Died: January 6, 1852; Paris, France
Primary field: Communications
Primary invention: Braille system

Early Life

Louis Braille (LEW-ee brayl) was the youngest child of Simon-René Braille, a harness and saddle maker, and Monique Braille. Braille's parents were literate—a fact worth noting since in the countryside east of Paris this was unusual for people of their social class, even relatively prosperous people like the Brailles. A bright and attractive child, Louis was adored by his brother and two sisters and his parents. As a toddler, he spent time in his father's workshop, watching Simon-René work while playing with his tools and supplies.

In 1812, three-year-old Louis accidentally blinded himself with one of the tools. In spite of this disability, when he reached the appropriate age his parents prevailed upon the parish priest to help enroll him in school. The local teacher quickly took note of Braille's intelligence and ability to memorize readily what the other pupils were able to write down. Braille was understood to be one of the brightest boys in the school, and his parents, priest, and teacher all determined to find a means to continue his education beyond what was available in their regional market town.

Braille's childhood in Coupvray was marked by the defeat of the Emperor Napoleon's army and subsequent occupation of the town by enemy soldiers. The difficult circumstances brought on by the occupation increased his parents' concern about how their blind son would support himself in later life. For this reason, on February 15, 1819, Braille's father took him to Paris to be admitted as a residential student at the Royal Institute for Blind Youth. The first modern school for the blind, the institute had been established three decades earlier by Valentin Haüy, a sighted person dismayed by the poor treatment accorded blind people. Haüy was determined to provide the blind with skills to support themselves by work rather than charity and saw literacy as central to his goal. He devised a system for embossing raised letters on heavy paper. These formed words that his blind students could feel, recognize, and therefore read. Haüy's educational program included training in both trades considered suitable for the blind and academic studies such as mathematics, geography, and Latin. He also encouraged talented students to pursue musical performance.

Life's Work

This was a time of rapid change in France, and Haüy's approach fared poorly during the revolutionary and Napoleonic eras. From 1801 until 1815, his school was housed in a charity institution for blind adults, and between 1806 and 1817 Haüy himself lived in exile in Russia. When the school finally moved back into its own quarters, the students found that they were living in a wretched building, several centuries old, dank, and with classrooms created by dividing up corridors. The new director, Sebastian Guillié, successfully revived Haüy's system of embossed books, but his poor treatment of the students only exacerbated the effects of the unsuitable building on their health. Upon his dismissal (for an affair

Louis Braille. (Library of Congress)

THE BRAILLE CODE

Louis Braille created the first truly practical system of tactile symbols that allowed the blind, using their fingers, to read with the comprehension and speed of sighted people reading print. He built on the efforts of two sighted people: Valentin Haüy, a philanthropist and educator who produced books with embossed letters of the alphabet for his blind students, and Charles Barbier, a military officer who devised a code of raised dots for transmitting messages and orders in the dark. Barbier's code used thirty-six phonetic symbols, each represented by a "cell" of two columns containing between one and six dots. The Braille code was unlike Haüy's embossed letters (which were the same shape as the printed alphabet) or Barbier's dots (which were phonetic). Using the sixty-three possible combinations of between one and six dots in a cell of two columns and three rows, the Braille code has a one-to-one correspondence with the letters of the alphabet and punctuation marks. The smaller cell size was readily read by touch, and one-to-one correspondence with letters of the alphabet allowed for easier written communication between blind and sighted people. Braille's system became dominant in France shortly after his death and subsequently spread throughout the world.

with a female teacher), Guillié was exposed as having lied about the students' nutritional status. Many were underweight and some—including Braille—were eventually to fall ill with tuberculosis.

In any case, Braille adapted quickly to his new home. His kind nature and native intelligence brought him friends among the students and recognition by the teachers and administrators. He learned to read using Haüy's embossed letters and regularly won prizes as the best student in one or another subject. Braille could tell, though, that many blind students had difficulty recognizing raised alphabet letters, and few learned, as he did, how to write with pen and ink. Even particularly adept students could not develop much speed reading embossed letters.

Braille's inventive genius was set in motion by an 1820 visit to the institute by Charles Barbier, a retired artillery officer who had devised a military code that used raised dots. Since the code could be read by touch, messages and orders could be decoded at night without a light that might reveal one's position to the enemy. Disappointed in his attempts to get the army to adopt his system, Barbier realized that it could be used by the blind. He demonstrated its use to Guillié, who agreed to test the code with his blind students. Braille was thus introduced to the idea of the blind reading with raised dots. He recognized the superiority of such a system over embossed letters, and he set out to produce a more accessible code than Barbier's.

Braille invented the Braille code while a teenager, working at it during both his free time at school and his summer vacations at home. By the time he published the code in a pamphlet in 1829, Braille had taught it to many of his fellow students, who confirmed that it enabled them to communicate in writing as no other system could. Meanwhile, in 1821, Alexandre Pignier replaced Guillié as director. Pignier paid attention to his students' interest in the Braille code and, although regulations prevented him from making it part of the formal curriculum, he allowed his students to study it on their own. He took particular interest in Louis Braille, and, upon the death of Braille's father in 1831, he promised that he would never abandon the blind young man.

As it turned out, Pignier was himself dismissed in 1842, the victim of intrigues by his assistant, Pierre Dufau. As director, Dufau tried to suppress the use of Braille's code and force on students his own modifications of the Haüy system. However, Dufau's assistant, Joseph Gaudet, noticing how well the students read and wrote using Braille, chose to publicly announce his support for the dots at the opening ceremonies for the institute's new building (where it remains in 2008, as the National Institute for Blind Youth). Publication of Gaudet's speech in pamphlet form provided the impetus the Braille code needed to lead, in 1854, to its adoption as the authorized system in France. Unfortunately, this was two years after Louis Braille had died.

During his twenties and thirties, Braille remained at the institute as a teacher, supplementing his income with a job as a church organist. A talented musician, his 1829 publication included a code for musical notation as well as the written alphabet. During the years that students at the institute informally (and sometimes surreptitiously) made use of his code, Braille continued to improve his system for music. He also undertook to invent a method for writing letters of the Roman alphabet using dots. Though this method was slower than writing the Braille code, Braille saw his raised-dot system as providing blind people the ability to communicate on paper with sighted people. In 1844, he met another talented blind inventor, Pierre-François-Victor Foucault, with whom he collaborated on a mechanical device, a predecessor to the typewriter, that produced raised-dot letters of the alphabet.

By the time the institute moved into its new home—a modern, salubrious building—Braille's tuberculosis had progressed to the point where it was incurable by the means available at the time. No longer able to maintain his regular schedule as a teacher, Braille spent several extended periods at home in Coupvray. While in Paris, he limited his work as an organist and reduced his teaching load. His condition became acute shortly before Christmas of 1851, and he succumbed a few weeks later, two days after his forty-third birthday.

Impact

Although Valentin Haüy was not the first to create a system for the blind to read by touch, no earlier attempt had ever been institutionalized. Braille's exposure to Haüy's method, and then Barbier's code, led him to create the first truly workable system for blind literacy. Readily understood by the blind and easily adaptable from French to other European languages, Braille was being used in the instruction of blind children in many western European countries by the end of the nineteenth century. The Braille code had a number of competitors (most based on principles derived from Braille) in the United States, and only in 1917 did it become the standard. In 1949, the government of India encouraged the United Nations Educational, Scientific, and Cultural Organization (UNESCO) to regulate Braille for use in all languages, regardless of writing system.

Until the development of sound recording and the subsequent adoption of discs and tapes for distribution to the blind by libraries, Braille and similar codes provided the only access to reading material for the blind. Braille literacy reached a peak in the middle of the twentieth century. More recently, sound recordings and specialized computer programs have led to a decline in Braille usage and the claims by some that Braille code is obsolescent. Among the organized blind, though, there remains great support for teaching Braille to visually impaired children beginning at the same age as the sighted learn to read print. In 2009, to mark the bicentennial of Louis Braille's birth, the U.S. Mint issued a commemorative one-dollar coin.

—*Edward T. Morman*

Further Reading

Bickel, Lennard. *Triumph over Darkness: The Life of Louis Braille*. Leicester, England: Ulverscroft, 1988. A competent and accurate account of Braille's life and influence. It tends toward the hagiographic and in florid language perhaps overemphasizes the devotion of the Braille family and Alexandre Pignier to the deposed French royal family and the Catholic Church.

Dixon, Judith, ed. *Braille into the Next Millennium*. Washington, D.C.: National Library Service for the Blind and Physically Handicapped, 2000. A collection of articles on the history and current status of tactile reading systems for the blind. Published in print and Braille.

Irwin, Robert B. "The War of the Dots." In *As I Saw It*. New York: American Foundation for the Blind, 1955. A firsthand account of how the Braille code eventually became the standard in the United States.

Mellor, C. Michael. *Louis Braille: A Touch of Genius*. Boston: National Braille Press, 2006. The print edition contains numerous beautiful illustrations that are described in detail in the Braille edition. The illustrations of the Braille and Barbier codes and of Foucault's invention clarify for the reader how they work. Although catalogued as a children's book by the U.S. Library of Congress, this is in fact a well-documented book based on primary materials, many of which are reproduced within it.

Roblin, Jean. *The Reading Fingers: Life of Louis Braille, 1809-1852*. Translated by Ruth G. Mandalian. New York: American Foundation for the Blind, 1955. This was originally published in French to commemorate the one hundredth anniversary of Braille's death. Accurate but occasionally hard to follow, this short work provides the English-speaking reader a sense of how Louis Braille has been viewed in France.

See also: Patricia Bath; Alexander Graham Bell.

GIOVANNI BRANCA

Italian engineer and architect

Branca's modern fame rests on his illustration of a steam machine in Le machine *(1629). In his own time, Branca was an accomplished architect, engineer, and writer; his two books, both published in 1629, attest to his ability to compile and present technical information to nonprofessional audiences.*

Born: April 22, 1571 (baptized); Sant'Angelo in Lizzola, Pesaro (now in Italy)
Died: January 24, 1645; Loreto (now in Italy)
Primary fields: Architecture; civil engineering
Primary invention: Steam turbine

EARLY LIFE

Giovanni Branca (joh-VAHN-nee BRAHN-kah) was born in Sant'Angelo in Lizzola, a small town in Pesaro (in the region of the Marches), in 1571. As an archival document attests, he was baptized there on April 22, 1571; his father was an otherwise undistinguished "maestro Niccolò." Nothing else is known about Branca's early life. Because Branca dedicated his *Manuale di architettura* (1629; manual of architecture) to Count Cesare Mamiani, who owned the fief adjoined to the castle of Sant'Angelo, some biographers have speculated that this nobleman supported the early education of Branca in Rome, the city to which he was connected throughout his adult life.

In Rome, Branca would have received his elementary education and the rudiments of the mechanical arts, which, in this period, involved the study of classic texts on architecture and mechanics, such as those by Vitruvius, Leon Battista Alberti, and Aristotle. However, the language as well as the technical aspects of his texts do not support the hypothesis that Branca received any advanced schooling or university training. Against this persistent historiographic supposition, it should be noted that the Marches benefited from a strong tradition of mathematical and engineering studies during the six-

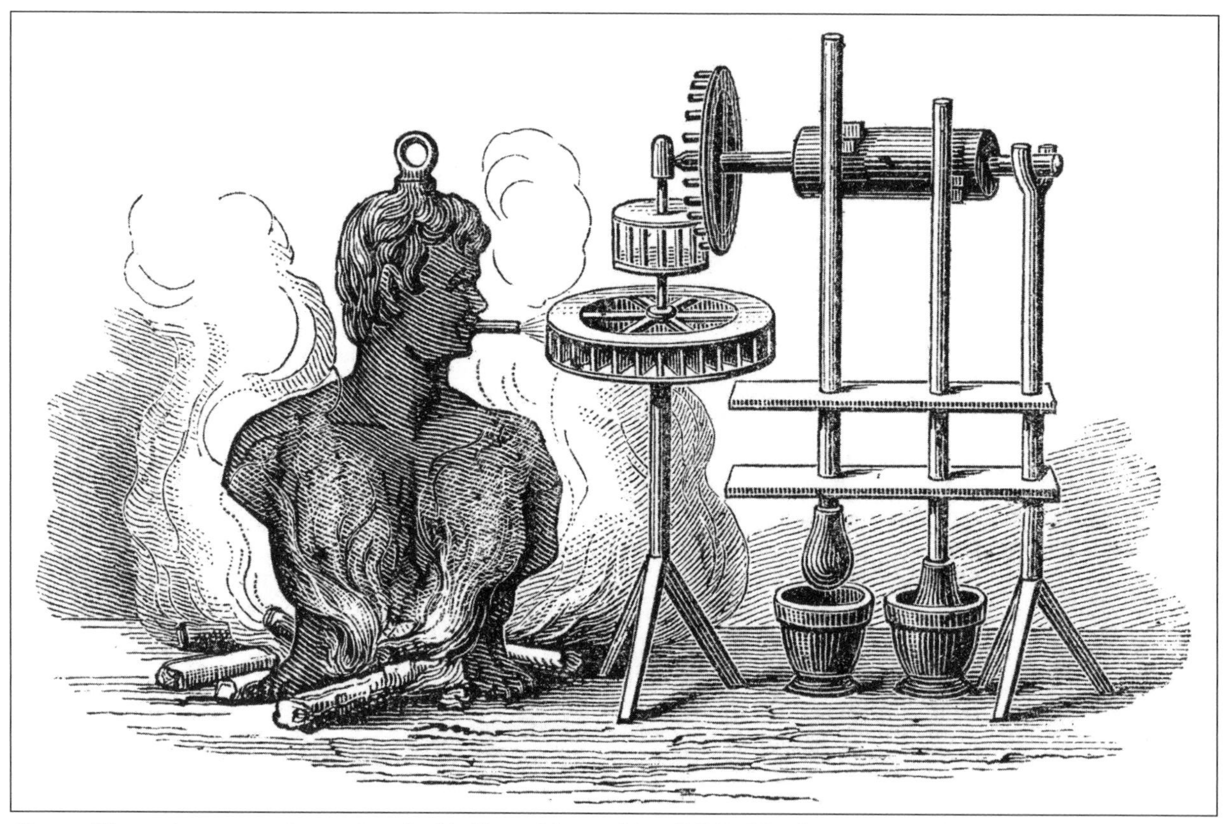

Giovanni Branca's steam engine, as described in his work Le machine *(1629).* (The Granger Collection, New York)

teenth century, epitomized by the fact that the court of Urbino was home to Federico Commandino and Guidobaldo del Monte.

The Wonderful Motor

Figure 25 in the first section of Giovanni Branca's *Le machine* (1629) is the illustration that made him famous in modern times. Many historians have seen in this machine an anticipation of the steam-powered machines that were developed during the eighteenth century. This assessment is more correct with respect to the steam turbine, which is primarily a twentieth century technology, than in relation to James Watt's steam piston machine. Branca's figure presents a boiler, a kind of pressure cooker, in which a set amount of water is turned into steam by the heat provided by coals burning underneath. The steam jet coming out of the mouth of the human-head-shaped lid is channeled through a pipe. The steam jet exiting from this pipe thrusts the blades attached to a drive shaft, producing rotary motion that is transmitted through a mechanism comprising three sets of gears. In the end, the rotary motion of the drive shaft produces the power to activate two pestles. After following the process of the machine's workings through the stations clearly labeled by letters in figure 25, the terse commentary explains that this *motore meraviglioso* (wonderful motor) is used to crush the ingredients necessary to produce gunpowder.

It should be noted that from the perspective of the history of technology, Branca's invention is indebted to the researches on the application of steam power pursued by Renaissance engineers, including Leonardo da Vinci. In their writings, they considered steam power, probably because Vitruvius referenced it in his *De architectura* (c. 20 B.C.E.; *On Architecture*, 1711), a text that circulated widely in the early modern period thanks to various editions and translations. Considering the design of the figure and the proposed machine from the standpoint of subsequent developments, Branca's machine emerges as a precursor not of the eighteenth century steam engines, which worked through a cycle and were usually based on pistons, but of the twentieth century steam turbines that, like his, harnessed directly the power of the steam.

Life's Work

After his baptismal certificate, the next surviving document on Branca mentions his 1614 appointment as "architect to the House of Loreto," a position he kept for the rest of his life. One of his first projects in this papal town outside of Rome, which was also an important pilgrimage site, concerned its aqueduct. Specifically, he was charged with correcting the engineering mistakes made to it by none other than Giovanni Fontana and Carlo Maderno, two leading architects of the Roman scene. In 1614, Branca was also granted Roman citizenship; rather than an honorific recognition, this title offered fiscal and legal advantages. In Loreto, in addition to supervising the building of the town's main church, Branca oversaw the maintenance and enlargement of the town's walls, including the addition of two pentagonal bastions to increase Loreto's defenses.

In 1629, Branca published in Ascoli (a large town in the Marches) his *Manuale di architettura*, an introductory manual of architecture for aspiring architects and builders. In the first three books of this manual, Branca covers building materials, the classical orders, and general instructions to design and build windows, vaults, stairs, chimneys, and other architectural elements. In the remaining three books, he explains the basic mathematical rules and principles needed by architects. The volume concludes with a series of thirty precepts and rules applicable to the problems of maintaining and changing the course of rivers, a subject on which Branca can claim primacy. Notably, unlike his other publication, this manual enjoyed considerable success, seeing several editions until 1789.

Published in Rome in 1629, *Le machine* presents seventy-seven figures and is divided into three sections, the first covering machines of diverse kinds; the second, pumps and hydraulic mechanisms; the third, siphons and compressed-air devices. On the page facing each illustration, there is a brief discussion (in both Italian and Latin) of the machine pictured, including its identification and application. As Branca states in the foreword, he does not claim to have invented many of the devices discussed. Generally speaking, *Le machine* belongs to the literary genre of the "teatri di macchine" (theaters of machines) that emerged during the second half of the sixteenth century. These were not engineering treatises but "coffee-table books" featuring illustrations of machines. Rather than explicating physical and mechanical principles, these books aimed at entertaining readers, as confirmed by the fact that their text and commentaries are often written in Latin, which at the time was not the language of practicing engineers but of the intelligentsia.

Within this genre, Branca's book distinguishes itself by the following features: It was the first non-luxury publication, it was a small octavo, and its figures are unsophisticated woodcuts. Evidently, Branca understood that this kind of publication had a wider market. Even though the steam machine, the invention for which this book and its author became most famous, is defined as a "wonderful engine"—a qualification partly hinting at the fact that it may not be a real machine—in other instances Branca illustrates models that certainly work in actuality, such as the water pump, a device to raise water. His ingenuity in employing raised water to perform work is demonstrated in figure 20. The Archimedean screw was a device commonly used to raise water; Branca "inverted" its principle: Water runs down the Archimedean screw cylinder, which, by turning, generates the power needed to operate a spinning wheel. Branca presents two applications of steam power. In addition to the steam machine, he envisioned a "smoke turbine": A wheel is powered by the fumes and hot air produced by a furnace and channeled through a long funnel-like chimney; a series of gears then transmits the motion to the cylinders of a rolling mill that can be used to strike medals or to thin metal bars.

Documents from the 1620's and 1630's reveal that Branca was granted lands as well as other public offices to administer the realty in Loreto, while also serving as judge and, eventually, "mayor" from July of 1644. He died on January 24, 1645, at the age of seventy-four.

Impact

Branca is representative of the Renaissance engineer-authors and inventors. His publication on machines epitomizes early modern engineering knowledge, both real and fanciful. Branca's steam turbine, for which he is famous, is not a practical device. It is based on working principles, but its realization and applicability was impossible because of the extremely precise and durable gears necessary to harness steam power at the pressure and speeds he envisioned. The machine is significant for continuing the intellectual thread that began with Hero of Alexandria (first century C.E.)—inventor of the aeolipile, the first steam engine—and that can be connected to the creation of modern steam machines. Because few of Branca's illustrations could be or were ever translated into three-dimensional working machines, the impact of his inventions was limited, serving above all as food for thought to stimulate thinking and research about these scientific principles and engineering solutions. In this respect, it is significant that two famous contemporaries owned copies of his machines book—the English natural philosopher Robert Hooke and the Italian architect and artist Gian Lorenzo Bernini.

—Renzo Baldasso

Further Reading

Keller, Alex. "Renaissance Theaters of Machines." *Technology and Culture* 19 (1978): 495-508. Tackles important intellectual issues concerning the history of the "theaters of machines" while also reviewing misconceptions about this genre that are frequently found in the older historiography on the history of technology.

_______. *A Theatre of Machines*. London: Chapman & Hall, 1964. In addition to an informative introduction and biographical accounts of Renaissance engineer-authors, this book presents a sample of illustrations from the "theaters of machines," including figures from Branca's work. The commentary is also illuminating.

Lefèvre, Wolfang, ed. *Picturing Machines, 1400-1700*. Cambridge, Mass.: MIT Press, 2004. Important collection of essays that examines the role of images and visual representation within the intellectual and cultural dimensions of the history of early modern science and technology. Useful for placing Branca's work within the scientific and technical context of the seventeenth century.

McPhee, Sarah. "Bernini's Books." *The Burlington Magazine* 142, no. 1168 (2000): 442-448. Describes and comments on the inventory of the library owned by the architect and artist Gian Lorenzo Bernini. The fact that Branca's *Le machine* is one of these 169 volumes is significant because it is testimony to the position of Branca's work within the intellectual environment of the mid-seventeenth century.

Thorndike, Lynn. *A History of Magic and Experimental Science*. Vol. 7. New York: Columbia University Press, 1958. Thorndike's two pages (617-618) on Branca's book demonstrate above all the difficulty modern historians have in dealing with his work, the technical dimensions of which are easily misunderstood and dismissed as daydreaming, while completely missing the importance of the popular dimension of machines design and of the "theaters of machines" as a literary genre.

See also: Archimedes; Ctesibius of Alexandria; Galileo; Hero of Alexandria; Robert Hooke; Al-Jazarī; Leonardo da Vinci; Thomas Newcomen; Charles Parsons; James Watt; George Westinghouse.

Jacques Edwin Brandenberger

Swiss French chemist and textile engineer

Brandenberger's goal of producing a stain-resistant cloth in the early 1900's was unsuccessful, but his experiments resulted in the invention of cellophane. Cellophane plays a large role in food preservation and safety, medicine, and other industries.

Born: October 19, 1872; Zurich, Switzerland
Died: July 13, 1954; Zurich, Switzerland
Primary fields: Chemistry; household products; packaging
Primary invention: Cellophane

Early Life

Little is known about Jacques Edwin Brandenberger's early life. He was born on October 19, 1872, in Zurich, Switzerland, and attended the University of Bern, where he majored in chemistry. In 1895, he graduated summa cum laude with a doctorate in chemistry. At age twenty-two, he was the youngest Ph.D. in Switzerland. After graduation, he moved to France, where he worked for a textile firm.

Life's Work

Around the turn of the century, Brandenberger was having dinner in a restaurant where someone at a nearby table had spilled a glass of red wine. While watching the wine stain spread, Brandenberger thought to design a waterproof cloth material. He based his work on that of English chemists Clayton Beadle, Charles Cross, and Edward Bevan, who in 1882 discovered that cellulose could be converted into soluble sodium cellulose known as xanthogenate by using sodium hydroxide and carbon disulfide. They then immersed the resultant material in an acid bath that converted it back to cellulose. Brandenberger initially experimented with rayon, a type of cellulose, in liquid form. However, the rayon made the cloth too stiff to work with and did not stick to it. Brandenberger's idea for waterproof cloth failed, but he noticed that the thin, transparent viscose film could be peeled off the cloth. He washed and bleached the film, and by 1908 he had successfully built a machine capable of mass-producing the product.

Brandenberger named his new product "cellophane," from the words "cellulose" and *diaphane*, the French word for "transparent." He published an article in the French magazine *Illustration* in which he discussed the multifarious uses for the new material. In 1913, Brandenberger founded La Cellophane, setting up its headquarters in Paris. The cellophane manufacturing plant was built in the nearby town of Bezons. During World War I, his company produced a large amount of cellophane that was used in the protective eye shields for gas masks. In 1911, Brandenberger patented his production methods and machines. Whitman's was the first American company to use cellophane. Starting in 1912, the candy company began wrapping its Whitman's Sampler

Cellophane

Cellophane, a staple of most modern-day kitchens, was invented by accident in 1908. The idea for waterproof cloth came to Jacques Edwin Brandenberger after he observed a wine stain on a restaurant tablecloth. Though he succeeded in producing a thin, clear film, he could not get it to stick to cloth. He eventually abandoned the waterproof cloth idea and focused on experimenting with the thin viscose sheet. After a decade of experimenting, Brandenberger successfully built a machine capable of mass-producing his cellulose sheets. He patented the production methods and machines in 1917.

Cellophane is made from wood, cotton, hemp, and other natural elements containing cellulose fibers. The cellulose material is dissolved in a solution of carbon disulfide and alkali. The resulting mixture is a liquid known as viscose. To convert the viscose back into cellulose, the solution is sent through a slit into an acid bath. Cellulose, and therefore cellophane, is made up of carbon, hydrogen, and oxygen.

In 1923, DuPont was sold the rights to manufacture and sell cellophane in North and Central America. DuPont scientist William Hale Charch and other researchers developed a process for making waterproof cellophane. Charch conducted more than two thousand experiments before finding the right mixture in 1927. Thus, DuPont began producing a wide line of regular and waterproof cellophanes—with different colors, thicknesses, and textures. DuPont also found ways to make cellophane production more cost-effective. Its scientists adapted machines to cut and fold the thin material. The chemical company also developed the adhesives to seal cellophane. With DuPont's aggressive marketing, cellophane became the common packaging for bread, cakes, cookies, and meats. The company sold cellophane as packaging for nonfood items such as toiletries and tobacco, and it established a department to come up with new uses for cellophane, such as holiday gift basket wrapping.

in the plastic. The new packaging kept out bugs and allowed the candy to be shipped nationwide for the first time.

Brandenberger was known for testing new or potential employees by giving them seemingly unsolvable tasks. Around 1921, he hired a young man on a probationary status. The employee was asked to turn a paper-bag-folding machine into one that would be able to make cellophane bags. Cellophane bags had to be made by hand, requiring a large workforce; Brandenberger envisioned a more effective method of production. After six weeks, the employee came to the conclusion that it was impossible to use the paper-bag-folding machine to make cellophane bags. He feared that he would be fired when he told Brandenberger this. Instead, Brandenberger commended him for having the courage to be honest and for being a hard worker, and the man kept his job.

Whitman's was the largest importer of cellophane until 1924. In 1923, La Cellophane licensed the U.S. rights to cellophane to the DuPont Cellophane Company, and the Delaware chemical company built its factory the following year. DuPont was given exclusive rights to La Cellophane's manufacturing processes and sales rights for North and Central America. In return, La Cellophane would hold the cellophane patent rights and sales rights for the rest of the world.

On December 13, 1947, the U.S. government filed a civil suit against DuPont, accusing the company of monopolizing interstate commerce of cellophane. It took six years for the district court of Delaware to make a ruling. Chief Judge Paul Leahy wrote the decision stating that DuPont did not violate the Sherman Antitrust Act. After reviewing the evidence—hours of testimony and more than seven thousand documents—Leahy felt that DuPont was acting as a competitor, not a monopoly: DuPont conducted market research, consumer surveys, developed new and better products (offering more than fifty types of cellophane), and looked for ways to cut costs.

In 1937, Brandenberger was awarded the Elliot Cresson Medal by the Franklin Institute of Philadelphia. Unlike some inventors, he was able to see how popular his invention became and the impact it had on the world. Besides its use in food packaging, cellophane is used in Scotch tape, some batteries, and Visking tubing for dialysis. Cellophane is also part of the manufacturing processes of fiberglass and some rubber products.

Brandenberger was able to retire comfortably and enjoyed collecting French antiques. He died on July 13, 1954, at the age of eighty-one. He had one daughter, Irma Marthe Brandenberger, who established a foundation in her father's name to honor people who have contributed to the welfare of humankind.

IMPACT

Cellophane is one of the most common packaging materials in the world. Fresh flowers, holiday gift baskets, packs of chewing gum, boxes of tea, and various types of candy are just a few examples of products that come wrapped in cellophane. Brandenberger's accidental discovery of cellophane revolutionized food storage and safety. Cellophane-wrapped meats and produce lasted longer and kept out bugs. The product also led to the development of other types of cellulose sheets, such as saran wrap. "Cellophane" has become part of the vernacular for any transparent, thin, plastic-type sheet. Cellophane has numerous applications, including medical equipment, scientific research, and rubber and fiberglass products. More than two thousand forms of cellophane are currently produced.

After the 1960's, cellophane use declined as similar products came on the market. Environmentalists raised concerns about carbon disulfide (used to produce cellophane), which can be a pollutant if it is not properly disposed of. Cellophane itself, on the other hand, is completely biodegradable.

—*Jennifer L. Campbell*

FURTHER READING

Aftalion, Fred. *A History of the International Chemical Industry*. Philadelphia: University of Pennsylvania Press, 1991. Discusses DuPont, the invention of cellophane, and the product's evolution.

Jones, Charlotte. *Accidents May Happen: Fifty Inventions Discovered by Mistake*. New York: Delacorte Books, 1996. In addition to cellophane, the author discusses Worcestershire Sauce, ice-cream floats, dynamite, and peanut brittle. Suitable for children from third to sixth grade.

Ndiaye, Pap. *Nylon and Bombs: DuPont and the March of Modern America*. Baltimore: The Johns Hopkins University Press, 2006. A history of DuPont that discusses cellophane and the company's aggressive advertising campaign, as well as improvements made to the product. Suitable for the general reader.

Porter, Glenn. "Cultural Forces and Commercial Constraints: Designing Packaging in the Twentieth Century United States." *Journal of Design History* 12, no. 1 (1999): 25-43. Investigates the effects of society on packaging design. One detailed case study examines DuPont and its aggressive advertising and marketing campaigns for cellophane.

Rutherford, Janice Williams. *Selling Mrs. Consumer: Christine Frederick and the Rise of Household Efficiency*. Athens: University of Georgia Press, 2003. Christine Frederick was a home-efficiency expert who found many ways to save time doing housework, and she wrote a column for *Ladies' Home Journal* that shared tips and advice for other housewives. Rutherford uses Frederick's life as a case study for examining the rise of consumerism in the United States.

Stocking, George, and Willard F. Mueller. "The Cellophane Case and the New Competition." *American Economic Review* 45, no. 1 (March, 1955): 29-63. Written by two economists, this article summarizes a 1947 lawsuit against DuPont stating that the company had a monopoly on the cellophane industry. Authors explain the details of DuPont's arrangement with La Cellophane, marketing and consumer research, and sales figures for cellophane.

See also: Wallace Hume Carothers; Richard G. Drew; Margaret E. Knight.

Walter H. Brattain

American physicist

Brattain, John Bardeen, and William Shockley are credited with what has been called the invention of the twentieth century, the transistor. Because of this tiny device, personal computers, cell phones, and hundreds of other electronic devices created a new age of productivity and telecommunications.

Born: February 10, 1902; Amoy, China
Died: October 13, 1987; Seattle, Washington
Also known as: Walter Houser Brattain (full name)
Primary fields: Communications; electronics and electrical engineering
Primary invention: Transistor

Early Life

Walter Houser Brattain (BRA-tihn) was born in Amoy, China, on February 10, 1902. His father, Ross, and mother, Ottilie, married after graduating from Whitman College in Walla Walla, Washington. Ross, a teacher, accepted a job in China teaching science and math. The three were there for a short time, and the family returned to Washington. Walter grew up on a large cattle ranch just south of the Canadian border.

In the fall of 1920, Brattain enrolled in Whitman College, majoring in physics and mathematics, and four years later he received a bachelor of science degree. He claimed that these were the only two subjects in which he excelled. He went to the University of Oregon for his master's degree (1926) and to the University of Minnesota for his Ph.D. (1929). While studying for his doctorate, he worked at the National Bureau of Standards (now the National Institute of Standards and Technology) in Washington, D.C., but decided that he preferred physics to engineering. Brattain met John Bardeen in Princeton, New Jersey, while Bardeen was working to complete his Ph.D. in theoretical physics at Princeton University. Robert Brattain, Walter's brother, was a classmate of Bardeen. Walter and John became fast friends and later became lab partners.

Life's Work

Bardeen and Brattain, along with William Shockley, would invent the transistor—essentially, a solid-state version of the triode vacuum tube. Compared to the vacuum tube, the transistor was very small, had an amazingly long life, consumed little power, and did not get hot. Were such a device possible (it took years to determine that it was), it would be an extremely valuable product for the telephone industry, which used thousands of vacuum tube amplifiers for long-distance service.

Brattain joined Bell Telephone Laboratories (Bell Labs) on August 1, 1929, after receiving his Ph.D. and began work with Joseph A. Becker, a research physicist at Bell Labs. Brattain spent most of his time studying copper oxide rectifiers. The two scientists hoped that they could make an amplifier by putting a tiny metal grid in the middle of the device, much as had been done with the triode vacuum tube. This did not work, but the experience provided valuable information regarding crystals and the theory of surface states in semiconductors.

In the years before World War II, Brattain was involved with the surface physics of tungsten and later silicon. He was sidetracked during the war, devoting his energies to developing methods of submarine detection.

Following the war, he returned to Bell Labs and was soon assigned to a new solid-state group organized by the president of Bell Labs, Mervin Kelly. The head of this group was William Shockley. Shortly thereafter, Bardeen joined the group. The three were ideally suited for the project. Bardeen was the thinker: He could examine an event and go beyond common understanding to explain it. Brattain was the experimenter: He could put together any contraption needed. Shockley was the visionary: He could look beyond the experiment and determine just what it might mean for the future.

Toward the end of 1947, a period often called "the miracle month," Brattain and Bardeen were still struggling to achieve amplification out of a semiconductor device. (Shockley was off pursuing a different approach.) Brattain was conducting an experiment that would supposedly explain how electrons acted on the surface of a semiconductor, and he was having trouble with condensation. Frustrated, he dumped the whole experiment into a beaker of water—taking care of the condensation. Suddenly, there was real amplification.

Bardeen suggested that somehow a metal point be pushed into the silicon surrounded by water. However, the contact point could not touch the water; it could only touch the silicon. Brattain solved the problem by coating the metal point with paraffin and pushing it into the silicon. With this, the apparatus worked; they had achieved amplification.

Over the following weeks, changes were made, and the results continued to improve. Germanium, rather than silicon, was used. The method used to get two gold point contacts just a fraction of a millimeter apart was quite ingenious. Brattain coated the edge of a draftsman's triangle with gold foil and then carefully sliced it through at one of the points. The first point-contact transistor had been made.

For a week, the two men kept the experiment a secret. On December 23, 1947, Bell Labs' management was briefed on the invention of the first solid-state amplifier. The patent dealing with the point-contact transistor was awarded to Brattain and Bardeen, and not to Shockley. However, several months later Shockley developed his own transistor—actually a much superior one, called the junction transistor. The three men were awarded the Nobel Prize in Physics in 1956.

Life for the three after the invention of the transistor was not smooth. Shockley was difficult to work with, and Brattain soon asked to be transferred to a different lab at American Telephone and Telegraph Company

THE TRANSISTOR

The transistor invented by Walter H. Brattain and John Bardeen in December, 1947, was called the point-contact transistor. One month later, William Shockley, the supervisor of the three-man group, invented the junction transistor. All three were awarded the Nobel Prize in Physics in 1956 for the invention of the transistor. Although the construction of the two types of transistors is different, they operate in essentially the same way.

In its basic form, the transistor's function is to take electric current (electrons), send those electrons from one element to another (in the case of a transistor, the emitter and the collector), and control the flow of those electrons with a third element (the base). A large current flowing between emitter to collector can be made smaller or larger by adjusting the current to the base. The result is amplification.

One example is simple amplification of an analog signal as might be used in a radio. Radio waves are extremely small; in order to be audible to humans, the waves must be amplified many times. An incoming radio signal is received by the radio's antenna, and the tiny electrical wave is sent to the base of a transistor. The resultant signal at the collector is identical in shape to the input signal at the base, except it is about one hundred times larger. It is now possible to apply this signal to the base of a second transistor and have the signal once again amplified about one hundred times. This process is continued until the resultant signal, the tone, is audible.

In another example, called switching mode, a transistor operates in one of two states: on or off. Digital computers utilize transistors that operate this way. By utilizing other electronic components, logic functions can be performed. Of great importance is the fact that these functions can be done very fast—millions of operations can be performed each second.

The electrons flowing in a transistor do not flow in a vacuum, as they would in a vacuum tube, but rather in a solid piece of germanium or silicon; hence the name "solid state." The theory of the transistor is extremely complicated, and a total understanding requires a knowledge of quantum mechanics. The materials used to make transistors (silicon and germanium, for instance) have four electrons in their outer orbits. It is possible to dope a piece of this element with molecules of a different element and combine several such pieces with very sophisticated technology. Then, as the electrons in the orbits of the several pieces flow (and they are in constant motion), the transistor effect is created.

(AT&T), where he stayed until retiring to take a teaching position at his alma mater. Bardeen left to work at the University of Illinois, where he could concentrate on physics theory; he would win a second Nobel Prize, for his work with cryogenics, in 1972. Shockley left AT&T to form Shockley Semiconductor Laboratory in Palo Alto, California.

Impact

The transistor has been called the most important invention of the twentieth century, largely because it made personal computers possible. There were, of course, computers before the transistor, but they were large, cumbersome, expensive, and hot. Their mean time between failure was very short. Communications channels (particularly with the telephone industry in mind) were expensive to build and difficult to maintain. All of this would change with the transistor. As improvements to the transistor were made, it evolved into the integrated circuit (invented by people who joined, and then left, Shockley Semiconductor Laboratory). Integrated circuits became smaller and faster, to the point where it is now possible to place several million on the head of a pin.

Transistors and the integrated circuits they made possible opened the way for cell phones, laptop computers, handheld computers, and global positioning systems. Today, telephones are able to indicate who is calling, and emergency service systems are able to pinpoint the location of accident victims. The Internet is accessible to millions of people, making it possible to communicate with anyone in the world. Indeed, every place on earth is equidistant from every other place on earth—all thanks to the transistor.

—*Robert E. Stoffels*

Further Reading

Fitchard, Kevin. "Reviving an Icon." *Telephony* 249, no. 2 (February 11, 2008): 15. An up-to-date story of Bell Labs, the home of the transistor. Offers considerable detail regarding the projects regularly handled and the results of the completed projects.

Perry, Tekia S. "Gordon Moore's Next Act." *IEEE Spectrum* 45, no. 5 (May, 2008): 38. The transistor evolved into the integrated circuit, and the integrated circuit evolved into the microprocessor. Gordon Moore, who worked under William Shockley at the Palo Alto laboratory, left with others to form Intel, the leading manufacturer of microprocessors.

Shockley, William. *Electrons and Holes in Semiconductors*. New York: Van Nostrand, 1950. An extremely complicated book that demonstrates the challenges presented in the invention of the transistor.

U.S. Department of the Army. *Basic Theory and Application of Transistors*. Washington, D.C.: Author, 1959. A training manual describing the theory and application of transistors. Somewhat simplistic but nevertheless worthwhile.

See also: John Bardeen; Seymour Cray; Nick Holonyak, Jr.; Gerald Pearson; Claude Elwood Shannon; William Shockley.

Karl Ferdinand Braun

German physicist

Braun developed the oscilloscope, which enabled researchers to see electrical waveforms in real time and was an important stepping-stone in the development of modern radars and of all-electronic television.

Born: June 6, 1850; Fulda, Hesse-Kassel (now in Germany)
Died: April 20, 1918; Brooklyn, New York
Primary field: Electronics and electrical engineering
Primary inventions: Wireless telegraphy; cathode-ray oscilloscope

Early Life

Karl Ferdinand Braun (BROWN) was born in 1850 in Fulda, a city in the principality of Hesse-Kassel, which would soon be incorporated into the militarily aggressive German kingdom of Prussia, and ultimately into the German Empire. Braun's father, Konrad Braun, was a civil servant working as a court clerk. His mother, Franziska Braun, née Gohring, was the daughter of the elder Braun's supervisor in the civil service.

After successfully completing the course of study in the local *Gymnasium*, or high school, Braun went to the University of Marburg to pursue a higher education. That path ultimately led him to the University of Berlin, where he earned his doctorate in 1872, writing a dissertation on the vibrations of elastic rods and strings. His work was interesting in its implications for thermodynamics, which at the time was still in its infancy and still largely confined to studies of high-temperature machines such as steam engines.

Life's Work

After completing his doctorate, Braun began to concentrate primarily on electrical phenomena. One of his earliest investigations was into the behavior of some metallic sulfide crystals, which conducted electricity only in one direction. His work would become the foundation for the development of the crystal detector, an early semiconductor device used in detecting and rectifying radio waves before the development of reliable vacuum tubes.

Over the next several years, he would move from one university to the next, always holding relatively prestigious positions in their departments of physics but never able to attain a stable appointment. That changed in 1895, when he finally returned to the University of Strassburg (modern Strasbourg), in Alsace, which at the time was part of the German Empire. He would continue to hold that position until his death and ultimately became so satisfied with it that he even turned down an offer of an endowed chair at the extremely prestigious University of Leipzig.

In the late 1890's, Braun became increasingly interested in the Crookes tube, an early prototype of the cathode-ray tube (CRT), which was a development of the diode originally developed by Thomas Alva Edison as part of research into why incandescent light bulbs were developing stains on the inside. By hanging a second element, or plate, inside the bulb, he was able to detect a current, which he named the Edison effect, but he could see no practical use for it, setting that work aside to pursue other projects with more immediate monetary rewards.

The Crookes tube modified the plate into a set of deflectors that could cause the cathode to emit a stream of electrons toward the far end of the tube, which could be coated with a phosphorescent material. The earliest forms of the CRT were instrumental in the discovery of the electron, which proved that electricity was particulate in nature rather than a fluid as experimenters as early as Benjamin Franklin had simply assumed, an assumption enshrined in terms such as "current" that were too deeply embedded in the discipline to be uprooted.

However, Braun saw additional potentials for the CRT, and by modifying it so that a fluctuating current could be imposed upon the plate voltage, he created the first oscilloscope. At last, scientists and engineers had a device that could display electrical waveforms in real time, which was extremely useful in the diagnosis of faults in complex electronic equipment. Even the basic phase reversal of alternating current (AC) could be observed on an oscilloscope, allowing engineers at power plants to see when a generator was lagging or otherwise malfunctioning.

Braun's first practical application of the oscilloscope was in radio transmission, when Guglielmo Marconi revealed that his transmitter would send signals only a few miles. By attaching an oscilloscope to the system, Braun was able to identify the upper limit on the Hertz oscillator, a key part of the antenna, by which further expansion of the spark gap actually decreased its output rather than increasing it. Braun then proceeded to design an entirely new type of antenna for Marconi's transmitter, removing the spark from the system by taking the antenna out of the transmitter circuit and having the signal be conveyed to the antenna by means of condensers, huge wire coils that transformed electricity into magnetic fields that would induce electrical current in the antenna. As a result, he was able to increase power and gain increased transmission distance in a fairly linear fashion. He also applied this discovery to Marconi's radio receiver, isolating the antenna from the detector circuits so it was less likely to pick up random static rather than the signal its user was seeking. As a reward for this breakthrough, Braun shared the 1909 Nobel Prize in Physics with Marconi.

His success with Marconi's transmitter ignited an interest in all aspects of radio transmission and detection. Braun developed a new kind of antenna that would transmit only in a single plane, unlike the earlier antennas that sent radio waves in all directions, rather like a spherical version of the ripples radiating outward from a rock thrown into a still pond. The unidirectional radio antenna was useful in sending a signal that was intended only for recipients in one particular area, for instance a military unit such as a squadron of ships at sea.

Braun also recognized the utility of radio in navigation. Although the development of the marine chronometer had greatly improved the accuracy of open-ocean navigation, its margin of error could still become deadly as ships approached dry land. Particularly if storms had thrown them off course since their last opportunity to take sun sightings and compare the local time to the reference time carried by the chronometer, ships could easily be thrown onto rocks when their navigators had placed them a mile or two away. Although lighthouses built along the coast could provide some warning for the most treacherous approaches such as Cape Hatteras or the Isles of Scilly, heavy rain or fog could obscure their lights until a ship was dangerously close. By contrast, radio waves passed untroubled through even the heaviest rain and fog. If one could establish a system of radio beacons along the shoreline, particularly near dangerous approaches and important harbor, sailors would have a readily available navigation tool no matter the weather.

In 1914, Braun became entangled in patent litigation in a U.S. court and as a result came to the United States. While he was there, he was also able to look into the various voice transmissions being pioneered by Reginald Aubrey Fessenden, Lee De Forest, Edwin H. Armstrong, and others. However, his age and resultant ill health delayed his testimony repeatedly, until the United States entered World War I in 1917. As a result, Braun was regarded as an enemy alien and prevented from returning to his native land, although his age and standing as an eminent scientist prevented any formal accusations of spying or internment.

Being trapped on the far side of the Atlantic, unable to contact his family and friends or to speak on behalf of German scientists as a result of the hostilities, was a very wearing situation for the elderly Braun, who had already experienced episodes of ill health. The final blow was a fall that broke his hip. Although he was hurried to the hospital, the injury refused to heal, leaving him bedridden. As it sunk through to him that he would never again be able to live an independent life, the will to live seeped out of him and he died in his Brooklyn apartment during the spring of 1918, with the end of the war still months away. Because the war made it impossible for his remains to be returned to his homeland, they were instead cremated so the ashes could be

THE OSCILLOSCOPE

In the earliest days of electricity, there was no way to directly display a waveform visually. Because scientists studying electrical phenomena frequently found it useful to have the waveforms displayed in visual form, early researchers laboriously hand-plotted the readings from a galvanometer on graph paper. However, rapidly changing readings could be missed, simply because of limits on human attention and reaction times. As a result, scientists developed various tools for plotting the waveforms mechanically. However, most of these devices used various kinds of pens or styli on paper, and while they did make a permanent record, they often ran into limitations related to the latency of mechanical systems.

When Karl Ferdinand Braun realized that the Crookes tube (an early prototype of the cathode-ray tube, or CRT), could be modified so that it would trace the waveform of an electrical signal across its flat end, he scored a major coup for all scientists and engineers working with electricity. Braun's oscilloscope provided them with a real-time indicator of a waveform's changes as they were occurring, which allowed researchers to observe events they might not necessarily want or be able to capture on a paper-based system.

Although Braun originally created the oscilloscope as an interesting demonstration of certain phenomena of electrical physics, he realized its practical use when radio inventor Guglielmo Marconi filed for a patent and had to reveal that his transmitter could only send a signal a dozen miles. Puzzled at this limited range, Braun contacted Marconi and as a result was able to investigate Marconi's equipment with his newly invented oscilloscope. As a result, Braun was able to identify several of the key factors that were limiting Marconi's success, in particular the loss of energy to sparking in the antenna. This collaboration led to Braun sharing the 1909 Nobel Prize in Physics with Marconi.

As the oscilloscope was adopted widely by scientists and engineers around the world, other uses for it were soon realized. Russian scientist and inventor Boris Rosing used a modified version of it to display his early television experiments, and Rosing's protégé Vladimir Zworykin would remember those works when designing the receiver for his own iconoscope television camera tube. As American and British military researchers developed radar as an air-defense technology, they used oscilloscopes modified to scan radially rather than horizontally to display the returns.

Another important use of the oscilloscope was in medical monitoring. As such devices as the electrocardiograph (ECG or EKG) and electroencephalograph (EEG) were developed to detect and display electrical activity of the heart and brain, respectively, doctors working in clinical situations often wanted to be able to see moment-by-moment activity levels rather than produce a permanent record. Thus, an oscilloscope was calibrated to show normal parameters for the physiological response being measured, so that medical personnel could tell at a glance whether a patient's heartbeat or other electrical activity was normal or awry.

Even in the digital age, the oscilloscope remained an important device, although increasingly CRT-based oscilloscopes gave way to ones using analog-to-digital conversion systems to display their readouts on flat-panel screens, generally a liquid crystal display (LCD). These solid-state digital oscilloscopes enjoy the advantages of lower power consumption, greater ruggedness, and better memory functions for the comparison of waveforms over time.

held safely until such time it was possible to transport them to Germany.

Impact

With the oscilloscope, Braun became the "father of the video display." The oscilloscope not only was immediately useful for physicists and electrical engineers studying the operation of circuits but also demonstrated the ability of the cathode-ray tube to display information in visual form. Thus, both Vladimir Zworykin and Philo T. Farnsworth turned to the CRT for their television receivers, and the developers of the minicomputer and microcomputer used the CRT to show data and operations. Although the CRT has been superseded by solid-state devices such as the liquid crystal display, those technologies became possible only because the CRT made television and personal computing profitable.

—*Leigh Husband Kimmel*

Further Reading

Davis, L. J. *Fleet Fire: Thomas Edison and the Pioneers of the Electric Revolution*. New York: Arcade, 2003. A history of the early days of electricity, culminating in the invention of radio.

Fisher, David E., and Marshall Jon Fisher. *Tube: The Invention of Television*. Washington, D.C.: Counterpoint, 1996. Includes information on Braun's CRT work as part of the prehistory of electronic television.

Kurylo, Friedrich, and Charles Susskind. *Ferdinand Braun: A Life of the Nobel Prizewinner and Inventor of the Cathode-Ray Oscilloscope*. Cambridge, Mass.: MIT Press, 1981. Book-length biography with in-depth coverage of Braun's life.

Lewis, Tom. *Empire of the Air: The Men Who Made Radio*. New York: Edward Burlingame Books, 1991. A history of the early days of radio. Places Braun in the larger context of the development of radio, from wireless telegraphy to commercial broadcasting.

See also: Edwin H. Armstrong; Sir William Crookes; Lee De Forest; Thomas Alva Edison; Philo T. Farnsworth; Reginald Aubrey Fessenden; Benjamin Franklin; Guglielmo Marconi; Vladimir Zworykin.

Wernher von Braun

German rocket engineer

Von Braun was one of the premier rocket scientists of the twentieth century. His work was responsible for Germany's V-2 rockets, several American rockets and missiles, and the Saturn V rocket that carried the Apollo astronauts to the Moon.

Born: March 23, 1912; Wirsitz, Germany (now Wyrzysk, Poland)
Died: June 16, 1977; Alexandria, Virginia
Also known as: Wernher Magnus Maximilian von Braun (full name); Baron von Braun
Primary fields: Aeronautics and aerospace technology; military technology and weaponry; physics
Primary inventions: Saturn V rocket; V-2 rocket

Early Life

Wernher von Braun (VAYR-ner fon BROWN) was born the second of three sons to Baron Magnus Maximilian von Braun, a Prussian farmer. In 1924, Baron von Braun and his family moved to Berlin when he accepted the position of Reich minister of agriculture, a position that he held until resigning in protest as soon as Adolf Hitler became chancellor of Germany. In school, the young Wernher von Braun showed an early aptitude for music, an interest that he retained for the rest of his life. Von Braun was enrolled in a prestigious French school, but he did not do well. He did particularly poorly in mathematics. His lack of interest in school led him to pursue other interests. It was at this time that he began an interest in rocketry that was to dominate the rest of his life. At age twelve, von Braun and his brother tied several sky rockets to the back of a wagon. After the rockets were lit, they propelled the wagon at a high rate of speed down a major Berlin street, bouncing off vehicles and pedestrians along the way. Despite being grounded, von Braun continued his rocket experiments. Von Braun's mother, though, encouraged his interest in rockets by introducing him to science-fiction novels and giving him a telescope.

Hoping for better performance, von Braun's parents transferred him to a boarding school at Ettersburg Castle, where he became a better student, though he still performed poorly in mathematics and physics. There, von Braun tried to read a book by rocket pioneer Hermann

Oberth. Unfortunately, he found the book to be filled with equations. He decided that he must learn physics and mathematics to understand the book. His hard work was rewarded, and he became an expert student in those areas.

In 1928, von Braun transferred to the Hermann Lietz School, another boarding school, but one well known for its technical training. There, von Braun became a mathematics tutor. Upon graduation, he moved to Berlin to receive technical training at the Federal Institute of Technology. Then, in 1934, von Braun received his Ph.D. in physics from the University of Berlin.

Life's Work

While still in school in Berlin, von Braun joined the Verein für Raumschiffahrt (VfR), the German spaceflight society. Together with other members of the group, he was able to experiment and construct increasingly powerful rockets. However, the cost of their work began to exceed what they could afford based on donations and their own funds. So, von Braun managed to secure funding from the German army in 1932 to construct even larger rockets. This money came with restrictions, though. The army wanted rockets to serve as ultra-long-range artillery. Some members of the VfR left because of this restriction. Von Braun wanted money to build rockets for space exploration, but money was not available for that. Money was available for weapons, though, and he apparently felt that the research and development for rockets used for weapons could eventually be turned toward peaceful applications.

The army wanted the rocket development work to be moved to a more secure site near Peenemünde, Germany. It was there, when von Braun was put in charge of a well-funded research team, that his work really began to take off. Von Braun began developing increasingly larger rockets, eventually resulting in the development of the alcohol-water- and liquid-oxygen-fueled Aggregat 4 (A-4) rocket. With the Nazi Party in power and war looming, the Nazis looked unfavorably on such a prominent facility as the Peenemünde rocket center being under the control of a non-party member. Under increasingly severe pressure, von Braun was finally forced to join the Nazi Party in 1937 or else have control of the facility taken from him. In 1940, von Braun was similarly given an ultimatum to either join the Schutzstaffel (SS) or be removed from his position. Von Braun relented, though he virtually never wore his uniform nor a swastika armband, and he remained critical of Nazi policies. In 1944, Hitler renamed the A-4 the Vergeltungswaffe 2 (V-2) rocket. The V-2 rocket was the first long-range military missile, capable of delivering a 2,000-pound warhead from Germany to London. The V-2 rocket accomplished this by powering itself into a ballistic arc that carried it just above Earth's atmosphere, making it the first rocket to achieve suborbital spaceflight. However, von Braun continued to promote peaceful space exploration. He was arrested by the Gestapo for comments made at a party declaring that his

The Saturn V Rocket

In 1961, President John F. Kennedy declared the goal of sending American astronauts to the Moon. In order to reach this goal, engineers needed to build a rocket far larger than any that had ever been constructed. Wernher von Braun and his team of rocket engineers had the task of designing the rocket that would do the job. The Saturn rocket family was the result of that work. The Saturn V rocket was the largest member of the family and was the culmination of von Braun's life's work. It was 364 feet tall and had a diameter of 33 feet. When fully loaded, it weighed in excess of 6 million pounds. It could carry a payload of over 250,000 pounds to Earth orbit and over 100,000 pounds to the Moon. No other rocket has yet matched this capability.

The Saturn V rocket consisted of three stages. The first stage, designated S-IC, was 183 feet long and was propelled by five massive rocket engines, each capable of providing 1.6 million pounds of thrust. The fuel for the first stage was RP-1 rocket fuel, basically a very highly refined form of kerosene. There was enough kerosene and liquid oxygen in the first stage of the Saturn rocket to fill more than fifty railroad tank cars. This propellant was burned within nearly three minutes of launch. The second stage, designated S-II, was 81.5 feet long and 33 feet in diameter. It was propelled by five J-2 engines using liquid hydrogen and liquid oxygen. The third stage, designated S-IVB, had one J-2 engine, also using liquid hydrogen and liquid oxygen as propellant. It was just under 59 feet long and 21 feet in diameter. The S-IVB stage was essentially the same as the second stage of the earlier Saturn 1B rocket.

A total of fifteen Saturn V rockets were produced. Three of these were launched into Earth orbit as test flights. Nine Saturn V rockets were launched with manned payloads to the Moon. Six of those payloads resulted in lunar landings. One Saturn V was used with its third stage modified to be the Skylab space station. The remaining two Saturn V rockets were never used, and portions of them are on display at various NASA centers.

Wernher von Braun. (NASA)

rockets would be far better used for peaceful purposes than as weapons.

Near the end of World War II, von Braun arranged for himself and several hundred other German rocket scientists to surrender to the United States. Upon their surrender, they were taken to Fort Bliss, Texas, where the U.S. Army put them to work developing missiles for the United States. Von Braun returned to Germany in 1947 to marry Maria von Quistorp. Their first child, Iris, was born in 1948. Though he was working for the U.S. Army building more weapons, von Braun continued to push for peaceful space exploration. He wrote a series of articles for *Collier's Weekly* in 1953 and 1954 expounding on the possibilities of manned space travel, space stations, and colonies in space. On April 15, 1955, Wernher von Braun became a naturalized U.S. citizen. In 1956, the Army created the Army Ballistic Missile Agency (ABMA) in Huntsville, Alabama, and von Braun was made its technical director. There, von Braun developed several more missiles, including the Jupiter missile and the Jupiter C missile.

While at ABMA, von Braun began work on plans to launch an artificial satellite into Earth orbit. However, in 1955, when the United States announced that it would launch a satellite during the International Geophysical Year of 1957-1958, von Braun's program was not selected to do the job. Rather, the Vanguard program was given priority. However, following the successful launch of two Sputnik satellites by the Soviet Union in 1957, and with the Vanguard program having difficulties, von Braun's team was given the green light to launch a satellite. They successfully launched Explorer 1, America's first artificial satellite, in January of 1958. Later that year, von Braun and ABMA became part of the newly created civilian space agency, the National Aeronautics and Space Administration (NASA).

Working with NASA, von Braun completed development of the Saturn 1B rocket, the largest rocket that had been built by the United States. He then headed the development of the Saturn V rocket, which eventually took American Apollo astronauts to the Moon. The Saturn V rocket remains the largest successfully operational rocket that has ever been built.

In March, 1970, von Braun was transferred to NASA headquarters. However, he never fit in with the Washington culture, and he felt ineffective. He retired from NASA in 1972 to begin work as vice president of engineering and development for Fairchild Industries. He was diagnosed with liver cancer in 1973 and colon cancer in 1975. He continued to work as best he could through his illness, but by the next year he was bedridden. He resigned from Fairchild on January 1, 1977, and died of cancer on June 16, 1977.

Impact

Von Braun was obsessed with rocketry from his early experiments with rockets as a boy. Oberth's book, *The Road to Interplanetary Space*, which he read as a schoolboy, was pivotal in influencing his choice of career in order to pursue his dream of building bigger and better rockets. His single-minded pursuit of this goal led him to become one of the most influential rocket scientists of the twentieth century. His V-2 rockets quickly became a feared weapon of war, though they came far too late in World War II to actually have much effect on the outcome of the war. His crowning accomplishment, though, was the Saturn V rocket, which was essential to the United States' manned exploration of the Moon. Furthermore, von Braun was a visionary and dreamer who truly believed that mankind needed to explore and colonize beyond Earth. He realized that education was key to successfully completing his goal. He was a champion of science education, continuing his educational activities until he became bedridden with cancer.

Von Braun was pressured into joining the Nazi party and the SS. He did not appear to share their agendas. Most likely, he joined solely for utilitarian purposes, as a means to continue his rocketry research. However, a number of people have not forgiven him for this decision, and while some have praised his integrity, others have long regarded him as a war criminal. He apparently knew that the SS was using slave laborers to build V-2 rockets, but he claims that he did not realize just how poorly they were treated and that his position in the organization was too low to influence any decisions regarding them. This claim has been disputed.

—*Raymond D. Benge, Jr.*

Further Reading

Bergaust, Erik. *Wernher von Braun*. Washington, D.C.: National Space Institute, 1976. A biography of von Braun written by a longtime associate shortly before his death. The book is organized around numerous episodes and issues in von Braun's life.

Bilstein, Roger E. *Stages to Saturn: A Technological History of the Apollo/Saturn Launch Vehicles*. NASA SP-4206. Washington, D.C.: National Aeronautics and Space Administration, 1996. Authoritative, very thorough, and readable description of the entire Saturn project, from first conceptions to the program spin-offs.

Neufeld, Michael J. *Von Braun: Dreamer of Space, Engineer of War*. New York: Alfred A. Knopf, 2007. A biography of von Braun that is very critical of his deals with the Nazi government to secure funding for his work.

Ward, Bob. *Dr. Space: The Life of Wernher von Braun*. Annapolis, Md.: Naval Institute Press, 2005. A biography of von Braun's life and work. Includes several photographs and an extensive bibliography.

See also: Robert H. Goddard; Burt Rutan; Henry Thomas Sampson; Konstantin Tsiolkovsky.

John Moses Browning

American engineer

Browning is history's most successful, prolific, and influential firearms inventor. His groundbreaking inventions established the basic functioning principles used in a wide spectrum of popular and seminal sporting rifles, shotguns, automatic pistols, and machine guns. These principles underlie almost all firearm designs produced and used to this day.

Born: January 21, 1855; Ogden, Utah
Died: November 26, 1926; Liège, Belgium
Primary field: Military technology and weaponry
Primary inventions: Colt .45 automatic pistol; single-shot rifle; gas-operated machine gun

Early Life

John Moses Browning was born in Ogden, Utah, to Jonathan Browning, a self-taught gunsmith and gunmaker from Tennessee. At age twenty-nine, Jonathan had moved to Illinois and converted to the Mormon Church. As a skilled gunsmith and "mechanic," Jonathan was an important contributor to the Mormons' self-sufficiency during their colonization of Utah. Jonathan was also polygamous, fathering twenty-two children with three wives. The eldest child with his second wife was John Moses Browning.

Jonathan was a talented gunmaker and inventor. He designed and built an unusual yet accurate and reliable breach-loading black-powder rifle called the "Harmonica rifle." In addition to gun construction and repair, Jonathan also tinkered with diverse and hopefully money-making projects including tool repair, brick making, and operating a tannery. Besides providing for a large family, dilettantism with projects, and inattention to business details, Jonathan proved to be an indifferent businessman. He did, however, pass on to his sons his tool skills and an understanding of firearms principles. John Moses, for example, constructed his first firearm at age thirteen. During his adolescent years, John did many of the shop's gun and tool repairs while Jonathan tinkered with his current fancy. As a result, at Jonathan's death John was the heir apparent to the family business.

Jonathan died in 1879, the year that John received his first patent. Family tradition claims that this was the upshot of a challenge by Jonathan that John should design a better breach-loading rifle than one then being repaired in the shop. The result was patent number 220,271 for a single-shot rifle that was strong, easy to use, reliable, and accurate. With Jonathan's shop, a patent, his own life savings, and his younger brothers as a workforce, John founded J. M. Browning and Brothers and began to produce the single-shot rifle.

Life's Work

As owner and manager of this new "factory," John discovered that it was difficult to maintain both quality and a profitable production schedule. Browning saw that running a gun-making enterprise was tedious and time-consuming. Browning was saved from these frustrations by the general manager of the Winchester Repeating Arms Company, Thomas Gray Bennett. After seeing one of the single-shot rifles, Bennett traveled in 1883 to Ogden to purchase production rights. As with most of his later designs, Browning sold the rights for a lump sum rather than for royalties, a deal that spared him from production work and made the purchasing company responsible for raising capital, running production, and assuring quality—which relieved Browning from the niggling details that interfered with inventing. Fortuitously, Browning had also just completed a design for a lever-action repeating rifle that was a considerable improvement over the existing Winchester action. Bennett's purchase of this new rifle, manufactured as the Winchester 1886 lever-action repeating rifle, established a relationship in which Browning became the primary designer of Winchester rifles.

Browning's inventions coincided with a revolutionary period in the evolution of firearm designs. The American Civil War had seen the new technology of fixed ammunition become popular, and firearms using fixed ammunition became increasingly common during the 1870's. Fixed ammunition is the combination of a bullet, gunpowder, some kind of primer, and a container as a single unit. Firearms operate by the burning of gunpowder that generates gases that propel the bullet. During this period, most of the fixed ammunition came with a metal case, usually made of brass. Brass was used because it is a soft and flexible metal that can easily stretch under the stress of heat and pressure from the gases generated by the burning gunpowder. The expanded brass forms a tight seal at the breach that prevents gas from spewing back into the shooter's face. This tight seal also results in increased pressures that allow less powder to give smaller projectiles better velocity, accuracy, and impact. Before the creation of fixed ammunition, loading required loose powder to be poured into the barrel through the muzzle, after which the ball or bullet was then seated with a ramrod. The breach was sealed to ensure no leakage of gas, but the end result was a loading and firing process that was slow, cumbersome, and prone to misfires. With reliable fixed ammunition, weapons could be conveniently loaded at the breach, and their spent cases could be rapidly ejected. Thus, fixed ammunition made repeating firearms feasible.

As long as muzzle-loading was the norm, firearm design remained generally stagnant. Once fixed ammunition was introduced, inventors designed systems like the lever action for rapid reloading, followed eventually by actions that were actuated and powered by the same gases used to propel bullets. A significant factor in this firearm development was the introduction in the 1880's of nitrocellulose-based gunpowder called "smokeless powder." Smokeless powder's different burning characteristics—most noticeably a longer and more consistent burn time—enabled designers to create firearms whose actions would be powered by the gases produced as the bullet passed down the barrel. Browning's great fortune was to be born during this time of change, so that he could invent systems like lever actions, pump actions, recoil actions, and gas-operated actions that could harness these new technologies. As a result, he designed 128 separate patents for actions that established the basic principles used in sporting and military firearms used across the world.

While Browning was a hard worker and designer, he did not work alone. His younger brother Matthew and his son John eventually added to some of John's designs both as designers and especially as testers. This was necessary because of John's method of designing. When an idea occurred to him, he immediately roughed out a working model to test. He did not make drawings and plans until he had a working prototype. Field testing of his designs was therefore of considerable importance. Browning created many outstanding designs, but they were optimized for function and not for mass production. Thus, when a company like Winchester purchased a Browning design, they often had to take out patents of their own for modifications to Browning's designs that would facilitate production processes.

Browning designed these operating systems as inspiration struck him, and when he had a working model in hand he would then approach a company to sell them manufacturing rights. Through that method, he eventually came to work with most of America's big arms companies. For a period of twenty years, he sold his creations to Winchester, during which time all of Winchester's new products were Browning designs. Ultimately, to protect its market share and to prevent competitors from getting new Browning actions, Winchester purchased but never produced thirty-four different Browning designs. When, however, in 1902 Winchester refused to buy Browning's new design for an automatic shotgun, Browning severed the relationship and sold the rights for this and other shotgun designs to Remington Arms. In a similar fashion, Browning sold his designs for automatic pistols to Colt's Patent Fire Arms Manufacturing Company and the European company Fabrique Nationale (FN), located in Herstal, Belgium. Browning sold his machine gun designs to Colt. During his life, Browning's patents came so rapidly that at one point he was applying for a new patent about every three months. Nevertheless, few of his designs are thought of as Brownings by users because the production companies sold weapons by their company brand names. Such famous firearms as the Winchester 94 lever-action rifle, the Colt .45 automatic pistol, and the Remington Model 11 shotgun are all Browning designs.

Impact

Browning was an independent inventor who grasped the firearm fundamentals taught by his father and had an intricate knowledge of the inner workings of mechanisms. When these skills were combined with a close attention to firearm principles and an inventive mind, the result was a plethora of firearms inventions. These inventions were focused on practicality and reliability and resulted in some of the best-known firearm designs of the nineteenth and twentieth centuries. Browning's designs included rugged and reliable lever-action rifles and shotguns, pump rifles and shotguns, automatic shotguns, recoil-operated automatic pistols, and machine guns. Among the best-known of Browning's designs is the Winchester 94 lever-action rifle, once touted as America's most popular hunting rifle. Among shotguns, the Remington Model 11 shotgun and superposed shotguns are seen as some of the best shotguns ever created. The Colt .45 automatic pistol, adopted by the U.S. Army, was used until 1985, while the .50-caliber M2 heavy machine gun that was adopted in 1921 and modified in 1932 is still in use. Military aircraft flying from the 1930's through the 1960's used Browning-designed .30- and .50-caliber machine guns and 37mm machine cannons. Because so many of these designs were seminal in nature, most firearms designs to this day derive from the principles identified and harnessed by John Moses Browning.

—*Kevin B. Reid*

The Colt .45 Automatic Pistol

While John Moses Browning's initial designs were focused on turning a principle into a working firearm, the finished products were characteristically simple, robust, reliable, and functional. A good example of this is the Colt .45 automatic pistol, officially known as the "U.S. Pistol, Automatic, Caliber .45, Model of 1911," which is commonly called the Colt Model 1911. The Model 1911 was an improved version of the Colt Model 1900, the first autoloading pistol produced in America.

The Model 1911 used a short-recoil system, in which the barrel and breach travel together a short distance to allow the bullet to pass the muzzle before the breach opens. This process is accomplished with a simple linkage between the barrel and the frame of the pistol. The breach is housed in a slide that moves backward and forward on rails. When a round is fired, the barrel and breach are initially locked together. The force of recoil forces the cartridge case back against the face of the breach. This drives the barrel and slide together for a short distance until the pivoted linkage between the barrel and the frame unlocks and disengages the barrel while the slide continues rearward. During this motion, a simple extractor grabs the empty cartridge case. As the slide continues backward, it compresses a recoil spring, cocks the hammer, and when it stops, ejects the empty cartridge case. Pressure from the recoil spring then pushes the slide forward. As it goes forward, the slide pushes a new round from the magazine into the chamber, the barrel pivots upward, and the breach locks into place. When the trigger is pulled again, the hammer falls, hitting the firing pin to fire the next round and initiate the cycle again. The mechanical elegance of this design is that each action performs multiple tasks.

The design of the Model 1911 coincided with the end of the Philippine-American War, in which U.S. troops faced natives who often continued to fight after sustaining numerous hits from lighter-caliber pistols. As a result, Browning chambered the new pistol for the .45 ACP (automatic Colt pistol) round. By combining a powerful round with a robust frame and a simple operating system, Browning created a weapon that was demonstrably effective and reliable in field conditions. This design was adopted by nations worldwide, including the United States, where it was issued from 1911 to 1985. The essential system used in the Model 1911 was also similar to later Browning automatic pistol designs such as the Browning Hi-Power, manufactured by FN. These two designs have served in armies in almost every Western nation as well as those nations supplied by the Western powers.

Further Reading

Browning, John, and Curt Gentry. *John M. Browning: American Gunmaker*. Garden City, N.Y.: Doubleday, 1964. Biography written by a historian and John Moses Browning's eldest son that offers family reminiscences and details of Browning's personal life combined with an academic understanding of how Browning's inventions shaped the world of small arms. This work also provides a comprehensive list of Browning's important designs.

Iannamico, Frank. *Hard Rain: History of the Browning Machine Guns*. Harmony, Maine: Moose Lake, 2002. A good introduction to the variety of models and modifications of Browning's .30- and .50-caliber machine guns.

Miller, David. *The History of Browning Firearms*. Guilford, Conn.: Lyons Press, 2006. A nicely illustrated introduction to the most significant and popular of Browning's firearm designs. Chapters organized by firearm types provide an understanding of the sheer number and diversity of Browning's designs.

See also: Samuel Colt; Sir James Dewar; Richard Gatling; Hudson Maxim; John T. Thompson.

William Bullock

American machinist

Bullock's invention of the web rotary printing press, with its increased speed of operation and efficiency, revolutionized the printing industry.

Born: 1813; Greenville, Greene County, New York
Died: April 12, 1867; Philadelphia, Pennsylvania
Primary field: Printing
Primary invention: Web rotary printing press

Early Life

William Bullock was born in 1813 and became an orphan at the age of eight when his father died; an older brother took over raising him. Early on, Bullock developed an interest in mechanics, and he spent his spare time reading on the subject. At the age of nineteen, he married Angeline Kimball in Catskill, Greene County, New York, and two years later he had his own business. In 1835, his first child, a son, was born. During this time, Bullock was not only operating his own machine shop but also experimenting with ideas for improving the traditional but tedious methods and equipment still in use in agriculture and construction. His first practicable invention was a shingle-cutting machine. Between 1838 and 1839, he traveled as far as Savannah, Georgia, to market the device, with no success.

Bullock went to New York City looking for more lucrative, satisfying work. His family was growing, with four sons and two daughters born between 1835 and 1847; his first son, however, had died at age two. While working in New York, Bullock designed several devices, most of which were related to agriculture. One was a lathe-cutting machine. Another was a cotton and hay press. Cotton and hay were important crops at that time, and farmers had to transport them over long distances to sell them. To make the crops easier to handle and transport, Bullock designed a press that could compress deseeded cotton and loose, bulky hay into manageable, compact bales, which the machine was also capable of tying together with wire or heavy twine.

Bullock also invented a grain drill, which was awarded a prize from the Franklin Institute of Pennsylvania in 1849. The device had a series of separate round disks that cut little trenches in prepared soil. From its seed hopper, it sent seeds through tubes into the trenches. Spike-toothed drags pulled the soil back into the trenches to cover the seeds. This invention eased the backbreaking labor of planting.

Life's Work

By 1850, Bullock and his family were living in Philadelphia, where he was editor of a newspaper, *The Banner of the Union*. Many of the existing printing presses had a flatbed construction and required considerable time and labor for a fairly limited circulation. Bullock began designing a hand-cranked wooden press, to which he later attached an automatic paper feeder. This device would become a crucial component of his most well-known invention, the web rotary printing press.

After Bullock's wife died in 1850, he moved his family back to Greene County, where he soon married Angeline's sister Emily. In 1853, when he became editor of a Whig Party paper, *The American Eagle*, his wife gave birth to a daughter, the first of six children they had together. Bullock continued to work on improving the printing press. He had an even greater incentive to develop an efficient printing press when the man who printed the Whig paper sold his business to a man who refused to print Bullock's paper. Determined to keep his paper going, Bullock built a wooden flatbed press with a self-feeder and began printing his paper himself.

By 1856, Bullock was ready to move on from Greene County. He sold his newspaper and moved to Brooklyn, New York, in 1857, where his son William was born that year. Bullock continued to work on improvements to his printing press, determined to make a machine that could not only print accurately and rapidly but also self-adjust and automatically feed paper. He sought to design a press that could print on both sides of a paper sheet. In 1858, when he felt that he had perfected certain aspects of his machine, he took out a patent on his automatic paper feeder.

Bullock moved to Pittsburgh in 1860, finally satisfied with his machine, which was called the web rotary printing press. Improving on Richard March Hoe's 1840's rotary press, Bullock designed his press to feed paper automatically instead of by hand, print on both sides of the paper, and cut and fold the sheets. His machine, a markedly improved press that made the printing process faster and less labor-intensive, could print as many as 12,000 sheets per hour. Newspaper publishers were quickly interested in the new press. In 1860, Bullock was called on to design one for the national publication *Frank Leslie's Illustrated Weekly*, and he built a complete working model for the *Cincinnati Times*.

Bullock went to England in 1862 to secure a British patent for his press, which was granted that year. In 1865, he built an improved cylindrical rotary printing press in Philadelphia that used a roll of continuous paper. This machine needed only three workers to operate it. Bullock continued to make modifications to his machines, until they could print as many as 30,000 sheets per hour.

On April 3, 1867, in Philadelphia, Bullock was working on one of his new presses that was to be used to print the *Public Ledger* newspaper, the city's most popular paper. As he was making an adjustment to the machine, he tried to kick one of the motor driving belts onto a pulley, but he miscalculated. His right leg was caught in the mechanism and badly crushed. Before he could be rescued from the machine, he suffered other injuries that

The Web Rotary Printing Press

Of William Bullock's several inventions, his web rotary printing press is by far his most significant and enduring. Though several other men made improvements on the press both before and after Bullock, the innovations he made in the nineteenth century were incorporated into the printing process well into the twentieth century. The printing press of Johann Gutenberg in the fifteenth century set the format for presses until the 1840's, when Richard March Hoe changed from the flatbed to the faster rotary press and used steam power instead of manual labor or the foot treadle to operate the mechanisms.

Bullock improved on Hoe's invention, which, though more advanced than Gutenberg's, still printed only one page at a time using a back-and-forth motion of the type bed. Bullock conceived of a machine that had two pairs of cylinders. Two stereotype (or type) cylinders held the raised letter type; two impression cylinders pressed the paper against the type to print the copy or images. Bullock's early machine moved the sheets of paper on tapes to the impression cylinder, which pressed the paper against the inked type. Later, he devised a way for the paper, in strips measuring five or six linear miles, to be rolled on huge rollers. The paper would pass through a spray to moisten it before printing, and it would be fed into the printing process.

As the type was printed on the roll paper, which was called a web, Bullock fashioned a mechanism that would cut the paper from the continuous roll by using a serrated knife attached to the cylinders. The knife, designed so that it rarely needed sharpening, cut the paper with fast strokes into newspaper page sheets. Once cut, the sheets were moved along by grippers and tapes to be delivered on belts and grabbed by automatic metal fingers as each sheet left the final printing cylinder. The press was also capable of folding the sheets into the final format. The earliest versions of the sheet cutting and delivery system were somewhat unreliable, but Bullock soon ironed out the problems. The improvements he made to his machine soon compelled other printers to use his press.

The increased speed of Bullock's press, its efficient use of the continuous roll of paper, and several other innovative changes he made eliminated the tedious hand-feeding of paper. When the stereotype printing process was invented, the rotary press process became even better. With it, type was produced in a flexible mold made of papier-mâché and could thus be bent to fit around the cylindrical forms that Bullock's press used. As a result, the web rotary printing press made it possible for newspaper publishers to produce more issues at a faster rate at less cost and for greater profit and popularity. Bullock's press was the beginning of the modern-day web-fed newspaper press.

would hamper his recovery. Gangrene developed in his leg, and amputation was considered the only option. He went in for the operation on April 12 and died during the procedure.

Bullock was buried on the North Side in Pittsburgh in the Union Dale Cemetery. Though he did not live long enough to enjoy the fruits of his inventions, he had passed on to a trusted workman and confidant many of his ideas for further improving his printing press. Because of that, modifications continued to be made to his presses, making them some of the most successful machines of the era.

Impact

Bullock's invention of the web rotary printing press marked the beginning of modern newspaper publishing. His machine achieved significant speed, and its automatic paper feeder using a continuous roll did away with the labor-intensive hand-feeding used by previous printing presses. The principles that form the basis of his innovative press were widely adopted for book and newspaper publishing for decades, until the second half of the twentieth century, when the computer caused yet another revolutionary change.

—Jane L. Ball

Further Reading

Harris, Elizabeth M. *Personal Impressions: The Small Printing Press in Nineteenth Century America.* Boston: David R. Godine, 2004. More than one hundred small printing presses and their makers are cataloged, described, and illustrated, giving an overview of the machines and the nineteenth century publishing industry. Useful in providing insight into the era during which Bullock worked.

McClelland, Peter. *Sowing Modernity.* Ithaca, N.Y.: Cornell University Press, 1997. Bullock is briefly discussed in his capacity as inventor of agricultural machines. A useful source on early American agricultural tools and equipment.

Thomas, Isaiah. *The History of Printing in America: With a Biography of Printers and an Account of Newspapers.* 2 vols. Whitefish, Mont.: Kessinger, 2008. Written by a leading early nineteenth century publisher and based on his personal research and knowledge of printers from 1640 to 1800, the book offers an important history of the printing "industry" of which Bullock was part.

See also: Johann Gutenberg; Richard March Hoe; Ottmar Mergenthaler; Jethro Tull; Eli Whitney.

Robert Wilhelm Bunsen

German chemist

Bunsen was involved in devising a laboratory burner that is named for him. Using the Bunsen burner to heat substances, he helped develop a spectroscope for identifying elements. He also discovered new methods to analyze gases and was a pioneer in the area of photochemistry.

Born: March 31, 1811; Göttingen, Kingdom of Westphalia (now in Germany)
Died: August 16, 1899; Heidelberg, Germany
Also known as: Robert Wilhelm Eberhard Bunsen (full name)
Primary field: Chemistry
Primary inventions: Spectroscope; Bunsen burner

Early Life

Robert Wilhelm Bunsen (RAH-burt VIHL-hehlm BUHN-sihn) was born in Göttingen, Kingdom of Westphalia (now in Germany), in 1811. He was the youngest of four sons from the marriage of Augustine Friedericke Gunsell and Christian Bunsen, who was the chief librarian and professor of languages at the University of Göttingen. Robert studied chemistry at Göttingen and received his doctorate at the early age of nineteen.

After graduating, he traveled throughout Europe on a government grant in the early 1830's. He met some of the leading scientists of the time, attended lectures given by prominent chemists, and established friendships and professional contacts that he would later draw upon when his own career became established.

In 1834, Bunsen returned to Göttingen to take a lecturing position at the university. His chemical research involved studying the element arsenic and its compounds, which were foul-smelling and poisonous substances. This was difficult and dangerous work, as the early laboratories had no ventilation fans to remove toxic gases. During this time, Bunsen discovered that an iron oxide compound was an effective antidote for arsenic poisoning.

Bunsen continued to work with dangerous arsenic compounds after he moved to the University of Kassel, in Germany, in 1836. To protect himself from the toxic fumes, he constructed a glass face mask that was attached to a long tube extending out a window for fresh air. Tragedy struck the chemist during an experiment when one of the compounds exploded. It shattered the mask, sending glass slivers into his right eye and blinding him. Bunsen stopped working on these dangerous compounds but was undeterred in his pursuit of scientific knowledge.

Life's Work

As a professor at the German University of Marsburg from 1839 to 1851, Bunsen turned to gas analysis and a study of blast furnaces used to manufacture iron. He was able to demonstrate that the iron ore industries in Germany and England were losing considerable fuel in their waste gases. By following Bunsen's advice, the companies were able to save considerably in their coal usage. He also recommended recycling gases to recover valuable by-products (such as ammonia) that were being lost. Bunsen went on to study other properties of gases such as their specific gravities and their absorption by liquids. On this topic, he would eventually publish his only book, *Gasometrische Methoden*, in 1857.

In 1852, Bunsen replaced the German chemist Leopold Gmelin as chemistry professor at the University of Heidelberg. A new laboratory building was constructed for Bunsen, and facilities included a system for piping coal gas into the building, to be used as fuel for laboratory burners. However, the burners of the day were very inefficient and could not generate high temperatures. They also burned with a yellow luminous flame that produced considerable smoke and soot. Bunsen (along with two coworkers, Peter Desaga, an instrument maker, and Henry Roscoe, a student) designed a more efficient burner consisting of a metal tube attached to a supporting base. A gas inlet at the bottom of the tube allowed the gas in, and holes drilled in the burner's tube allowed the gas and air to mix in just the right proportion before combustion. The result was a nonluminous (pale blue) flame that was cleaner and hotter. A sliding metal cover over the holes allowed the flame to be controlled.

With Bunsen's growing reputation as a fine experimentalist and teacher, the University of Heidelberg attracted the best students in Europe as well as other illustrious scientists of the period. In 1859, Bunsen began collaborating with the Prussian physicist Gustav Kirchhoff.

Robert Wilhelm Bunsen. (Popperfoto/Getty Images)

Bunsen had observed that compounds containing metals gave off specific colors when heated in the hot flame of his Bunsen burner. For example, sodium chloride (ordinary table salt) produced a brilliant yellow colored flame, as did other compounds of sodium. This meant that metals could be detected by studying the flame colors produced when they burned. As a result, Bunsen went on to discover two new elements, the somewhat rare metals cesium and rubidium, in 1861.

A century before Bunsen's work, Sir Isaac Newton had shown that passing white light through a triangular glass prism could separate it into the visible colors seen in a rainbow. Working with Kirchhoff, Bunsen constructed a device that could analyze the light emitted from burning elements. In 1859, the two made a primitive spectroscope and used it to study the light emitted from burning metals in the hot Bunsen burner flame.

When passed through a prism in the spectroscope, the light was broken down into its constitute colors and appeared in the form of a series of lines. The pattern of lines was unique for each element, and Bunsen had found a chemical analysis method to identify elements. This discovery led to a new field of science called spectroscopy.

THE SPECTROSCOPE

Prior to the discovery of the spectroscope, chemical tests were used to identify each of the known chemical elements. As an increasing number of elements were being discovered during the nineteenth century, the spectroscope became a useful tool to quickly characterize elements since each has a unique chemical "fingerprint."

This fingerprint appears in the form of dark lines, representing absorbed light, as well as a series of colored lines from the emitted light when elements or compounds are heated to a high enough temperature. For example, lithium produces a red light, copper is green, and potassium is violet. To the eye, this light appears to be composed of just one or two colors. However, when passed through a prism and focused with a set of lenses, the light emitted from a burning element can be broken down into a series of distinct lines. The existence of these lines had previously been observed in sunlight, but their origin was uncertain.

Robert Wilhelm Bunsen and Gustav Kirchhoff enclosed their device in a box to prevent interference from other sources of light and attached a viewing telescope to see the lines. Their early version of the spectroscope proved to be a satisfactory way to analyze flame colors. The technique proved to be sensitive for very small sample quantities and could detect microgram amounts of many elements. It would later be determined that the line spectra could be related to electron transitions in atoms.

Bunsen also used this technique to study light from the Sun and suggested the instrument could be used to identify the solar composition as well as light from more distant stars. In 1888, the spectroscope was available commercially.

Bunsen's interest in light also led to research in photochemistry, the study of chemical reactions which are initiated on exposure to light. He studied the reaction between the gaseous elements hydrogen and chlorine, and he showed that the extent of reaction depended on the amount of light the mixture was irradiated with. He also had an interest in electricity and developing new batteries. He invented the Bunsen battery in which he replaced expensive platinum electrodes with cheaper carbon and zinc.

In addition to his fine experimental skills, Bunsen was highly regarded as a teacher. He would often spend the entire day in the laboratory working and teaching beside his students. He never married, and his life was centered on his research and his students. Many of them, such as Dimitry Ivanovich Mendeleyev, who is generally credited for organizing the modern periodic table of elements, would themselves go on to become famous. Bunsen died peacefully at the age of eighty-eight.

IMPACT

The Bunsen burner became an important tool in all chemical laboratories. It provided students and researchers with a high-temperature flame needed to perform many new reactions, tests, and analyses. Bunsen's other inventions such as the filter pump, vapor calorimeter, photometer, and effuser were also used as experimental tools. The Bunsen battery helped other scientists in their areas of electrochemical research. With its inexpensive carbon and zinc electrodes, it could be considered an early precursor of the modern alkaline battery.

Although Bunsen is known mostly for the burner named after him, his work on the light emitted from burning elements in a flame led to the development of the spectroscope. This had enormous impact in chemical analysis and the discovery of new elements. Shortly after Bunsen discovered cesium and rubidium, William Crookes of England used the spectroscope to discover the metal thallium. Four other elements, indium, gallium, scandium, and germanium, were subsequently found by this method. In 1868, spectroscopic analysis of the solar spectrum revealed the presence of helium in the Sun, the only element to have been detected on a nonterrestrial body before being discovered on Earth. Studying the light from distant stars became a standard technique for identifying their elemental composition.

The ability to produce colors in the high-temperature flame of a Bunsen burner became an important teaching tool. Detecting and distinguishing metals by their flame colors became a common laboratory exercise in most basic chemistry classes. The aesthetic quality of flame colors was also incorporated into the fireworks and other industries. With various metal compounds mixed with gunpowder, colorful fireworks and skyrockets have delighted crowds around the world. Other applications of elements in colored lights include neon in signs, the yellow glow of sodium vapor used to illuminate highways, and the bright red of strontium in emergency flares.

—*Nicholas C. Thomas*

FURTHER READING

Curtis, Theodor. "Robert Bunsen." In *Great Chemists*, edited by Eduard Farber. New York: Interscience Publishers, 1961. An interesting account of Bunsen's life and his contributions to science.

Farber, Eduard, ed. "Bunsen's Methodological Legacy."

In *Milestones of Modern Chemistry*. New York: Basic Books, 1966. Contains a translation of the initial paper on the spectroscope, Bunsen's collaboration with Kirchhoff, and subsequent element discoveries.

Ihde, Aaron J. *The Development of Modern Chemistry*. New York: Dover, 1984. An account of the development of chemistry, with a description of Bunsen's collaboration with Kirchhoff.

Jensen, William B. "The Origin of the Bunsen Burner." *Journal of Chemical Education* 82 (2005): 518. A short account of Bunsen's discovery, with many references to other earlier articles about Bunsen from the *Journal of Chemical Education*.

Russell, Colin A. "Bunsen Without His Burner." *Physics Education* 34 (1999): 321-326. Describes Bunsen's major contributions in areas such as gas analysis and spectroscopy.

Schwarcz, Joe. "The Man Behind the Burner." *Canadian Chemical News*, p. 10. An easy-to-read account of Bunsen's role in the discovery of the burner.

Weeks, Mary E. *Discovery of the Elements*. Whitefish, Mont.: Kessinger, 2003. A collection of articles published in the *Journal of Chemical Education* telling the story of the discovery of the chemical elements, including several found by Bunsen's spectroscope method.

Williams, Kathryn R. "A Burning Issue." *Journal of Chemical Education* 77 (2000): 258-259. A nice description of Bunsen's involvement in the development of the burner named for him.

See also: Sir William Crookes; Joseph von Fraunhofer; Heike Kamerlingh Onnes; Dimitry Ivanovich Mendeleyev; John Tyndall.

LUTHER BURBANK

American horticulturist and botanist

Not educated as geneticists are today, Burbank considered himself a plant breeder. He made important innovations concerning many garden plants and did pioneer work in the development of the true-breeding species hybrid.

Born: March 7, 1849; Lancaster, Massachusetts
Died: April 11, 1926; Santa Rosa, California
Primary fields: Agriculture; horticulture
Primary inventions: Russet Burbank potato; plant breeding

EARLY LIFE

Luther Burbank was the son of Samuel Walter Burbank, a farmer from Lancaster, Massachusetts, and Olive Burpee, from the same family that produced the well-known seed grower W. Atlee Burpee. Olive also loved gardening and was skilled at making things grow. Luther was a small, slightly built boy who preferred reading to physically demanding activities, although he did enjoy ice skating. As a young boy, he developed his interest in plant breeding from watching his older brother George grafting apple trees. Shy and reticent, Luther showed his penchant for invention at the age of sixteen when he made a wall clock and also a set of dumbbells for his high school gymnasium.

After his elementary schooling, Burbank entered Lancaster Academy in the fall of 1864. The academy was

Luther Burbank. (Library of Congress)

THE RUSSET BURBANK POTATO

Luther Burbank worked before the period in which horticultural discoveries could be patented. Therefore, the patents awarded him after his death do not describe his procedures in detail, nor do the field notes that he made give the kind of details that facilitate a step-by-step explanation of his breeding practices. One of his most famous discoveries came very early in his career, while he was still working in Massachusetts. His development of the potato that came to be known as the Russet Burbank exemplifies his characteristic way of working. His aim here, as generally, was down-to-earth production of improved plants that served to nourish humans and satisfy their desires for beauty.

As he admitted, his work on the potato involved a stroke of good fortune. Growers of potatoes knew that potatoes, which are normally propagated by planting the "eyes" that grow on the tubers at some point after they are harvested, sometimes will generate seed pods on the potato skin. This development is quite rare, however, and the seed pod that Burbank found on an Early Rose potato was the first and only one that he ever encountered. The Burbank potato owed its existence to this rare development. What separated him from all the farmers who had witnessed seed pods on potatoes was his careful application of Darwinian theory, his curiosity, and his intuition.

From this pod he carefully raised twenty-three seedlings; from the most flourishing of these, he grew what came to be called the Burbank potato. He gathered twenty-three of these small seedlings and isolated the best ones, and the potato that came to be called the Russet Burbank was a "sport," or unusual deviation, from one seedling—one that in this case grew unusually well. Because Burbank understood the process of natural selection as elaborated by Charles Darwin, he knew how to proceed. The forces of nature would sometimes isolate, and thus create the opportunity for, favorable variations in the offspring of living plants and animals. Burbank could do this in his garden because he could anticipate this modification of offspring. As Burbank often noted, it was not simply recognizing the possibility of how a better potato or other plant might be produced but a long process of tending the improved version through successive generations thereafter that brought about success.

The Burbank potato became a principal crop in Idaho and now is often called the Idaho potato. It is difficult to determine which is the most popular variety of potato today, but this one certainly remains one of the most popular and has been found particularly well suited to one of America's favorite food items: French fries. The russet potato—like many other fruits, vegetables, and flowers developed by Burbank—remains a great favorite many decades after his death.

regarded as a preparatory school for universities such as Harvard and Yale, but Luther completed only four years of the five-year program and did not attend college. To a large extent, he educated himself. His favorite authors were Charles Darwin, Henry David Thoreau, and Alexander von Humboldt. He referred to these three as his "book influences." The book that intrigued him most was Darwin's *The Variation of Animals and Plants Under Domestication* (1868).

A short period of medical studies under a local doctor did not satisfy him, but he yearned for the opportunity to grow plants. He was able to purchase a seventeen-acre field in the local area in 1871. It had unusually fine soil for New England, and he soon began truck gardening. At this point, he undertook this profession less as a business than as an opportunity to make experiments in the culture of plants.

LIFE'S WORK

Like many other gardeners, Burbank observed that plants even in the same row grow differently, some being clearly superior to others. Grasping the importance of Darwinian thought and applying it to plant breeding, he began to stimulate modifications that nature might or might not bring about over centuries. Although Burbank's seventeen acres were very good land for New England, Burbank knew that California provided far greater opportunities for a plant breeder. In 1875, when he was only twenty-six, he moved to Santa Rosa, California, a place he described as "the chosen spot of all this earth." In California he could generate throughout the year the conditions that would allow him to make improvements to many varieties of plants.

Burbank's early and famous work on the russet potato is discussed in the accompanying sidebar. He spent much of his time and patience on fruits and flowers. His aim was to improve plants by applying the principles of natural selection and to achieve new varieties by grafting and crossing plants that he acquired from sources both domestic and foreign. He claimed that he could conduct as many as three thousand experiments at one time and that from the tens of thousands of varieties that he crossbred, hundreds were successful. He was credited with over eight hundred new varieties of plants.

One of his favorite trees was the plum tree. In the 1880's, he gathered plum seedlings from Japan and many from European and American sources. The varieties that he developed include the Wickson, Golden, and Satsuma, the last based on a Japanese plum. He developed one variety of plum without pits. Working with many sweet plums that were particularly suitable for drying into prunes, he greatly extended the making of prunes. He crossed plums and apricots and developed the plumcot tree.

Berries were another special interest. Burbank made many crosses of raspberries, blackberries, and dewberries over several decades to combine the virtues of each. He summed up this work in an eight-volume work on small fruits in 1921. Among his most celebrated flowers is the Shasta daisy, which he developed by crossing American and European varieties of field daisies and crossing the resulting hybrid with a Japanese daisy. One of his unusual inventions that exemplified the practical nature of his work is a thornless cactus, produced as food for cattle on desert ranges with limited vegetation.

At a 1909 meeting of the American Breeders' Association, Burbank spoke on "Another Mode of Species Forming," a rather vague title that set forth ideas on "the true-breeding species hybrid" that was little understood by breeders at the time. He emphasized not the mere crossing and selection but what he called "the real work" of sustained attention to successive generations of plants.

Aside from his lack of a scientific background, Burbank was faulted by his critics for several of his practices. He failed to report his activities to horticultural or scientific meetings, and he did not submit articles to scientific journals for publication. He did not describe his plants in a scientific way with proper Latin designations but in the manner of a nurseryman writing for the general public. He was criticized for his self-promotion and his sometimes exaggerated claims concerning his accomplishments. He could be careless with numbers, once referring to having planted four thousand *varieties* of seedling potato when he had actually planted that number of *individuals*. He enjoyed the fame that he achieved and did not bother to correct the misleading information of the sort that often circulates when people of limited knowledge recount the achievements in complicated fields of endeavor.

He disappointed his customers also, who sometimes could not approximate in their gardens the results that he obtained in Santa Rosa, his optimum "chosen spot." Generally, however, his perseverance over a career that lasted fifty-five years resulted in improved fruits and flowers that have remained favorites with gardeners throughout the world.

Burbank was a private man and stubbornly resisted visitors when he was working. He married twice, to Helen Coleman in 1890 (that marriage ending in divorce six years later), and to Elizabeth Waters in 1916. She survived him. He had no children with either of his wives.

Impact

The impact of Burbank's work has been substantial. His enormous popularity aroused jealousy among his compatriots, most of whom had professional training far beyond his own. He began his work before genetics became a recognized science, but long before his career was over he alienated scientifically trained geneticists, whose harsh assessments were sometimes justified. There is no doubt that with more training he would have understood why his unsuccessful attempts, such as his inability to produce a yellow sweet corn, were failures. Although he did not lie about his achievements, he tended to exaggerate them. He certainly was not what many people believed him to be: the plant breeder of all plant breeders.

On the other hand, the institutions that were formed in his name, the Luther Burbank Press, which published his writings, and the Luther Burbank Company, which sold his products, were important influences on his profession. These successes made scientists realize that organizations could be formed to promote biological advances and legislatures and foundations enlisted. For ordinary consumers, Burbank's name was magical. People who recognized horticultural contributions would be more inclined to support such endeavors. Specifically, his work on tree breeding encouraged the U.S. Department of Agriculture to enter into the improvement of forest trees. The general public, unconcerned about how "unscientific" he was, appreciated the plants that he developed.

—Robert P. Ellis

Further Reading

Beeson, Emma Burbank. *The Early Life and Letters of Luther Burbank*. San Francisco: Harr Wagner, 1927. Shortly after Burbank's death, his sister produced this important source of information about the development of Burbank's career.

Brown, Jack, and Peter Caligari. *An Introduction to Plant Breeding*. Ames, Iowa: Blackwell, 2008. Comprehensively presents the activity that Burbank was practicing during most of his working time. It is highly recommended for people wishing to study or research plant breeding.

Burbank, Luther. *Luther Burbank: His Methods and Discoveries and Their Practical Application*. New York: Luther Burbank Press, 1914-1915. Contains the author's field notes, which are the closest the reader can come to studying his work systematically.

Dreyer, Peter. *A Gardener Touched with Genius: The Life of Luther Burbank.* New York: Coward, McCann & Geoghegan, 1975. Dreyer's book credits Burbank's successes but does not hesitate to acknowledge his shortcomings.

Howard, Walter Lafayette. *Luther Burbank: A Victim of Hero Worship.* New York: Stechert, 1945. As far back as 1945 it was possible for Howard to show how Burbank was in a sense undone by the enormous acclaim that many critics regarded as unjustified. Geneticists and plant breeders eventually began to cease even mentioning him in their publications.

Kraft, Ken. *Luther Burbank: The Wizard and the Man.* New York: Meredith Books, 1967. The author was able to spend much time in Santa Rosa, California, where Burbank spent most of his working life, interviewing people who knew Burbank.

Tornqvist, Carl-Erik. *Plant Genetics.* New York: Chelsea House, 2006. The work that Burbank did is now performed by geneticists. This book does not mention Burbank but clearly presents geneticists's methods with plants.

See also: George Washington Carver; Joseph Monier; Jethro Tull.

William Seward Burroughs

American bank clerk

Burroughs invented, produced, and sold the first practical adding machine. It was the first key-operated calculator that printed entries and sums. His work also led to the creation of a company that became the market leader for decades.

Born: January 28, 1855; Auburn, New York
Died: September 15, 1898; Citronelle, Alabama
Primary field: Business management
Primary invention: Adding machine

Early Life

William Seward Burroughs was born in Auburn, New York, on January 28, 1855. His father, Edmund Burroughs, was a machinist, inventor, and tool manufacturer. During his childhood, William tinkered in his father's machine shop. At the age of fifteen, William began working as a bank clerk. Many historical accounts tell of the young Burroughs's long, tedious days of calculation at his job, which he held for several years. However, records show that he also worked as postal clerk, box maker, and planer in Auburn. Burroughs himself told such tales in early interviews. It is probable that this story would have helped sell machines to what he saw as the primary market—banks.

In the late 1870's, Edmund Burroughs moved to St. Louis. William had been urged to move to a warmer climate, and he followed his father with his family in 1882. William had married Ida Selover in 1879, and they eventually had four children. Their grandson, William S. Burroughs, became the famous Beat writer. After moving to St. Louis, William worked various jobs that gave him experience in manufacturing. He invented various items, including a folding chicken coop, before concentrating on designing an adding machine.

Life's Work

In St. Louis, Burroughs worked for a time in his father's machine shop, where he met many inventors, including possibly Frank Stephen Baldwin, who had invented a calculator mechanism (1872), which Burroughs may have seen. Burroughs's goals for his machine were to speed up the process of calculation, make it more accurate, and to provide a written, or permanent, record of financial transactions. His original idea was for a large desktop machine, but he also wanted to automate an accounting clerk's function.

Burroughs went through many ups and downs while he worked on his machine, sometimes having to interrupt his work to earn money another way. His health suffered at times, as he worked late into the night and often into the early morning. Burroughs eventually met some St. Louis businessmen who were interested in his ideas for the adding machine. In 1884, Thomas Metcalfe and Richard M. Scruggs of the St. Louis dry goods firm Scruggs, Vandervoort, and Barney invested in Burroughs's project. Burroughs used the funds to rent bench space in the workshop of Joseph Boyer, an inventor.

Burroughs built his first machine that year and filed for a patent in 1885. His patents were the first in what would become a common patent class of the "adding and listing machine." Burroughs's first machine printed only the final totals and not the numbers entered. In 1886, he filed another patent for a machine that printed both the numbers entered and the results. Both patents were granted on the same day in 1888. In the meantime, Burroughs, Metcalfe, Scruggs, and St. Louis merchant William Pye organized the American Arithmometer Company.

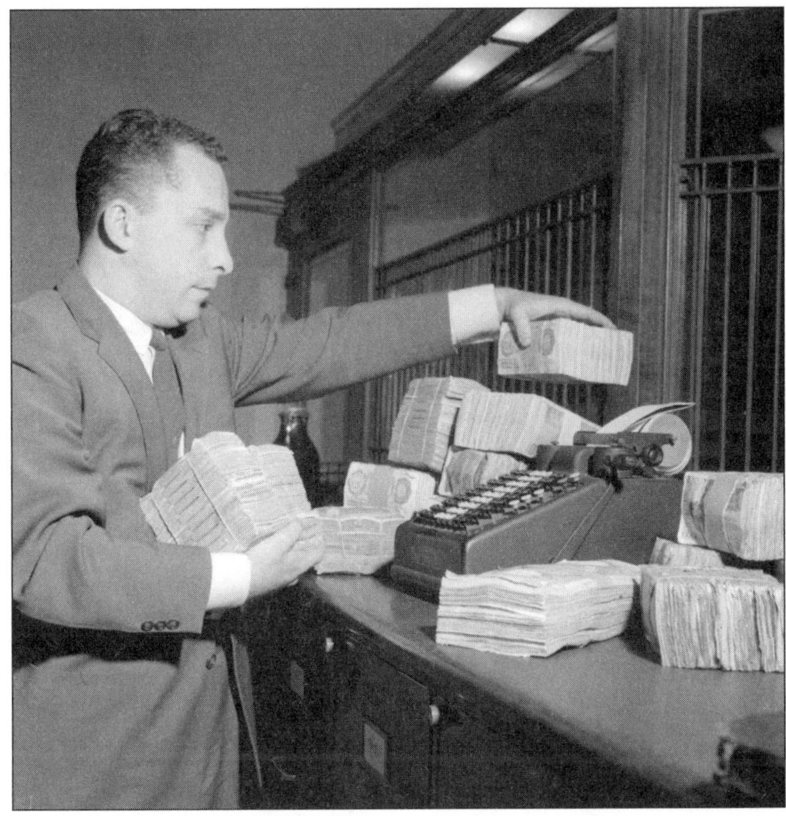
A man uses a Burroughs adding machine to count currency in 1956. (Getty Images)

Burroughs's backers may have pressured him to rush the machines to market, and the devices did not hold up well under daily use. These machines proved impractical. The force with which the operator pulled the handle on the machine could change the results. Burroughs reportedly took this first set of defective machines and threw them out the storeroom window. Within a short period of time, he had discovered the answer to the problem. He used a dashpot, which allowed the machine to operate smoothly even if the operator improperly used the handle. In 1892, Burroughs was granted a patent for the first fully functional, reliable, and practical adding machine. Large-scale production of the machines began, and his company ordered one hundred machines to be produced by the Boyer Machine Company—the same company from whom Burroughs rented shop space. The American Arithmometer Company took over production in 1895.

Burroughs championed the use of fully interchangeable parts, which sped up production and made repairs easier for mechanics in the field. The demand for these types of commercial machines was spurred by a growing economy and increasingly large businesses in the late nineteenth century. The Industrial Revolution had made the mass production of these machines possible.

The Burroughs Registering Accountant, as the adding machine became known, was widely successful, particularly in banking and insurance offices. It far outsold every other calculator on the market. The machine allowed clerks to add numbers much faster and more accurately than hand calculation. A lesser-paid clerk with an adding machine could do more and better work than a better-paid clerk calculating by hand.

Because of his continual health problems, Burroughs retired in 1897. The next year, he died from tuberculosis. By the time of his death, more than one thousand of his machines had been sold. Burroughs had shown not only the technical skill to design and build his adding machine but also the skill to manufacture and market it. Though he produced and sold machines in both the United States and Great Britain, he died before he could witness the full impact of his machine. In 1904, the American Arithmometer Company moved from St. Louis to Detroit. The company changed its name to Burroughs Adding Machine Company in 1905. By 1926, more than one million machines had been sold.

Impact

Burroughs's machine was the first to combine the printing of totals and the printing of entries. Each function had appeared separately in patents, but not together. His was the most important and most popular of the several adding machines that came onto the market in the late nineteenth century. These early machines had to meet and beat the standards set by companies that had hired men trained as rapid "human calculators." Once the machines were available and proved that they could perform more accurately and faster than these employees, companies began to hire less well-trained, and thus less costly, workers.

With Burroughs's machines, companies could certainly perform calculations more quickly and keep records more current. However, the machines also allowed companies to do things they had not been able to do before because of sheer volume and the lack of cost-effectiveness. Insurance companies could create and maintain more and better charts, statistics, and records. The railroad industry could monitor its vast and growing operations. The machines also led to better bookkeeping practices with current, accurate, and more permanent records.

Burroughs was an inventor-entrepreneur who built the foundation for a strong company that far outlived him and dominated the market. The Burroughs Adding Machine Company continued to improve his design after his death, but his fundamental design remained the basis for decades. All the key mechanical innovations were patented before 1900. Burroughs's machine was the first to include both a keyboard (for entries) and a printer (for results) and that was reliable and practical for use in business. His company was a founding member of the office equipment industry. The company, renamed the Burroughs Corporation in 1953, typified the technology, practices, and marketing of the industry. Burroughs Corporation managed to survive and even thrive despite heavy competition, and it was the only adding machine company to successfully transition into the computer age.

—*Linda Eikmeier Endersby*

The Adding and Listing Machine

The patent for the Burroughs Registering Accountant was granted in 1892. It became one of the most popular and well marketed of the adding machines. The success of the machine depended on not only the mechanical aspect but also the sales aspect. While the early Burroughs machines were simply encased in wooden boxes, later ones were partially encased in glass. The latter kind enabled salesmen to show the machine's inner workings and impress potential buyers with the mechanics. Salesmen trained buyers how best to use the machine, including changes in bookkeeping practices that would take advantage of the machine's mechanics.

The machine featured keys used to set digits and a crank that, when pulled, entered the numbers. The keyboard had nine rows of keys, one for each digit (1-9). Numbers were entered by pushing one digit in each column. A zero was represented by no keys pressed down in a column. After pressing down the keys, the operator pulled the crank forward, which caused the entry to print. Releasing the crank added the number to those already entered.

The machine printed by feeding paper from a roll between type and a printing roll (similar to a modern typewriter). An ink ribbon was interposed between the type and the paper. The type then pressed against ribbon, paper, and printing roll and produced an imprint.

The machine had several safeguards against improper operator usage. For example, it had a "locked keyboard," which froze if an operator tried to push two keys in the same column. When a key was pressed, it stayed down so that the operator could verify the entry before pulling the handle on the side of the machine. The dashpot, or governor, was a cylinder partially filled with oil that worked up and down on a plunger. Whatever the force of the pull, the dashpot moderated it before it reached the calculating mechanism. The dashpot smoothed the machine's operations even with improper usage by the operator.

The Burroughs Adding Machine Company (later Burroughs Corporation) produced several machines with more advanced features after William Seward Burroughs's death. These enhancements included electrification and adding an additional adding mechanism. However, the machines were based on Burroughs's fundamental design; all the major innovations in the adding machine field had been made before 1900.

Further Reading

Coleman, John S. *The Business Machine, with Mention of William Seward Burroughs, Joseph Boyer, and Others, Since 1880*. New York: Newcomen Society in North America, 1949. Interesting and dramatic account of Burroughs and his machine. Focuses on mechanical and commercial rather than personal details. Illustrations.

Cortada, James W. *Before the Computer: IBM, NCR, Burroughs, and Remington Rand and the Industry They Created, 1865-1956*. Princeton, N.J.: Princeton University Press, 1993. Focuses on later history of the Burroughs Corporation. Provides some details on Burroughs's work as well as the long-term impact of his work. Illustrations, notes, tables, index.

Ifrah, Georges. *The Universal History of Computing: From the Abacus to the Quantum Computer*. New York: John Wiley & Sons, 2001. Short section on the

Burroughs machine. Provides an overview of the historical context in which Burroughs worked. Illustrations, references, bibliography, index.

Kidwell, Peggy Aldrich. "The Adding Machine Fraternity at St. Louis: Creating a Center of Invention, 1880-1920." *IEEE Annals of the History of Computing* 22, no. 2 (2000): 4-21. Provides information on Burroughs as well as the historical context in which he invented the first practical adding machine. Details on several other inventors in the St. Louis area who contributed to the development of the commercial adding machine industry. Illustrations, references.

Martin, Ernst. *The Calculating Machines: Their History and Development.* Translated and edited by Peggy Aldrich Kidwell and Michael R. Williams. Cambridge, Mass.: MIT Press, 1992. Detailed description of the workings of the Burroughs machine and others of the same era. Some information on Burroughs's life. Illustrations, index.

Turck, J. A. V. *The Origin of Modern Calculating Machines: A Chronicle of the Evolution of the Principles That Form the Generic Make-up of the Modern Calculating Machine.* Chicago: Western Society of Engineers, 1921. While dated to some extent, this book provides detailed technical discussion of Burroughs's patents and machines and gives historical context by describing other machines of the era. Illustrations, subject index.

See also: Ted Hoff; Herman Hollerith; Jack St. Clair Kilby; John William Mauchly; Konrad Zuse.

David Bushnell

American engineer

During the Revolutionary War, Bushnell designed and built the first attack submarine in the history of warfare. While it failed in its original objective against the British navy, it would have a significant impact on submarine technology.

Born: August 30, 1742; Saybrook, Connecticut
Died: 1824; Warrenton, Georgia
Also known as: David Bush
Primary fields: Military technology and weaponry; naval engineering
Primary invention: Bushnell's submarine

Early Life

David Bushnell was born and raised on a farm near the town of Saybrook, Connecticut. His Bushnell ancestors had emigrated from England in 1639, just over a century before he was born. Between chores on his father's hardscrabble land, young Bushnell read voraciously about all kinds of gadgets and how they worked. Construction techniques also fascinated him. He hoped to deepen his understanding of science and technology at nearby Yale College (later Yale University), but lack of funds made this unattainable until he inherited a modest bequest upon his father's death.

When Bushnell finally reached the Yale campus in 1771, he was, at the age of thirty-one, by far the oldest in his class. He excelled in science and mathematics to the extent that his science professor allowed him to conduct unsupervised experiments. Bushnell had become intrigued by gunpowder for its potential military uses at a time when relations between the American colonies and the British mother country were coming under increasing strain. Finally, after many attempts, Bushnell managed to detonate underwater two pounds of gunpowder sealed in a wooden keg and detonated by a waterproof fuse. Bushnell had next to find the best means for deploying this weapon, as necessary, against the British navy.

In early 1775, Bushnell's senior year, the intensifying dispute between the colonies and England had come to flashpoint with skirmishes at Lexington and Concord in Massachusetts. Alienated by British taxation policies and by arbitrary interventions in colonial affairs, local militias were mobilized and mounted a full rebellion against their British rulers.

Life's Work

Immediately following graduation in June, 1775, Bushnell returned to the family homestead in Saybrook. Over the next year, he built and tested at his own expense a small submarine that he had designed while still at Yale. He found locally most of what he needed. Most important, he began with two large slabs cut from the trunk of an oak tree. Craftsmen then hollowed out these pieces and trimmed them to match like mirror images. They were then fitted together and sealed with tar along the seam where they came together. A band of iron was

David Bushnell's Turtle, *the first attack submarine.* (NOAA)

nailed to the seam to complete the waterproofing of the craft. The result was an oval-shaped wooden cockpit or cabin that Bushnell dubbed the *Turtle* because of its resemblance to two fused tortoise shells standing on end.

The *Turtle*'s cabin measured a little over seven feet long, six feet high, and three and a half feet wide at the middle. These dimensions allowed barely enough room for one operator, who entered through a small hatch at the top of the cabin. He sat on a wooden beam facing a whole array of devices such as valves, peddles, pumps, and shafts necessary to run the submarine. Fixed outside on the submarine's back was a wooden keg with a capacity of up to 150 pounds of gunpowder. By the summer of 1776, the *Turtle* was fully tested and ready. The American military commander George Washington had learned of Bushnell's secret project and authorized its use against the British fleet that was blockading New York harbor.

American forces defending New York City were surrounded by a veteran British army supported by warships anchored nearby. Naval cannons from the harbor regularly raked the American positions. British strategy was to take New York City and overrun the Hudson River Valley, which would split the American colonies in two. General Washington wanted the *Turtle* to disrupt the blockade of New York harbor by harassing the enemy fleet.

The *Turtle* was secretly ferried down the Connecticut River from Saybrook and poised for a strike at the British ships. However, on the eve of the attack, in August, 1775, David's brother, Ezra, fell ill with a high fever and was incapacitated for several weeks. The submarine was withdrawn, pending the training of a substitute pilot. David Bushnell himself lacked the physical strength to operate it.

A replacement named Ezra Lee was found and given accelerated training. By the evening of September 6, 1776, the *Turtle*, piloted by Lee, departed Manhattan Island and made its way slowly toward the enemy fleet. Using a pedal to work a propeller, Lee peddled the *Turtle* slowly toward its target, the HMS *Eagle*, the flagship of the fleet. The *Eagle* was a formidable frigate with its sixty-four guns pointed in all directions. To sink or damage it would have been a severe blow to British morale.

Half-submerged, the *Turtle* approached the *Eagle* while carefully observing it through a small conning tower. Lee then fully submerged by taking on water by means of a foot valve. Next, he maneuvered and stabilized the *Turtle* under the *Eagle*'s hull by using a horizontal propeller with one hand while steering with the other. A long, wood screw located outside at the top of the submarine was to drill a hole in the *Eagle*'s hull by turning into it. The 150-pound keg of gunpowder on the back of the submarine would then be drawn to the *Eagle* by an attached rope. The charge was to be fixed in the drill hole, and the rope would automatically draw the explosive container until it rested hard against the hull. An improvised clockwork timer would be set to detonate a fuse to the gunpowder once the *Turtle* was well clear of the ship.

The operation worked as planned until it came to drilling the hole. Unknown to Bushnell, the *Eagle*'s hull had a reinforcing iron bar at the point where the wood drill tried to penetrate. After several maneuvers to find vulnerable places on the hull, Ezra Lee, exhausted from his long ordeal, aborted the mission as dawn approached and headed back to shore. En route, he jettisoned the keg of gunpowder that exploded harmlessly in the bay.

Subsequently, Bushnell attempted two other attacks, neither of them successful. The failures were not due to the submarine's performance but related mostly to poor judgment and simply bad luck. Bushnell spent the rest of the war designing improved sea mines. His life after the war is something of a mystery, as he disappeared. As became clear only after his death in 1824, Bushnell had gone to rural Georgia, changed his name to David Bush, and lived out his days as a schoolteacher and physician. He never married.

Impact

The *Turtle* was far more than a curious fantasy of an eccentric and secretive tinkerer. Bushnell built a fully functioning submarine replete with ingenious devices and capable of delivering a lethal charge of explosives to seaborne targets. Due to Bushnell's work as an American patriot during the Revolutionary War, the "water machine" became more widely recognized as a potentially deadly new weapon of naval warfare.

Bushnell was an innovator. He was the first, for example, to successfully use pumps to fill empty ballast tanks, which allowed the submarine to submerge and resurface. This principle is still in use today, as is his idea of the screw propeller to guide the submarine. Also of significance was Bushnell's discovery of how to make waterproof powder kegs that could be detonated with a waterproof fuse either on or under the water. Here can be found the genesis of the sea mine or torpedo so well known in modern naval operations. Finally, Bushnell is credited with constructing the first documented example of a submarine actually used for combat operations. Robert Fulton's celebrated *Nautilus* submarine, completed in 1801, sported a conning tower, screw propellers for propulsion, and a procedure for detonating explosives against ships' hulls.

Frequent descriptions of Bushnell as the "father of submarine warfare" need qualification. Many of his ideas and techniques regarding the submarine came from European sources. Nonetheless, Bushnell skillfully adapted these materials to his own purposes. He was an innovator in several respects as well as a transmitter of submarine lore to future generations.

Bushnell's lack of success in his time has been described as a kind of "fertile failure" in that what he achieved would resonate. Despite the vast differences between the submarine technology of the eighteenth cen-

Bushnell's Submarine

David Bushnell left no drawings of his design of the *Turtle*, but many details have been reconstructed from a long letter he sent Thomas Jefferson in 1787 regarding his submarine. There are also contemporary accounts by others and a number of physical reconstructions of it over the years by naval buffs.

The *Turtle* was operated almost completely by the hands and feet of the pilot. Working the propellers alone over any distance required a strength and stamina that the rather frail Bushnell did not have. Aboard the craft itself, there were so many different tasks to be performed, sometimes simultaneously, that the pilot often needed the dexterity and concentration of a kind of one-man band.

The *Turtle* was driven through the water by two hand-cranked screw propellers. One was for vertical movement when the vessel was submerged, the other for movement forward, either on or below the surface. The forward propeller was supplemented by a rudder and tiller. Each propeller, vertical and horizontal, had a set of four blades, two on each side. They resembled the blades of a windmill and functioned like oars in the water. There might also have been a foot treadle to peddle the craft, similar to the action of a spinning wheel. The submarine had a top speed of four knots.

The second system essential to the *Turtle*'s operation involved the use of pumps, valves, and air vents. The submarine submerged by drawing water into the cabin, and it ascended by pumping the water out with two hand pumps. The amount of water let in determined how deep the craft could go—about twenty feet being the maximum. A cork barometer devised by Bushnell registered the depth at any point.

During the process of submersion, water must at times have reached almost to the knees of the pilot seated on his bench. Foot-operated valves and water pumps located at the lower front and back of the cabin were designed to drain the water out when it was time to resurface. In an emergency, a ballast of two hundred pounds of sand at the bottom of the cabin could be released. Finally, the *Turtle* had an air supply of thirty minutes maximum. It could be replenished by surfacing far enough to allow a snorkel-like device at the top of the cabin to take in air through three small sealable air vents.

Such features, along with others noted earlier, combine to make the *Turtle* a remarkable achievement and a benchmark event in the history of submarines.

tury and that of the present, with its nuclear-powered submarines and their nuclear missiles, there is still a sense in which modern submarines remain lineal descendants of the *Turtle*.

—*Donald D. Sullivan*

FURTHER READING

Diamant, Lincoln. *Dive! The Story of David Bushnell and His Remarkable 1776 Submarine (and Torpedo)*. Fleischmanns, N.Y.: Purple Mountain Press, 2003. A brief but lively overview of the *Turtle* episode. Especially effective in the use of direct quotes and contemporary documents relating to the event. Illustrations, bibliography.

Lefkowitz, Arthur S. *Bushnell's Submarine: The Best Kept Secret of the American Revolution*. New York: Scholastic, 2006. Written with a "you-are-there" sense of immediacy. Occasional one-page side discussions on related topics add a valuable dimension. Illustrations, index.

Parrish, Thomas. *The Submarine: A History*. New York: Viking Press, 2004. One of the best general histories of submarines to date. Traces the transformation of the submarine from a kind of exotic curiosity (Bushnell's *Turtle* in 1776) to the nuclear submarine of 2000, a core element of modern naval warfare. Illustrations, bibliography, index.

Roland, Alex. *Underwater Warfare in the Age of Sail*. Bloomington: Indiana University Press, 1978. Traces the history of the submarine from the early seventeenth to the later nineteenth centuries, including the U.S. Civil War. Chapters 6 and 7 relate Bushnell's achievement to the broader history of submarine technology and warfare. Disputes the originality of Bushnell's submarine. Illustrations, bibliography, index.

Wagner, Frederick. *Submarine Fighter of the American Revolution: The Story of David Bushnell*. New York: Dodd, Mead, 1963. Still the only full-scale scholarly biography of Bushnell. Efficiently builds suspense toward the climactic event of the *Turtle*'s attack on the English flagship. Illustrations, bibliography.

See also: Robert Fulton; John Philip Holland.

NOLAN K. BUSHNELL

American electrical engineer

As the cofounder of Atari and a leading developer of some of the earliest interactive video games, Bushnell is widely considered to be the "father of the video game industry."

Born: February 5, 1943; Clearfield, Utah
Also known as: Nolan Kay Bushnell (full name)
Primary field: Electronics and electrical engineering
Primary invention: *Pong*

EARLY LIFE

Born to a Mormon family in Clearfield, Utah, Nolan Kay Bushnell had a well-rounded childhood. He enjoyed science, especially electronics, as well as debating, and sometimes used gadgetry to play practical jokes on classmates and neighbors. At age fifteen, after his father died, Bushnell took charge of some of his father's uncompleted cement construction projects. Entering the University of Utah in 1962, Bushnell participated in many school activities, and he discovered that the university possessed a computer, which was rare at that time. Although he was an undergraduate engineering student, he befriended some advanced computer science students and was allowed to work with the school's computer, one of the few computers with a monitor screen. One of their favorite pastimes was playing *Spacewar!*, considered to be the first computer game, written by Steve Russell and other scientists at the Massachusetts Institute of Technology (MIT). The game was known primarily in academic circles, especially among students who had access to the expensive computers at their respective research institutes and labs. Bushnell also learned to program in FORTRAN and other languages.

In the evenings while attending college, Bushnell worked at an amusement park not far from Salt Lake City. He made a connection between this experience of entertainment as a business and the esoteric game that he and his classmates loved so much. At this time, computers were completely beyond the reach of consumers, but Bushnell already envisioned a product that might someday bridge the gap between the multimillion-dollar lab computers at the university and the electromechanical arcade games (such as pinball) that were already a familiar part of popular culture. Bushnell, who admired the Walt Disney Company's creative use of technology, had hoped to work for the company. After graduating, however, he was hired as a research engineer by Ampex, an electronics company in California.

At Ampex, Bushnell met another engineer, Ted Dabney, who shared his interests. They decided to make a coin-operated game using parts available to them through Ampex and other sources. Their game, *Computer Space*, was essentially derived from *Spacewar!* but modified to run on dedicated hardware assemblies. Bushnell and Dabney left Ampex and sold the game to Nutting Associates, a manufacturer of coin-operated arcade game machines. Nutting went into production with *Computer Space*, and many units were constructed. However, Nutting did not present the game to an appropriately sophisticated audience; average consumers found that it was too difficult to learn. Bushnell and Dabney grew frustrated with Nutting and decided to form their own company.

Life's Work

Bushnell and Dabney initially named their company "Syzygy," using an astronomical term, but in 1972, soon after parting ways with Nutting, they registered the name Atari. In the traditional Japanese game *go*, one of Bushnell's favorite games, the expression "atari" is used when a player has his opponent's pieces surrounded. To help fund their new enterprise, which they started with only $500, Bushnell and Dabney repaired pinball machines and other arcade games, thus maintaining contact with a group of potential customers for their new technology. Having observed Nutting's experience with the marketing of *Computer Space*, Bushnell decided to make a game that would be easy enough for beginners to enjoy. One of the first new employees hired by Bushnell and Dabney was Al Alcorn, another engineer who had worked at Ampex. To give him experience in designing dedicated transistor-to-transistor logic devices, Bushnell asked Alcorn to make a simple ball-and-paddle game. Although the assignment was originally intended as a kind of exercise, Alcorn took the assignment very seriously. As the new device took shape, Bushnell recognized its potential, and the team added additional features. The resulting product was named *Pong*, and it became an immediate success. Bushnell decided that Atari would do the manufacturing as well as the design.

To meet the demand for *Pong*, Bushnell expanded Atari's facilities. Because the game's logic structure was revealed visually by the physical connections between its components, many competitors created their own versions. Although the market was soon flooded with imitations, Atari created variations of *Pong* and eventually created new games based on similar technologies. *Space Race*, the company's next game, was released in 1973 and quickly copied by Midway. The frenzied accelerating corporate competition, with innovation followed by imitation, resembled the accelerating pace of the games themselves. As Atari expanded, Bushnell and his young employees maintained a casual atmosphere that rejected the formality of other companies. The most well-known former Atari alumni are Steve Jobs and Steve Wozniak, who struck out on their own to form Apple Computer after having first invited Atari to invest in their idea of marketing personal computers.

Nolan K. Bushnell. (AP/Wide World Photos)

Because distributors in the coin-operated games business tended to rely on individual manufacturers, Atari's many competitors were able to grab segments of the market. As a way of working around this, Bushnell created a second highly successful company, Kee Games, which sold variations of Atari's products under different names. As microprocessors increased in power and lowered in cost, it became more possible to use programmed rather than hard-wired game logic. In 1975, Sears marketed Atari's home console version of *Pong* using a single chip that contained all of the logic required. Atari was purchased by Warner Communications in 1976, and Bushnell, who stayed with the company for some time after that, made millions of dollars of profit.

Bushnell's next important venture was Chuck E. Cheese, which he had developed for Warner while still at Atari. Chuck E. Cheese focused on family entertainment by combining pizza and soft drink service with video game arcades and entertainment by animatronic characters. He purchased the company from Warner in 1977 and left in 1984. By this time, Bushnell was involved in multiple projects and activities, including investments with the Catalyst Technologies Venture Capital Group, which he had founded in 1981 and which supported many new initiatives in game technology, robotic toys, and entertainment. Another of his companies is uWink (founded in 2000), which also combines dining and gaming experiences. Bushnell has appeared on documentary programs, and in 2005 he appeared as a judge in several episodes of the reality show series *Made in the USA*.

IMPACT

Atari ultimately had difficulties in maintaining its economic momentum, but Bushnell's combination of technical knowledge, creative imagination, and entrepreneurial risk-taking continued in the industry that he had helped to establish. As a direct result of the activities of Bushnell (along with his many competitors and imitators), both coin-operated video game stations and in-home game devices connected to television sets became an important and familiar part of popular culture throughout the world. Within the entertainment industry, his use of electronics to control full-size characters in restaurant settings extended Disney's theme park animatronics concepts into new environments.

PONG

Pong was the first commercial video game to achieve widespread popularity. There were two slightly earlier but less successful inventions that introduced certain features brought together in *Pong*. The first was Nolan K. Bushnell and Ted Dabney's *Computer Space*, released by Nutting Associates in 1971. *Computer Space* was a coin-operated self-contained video game that used hard-wired discrete logic gates made from inexpensive components (rather than a program running on a central processing unit) to achieve a complex level of interactivity. The second preceding invention was the first home video game console: the Odyssey Home Entertainment System, created by Ralph Baer and released by Magnovox in 1972. The Odyssey also used inexpensive components, transistors and diodes, in a system connected to a television set. The Odyssey would play several different variations of a simple paddle game, with cartridges inserted to activate the games.

Meanwhile, Bushnell and his new engineer Al Alcorn, who had left Nutting, continued to perfect transistor-to-transistor circuits for their coin-operated games. Later in 1972, Atari released *Pong*, after testing a prototype in a local bar. Although it was essentially a stand-alone two-person paddle game simulating table tennis, *Pong* included several innovative features that distinguished it from *Computer Space* and the Odyssey. Like *Computer Space*, there were separate circuits for the various functions of the game. In this case, there were circuits to keep track of the positions of the paddles and the ball (by counting scan lines), circuits to handle paddle input from the knobs, a digital counter to keep score, and circuits to change voltages that generated the patterns of light and darkness between each scan cycle on the TV screen. As the game progressed, the speed of the ball would increase, resulting in an increase in the level of challenge. Each of the paddles was divided into areas that would affect the angle of deflection when the ball was contacted, adding an exciting level of realism. As another innovative touch, some of the waves created by the voltage changes in the device were amplified and sent to a speaker to create the characteristic impact sound selected by Bushnell. The combination of increasing speed, changes in the ball's deflection angle, scorekeeping, and sound created an unprecedented level of interactivity.

Ironically, it was a mechanical feature that caused the first problems with the new invention. When the prototype was being tested in a consumer setting, Alcorn received a call to let him know that the machine had stopped working. When he investigated, he found that the machine's very popularity had caused the malfunction. Like the pinball machines that preceded it, *Pong* had a coin collector, which had overflowed. Aside from its technical innovations and efficient design, the psychological dimension of user engagement ushered in a new art form. *Pong* exemplified Bushnell's game design philosophy, which dictates that a game should be easy to learn but difficult to master.

Bushnell also played a role in an ongoing argument over the future of technology. Alan Mathison Turing, a pioneer in the earliest days of computing, had envisioned a flexible approach in which a single computer would be programmed to do many divergent tasks. In some ways, by creating dedicated hardware for gaming, Bushnell and his associates challenged the multiple-function approach envisioned by Turing. Atari's famous rejection of Steve Jobs's offer to have the company invest in the development of personal computers is another example of Bushnell's approach. With the passage of time, personal computers did become important as gaming platforms, but dedicated gaming hardware also continued to develop and to play a large role in consumer culture as the home console market expanded and diversified.

—John E. Myers

FURTHER READING

Cohen, Scott. *Zap! The Rise and Fall of Atari*. New York: McGraw-Hill, 1984. Focus is on the individual company, including its transformations after being purchased by Warner Communications. Includes information about the major figures and their relationships. List of primary sources (individual people), bibliography, index.

DeMaria, Rusel, and Johnny L. Wilson. *High Score! The Illustrated History of Electronic Games*. New York: McGraw-Hill/Osborne, 2002. Comprehensive, chronological approach, including personal accounts, photographs, and descriptive summaries, including detailed coverage of Bushnell and Atari. Full-color illustrations of game graphics and hardware. Image credits, index.

Jones, George. *Gaming 101: A Contemporary History of PC and Video Games*. Plano, Tex.: Wordware, 2004. Includes treatment of the business strategies, corporate competition, and marketing of game development, with emphasis on the early years of the industry. Illustrated.

Kent, Steven L. *The Ultimate History of Video Games: From Pong to Pokémon and Beyond—The Story Behind the Craze That Touched Our Lives and Changed the World*. Roseville, Calif.: Prima, 2001. Descriptive approach, augmented by extensive quotations from relevant figures. Includes accounts of corporate competition and trends within the industry. Source notes, index.

Poole, Stephen. *Trigger Happy: Video Games and the Entertainment Revolution*. New York: Arcade, 2000. An aesthetic and critical approach positions video games in relation to other art forms such as film, and describes their evolution in these terms. Bushnell is referenced for his philosophical influence as well as his more direct contributions. Bibliography, index, black-and-white examples of game graphics.

See also: Bill Gates; Steve Jobs; Ken Olsen; Alan Mathison Turing; Steve Wozniak.

CAI LUN
Chinese court official

Cai Lun is credited with inventing the process of papermaking by suspending mashed fibers in water, screening out the water, and drying and polishing the remaining sheets. This basic process remains the same today.

Born: c. 50 C.E.; Guiyang (now Leiyang, Hunan Province), China
Died: c. 121 C.E.; China
Also known as: Jingzhong; Ts'ai Lun (Wade-Giles)
Primary field: Manufacturing
Primary invention: Paper and papermaking

EARLY LIFE

Little is known about the early life of Cai Lun (si loon) beyond the date and place of his birth. From his later career at the Chinese imperial court, however, it is possible to infer some further elements of his childhood and youth. Cai Lun lived during the Eastern, or Later, Han Dynasty. This was the first dynasty in which China was united in culture and government under a far-reaching imperial establishment. To manage such an extensive empire, the court needed a large number of competent administrators. Chinese court officials were always on the lookout for able young men to join their ranks. Of prime importance to ambitious young men were intelligence and a good education. More than nine thousand characters existed in the written Chinese language at this time, and many years of study were needed for proficiency. It is likely that Cai Lun came from a comfortably situated family, if not a wealthy one, and that he attended either a government or a private school. When he entered imperial service at about the age of twenty-five, he would have already gone through years of study and must have ranked well in his examinations.

LIFE'S WORK

Cai Lun began his service as court eunuch about 75 C.E. His initial duties are not known, but they probably included a component of secretarial work. Most of his assignments would have been administrative rather than purely scientific. However, he seems to have been genuinely interested in the pursuit of knowledge. He was known as a serious and careful man who in his leisure hours would seclude himself in his quarters to study. Like any political center, the Han imperial court was rife with factions and with individuals jockeying for power. To survive and advance in this setting as he did, Cai Lun also had to navigate the dangers of imperial politics and make powerful friends.

His abilities were recognized by a series of promotions. By 97, he was appointed inspector of works. In this post, he oversaw the production and improvement of swords, weapons, and other devices. Perhaps his interest in manufacturing processes was already evident.

His experiments with papermaking seem to have been spurred both by his own curiosity and by necessity. The Eastern Han Dynasty was the heir of a long tradition of written language. The earliest traces of writing found in China were inscribed on a variety of natural materials: bone, stone, clay, and metal. These were substances especially suited for recording messages aimed at future generations as well as the writer's contemporaries. However, the Han Dynasty faced the complex problem of governing a population of some sixty million people. Just keeping up with its ordinary business required much written communication. Most of such writing was done either on sheets of silk or on wooden or bamboo strips. The writing implement used was a small brush. Learning to wield it gracefully was an integral part of learning to write the ideographic characters.

Both silk and wood had major drawbacks as writing surfaces. Silk, which was used for most official documents, was expensive and fragile. The brushed ink strokes also bled through it, so only one side of the silk sheets could be used. Bamboo and wooden strips were more substantial, but heavy and bulky. For longer texts, books were created by binding or strapping together a series of strips so each could be unfolded as the reader came to the bottom of the previous strip. Wood strips were used for the majority of ordinary messages.

Clearly there was a need for another medium for the written word. It must be noted that Chinese did have a word for paper, *chi*, before Cai Lun's invention of papermaking. In 102, the imperial consort Teng, one of Cai Lun's sponsors, requested that samples of *chi* be sent to her from various regions. *Chi* is also mentioned even earlier. Archaeologists have determined that *chi* appears to have referred to coarse pieces of treated hemp fibers, although thin mulberry bark is also a possibility. The use of these substances was no doubt known to Cai Lun when he began his experiments.

It is not known how long it took him to work out the process, how many assistants he had, or whether he did the work at court or at his home in Leiyang, where a stone mortar was exhibited in later years as the one he used in papermaking. Also, there is no "recipe" for the proportions of the different fibrous materials that made up the finished product. The basic facts of his invention were recorded by court historians. Taking a mixture of materials—including hemp ends, tree bark, and scraps of fish net—he perhaps presoftened them, then crushed them into tiny fragments and suspended the mix in water. This wet pulp was then spread evenly on a screen of cloth or bamboo and dried in the sun. Once totally dry, it emerged as a new substance, paper, which could be peeled off the screen and polished to a relatively smooth surface with a stone.

Cai Lun presented a report on his papermaking process to Emperor He in 105 It was immediately recognized as an important advance, and Cai Lun won imperial commendation for his work. Even though some of the materials and steps of the process were already in use, he had brought them together to create a new product with superior qualities and a huge number of possible uses.

Even so, his invention did not revolutionize written communication overnight. Existing materials continued to be used for many books and messages. In fact, when an official version of the classical texts was commissioned by the emperor in 175, it was engraved on stone tablets. (This medium, however, made it possible for scholars to take rubbings of the engraved works on paper, for their own use.) Paper's use for written messages seems to have begun soon after Cai Lun's disclosure of the papermaking process, but paper did not replace other materials in China for many years. The earliest authenticated example of paper containing writing was found in 1942 at the ruins of a frontier watchtower that was manned during the Han era. Members of the Chinese Academy who discovered it dated it to between 109 and 110, just before the watchtower was destroyed. The paper, made of vegetable fibers, contains some twenty characters. Its existence suggests that Cai Lun's techniques spread fairly quickly. Other practical uses for paper, including serving as a wrapping material, toilet tissue, and even as clothing, were also adopted rapidly in China.

Cai Lun himself continued his career as a courtier and imperial administrator. In 114, he received the title of marquis; this was a select status outranked only by certain kinsmen of the emperor. Among other privileges, it entitled him to the income from three hundred dwellings. He was also appointed a chief, or chamberlain, of the palace. In 117, he was named to head a project to reconcile differing versions of the "books of history." His papermaking endeavor seems to have been picked up and carried on by others. His apprentice Zo Po added improvements to the process. One source credits Cai Lun with setting up a paper factory in Turkestan. It does seem likely that, once familiar with this new product, the Han authorities would encourage its large-scale production.

Unfortunately, the palace intrigue that helped in Cai Lun's rise also brought about his downfall. He was strongly supported by Dowager Empress Teng, the same

PAPER AND PAPERMAKING

The basic components of paper are simple. Starting with organic materials of vegetable origin, small strips or pieces are sometimes pretreated to soften them, then are put through a process to disrupt the natural structure and rebond the fibers through a process similar to felting. When this process is done by hand, after water is added the pulp is beaten by a stone, a wooden mallet, or another implement. Sometimes animal-powered mallets are used. Mechanization allowed larger batches to be processed at once, with devices pulverizing the material without using direct human effort. The Hollander beater, for example, was first devised in the Netherlands in the seventeenth century. It used wind power to turn heavy cylinders with multiple teeth over and over in a huge tub, mashing wet fibers into pulp.

After the mixture is the right consistency, it is spread or poured to cover a flat surface evenly. This can be as small as Cai Lun's hand screens or, as in today's factories, the size of a small playing field. The next step, extracting the liquid, in early modern times was largely accomplished by pressing the mixture down with heavy wooden or metal presses. Used repeatedly, they would remove most of the pulp's 99 percent component of water. The resulting sheets were then hung or spread in a drying loft to air-dry completely. With modern papermaking machines, heavy cylinders serve as presses and, once the paper comes off these rollers, it is ready for processing into the designated final product.

Contemporary paper mills are automated, so their controls can be adjusted to produce papers of varying thickness, texture, sheet size, absorbency, and other traits. Chemical treatments are usually added during the process. An immense variety of paper products with diverse qualities and uses now roll out of paper mills over the world. Cai Lun's invention has proved uniquely essential to modern civilization.

woman who had taken an interest in his papermaking venture. After her death, he was implicated in a threat to her rival, the new empress. Rather than being executed, he was allowed to bathe, dress in his finest formal robes, and take poison. He died in 121.

Impact

The importance of Cai Lun's invention can hardly be overstated. Paper serves many purposes. For most of these, any substitute substances have significant drawbacks. Paper is reasonably durable, light, biodegradable, absorbent, and capable of being made from a variety of natural vegetation. It can be manufactured so cheaply that almost everyone can use it. Unlike electronic communications methods, records kept on paper can be made, retrieved, and read or viewed without any intervening device. Under the right conditions, they can be kept intact for long periods of time without being made inaccessible by newer technology. A world without paper is now almost impossible to imagine. It remains of huge importance for conveying written and printed information, but it also forms part of the everyday environment in many other ways.

The technology and use of paper spread rapidly through China and the rest of East Asia in the first few centuries after Cai Lun reported his invention. Samarqand became a paper-manufacturing town following a battle fought there when two Chinese papermakers taken prisoner offered knowledge of their craft in exchange for their freedom. Papermaking knowledge spread along the Silk Road and met with many innovations in an Arab world newly flourishing with commerce and conquest. Paper was first introduced into Europe in Spain, by the Moors, and Italian papermakers were also operating by the end of the thirteenth century. The craft spread slowly to the rest of Europe, because it was viewed with some suspicion during the transition from medieval to modern times. However, paper was so integrally important to the spread of the printed word, and to the needs of a society in which literacy and record keeping were increasingly important, that by the sixteenth century it was being produced and used in most European countries. Today, it is hard to find a corner of the world where paper is unknown.

—*Emily Alward*

Further Reading

Asunción, Josep. *The Complete Book of Papermaking*. New York: Lark Books, 2003. Lavishly illustrated book primarily focused on hand papermaking methods and devices. Contains unique information on the early development of paper technology.

Farley, Jonathan. "Paper: Its Past, Present, and Potential." *Curtis's Botanical Magazine* 19 (February, 2002): 2-7. An overview that ranges from before Cai Lun to the European medieval period.

Hunter, Dard. *Papermaking: The History and Technique of an Ancient Craft*. 1947. 2d ed. New York: Dover, 1978. Intensively researched history of the process and industry around the world. Photographs, glossaries, chronology of paper-related events, anecdotes involving historic figures' relationship to papermaking.

Tsien, Tsuen-Hsuin. *Paper and Printing*. Vol. 5, part 1 in *Science and Civilisation in China*, by Joseph Needham. New York: Cambridge University Press, 1985. The major resource in English on the history of paper in China. Meticulously researched, with multiple bibliographies. Written for the scholar but accessible to the general reader.

See also: Johann Gutenberg.

Robert Cailliau

Belgian electrical engineer

In collaboration with Tim Berners-Lee, Cailliau invented the World Wide Web, which revolutionized communication and information sharing throughout the world. First developed as an essential tool for the scientific community, the World Wide Web soon became a technology available to everyone.

Born: January 26, 1947; Tongeren, Belgium
Primary field: Computer science
Primary invention: World Wide Web development

Early Life

Robert Cailliau (roh-BEHR ki-JIOH) was born on January 26, 1947, in Tongeren, Belgium, located north-northwest of Liège. Although his name appears to be French, he comes from a Flemish family that traces its residency in Flanders back to 1602. Cailliau grew up speaking a Dutch dialect. In 1958, his family moved to Antwerp, and he attended the Rijks Atheneum school. After graduating from secondary school, he attended Ghent University, where he had his first experience working with human-machine interfaces in a lab class for mechanical engineering. In 1969, he graduated from Ghent University with a degree in electrical and mechanical engineering. He then worked at the university until he attended the University of Michigan to further his studies. In 1971, he completed a master of science degree at the university. His area of specialization was computer, information, and control engineering, with a concentration in operating systems and programming languages. In 1972, he returned to Ghent University. The following year, he did his military service in a post at the Belgian Royal Military Academy. While at the academy, he began writing FORTRAN programs, in which he simulated troop movements.

Life's Work

In 1974, Cailliau accepted a position at the European Council for Nuclear Research (later renamed the European Organization for Nuclear Research), known as CERN, in Geneva, Switzerland. Cailliau held positions in four different departments while at CERN. His first position was as a member of the team working on the control system of the Proton Synchrotron accelerator. During this time, he met Tim Berners-Lee, who was working for CERN as a contract programmer. From 1986 to 1989, Cailliau was head of Office Computing Systems at CERN. He was chosen for this post because of a text-processing system that he had written with a friend. During this time, he began considering the creation of a hypertext system that would connect all of the documentation over the CERN network.

In 1989, CERN was restructured, and this change enabled Cailliau to begin seriously working on a hypertext system. For some time, Cailliau worked on the idea by himself, as no one else at CERN was really interested in it. However, Berners-Lee was already working on similar ideas. The two men collaborated and developed a project that Berners-Lee had begun at an earlier date, "Information Management: A Proposal," which was renamed "WorldWideWeb." They received approval from CERN to spend a year developing the project. Working under Mike Sendall, Cailliau and Berners-Lee developed a network hypertext system. By the end of 1990, their system was introduced as the World Wide Web. It quickly won the support of physicists, and on April 30, 1993, CERN, at the insistence of Cailliau, put the World Wide Web in the public domain.

In 1993, Cailliau joined a group from Fraunhofer Gesellschaft in working on a Web-based project under the auspices of the European Commission. He also began planning the first International WWW Conference, which took place in May, 1994, at CERN. The conference was well attended, and its success resulted in the formation of the International World Wide Web Conference Committee, which organized annual conferences. Cailliau served on the committee from 1994 to 2004.

In 1994, in conjunction with the European Commission, Cailliau started the Web for Schools program, which was the initial step to establishing the Web as a resource to be used in educational programs in the European Union. He was also instrumental in setting up the World Wide Web Consortium (W3C), which oversees the standards of the World Wide Web. Cailliau transferred the Web technologies from CERN to the consortium. His work at CERN was involved with the CERN intranet services.

Cailliau then moved to another division of CERN. During the time he spent trying to convince various individuals of the value of the Web, he became keenly aware of the difficulty of introducing new ideas to people. In 2000, he published *How the Web Was Born: The Story of the World Wide Web* with James Gillies of CERN.

THE WORLD WIDE WEB

The concept of the World Wide Web (WWW) was the result of the need of scientists worldwide to be able to communicate quickly and easily with each other and to access information. The European Organization for Nuclear Research (CERN) was the site at which the research and development of the concept began. The CERN laboratories served as a focal point for scientists working in universities and national laboratories throughout the world. Many of these scientists spent some time actually working at CERN, but most of their work was done in their home countries; therefore, they needed to contact each other quickly from wherever they happened to be.

In 1989, the first proposal for the World Wide Web was presented by Tim Berners-Lee, a computer scientist who had joined CERN as an independent contractor in 1980. At that time, he developed a prototype system based on the concept of hypertext to make it easier for research scientists to share and update information. The system was called Enquire. His 1989 proposal used many of the ideas he had utilized in Enquire. Robert Cailliau, also a CERN scientist, was experimenting with this same idea of establishing a network for scientists who had worked at CERN to communicate easily once they returned home and to be able to access what Cailliau called an "automatic library." Cailliau and Berners-Lee began working together and in May of 1990 presented a refined version of the 1989 proposal. The proposal was approved by their manager, Mike Sendall, and they began developing the World Wide Web. By the end of the year, they had written prototype software for a basic system. Berners-Lee built the first Web browser and editor, which he developed on the NEXTSTEP operating system, and the first Web server, called "httpd" (hypertext transfer protocol daemon). All of the first Web servers were in European physics laboratories, making the Web available to a limited number of users.

In 1991, the Web became accessible to a large number of research and university laboratories in Europe. Then, in December, 1991, the first U.S. Web server came online at the Stanford Linear Accelerator Center in California. In 1993, the development of reliable, user-friendly browsers for personal computer (PC) and Macintosh computers provided the impetus necessary for a significant increase in Web servers and users. On April 30, 1993, CERN placed the World Wide Web in the public domain, and in 1994 the first International World Wide Web Conference took place. CERN determined that it was no longer the proper base for Web development and proposed that an international consortium be established in collaboration with Massachusetts Institute of Technology (MIT). The French National Institute for Research in Computer Science and Controls took over for CERN. In January, 1995, the World Wide Web Consortium (W3C) was founded to oversee and advance the development of the Web. Berners-Lee left CERN at the end of 1994 to work on the consortium at MIT.

Cailliau then became head of CERN's External Communications division. He remained in this position until his early retirement in 2005.

After retiring, Cailliau began sharing his knowledge as a speaker at conferences. He has also devoted his time to teaching programming to children and adolescents with severe learning and/or social disabilities through the Internet-based educational charity Not School. He uses Revolution, a programming language that started as MetaCard, to teach his students. Cailliau has also been working on a major project that deals with a Hyperbook-generating program he calls iAlbum.

Cailliau has received numerous awards and recognitions for his scientific work. In 1995, he was chosen as the recipient of the ACM Software System Award along with Tim Berners-Lee. In 1999, he received the Plantin Prize awarded by Antwerp and was given an honorary doctorate by Southern Cross University in Australia. In 2000, he received an honorary doctorate from Ghent University. In 2001, once again with Berners-Lee, he was the recipient of the Médaille Genève Reconnaissante. In 2004, King Albert II of Belgium awarded him the Commander in the Order of King Leopold. Cailliau was given honorary citizenship in the city of Tongeren in 2006.

IMPACT

Cailliau played an important role in making the concept of the World Wide Web a reality. Working with Berners-Lee, he convinced CERN to back the project. Then, in 1993, he was instrumental in persuading CERN to place the World Wide Web in the public domain. His efforts brought about the International World Wide Web Conference series, an annual event bringing together researchers and computer scientists. He has been one of the major proponents for using the Web as an educational tool both in the schools, with programs such as Web for Schools, and totally online, such as Not School.

—*Shawncey Webb*

Further Reading

Berners-Lee, Tim. *Weaving the Web: The Original Design and the Ultimate Destiny of the World Wide Web by Its Inventor*. New York: HarperCollins, 2000. Concentrates more on the Web than on its creators. Appendix, glossary, index, and text of "Information Management: A Proposal."

Gillies, James, and Robert Cailliau. *How the Web Was Born: The Story of the World Wide Web*. New York: Oxford University Press, 2000. Story of the Web through 1990, with details about the people involved in its creation. A scholarly work, but cased in a narrative form. Plates, figures, time line, bibliography, epilogue, index.

Hafner, Katie, and Matthew Lyon. *Where Wizards Stay Up Late: The Origins of the Internet*. New York: Simon & Schuster, 1996. Tells the tale of the birth of the modern Internet, beginning with the launch of Sputnik and the Defense Department's Defense Advanced Research Projects Agency (DARPA) network projects.

Naughton, John. *A Brief History of the Future: From Radio Days to Internet Years in a Lifetime*. Woodstock, N.Y.: Overlook Press, 2000. Surveys the great minds who contributed to the birth of the Internet. Glossary, index.

Solomon, Gwen, and Lynne Schrum. *Web 2.0: New Tools, New Schools*. Eugene, Oreg.: International Society for Technology in Education, 2007. A useful book that discusses the teaching potential of the Internet. Appendixes and index.

See also: Tim Berners-Lee; Vinton Gray Cerf; Philip Emeagwali; Bill Gates; Bob Kahn; Robert Metcalfe; Larry Page.

John Campbell

Scottish naval officer

Campbell, an exemplary British naval officer of the eighteenth century, was critical in the development of the nautical sextant, an instrument that precisely measures angular distance of celestial objects from the horizon to chart location. Since its inception, the sextant has become essential for marine navigation.

Born: c. 1720; Kirkbean, Kircudbrightshire, Scotland
Died: December 16, 1790; London, England
Primary fields: Maritime technology; navigation
Primary invention: Nautical sextant

Early Life

John Campbell was born in the parish of Kirkbean in Kircudbrightshire, Scotland, around the year 1720. His father, also named John, was the minister of the local parish. Campbell began his naval career as an apprentice on a coasting vessel. Shortly thereafter, he joined the British Royal Navy and in 1740 became midshipman on the *Centurion*. The *Centurion* sailed in Commodore George Anson's fleet in its famous circumnavigation around the globe; Anson would advance Campbell's career at every opportunity. With outstanding sailing skills and devotion to the navy, Campbell quickly rose through the ranks. In 1743, he was appointed master and in 1745 lieutenant. In 1749, he was promoted to post captain of the *Bellona*, a frigate. Among seamen, Campbell would earn an almost unrivaled reputation as an astronomer and navigator, two arts linked in maritime journeys. He was also commended for his abilities as a naval officer.

Life's Work

Campbell's first recorded efforts at advancing the art of navigation by the stars—as mariners had been doing since the first oceanic journeys—were in relation to the octant. About 1747, he was the first person known to employ the octant designed by John Hadley to measure at sea the angle of distance between the Moon and the stars. Given his success, Campbell was asked in 1752 by the Board of Longitude (created in 1714 to solve the problem of finding longitude at sea) to test the new lunar tables and circular repeating instrument of German geometer and astronomer Tobias Mayer. Appointed the captain of the *Essex* gunboat in 1757, Campbell successfully carried out the experiment. However, he found Mayer's circular repeating instrument cumbersome in comparison with the wooden Hadley octant. Campbell's trials led him to suggest important modifications to the octant. He suggested that the instrument's arc be extended from 45° to 60° so that its range of measurement would be increased from angles up to 90° to angles up to 120°. He also suggested that, to increase the stability of the navigational instrument, its frame be changed from wood to brass. Finally, he made better use of the telescopic sights.

When the renowned instrument maker John Bird employed Campbell's suggestions in 1759 to make a measuring instrument of eight inches radius with a brass frame, the first marine sextant had come into existence. The sextant built from Campbell's suggestions was such a success that it became the standard maritime charting instrument for the next two centuries. It was particularly successful in determining longitude by observing lunar distances according to methods developed by Royal Astronomer Nevil Maskelyne. The sextant allows for precise locating of one's position at sea by measuring the altitudes of the Moon, Sun, planets, or stars above the visible oceanic horizon. Technically, it works by measuring the angle between two points by bringing the direct image from one point and a double-reflected image from another point into alignment. The angular reading is taken from the sextant's arc to measure both longitude and latitude. Yet for all of its precision and working parts, Campbell's sextant was only one-third the weight of the Mayer circle. Edward Troughton improved Campbell's sextant in 1788 by patenting a lightweight double frame. Unlike some of its predecessors, the sextant could be used both day and night. The shades allowed for dimming bright objects; calculation of the stars could be made even when the horizon was not visible.

The ships that Campbell commanded took part in several victorious sea battles. In November, 1759, Campbell and his lifelong mentor, Admiral George Anson, personally informed the king of the British victory at Quiberon Bay. On May 24, 1764, Campbell became a member of the learned Royal Society. As a Royal Society fellow, he carried out a sea trial of John Harrison's longitude marine clock on the *Dorsetshire*, which Campbell had commanded since 1760. Harrison's "chronometer" would eventually win the prize of £20,000 offered by the Board of Longitude. In March, 1765, Campbell visited the Royal Observatory in Greenwich, England. On November 19, 1767, he was appointed a member of the Royal Society's Transit Committee to arrange for global measurements of the June 3, 1769, transit of Venus.

At a Royal Society council meeting on December 3, 1767, it was suggested that Campbell, as a "lover of astronomy," captain a ship to the South Pacific for this purpose. He apparently declined, but at a council meeting on May 5, 1768, he suggested that Captain James Cook lead the expedition. The Admiralty had already instructed the Navy Board to outfit a ship for this venture, and on August 25, 1768, Captain Cook launched his famous voyage of discovery on the *Endeavour*. (Cook named a New Zealand cape for Campbell.) Campbell was also instrumental in the rise of William Bligh, who captained his first ships in Campbell's service. Campbell commanded several additional ships until January 23, 1778, when he was promoted to vice admiral. Two months later, he became first captain of the *Victory*.

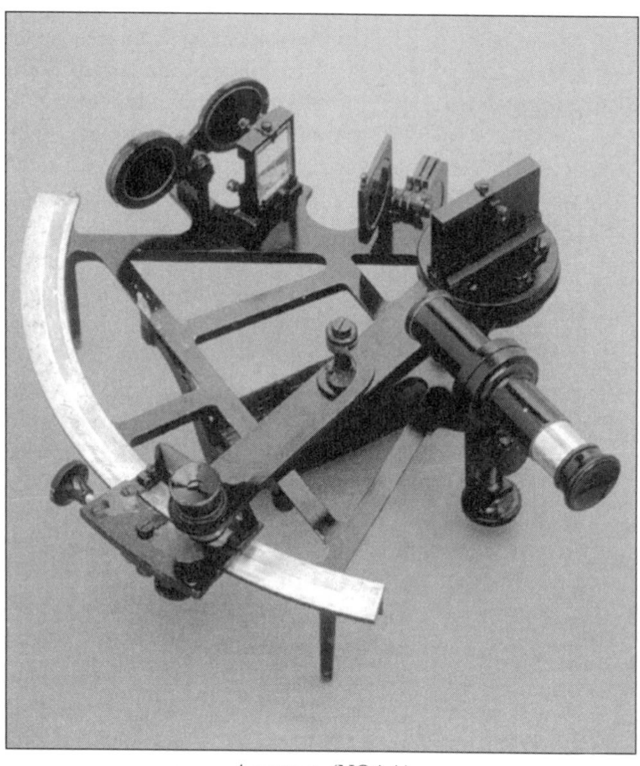

A sextant. (NOAA)

In 1782, Campbell was appointed governor and commander in chief of the English colony on Newfoundland. By all accounts, he was an enlightened and productive governor. For example, he allowed religious freedom for all of Newfoundland's inhabitants. As a result, Newfoundland's Catholic bishop authorized the construction of a chapel. Campbell also established a public wharf and storehouses for the benefit of the Newfoundland residents. As governor, he continued his navigational trials, testing the chronometer of Thomas Mudge and ascertaining the longitude of Newfoundland. Campbell retired to England in 1786. He died at his house at Charles Street, Berkeley Square, London, four years later, perhaps survived by his wife.

Impact

Campbell made a lasting impact on navigational history with the development of the nautical sextant. It is perhaps excessive to call Campbell the inventor of the sextant, as it is an instrument that evolved from its eighteenth century predecessors, most notably the quadrant and the octant. In addition, it was the great skill of English crafts firms and instrument makers—such as John Bird, who constructed the sextant from Campbell's suggestions—that made progress in marine instrumentation possible. Nevertheless, Campbell's improvements to the arc scale, frame, and sights of the octant were decisive in creating the essential navigational instrument for the modern sailor—the nautical sextant.

Campbell's insight followed from the two central marks of his career—his outstanding seamanship and his expertise in astronomical navigation. Throughout his career as sailor, captain, admiral, and governor, Campbell was noted for courage, integrity, and seamanship. His astronomical ability was such that the Board of Longitude repeatedly asked him to carry out trials at sea of the latest navigational instruments. The success of such experiments were critical to the Royal Navy as it was becoming a worldwide power. In turn, Campbell was able to use the results of his sea trials and his acquired experience to develop the sextant.

The British navy of the eighteenth century was the most powerful force at sea that the world had ever seen and the critical military branch of the British Empire spanning the globe. Certainly, many factors contributed to the success of the Royal Navy—the stable political institutions of Great Britain, its advances in industry and technology, successful scientific and bureaucratic institutions such as the Board of Longitude, the fine workmanship of shipbuilders and instrument makers—but not to be underestimated are the contributions of sea captains like Campbell who combined outstanding seamanship, devotion to service, astronomical knowledge, and scientific curiosity. The result was the invention of the nautical sextant.

Although invaluable to ocean travel, the sextant has been used in other fields. The sounding sextant is constructed for horizontal rather than vertical use and is used in hydrographic surveys. The surveyor's sextant is used on land for horizontal angular measurements. Box sextants are also used by surveyors.

—*Howard Bromberg*

The Sextant

The sextant was the chief navigational tool for maritime transport for two centuries. It is an ingenious device for finding one's position on the sea by measuring the angle of a celestial body above a horizontal line of reference. The measurement of the angle and the elapsed time is used to chart a position line on a nautical chart. For the entire history of ocean travel, mariners have needed an accurate method to locate their positions by the only constant observable to them—the stars. With advances in maritime science, navigators began using some kind of astronomical instrument to map their positions according to the Sun, Moon, planets, and stars. The sextant developed from and improved upon these astronomical instruments.

Over the course of history, marine navigators have variously used latitude hooks, kamals, astrolabes, balestillas, cross-staffs, back-staffs, nocturnals, and quadrants for this purpose. Similar to the principles that led him to invent the reflecting telescope, Sir Isaac Newton had already suggested the idea of making use of moving mirrors as reflecting instruments. Newton's idea of doubly reflecting mirrors allows for subtracting the motion of the sextant from the reflection. The eighteenth century octant was the direct forerunner of the sextant. John Hadley and Thomas Godfrey had independently developed effective marine octants around 1731, both employing double-reflecting mirrors. John Campbell's modifications transformed the octant into the most successful ocular instrument in the history of marine navigation—the sextant.

The name "sextant" is derived from the Latin *sextus*, or sixth part of a circle. Prototypes of the instrument had been used by astronomers since the sixteenth century. The famous astronomer and compiler of celestial data Tycho Brahe had developed a forerunner of the sextant, but it was with Campbell that the nautical sextant took final shape. The sextant enables sailors to calculate their longitudinal and latitudinal position based on precise measurements of the angles of celestial objects. The sextant also makes use of the innovation of the double-reflecting mirrors. The sextant combines two mirrors or prisms, a telescopic sighting tube, an arc scale, and a shaded micrometer. The observer adjusts the components to measure the angle of a celestial object—the Moon, Sun, planet, or star—compared to the horizon. With the measurement calculated by a time frame, it is possible to achieve highly accurate readings of the latitude and longitude based on the perceived movement of the celestial object. The sextant was often used with the chronometer, a precision time-measuring device. Compared with its predecessors, the sextant was sturdy, lightweight, portable, and extremely accurate, even on a moving ship. With its invention, mariners had the ideal tool for charting their positions. Even with the increasing use of electronic locating devices, the sextant remains an important navigational tool.

Further Reading

Bauer, Bruce. *The Sextant Handbook: Adjustment, Repair, Use and History*. Camden, Maine: International Marine, 1992. A guide to every aspect of the sextant.

Bowditch, Nathaniel. *The American Practical Navigator*. Bethesda, Md.: Paradise Cay, 2002. One of the most historic and famous navigational texts, in use by sailors and continually updated and revised by the U.S. Navy since 1802. Book 1, chapter 16 contains a full treatment of the marine sextant.

Collingridge, Victoria. *Captain Cook: A Legacy Under Fire*. Guilford, Conn.: Lyons Press, 2002. Revisionist account of Cook's discoveries that recounts Campbell's connection to the *Endeavour*'s travels.

Cotter, Charles. *A History of the Navigator's Sextant*. Glasgow, Scotland: Brown, Son, and Ferguson, 1985. Comprehensive history ranging from the ancient astrolabe to modern aviation "bubble" sextants. Cotter attributes the first sextant to Campbell's suggestions, adding that subsequent navigators are thereby in his debt.

Dash, Joan. *The Longitude Prize*. New York: Farrar, Straus and Giroux, 2000. Prizewinning book for younger readers that narrates the story of the Board of Longitude and its £20,000 prize for determining longitude, and Campbell's contributions thereto.

Howse, Derek. *Greenwich Time and Longitude*. London: Philip Wilson, 2003. History of world standard Greenwich time recounts Campbell's contributions to the accurate measuring of lunar distances at sea.

Rollman, Hans. "Richards Edwards, John Campbell, and the Proclamation of Religious Liberty in Eighteenth Century Newfoundland." *Newfoundland Quarterly* 80, no. 2 (1984): 4-12. Rollman, a professor of religious studies in Newfoundland, recounts Campbell's contribution to religious tolerance.

Syrett, David, and R. I. DiNardo. *The Commissioned Sea Officers of the Royal Navy, 1660-1815*. London: Scolar Press, 1954. Volume 1 of the Occasional Publications of the Navy Records Society. Offers authoritative information about ranks and careers of Royal Naval officers.

Williams, Glynn. *The Prize of All the Oceans: Anson's Voyage Around the World*. New York: Viking Press, 2000. Absorbing story of Anson's voyage around the world in its battles against Spain. Campbell gained valuable experience under Anson's mentorship sailing with the fleet.

See also: Martha J. Coston; Nils Gustaf Dalén; John Harrison; Jesse Ramsden; Elmer Ambrose Sperry.

Marvin Camras

American electrical engineer

Camras invented a magnetic tape recording process widely used in electronic media, including music and motion-picture sound recording, audio and videocassettes, floppy disks, and credit card magnetic strips.

Born: January 1, 1916; Chicago, Illinois
Died: June 23, 1995; Evanston, Illinois
Primary field: Electronics and electrical engineering
Primary invention: Magnetic tape recording

Early Life

Marvin Camras was born in Chicago, Illinois, on New Year's Day, 1916. From early childhood, he was fascinated by technology. At the age of four, he built a flashlight, and he later designed a working telephone so he could talk with his cousin William. After high school, Camras attended the Armour Institute of Technology (now the Illinois Institute of Technology, or IIT), where he studied electrical engineering. At that time, his cousin was hoping for a career in opera.

Camras searched for a way to record his cousin's voice. Drawing upon the work of Danish inventor Valdemar Poulsen (1869-1942), whose telegraphone was an early device for recording sounds magnetically, Camras tried using magnetized piano wire to record his cousin's singing. In early attempts, the wire twisted during playback, distorting the sound. Camras kept working on his invention and eventually found a solution. He designed a magnetic recording head that would surround the wire but not actually touch it. The results were impressive, at least in terms of recording quality. When Camras demonstrated the wire recorder for his professors at the Armour Institute of Technology, they were so impressed with the clarity of the sound reproduction that they offered Camras a position at the Armour Research Foundation. William, apparently, was less impressed: After hearing the playback of his voice, he gave up his plans for a singing career.

Life's Work

Marvin Camras received his bachelor of science degree from the Armour Institute of Technology in 1940, during the final years of the Great Depression. Unlike many new graduates of that time, he was fortunate to have a job waiting for him upon graduation. Camras's professors encouraged him to keep working on his wire recording techniques at the Armour Research Foundation, which in 1940 merged with the Lewis Institute to become the Illinois Institute of Technology, while earning his master's degree. Camras completed his M.S. in 1942.

In December, 1941, Camras submitted his first patent for a "Method and Means of Magnetic Recording." It was approved in 1944. By this time, the United States had entered World War II, and Camras's work attracted the attention of the military. An article published in *Time* magazine in 1943 discussed the potential wartime benefits of Camras's "highly portable little gadget," a wire recorder approximately the size of a typewriter and weighing ten pounds. Far less bulky than earlier recording devices, the magnetic wire sound recorder Camras developed was seen as a way for newscasters to record live broadcasts from the scene of battle. The article noted that Camras, described as a "stocky, shy 27-year-old," would receive a 25 percent royalty for each recorder sold.

During World War II, Camras's wire recorders were used by the armed forces for training and intelligence purposes. The Navy used his recorder during submarine pilot training to simulate depth-charge attacks. The Army also used Camras's "Model 50" recorder for a special military disinformation program kept secret until after the war. To divert the attention of enemy forces, battle sounds were recorded and amplified, then played in locations where the D-Day invasion was not going to take place.

After the war, Camras continued working on recording techniques but switched his medium from wire to a thin, flexible yet durable tape. After experimenting with many different methods to magnetize the tape, he developed a ferric oxide "paint." This coating, whose particles would align uniformly when magnetized, created an ideal recording surface. This innovation proved to be an enormous commercial success, making "tapes" of one sort or another (audio, video, even computer) a nearly ubiquitous household item. In his *Magnetic Recording Handbook* (1988), Camras describes the introduction of a home tape recorder in 1946; as postwar prosperity increased the market for consumer goods, such products and their accessories became a multimillion-dollar industry.

Continuing to innovate, in 1949 Camras invented high-frequency bias recording, a method of using high-frequency sounds to sensitize magnetic tapes, allowing for a clear, almost distortion-free reproduction of sound. Camras describes the complex process in depth in his *Magnetic Recording Handbook*. Some of his other inventions included patents in methods of stereo tape recording, multitrack recording, motion-picture soundtrack recording, and an early prototype (1950) of a videotape recorder. In all, Camras patented more than five hundred inventions, largely in the field of electronics. Among the corporations that licensed his patents were General Electric, Minnesota Mining and Manufacturing (3M), and Eastman Kodak.

Despite his many successful inventions, Camras never attained great wealth. Yet he clearly loved his chosen field. His work with the IIT Research Institute continued

Marvin Camras sits in front of his magnetic tape recorder and other sound recording equipment. (Time & Life Pictures/Getty Images)

through 1987, and he continued to teach electrical engineering at the Illinois Institute of Technology until 1994, when he was well into his seventies. Camras was awarded an honorary doctorate from IIT in 1968. He was inducted into the National Inventors Hall of Fame in 1985 and was also awarded the prestigious National Medal of Technology from President George H. W. Bush in 1990.

Camras lived for most of his adult life in Glencoe, Illinois. In his private life, the pioneer of sound recording techniques enjoyed playing the harmonica and making violins and violas. Some of the instruments he designed were used by his daughter, Ruth Camras Prickler, a musician and music teacher, and son-in-law, Charles Prickler, head of the Chicago Symphony Orchestra. Marvin Camras died of kidney failure on June 23, 1995. He was survived by his wife of many years, Isabelle Pollak Camras, four sons, a daughter, and six grandchildren. In an obituary published in *The New York Times*, Ray Dolby, the chairman of Dolby Laboratories, Inc., maker of professional sound equipment, praised Camras's contributions to the field of sound recording, calling him "a legend" whose basic designs and discoveries are still used in tapes and recorders.

Magnetic Tape Recording

Marvin Camras was not the first person to invent a technique for sound recording. His magnetic wire recorder, first designed in the late 1930's and accepted for patent in 1944, drew upon the work of earlier inventors, especially Valdemar Poulsen. Camras's unique contribution made the process easier, better, and ultimately more accessible. His wire recorder used a magnetic recording head that surrounded the wire, preventing tangling and providing a superior sound. Camras went on to improve his original invention by creating magnetic coated tape that could be used instead of wire. Coated magnetic tape became the medium of choice for professional music and film recording equipment as well as home audio and videotape. Both the internationally famous rock band making a multitrack recording and the high school student taping an oral history interview on a minicassette recorder have Camras to thank for the technology that makes these recordings possible.

Magnetic tape recording takes many forms, but the basic mechanism remains the same: A tape that has been coated with magnetically active particles, typically ferric oxide and chromium dioxide, is passed through one or more magnetic tape heads. In essence, the particles coating the tape operate as small, individual magnets. The tape head operates as a magnetic field. As the tape passes around the head, the magnetic particles are activated and realigned. The process creates a magnetic pattern that remains on the tape until it is erased or rerecorded.

Camras's magnetic tapes and their coatings were for many years, and to some extent still are, the basis of most entertainment and data recording and storage in the United States and worldwide. While the magnetic recording process was originally developed for audio recording, later developments allowed it to be used for video recording, combining images and sound. The technology was also adapted for use in computer disks and magnetic credit card strips.

Camras's original wire recorder was used for strategic and training purposes during World War II, showing the versatility of the medium. The greatest impact of the magnetic recording technology, however, was on the broadcast and entertainment industries. Instead of a live radio or television broadcast, programs could be prerecorded and played, then replayed, at a later date. Instead of recording a song in one take, as musicians did in the early years of records, magnetic recording allowed songs to be created in multiple tracks and later mixed and edited into a single production. Some of the most innovative and acclaimed popular recordings of the rock era, such as the Beach Boys' *Pet Sounds* (1966) and the Beatles' *Sgt. Pepper's Lonely Hearts Club Band* (1967), could not have been created without multitrack recording.

Impact

Camras invented the magnetic tape recording method that became the basis of most electronic media, including audio and videocassettes, computer floppy disks, and credit card magnetic strips. His design of a magnetic tape head, used first in wire recorders and later in tape recorders, greatly simplified the recording and playback process and improved sound quality. His later work in high-frequency bias recording, multitrack recording, and related technologies further refined the clarity of sound reproduction. Camras's simple invention, born out of a desire to record a relative's singing, became a fundamental part of the multibillion-dollar music, film, and computer industries. Yet Camras himself shunned the spotlight, living a life marked by stability and continuity, working, teaching, and raising a family in the same midwestern community where he lived for most of his life.

Camras spent an impressive fifty-year career at the Armour Research Foundation and the Illinois Institute of Technology, where he taught from the 1940's until 1994. During those years, he earned more than five hundred U.S. and international patents for his work. His professional honors included the National Inventors Hall of Fame, the National Medal of Technology, and fellowships in the Institute of Electrical and Electronics Engineers (IEEE) and American Association for the Advancement of Science (AAAS).

—*Kathryn Kulpa*

Further Reading

Camras, Marvin. *Magnetic Recording Handbook*. New York: Van Nostrand Reinhold, 1988. Profusely illustrated with photographs and diagrams, this is a scholarly study of the history, theory, and technology of magnetic recording. Camras describes recording techniques and media, covering his own contribution as well as those of scientists who preceded and followed him. Illustrations, bibliography, index.

_______, ed. *Magnetic Tape Recording*. New York: Van Nostrand Reinhold, 1985. Anthology of scholarly articles on the technology of sound recording. Includes Camras's original 1941 patent application. Illustrations, citation index, subject index.

Gilpin, Kenneth N. "Marvin Camras, 79, Inventor in Tape Recording." *The New York Times*, June 28, 1995, p. B8. Obituary article provides a summary of Camras's life and scientific contributions.

McGrath, Kimberley A., and Bridget Travers, eds. *World of Invention*. Detroit, Mich.: Gale Research, 2001. 2d ed. Includes a short biographical sketch of Camras's life and a summary of his innovations in the field of magnetic recording. Bibliography, index.

Morton, David. *Off the Record: The Technology and Culture of Sound Recording in America*. New Brunswick, N.J.: Rutgers University Press, 2000. Lively, well-documented study of the history of recording in the United States, covering both technological and cultural aspects of sound recording. Illustrations, bibliography, index.

Raichel, Daniel R. *The Science and Applications of Acoustics*. New York: Springer Science & Business Media, 2006. A scholarly study of the fundamentals of acoustics. Chapter 19, "Sound Reproduction," is of particular interest, placing Camras's contribution in the context of other recording techniques.

"Wire for Sound." *Time*, May 17, 1943. Contemporary news article about Camras's work for the military discusses possible wartime uses for his magnetic recording device.

See also: Alexander Bain; Semi Joseph Begun; Charles P. Ginsburg; Peter Carl Goldmark; Les Paul; Alan Shugart; Charles Wheatstone.

Chester F. Carlson

American physicist

Carlson invented xerography, a dry-copying process using electrostatic methods to reproduce documents and images on plain paper. The principles he outlined in his first patent applications remain fundamental to all existing plain-paper photocopiers and laser printers. Xerox copiers transformed the way business offices operated.

Born: February 8, 1906; Seattle, Washington
Died: September 19, 1968; New York, New York
Also known as: Chester Floyd Carlson (full name)
Primary field: Printing
Primary invention: Xerography

Early Life

All four of Chester Floyd Carlson's grandparents immigrated to the United States from Sweden in the mid-nineteenth century. His mother, Ellen Josephine Hawkins, and his father, Olof Adolph Carlson, both suffered from tuberculosis; a severe case of spinal arthritis incapacitated his father. Family poverty forced eight-year-old Carlson to begin seeking odd jobs; by high school, he was the main family provider, earning $50 to $60 a month. His mother died in 1923, leaving the high school junior the sole support of his father until he died in 1932.

Carlson enrolled in a work-study program at Riverside Junior College in Riverside, California, in 1925, alternating six weeks of classroom with six weeks of work. Completing the four-year program in three years, he was admitted to the California Institute of Technology as a junior, graduating with a physics degree in 1930. In that Depression year, his applications were ignored by more than eighty companies before Bell Telephone Laboratories in New York City hired him as a laboratory technician.

Repetitive lab work bored Carlson, who arranged a transfer to the company's patent department. After Bell fired him in 1932, he found a position with a patent attorney. In 1934, Carlson became a registered patent attorney based on his work experience as a patent clerk, although he could not practice in court. That year, Carlson joined the patent office of P. R. Mallory & Company, rising to manager of the patent department before resigning eleven years later. He married Elsa von Mallon in the fall of 1934. In 1936, Carlson enrolled in night classes at the New York Law School, spending his weekends studying at the public library. He received an LL.B. in 1939 and was admitted to the bar in 1940. The first marriage was not a success; the couple divorced in 1945, and Carlson married Dorris Helen Hudgins in 1946.

Carlson suffered from writer's cramp while copying long passages by hand from law books he could not afford to buy. He was irritated by the difficulty of producing error-free, multiple copies of patent specifications using carbon paper, and he knew how much it cost to have engineering drawings reproduced in special photocopy shops. The world, he decided, needed an office copier to perform these tasks. While reading law at the public library, he also surveyed scientific literature on copying and believed he found a unique solution.

Life's Work

Others also sought to produce convenient copiers, most investigating chemical and photographic possibilities. Carlson rejected those approaches, knowing he would be competing with large corporations, such as Eastman Kodak, employing squadrons of engineers and scientists. Instead he turned to physics, searching for a process that would produce images on plain paper without using chemicals. He discovered an article by a Hungarian scientist describing experiments using electrostatic principles to produce an image by directing a beam of ions to a rotating drum covered with insulating material.

Uniquely, Carlson conceived the idea of combining the properties of electrostatics with photoconductivity. No one else anywhere thought of this as a way to copy documents. He proposed using light to clear electrostatic charges from non-image areas on a plate. This needed a material that acted as an electrical conductor in light and an electrical insulator in the dark. If light shone an image of a printed page on an electrostatically charged plate covered with such material, the charge would be removed from the blank areas of the plate, leaving only the image charged. Dusting the plate with an opaque powder of the opposite charge would create a negative image that could be transferred to a sheet of paper, producing an exact copy of the original.

Carlson filed a patent application describing his idea in 1937. He elaborated it the following year, incorporating what he had learned in experiments. Carlson had difficulty making his idea work until he hired a refugee German scientist in October, 1938; the two produced the first xerographic image on October 22. In 1942, Carlson received an expanded patent establishing the foundation principles of what later became called xerography and that are basic to all xerographic machines.

Approaches to over twenty major manufacturing corporations during the next six years aroused little interest; International Business Machines (IBM) considered but decided against pursuing his invention. In 1944, the Battelle Memorial Institute of Columbus, Ohio, agreed to develop commercial applications of Carlson's process. The history of the next sixteen years demonstrates how difficult it can be to translate a brilliant invention into a commercially successful product, requiring the work of dozens of scientists and engineers before introduction of the Xerox 914 in 1960.

Battelle, a well-known and successful industrial research organization, had no more success than the obscure inventor in interesting a large corporation in Carlson's patent. Only the Haloid Company, a small manufacturer of photographic paper in Rochester, New York, requested a license, which Battelle granted in 1946 despite serious doubt that Haloid had the resources to finance needed research. Meanwhile, Battelle scientists discovered a better insulator to coat the plate involved in Carlson's process and found more efficient chemicals to carry out the complex procedures needed to produce an image.

As Haloid became central to the development of his patents, Carlson moved to Rochester in 1949 as a consultant. Unlike inventors who contribute to many fields, Carlson concentrated on xerography; of his forty-two patents, all but two dealt with copying.

Haloid's 1949 Model A machine proved a failure as an office copier. It was big, clumsy, and required many manual operations. However, when users of lithographic machines discovered that it cut costs of creating a master copy by almost 90 percent, companies employing lithographic machines began adopting it. Copyflo machines introduced in 1954 used xerographic principles to print from microfilm. Neither machine was the office copier that Carlson had envisioned.

The president of Haloid, Joseph C. Wilson, proved as fixated on the concept of a plain-paper office copier as Carlson and effectively bet his company on achieving that goal, spending on research during the 1950's more than his company's entire earnings. Recognizing his company's limited experience with machinery production, Wilson asked IBM to manufacture and market the machines. IBM hired the renowned Arthur D. Little consulting company for advice; the company concluded that a desk-sized machine costing $2,000 to produce could not compete with currently available chemical-based desktop copiers priced as low as $99.50 and predicted that the market would be limited to a few thousand units. IBM rejected participation.

Wilson pushed doggedly ahead, buoyed by the results of a 1959 field test that placed a half-dozen machines with Rochester companies to discover problems that needed fixing. Difficulties seemed endless, as the copiers broke down repeatedly, but when Haloid tried to retrieve its machines, no tester wanted to give them back. Wilson decided to begin selling; the first commercial Xerox 914 (9″ × 14″ was the largest sheet of paper it could use) shipped in March, 1960.

Patent lawyer Carlson had kept a close watch on royalties from his invention. One estimate puts his eventual wealth at $150 million. Carlson spent his last years anonymously giving money to charities and civil liberties organizations. His wife's will (they had no children) completed the process of giving away his fortune to groups he admired. On September 19, 1968, Carlson died of a heart attack.

Impact

Despite skepticism over Haloid's advertising claims, and reliability problems that plagued Xerox machines for years, the 914 was a runaway success. *Fortune* magazine called it the most successful product ever marketed in America. It transformed the way every office in the world operated. Customers enthusiastically invented uses for the machines that even Carlson never anticipated. As profits poured in, the Haloid Company renamed itself Xerox. Royalties made Battelle one of the nation's wealthiest research organizations and Carlson a multimillionaire.

A federal official, asserting that copying on plain paper was impossible, wrote warning Xerox to desist; Xerox's lawyer responded by copying the letter on a brown paper bag, which he returned to sender. When a Xerox television ad showed a child making a copy for her father, the Federal Trade Commission sent an investigator to see if a midget had been sneaked into the commercial, as it seemed hard to believe that a child could work such a complicated machine.

Xerox solved the price difficulty that had seemed insuperable to business consultants by leasing the machines and metering use. Charging five cents per plain-paper copy, Xerox wiped out existing copiers using more expensive, chemically treated paper that made hard-to-read copies that often smelled bad and tended to curl as they aged.

Xerography

When Chester F. Carlson tried to find a sponsor for his invention, he had no model to show. All he had was a crude, six-step process he demonstrated unsuccessfully to IBM but with greater success to Battelle: He coated a smooth plate with a layer of dielectric material, then applied an electrostatic charge to the coated plate; placing a printed page facing the plate, he used a bright light to shine an image of the document on the plate, releasing the charge on the plate where light struck unshaded areas; the plate was dusted with a charged powder, revealing the image; the image was transferred to a sheet of paper, where the image was fused by heat.

Carlson's demonstration involved difficult manual steps and produced fuzzy copies. What fired the imagination of the men at Battelle and Haloid was realizing that, by combining the principles of electrostatics and photoconductivity, Carlson had come up with a truly new and revolutionary procedure that made copies without using either photography or printing with ink.

Transforming Carlson's process into an office-sized copier engaged the talents of many scientists and engineers. Battelle chemists discovered that coating the plate with selenium greatly increased the sensitivity of the plate. Using optical projection of the image to the plate permitted copying two-sided originals and books. More efficient chemicals were found for the powder or toner that revealed the image. A cylinder proved better than a flat plate for transferring the image, which introduced new complexities to the projection system. The temperature needed to fuse the toner was high enough to occasionally start fires: The early 914 models came with fire extinguishers, which salesmen renamed "scorch eliminators."

Carlson wanted an automatic desktop copier, but cramming everything into such a small compass was beyond the engineering and manufacturing skills of Haloid. The first commercial xerographic machine, the Model A, was room-sized and required many hand operations. Slowly, engineers learned how to automate the process, but squeezing all steps into a desktop-sized box proved too much for 1950's technology; Haloid settled for the desk-sized 914. Research since 1960 has improved the reliability and reduced the size of xerographic machines. However, all xerographic machines still depend upon the six-step process Carlson invented in 1938.

New uses proliferated. In offices where it had been the practice to use routing slips to circulate memoranda, personal Xerox copies now went to every recipient. Making copies of copies became common. Even the annoying frequent breakdowns of the early examples actually proved advantageous. It was cost-effective to rent several machines, ensuring a functioning copier available when needed; the presence of more machines encouraged making even more copies.

—*Milton Berman*

FURTHER READING

Brooks, John. *Business Adventures: Twelve Classic Tales from the Worlds of Wall Street and the Modern American Corporation.* New York: Weybright and Talley, 1969. Reprints Brooks's April 1, 1967, *New Yorker* article describing the enthusiastic reception of the 914 copier and the ingenious, unforeseen ways it was used.

Ellis, Charles D. *Joe Wilson and the Creation of Xerox.* Hoboken, N.J.: John Wiley & Sons, 2006. Laudatory biography of Wilson as a business and community leader, whose skills and leadership Ellis claims were indispensable to the success of xerography.

McKelvey, Blake. *Business as a Profession: The Career of Joseph C. Wilson, Founder of Xerox.* Rochester, N.Y.: Office of the City Historian, 2003. Credits Wilson's managerial and negotiating skills with guiding development of commercial applications of xerography.

Owen, David. *Copies in Seconds: How a Lone Inventor and an Unknown Company Created the Biggest Communication Breakthrough Since Gutenberg—Chester Carlson and the Birth of the Xerox Machine.* New York: Simon & Schuster, 2004. A lively account of Carlson's life and work based on interviews with his widow and previously inaccessible manuscripts.

Pell, Erik M. *From Dreams to Riches: The Story of Xerography.* Rochester, N.Y.: Erik M. Pell, 1998. Self-published book by a physicist who worked at Xerox from 1961 to 1978 provides a detailed technical account of the development of xerography.

See also: William Seward Burroughs; Lewis Waterman.

WALLACE HUME CAROTHERS

American organic chemist

Carothers conducted innovative polymer chemistry research to create synthetic rubber and nylon, stronger than natural materials, which were industrially developed for widespread distribution in consumer and military products. His investigations helped professionalize polymer chemistry as a scientific field.

Born: April 27, 1896; Burlington, Iowa
Died: April 29, 1937; Philadelphia, Pennsylvania
Primary field: Chemistry
Primary inventions: Nylon; synthetic rubber

EARLY LIFE

Wallace Hume Carothers, born on April 27, 1896, in Burlington, Iowa, was his parents' first child. His father, Ira Hume Carothers, taught penmanship at the local Elliott's Business College. His mother, Mary McMullin Carothers, named her son Wallace to honor her mother's maiden surname. By the time of the 1900 U.S. Census, the Carothers were living in Mount Pleasant, Iowa, before moving to the state capital, Des Moines, when Ira was hired by Capital City Commercial College.

Carothers and his two younger sisters and brother attended United Presbyterian Church services with their parents, who were devout members of that denomination. He took classes at North High School and collected water meter data and worked in the city library's reference section for income. Science intrigued Carothers, who read Robert Kennedy Duncan's books discussing chemistry and built a chemistry laboratory in his bedroom.

After his 1914 high school graduation, Carothers completed the year-long business curricula at Capital City Commercial College, where his father had been promoted to vice president. Tarkio College, a four-year Presbyterian-affiliated school in northwest Missouri, sought students for its Commercial Department. Hoping to please church leaders, Carothers's father selected Wallace and another student to travel to Tarkio in September, 1915. Carothers earned tuition money as an assistant in the Commercial and English departments and as Tarkio president Reverend J. A. Thompson's private secretary.

Although Carothers took business courses, he sought a scientific education and within two years completed every chemistry class Tarkio offered. Department head Arthur McCay Pardee, who had been taught by Duncan, loaned Carothers his chemistry texts, which expanded Carothers's understanding of organic chemistry and German chemical research. Carothers devoted his laboratory work to investigating carbon. Disqualified for World War I service because of his goiter, Carothers taught chemistry at Tarkio, starting in 1918 when Pardee left for war work, until 1920 when he received his bachelor of science degree.

Wallace Hume Carothers. (Hagley Museum and Library)

Life's Work

Because Carothers aspired to become a professional chemist, he traveled to Urbana, Illinois, to enroll in graduate school at the University of Illinois, which Pardee had suggested would offer Carothers a challenging organic chemistry program. Roger Adams mentored Carothers and provided professional support throughout Carothers's career. After Carothers received his master of science degree in 1921, he taught chemistry courses at the University of South Dakota at Vermillion.

The next year, Carothers started doctoral work at the University of Illinois. In 1923, he published his first paper in the *Journal of the American Chemical Society*. Carothers completed his dissertation, "Platinum Oxide as a Catalyst in the Reduction of Organic Compounds," and received his Ph.D. in 1924. He remained at the university to teach until 1926. While at Illinois, Carothers endured intense emotional despair and purchased cyanide, telling people he might kill himself with the poison.

When Harvard University sought an organic chemistry instructor, Adams endorsed Carothers for that position. At Harvard, Carothers started investigating chemistry associated with polymers and large molecules. He preferred pure, not applied, science and did not actively seek industrial or commercial use of his findings. His research, however, attracted chemists' attention at both academic and industrial laboratories. Charles M. A. Stine, director of the chemical department at E. I. du Pont de Nemours and Company, contacted Carothers while searching for an exceptional organic chemist to develop synthetic materials for DuPont to produce. Carothers accepted, as he disliked teaching and considered focusing on research with a team of skilled chemists preferable.

Carothers moved to Wilmington, Delaware, and started his DuPont duties as research director on February 6, 1928. DuPont managers told Carothers to consider how his chemists might make synthetic rubber, needed because natural rubber was not easily obtainable, with an acetylene polymer. Intrigued by Hermann Staudinger's polymer work in Germany, Carothers tested that chemist's provocative 1920 hypothesis that polymers chemically consisted of long chains of large molecules.

In April, 1930, during their investigations to prove Staudinger's theory, the DuPont chemists developed the synthetic rubber neoprene from polymerized chloroprene made from acetylenes. DuPont trademarked that synthetic rubber as Duprene and commercially manufactured it, noting its resiliency to temperature extremes. In 1931, *Chemical Review* printed Carothers's paper "Polymerization," which discussed significant publications regarding polymer chemistry and explained related terminology and information to aid other chemists to pursue investigations in that emerging field. Carothers was associate editor of the *Journal of the American Chemical Society* from 1929 to 1937 and also edited the annual *Organic Syntheses* in the early 1930's.

After developing synthetic rubber, Carothers attempted to create synthetic polyester fibers with sebacic acid and ethylene glycol in his laboratory. When colleague Julian Hill removed a glass stick he had inserted into a polymer, some of the polymer stuck to the stick, stretching without snapping as he stepped away. The polymer threads remained pliable and strong when dried and cooled but dissolved in moisture and heat.

Carothers decided to pursue another project, creating the synthetic scent Astrotone. Elmer K. Bolton, who had succeeded Stine when he was promoted, pressured Carothers to continue his synthetic fiber investigations. In 1934, Carothers resumed research with large molecules from amines instead of glycols in an attempt to create fibers which were more durable when heated. He also explored the role of condensation in polymerization. Carothers and his chemists successfully made synthetic fibers on February 28, 1935. Fluent in German, Carothers met Staudinger at the September, 1935, Faraday Society meeting in England to discuss their work with macromolecules.

Despite Carothers's achievements, including approximately fifty DuPont patents identifying him as inventor and an invitation to head the University of Chicago's Chemistry Department, he perceived himself as inept, agonized that his synthetic fiber was useless, and doubted his capabilities. Carothers's intense work ethic, a failed romance, and alcoholism conflicted with his emotional stability. His ever-present cyanide vial and erratic actions alarmed DuPont managers and coworkers, who tried to reassure the fragile Carothers regarding his scientific merits and reduced his workload. In the summer of 1934, Carothers received psychiatric treatment at a Baltimore hospital.

On February 21, 1936, Carothers married Helen Everett Sweetman, a DuPont chemist who worked in the Patent Department. Four months after their wedding, she arranged for him to be admitted to a Philadelphia mental institution for several weeks. That year, the National Academy of Sciences chose Carothers as that group's first organic chemist member who researched for an industrial employer.

On April 9, 1937, Carothers filed a patent for DuPont describing his synthetic fiber. His depression had deepened when a sister died in January, 1937, and his wife revealed she was pregnant despite Carothers's insistence they not have children because of his mental instability. In late April, 1937, Carothers retreated to a Philadelphia hotel room, where authorities found his cyanide-poisoned body.

Nylon

Wallace Hume Carothers and his research team at DuPont investigated several chemical possibilities to create the first synthetic fibers before focusing on polyamides—polymers consisting of carbon, hydrogen, nitrogen, and oxygen molecules. The chemists made what Carothers referred to as a superpolymer when acids and alcohols, specifically molecules of adipic acid and hexamethylenediamine, both containing six carbon atoms, reacted. The chemists removed water from this superpolymer and pulled it into a thin flexible filament similar to silk threads but stronger. Carothers and DuPont personnel referred to that synthetic fiber as polyhexamethyleneadipamide, polymer 66, and fiber 66, before DuPont formally called it nylon—chosen from possible names DuPont workers suggested, including "Wacara" to honor Carothers.

DuPont, eager to manufacture nylon, began researching techniques and equipment to spin nylon filament, investing $8 million in a Seaford, Delaware, factory to make nylon yarn. Consumers bought approximately four million nylon stockings when stores initially sold nylon products in May, 1940. Before nylon presented options, U.S. manufacturers invested $70 million yearly in silk from Japan to make hosiery.

During World War II, nylon reinforced Allied troops' military equipment. Nylon strengthened uniforms, parachutes, and tents, and was used for aircraft tires and fuel tanks, ropes, and medical supplies. Some soldiers used nylon mosquito tents, while others were protected by nylon flak jackets. In 1945, DuPont produced 25 million pounds of nylon for wartime needs.

Nylon became DuPont's main income source after the war. The company increased nylon production to meet domestic demands and created almost 100 million pounds of nylon in 1949. Nylon became a popular fabric for clothing, expanding material choices and fashion possibilities. Other common products consisting of nylon are carpets, fishing lines, and toothbrushes.

The success of nylon motivated many chemists to make additional synthetics that had nylon's durability and versatility. Since nylon's invention, some scientists improved nylon by chemically designing it for specific uses. Others appropriated chemical knowledge used to produce nylon, supplemented with such technologies as computers, to expand polymer uses for medicine or invent such materials as Kevlar.

Impact

Carothers died without knowing how significant his synthetic fiber invention would become. His chemical innovations initiated industrial activity specifically devoted to manufacturing and selling nylon and neoprene. His inventions assisted economic recovery as the Depression ended and injected millions of dollars, then billions in later decades, into the U.S. and global economies, as well as increasing domestic and foreign trade as synthetics were incorporated in more products. DuPont employees, executives, and stockholders profited from Carothers's inventions; many became wealthy, and DuPont was able to invest in additional research while seeking a similar extraordinary invention as nylon.

In addition to enhancing economic conditions, Carothers's inventions and investigations advanced professional recognition of polymer research as an emerging branch of industrial chemistry. His successful work with macromolecules caused many chemists to reconsider their previous rejection of Staudinger's theories and pursue similar research. Industries sought chemists to investigate how to create synthetics with polymers to meet specific manufacturing and consumer needs and demands, escalating production. Staudinger noted that Carothers's successes with polymers and macromolecules contributed to acceptance of his research, which won him the 1953 Nobel Prize in Chemistry. Carothers's DuPont colleague Paul John Flory was awarded a Nobel Prize in 1974 for macromolecular research. If Carothers had lived longer, he might have also received a Nobel Prize for his groundbreaking work.

Although Carothers did not attain public fame during his lifetime, his inventions, primarily nylon, earned him posthumous acclaim. Nine years after Carothers's suicide, his DuPont colleagues named a nylon research laboratory located at Wilmington in his honor. The National Inventors Hall of Fame selected Carothers for induction in 1984. *The Wall Street Journal* profiled Carothers in May, 1989, as a significant figure in the history of U.S. commerce. In 1990, *Life* magazine listed Carothers among notable twentieth century Americans. In August, 1998, *U.S. News & World Report* declared that Carothers and nylon represented outstanding twentieth century innovation. The American Chemical Society and Chemical Heritage Foundation commemorated a Carothers centennial in April, 1996, and the laboratory where Carothers invented nylon was declared a historical chemical landmark four years later.

—*Elizabeth D. Schafer*

Further Reading

Furukawa, Yasu. *Inventing Polymer Science: Staudinger, Carothers, and the Emergence of Macromolecular Chemistry*. Philadelphia: University of Pennsylvania Press, 1998. Places polymer research developments in context with scientific and public perception of chemistry's role during World War I and the interwar period and analyzes Carothers's influence on academic and industrial chemistry.

Handley, Susannah. *Nylon: The Story of a Fashion Revolution—A Celebration of Design from Art Silk to Nylon to Thinking Fibres*. Baltimore: The Johns Hopkins University Press, 1999. Textile scholar summarizes Carothers's research and DuPont's production and distribution of nylon, examining how consumers responded to nylon and how synthetics transformed the clothing industry.

Hermes, Matthew E. *Enough for One Lifetime: Wallace Carothers, Inventor of Nylon*. Washington, D.C.: American Chemical Society and the Chemical Heritage Foundation, 1996. Former DuPont researcher Hermes consulted archival records and Carothers's family, coworkers, and associates for this detailed account. Includes appendix of chemical formulas associated with Carothers's research and photographs from Carothers's relatives and friends.

Hounshell, David A., and John Kenley Smith, Jr. *Science and Corporate Strategy: DuPont R&D, 1902-1980*. Cambridge, England: Cambridge University Press, 1988. Discusses Carothers's career at DuPont during the 1930's and how management controlled his pure research interests by insisting he focus on such goals as producing marketable synthetics.

Kinnane, Adrian. *DuPont: From the Banks of the Brandywine to Miracles of Science*. Wilmington, Del.: E. I. du Pont de Nemours and Company, 2002. Comprehensive illustrated corporate history notes the impact of the Depression on DuPont's research, particularly the emphasis on commercial applications, and Carothers's reactions to this policy.

Raber, Linda R. "Landmark Honors Carothers' Work." *Chemical and Engineering News* 79, no. 4 (January 22, 2001): 108-109. Quotes text of plaque placed at Carothers's DuPont laboratory when the American Chemical Society named it a historic chemical site in 2000, providing a list of speakers at the unveiling and a synopsis of Carothers's work.

See also: Charles Goodyear; Stephanie Kwolek; Charles Macintosh; Theodor Svedberg.

Willis Carrier

American engineer

Deemed by Time *magazine as one of the one hundred "Most Important People of the Century," Carrier was instrumental in the development of one of the most significant and quintessential inventions of the last hundred years, the air conditioner.*

Born: November 26, 1876; Angola, New York
Died: October 9, 1950; New York, New York
Also known as: Willis Haviland Carrier (full name)
Primary field: Mechanical engineering
Primary invention: Air conditioner

Early Life

Born the only child of older parents, Willis Haviland Carrier was the direct descendant of a prominent New England family that included an ancestor hanged by the Puritans during the notorious Salem trials of the seventeenth century. Carrier's father was a farmer, and his mother a "birthright" Quaker. Carrier grew up surrounded primarily by adults, including his grandparents and a great-aunt. Lacking siblings, he spent a great deal of time tinkering with any gadget he could find around the house. Surprisingly, however, he struggled with even the most fundamental math in school, having to slice apples into various parts so he could understand fractions. Although he was not regarded as a particularly motivated or industrious child, his marks in secondary school were sufficient to gain him a scholarship to Cornell University in Ithaca, New York. There Carrier studied electrical engineering while earning his room and board by stoking furnaces, mowing lawns, and taking in his classmates' laundry.

Willis Carrier in 1915. (Courtesy, Carrier Corporation)

Shortly after graduating from Cornell with a master's degree in 1901, Carrier landed his first professional engineering job. At the Buffalo Forge Company, he initially designed commercial heating systems to dry lumber and coffee. Within months after joining the company's research department, he had worked out a series of accurate tables used to calculate how much surface area would be needed to heat a given space. This, his first of many contributions to climate-control technology, saved Buffalo Forge $40,000 and catapulted Carrier to head of the department. He had overcome his childhood difficulties with math through rote trial-and-error experimentation and perseverance, traits that would soon lead him to develop one of the twentieth century's most important inventions.

Life's Work

Also while with Buffalo Forge, Carrier made several important discoveries related to industrial heating and humidity control and made his first forays into the industrial application of cooling methods. In 1902, he worked with Brooklyn, New York, printer Sackett-Wilhelms to control the excessive humidity that had previously wreaked havoc on the delicate conditions required for quality color printing. Not only did the "dew-point control" device he designed control humidity, but it also cooled interior air. Carrier had in effect designed the world's first mechanical air-conditioning system. He promptly applied for the first of what would eventually become hundreds of U.S. patents, for a mechanism that created a spray mist to regulate the air in a public ventilating system. His "manufactured weather" system was first installed at La Crosse National Bank in La Crosse,

The Air Conditioner

Although Stuart Cramer of Charlotte, North Carolina, originally coined the term "air conditioning" for a process he patented in 1906, it was Willis Carrier who is responsible for making the term widely known. The "dew-point control" device he conceived in 1902, through which moisture and ventilation are combined mechanically to control humidity and air temperature, is the basis for all modern air-conditioning systems. The air conditioner as it is known today works on basic principles not unlike the age-old practice of placing wet cloths in an open passageway to cool the area inside it. In the mechanical application, a chemical refrigerant is pushed through a series of evaporator coils. Hot air from the interior space is then forced over the coils via an intake fan. The refrigerant, which begins in a volatile liquid form, evaporates as it is exposed to the air and absorbs the desired amount of heat. Eventually the cooling air reaches its saturation point, causing the water within it to condense on a set of metal blades placed just above the evaporator coils. These blades, or fins, allow the moisture removed from the "conditioned" air to drain away while the cooled air is rereleased into the space. After the refrigerant fully vaporizes, it is fed into a device called the compressor. The compressor then forces the evaporated gas through a set of condenser coils, which are exposed to the outside air. This allows the refrigerant to return to a liquid form and release the heat it has absorbed through an exterior exhaust system.

The chemical composition of the refrigerants first used was for some time a significant obstacle to the air conditioner's functionality. Carrier's first air conditioner used a highly toxic and flammable refrigerant such as methylene chloride. Although this substance was initially considered acceptable for industrial cooling applications, it proved too hazardous for reliable home use. In 1928, Thomas Midgley, Jr., developed Freon, the first chlorofluorocarbon (CFC) refrigerant. Much more stable than the chemicals initially used in air conditioning, Freon (or R-11, as its producer DuPont called its first variant) paved the way for the safe and cost-effective use of air conditioning in homes, businesses, and other public places. In recent decades, however, CFCs have been found to cause significant hazards of their own. CFCs that have been gradually allowed to escape into the atmosphere are known to deplete the ozone layer, and their production and use have been curtailed if not prohibited in many countries throughout the world. The ozone-friendly alternative Puron (R-410A), which was developed in the mid-1990's, is now used as the primary refrigerant in today's more contemporary air conditioners and climate-control systems.

Wisconsin. In 1906, Carrier devised methods to help a South Carolina textile mill control the temperature of dangerously overheating fabric spindles, which led to his discovery of the "law of constant dew-point depression." He subsequently used this principle to design the automatic temperature control system, for which he was awarded his second patent. Carrier's engineering paper "Rational Psychrometric Formulae," published in 1911, laid the theoretical foundations of modern air-conditioning design.

While Carrier worked at Buffalo Forge, his potential for advancing the development of climate-control technology seemed limitless. However, in 1914, a setback occurred that influenced how Carrier did business for the rest of his life. At the prompting of frugal and shortsighted financiers, the company dismantled its engineering department, seeing no further need to put its resources into product development or innovation. Carrier and several other engineers were let go. Disgruntled but undeterred, he and Buffalo Forge salesman Irving Lyle raised $35,000 capital and formed their own company. Prior to Carrier Engineering Corporation, air conditioning had been regarded primarily as an industrial application. The cooling of machines, not people, was viewed as the only feasible commercial use for interior cooling devices. However, Carrier and his new partners saw vast potential in the development and production of air-conditioning systems for indoor temperature and air-quality control.

One major obstacle to cooling public spaces safely, however, was the flammable refrigerants used to cool industrial machines. In 1922, Carrier developed the first nonflammable coolant, as well as the first centrifugal refrigerating machine—the nexus of the two technologies that finally made safe and cost-effective air conditioning possible. By the mid-1920's, Carrier's new machine, propelled by the refrigerant methylene chloride, made his air-conditioning systems feasible for public use. The celebrated Grauman's Metropolitan Theater in Los Angeles, in addition to a handful of comparably sized theaters in Texas, became his first commercial clients. Also, by 1928, Carrier was able to expand the scope of his company's offerings, installing the first large-scale air-conditioning system in the twenty-one-story Milam

Building in San Antonio. In the same year, Carrier also made available the first home air-conditioning unit, which was gas-powered.

Carrier Corporation enjoyed monumental success even during the Great Depression, attesting to the fundamental appeal and prescience of its founder's inventions. In 1932, Carrier installed his first "centralized" air-conditioning system in Philadelphia's thirty-two-story Savings Fund Society Building. His ingenious design, which placed its cooling plant in the center of the building so as to allow efficient air flow equally to all floors both above and below the housing, remains the method by which high-rise buildings are cooled even today. Air conditioning was the toast of the renowned 1939 New York World's Fair. Through the 1930's and 1940's, Carrier continued to develop and introduce a host of innovations that led, in the subsequent decades, to making air conditioning as commonplace and essential as indoor plumbing or electricity.

Perhaps less well known, but just as significant, were the industrial temperature and air-quality control systems Carrier continued to develop and market until his death in 1950. As early as 1929, he had designed the air-conditioning system for the Morro Velho gold mine in Brazil that made deep-shaft mining possible. This development made the extraction of deep ground commodities as diverse as coal, diamonds, and rare minerals more feasible and efficient than had ever been thought possible.

Impact

Carrier was a remarkable figure. Although he died in 1950 just as the age of modern climate control was getting under way, his invention has affected the course of human development in the last half century in ways that only a handful of other technological innovations can claim. By controlling the unwanted heat and humidity often created as a by-product of large-scale manufacturing processes, Carrier's technology allowed countless industries to become more efficient. Modern cooling and climate control has paved the way for people to live, assemble, and interact in spaces never before dreamed of—including indoor theaters, concert halls, stadiums, and shopping malls. Without air conditioning, modern high-rise office complexes, hospitals, and apartment buildings would not be possible. Countless lifesaving drugs, chemical formulations, and industrial processes owe their existence to the precise climate control afforded by the technologies designed and marketed by Carrier.

Although seldom celebrated as an entrepreneur or business figure, Carrier also merits mention as one of the twentieth century's most important industrialists. Not only did he invent the device that makes much of modern industry possible, but he also founded and operated one of the world's largest corporations for over three decades. Affectionately dubbed "The Chief" by his employees, Carrier led Carrier Corporation until his death, and the company remained the largest independent heating and cooling business in the world until 1979, when it became a division of international conglomerate United Technologies. Carrier's products are still sold in 172 countries on six continents, a testament not only to the technological genius but also to the business acumen of one of the most important industrialists of the last hundred years.

—*Gregory D. Horn*

Further Reading

Bridgman, Roger. *One Thousand Inventions and Discoveries*. New York: Dorling Kindersley, 2002. A collection of articles about the modern world's most influential technological developments. Includes a colorful, engaging biography of Carrier as well as a highly accessible explanation of how air conditioning works. Focuses on the impact of Carrier and his most famous invention on contemporary life. Illustrations, bibliography, index.

Ingels, Margaret. *Willis Haviland Carrier: Father of Air Conditioning*. 1952. Reprint. New York: Arno Press, 1972. Perhaps the only book-length biography of Carrier, this work provides a rare glimpse into the inventor's childhood and early adult life, probing the forces that shaped his remarkable character, drive, and genius. Also provides many employee anecdotes and personal accounts related to Carrier's years as head of Carrier Corporation. Illustrations, index.

Langley, Billy C. *Fundamentals of Air Conditioning Systems*. 2d ed. Lilburn, Ga.: Fairmont Press, 2000. Technical text on the theory, design, and function of modern air-conditioning systems. Illustrations, bibliography, index.

McQuiston, Faye C., J. D. Parker, and J. D. Spitler. *Heating, Ventilating, and Air Conditioning Analysis and Design*. 6th ed. Hoboken, N.J.: John Wiley & Sons, 2005. Additional text on the air-conditioning technology. Focuses on the historical development of modern air-conditioning methods, including a section on Carrier's contributions to the science of climate control. Illustrations, bibliography, index.

Panati, Charles. *Panati's Extraordinary Origins of Ev-*

eryday Things. New York: HarperCollins, 1989. Similar to the Bridgman book, an anthology filled with information about the development of several significant modern inventions and technological processes. Contains some biographical references to Carrier but concerns itself primarily with describing the design and function of the modern air conditioner. Illustrations, bibliography, index.

See also: Frederick McKinley Jones; Roy J. Plunkett.

George R. Carruthers

American astrophysicist

Carruthers designed and built the first space-borne ultraviolet light detector and camera and made the first measurements of ultraviolet emission from sources beyond Earth.

Born: October 1, 1939; Cincinnati, Ohio
Also known as: George Robert Carruthers (full name)
Primary fields: Aeronautics and aerospace technology; physics
Primary invention: Far-Ultraviolet Camera

Early Life

George Robert Carruthers was born to Sophia and George Carruthers on October 1, 1939, in Cincinnati, Ohio. His father was a civil engineer with an interest in astronomy. Young George received most of his primary education in the town of Milford, Ohio, where the family moved when he was seven. He grew up in the exciting first years of space exploration, when the idea of space travel was fanned by science-fiction books and films. His father encouraged him to learn about science and technology and fostered his son's interest in model rockets and astronomy. The boy built his first telescope at the age of ten.

Two years later, the Carruthers family suffered a great loss when George's father died suddenly, leaving the mother and four children. They moved to Chicago, Sophia Carruthers's hometown, in 1951, and George continued his education there, graduating from Englewood High School in 1957. Chicago offered excellent opportunities to learn about science because of its outstanding museums, especially the Field Museum of Natural History, the Museum of Science and Industry, and the Adler Planetarium, and George took advantage of these opportunities. His enthusiasm for space science was reflected in his joining the Chicago Rocket Society. Through his school, he entered several science fairs in which he received recognition for his scientific knowledge and inventiveness.

Following high school, Carruthers entered the University of Illinois, concentrating on physics, aeronautical engineering, and astronomy. After graduating in 1961 with a bachelor of science degree, he stayed on at Illinois for graduate work, obtaining a master's degree in the following year and a Ph.D. in 1964. His doctorate was in aeronautical and astronautical engineering. During his graduate career, he carried out several important experiments dealing with plasmas, especially in relation to plasma rocket engines and spacecraft reentry problems.

Life's Work

Carruthers's began his scientific career at the Naval Research Laboratory in Washington, D.C. He joined its rocket research group immediately after receiving his Ph.D., first as a National Science Foundation postdoctoral fellow and later as a research physicist in the Naval Research Laboratory's Hulburt Center for Space Research.

By 1964, space science had become a major activity in the United States. Orbiting spacecraft proliferated, and new opportunities for studying the planets and stars were opening up. One of these opportunities was the study of ultraviolet (UV) radiation emitted by cosmic sources. Ultraviolet light is absorbed by Earth's atmosphere, and ground-based scientists had not been able to detect it. Carruthers was interested in finding a good way to detect, measure, and study ultraviolet light from space. He carried out some experiments with suborbital sounding rockets, which reached high enough above most of the atmosphere to detect the ultraviolet light. In 1966, Carruthers's newly invented ultraviolet detector was successfully flown on a sounding rocket. In 1969, he patented the design for an ultraviolet camera, which was called an "Image Converter for Detecting Electromagnetic Radiation Especially in Short Wave Lengths." Subsequent experiments led to a major achievement in 1970 when his rocket-borne camera detected molecular hydrogen in space for the first time. Astronomers knew that hydrogen was abundant in the universe, as atomic hydrogen could be detected from the ground and was clearly the most common atom in space. However, in its molecular form, it had never been seen before, and Carruthers's camera proved an important new window into the universe.

Carruthers's results from rocket flights were impressive, especially considering the very short time the camera was above the atmosphere. To get better results, it was realized that the ultraviolet camera should be mounted on a telescope on a firm platform in space so that longer exposures could be made. The first opportunity for this came in 1972, when the Apollo 16 crew set up the Far-Ultraviolet Camera/Spectrograph on the lunar surface. Carruthers was the principal investigator and chief engineer for the experiment. The telescope and camera worked well, and the scientific results were superb, including UV images and spectroscopic data for both Earth atmospheric studies and stellar astrophysical measurements. In 1974, a backup camera from the Apollo mission was taken into space to be used on Skylab 4. Several experiments were carried out, including a first look at the UV light from a comet, as Comet Kohoutek was near the Earth at that time.

While satellite and lunar experiments were undoubtedly very productive, they were also very expensive and rarely available. For that reason, during this era Carruthers continued to use sounding rockets, which were much cheaper and more available, for science and engineering experiments. For instance, he was able to take advantage of the 1986 passage of Halley's comet to obtain some important ultraviolet observations of the hydrogen emission from the corona (the outer atmosphere) of this most famous comet.

In the 1990's, Carruthers was involved in using the Air Force's Advanced Research and Global Observation Satellite (ARGOS) for orbital study of the Earth's far-outer atmosphere, the electrically charged ionosphere and the neutral outer layers. His group developed a number of highly effective UV instruments for ARGOS deployment.

THE FAR-ULTRAVIOLET CAMERA

The best-known of George R. Carruthers's inventions is the Far-Ultraviolet Camera, which Apollo 16 astronauts took to the Moon in 1972 to observe the ultraviolet (UV) light from several important astronomical objects. The experiment consisted of a miniature observatory, which included a telescopic camera, an altazimuth mounting, a table, and a tripod—all of which weighed twenty-two kilograms. The electronographic camera used a cesium iodide cathode to display the UV light and a film cartridge to record it. The telescope aperture was three inches in diameter, and the design was that of a Schmidt telescope with a focal ratio of f/1. The small observatory was mounted in the shadow of the Apollo Lunar Module in order to avoid direct sunlight and to have proper thermal conditions.

The astronauts operated the telescope according to a carefully determined plan, having practiced with the device on Earth. However, the Lunar Module had landed on a slope, so that if the telescope were set up as planned, its mount would be tilted, making the preplanned pointings incorrect. A resourceful astronaut solved that problem by jamming one of the tripod legs deeply into the lunar soil, leveling the telescope successfully. The astronauts were scheduled to adjust the direction of the telescope periodically to point it toward different objects. The telescope-camera design allowed it to record both UV images and spectra. In the latter case, the UV light was spread out into its different wavelengths. At the end of the mission, astronauts removed the film cartridge and brought it back to Earth. The telescope and camera were left on the Moon.

This experiment had an important impact on both astronomy and geophysics. Most of the objects studied had never before been imaged in the ultraviolet part of the spectrum. With Carruthers's camera, the Earth's outer atmosphere and its hydrogen-glowing geocorona were seen in excellent perspective. The nearby stars were recorded, and it was possible to measure accurately the temperatures of very hot stars for the first time, as they emit most of their radiation in the ultraviolet. Radiation from intergalactic hydrogen was seen for the first time, and the structure of the Milky Way was revealed in a new way. Even other galaxies were targeted. One of the most spectacular images was one showing the Large Magellanic Cloud, a neighbor galaxy 170,000 light years away, which was revealed to be lit up like a Christmas tree by the many UV-emitting hot stars spread across its face.

IMPACT

Carruthers was a pioneer in the field of ultraviolet astronomy. His Far-Ultraviolet Camera, set up on the Moon's surface by the Apollo 16 astronauts, produced about two hundred UV pictures of the Earth's far-outer atmosphere and deep-space objects. For the first time in history, his device detected hydrogen in deep space, and it accurately measured the energy output of very hot stars.

Carruthers has had a strong interest in teaching young people about science and its applications. In addition to talks to students at several universities, he is active in the work of Science, Mathematics, Aerospace, Research, and Technology (SMART), a group of scientists and engineers who provide training workshops for black teachers and students. Of the many awards that Carruthers has received, the most notable are the Arthur S. Fleming Award (1971), the Exceptional Scientific Achievement Award (1972), an honorary doctorate from Michigan Technical University (1973), the University of Illinois Alumni Award (1975), the Samuel Cheevers Award (1977), the Black Engineer of the Year Award (1987), and election to the National Inventors Hall of Fame (2003).

—*Paul W. Hodge*

Further Reading

Barstow, Martin A., and Jay B. Holberg. *Extreme Ultraviolet Astronomy*. New York: Cambridge University Press, 2003. This technical book provides a complete history of the development of ultraviolet astronomy, which was pioneered by Carruthers. It includes details of the early years of ultraviolet astronomy, when sounding rockets carrying Carruthers's detectors provided the first extraterrestrial detections of UV sources.

Carruthers, George. "Apollo 16 Far-Ultraviolet Camera/ Spectrograph: Instruments and Operations." *Applied Optics* 12 (1973): 2501-2508. The ingenious and eminently successful Apollo 16 Far-Ultraviolet Camera, the first (and so far only) telescope to be used on the Moon, is described in detail. There are good diagrams and useful engineering details, but the paper is at a technical level.

_______. "Television Sensors for Ultraviolet Space Astronomy." In *Astronomical Observations with Television-Type Sensors*, edited by J. W. Glaspey and Gordon Arthur Hunter Walker. Vancouver, B.C.: Institute of Astronomy and Space Science, University of British Columbia, 1973. This is probably Carruthers's most important paper about his design and its relation to other instruments used for ultraviolet astronomy. It is fairly technical but well written, and it provides an excellent introduction to the engineering details of these kinds of instruments.

Henderson, Susan K., Stanley P. Jones, and Fred Amram. *African-American Inventors II: Bill Becoat, George Carruthers, Meredith Gourdine, Jesse Hoagland, Wanda Sigur*. Mankato, Minn.: Capstone Press, 1998. This short book is intended for high school-age readers. It provides the basic facts about the lives of five outstanding black inventors.

Kessler, James H., J. S. Kidd, Renée A. Kidd, and Katherine A. Morin. *Distinguished African American Scientists of the Twentieth Century*. Phoenix, Ariz.: Oryx Press, 1996. This encyclopedic book covers the lives and accomplishments of one hundred African American scientists and inventors. Its 392 pages are full of biographical data, arranged alphabetically and including a photograph of each person. Carruthers's biography is four pages long. The book was written for young readers in clear and rather plain language.

Orloff, Richard W., and David M. Harland. *Apollo: The Definitive Sourcebook*, New York: Springer Praxis Books, 2006. As the developer of the first telescope to be deployed on the surface of the Moon, George Carruthers was an important figure in the scientific success of the Apollo program. This thick and authoritative source book provides comprehensive accounts of each of the Apollo flights and summarizes the science attained. Its 633 pages are densely packed but are written in reasonably nontechnical language.

See also: Bernhard Voldemar Schmidt; Valerie L. Thomas.

Edmund Cartwright
British clergyman

Cartwright's creation of the power loom was one in a series of significant eighteenth century inventions that revolutionized textile manufacturing, especially cotton textiles, in England and is considered part of the Industrial Revolution, which transformed England's socioeconomic structure.

Born: April 24, 1743; Marnham, Nottingham, England
Died: October 30, 1823; Hastings, Sussex, England
Primary fields: Business management; manufacturing
Primary invention: Power loom

Early Life

Edmund Cartwright's (KAHRT-rit) early life is not that well documented. His father, William, was a landowner in Nottinghamshire, England. William and his wife, Alice, had thirteen children, and Edmund was the fourth son. Edmund attended Wakefield Grammar School, graduated from University College, Oxford University, and was elected to a fellowship at Magdalen College, Oxford University, in 1764. He published a long poem, "Armine and Elvira," in 1770 and "Prince of Peace" in 1779. He pursued a career in the Church of England and became rector at Goadby, Marwood, Leicestershire, in 1779 and prebend of Lincoln Cathedral. Edmund's brother, Major John Cartwright (1740-1824), was a supporter of political reform during the reign of George III (r. 1760-1820). However, Edmund's fame was not to come from preaching, poetry, or politics; it came from inventing—an unexpected development considering his background and training. Edmund was married twice, first to Alice and then to Susannah after Alice's death.

Life's Work

Textile production in England had long been a significant sector of the economy. Because of the large number of sheep in England, the production of woolen cloth provided work for many villages through a process variably called the domestic or putting-out system or the cottage industry, whereby a cloth merchant would drop off raw wool to villagers who owned spinning wheels and handlooms. Inhabitants turned the raw wool into thread and bolts of cloth and then received payment from the merchants. The people worked at their own pace, with their families and at home. Working with family and friends to supplement their agricultural income became a social as well as an economic activity. All this would begin to change in the eighteenth century as the factory system developed, causing people to commute to work instead of working at home and to become subject to "industrial discipline" by being at work at an appointed time, only having an allotted time for meals, and receiving corporal punishment. There was also extensive reliance on child and woman labor.

The series of inventions started with John Kay's flying shuttle (1733), which allowed weavers to weave more quickly. Cotton began to become the preferred material to work with because of England's connections to the colonies of the American South, Egypt, and India. Because of the flying shuttle, weavers outpaced the spinners, and it was not until 1764 that James Hargreaves's spinning jenny allowed spinners to produce more thread and catch up to the weavers. In 1769, Richard Arkwright invented the spinning frame, also known as the water frame, which spun multiple threads into yarn; the large machine was powered by water and had to be housed in a building by a stream—in effect, a factory. Samuel Crompton in 1779 combined the spinning jenny and the water frame to create what is basically the modern spinning device—the spinning mule, or water mule.

In 1784, while Cartwright was on vacation at Matlock, Derbyshire, he met with a group of businessmen from Manchester, and they discussed the textile industry and the problem that resulted from Arkwright's water frame: Though the machine spun a great quantity of thread, it was difficult to weave the thread quickly into cloth. This meeting led to Cartwright's visit to Arkwright's textile mill in Derbyshire to view textile manufacturing firsthand. Cartwright was inspired to invent a weaving machine to complement the water frame. The first version that was produced with the help of a carpenter and blacksmith was modified, and Cartwright was awarded a patent for the device in 1785. The power loom was a very large, complex steam-powered machine that took two people to operate. The basic design was modified by Cartwright and other inventors to allow the machine to stop when the thread broke and to remove the finished cloth by rolling it off when the process was complete.

The relatively open social structure in England enabled a clergyman to become a textile entrepreneur by attempting to profit from his own invention. Although Cartwright built his own textile factories with steam-powered looms at Doncaster in 1787, he was not a successful businessman, declaring bankruptcy and shutting down in 1793—an apparent failure at age fifty. This also caused hardship for his brothers and sisters who had invested in his textile ventures. He did sell four hundred of his power looms to another manufacturing company, but that factory burned down. Local authorities and subsequent historians have suspected that arson on the part of disgruntled weavers may have been the cause of his factory's destruction. Before the mechanization of textile production, weavers were highly skilled artisans; now they had been reduced to fixing broken threads on machines or removing bolts of finished cloth from the power looms. This loss of prestige and even loss of employment caused many textile workers to petition authorities for redress, while others resorted to violence—smashing textile machinery, burning factories, and engaging in riots.

Cartwright continued tinkering and was awarded several additional patents. In 1790, he patented a woolcombing machine, and in 1792 he invented a machine for making rope. Finally, in 1797, he received a patent for an alcohol engine, similar to a steam engine in concept but using alcohol rather than water. One can understand the lack of success for this last device, as alcohol is more expensive and harder to obtain than water. In 1801, Parliament extended his patent for the power loom for an additional fourteen years, but in the following year, a textile manufacturer, William Horrocks, received a patent for an improved version of Cartwright's power loom that increased productivity. In 1807, Cartwright petitioned Parliament for recognition of the importance of his invention and for some monetary compensation. Robert Peel, a prominent member of the House of Commons and a wealthy textile manufacturer, supported this petition, and in 1809 Parliament voted a sum of £10,000 in recognition of the benefits that the power loom had bestowed upon England. This substantial payment helped Cartwright satisfy serious personal debt, as recent projects of his such as interlocking bricks and incombustible floorboards failed to come to fruition.

Cartwright had earned a doctor of divinity degree from Oxford University in 1806, and with his grant of money from Parliament he purchased a farm in Sevenoaks, Kent, where he lived a quiet, unassuming life. He died at Hastings, Sussex, and was buried at Battle, Sussex.

IMPACT

The power loom, along with the other textile inventions, produced major structural changes for all levels of British society. For the individual, factory work replaced working at home; families—husband, wife, and children—often ended up working in the factory, until the Factory Acts of the nineteenth century regulated working hours and conditions and banned work by children under certain ages. Many skilled artisans were reduced to textile workers who performed monotonous and even dangerous tasks in noisy factories that were hot in summer and cold in winter. There was no accident insurance

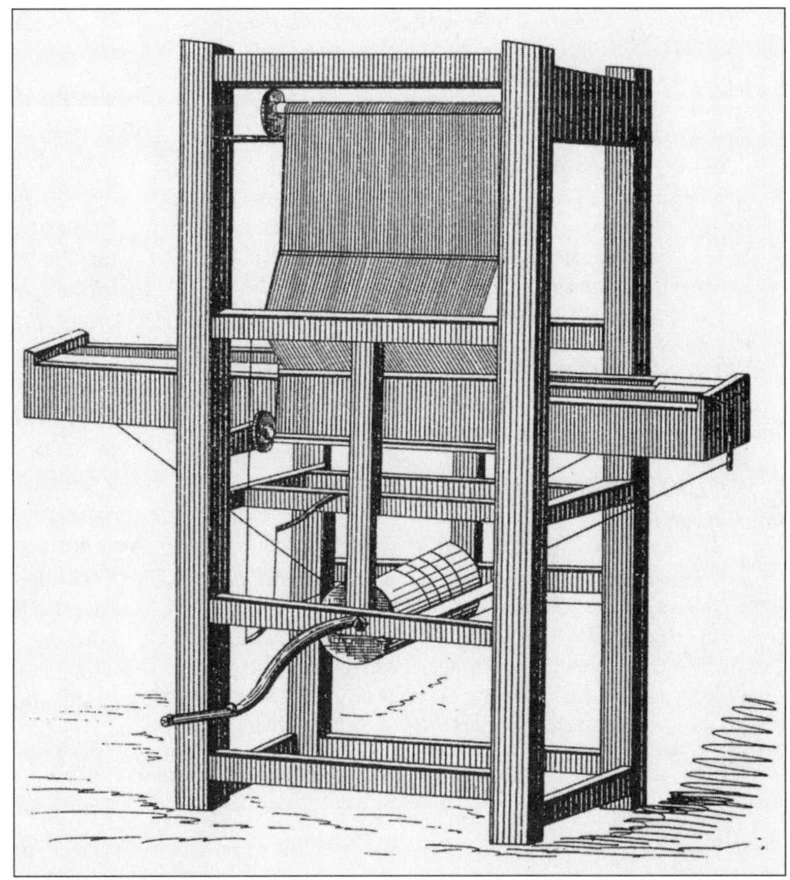

Edmund Cartwright's power loom, patented in 1785. (The Granger Collection, New York)

or workers' compensation, so workers who were injured often lost their jobs. However, manufactured clothing became cheaper because cotton was easier to work with, and it was easier to care for and could be dyed various colors. Slowly, real wages rose, allowing workers to purchase manufactured products. Middle-class factory owners gained wealth, and during the nineteenth century they began to push for political power commensurate with their newly acquired wealth.

Localities changed because of the development of textile mills. It is estimated that there were more than two thousand power looms in England in 1810. As people left the countryside because of agricultural unemployment caused by the enclosure movement that forced farmers of smaller parcels off their land, they moved to work in textile mills, causing those industrial areas to explode into massive cities of several hundreds of thousands of inhabitants within a few decades. Such rapid urbanization brought significant problems: overcrowded slums of substandard housing, pollution, crime, prostitution, and disease. For example, Manchester grew in population from about 25,000 in 1772 to almost 370,000 by 1850.

England became known as "the workshop of the world" and increased its economic power many times over, especially through exports of textiles and other items produced by factory labor. Until the late nineteenth century, England's exports were larger than the combined exports of a number of European countries. England's influence in India through the East India Company expanded because of the export of manufactured cotton textiles to India that nearly ruined India's own hand-produced textile industry. In the twentieth century, Mohandas Gandhi's protest movement against British domination of India included ritual spinning of cotton thread to promote economic self-reliance and political independence.

—Mark C. Herman

THE POWER LOOM

Edmund Cartwright noted that the weaving process had three components that followed one another and that it would not be difficult to create a machine that would replicate these movements. He came to these conclusions in spite of the fact that the Manchester businessmen with whom he discussed the textile industry believed that it was impossible to create a mechanical weaving machine. Cartwright's original notes and drawing apparently do not exist, so the exact nature of his creative process cannot be reproduced or described except in the general summary he mentions in his writings. The warp portion was placed in a perpendicular fashion, and the shuttle was moved by springs attached to a cylinder under the loom. Cartwright noted that the springs were extremely strong and that it required the strength of two men to work the loom, but the pace of weaving was very slow. Because of the tension in the springs, the two men tired quickly; thus, the loom could only be operated for a brief period.

The biggest modification that Cartwright made was to reposition the warp horizontally and add a drive shaft to connect it to a power source, so that the strong springs could move the shuttle. Apparently, the first power source used was a bull, then the much more practical and efficient steam engine. Among the problems that Cartwright faced was patent infringement, which involved him in lawsuits to protect his invention from piracy.

FURTHER READING

Stearns, Peter N. *The Industrial Revolution in World History*. 3d ed. Boulder, Colo.: Westview Press, 2007. A broadly focused survey that provides the context for Cartwright's invention and is strong on the effects of mechanization in the textile industry.

Strickland, Mary, and Jane Margaret Strickland. *A Memoir of Edmund Cartwright: A Memoir of the Life, Writings, and Mechanical Inventions of Edmund Cartwright*. 1843. Reprint. New York: A. M. Kelley, 1971. Although an older work, this book contains the most complete biographical information about Cartwright and captures the immediacy of his achievement, as it was published shortly after his death.

Weightman, Gavin. *Industrial Revolutionaries: The Creation of the Modern World, 1776-1914*. London: Atlantic Books, 2007. This work is strong on the importance of the individual inventors and entrepreneurs and the social and economic impacts of industrialization.

See also: Sir Richard Arkwright; James Hargreaves; John Kay.

George Washington Carver

American agriculturalist

Carver is most famous for the large number of by-products that he derived from the peanut, sweet potato, and several other crops, but his achievements in the revivification of Southern agriculture and the advancement of African American education were also notable.

Born: July 12, 1861?; near Diamond Grove (now Diamond), Missouri
Died: January 5, 1943; Tuskegee, Alabama
Also known as: Plant Doctor
Primary fields: Agriculture; chemistry; food processing
Primary invention: Peanut milk and other by-products of sweet potatoes and peanuts

Early Life

The person who came to be called George Washington Carver was born a slave, and because documentation about slaves tended to be thin, considerable uncertainty exists about his early life. He took his last name from his owners, Susan and Moses Carver, and in later reminiscences he stated that he had been born near the end of the Civil War, though some scholars give dates as early as 1860 or 1861 and others opt for 1865. Material issued by the George Washington Carver National Monument gives his birth date as July 12, 1864. His mother, Mary, had a previous son, Jim, and his father, according to Carver, was a slave on a neighboring farm who had been killed in an accident. What is certain is that George grew up in Missouri on the Carver farm, located near a diamond-shaped stand of trees in the village of Diamond Grove.

A tragic event that influenced George's life occurred when he and his mother were kidnapped by Confederate raiders and taken to Arkansas. Eventually, Moses Carver was able to locate George and barter him back in exchange for a racehorse, but Mary was never found and was assumed to have died. After the end of the Civil War, George and his brother Jim were adopted and raised by the Carvers. Because of his frail health, George worked at household tasks rather than in the field, but, as a young boy, he exhibited a deep curiosity about nature, and he collected wild plants and raised them in his own garden. His skill in nursing sickly plants to health led to his being called the "Plant Doctor."

George's early education occurred at a church school, and he became a Christian when he was ten years old. After his prayers for improved health were answered, his faith in a benevolent Providence solidified and became a defining characteristic throughout his life and scientific career. As a teenager, wishing to further his education, he was allowed to attend a school for "coloreds" in Neosho. He then led a peripatetic existence until he was finally able to get a high school education in Minneapolis, Kansas, where he worked in a laundry and added "Washington" as his middle name to distinguish himself from another George Carver.

After being rejected by a college because of his race and after a failed attempt at farming on the Kansas frontier, he moved to Iowa, where he enrolled at Simpson College as its first African American student. There he met Etta Budd, an art teacher who encouraged him to switch from art to botany and to transfer to Iowa State College of Agriculture and Mechanic Arts (now Iowa State University), where her father was a professor of horticulture. In 1891, he became the first African American to be accepted by Iowa State. By working in the agricultural laboratory, he was able to pay his college costs while also doing well in his academic subjects. His thesis for his bachelor's degree centered on his experiments with plant hybrids. In 1894, he became the first African American to graduate from Iowa State. He remained at Ames to obtain his master's degree, following which he accepted an offer to become the college's first black faculty member. He taught botany and conducted plant experiments, while managing the college's greenhouse.

Life's Work

Booker T. Washington, who had founded the Tuskegee Normal and Industrial Institute for Negroes (now Tuskegee University) in 1891, had learned of Carver's achievements, and in 1896 he invited him to head Tuskegee's Department of Agriculture. Carver accepted and traveled to Alabama, beginning what would become a forty-seven-year association with this institution. Initially, he was confronted with challenges, such as the department's meager facilities of a barn and a few farm animals. By scavenging the institute, he was able, using his improvisatory skills, to create and equip an agricultural laboratory, which became the site of his and his students' research. He also had to overcome the negative attitude of faculty members who disparaged agricultural work, associating it with sharecropping, but Carver made his first important contributions by showing sharecroppers and other small farmers how to improve their harvests.

For decades, Southern farmers had been growing cotton and tobacco with diminishing returns, and Carver recognized that their problems were due to soils that had become seriously depleted in nutrients. Through his experiments, bulletins, and visits, he was able to convince an increasing number of farmers to alternate their plantings of cotton with such leguminous plants as peanuts, which enriched the soil with nitrogenous compounds. He was rewarded for his efforts when the state of Alabama passed a bill to support an Agricultural Research Station at Tuskegee. From 1903, when his peanut studies began, until 1915, when Booker T. Washington died, he developed many recipes that contained peanuts and many by-products that he derived from peanuts. The farmers who followed Carver's advice were so successful that their high yields created a problem, for when markets became saturated with peanuts, their price dropped. This stimulated Carver's inventiveness, and he developed a large number of uses for the excess peanuts. To farmers and members of the peanut business he became known as the "Peanut Man."

In 1916, Carver published what turned out to be his most popular bulletin. It was on 105 ways of preparing the peanut for human consumption. For example, the fifty-first recipe was for peanut butter, which led some to the erroneous conclusion that he was its inventor. He had already derived many products from soybeans and sweet potatoes, but the favorable response to his recipes led him to discover many other uses for the peanut. Over the years, several authors have claimed that Carver derived more than three hundred products from the peanut, but later scholars questioned this claim. Because Carver publicized his discoveries through bulletins, speeches, and demonstrations, and because he kept inadequate laboratory notebooks and eschewed publication in scientific journals, it has been difficult to substantiate many of his discoveries. However, studies have shown that his lists contain redundancies, unoriginal products, and products that are simple combinations of previously known materials. When these are removed, the list contracts to about a hundred. These include such food products as cheeses, milk and meat substitutes, and flour; such cosmetics as face powder, face and hand lotion, and shampoo; and such general products as medicines, dyes, paints, and stains. Carver's methods were largely trial and error. Using chemical solvents, he would extract materials from his peanut plants and then combine these extracted materials with other substances in the hope of creating a useful product. He published his most interesting results in his bulletins and exhibited his food and cosmetic products at state fairs and other venues, but, as his later critics have pointed out, not one of these became a successful commercial product. Nevertheless, his ability to make so many things from the peanut excited the public imagination.

George Washington Carver during his early years at Tuskegee University. (Library of Congress)

After Washington's death, Carver formed a close friendship with his successor, Robert Russa Moton. Moton's tenure as president lasted to 1935, and during this time Carver, now free from classroom and administrative obligations, was able to devote himself fully to agricultural research. His studies of soils and his investigations of such crops as sweet potatoes, soybeans, and pecans led him to make a large number of products. For example, he most famously derived 118 products from the sweet potato, but, as with the peanut, scholars have found repetitive and unoriginal entries and have reduced the list to forty uses—including his recipes for sweet potato flour, starch, and sugar bread.

Although Carver did not singlehandedly revolutionize Southern agriculture by his advocacy of the peanut, sweet potato, and other crops, the American peanut business prospered because of his example and the work of many others. The U.S. peanut business became so large that it felt threatened when China-grown and Japan-processed peanuts undersold the U.S. product. In 1921, Carver, testifying in favor of a protective tariff before the House Ways and Means Committee, helped persuade its members that the American peanut industry was well worth saving, and a tariff on imported peanuts became the law. His successful appearance before Congress increased his fame, and he received many invitations to speak around the country as well as several job offers—including one from Thomas Alva Edison—all of which he refused, preferring to remain at Tuskegee.

In 1923, he agreed to lend his expertise and name to a company that was being formed to develop commercially some of his agricultural derivatives. The Carver Products Company would actually manufacture no products but sell some of Carver's processes to concerns that did. With this in mind, Carver, for the first time in his career, had to patent his products and processes: On January 6, 1925, he was granted a patent for cosmetics and his process for making them; on June 9, 1925, he received a patent on paints and stains along with the processes for making them; and on June 14, 1927, he obtained another patent on his formulas for making paints and stains. With the incorporation of the company bearing his name, Carver garnered much favorable publicity, but the company was insufficiently capitalized and poorly managed, and it eventually failed. Similarly, the Carver Penol Company was founded a few years later to market Carver's discovery of an emulsion of creosote and peanut juices. Physicians had long used creosote as an antiseptic and a remedy for bronchitis, but it had a nauseating taste. Carver's idea was to create a palatable mixture that would synergistically combine the medicinal properties of creosote and the nutritive values of peanuts. Carver called the combination Penol, and he tried it on himself. He found its taste pleasant, and it cured him of a persistent cough. Some physicians tried it on their patients and reported successes. By the mid-1920's, some prominent

Peanut Milk

George Washington Carver's discovery of peanut milk contributed to his fame as the "Peanut Man." He certainly had dreams for its commercial success. He did not see it as a substitute for cows' milk but as an important new supplement to the human diet. The peanut was rich in protein and other nutrients, and he hoped that it might also serve as a replacement for those unable to consume cows' milk.

As with many of his other inventions, Carver created peanut milk by a process of trial and error. He knew that peanuts contained a high percentage of oil and that they also contained varying amounts of proteins, carbohydrates, and fats. His peanut milk was an emulsion of these oils, fats, proteins, and carbohydrates. In fact, he made several kinds of peanut milk by varying the proportions of some of these components and by adding water. Like oil in vinegar, peanut oils in water formed an emulsion, a suspension of tiny globules, since the two liquids are immiscible. Carver, who first made peanut milk in 1919, was very happy with his creation, using it to make tasty bread and creamed vegetables.

On September 22, 1919, Carver informed Dr. Robert Russa Moton, Tuskegee University's president, of his discovery, and Carver began to publicize his new product in speeches. This information soon reached members of the peanut industry in Alabama, and Carver was invited to speak about peanut milk and his other peanut derivatives at a 1920 meeting of the United Peanut Association in Montgomery, Alabama. When he arrived, he, as a black man, was not allowed to enter the convention hall by the front entrance, but he was finally allowed to reach the meeting hall through a rear entrance. He then lectured the delegates about the virtues of peanut milk, which, he stated, could be made more quickly and efficiently than a cow produces milk. His talk was enthusiastically received, and several delegates wanted to facilitate the commercial development of peanut milk. However, Carver's hopes for its commercialization were frustrated when he learned of a patent for peanut milk that had been filed in England in 1917. Carver believed that his product was superior to the English version. He went on to make thirty-two kinds of peanut milk, but he never patented any of his formulas. Nevertheless, Carver's advocacy of his creations proved to be beneficial for the peanut industry, since it was his life and personality, not his peanut milk, that ultimately excited the public.

businessmen formed the Carver Penol Company and raised sufficient capital to construct a small factory to make bottles of Penol. The company lasted into the 1930's, but because of poor sales and a Food and Drug Administration (FDA) report in 1937 that invalidated Penol's nutritional and medical claims, the Carver Penol Company eventually failed.

During the 1930's, Carver became an important part of the chemurgy movement, which advocated the development of commercial chemicals from agricultural products. In 1937, he attended two chemurgy conferences, at one of which he met Henry Ford, and they became friends. In fact, Ford and other important members of this movement considered Carver to be its "patron saint." Despite his growing fame and influence, he witnessed his work at Tuskegee decline because of lack of funding brought on by the Great Depression. He was also old, and his health began to fail. In 1941, Ford came to Tuskegee to dedicate the George Washington Carver Museum, and Carver himself established a foundation to continue his work at Tuskegee. After a fall down a flight of stairs, he was hospitalized, and he died from various complications, including anemia, early in 1943. He was buried near Booker T. Washington at Tuskegee, and his epitaph epitomized an idealized view of his life: "He could have added fortune to fame, but caring for neither, he found happiness and honor in being helpful to the world."

Impact

Even though Carver patented only three from his lists of more than five hundred crop derivatives, recipes, and by-products, he became famous as an agricultural inventor. His accomplishments had a significant influence on the African American community, and he received the Spingarn Medal of the National Association for the Advancement of Colored People (NAACP). His contributions to Southern agriculture were honored by the Roosevelt Medal in 1939. Posthumously, his honors multiplied with his election to the Hall of Fame for Great Americans (1977) and his induction into the National Inventors Hall of Fame (1990). He was commemorated in two U.S. postage stamps (1947 and 1998), a Polaris submarine was christened the USS *George Washington Carver*; and his Missouri home was made into a national monument.

The glorified story of Carver's rise from a slave to a great scientist fascinated the public of all races, and *Time* magazine called him the "Black Leonardo," because, like da Vinci, he contributed not only to science but also to art (he was an accomplished painter). After his death, hagiographies written for children and general audiences established the image of Carver as a saintly scientist and inventor whose advocacy of the peanut had helped save Southern agriculture. In recent decades, as scholars have corrected the errors in this idealized portrait, Carver's influence has lessened, particularly among scientists. Because he did not participate in meetings of professional scientific organizations and failed to publish his results in refereed journals, his discoveries and inventions have been criticized. His status among business historians has also diminished as it has become widely known that not one of his agricultural by-products ever achieved commercial success. On the other hand, in an age of increasing environmental sensitivity, some scholars have praised Carver's support of sustainable agriculture at the local level, where efficient use is made of all parts of crops. Enlightened scholars now view Carver more as a naturalist than a scientist, someone whose religious beliefs ally him with modern holists rather than with reductionists and industrialists. Ultimately, his motivating vision was of a multiracial America in which carefully conserved land supported people living modestly, healthily, and happily.

—*Robert J. Paradowski*

Further Reading

Erbach, Donald C., and L. Frank Flora. "Biobased Products: America's Second Green Revolution." *Agricultural Research* 50 (April, 2002): 2. This editorial traces the "second agricultural green revolution" that is underway in the early twenty-first century to George Washington Carver's work almost a century ago.

Gates, Henry Louis, and Cornel West. *The African-American Century: How Black Americans Have Shaped Our Country*. New York: Free Press, 2000. Discusses Carver's achievement in the chapter on the second decade of the twentieth century. Bibliography and index.

Graham, Shirley, and George D. Lipscomb. *Dr. George Washington Carver, Scientist*. New York: J. Messner, 1944. This early biography, introduced by messages from President Franklin D. Roosevelt and Vice President Henry A. Wallace, presents an idealized biography accessible to young readers and general audiences. Illustrated, appendixes, and index.

Holt, Rackham. *George Washington Carver: An American Biography*. Rev. ed. Garden City, N.Y.: Doubleday, 1963. Carver chose Holt to write his authorized biography, and this account is enlivened by material from the author's interviews with Carver, his friends, and colleagues. Bibliography and index.

Kremer, Gary R., ed. *George Washington Carver: In His Own Words*. Columbia: University of Missouri Press, 1987. The editor has collected important and interesting letters and speeches of Carver. Bibliography.

McMurry, Linda O. *George Washington Carver: Scientist and Symbol*. New York: Oxford University Press, 1981. Using extensive primary and secondary sources, the author attempts to discover the real man and separate him from his idealized portrayals. Forty-four pages of detailed notes and an index.

See also: Henry Ford; Percy Lavon Julian; Eli Whitney.

George Cayley

British aeronautical engineer

Cayley founded the science of aeronautics by identifying the controlling forces on an airplane in flight. He designed and flew a fixed-wing glider airplane that lacked only two modern innovations: movable wing flaps (ailerons) for roll control, and a power plant.

Born: December 27, 1773; Scarborough, Yorkshire, England
Died: December 15, 1857; Brompton, Yorkshire, England
Primary field: Aeronautics and aerospace technology
Primary invention: Monoplane glider

Early Life

George Cayley was born in Scarborough in Yorkshire, England, on December 27, 1773. His mother, Isabella Seton, was from a prominent family that was distantly related to Anne Boleyn, one of the unfortunate brides of Henry VIII. His father was Thomas Cayley, and his grandfather, also of the name George Cayley, was the fourth baronet of Brompton. ("Baronet" is a hereditary title reserved for commoners, superior to all orders of knighthood other than the Order of the Garter, but inferior to full barons.) Thomas, in turn, became the fifth baronet of Brompton at the age of sixty-two when Sir George the elder died. The younger George Cayley inherited the title eighteen months later upon Sir Thomas's death in 1792.

Family lore says that the young Cayley had an intense interest in mechanical devices and was allowed to spend a great deal of time annoying the village watchmaker. Cayley was primarily educated through the services of two tutors. The first was George Walker, minister of High Pavement Chapel in Nottingham and fellow of the Royal Society of London for the Improvement of Natural Knowledge, Great Britain's premier learned society. It stood at the center of the scientific discoveries and technological developments of the time. Through Walker, Cayley felt the influence of Britain's finest minds. Walker also possessed strongly liberal ideas in both politics and religion; presumably, Cayley was influenced by these ideas as well. Cayley's mother chose George Cadogan Morgan, very similar to Walker in many ways, to be Cayley's tutor starting in 1792. The Walker influence quite likely continued throughout Cayley's life: He married Sarah Walker, George's daughter, in 1795.

Cayley's accession to the baronetcy of Brompton brought him large estates, significant wealth, and important responsibilities. The rest of Cayley's life would be an equal mixture of agricultural management, political leadership, scientific research, and engineering projects. One measure of his genius was his skill at filling these roles.

Life's Work

Cayley's interest in flight started at a young age. He began, like so many others before him, by studying the flight of birds. Previous investigators thought of human or mechanical flight almost exclusively in terms of flapping wings, always based on the mistaken belief that bird wings flapped simultaneously downward to generate lift and backward to generate thrust. Designs for flying machines, such as Leonardo da Vinci's ornithopter, relied on this thinking. One of Cayley's earliest scientific observations was that birds flap their wings downward only but warp their wings to achieve forward thrust.

An engraved silver medallion produced by Cayley in 1799 shows an aircraft design on one side that incorporated a fixed wing for the generation of lift and a separate mechanism for the generation of thrust. Cayley, for the first time in aeronautical history, divorced the generation of lift from the generation of thrust. This became a central tenet of aeronautical development over the next century, finally achieving reality with the success of Orville and Wilbur Wright in 1903. (Simultaneous generation of lift and thrust from a rotating wing was eventually realized in the development of the helicopter.) The other side of the medallion shows the aerodynamic force on an in-

THE MONOPLANE GLIDER

George Cayley's most sophisticated aircraft design appeared in *Mechanics Magazine* on September 25, 1852. Called the "governable parachute," it was in fact a human-carrying glider. Cayley regarded gliders and parachutes to be of the same class since they rely solely on gravity for maintaining airspeed. This 1852 glider design, though probably never built and flown, was thoroughly modern in concept and approach to flight.

Airplanes have three independent degrees of freedom: pitch, the motion of the nose up or down in a vertical plane; yaw, the motion of the nose to the right or left in a horizontal plane; and roll, a rotation to the right or left about an axis stretching from nose to tail. Pitch is controlled by the elevators. Yaw is controlled by the rudder. Roll is controlled by the ailerons.

Nominal flight configuration has pitch, yaw, and roll all equal to zero. This is level flight with the nose pointed in the direction of travel. A stable airplane, one safe and comfortable to fly, spontaneously returns to nominal flight if disturbed; an unstable airplane spontaneously tends to dangerously increasing values of one or more of these motions if disturbed.

Cayley's aircraft, the 1852 design among them, were the first in history inherently stable in pitch and roll in straight or slightly curved flight, and the first equipped with pilot-controlled elevators and rudders. Rudder and elevator were combined into a single cruciform tail. Both were movable, giving the pilot true control over the aircraft.

The 1852 design incorporated dihedral wings for built-in roll stability, but it did not include ailerons or any alternative way of changing the shape of the wings, making the glider difficult to steer. Fixed-wing designs such as Cayley's have no way of initiating or controlling roll and therefore cannot initiate banking turns. While capable of true flight in a straight line, they can accomplish turns only with great difficulty and are not truly navigable in the air.

Cayley's 1852 design had no onboard propulsion. Other earlier designs incorporated movable flappers separate from the fixed wings to generate thrust in the manner of birds. Cayley knew of the propeller but believed his flapper approach to be superior. Overall, the propeller receives very little mention or regard in Cayley's writings. Further, Cayley's power plant designs were crude and ineffective—understandable at a time when the science of thermodynamics and the technology of heat engines were both in their infancy.

clined plane functioning as a fixed wing. The force is properly resolved into the two components of lift and drag, demonstrating that at this early date, Cayley possessed a full appreciation of the fixed wing and its application to flight.

Cayley, like others before him, investigated these forces experimentally for insight into the physics of flight. In the 1820's, he used the whirling-arm apparatus invented by Benjamin Robins in 1742. This continued to be the instrument of choice for the testing of airfoils and for measurements of lift and drag until the Wright brothers adopted and improved the wind tunnel, an 1871 invention of Francis Wenham and John Browning.

Cayley designed, built, and flew his first engineered glider in 1804. Although only a small handheld model (one meter long) and childish to modern eyes, it was the first aircraft in history possessing a fixed wing and adjustable tail consisting of a combined elevator and rudder.

Cayley published a tripartite paper, "On Aerial Navigation," in the *Journal of Natural Philosophy, Chemistry and the Arts* in November of 1809, February of 1810, and March of 1810. This paper was the first to document that flat surfaces inclined to the wind generate lift; that curved (cambered) surfaces do so more efficiently; and that lift is caused by a low pressure region above the wing. The paper also contains the first discussion of flight control achieved through vertical and horizontal tail surfaces and announces the first successful flight of a full-sized glider, flown unmanned at Cayley's estate in 1809.

From 1810 to 1845, Cayley's energies were consumed by other activities. He resumed his aeronautical research in 1848. His first manned aircraft flew in the spring of 1849. Cayley reported that some of the flights took place with a boy of ten years age on board. A second, presumably larger version of this aircraft flew with a man on board in 1853.

Cayley also patented an early version of the modern caterpillar tractor, experimented with hot air heat engines, built a crude one-cylinder internal combustion engine using gunpowder as fuel, and built the first movable artificial hand. He died in 1857 at the age of eighty-three.

IMPACT

Cayley's first publication on aerial flight garnered a small audience. It was reprinted several times during the later half of the nineteenth century. Cayley published his most important paper in *Mechanics' Magazine*, dated September 25, 1852. Despite the large readership of this periodical, Cayley's paper was immediately forgotten. His other inventions and innovations suffered similar fates.

Nevertheless, the unsung Cayley is sometimes credited as the "father of aviation," and rightly so. It was his pioneering work that paved the way for the Wright brothers' historic flight in 1903. Notably, Cayley discovered that the means of generating lift should be separated from the means of generating propulsion. His aircraft were the first in history that were inherently stable in pitch and roll in straight or slightly curved flight, and the first equipped with pilot-controlled elevators and rudders.

No one else combined all of Cayley's innovations in aerial flight until after the Wright brothers. Unlike Cayley, the Wrights chose a statically unstable configuration. In this regard, they took a step backward from Cayley's use of a rudder. Instead, they used wing warping (the generation of adequate thrust using an internal combustion engine) to initiate and control roll. This required constant input from the pilot to maintain control of the aircraft but also allowed the plane to execute banking turns. Further, the Wright brothers used a forward elevator in a canard configuration to achieve pitch control. A separate rudder in the rear controlled yaw. Airplane development subsequent to the Wright brothers returned to statically stable configurations closer to Cayley's approach.

Finally, the Wrights embraced the propeller. They were the first to analyze it as a "rotating wing," and as a result they were the first to wring enough thrust out of it for manned aerial flight. The Wright brothers also had the internal combustion engine to adapt to their needs. Wing warping and an efficient aerial propeller finally made it possible for the Wrights to make Cayley's dream of manned aerial flight a reality.

—*Billy R. Smith, Jr.*

Further Reading

Anderson, John D., Jr. *Introduction to Flight*. 4th ed. Boston: McGraw-Hill Higher Education, 2000. Chapter 1, "The First Aeronautical Engineers," contains an appreciative summary of Cayley's work by an accomplished aerospace engineer and teacher. Although the book itself is an introductory aerospace engineering college text, this chapter is primarily historical and well within the grasp of an intelligent reader. The chapter is illustrated and contains a bibliography.

Dee, Richard. *The Man Who Discovered Flight: George Cayley and the First Airplane*. Toronto: McClelland & Stewart, 2007. The only biography of George Cayley currently in print in North America. Bibliography, index.

Jakob, Peter L. *Visions of a Flying Machine: The Wright Brothers and the Process of Invention*. Washington, D.C.: Smithsonian Institution Press, 1990. The author briefly describes Cayley's accomplishments while setting the historical context for the Wright brother's research. Illustrated, chapter notes, bibliography, and index.

Pritchard, J. Laurence. *Sir George Cayley: The Inventor of the Aeroplane*. New York: Horizon Press, 1962. The first full biography of George Cayley. Chapter notes, index.

See also: ʿAbbas ibn Firnas; Emile Berliner; Sir Christopher Cockerell; Glenn H. Curtiss; Robert H. Goddard; Samuel Pierpont Langley; Bill Lear; Louis-Sébastien Lenormand; Leonardo da Vinci; Edwin Albert Link; Paul B. MacCready; Joseph-Michel and Jacques-Étienne Montgolfier; Hans Joachim Pabst von Ohain; Burt Rutan; Igor Sikorsky; Robert Stirling; Charles E. Taylor; Andrei Nikolayevich Tupolev; Faust Vrančić; Sir Frank Whittle; Sheila Widnall; Wilbur and Orville Wright; Ferdinand von Zeppelin.

Vinton Gray Cerf

American computer scientist

Cerf is one of a handful of individuals (along with Leonard Kleinrock and Bob Kahn) who is most frequently called the "father of the Internet." While a professor at Stanford, Cerf codesigned the packet network interconnection protocols that would come to be known as TCP/IP, which helped pave the way for the Internet.

Born: June 23, 1943; New Haven, Connecticut
Primary fields: Communications; computer science
Primary invention: Transmission Control Protocol/ Internet Protocol

Early Life

Vinton Gray Cerf was born six weeks premature on June 23, 1943, in Connecticut while his father was overseas serving in the Navy in World War II. After a brief stay in Tennessee, the Cerf family settled in California. Cerf's hearing loss became evident as early as nine years of age, yet he did not require hearing aids until he was in junior high. Cerf stood out from his fellow high school students because he regularly wore a coat and tie. He was also an avid reader of science fiction and fantasy and, as a student, fell in love with algebra. In 1961, he graduated from Van Nuys High School and headed to Stanford University.

Cerf obtained a bachelor's degree in mathematics from Stanford. After graduation, he took a job at International Business Machines (IBM) as a systems engineer supporting the programming language QUIKTRAN, an interactive FORTRAN time-sharing service. After just two years, he decided to return to graduate school at the University of California, Los Angeles (UCLA), where he earned his master's degree in 1970 and his doctorate in computer science in 1972. Cerf's doctoral thesis was based on work he did with the "Snuper Computer," the Defense Department's Defense Advanced Research Projects Agency (DARPA) project that was aimed at allowing one computer to remotely observe the operation of another. As a result of his work with the Snuper Computer, Cerf began work with the Network Measurement Center at UCLA, a program designed to performance-test network traffic flow. During his time at UCLA, Cerf worked with Leonard Kleinrock and, in 1969, was a member of the group of graduate students who connected the first computer to a "switch," another computer that would serve to route data from one host computer to another.

This was the first step in building the Advanced Research Projects Agency Network, ARPANET, which was the first packet-switched network and the forerunner of the Internet. By connecting the computer to the switch, the two computers could "talk," or network, with each other. Thus, on September, 2, 1969, Cerf, Kleinrock, and others succeeded in hooking their UNIX computer to a refrigerator-sized switch known as an Interface Message Processor (IMP). This successful test allowed the group to connect UCLA's computer to Stanford's on October 20, 1969. Although the system crashed on the first attempt, the first two nodes of ARPANET had been joined.

During his tenure at UCLA, Cerf met Bob Kahn, who was designing the hardware backbone for ARPANET. Kahn and Cerf worked together to measure the data flow through the fledgling network. After receiving his doctorate from UCLA, Cerf accepted a position as assistant professor at Stanford in 1972. While at Stanford, he began engaging in research on packet network interconnection protocols. He also began working with Kahn on the Department of Defense's ARPANET project. The pair were attempting to establish communication protocols for the fledgling network.

Life's Work

At its inception, ARPANET was more of an idea than an actual network of connected computers. The main problem was that each of the sites had different computers, each computer was the size of a refrigerator or larger, and each computer operated in its own specialized language. Because of this problem, the communication between computers had to be mediated by a third computer called an Interface Message Processor. The initial challenge that DARPA faced was to have IMP allow for packets of data, or "datagrams," that had been created on different machines through different computing languages to seamlessly flow from the point of origin to the intended destination without data loss or corruption.

The answer to this problem was a set of protocols that have come to be known as the Internet Protocol Suite. In 1969, Cerf led the way in writing the original transmission protocols for ARPANET, which were known first as Telnet (protocols that allowed remote log-ins) and by early 1970 as a complete set of protocols known as Network Control Protocols (NCPs). However, by 1972, Cerf and Kahn, who was hired by DARPA in 1972 to work on radio and satellite packet networks, realized that a new set of protocols were needed. Within a year, Cerf and Kahn had developed a new Internet Protocol (IP), in which any differences between sending and receiving networks were hidden behind the IP itself. This new approach meant that since the network was not responsible for the reliability of the data, the sending and receiving machines would have to find ways to ensure data validity.

In 1973, Cerf and Kahn presented a paper outlining their new protocols to the International Networking Group. By May, 1974, they published "A Protocol for Packet Network Intercommunication," which described the initial version of Transmission Control Protocol (TCP). By 1976, Cerf was hired away from Stanford to work as the program manager for packet radio, packet satellite, and other related research programs on the DARPA Internet. In October, 1977, the pair demonstrated a protocol that linked three separate networks—Packet Radio Net, ARPANET, and SATNET—to the University of Southern California's Information Sciences Institute. The packets of data were transmitted 94,000 miles with no loss of data. This was the first demonstration of the TCP aspect of the new protocols.

In 1978, Cerf and his colleagues continued refining the protocols by separating the IP from the TCP to create a multilayered protocol that was more reliable and stable than the original TCP had been. This approach reduced the problem of conflicts between networks and programming languages to a negligible issue.

The original protocol designs for NCP had envisioned connecting a total of just 256 network hosts. By March, 1982, the Department of Defense had made TCP/IP the standard protocol for all military networking. One year later, the final NCP-to-TCP/IP transition took place, and there were just a few hundred host computers on the network. Ten years later, thanks in part to Cerf's linking MCI Mail, the first commercial e-mail system, to the Internet, the number of hosts had grown to over 1.3 million.

Although TCP/IP undergoes continual evaluation and change through its "requests for comments" (RFC) pro-

Internet pioneer Vinton Gray Cerf, seen here in 1999, codeveloped TCP/IP, a suite of computer networking protocols that became the language of the Internet. (Getty Images)

TCP/IP

Transmission Control Protocol/Internet Protocol (TCP/IP) is a suite of protocols, or a common language, allowing for the management of the transmission of information between interconnected computers and interconnected networks. Using TCP/IP, the network, rather than the individual computers that make up the network, becomes responsible for routing the packets of data. Designed primarily by Vinton Gray Cerf and Bob Kahn, the TCP/IP suite was established to determine a specific format for each packet of data that would be transmitted across the network as well as the protocols that determined how those packets would travel to their destination and be reconstructed once they arrived.

Although the protocols are generally thought of as one unit, the TCP and the IP serve different functions in the transmission of data across a network. IP's primary task is the actual routing of the packets from their point of origin to their destination. This task is accomplished by addressing and forwarding the individual packets. To accomplish this, each "end host," or computer hooked up to the Internet, is assigned a distinctive IP address. The IP address is a 32-bit number (which may, due to the demand for IP addresses, become a 128-bit number in the future) that identifies the network, subnetwork, the host, and the specific machine to which a packet should be routed. By way of comparison, the packet is an envelope containing a chunk of the data being sent and the IP address is the mailing address of the intended recipient.

The packets themselves are chunks of bytes that are created when the original file—which can be a Web page, an image, a sound, or a video—is broken up into smaller pieces. Each packet is made up of a header, which contains the IP address and routing information, and the body, which is the TCP data. The TCP data will later be reassembled to re-create the original file.

IP's service, by itself, is unreliable—in that it only makes sure that the packets get to the address. IP does nothing to guarantee the accuracy or validity of the contents when they arrive. IP does not protect against data corruption, lost packets, packets arriving in the wrong order, or packets being duplicated en route. Ensuring reliability is the role of TCP, which guarantees reliable delivery of data by monitoring and controlling the packets as they flow through the network. Upon reassembly, the packets are checked for errors and put into the proper order; if necessary, a call is sent back to the host machine to resend any lost packets. Once TCP has re-created the original file, it sends that file to the application program that requested the file from the original host.

If everything is working properly, in less than a second TCP delivers the file an application has requested from a remote host halfway around the globe. TCP is utilized by the Internet's hottest applications, ranging from the World Wide Web and e-mail to streaming media and online gaming.

cedures, the protocols themselves have remained remarkably unchanged. Future versions may require larger bit sizes for IP addresses or may incorporate stronger algorithms for data correction or error detection, but the heart of the protocols continues to withstand scrutiny and deliver data quickly and efficiently.

Impact

Only rarely does an innovation lead to fundamental changes to the means by which entire populations communicate. TCP/IP was one of those innovations. By creating the protocols that allowed computers and networks to be linked together, Cerf, Kahn, and their colleagues opened the floodgates for the innovations that followed such as the World Wide Web, Web browsers, and search engines. The protocols that comprise TCP/IP serve as the rules of the road upon which the information highway was made navigable and colonized. The TCP/IP turned ARPANET into the Internet, as the NCP and other competing protocols simply were not capable of handling the sheer volume of traffic that occurred as ARPANET evolved into the Internet.

—*B. Keith Murphy*

Further Reading

Abbate, Janet. *Inventing the Internet*. Cambridge, Mass.: MIT Press, 2000. Abbate's history of the Internet provides a clear explanation of the workings of the technology that came together to create the "information superhighway." What makes this work valuable is that she also takes the time to introduce the reader to the people behind the technology, including Vinton Cerf.

Hafner, Katie, and Matthew Lyon. *Where Wizards Stay Up Late: The Origins of the Internet*. New York: Simon & Schuster, 1996. An incisive portrait of the development of the Internet, this work illuminates the key characters, including Cerf, who played the essential role in bringing the information highway to life.

Stefik, Mark, ed. *Internet Dreams: Archetypes, Myths, and Metaphors*. Foreword by Vinton Cerf. Cambridge, Mass.: MIT Press, 1996. This volume of essays addresses the way people think of the Internet and what that conception means about society. In addition to Cerf, contributors include Vannevar Bush.

See also: Tim Berners-Lee; Robert Cailliau; Philip Emeagwali; Bob Kahn.

Georges Claude

French chemist

Claude's development of the neon sign illuminated the commercial landscape in developed countries throughout the world. His signs enabled businesses to attract customers just as easily at night as during the day.

Born: September 24, 1870; Paris, France
Died: May 23, 1960; Saint-Cloud, France
Primary fields: Chemistry; electronics and electrical engineering
Primary invention: Neon lighting

Early Life

Georges Claude (zhawrzh klohd) was born into a middle-class family in Paris, France. His father was assistant director of the Manufactures des Glaces de Saint-Gobin. Claude attended the École de Physique et de Chimie Industrielles de Paris. While studying there, he was a student of biophysicist Jacques-Arsène d'Arsonval, who in 1881 proposed generating electric power by utilizing the temperature difference between the warm surface water of the ocean and the deep ocean water. D'Arsonval did not do any experiments to verify his theory, but he did give Claude an idea for later research. The process is now known as ocean thermal energy conversion (OTEC). Claude graduated in 1886 and obtained a position with the municipal electricity works of Paris. While working with a high-tension wire, he was involved in a near-fatal accident. This experience prompted him to develop improved safety measures.

Life's Work

In 1897, Claude made his first major contribution as an industrial chemist. He invented a means by which acetylene, an extremely dangerous flammable gas, could be transported at greatly reduced risk by dissolving it in acetone. His method resulted in an expansion of the acetylene industry. In 1902, he successfully developed a process for producing liquefied air in the large quantities for industrial use. His process, which he patented, employed separation by fractional distillation. That year, in partnership with businessman Paul Delorme, Claude established the corporation L'Air Liquide. Claude supplied liquid oxygen to the Scottish chemist Sir William Ramsay, known for his extensive research on inert gases, and Claude himself began studying such gases. In addition, he devised improved methods for generating power from the energy released by liquid oxygen when it is reconverted into gas. His method became known as the Claude cycle. As early as 1910, he advocated the use of liquid oxygen in iron smelting, but his idea found little support until after World War II.

Claude continued to study and experiment with inert gases. His experiments with neon led him to discover, in 1910, that a sealed tube filled with the gas emitted a bright red-orange light when electricity ran through it. He also developed a way to purify the neon in the tube by using a charcoal filter. Claude next invented the neon lamp, which he exhibited at the Paris Motor Show on December 11, 1910.

Claude elaborated his work on neon-filled tubes, bending them to form letters and pictures and combining these tubes to make signs. The first neon sign was displayed at a Paris barbershop in 1912. He obtained international patents on his invention and founded the Claude Neon Company. His nephew André Claude served as director of the company and later developed the fluorescent light. Georges Claude's neon signs quickly became popular in the advertising community. In 1923, he sold two signs to Earle C. Anthony, owner of the Packard car dealership in Los Angeles. The "Packard" signs were the first neon signs in the United States, where neon signage became a fixture of the culture. In 1929, the first neon sign appeared in Las Vegas, Nevada, at the Oasis Café. However, manufacturing the signs in France and shipping them to the United States proved to be unsatisfactory in terms of time and transport, so Claude sold the licensing rights for the manufacture of neon tubing in the United States to the Federal Sign and Signal Company of Chicago. In 1937, Claude entered into a franchise agreement that established Claude Neon in Johannesburg, South Africa. Neon signs were manufactured in various places around the world, and Claude became a very rich man.

During the time that Claude was experimenting and developing the neon lamp and neon sign, he was also doing research in other areas. Around the time of World War I, he discovered a method for producing liquid chlorine, used in poison gas. In 1917, basing his work on that of French chemist Henri Le Châtelier, Claude invented an economical process that used high pressure to synthesize ammonia. In 1924, he was elected to the Académie des Sciences.

In 1926, using concepts proposed by his former teacher D'Arsonval, Claude began investigating ocean thermal energy conversion. In Cuba in 1930, he built the first prototype plant employing the technology. Using a low-pressure turbine, he successfully produced 22 kilowatts of electricity. In 1935, he purchased a cargo ship, *La Tunisie*, which he anchored just off the coast of Brazil, aboard which he built another plant. However, both plants were destroyed by inclement weather and rough seas before they could prove Claude's project economical and practical.

During World War II, Claude served as scientific adviser to Marshall Philippe Pétain's Vichy government. At the end of the war, Claude was accused of collaboration with the Nazis and charged with helping to design the V-1 rocket. The latter charge was dropped. In 1945, he was sentenced to life in prison, expelled from the Académie des Sciences, and deprived of the honors he had received for his scientific work during World War I. His friends immediately began efforts to secure his release, which came in 1949. During the last years of his life, he returned to investigating OTEC. Claude died on May 24, 1960, in Saint-Cloud, France, at the age of eighty-nine.

THE NEON SIGN

After supplying liquid oxygen to Scottish chemist Sir William Ramsay, Georges Claude became interested in studying inert gases. In 1910, he discovered that a sealed tube filled with neon produced a bright red-orange light when electric current ran through it. Following his discovery, Claude invented a neon lamp. He then discovered how to bend the tubes and form letters, which became neon signs.

Hollow glass tubes are used for making neon signs. Lead glass tubes are the type most commonly used. They usually have a diameter ranging from eight to fifteen millimeters. Lengths of the tubes vary. The tubes are scored with a file before they are heated; this enables the glass bender to snap or break them at the desired lengths after they have been heated. The tubes are then heated in sections until they become malleable and can be bent into the desired shapes. Next, they are lined up with a graphics or lettering pattern to be used for the sign.

Once a tube is finished, an electrode is welded to each end. These electrodes are made of lead glass and have a metal shell. Two wires extend beyond the electrode so that the sign wiring can be attached later. It is extremely important that all of the welds and seals are secure without any leaks.

The finished tubes are then processed. First, each tube is attached to a manifold attached to a vacuum pump. The tube is evacuated of air until it reaches near-vacuum. While this process occurs, a high current of electric charge is forced through the tube by way of the wires protruding from the electrodes. This process, known as bombarding, heats the glass tube to a temperature of several hundred degrees Celsius, producing a very clean interior of the glass tube at a high vacuum. The tube is left attached to the manifold and allowed to cool. It is then filled with neon, argon, or a mixture of gases.

Claude's neon signs brought a new energy to the commercial districts of cities and even to residential neighborhoods, where local shops displayed these blazing, attention-grabbing signs. Light and color became essentials of outdoor advertising.

IMPACT

Claude made important contributions in a variety of fields. His method of safely transporting acetylene by dissolving it in acetone enabled industries involved in operations such as chemical synthesis and welding to increase their use of the gas and thus improve their production. Claude's process for producing large quantities of liquid air made its use in industry practical. His research into ocean thermal energy conversion laid the groundwork for later investigation into this environmentally friendly technology. Claude's research into methods of making poisonous gases significantly changed warfare during World War I.

Claude's most important impact was, however, in the advertising industry. His invention of the neon light and its use in signs revolutionized advertising. His neon signs were bright and attractive; they made the old painted signs appear dreary and obsolete. Neon signs appeared outside of car dealerships, restaurants, movie theaters, and almost every type of establishment imaginable. Undoubtedly, the neon sign played an extremely important role in the development of the entertainment industry in Las Vegas.

—*Shawncey Webb*

Further Reading

Block, Mark P., and Robert Block. *Las Vegas Lights*. Atglen, Pa.: Schiffer, 2002. A history of the development of neon signs and their importance in American advertising, especially in entertainment and Las Vegas. Portrays the impact of neon signs through 235 images.

Davidson, Len. *Vintage Neon*. Atglen, Pa.: Schiffer, 1999. Authored by the founder of the Neon Museum of Philadelphia, the book includes photographs with commentary by shopkeepers, manufacturers, and others involved with neon signs. Offers a good panoramic view for understanding how Claude's invention of the neon sign changed the landscape of America, lighting it with bright cowboys, cars, bowling pins, and other figures.

Miller, Samuel. *Neon Techniques*. Edited by Wayne Strattman. Cincinnati: ST Media Group International, 1997. First published in 1935, the book gives detailed descriptions and explanations of design and fabrication of neon signs. Discusses techniques of bending and filling tubes. Explains various means of producing electrical discharge. Somewhat technical but clear.

Takahashi, Masayuki Mac. *Deep Ocean Water as Our Next Natural Resource*. Translated by Kazuhiro Kitazawa and Paul Snowden. Tokyo: Terra Scientific, 2000. Recounts details of the plants Claude constructed and the methods he applied to produce electricity. Discusses why his project met with failure.

See also: Fritz Haber; Dimitry Ivanovich Mendeleyev.

Josephine Garis Cochran

American engineer

Cochran patented the dishwasher that provided the basic design for the modern dishwasher. She also opened her own manufacturing facility, Cochran's Crescent Washing Machine Company, which later became KitchenAid.

Born: March 8, 1839; Ashtabula County, Ohio
Died: August 3, 1913; Chicago, Illinois
Also known as: Josephine Garis (birth name); Josephine M. Fitch
Primary field: Household products
Primary invention: Dishwasher

Early Life

Josephine Garis Cochran (KAHK-rehn) was born to Irene Fitch and John Garis in the spring of 1839 in Ashtabula County, Ohio (some sources say Valparaiso, Indiana). Her family involvement with engineering was influential to her education when she was young. Her maternal grandfather (possibly her great-grandfather), John Fitch, patented what is reportedly the first steamboat in 1791. Her father served as an engineer consultant who worked in both Ohio and Indiana supervising saw and textile mills along the Ohio River. He took the young Josephine with him during some of his travels, influencing her views of manufacturing facilities and engineering. John Garis is also credited with inventing a hydraulic pump system that drained marshes, an invention that probably led to a later consulting job on the building of Chicago in the 1850's.

When Josephine's private Indiana high school burned down, she moved to central Illinois to live with a sister. There, she met William A. Cochran, a local civil servant, and married him on October 13, 1858, at the age of nineteen. Reports say that she added an *e* to "Cochran" after his death in 1883. They had one child, a son named Hallie, who died at the age of two. The Cochrans were founding members of the First Congregational Church in Shelbyville, Indiana. During the last years of his life, William Cochran was ill and in debt—factors that contributed to Josephine Garis Cochran's push to finish her invention, the dishwasher.

Life's Work

Cochran's decision to invent a dishwashing machine was reportedly influenced by her irritation with the way her servants were handling her heirloom china. Observing chips and breaks in dishes that had been passed down since the 1600's, she began washing the dishes herself. Since she detested this job, she decided to invent a ma-

The Dishwasher

Josephine Garis Cochran's lack of formal mechanical training may have been a problem for some, but her technological acumen was strong enough to make her into a brilliant businesswoman who threw aside expectations for women in her time to become the inventor of the forerunner of the modern dishwasher. Her experiments with water pressure washing of dishes to preserve her time and her china led to her invention. Her innovations included racks that were moved manually and, later, mechanically, racks that moved back and forth, and racks that revolved. In early models, hand-pumped water was poured over dishes held in stationary racks. Later models were motorized, spraying hot water and soap onto moving racks. Before her invention, it was thought that mechanized scrubbing was the only way to effectively clean the dishes.

The Garis-Cochran Dish-Washing Machine worked so well that it sold in large quantities to hotels and restaurants across the United States, with the inventor herself traveling to cities such as St. Louis, Cleveland, and New York to sell her product. Her salesmanship was direct and bold, earning her a strong business reputation. Though her early dishwashing models were too large and expensive for general home use, Cochran invented a smaller model that would work in the home, and she creatively marketed it as a place to hide dirty dishware, appealing to a large number of homemakers (though the average home would not be able to afford one for decades).

As she built her business, Cochran and her machine became linked to several manufacturing companies. Her own factory, Cochran's Crescent Washing Machine Company, was invested in by Tait Manufacturing in Decatur, Illinois. The investments allowed her to make renovations to her machine, leading to a second patent in 1900. Her company was purchased by Hobart in 1926 and was later turned over to KitchenAid, which was acquired by Whirlpool Corporation in 1986.

chine to do the work for her. Testing ideas for the machine, she streamed water over the dishes in the sink to see how clean the dishes would become.

As her idea progressed, she turned the woodshed behind her house into a workshop. George Butters, a mechanic for the Illinois Central Railroad, became her assistant in the design and building of her project. One of her goals in designing the early dishwashing machine was to avoid power-driven, motorized brushing of the dishes. They started with a washtub construction that would contain the dishes and keep the soap and water from spraying all over the kitchen. As a result, a copper boiler became the central piece to the new machine. The boiler was built into a large frame, and racks were placed inside to hold the dishes. Reports vary on whether the racks were made of wood or wire, with wire being the predominantly accepted material, at least for the later models. The early model, made with wooden racks, worked with a hand pump that sprayed hot water and soap against the dishes that were set into the individual racks.

Cochran applied for a patent and was awarded one on December 28, 1886. Her machine was officially called the Garis-Cochran Dishwasher (also known as the Garis-Cochran Dish-Washing Machine). The idea of a dishwashing machine was not new; a hand-cranked wooden machine had been patented by Joel Houghton in 1850. Other inventors had applied for patents as well, but whereas their models were based on the motorized scrubbing of the dishes, Cochran's used a water pressure wash.

Cochran's first models after the patent were manufactured by local machine shops and sold for between $100 and $150 apiece. The size and price were prohibitive to home owners, so Cochran sold them to hotels and institutions. Her first sale was to the Palmer House, a prestigious Chicago hotel. She later sold to the Sherman House, another upscale Chicago hotel, as well as other large businesses. The dishwashing machine was under almost constant revision; Cochran worked to make it more efficient and more marketable. To reach the home market, she advertised the dishwasher as a good place to store dirty dishes, hiding them from sight. Then, in 1888, she sold a machine that reportedly was able to wash 120 dishes per minute.

In 1889, Cochran opened her own manufacturing facility, which she called Cochran's Crescent Washing Machine Company. Her early assistant, George Butters, became the foreman, and three other employees were hired to build the commercial washers. The company made several models and sizes. One model held dirty dishes in racks that were placed inside a boxlike container where hot soapy water was hand-pumped over the dishes. The operator would need to pour clean hot water afterward to rinse them. A motorized version was also manufactured. In this machine, dishes were placed in racks that moved back and forth while water sprayed up from underneath. This version was easy enough to operate by anyone. A motor was made to be connected to the side, but this required an extra purchase.

At the 1893 World's Columbian Exposition (World's Fair) held in Chicago, Cochran made her real break into sales. While displaying her machine and marketing it herself, she loaned nine dishwashers to other businesses at the exposition. The approval was overwhelming, and she sold the same number of machines. This began her busiest time in the business.

Over the next decades, the Garis-Cochran Dishwasher evolved several times. In 1900, Cochran registered for a patent on the new model that moved dishes back and forth. There was also a version that rotated the racks of dishes and then drained into a sink. Cochran herself became quite a businesswoman, traveling around the country selling her machines. It is reported that she even traveled into her seventies. She died in 1913 at the age of seventy-four.

IMPACT

The Garis-Cochran Dish-Washing Machine is the forerunner of the modern dishwasher. The pressure washing system that utilized hot water, soap, and air drying kept dishes from being damaged in the washing process. Cochran's innovation took off at the 1893 World's Columbian Exposition, leading to many imitations of her machine, none of which were as good. Cochran spent the middle and later years of her life inventing, building, and selling her dishwasher to institutions that could afford and house it. Her machine was so efficient that it replaced up to three-quarters of the kitchen staff in larger restaurants and hotels.

Though lacking technical training, Cochran was an innovative woman who took a chance on building a dishwashing machine. She boldly sold her invention, going on cold calls to businesses herself and modeling it herself at the 1893 World's Fair.

Cochran wanted to build a machine that would lessen the household workload of women, and this dream became a widespread reality after her death. By the 1940's, Cochran's idea had been downsized to a dishwasher that would become popular in the home. A version of this dishwasher is still manufactured and used today.

—Theresa L. Stowell

FURTHER READING

Casey, Susan. *Women Invent: Two Centuries of Discoveries That Have Shaped Our World.* Chicago: Chicago Review Press, 1997. This simple, straightforward book, written at a child's reading level, traces the history of a handful of female inventors, from conception of their ideas through the actual manufacturing and sale of their products. The author also addresses general questions about inventing and patenting a product.

Fenster, J. M. "The Woman Who Invented the Dishwasher." *American Heritage of Invention and Technology* 15, no. 2 (1999): 54-61. Provides a strong overview of Cochran's life and invention. Fenster provides a detailed tracing of her life, including information on her parents and husband and their influence on her. The article also includes information on her manufacturing and sales processes.

Karwatka, Dennis. "Josephine Cochrane Invents the First Practical Dishwasher." *Tech Directions* 59, no. 10 (2000): 12. Karwatka provides a brief but thorough description of Cochran's dishwasher and how it worked. He also includes a copy of an 1895 advertisement for the machine that provides interesting, pertinent details about the machine.

Vare, Ethlie Ann, and Greg Ptacek. *Patently Female.* New York: Wiley, 2002. Starting with the first patent ever awarded to a woman, this book traces largely unknown female inventors. For some female inventors, the authors provide a connection to famous male figures who may have taken or received credit for the women's concepts and works. The authors do not always provide specific dates.

See also: Beulah Louise Henry; James Murray Spangler; Percy L. Spencer; Earl S. Tupper.

Sir Christopher Cockerell

English engineer

Cockerell became world famous for his invention of the hovercraft, but he had earlier made a highly significant contribution to the British war effort in World War II, developing radio communication and navigation devices for use in the Royal Air Force and the Fleet Air Arm. He also made some notable early contributions to the development of prewar television technology.

Born: June 4, 1910; Cambridge, England
Died: June 1, 1999; Sutton Scotney, Hampshire, England
Primary fields: Aeronautics and aerospace technology; mechanical engineering; navigation
Primary invention: Hovercraft

Early Life

Christopher Sydney Cockerell was the only son among the three children of Sir Sydney Carlyle Cockerell (1867-1962), the director of the Fitzwilliam Museum in Cambridge, England, and his wife, Florence Kate (1872-1949). Christopher never got on with his father, who had once been William Morris's secretary and to whom his son's interest in the practicalities of engineering always seemed vulgar. Christopher had a much better relationship with his mother, a talented artist and illuminator. His father's literary interests were reflected in the visitors to the family home, who included George Bernard Shaw, Joseph Conrad, Siegfried Sassoon and T. E. Lawrence, but the only conspicuous interest that Christopher showed in these worthies was in Lawrence's motorcycle. A succession of governesses hired to teach him at home despaired of diverting his interests into more "acceptable" channels; he became passionately interested in radio, building his own TV set, and built a steam engine to power his mother's sewing machine—which she refused to use.

After attending Lydgate House Preparatory School in Hunstanton for three years (1921-1924)—where he built a radio set for the school—he went on to Gresham's School in Holt, where he met W. H. Auden and built another radio. Cockerell went on to study engineering at Peterhouse College, Cambridge, spending much of his spare time working on motorbikes, winning several prizes for racing. He often stayed during vacations with Captain Edward George Spencer-Churchill, from whom he picked up a fascination with antiques and shooting. His father was disgusted when the young man spent the £20 he was given for his twenty-first birthday on a Mauser rifle with a telescopic sight and silencer.

Life's Work

After graduating from Cambridge, Cockerell initially went to work for W. H. Allen and Sons of Bedford as a pupil engineer, but he soon returned to Cambridge to do research on radio and electronics. In 1935, he joined the Marconi Wireless Telegraph Company, working at the company's Writtle site near Chelmsford. He worked on the first outside broadcast vehicle used by the British Broadcasting Corporation (BBC), and he helped develop the shortwave aerials that began transmitting TV signals from Alexandra Palace. In 1937, however, his career took a crucial turn when he was promoted to head of Aircraft Research and Development. On September 4 of that year, he married Margaret Elinor Belsham.

Cockerell's last prewar commission for Marconi was to develop a radio direction-finder for the Cunard liner *Mauretania*. When war broke out, he was immediately approached to develop similar equipment for use in aircraft. Great Britain's bombers were in dire need of better communication and navigation equipment, and Cockerell immediately came up with a prototype system that was rushed into production in a matter of weeks. The system proved invaluable in helping bombers make their way home after raids, and it made a vital contribution to the conflict between the Royal Air Force (RAF) and Germany's Luftwaffe, in which the RAF's initial disadvantage was eventually reversed.

With the assistance of the firm of E. K. Cole, Marconi manufactured some 120,000 R1155 receiver units and some 55,000 T1554 transmitters during the war; Cockerell always regarded this as the most important achievement of his career. He also helped produce a universal display unit for the Royal Navy that integrated radar information with other instrumentation, and he developed a beacon that allowed Fleet Air Arm pilots to return safely to their carriers. In the run-up to D Day, he developed an apparatus, code-named "Bagful," that allowed the RAF to locate and map all the German radar stations in northern France.

When the war was over, Cockerell continued to work on equipment for both military and civil aircraft, developing improved navigation systems and apparatuses for positioning aircraft during their final approach to landing. He refused further promotions because he wanted to

Hovercraft inventor Sir Christopher Cockerell, center, with pilot Peter Lamb, left, and Saunders Roe designer Richard Stanton-Jones with an early model of the SR-N1 hovercraft in 1959. (Popperfoto/Getty Images)

maintain the level of his practical involvement. In 1948, he moved to the Marconi research laboratories at Great Baddow, near Chelmsford, but resigned in 1951 because he wanted to be able to follow up his own initiatives more freely. His wife's inheritance from her father had been invested in a boat-building business at Oulton Broad, near Lowestoft, and Cockerell went to work for the company designing motorboats. He soon became interested in the possibility of minimizing the resistance of the water to a boat's progress by floating the vehicle on a cushion of air. In December, 1955, he filed a patent for his hovercraft design.

Cockerell could not get industrial backing to develop the hovercraft, and the Admiralty was not impressed either, although the Ministry of Supply was instructed to put it on the secret list. Saunders Roe, on the Isle of Wight, undertook to build a prototype for the ministry and reported favorably on its progress in 1958, at which point the company was commissioned to build a much larger 400-ton model for potential use as a cross-channel ferry. It proved impossible to maintain secrecy, and the project was declassified. The National Research and Development Corporation (NRDC) then provided financial support, forming a subsidiary company, Hovercraft Development Ltd., in January of 1959. Although the company's offices were initially located in Cockerell's home in East Cowes, Cockerell was merely a director and technical consultant, while the chairman and managing director was the NRDC's Dennis Hennessy. When the company moved across Southampton Water to Hythe in 1960, Cockerell bought a house there, where he lived for the rest of his life.

The Saunders Roe model SR-N1 was shown to the press on June 11, 1959, causing something of a sensation.

On July 25, it made a channel crossing, fifty years to the day after Louis Blériot's first aerial crossing. An experimental track for hover trains was set up near Cambridge. Hovercraft Development eventually filed some two hundred patents, fifty-nine of them in Cockerell's name. Licences to build hovercraft were granted to various companies, including Saunders Roe, Vickers, Folland, and Cushion Craft in the United Kingdom; Bell Aircraft in the United States; and Mitsui and Mitsubishi in Japan. The various British enterprises were soon merged into the British Hovercraft Corporation—a move strenuously opposed by Cockerell, who believed (correctly, as it turned out) that the merger would stifle innovation. He resigned from the new entity on March 23, 1966. He was knighted in 1969 for his contributions to engineering.

In the 1970's, Cockerell became very interested in the possibility of developing technologies of renewable energy that would outlast intrinsically limited supplies of coal and oil. He and Edwin Gifford, with whom he had previously worked on hovercraft development, formed a company called Wavepower Ltd. to exploit a number of patents that Cockerell took out for devices to produce electricity from the energy of waves. The prototypes worked, but the electricity they produced was far more expensive than conventionally generated electricity, and the company had to be wound up in 1982.

By this time, Cockerell was in his seventies, and he was unable to initiate a further phase of his remarkable career, but he remained very active as a public figure, firing off scores of letters to the press and various institutions, frequently complaining about the low status of engineers in British society and the fact that the British education system was turning out "half-educated people" with no appreciation of science and technology. He died in 1999 in Sutton Manor Nursing Home in Hampshire and was survived by his two daughters, Anne and Frances.

Impact

Cockerell became famous as the archetypal British inventor of the twentieth century, and the hovercraft became—somewhat ironically, as things turned out—a key example of British technological ingenuity. The hovercraft failed to live up to his hopes, at least in the fact that its development was far more successful outside Britain than within, and proved to be of peripheral value in a relatively limited range of contexts.

The Hovercraft

While working for a motorboat company, Christopher Cockerell began to consider the possibility of reducing the friction between the water and a boat by floating the vehicle on a cushion of air. This idea led him to invent the hovercraft, an amphibious vehicle that can hover above both water and land. The hovercraft's large fan directs air under the vehicle, inflating the flexible "skirt" and generating lift. The skirt not only prevents air from escaping but also allows the vehicle to clear obstacles. A proportion of fan-generated air is expelled at the back of the craft to generate thrust.

On December 12, 1955, Cockerell filed for his first hovercraft patent. Various earlier attempts had been made to build a hovercraft before his success. He was almost beaten to it by Colonel Melville W. Beardsley, who built a prototype for the U.S. Navy in 1959 and to whom Hovercraft Development Ltd. had to pay a large sum for his U.S. patents. The SR-N1 model, demonstrated in the same year, was initially impractical because its hovering height of one foot caused problems when the waves were higher than two feet. The machine only became viable when it was fitted with a flexible skirt, devised by Denys Bliss. The skirt, made of nylon-reinforced rubber, enabled the hovercraft to cope with considerably higher seas.

The first passenger-carrying hovercraft was the Vickers VA-3, which operated along the North Ales coast. Cockerell, Edwin Gifford, and Don Robertson formed Hovertransport Ltd. in 1964 to operate a ferry across the Solent, between Southsea in Hampshire and Ryde in the Isle of Wight, but British Rail decided to buy the first craft—the SR-N4—for use as a cross-channel ferry. Six of them were built for that purpose, four of which were widened and two lengthened as well. The last two, which could carry sixty cars and more than four hundred passengers, continued to operate as cross-channel ferries until they were decommissioned in October, 2000, being unable to withstand competition from the Channel Tunnel and fast catamarans known as SeaCats. The SR-N6 went into service between Southsea and Ryde, carrying thirty-six passengers, and that route was still in use in the twenty-first century, operated by two 98-seater AP1-88s.

The hovercraft was more ingeniously exploited by the U.S. Navy, which retained its interest in its potential after Beardsley's work was superseded and Bell Aircraft began producing the craft under license from Saunders Roe. Hovercraft operated successfully in the Mekong Delta during the Vietnam War and were used as tank-landing craft in the Gulf War. Interest was also maintained in Japan, where a hovertrain was installed at Narita International Airport.

Cockerell was quite right to regard his war work as the greatest achievement of his career. He played no small part in saving Britain from an invasion by air that would have changed the history of the twentieth century dramatically had Nazi Germany succeeded, and he also made a key contribution to facilitating the counterinvasion of northern France that eventually brought the war in Europe to an end. Of all the many inventors and engineers who played a part in the war effort, there was probably none whose summary contribution was more important than Cockerell's.

—*Brian Stableford*

Further Reading

Johnson, P. S. *The Economics of Invention and Innovation: With a Case Study of the Development of the Hovercraft*. London: M. Robertson, 1975. An interesting analysis of the difficulties of exploiting Cockerell's key invention.

Wheeler, R. L. "Sir Christopher Sydney Cockerell." In the *Oxford Dictionary of National Biography*, edited by H. C. G. Matthew and Brian Harrison. New York: Oxford University Press, 2004. A succinct but comprehensive biography.

_______. "Sir Christopher Sydney Cockerell CBE, RDI, 4 June 1910-1 June 1999." *Biographical Memoirs of Fellows of the Royal Society* 47 (November, 2001): 69-89. A more leisurely biography than the same author's entry for the *Oxford Dictionary of National Biography*. Covers the same ground in slightly more detail.

See also: Sir Robert Alexander Watson-Watt; Sir Frank Whittle.

Stanley Norman Cohen

American geneticist

Cohen, along with Herbert Wayne Boyer, was the first scientist to create a functional recombinant DNA molecule. This signal achievement forms the bedrock of modern genetic engineering and gave rise to the multibillion-dollar field of biotechnology.

Born: February 17, 1935; Perth Amboy, New Jersey
Primary fields: Biology; genetics
Primary invention: First recombinant DNA organism

Early Life

Stanley Norman Cohen was born in Perth Amboy, New Jersey, just across Arthur Kill from the southern tip of Staten Island, New York. He attended Rutgers University, graduating in 1956 with a bachelor of science degree in biological sciences. In 1960, he earned his medical degree from the University of Pennsylvania School of Medicine. Following postdoctoral work, Cohen joined the faculty at the Stanford University School of Medicine in 1968, where he held teaching and research positions as a professor of genetics and medicine.

By 1972, Cohen had begun work on the problem of antibiotic resistance in bacteria. Several genes coding for such resistance had previously been found on bacterial plasmids. Plasmids are small, extrachromosomal, circular bits of DNA with the capacity to be passed, intact, between different bacteria. In other words, the plasmids and their genes are mobile. Bacteria without antibiotic resistance could, under certain conditions, become resistant simply by picking up a resistance plasmid from another resistant bacterium. Although there are different mechanisms that confer resistance in bacteria, researchers had deduced that the genes for these mechanisms seemed to be passed in the same manner on plasmids. Cohen was interested in isolating these resistance genes so that he could insert them into *Escherichia coli* (*E. coli*), a common, well-characterized intestinal bacterium, and so further study the mechanisms of transmission.

At about this time in the late 1960's and early 1970's, several other research groups were working on the isolation and description of a group of enzymes called restriction enzymes. Herbert Wayne Boyer, from the University of California, San Francisco, was one such researcher working on restriction enzymes. These enzymes have the ability to recognize specific, short sequences of DNA and cut them, leaving either sheared off "blunt ends" or staggered "sticky ends." These ends of DNA can be matched up to complementary ends of different pieces of DNA and "glued" back together by another enzyme called DNA ligase. Most scientists in the field recognized that such enzymes could be a very valuable tool for dissecting various DNAs and studying them.

Cohen and Boyer met at a research conference in

1972 and discussed their work. From this discussion rose a collaboration that forever altered the fields of biological and medical research.

Life's Work

In order to understand how genes and their protein products work, it is generally necessary to isolate those genes away from the original systems in which they are found. Though this sounds reasonably simple today, this was a major hurdle facing Cohen and most researchers in the early 1970's. The key was to first isolate one gene from many and then graft it into a known and reasonably controlled biological environment that would allow predictable manipulation of that gene. Researchers were looking for a practical solution to a very real problem, and this is what the collaboration between Cohen and Boyer delivered.

Three things were needed in order to make a system that would be useful for further work in genetics. First, a way had to be found to get a specific piece of DNA into a living organism; in other words, scientists had to find a way to make recombinant DNA. Next, that DNA had to be made to replicate, or copy, itself in order to generate large amounts of the desired product. Finally, researchers had to be able to determine which cells received DNA (and so were "transformed" by that new DNA) and which cells did not; researchers had to "mark" the cells in some way so that the cells could be "selected." With Boyer's restriction enzymes and Cohen's work on plasmids, they succeeded in creating the first recombinant plasmid (pSC101), using it to transform *E. coli* cells in the presence of simple salts that facilitated plasmid transfer. Antibiotic resistance itself was used as a marker for selection. At its simplest, this system is the basis for all genetic engineering performed in the research laboratory today. The greatest utility of the system is that DNA from any organism, from human to mouse to corn, can be inserted into a bacterial plasmid for further study.

Stanley Norman Cohen. (©The Nobel Foundation)

Even before Cohen and Boyer published their collaborative work, Boyer presented the preliminary findings at the Gordon Conference on Nucleic Acids in June of 1973. The news was well received, but before the conference was even over some had expressed concerns about the safety of creating functional recombinant molecules, particularly if these novel genetic elements were then inserted into such an easily grown organism as a bacterium. From its inception, then, genetic engineering has had to weigh the merits of utility against the dangers of ill use. In the early 1970's, little was known about what, if any, dangers recombinant molecules might hold, and the issue split the scientific community. Cohen and Boyer were among the first cosigners of letters calling for a voluntary moratorium on certain types of research, at least until more was known. Other scientists scoffed at the perceived danger. Within a few short years, in 1975 the National Institutes of Health (NIH) formed the Recombinant DNA Advisory Committee (RAC) to include both scientists and the public in the debate. By 1976, the NIH had issued the *Recombinant DNA Research Guidelines*, which continue to guide research practices to this day. The *Guidelines* ensure that dangerous genetic combinations are restricted to laboratories to prevent them from "escaping" into nature, but as technological abilities have grown, new controversies continue to arise. Many modern ethical arguments focus not on *doing* genetic research but rather on the *applications* of it. Human cloning, even only of tissues, is probably one of the most hotly debated of the technologies to have come from Cohen and Boyer's original work.

Today, Cohen continues his work on the genetics of antibiotic resistance. His other research interests include

RNA decay and the growth of mammalian cells. Recently, work in the Cohen laboratory has produced GABRIEL, a bioinformatics program used in the analysis of DNA microarrays, which can be used to investigate the expression of thousands of genes at the same time.

Cohen has earned many awards over the years for his work in the field of genetics, including the Wolf Prize in Medicine in 1981 and the National Medal of Science in 1988. Along with Boyer, Cohen has won the National Medal of Technology (1989), the Lemelson-MIT Prize (1996), and the Shaw Prize in Life Science and Medicine (2004). Cohen was elected to the National Academy of Sciences in 1979 and was inducted into the Inventors Hall of Fame in 2001.

Recombinant Plasmids

In 1979, Stanley Norman Cohen and Herbert Wayne Boyer filed for and received the U.S. patent for the "Process for Producing Biologically Functional Molecular Chimeras." The patent explains how the two men and their coworkers created functional recombinant molecules that produced a novel product they wanted.

Plasmids are small, extrachromosomal, circular deoxyribonucleic acid (DNA) molecules that are found in many bacteria and that are capable of self-replication (copying). Intact genes put into these plasmids will be copied and expressed just as any other "natural" gene found on the plasmid. To produce a recombinant plasmid according to the methods developed by Cohen and Boyer, one first takes the chosen gene and removes it from whatever DNA strand it inhabits by cutting it out with a restriction enzyme (typically a restriction enzyme that creates "sticky ends"). Then, the bacterial plasmid is treated with the same restriction enzyme. The two DNAs are mixed together and DNA ligase is added. The sticky ends match up, and the ligase "patches" the strands together to reconstitute a complete plasmid, only now the plasmid is a recombinant. Host cells, such as *Escherichia coli* (*E. coli*), when exposed to calcium chloride (a simple salt), become more permeable to molecules outside their cell walls. When these salt-treated cells are mixed with DNA under the correct conditions, the DNA enters the cells. Once the cells have recovered from this transformation procedure, they begin to manufacture the protein products specified by the recombinant plasmid. To separate these bacterial "factories" from bacteria that did not take up recombinant DNA during transformation, some sort of selection mechanism is used. In Cohen's system, the recombinant plasmids all carry an antibiotic resistance gene, such as that coding for tetracycline resistance. After transformation, exposure to tetracycline in the growth media will kill off all cells that did not take up recombinant DNA. In this way, only the correctly transformed cells are kept, grown, and their recombinant products recovered.

This technique allows a researcher to express the product for any gene he or she cares to study. Insertion of the gene for human insulin into a bacterial plasmid allowed Genentech, the company founded by Boyer, to mass-produce human insulin for the treatment of diabetes. Engineered human insulin works better in patients than animal-produced insulin, thus providing better treatment outcomes for patients. Human insulin was only the first of a long list of synthetic medicines produced by recombinant DNA technology.

Impact

The collaborative work of Cohen and Boyer laid the foundations for genetic engineering, and as such their work comes next in importance only to the discovery of the structure of DNA itself by James D. Watson and Francis Crick. Cohen and Boyer's relatively simple method for creating and expressing recombinant DNA molecules in bacterial host cells spawned an expansion of research opportunities at university and governmental levels and launched the biotechnology industry. Their patents alone generated millions in royalties, and subsequent patents in biotechnology based on their work have generated billions. Boyer himself went on to cofound Genentech, one of the largest biotechnology companies in the world and the original creator of the first human insulin ever produced from recombinant DNA.

Genetic engineering finds applications in almost all scientific disciplines. Many modern medicines are produced from genetically modified bacteria. Many plants and some animals have also been modified to produce genetically modified foods or plants resistant to disease. Recombinant organisms are used to produce numerous industrial chemicals, dyes, biofuels, and synthetic materials. Engineered plasmids allowed a global collaboration on the mapping of the human genome and the genomes of many other living organisms. Detection of genetic diseases, cleaning up oil spills, and gene therapy for the curing of diseases also owe their success to the methods of Cohen and Boyer. It is not outrageous to claim that without their work, most modern biological and medical research could not take place.

—Elizabeth A. Machunis-Masuoka

Further Reading

Chang, Annie C. Y., and Stanley N. Cohen. "Genome Construction Between Bacterial Species *In Vitro*: Replication and Expression of *Staphylococcus* Plasmid Genes in *Escherichia coli*." *Proceedings of the National Academy of Sciences of the United States of America* 71, no. 4 (April, 1974): 1030-1034. Describes the creation of pSC101, the first recombinant plasmid shown to be capable of expressing (producing) protein from DNA of one organism within cells of another species.

Cohen, Stanley N., Annie C. Y. Chang, Herbert W. Boyer, and Robert B. Helling. "Construction of Biologically Functional Bacterial Plasmids *In Vitro*." *Proceedings of the National Academy of Sciences of the United States of America* 70, no. 11 (November, 1973): 3240-3244. Describes the critical first steps in the use of restriction enzymes for the creation of the first-ever recombinant DNA molecule.

Espejo, Roman, ed. *Biomedical Ethics: Opposing Viewpoints*. Opposing Viewpoints Series. San Diego, Calif.: Greenhaven Press, 2003. Genetic engineering and biotechnology have generated as much controversy as utility since the first plasmids were generated in the 1970's. This book gives both pro and con arguments for many of the applications of Cohen's original work as they apply to medical technologies such as human cloning and genetic research. Periodical and book bibliographies, discussion questions, and contact information for various bioethical organizations.

Fumento, Michael. *Bioevolution: How Biotechnology Is Changing Our World*. San Francisco, Calif.: Encounter Books, 2003. It is almost impossible to catalog all the ways in which biotechnology affects modern life, but this book provides a good starting point, ranging from "Miracles in Medicine" to "Biotech Brooms." Techniques and ethical issues are clearly presented. Endnotes with bibliographic information.

Krimsky, Sheldon. *Genetic Alchemy: The Social History of the Recombinant DNA Controversy*. Cambridge, Mass.: MIT Press. 1982. Provides an excellent chronology of the key events and primary documents of the initial controversies arising from the work of Cohen and Boyer. Extensive endnotes and bibliographic information.

See also: Herbert Wayne Boyer; Kary B. Mullis.

Samuel Colt

American industrialist and manufacturer

Colt created the mass-produced revolver, the first practical multishot firearm. The revolver was easy to carry for self-defense and was used as a weapon during the nineteenth century Indian wars.

Born: July 19, 1814; Hartford, Connecticut
Died: January 10, 1862; Hartford, Connecticut
Also known as: Colonel Colt
Primary fields: Manufacturing; military technology and weaponry
Primary invention: Colt revolver

Early Life

As a child, Samuel Colt's prized possession was an old cavalry pistol, which he taught himself to repair. His mother, Lucretia, died when he was six. His father, Christopher, remarried in 1823, and within a year the stepmother had sent Samuel to work on a farm. After a year on the farm, he moved to Ware, Massachusetts, to work in the new dyeing and milling factory his father had built, one of the first in the United States.

For a while, Samuel attended Amherst Academy, a boarding school in Massachusetts. He withdrew from the school after he fired a cannon in defiance of a teacher's order. The sixteen-year-old then set to sea, serving as a cabin boy on the brig *Corvo*, which visited Calcutta and London. According to legend, he observed the ship's wheel, saw how it could be locked into place, and decided that a similar locking mechanism could be used on a revolver firearm.

Upon his return to America, he began raising funds for the revolver project. He traveled the country as the "celebrated Doctor Coult of New York, London, and Calcutta," putting on exhibitions where spectators could consume "exhilarating gas" (nitrous oxide). He worked with thirteen gunsmiths or gunmakers to construct exemplars of the designs he had imagined. In 1835, at age twenty-one, he traveled to England to obtain a British patent for his revolver and obtained parallel French and American patents shortly thereafter.

Life's Work

Colt set up the Patent Arms Manufacturing Company in Paterson, New Jersey. The factory made revolving handguns, rifles, carbines (short rifles), and shotguns. Its first product was a small .34-caliber five-shooter pistol, produced in 1837. In 1838, Major General Thomas Jessup ordered fifty Colt revolver rifles for use in the ongoing Second Seminole War in Florida. Years later, General William Harney wrote that the Colts had been the decisive reason for the U.S. victory.

Samuel Colt. (Library of Congress)

Colt firearms were popular with the military of the newly independent Republic of Texas, and in 1841 Colt finally obtained orders from the U.S. Army and Navy. However, overall sales were slow, and Colt was a poor manager, so in 1842 the Paterson factory shut down. Captain Samuel Walker, of the U.S. Regiment of Mounted Riflemen, had learned about Colt firearms during the Seminole wars and from his service as a Texas Ranger (the state police force of the Republic of Texas). In 1846, during the Mexican War, General Zachary Taylor ordered Walker to procure Colt guns for the U.S. Army in Mexico. Colt incorporated suggestions from Captain Walker to improve the front and rear sights, install a lever for easier loading, and reconfigure the grip. The Army ordered one thousand six-shooter handguns, in .44 caliber, and Colt was back in business.

The 1849 California gold rush increased civilian demand for the guns and established the Colt name as synonymous with the American West. Colt traveled tirelessly to promote his products. In 1850, he was commissioned as a lieutenant colonel in the Connecticut State Militia, a title that made it easier for him to obtain sales meetings with foreign dignitaries.

Revolvers began to achieve mass popularity in England after Colt displayed his guns at London's 1851 Great Exhibition of the Works of Industry in All Nations, held at the Crystal Palace. The British army and navy bought large quantities, including over twenty thousand revolvers in 1854-1855 for use in the Crimean War. Colt's Pimlico factory in London was the first foreign factory opened by an American, although the factory closed a few years later because of British competition.

By the time the British were suppressing the Indian Mutiny of 1857-1858, the favored British revolver was the one invented by the Briton Robert Adams. (Colt's relevant patents expired in Britain in 1849, but not until 1857 in the United States, so competition came to the United Kingdom sooner.) The Adams revolver was double-action: pulling the trigger would not only fire the cartridge but also recock the hammer, and thereby rotate the cylinder. Although the Adams revolver was less accurate than the Colt, especially at longer distances, the British preferred its faster rate of fire.

To make guns for the Mexican War, Colt had subcontracted the job to a factory in Whitneyville, Connecticut, owned by Eli Whitney, Jr., son of the inventor of the cotton gin. The younger Whitney taught Colt a great deal about industrial mass production. Colt applied Whitney's ideas and advanced them (thanks in part to his brilliant employee Elisha K. Root), first at a factory that Colt

The Colt Revolver

The oldest surviving revolver dates to 1597. Before Samuel Colt's revolver, the most common multishot handgun was the large and awkward pepperbox; it could fire four to six rounds, with each round having its own barrel and firing chamber. Single-barrel revolvers had already been conceptualized and manufactured based on the principles of Captain Artemus Wheeler, who patented a flintlock revolver carbine in 1818. Such revolvers were improved and commercialized by Elisha Collier, but the Collier guns did not work well. He shut down his firearms business in 1828.

Colt made a reliable revolver that could use percussion cap ammunition (the most advanced ammunition of the time) and whose cylinder did not need to be rotated by hand. It was the first mass-produced revolver. The original Colt revolvers were all single-action—that is, the shooter would use his thumb to pull back, or cock, the hammer into a fixed position. The act of cocking the hammer would engage the pawl (a lever connected to ratchets on the cylinder). The ratchet motion would index the cylinder, bringing the next cylinder chamber into alignment with the barrel. When the hammer was cocked, a lever locked the cylinder into alignment with the barrel. Pulling the trigger would drop the hammer, which would hit the percussion cap, igniting the gunpowder, which would propel the lead bullet down the barrel and toward the target. To fire the next shot, the shooter would start the process again by thumb-cocking the hammer.

The cylinder was mounted on a central rod (arbor), to which the barrel was also mounted, and was locked onto the frame by a pin that fit into holes in the barrel and arbor. The cylinder was partitioned so that the percussion cap for one round was isolated from all the other percussion caps. This usually prevented the flash of a single percussion cap from igniting any other percussion cap. Later models by Colt chamfered the cylinder chamber mouths. The chamfering deflected outward the escaping gases from the gunpowder explosion, further reducing the risk that the gas would ignite the percussion cap in an adjacent chamber.

rented in Hartford, and then in the massive Hartford factory he built in 1855.

Before Colt, firearms were built one at a time by gunsmiths who made individual parts as they went along. Colt brought standardized production to firearms manufacture. At the Hartford factories, all parts were made by semiskilled laborers using machine tools, Because each part was made within defined tolerances, the various parts could be readily assembled into a completed firearm. Each gun was the product of several hundred standardized machine operations—as well as dozens of precise inspections. The uniform sizing of interchangeable parts meant that customers could order spare parts, or replacements for broken parts, which would be certain to fit their own gun.

After the London exhibition, the British came to Colt's factory to study what was called "the American system": production lines producing high volumes of high-quality products based on precisely engineered interchangeable parts. Although European tradition insisted that lovely objects could only be created by expert craftsmen working slowly, Colt's mass-produced guns had beautiful form, finish, and colors—some guns with a style that anticipated Art Deco.

While textile mills in New England treated workers as interchangeable inputs who could be discarded or used up, Colt treated his employees well. To maintain the highest quality in work, he limited shifts to ten hours per day, plus a full one-hour lunch break. Sanitation standards at the factory were high, with wash basins, towels, soap, and hot and cold water. Near the factory, Charter Oak Hall was perhaps the first employer-built social center in America, with games and reading material. Charles Dickens, a harsh critic of social injustice in England, praised Colt's factory in an 1854 issue of Dickens's magazine *Household Words*. Colt also imposed high standards on his outside contractors, severing relationships with contractors who imposed long hours or who did not pay well. He saw high employee morale as essential to mass production of high-quality products.

An innovative marketer, Colt was apparently the first to use the phrase "new and improved" in advertising. Celebrity endorsements, particularly from military figures such as future U.S. presidents Zachary Taylor and Franklin Pierce, were also a major element in his promotions. Colt worked very hard all his life and eventually worked himself to death, falling prey at age forty-seven to a cold, his condition having been weakened by several years of what might have been rheumatic fever, gout, or malaria. Although Colt died in 1862, his company, with several changes of official names and owners, continues in business to this day and has produced many other innovations in handguns and rifles, and in industrial manufacturing. Among the most notable post-1862 Colts are the 1873 Peacemaker revolver and the Model 1911 self-loading pistol. The latter gun, with slight modifications, is widely produced today and is still regarded by many experts as the best self-defense gun.

Impact

Before the invention of the Colt revolver, warring Indians could fire several arrows in the time it took a white soldier to fire and reload a single shot from a gun. At "Hays' Big Fight" in July, 1844, fifteen mounted Texas Rangers (led by Captain John Coffee Hays and including Samuel Walker) faced eighty mounted Comanches at a tributary of the Pedernales River. At the time, the Comanches were the greatest light cavalry in the world. Nevertheless, the Texans had Colt's revolvers, and the battle ended with half the Comanches killed or wounded. The Colt handgun not only provided firepower superiority over the Indians but also could readily be fired one-handed by a horseman. It changed the balance of power and was the foundation of white victories over the Indians in Texas and many other places in the West.

During the American Civil War, Colts were the most common revolver on both sides. As in most wars, handguns were carried mainly by officers. Colt's factory manufactured about 200,000 revolvers during the war, selling 127,000 to the U.S. Army and the rest to individual purchasers in the Union. In the 1861-1866 period, Colt's firearms accounted for 39 percent of U.S. government firearms acquisitions (mostly the Army Model handgun).

Even more significant, Colt's six-shooter was small enough to be carried routinely by a civilian and had enough firepower for a small person to defend him or herself against a group of larger assailants. For the first time ever, no longer were a group of large males the almost-sure winner of a violent confrontation with a woman or a smaller man. After the Civil War, a popular saying was "Abe Lincoln may have freed all men, but Sam Colt made them equal." The Colt revolver was one of the greatest advances of self-defense in all of human history.

—*David B. Kopel*

Further Reading

Boorman, Dean K. *The History of Colt Firearms.* New York: Lyons Press, 2001. Coffee-table book with many beautiful photographs, covering all Colt firearms from the 1830's to the present.

Edwards, William B. *The Story of Colt's Revolver.* Harrisburg, Pa.: Stackpole Press, 1953. An impressively thorough biography, replete with extensive correspondence to and from Colt, copies of patents, government documents on the testing and purchase of Colt guns, and product advertisements.

Houze, Herbert G., et al. *Samuel Colt: Arms, Art, and Invention.* New Haven, Conn.: Yale University Press, 2006. A beautiful book with hundreds of photographs of firearms, the manufacturing process, paintings, the Colt family tree, and other Colt memorabilia, assembled for a special Colt exhibit at the Wadsworth Atheneum in Hartford. The book also contains extensive text, well-researched and footnoted, about Samuel Colt and the business he built.

Wilson, R. L. *Colt: An American Legend.* New York: Abbeville Press, 1985. The official history of Colt firearms. Serial number tables for all models. Lavishly illustrated with over four hundred pictures and aimed mainly at collectors.

See also: John Moses Browning; Richard Gatling; Samuel F. B. Morse; John T. Thompson; Eli Whitney.

William Fothergill Cooke

English electrical engineer

Cooke was one of the chief pioneers of telegraphy in Great Britain, working in collaboration with Charles Wheatstone. Although most commentators consider that Cooke's contribution to the partnership was more on the business side than on the scientific side, Cooke certainly did not see it that way himself.

Born: May 4, 1806; Ealing, Middlesex, England
Died: June 25, 1879; Farnham, Surrey, England
Also known as: Sir William Fothergill Cooke
Primary fields: Communications; electronics and electrical engineering
Primary invention: Electric telegraph

Early Life

William Fothergill Cooke was one of the four children of William Cooke, a surgeon, and his wife, Elizabeth Ann (née Fothergill). The elder William Cooke was elected as physician to Durham Infirmary in 1822—a post that he held until 1842. The younger William was therefore sent to Durham School, having presumably received his earlier education in Ealing for two years before going up to Edinburgh University. He did not graduate but went into the Indian army, becoming an ensign; he resigned his commission after five years after returning to England suffering from ill health.

Following his return from India, Cooke decided to follow in his father's footsteps, and he studied anatomy in Paris, where he developed a remarkable facility for making dissection models in colored wax. That skill won him an invitation to visit the Anatomical Institute in Heidelberg, Germany, and while he was in that city he attended a demonstration given on March 6, 1836, by the professor of natural philosophy at Heidelberg University, Geheime Hofrath Moncke, of a telegraph apparatus based on a design by the Russian baron Pavel Schilling.

Cooke immediately realized the potential of the technology, especially in connection with the railway systems then in their early development, and he also realized that a race had begun to develop a commercially viable system. He promptly abandoned his medical studies in order to devote himself to telegraphy, returning to England in April, 1836, and began experiments in collaboration with a solicitor named Burton Lane. He commissioned an apparatus for exhibition from a clockmaker in Clerkenwell, who might well have been the same one who employed Alexander Bain, the inventor of the chemical telegraph, when the latter arrived in London the following year.

Cooke could not get his initial apparatus to work over long distances. He appears to have been ignorant of the implications of Ohm's law relating to electrical resistance, and he could not understand why his signals lost strength as they traversed the connecting wire. He sought help from Michael Faraday and Peter Roget of the Royal Society, but they could not offer him a practical solution to the problem. Roget referred him to Charles Wheatstone, who was then trying to develop a telegraph apparatus of his own; the two met for the first time on February 27, 1837, and formed a formal partnership of collaboration in May of that year.

Life's Work

Cooke had already been in negotiation with the Liverpool and Manchester Railway Company for the use of telegraphy in signaling before he formed his partnership with Wheatstone, but it was not until Wheatstone solved the problem of long-distance transmission that the partners were able to produce their first workable system. The device was patented on June 12, 1837. Using a twelve-mile wire, Robert Stephenson helped Cooke set up a test between London's Euston Station and Camden Town Station. Various other railway companies tested the device, but it was deemed to be too expensive to be useful.

The principal problem with the initial Cooke-Wheatstone model was that it used five signaling needles and line wires in order to set up sufficient combinations of signals to encode the twenty-six letters of the alphabet. Cooke and Wheatstone developed a two-needle model in 1838, but it was still too costly. The American inventor Samuel F. B. Morse was a year behind them in filing his own key patent for a telegraph system, but he was quicker to adopt a binary code developed in Germany by Carl August von Steinheil and thus obtained a narrow lead in making telegraphy economically viable. It was not until Cooke and Wheatstone produced and patented a single-needle apparatus in 1845 that the application finally became economically viable; it was then swiftly adopted by all the railway companies in Great Britain.

On June 5, 1838, Cooke married Anna Louisa, the daughter of Joseph Weatherly, a solicitor from Rotherham; they had one daughter. By that time, Cooke and Wheatstone were already somewhat at odds, and they eventually fell out in spectacular fashion in 1841 over the question of entitlement to the credit for their achievements. Their quarrel dragged on long after the dissolution of their formal partnership. The dispute was taken for arbitration, Sir Marc Isambard Brunel representing Cooke and Professor John Frederic Darnell representing Wheatstone; their carefully mediated decision that Cooke and Wheatstone were equally responsible for the invention of the telegraph satisfied neither of the contending parties.

Wheatstone and Cooke clashed again when Cooke and John Lewis Ricardo—the nephew of the famous economist David Ricardo and the chairman of the North Staffordshire Railway—set up the Electric Telegraph Company in 1846, initially with Wheatstone's cooperation. The formation of the company was complicated by claims from several other inventors who had patented relevant devices, most notably Alexander Bain. A parliamentary commission had to be appointed to sort out the various claims; although Bain was compensated to the tune of £7,500 and Wheatstone to the tune of £33,000, Cooke was the big winner, his patents eventually being bought by the company for £120,000. The company went on to become a great success; it eventually merged with the International Telegraph Company in 1856.

The dispute between Cooke and Wheatstone went into a further phase when Cooke published a combative pamphlet in 1854 entitled *The Electric Telegraph: Was It Invented by Professor Wheatstone?*—a question to which he replied, resoundingly but probably inaccurately, in the negative. Wheatstone replied in kind the following year, but he did not have Cooke's mastery of the polemic style, and he only prompted further assertive publications from Cooke in 1856, 1857, and 1866.

Cooke attempted to obtain extensions of his early patents, but the Privy Council decided that he had been sufficiently remunerated and refused the extension. Without the ingenious Wheatstone to assist him, he made no headway with further inventions of his own, but he had already made his mark. He and Wheatstone jointly received the Albert Gold Medal of the Society of Arts in 1867, and Cooke was knighted in 1869, a year after Wheatstone. Cooke began investing in mining enterprises in North Wales in the hope of increasing his fortune, but he lost it instead and was reduced to relative poverty. He was granted a civil list pension in 1871, but he ended up living with his son-in-law, in whose home he died in 1879. His wife survived him, living until 1891.

IMPACT

It is impossible to separate Cooke's impact on the history of technology from that of his collaborator Charles Wheatstone. Wheatstone undoubtedly had some justice in his claim to be due the larger share of the credit for the inventive component of their joint enterprise, but he was

THE ELECTRIC TELEGRAPH

The principle of telegraphy is relatively simple. A transmitting device in which a needle is moved by an electromagnetic field, making intermittent contacts, produces signals that are transmitted through a copper wire to a distant receiver, which reproduces the signals in some decodable form, usually as sounds. The possibility had been pointed out by Pierre-Simon Laplace and further popularized by André-Marie Ampère before numerous inventors began to produce actual models; Pavel Schilling's was not the first, but it was by far the most widely publicized. William Fothergill Cooke and Charles Wheatstone were not the only Englishmen working on the problem in 1837-1838, but the Devonshire surgeon Edward Davy did not follow through with his model, leaving them a clear field in Great Britain, although their slowness in developing a single-needle system using a binary code disadvantaged them relative to Samuel F. B. Morse in the United States. Cooke and Wheatstone first developed a five-needle telegraph system to indicate the alphabet, but the device was not economically viable compared to Morse's simpler single-needle system, which used a system of dots (short signals) and dashes (long signals) to represent letters. Cooke and Wheatstone finally produced and patented a single-needle apparatus in 1845.

The patterns of the technology's development differed markedly between the United States and Europe because geography imposed different priorities. Railway systems were developed more rapidly in the compact countries of Western Europe, and it was entirely natural for Cooke and Wheatstone to give initial priority to railway signaling, while the vast open spaces of America meant that the primary emphasis had to be more narrowly devoted to the long-distance transmission of information. Within a relatively short space of time, however, transatlantic cables were laid and telegraphy became a key mode of communication between as well as within continents. The technology swiftly revolutionized communications in news, business, and warfare, and everyone who had a significant hand in its development had good claims to have played an important role in the development of modern civilization.

always ready to appropriate the work of others into his own devices and might have overestimated the value of his personal contribution. Cooke certainly overestimated, or at least overrepresented, his technical contribution. Nevertheless, the fact remains that it was Cooke who saw and felt the urgency of pushing through the original idea, and it was certainly Cooke's business acumen rather than Wheatstone's technical ingenuity that succeeded in establishing their apparatus as the standard model in Britain. If Cooke was overcompensated by the Electric Telegraph Company by comparison with the other claimants, at least he had the good grace to throw the money away on reckless investments. The telegraph itself went on to have a tremendous impact on nineteenth century communications, not merely in connection with railway signaling but also in the general transmission of information.

—Brian Stableford

Further Reading

Bowers, Brian. "Inventors of the Telegraph." *Proceedings of the Institute of Electrical Engineers* 90, no. 3 (March, 2002): 436-439. A brief but scrupulous attempt to weigh up the relative contributions of Cooke, Wheatstone, and Morse to the early development of telegraphic technology.

Burnley, James. "Sir William Fothergill Cooke." Revised by Brian Bowers. In the *Oxford Dictionary of National Biography*, edited by H. C. G. Matthew and Brian Harrison. New York: Oxford University Press, 2004. A brief and rather scanty biographical sketch, to which relatively little was added for the benefit of the new edition; it draws a good deal of information from a memoir by Latimer Clark and seems to regard the data given in Cooke's own self-serving pamphlets with some suspicion—as does Munro.

Hubbard. Geoffrey. *Cooke and Wheatstone and the Invention of the Electric Telegraph*. London: Routledge, 2008. A new edition of a book initially published in 1965 that offers a definitive account of the problematic relationship between Cooke and his collaborator, and their joint contribution to the development of telegraphy in Britain. Endeavors to strike a judicious balance in assessing the two men's rival claims and is more successful in that regard than most earlier accounts.

Morus, I. R. "'The Nervous System of Britain': Space, Time and the Electric Telegraph in the Victorian Age." *British Journal of the History of Science* 33, no. 4 (2000): 455-476. A comprehensive account of the development of telegraphy in Britain. Better informed and better balanced than Munro but not as broad in its scope.

Munro, John. *Heroes of the Telegraph*. Whitefish, Mont.: Kessinger, 2004. A new edition of a popular work first published in 1883 that relegates Cooke's biography to an appendix while granting Wheatstone a chapter because, in Munro's opinion, Wheatstone was a "man of science" and Cooke a mere businessman—a prejudice that many other historians of science have shared but that might not be entirely just.

See also: Alexander Bain; Michael Faraday; Samuel F. B. Morse; Charles Wheatstone.

William David Coolidge

American engineer and physicist

Coolidge is best remembered for developing the ductile tungsten filament for lamps in 1911 and for creating the Coolidge tube, which improved the operation of Wilhelm Conrad Röntgen's X-ray machine. He was also instrumental in developing polymeric materials and silicones that became essential components of electronics after World War II.

Born: October 23, 1873; Hudson, Massachusetts
Died: February 3, 1975; Schenectady, New York
Primary fields: Electronics and electrical engineering; physics
Primary inventions: Ductile tungsten; Coolidge tube

Early Life

William David Coolidge was born in Hudson, Massachusetts, a town about twenty-five miles from Boston, on October 23, 1873. The son of Albert Edward Coolidge, a small farmer and shoemaker, and Mary Alice Shattuck Coolidge, a dressmaker, William was descended from an illustrious family that had arrived in Boston in 1630 and numbered among its members Calvin Coolidge, the thirtieth president of the United States. William, nicknamed Will, received his primary education in a humble one-room school where a single teacher worked hard to educate students of all grade levels together. The limits of his education, however, did not keep him from excelling; he showed exceptional abilities not only in his studies but also in sports and other outdoor activities, such as hiking and fishing. Fascinated by photography, Coolidge built his own camera while he was still in elementary school and outfitted a darkroom in his parents' house; this childhood passion remained his most enjoyed hobby over the entire course of his life.

After finishing elementary school, Coolidge went on to Hudson High School, where he excelled in mathematics and physics, graduating as valedictorian of his class of thirteen students. Because of his family's limited financial resources, after graduation he took a job in a factory that manufactured rubber garments instead of going to college. Fortunately, a friend suggested that he apply for a scholarship at the local college known as Boston Tech, which was, in fact, the Massachusetts Institute of Technology (MIT). His excellent high school grades combined with his mechanical and electrical skills won him the award, and in September, 1891, at age seventeen, Coolidge entered MIT. Studying electrical engineering, chemistry, physics, and modern languages, he was immediately impressed by his chemistry professor, Willis R. Whitney, who in turn was delighted to have such a dedicated student.

During the summer of his junior year at MIT, Coolidge earned an internship at Westinghouse Electric in Pittsburgh, Pennsylvania. His experience at Westinghouse taught him that he was not well adapted to conducting engineering research in a company setting; he was much better suited to laboratory experimentation. When he graduated in 1896, with the encouragement of Professor Whitney, Coolidge applied for a scholarship to go to Leipzig, Germany, to study physics under the guidance of Gustav Wiedemann and Paul Drude. Accepted into the program, he financed his adventure through a combination of a scholarship and money borrowed from a friend. The investment turned out to be a good one; in just three years, Coolidge completed his studies and received his doctorate in physics.

Life's Work

With his impressive record at Leipzig, where he had earned his Ph.D. with the highest possible grade, Coolidge was offered a teaching position in the Physics Department at MIT. For the next five years, he taught, assisted professor of chemistry Arthur Amos Noyes, and continued to work with his mentor, Whitney.

Whitney was in charge of the new General Electric (GE) Research Laboratory in Schenectady, New York, and so was able to offer a position there to Coolidge, whose potential for research he had cultivated and highly respected. After a successful negotiation in which Coolidge secured a salary that was twice what he had been earning at MIT and gained the right to use half his time (and the laboratory's equipment) for his personal research, Coolidge accepted the position. Beginning in 1905, one of his first projects focused on improving Thomas Alva Edison's lamp; his work resulted in the creation of a light bulb that was three times more powerful than Edison's. The profits that General Electric real-

The Coolidge Tube

The Coolidge tube is a glass tube in which X rays are produced. William David Coolidge, impressed by Wilhelm Conrad Röntgen's discovery of X rays, set out to build a machine that could produce the high voltages indispensable to obtaining them. Basing his mechanism on Röntgen's work, Coolidge produced a device in which air was contained at low pressure in a tube where its positive ions struck the cathode, generating electrons that in turn struck the anode, generating X rays. His machine was sufficiently successful to be purchased by a local physician for X-ray diagnosis.

A decade later, while working on ductile tungsten and molybdenum in 1909, Coolidge experimented with these two chemicals to see if they could be used as X-ray targets. Three years later, after tungsten had been used successfully to mass-produce Mazda C bulbs, Coolidge tried to use solid tungsten as the cathode and anode of an X-ray-generating tube that replaced low-pressure gas with a vacuum. Working with his colleague Irving Langmuir, Coolidge had realized that the hot metal of the cathode in a vacuum emits electrons (this effect had been studied previously by Thomas Alva Edison, who called it the "Edison effect"; today scientists use the term "thermionic emission"). By heating the cathode in his tube, Coolidge could generate X rays more reliably than was the case with the previous system using low-pressure gas.

Different Coolidge tubes were produced according to their intended uses. The first tube that was produced immediately proved itself to be useful for dental diagnosis and found a ready market. Further development of larger units extended the popularity and application of Coolidge tubes in radiology. During World War I, Coolidge was asked to create portable units to be used in field hospitals. Later, when physicians hoped to extend the use of X rays for deep therapy, Coolidge successfully developed a process to increase the voltage of his tubes while keeping the target cool by irrigating it with a flow of cold water.

ized from this extremely popular innovation more than justified both Coolidge's salary and the company's massive investment ($116,000) in the construction of the laboratory.

Financially secure in his new position, on December 30, 1908, Coolidge married Ethel Woodward, the daughter of the president of a local bank. Their marriage produced two children, Elisabeth and Lawrence, but ended in tragedy when Ethel died in 1915 of an infectious disease. Soon after, Coolidge hired Dorothy Elisabeth MacHaffie, a nurse, to care for his two young children. Within a year, Coolidge married her.

At the laboratory, Coolidge continued to search for ways to improve the light bulb, experimenting with different substances to be used as filaments, until a lamp using tungsten was produced in Austria. Although the tungsten filament produced a very bright light, researchers in Europe and at General Electric were confronted with a major problem: The brittleness of the filament rendered the bulb extremely fragile. After three years of intense research, Coolidge discovered a method to make tungsten ductile (capable of being drawn out into a very thin wire or thread) at room temperature through the addition of 1 percent of thorium. The result was a flexible, durable filament that was so thin that a single pound of tungsten made a wire 8.5 miles long and would be sufficient to produce twenty-three thousand bulbs. This new incandescent lamp was produced in 1911.

Two years earlier Whitney had hired Irving Langmuir, who had worked on heat transfer in gases at high temperatures. Langmuir suggested that Coolidge could double the light output of his bulbs by replacing the vacuum previously used with an inert gas. The collaboration between Langmuir and Coolidge resulted in the production of General Electric's best-selling Mazda C light bulb.

In the months following the development of ductile tungsten, Coolidge explored its application to a variety of problems, employing it to replace platinum in telegraph keys, auto ignitions, and other equipment controls. His most significant discovery, however, came when he used the tungsten to make a source of X rays that was dramatically more dependable than previously available sources. Wilhelm Conrad Röntgen, a German physicist, had discovered X rays in 1895, and Coolidge had met Röntgen briefly when he was studying in Leipzig. There was a certain parallel between the development of the bulb Coolidge had worked on and the bulb that Röntgen used to produce X rays. Coolidge's idea, for which he received a patent in 1913, was to replace the low-pressure gas in Röntgen's X-ray-generating tube with a vacuum in which a thick tungsten filament, when heated by an electric current, would generate a continuous and ample stream of electrons. This invention, which became known as the Coolidge tube, was hailed as a breakthrough that could produce electrons "in the same quantity every second as a ton of radium." The value of the Coolidge tube in improving X-ray diagnosis was immediately recognized by both physicians and the scientific community. Coolidge received the Rumford Prize of the American Academy of Arts and Sciences in 1914 for his experimental achievements on "ductile tungsten and its application in the production of radiation."

With the onset of World War I, Coolidge and the GE Research Laboratory plunged into the vital scientific support of the war effort. Coolidge's development of portable X-ray machinery immeasurably improved battlefield diagnoses of injuries and saved countless Allied lives, but his greatest contribution came when GE, the Submarine Signalling Company, and Western Electric collaborated to produce an effective submarine detection system based on sealed rubber binaural listening tubes—"C tubes"—that Coolidge produced. Supplied with these devices in 1918, Allied navies were able to end the dominance of German U-boats in the Mediterranean, an important factor in the ultimate Allied victory.

On November 1, 1932, after the economic pressures of the Great Depression had overwhelmed the retiring Willis Whitney, Coolidge became director of research at the GE Research Laboratory, where he took on the challenge of ensuring the laboratory's survival in hard times. Through remarkably careful management, Coolidge succeeded, and by 1940, as the economy improved, he began to envision his own retirement. Unfortunately, world events interfered, and Coolidge decided to stay at his post for the duration of World War II. A member of President Roosevelt's Advisory Committee on Uranium, Coolidge was involved in the development of the atomic bomb, bringing valuable practical engineering skills to the project. Coordinated with other institutions through the government's Office of Scientific Research and Development, Coolidge and the GE Laboratory also contributed to the development of microwave radar as well as radar and radio countermeasures.

With the end of the war finally in sight, Coolidge finally retired on January 1, 1945. Retirement, however, did not end his intellectual activity. Blessed with remarkably good physical and mental health, Coolidge continued to visit the GE Laboratory, advising the next generation of researchers there until shortly before his death, at 101 years of age, in 1975.

Impact

Coolidge is remembered for his development of ductile tungsten and for the invention of the Coolidge tube, which revolutionized radiology; he is also remembered for his development of essential technological applications that helped to win both world wars. During his lifetime, Coolidge was awarded eighty-three patents and received numerous prestigious honors, such as the Washington Award of the Western Society of Engineers (1932), the John Scott Award granted by the City Trusts of the City of Philadelphia (1937), the Faraday Medal of the Institution of Electrical Engineers of England (1939), the Duddell Medal of the Physical Society of England (1942), the Franklin Medal of the Franklin Institute (1944), the first K. C. Li Gold Medal for the Advancement of the Science of Tungsten by Columbia University (1951), the Röntgen Medal (1963), and the Climax Molybdenum Wedgwood Medallion (1973). In 1972, Coolidge was the first recipient of an annual award named in his honor, the William D. Coolidge Award, presented by the American Association of Physicists in Medicine.

Even though Coolidge made such essential discoveries, he always stressed that they had been the fruits of intense labor by a team of researchers at the laboratory and could not possibly be attributed to his work alone. He was regarded by his colleagues as an honest, quiet, modest, and energetic man.

—*Denyse Lemaire and David Kasserman*

Further Reading

Evans, Harold. *They Made America: From the Steam Engine to the Search Engine—Two Centuries of Innovators*. Boston: Little, Brown, 2004. Chronicles the work of seventy American inventors and entrepreneurs, focusing on the impacts of their work and their roles as visionaries on the modern world.

Hughes, Thomas. *A Century of Invention and Technological Enthusiasm, 1870-1970*. Chicago: University of Chicago Press, 2004. Provides comprehensive information about inventors in the United States and the roles that prominent laboratories, such as General Electric Research Laboratory, have played in their discoveries.

Liebhafsky, Herman. *William David Coolidge: A Centenarian and His Work*. New York: John Wiley & Sons, 1974. Presents a detailed, complex portrait of Coolidge and his family, drawing on the scientist's personal journals and papers. Particularly interesting are the notes that Coolidge took daily in his laboratory.

Miller, John. *Yankee Scientist: William David Coolidge*. Schenectady, N.Y.: Mohawk Development Service, 1963. Provides biographical information as well as discussion of Coolidge's achievements and inventions.

Van Dulken, Stephen. *American Inventions: A History of Curious, Extraordinary, and Just Plain Useful Patents*. New York: New York University Press, 2004. Presents brief overviews of a large number of American inventions from two centuries of U.S. Patent Office records. Includes illustrations.

See also: Thomas Alva Edison; Irving Langmuir; Wilhelm Conrad Röntgen.

Martin Cooper

American electrical engineer

In spearheading two decades of research into developing the first mobile (entirely wireless) telephone, Cooper, an electrical engineer working at the time for Motorola, revolutionized telecommunications for both personal and corporate use by investing phone users with unprecedented freedom and mobility.

Born: December 26, 1928; Chicago, Illinois
Primary fields: Communications; electronics and electrical engineering
Primary invention: Mobile phone

Early Life

Martin Cooper was born the day after Christmas in 1928. An inquisitive child, fascinated by the family's cathedral radio and by the telephone on the parlor wall (he dismantled both devices and reassembled them with ease), Cooper determined early on that he would study electronics. He attended the nearby Illinois Institute of Technology (IIT), founded only a decade earlier and considered a cutting-edge facility for students eager to help convert the considerable body of war technology into useful (and revolutionary) peacetime applications.

After graduating with honors in 1950 with a degree in

electrical engineering, Cooper enlisted in the Navy that year, certain that defense technologies represented the most comprehensive application of new theories in electronics, communications, and computer technology. During a four-year stint, Cooper served on a submarine and two destroyers, learning with remarkable proclivity the ships' massive electronic communications systems. Returning to Chicago, Cooper was hired by Motorola in 1954 and placed in the systems division, in charge of developing portable communications products. Gifted with an intellectual curiosity (he was later inducted into Mensa, the high-IQ society), while he worked at Motorola he also completed his master's degree in electrical engineering at IIT (1957). During his tenure, research into mobile communication was centered on providing vehicular phones for police, firefighters, and paramedics. Although gratified by providing new technologies for such service occupations, Cooper was restless, certain that mobile communications could ultimately be provided to the consumer, that communications could be freed from land wires that bound communication to a particular home or business. In the late 1960's, he was placed in charge of Motorola's division of cellular research aimed at developing a prototype of just such a device.

Life's Work

Historically, the foundation premise for wireless communication actually dates to before World War I, when American Telephone and Telegraph (AT&T), for most of the century the communications monopoly in the United States, vetoed in-house proposals to develop the technology, fearing it would compromise its monopoly on land-wire service. It would be more than three decades (1947) before Bell Laboratories, a massive conglomerate with government-funded research facilities, drew up preliminary drafts of a wireless cellular network in which portable phones in cars would use a matrix of cells, or small overlapping service areas, to pass a signal along using elevated base stations with microwave antennas, a structured network of cells to help citywide emergency services. Initial success in the mid-1950's encouraged

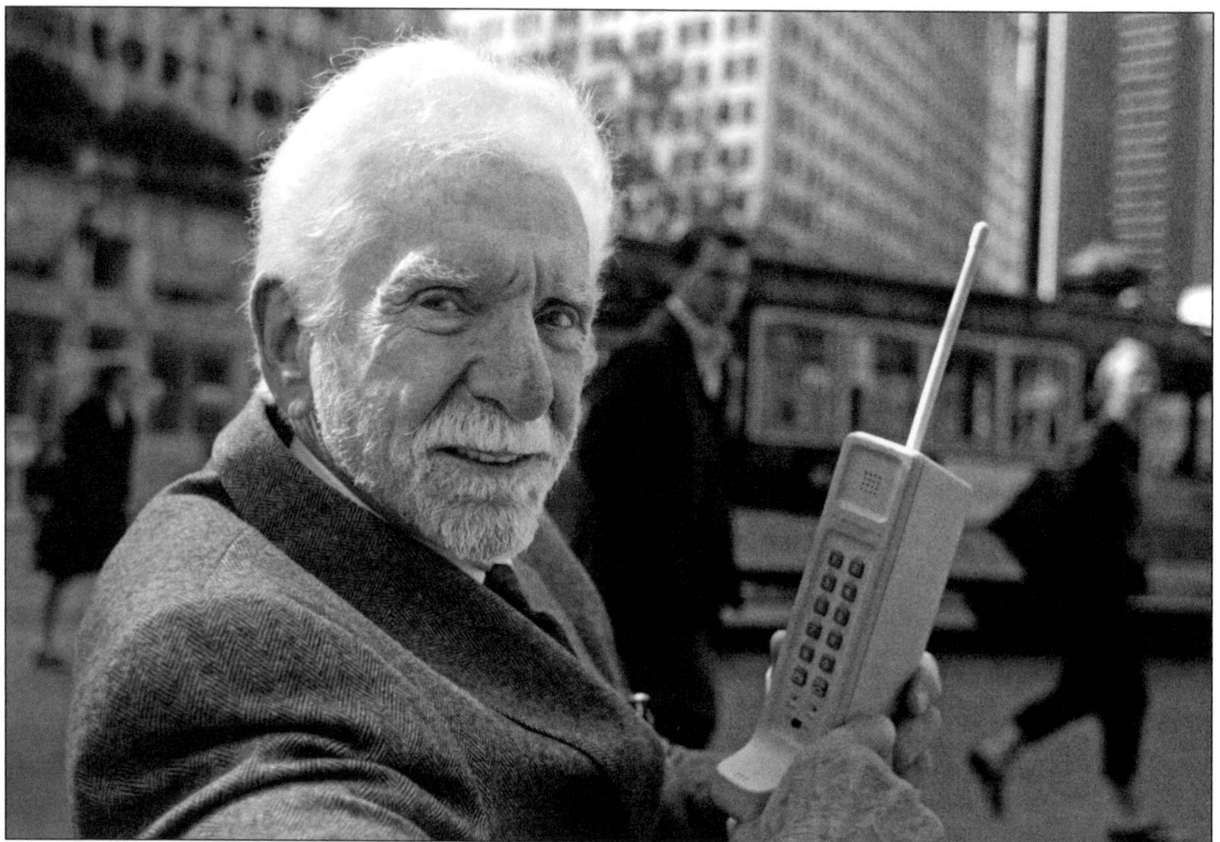

Martin Cooper holds a Motorola DynaTAC 8000X (1973), the first handheld cellular telephone. (AP/Wide World Photos)

development of a theory that using smaller cells—that is, decreasing the range of service—would significantly increase the volume of signals the system could manipulate (the signal could be tracked and switched from one base to another) and thus make possible, at least theoretically, handheld cellular phones.

It was upon this body of research that Cooper directed his Motorola team. At the time, Motorola was considered a minor presence in the communications industry without the resources of Bell, but this did not deter Cooper, whose vision of a personal phone provided the visionary energy for the project (with typical self-deprecating humility, he would later claim the idea came to him from watching *Star Trek* and the *Enterprise* crew's communicators). On April 3, 1973, Cooper flew to New York City with a prototype portable phone, intending to demonstrate it for the Federal Communications Commission (FCC) at the Manhattan Hilton. In what has become a legend in the communications history of the twentieth century, Cooper paused a moment on his way to the meeting and, there on the sidewalk, amid pedestrian traffic and against the noise of a Manhattan afternoon, calmly pulled out the Motorola DynaTAC 8000X (Dynamic Adaptive Total Area Coverage), the bulky (close to two and one-half pounds and about the size of a brick) prototype. Without fanfare, he made the first cellular phone call. The phone set transmitted the signal off a base station positioned atop the nearby Burlington Consolidated Tower. Cooper heard the familiar ringing. As he would relish telling for years, he had called the competition at rival Bell Labs.

There were of course significant challenges before that prototype could be introduced to a mass market. By some estimates, Motorola alone spent more than $100 million in research. Within five years, a prototype system able to service a little over two thousand customers was piloted in Chicago. Over the next ten years, communications technology (largely credited to Bell Labs) addressed the construction of thousands of cell stations to transmit signals. In 1983, the FCC granted Motorola permission to market the DynaTAC 8000X, which was 10 inches long, was rectangular, and weighed 28 ounces. Initial talk time (roughly thirty-five minutes before recharging) was significantly increased, and the cost came down as parts were standardized and durability significantly increased, although the cost of the 1983 unit was still $3,500.

The impact of the so-called radio telephone system was immediate, and Cooper was singled out as the "father of the cell phone," although he was clear that his work rested on the efforts of the skilled team at Motorola. Consumer demand was historic—the phones were hailed not only as a status symbol but also as a necessary ele-

CELLULAR PHONES

It is difficult today to appreciate the groundbreaking work of Martin Cooper's team—his prototype appears clunky and looks more like a shoe phone—largely because of the breakneck speed of technological evolution that so quickly reshaped his cellular phone. (Cooper famously observed that within a decade of the phone's first use, he had become not the father but the grandfather of the cell phone.) When it is recalled that in 1973, when Cooper made his first call, phones still had cords and the global communications network relied entirely on land wires, the audacity of Cooper's research team can be appreciated. The initial design called for entirely redesigning the shape of the phone itself as well as conceptualizing a computer system and the physical infrastructure to support the phone. Creating the prototype cellular phone was enormously challenging for Cooper's research team, as no model of such a device actually existed. All the technology and all the innovations were done specifically for the test model (although much of the initial work relied on patents Motorola already held in two-way radio transmitters and semiconductors).

The DynaTAC 8000X (Dynamic Adaptive Total Area Coverage) prototype was based on the premise that a caller's signal would be switched from one coverage area (cell) to another as the user moved. The earliest models of the cellular phone were little more than elaborate battery-operated walkie-talkies, or, more precisely, radios that sent and received radio frequencies and depended on base stations to relay the signal. As Cooper envisioned expanded use, however, low-powered transmitters in each cell would allow frequencies to be reused simultaneously in other nearby cells—thus eliminating the problem faced by earlier car phones of long waits for signals to be relayed. Computerized network equipment tracked the signal, and antennae transmitted the signal like a radio station. The same computerized tracking system maintained the signal's integrity amid other cell calls, those signals handed off through the network of directional antennae. As Cooper and his team had envisioned, as cell phone use inevitably increased, the system could accommodate virtually unlimited signal transmission by making the cell regions themselves progressively smaller, thus enabling more signals but still maintaining necessary clarity.

ment for safety. Businesses quickly saw the potential for converting previously dead time to productivity. By the end of the 1980's, close to two million customers were using cellular service. Cooper, now a visionary in the field, left Motorola (at the time of his departure, in addition to the cell phone work, he had been credited with important breakthrough work in high-capacity paging terminals and radio pagers) to cofound Cellular Business Systems. When he sold the firm to Cincinnati Bell, Cellular Business Systems had secured a remarkable 70 percent of the cellular industry as its customers.

In 1992, although in his mid-sixties, Cooper started his own communications company, ArrayComm, headquartered in San Jose, California. Certain that cell phone technology could be made far more accessible, efficient, and economical, Cooper spearheaded research into next-generation smart antenna software technology able to manage a higher traffic of calls more efficiently. Tireless in his promotion of wireless communication and a savvy entrepreneur with an intuitive appreciation for the dynamics of marketing, he became a sought-after motivational speaker in both management and communication theory. (He devised Cooper's law, which mathematically projected that since Guglielmo Marconi's initial transmission in 1895, the number of radio frequency conversations that can be concurrently conducted in a specific area had doubled every thirty months.) In addition, Cooper served on trade missions on behalf of the United States to introduce communication innovations in market-friendly countries, most notably China.

Impact

The cell phone reoriented not only the telecommunications industry but society as well. Like other groundbreaking inventions—among them the telephone, the car, and the airplane—the cell phone redefined the conception of how people define spatial society itself. By liberating the communications process from land wires, by putting communication freedom literally in the hands of the consumer, the cell phone created an entirely new conception of the global community. Phones were now about people, not places. Its most obvious impact has been felt in emergency conditions and the quick notification of appropriate help.

In addition to saving lives, cell phones have dramatically reconstituted the notion of accessibility: Conversations routinely are conducted with generous frequency, and despite a growing chorus of social commentators who see the increased chatter as trivializing the communication dynamic, the impact has been dramatic. The generation born after 1985 cannot imagine being bound to landline phones. As the cell phone has become less cumbersome and more versatile (permitting text messaging, Internet connections, e-mail delivery, digital photography, and game technologies), it is positioned to become the most important communication innovation since the telegraph. Of course, its prevalence has brought problems. In an effort to decrease the number of traffic accidents and fatalities linked to handheld cell phone use while driving, various states have introduced legislation restricting drivers from using the handheld devices. Establishments have created "quiet zones" to limit where cell phones can be used. Security issues have only begun to be addressed, given the massive amounts of data being freely transmitted. In addition, concerns have been raised over long-term exposure to cell phone radiation and its possible link to the development of brain tumors.

As Cooper tirelessly pointed out, the next generation of cell phone communications must work on more efficient relays and fewer dropped calls. The technology will become more transparent—that is, more complex yet manageable with fewer instructions. As Cooper sees it, the second wireless revolution will focus on low-cost data delivery, open access by using powerful cells in more places rather than relying on the current tower-to-tower transfer (the antennae create environmental dissonance and have raised the ire of nearby residents and generated concerns from pilots), and allowing the free market to bring the cost of the technology (and the calling programs) within the reach of virtually everyone. Conservative estimates, as of November, 2007, place the number of cell phone users worldwide at 3.3 billion.

—*Joseph Dewey*

Further Reading

Agar, Jon. *Constant Touch: A Global History of the Mobile Phone*. Cambridge, England: Icon, 2005. A quick and accessible look at the most pertinent elements of the technology. A good place for those not versed in electronics and communication technology to appreciate the evolution of the technology itself. Illustrated.

Glotz, Peter. *Thumb Culture: The Meaning of Mobile Phones for Society*. Bielefeld, Germany: Transcript, 2005. Dispensing entirely with academic dressing, the study investigates the pop culture response to the cell phone, particularly its emphasis on the emerging generation born in the mid-1980's whose conception of individuality and private space has been so significantly altered.

Goggin, Gerard. *Cell Phone Culture: Mobile Technol-*

ogy in Everyday Life. New York: Routledge, 2006. A dense and researched investigation that positions the cell phone within a complex of other technological innovations (most prominently the telegraph and the car) to test the potential impact of technology on how people conceive of the dynamics of work, family, community, and culture.

Ling, Rich. *The Mobile Connection: The Cell Phone's Impact on Society*. San Francisco, Calif.: Morgan Kaufmann, 2004. A witty, accessible, and anecdotal investigation into the impact of the invention, most notably on how people define a community, with particular emphasis on privacy and security. A sociologist, Ling is one of the invention's most published and respected commentators.

See also: Alexander Graham Bell; Ivan A. Getting; Elisha Gray; Alfred J. Gross; Guglielmo Marconi.

Peter Cooper

American industrialist

An industrialist, philanthropist, educator, and political reformer, Cooper patented farsighted inventions throughout his life. He improved processes for making glue, iron, and steel; first demonstrated the capabilities of the steam locomotive on American railways; and experimented with prototypes for a flying apparatus and endless-chain machines.

Born: February 12, 1791; New York, New York
Died: April 4, 1883; New York, New York
Primary fields: Food processing; household products; industrial technology; manufacturing; railway engineering
Primary inventions: Steam locomotive; glue-making process

Early Life

Peter Cooper was born in New York City in 1791. He was the fifth of nine children born to John and Margaret Campbell Cooper. Shortly after Peter's birth, John moved the family to Peekskill, New York, which is located on the Hudson River, about an hour north of Manhattan. John Cooper opened a general store and engaged in numerous homespun trades. Peter attended a Peekskill school for only a short period; his lack of a formal education would trouble him his entire life. At an early age, Peter, like many inventors, exhibited mechanical genius and a talent for making things with his hands. Assisting his parents in their chores, Peter became skilled at hatmaking, cobbling, and wagon making and built a crude washing machine out of barrels and wheels.

At age seventeen, Cooper moved to Manhattan, where he was an apprentice to the carriage-building firm of Burtis and Woodward for four years. During this period, Cooper invented a machine for mechanically mortising the hubs of carriage wheels and a machine for drawing power from the tides. After his apprenticeship, he bought a business manufacturing cloth-shearing machines. With Cooper making various improvements to the machines, the business was a success, and he felt sufficiently prosperous to marry Sarah Bedell on December 18, 1813. The first of their six children was born the following year. On March 27, 1815, Cooper patented a pendulum-swinging, musical cradle he had made for his son. He also entered the cabinet-making and grocery businesses.

Life's Work

In 1821, Cooper purchased a struggling glue factory located at Fourth Avenue and Thirty-third Street in Manhattan for $2,000. Refining and patenting various glues and glue-making processes, Cooper soon offered the finest glue products in the United States, rivaling the expensive imports from England and France. Soon, Cooper added an improved make of isinglass, neat's-foot oil, whiting, cement, and the first packaged table gelatin to his successful line of manufactured products. In 1849, Cooper relocated the factory to Maspeth in Queens County. The profits from the factory provided Cooper with his first fortune. Meanwhile, his daily activities and interests led him to other inventions. He invented a blade-revolving lawn mower, a torpedo for proposed use by the Greeks in their rebellion against the Turks, and even an experimental flying machine (which exploded, endangering Cooper and his youngest brother, Edward, who was assisting him). Peter also obtained patents for improvements in constructing steam boilers, grinding marble tabletops, and transporting salt.

During this period, Cooper was absorbed by the quest to build machinery that would lose as little energy as possible in operation. For example, he realized that a revolving crank lost energy at the two inert points in its wheel. He patented a system of rotating steam pistons to try to

A New Process for Making Glue

Peter Cooper's glue factory was his first great success and the lifelong basis of his fortune. It succeeded because Cooper invented a better process for making glue, allowing him to produce the highest quality glues at low prices. As U.S. patent law allows for innovative industrial methods to be patented, Cooper received a patent on April 29, 1830, for his new method. Glue was historically made by boiling animal matter until glue oozes out. The water holding this glue was called foot water. Cooper's patented method improved the process for evaporating the foot water to distill the glue. Cooper replaced the open boiler traditionally used for evaporating foot water with a double-basin method derived from kitchen techniques. He built a brick furnace with a flue leading to two basins, one placed above the other. The furnace applied heat to the water in the lower basin through the flue. The foot water was poured into the upper basin. The boiling water in the lower basin evaporated the foot water to the right consistency. This double-basin method made for a more standard evaporation and thus a finer-grained glue. With this process, Cooper could produce ten well-defined grades of glue. He developed a system of grading for glue quality that was adopted and widely used in the glue industry. Cooper's success with his glue factory illustrates well how innovative and ingenious ideas for industrial production, protected by patents, can lead to commercial and economic success.

solve this problem. He also formulated a concept of an endless chain as a way to power machines with their own momentum. He applied this concept to improve methods of filling a creek with sand in a chain of boxcars and to carry iron ore from mines to forges in a chain of buckets. More ambitiously, he proposed endless-chain techniques for hydraulically propelling boats, driving locomotives, and powering the elevated trains of New York City. Although not all of these ideas met with success, they do demonstrate the fertility of Cooper's mind in wrestling with perennial problems of technology and science. His concept of an endless chain can be seen as a precursor to the conveyor belt.

In 1828, Cooper purchased three thousand acres in Baltimore in anticipation of the launch of the Baltimore and Ohio Railroad, the first in the United States. Finding suitable timber and iron ore on the property, he built kilns for turning the wood into charcoal and a furnace for smelting iron. Dissatisfied with the slow progress of the railroad, in 1830 he constructed an experimental steam-operated locomotive that he called *Tom Thumb. Tom Thumb* was a four-wheel locomotive with a vertical steam boiler, improvised boiler tubes made from rifle barrels, and a blower pulley. Its success demonstrated the possibilities of steam locomotives and brought Cooper national fame; the sale of his Baltimore properties and iron mill brought him a second fortune. He then built an iron foundry on Thirty-third Street near Third Avenue in Manhattan. Cooper made innovative use of the hot-blast method and anthracite coal to "puddle," or stir, the liquid iron mixture. In addition to railroad tracks, the foundry manufactured various kinds of wire, including the suspension wire used for the Niagara Falls Bridge. Moving the foundry to New Jersey, Cooper became one of the largest iron producers in the country. In the 1850's, the foundry began producing structural iron beams used for the new architecture of skyscrapers. The foundry later pioneered the open hearth process for making steel. With his mix of successful industries, Cooper was the leading manufacturer in New York.

The year 1828 also marked Cooper's entry into the public life of New York City, where he served as an alderman from 1828 to 1831 and from 1840 to 1841. As a public official, he assessed and made recommendations as to technological issues facing the city's water supply and pedagogical issues facing the public school system. In 1855, his daughter Amelia married Abram Hewitt, who became an indispensable partner in Cooper's enterprises. The Cooper and Hewitt firm backed numerous major ventures, including Cyrus Field's transatlantic cable, which was completed in 1858.

Cooper's enthusiasm for technology and invention had an almost religious dimension. In the short autobiography he dictated from February 20 to April 17, 1882, Cooper spoke of science as the law of God by which humankind would be drawn into a peaceful and prosperous future.

Motivated by his belief in scientific progress as the wellspring of human life, and conscious of the difficulties posed for him by his lack of education, Cooper decided to use his fortune to build a free college of technology in New York City. He began building the school in 1853 on a city block he acquired bordered by Seventh Street, Astor Place, and Third and Fourth Avenues. The imposing edifice featured many of Cooper's farsighted architectural ideas, such as leaving a shaft for a yet-to-be-invented elevator. The Cooper Union for the Advancement of Science and Art opened on July 1, 1858. It had a night school of arts and sciences, a school of design for women, a library, and a program of public lectures and forums. All branches were free and were endowed by Cooper, his brothers and children, and philanthropist friends of Cooper and Hewitt such as Andrew Carnegie.

In his last decades, Cooper concentrated increasingly on philanthropy and politics. In 1863, he became president of the Citizen's Association, dedicated to reforming the machine politics of Boss Tweed's New York City. In 1876, Cooper was the Greenback Party's first candidate for president of the United States. Cooper had become a national advocate for paper money ("greenbacks") to replace gold and silver as the nation's chief currency, with the paper money to be issued, regulated, and backed by the federal government. The chief plank of his Greenback Party platform was the elimination of the gold standard, a proposal popular with workingmen. Although this proposal was much derided in its day, it would become America's monetary policy in the twentieth century. Cooper continued taking out patents to the end, including ones for powdering eggs and for propelling elevated railway cars. In 1883, Cooper died at the age of ninety-two, one of the most acclaimed citizens of New York City.

Impact

Cooper is the quintessential early American inventor and industrialist. Without a formal education, Cooper relied on his mechanical genius, his ingenuity, and his industry. Many of his ideas lacked a scientific basis, and some proved fruitless, although even then he often showed an intuitive grasp of some fundamental mechanical principle—endless-chain devices, a flying machine, elevators—that would be realized decades later. Where his ideas had a practical basis and were based on his powers of observation and of everyday mechanics, they rarely failed. In his manifold enterprises, he patented machines and processes, improved technology, and perfected industrial methods. His array of inventions was at the heart of his various businesses—glue making, iron smelting, steel production—and of the fortunes he accumulated. His industries were an important component in the success of American business. His patent for table gelatin would be acquired by manufacturer Pearle Wait and renamed "Jell-O," becoming one of the famous American food products of the twentieth century. When the first railroad track was laid down by the Baltimore and Ohio Railroad in 1827, there was uncertainty as to the best way to economically power the train. Cooper's *Tom Thumb* prototype engine demonstrated the capabilities of the steam engine locomotive for commercial transportation. Steam engines would become the chief engine for railroad traffic for the remainder of the nineteenth century.

If his lack of education hampered his scientific work, it also spurred his grandest philanthropic venture. Cooper established the Cooper Union for the Advancement of Science and Art as a free institution so that students with little means could receive a superior education. With great foresight, he provided for the education of women as well. Cooper Union immediately showed its importance for the nation on February 27, 1860, when the Republican candidate for president, Abraham Lincoln, delivered one of the most important speeches of his career in its Great Hall. In the century and a half since, Cooper Union has continued to play a vital role in New York City, while providing a superb education to tens of thousands of promising scholars.

—*Howard Bromberg*

Further Reading

Beckert, Sven. *The Monied Metropolis: New York City and the Consolidation of the American Bourgeoisie 1850-1896*. New York: Cambridge University Press, 2003. Academic study of New York City's economic elites in the nineteenth century. Describes Cooper's frugal, hardworking, down-to-earth lifestyle as the city's richest manufacturer.

Burrows, Edwin, and Mike Wallace. *Gotham: A History of New York City to 1898*. New York: Oxford University Press, 1999. This immense panorama of New York City history recounts the important role that Cooper's industrial inventions and innovations played in the economic growth of the city.

Dunn, Gano. *Peter Cooper: A Mechanic of New York*. New York: Newcomen Society, 1949. Booklet with drawings and speeches contemporary with Cooper.

Girko, Miriam. *The Lives and Times of Peter Cooper*. New York: Thomas Crowell, 1959. Engaging narrative geared to younger audiences. Includes a chronology and drawings of six of Cooper's original patent grants.

Nevins, Allan. *Abram S. Hewitt, with Some Account of Peter Hewitt*. New York: Harper Brothers, 1935. A joint biography of Cooper and his son-in-law Hewitt by one of America's leading historians. Drawing on original papers, Nevins's account, although older, is an engaging and incisive depiction of Cooper's manifold careers. Includes an interesting appendix accounting for the growth of Cooper's fortune.

See also: Joshua Lionel Cowen; Peter Cooper Hewitt; Richard March Hoe; Elmer Ambrose Sperry; James Watt.

Martha J. Coston

American engineer

Coston developed a pyrotechnic signaling device and code system for use at sea. For more than a century, Coston flares saved lives and property. They also gave the North a strategic edge during the American Civil War.

Born: April 10, 1828; New York, New York
Died: January 12, 1904; Washington, D.C.
Also known as: Martha Jay Coston (full name); Martha Hunt (birth name); Martha Jay Scott Coston
Primary fields: Communications; maritime technology; military technology and weaponry; navigation
Primary invention: Signal flares

Early Life

Martha Jay Coston was born in New York City in 1828 to John Scott and Rebecca (Parks) Hunt of Baltimore. Her father died when she was young, after which her mother moved the family from Baltimore to Philadelphia. As a girl, Martha enjoyed learning and preferred quiet times with her mother to the boisterous company of her elder siblings.

When she was fourteen, Martha met Benjamin Franklin Coston, an up-and-coming scientist five years her senior. He had a reputation as a prodigy; not yet twenty, he had invented a submarine vessel capable of staying submerged for eight-hour periods thanks to a chemical process that supplied breathing air. Benjamin and Martha became friends, and the young inventor took to visiting the schoolgirl at home and helping her with her studies.

The two obtained permission from Martha's mother to marry once Martha turned eighteen. In 1844, they decided to wed in secret, but the sixteen-year-old Martha could not hide the marriage from her mother for long. After reconciling with Martha's family, the newlyweds relocated to Washington, D.C. There Benjamin assumed an appointment as master in the service and head of the Washington Navy Yard laboratory.

The Costons flourished in the nation's capital, forming many social and political connections. However, in 1847, Benjamin resigned from the Navy, due in part to a disagreement with the government over his pay and position, as well as in part to a decline in health related to occupational chemical exposure. Benjamin, Martha, and their three young sons relocated to Boston, where Benjamin became president of a gasworks.

Not long after the birth of their fourth boy, Benjamin became severely ill. Martha cared for her husband for three months before his death on November 24, 1848. Martha and the family moved back to Philadelphia to live with her mother, soon after which her infant son died. Martha then turned to the care of her ailing mother, who after a protracted illness also died.

Life's Work

While tending sick family members, the young widow Coston had paid little attention to money matters. Medical and funeral expenses, coupled with her naïve trust in relatives and her husband's business associates, had drained her finances. Hoping to find something of value, Coston combed through her husband's papers. There she found notes on an uncompleted invention, one involving the use of coded combinations of colored fire to be used for remote communications at sea.

Coston remembered that her husband had tried making some test flares during his work at the Washington Navy Yard. After locating and retrieving the flares, she gave them to a trusted high-ranking naval officer for testing. While she awaited the results, illness claimed the life of yet another of her sons.

On the heels of this tragedy came the unwelcome news that her husband's flares had proved to be useless. However, Secretary of the Navy Isaac Toucey assured her that the concept was an excellent one. He encouraged her to perfect the invention, offering her use of the naval laboratory's personnel and resources. When those yielded no positive results, Toucey told Coston that, if she could find someone to make a working flare, the Navy would pay her expenses.

The young widow spent the next decade trying to realize her husband's concept, hiring and dismissing a series of chemists and conducting her own experiments. To carry out her husband's coded signaling plans, she needed to be able to produce three distinct, brilliant, and lasting pyrotechnic colors. She eventually managed to create intense, bright white and red flares, but a third color eluded her. (In a spirit of patriotism, she was striving for blue.)

A breakthrough came in August, 1858. America's top pyrotechnists were gathered in New York City to create a mammoth fireworks display celebrating the first transatlantic cable communication, a message sent by Queen Victoria to President James Buchanan. Among the convened fireworks experts, Coston found the technical

COSTON PYROTECHNIC NIGHT SIGNALS

Martha J. Coston's flares were metal cartridges packed with a proprietary chemical composition that burned with brilliant, distinct colors. The original standard set of Coston signals was made up of twelve pyrotechnic cartridges. Three would burn in a single color (red, white, or green), and six would burn in differing combinations of two of the colors; these flares represented numbers 1 through 9. The one flare including all three colors represented the number 0. Rounding out the set were a preparatory cartridge *P* (white-red-white) and an assent cartridge *A* (red-white-red). The cartridge cases were painted to indicate the color of the pyrotechnics.

To convey a message—for example, "cease fire"—the sender would set off the *P* flare, and the receiver would acknowledge readiness by responding with the *A* flare. Because the numeric code for "cease fire" was 3-1, the sender would then set off the cartridge corresponding to 3 (white then green) immediately followed by the cartridge representing 1 (white).

Users of the earliest Coston signals fitted the cartridge into a manual holder, ignited the flare by hand, and held it aloft until the flame was spent. By the early 1860's, a pistol-type holder had emerged (inventor unknown) that lit the cartridge by means of an exploding percussion cap. Coston's 1871 patented improvement to the original flare included a redesigned holder and a self-igniting outer casing for the cartridge. Twisting the handle and cartridge casing in opposite directions caused a built-in match to be struck, lighting the flare. Other improvements included elder son Henry Coston's aerial signaling system (patented in 1877), in which a pistol-type igniter and holder launched the pyrotechnics high in the air.

Before Coston's flares, ships at sea could communicate at a distance with other vessels or onshore personnel using a variety of coded signals involving flags, colored lanterns, rockets, or flashes from a fired pistol. What set the Coston flares apart was their effectiveness at night and under rainy, foggy, and smoky conditions; the ease with which their messages could be understood; and the distance at which they were effective (when ignited, the flares could be seen from ten or more miles away, depending on visibility conditions and the size of the flare used). Their resistance to spontaneous combustion made them safer than other, more unstable signaling pyrotechnics.

The flares proved themselves time and time again during the Civil War. Countless nighttime efforts to slip past Union blockades were foiled thanks to ship-to-ship communication via Coston flares. Battles were coordinated using the flares, notably the Union's successful and strategically significant January, 1865, attack on the Confederate garrison at Fort Fisher, North Carolina.

During and after the war, the flares aided search and rescue efforts. In December, 1862, when the ironclad warship USS *Monitor* sank in a storm off Cape Hatteras, Coston flares brought rescuers to the scene. The flares saved lives in unexpected ways, too: Coston's autobiography tells how Arctic explorers used theirs to chase wolves from their camp.

know-how she needed. Within months, she had her third color (blue being prohibitively expensive, she settled for green) and a reliable, functioning flare.

Coston was granted U.S. Patent number 23,536 for her "Pyrotechnic Night Signals" in April, 1859. She filed as administrator for B. Franklin Coston, crediting her husband rather than claiming the invention as her own. (One of the witnesses was a J. Quincy Adams—possibly President John Quincy Adams's lawyer grandson, as the president himself had died over a decade earlier.) Coston was one of only five women to receive a patent in 1859, and the only one whose invention was of a nondomestic nature.

Later that year, she also obtained patents in England, France, the Netherlands, Austria, Denmark, Italy, and Sweden and sold three hundred trial flares to the U.S. Navy for approximately $5,000. Navy vessels equipped with the trial flares would make overwhelmingly favorable reports over the next two years on the invention's effectiveness.

Beginning in the summer of 1859, Coston paid extended visits to England and France to interest the navies of both countries in the use of her flares. She returned to the United States in early 1861, shortly before the presidential inauguration of Abraham Lincoln and the beginning of the Civil War. Lincoln's call that year for a blockade of all U.S. ports resulted in a pressing demand for the flares. Based on the success of the trial flares, Congress paid Coston $20,000 for rights to the patent for use by the Navy and contracted with her to produce the flares. She initially hired a manufacturer to fulfill the orders to her specifications, but in later years she and her sons took over the business of manufacturing the flares.

In January, 1863, Coston set sail for Europe, where she would spend the next several years marketing her invention while mingling with society, nobility, and royalty. In 1867, the French government (after a protracted but fruitless effort to reverse engineer the invention) purchased the rights from her to manufacture the flares for use by France's military. In June, 1871, Coston was granted a U.S. patent (number 115,935), this time under her own name, for a new invention: an improvement to the flares that enabled the user to ignite a Coston signal by twisting its handle.

Coston moved back to the United States in 1873, by which time Italy, Denmark, and the Netherlands had officially adopted the flares. America's Civil War had ended eight years earlier, and the Coston family's domestic marketing efforts turned to civilian use of the flares by passenger ships, yachts, the U.S. Merchant Marine, and the Life-Saving Service (later the Coast Guard).

Coston detailed her experiences as a wife, widow, inventor, and traveler in her 1886 autobiography *A Signal Success*. She died in 1904. The Coston Signal Company (renamed the Coston Supply Company in 1927) remained in operation at least until the mid-1980's.

Impact

Coston labored for years to bring her husband's idea to fruition. Her efforts yielded untold savings in lives and property. For more than a century, her flares were used around the world by military, civilian, and commercial watercraft in distress to call for aid. With the flares, onshore personnel warned ships away from hazardous conditions. Similar signaling devices inspired by Coston's flares are still in use today and are considered standard marine safety equipment.

Coston's well-timed success in perfecting the invention meant that the North entered the Civil War equipped with the new flares. Coston's signaling device may not have been the deciding factor in the war, but it certainly was a strategic advantage for the Union's naval forces, and the part it played in planning and executing battles may have helped to bring the war to a close that much sooner.

As a nineteenth century woman working in a traditionally male field, Coston encountered her share of resistance, and sometimes even overt hostility. Yet she persisted, determined to support herself and her family, contribute to her country's welfare, create a quality product, and earn a fair price for it. Her story was an inspiration for women entering the twentieth century, and it still inspires today.

—*Karen N. Kähler*

Further Reading

Coston, Martha J. *A Signal Success: The Work and Travels of Mrs. Martha J. Coston—An Autobiography*. Whitefish, Mont.: Kessinger, 2007. A recent reprint of Coston's 1886 autobiography, the most detailed available source on Coston's life and career. Spans her life from girlhood through the 1880's. Coston describes the process of perfecting and patenting the flares (without divulging trade secrets) and provides several examples of their use, along with numerous testimonials from military officers. Illustrations.

Drachman, Virginia G. *Enterprising Women: 250 Years of American Business*. Chapel Hill: University of North Carolina Press, 2002. The second chapter devotes a section to Coston, focusing on her evolution as a businesswoman and her efforts to gain a foothold in the traditionally male realm of maritime technology. Illustrations, index.

Macdonald, Anne L. *Feminine Ingenuity: Women and Invention in America*. New York: Ballantine Books, 1992. Discusses Coston and her work in the context of other American women inventors and their inventions. Includes a schematic of Coston's 1871 twist-ignition improvement to the pyrotechnic night signals. Bibliography, patents list, index.

Pilato, Denise E. *The Retrieval of a Legacy: Nineteenth Century American Women Inventors*. Westport, Conn.: Praeger, 2000. Chapter 4, "The Civil War: Impetus to Inventing Women," includes a good biography on Coston drawn largely from the inventor's own writing. Notes, bibliography, index.

Vare, Ethlie Ann, and Greg Ptacek. *Mothers of Invention: From the Bra to the Bomb, Forgotten Women and Their Unforgettable Ideas*. New York: William Morrow, 1988. The chapter on "Unsung Heroines" provides an excellent overview of Coston's life, her inventions, and the obstacles she faced as an enterprising woman in the nineteenth century. Index.

See also: John Campbell; Nils Gustaf Dalén; John Harrison.

Frederick Gardner Cottrell

American chemist

Although electrochemists remember Cottrell best for the Cottrell equation, which is important in chronoamperometry (a measuring technique for electrochemical analysis), he is most famous for inventing the electrostatic precipitator for removing suspended particles from gases, thus abating smoke pollution from power plants and dust from cement kilns.

Born: January 10, 1877; Oakland, California
Died: November 16, 1948; Berkeley, California
Primary field: Chemistry
Primary invention: Electrostatic precipitator

Early Life

Frederick Gardner Cottrell was the son of Henry and Cynthia L. Durfee Cottrell, a *Mayflower* descendant. As a young boy, he was fascinated with photography, as was his father. With money earned from chores, he bought a small printing press and printed business cards for various services, including installing electric doorbells. He started a magazine about scientific progress, *Boy's Workshop*; one article on the deposition of dust by electrical aid was written when he was thirteen. He received his early education at the Horton School in Oakland, California, and after two years at Oakland High School, he passed the entrance examination into the University of California, Berkeley, from which he graduated in three years.

Before becoming a teacher at Oakland High School, Cottrell was an assistant to the professor of chemistry at the university. Living frugally and saving money from his teaching job and a weekend job as laboratory assistant at the university provided him the means to do postgraduate work in Germany at the University of Berlin and the University of Leipzig, where he earned his Ph.D. (summa cum laude). Upon his return to California, he joined the faculty at the University of California, Berkeley. In 1904, he married Jessie M. Fulton, whom he had met in a botany class in high school. During this time, Cottrell's father died, and his two children died in infancy.

Life's Work

After Cottrell's father died, he was left with several relatives to support, so without a definite plan, he turned to research in the hope of inventing something quickly in order to make money. One idea came to him on recalling problems reported by former classmates who had become miners. Miners, as well as manufacturers of cement, explosives, and chemicals, realized that dust, smoke, and vapor from kilns, furnaces, and smelting were damaging the environment up and down the West Coast. The filters available were ineffective, so Cottrell determined to find some new method to solve the problem. He remembered reading about an experiment by the English physicist Sir Oliver Lodge in which electrical precipitation had been used, although unsuccessfully. Nevertheless, applying the principle, Cottrell spent $20,000 and five years developing a precipitator that would remove more than 98 percent of the dust.

A large lead-smelting company whose existence was threatened with an injunction consulted Cottrell; within a few months, electrostatic precipitators were installed, and the company's problem was solved. The word spread, and other smelting plants consulted him, as did the Southern Pacific Railroad, which sought a way to re-

Frederick Gardner Cottrell. (Library of Congress)

THE ELECTROSTATIC PRECIPITATOR

While trying to think of some invention that would enable him to gain funds sufficient to support relatives after his father died, Frederick Gardner Cottrell happened to recall hearing some former classmates who had become miners complaining about the damage being caused by smoke, dust, and vapor, and about the millions of dollars that firms were spending to settle lawsuits or to buy up large tracts of land to stop complaints of citizens in the area. He determined at that moment to devise a new method of dealing with the pollution. He also recalled reading about the work of an English physicist, Sir Oliver Lodge, who had tried unsuccessfully to clean the air using electrical precipitation. Applying the general principles of this earlier work, Cottrell spent five years and some $20,000 in developing a complicated machine that would remove over 98 percent of the pollutant.

A lead-smelting company that was being threatened with injunctions by area farmers heard of his invention and called Cottrell in; soon, similar firms everywhere were seeking Cottrell's help. Meanwhile, Cottrell was discovering other uses for his electrostatic precipitator. The Southern Pacific Railroad needed to find a way to remove emulsifying water from petroleum in the oil pipelines it operated. The same principle used in cleaning the air worked: a current was run through the emulsified oil, separating the water from the oil. His precipitator also proved effective in recovering one hundred tons of cement particles as well as reclaiming potash at a cement plant. The devices, also known as cottrells, are also used to enable power plants to burn pulverized coal without creating illegal levels of smoke emission, to reclaim gold and silver, to apply sand to an adhesive surface to make sandpaper, and to attract flock to a rubber base to make carpet.

While adaptations are necessary to address different problems, the electrostatic precipitator works by recognizing that fine droplets and solid particles in smoke, for example, are held in suspension by repelling electrical charges on their surfaces. The device neutralized the charges on a suspended material and causes it to precipitate.

The first patent for Cottrell's electrostatic precipitator was issued on August 11, 1908. The expense this device has saved in abating pollution and reclaiming various materials makes it invaluable. Companies that install cottrells find that they pay for themselves quickly in terms of the value of the materials that the precipitated solids are able to recover.

move emulsifying water from petroleum in the pipelines it operated. Cottrell was able to reclaim potash from cement particles in a cement plant. In 1907, he applied for a patent for his electrostatic precipitator, which came to be known simply as a "cottrell." Over time, the devices made it possible to burn coal without creating illegal levels of smoke emission, to reclaim large amounts of gold and silver for government mints, to apply sand to an adhesive surface to make sandpaper, to attract flock to a rubber base to make carpet, and to remove arsenic from sulfuric acid for a DuPont installation in California.

In 1911, Cottrell became chief physical chemist for the U.S. Bureau of Mines, and he advanced to the position of director in 1919. During his brief time in that position, he worked in World War I programs to develop processes by which nitrogen could be fixed for explosives and to distill helium from air for use in lighter-than-air craft. The following year, however, he became chairman of the Division of Chemistry and Chemical Technology of the National Research Council, while continuing as a consultant for the Bureau of Mines. Between 1922 and 1930, Cottrell served as director of the Fixed Nitrogen Research Laboratory of the U.S. Department of Agriculture.

Although financing the experiments that would result in the electrostatic precipitator had been a challenge, the profits from its manufacture could have made Cottrell a wealthy man. However, he felt that he should use some of the profit to support scientific research, so in 1912 he founded the Research Corporation with the help of Charles Walcott, then secretary of the Smithsonian Institution. The foundation was set up to receive income from his patents and those of other inventors; the funds were then distributed to university researchers in the physical sciences as seed money. Some successful recipients who were funded include Ernest Orlando Lawrence, who developed the cyclotron and was later awarded the Nobel Prize in Physics; Robert H. Goddard, a pioneer rocket scientist whose work laid the experimental foundation for rockets used in World War II and for modern spacecraft; Robert R. Williams, who, after turning his patents for the volume production of vitamin B_1 over to the foundation, saw the price of the vitamin reduced from ten dollars per gram to a few cents; and James Van Allen, who used a small grant to study radiation surrounding the earth, with the result that the Van Allen radiation belt he discovered became known worldwide.

While Cottrell downplayed the praise given him for

choosing to help other scientists over gaining a personal fortune, numerous awards were conferred on him in recognition of his achievements. In 1919, he was awarded the Perkin Medal by the Society of Chemical Industry. The next year, the Chicago section of the American Chemical Society selected him to receive the Willard Gibbs Medal, given to eminent chemists whose work has enabled everyone to live more comfortably and to understand the world better. In 1927, the University of California conferred upon him an honorary LL.D. Two honors came his way in 1937: He was given the Gold Medal of the Mining and Metallurgical Society of America and the Washington Award, given by the Western Society of Engineers. The following year, he was the recipient of the Melville Prize Medal. In 1943, the American Society of Mechanical Engineers honored him with the Holly Medal. He also garnered the Medal of the American Institute of Chemists.

Cottrell was a member of numerous professional organizations and honor societies, including the National Academy of Sciences, the American Institute of Mining Engineers, the American Association for the Advancement of Science, and the American Electrochemical Society. He was inducted into Phi Beta Kappa, Sigma Xi, and Alpha Xi Sigma.

Impact

Cottrell was driven throughout his distinguished career by an energetic pioneering drive in physical chemistry and industrial engineering as well as by a strong and persistent sense of the social significance of scientific and engineering advances. He had a strong belief in the social responsibility of a scientist or engineer, and he held a strong and steadfast conviction about the intrinsic value and the human utility of research.

When Cottrell undertook to find a way to remove suspended particles from gases and thereby perform pollution abatement, a project at which an earlier scientist had been unsuccessful, he came up with a device that would later be found in industrial plants throughout the world. Considered to be an indispensable item because it can cleanse a factory's exhaust of dust and chemicals that otherwise would poison streams and crops and pollute the air, the electrostatic precipitator came to be known simply as a cottrell. If his electrostatic precipitator were his only major contribution to science and engineering, that would still have made him worthy of recognition, but many remember him best for his creation of the Research Corporation in 1912. He set up this foundation to receive his own patents as well as those of other public-spirited inventors. With the funds generated, he distributed seed money to university researchers in the physical sciences. The organization prefers to help young scientists who need funding for their first major projects. Cottrell himself said, "Bet on the youngsters. They are long shots, but many will pay off."

—Victoria Price

Further Reading

Cameron, Frank T. *Cottrell: Samaritan of Science*. 1952. Garden City, N.Y.: Doubleday, 1993. Reprinted biography highlights Cottrell's life and his philosophy about the social responsibility of the scientist as manifested in dedicating one's career to the enlistment of science in the service of society.

Cornell, Thomas D. *Establishing Research Foundation: A Case Study of Patents, Philanthropy, and Organized Research in Early Twentieth-Century America*. Tucson, Ariz.: Research Corporation, 2004. Outlines the background and development of Cottrell's Research Corporation; notes its distinctive historical role in addressing the new social problem brought on by the rapid industrial growth in the United States—pollution. Emphasizes Cottrell's main objective of rendering public service, not making a profit.

Dodgson, Mark, David M. Gann, and Ammon Salter. *The Management of Technological Innovation: Strategy and Practice*. New York: Oxford University Press, 2008. Explains why technological innovation is important, provides a business context for the management of technological innovation, identifies types of technological innovation and discusses its changing nature, and treats innovation strategy. Acknowledges Cottrell and his work with his Research Corporation.

Manchester, Harold. *New Trail Blazers of Technology*. New York: Charles Scribner's Sons, 1976. The author, who had known Cottrell personally, devotes chapter 1 to a readable account of Cottrell's life in addition to commentary on the importance of his work and his development of the electrostatic precipitator, which came to be known by the developer's name. Describes how Cottrell's Research Corporation came into being and explains its unique importance in terms of helping young scientists who might not have received adequate notice from other foundations and organizations.

See also: Meredith C. Gourdine; John Tyndall.

Jacques Cousteau

French oceanographer and engineer

Cousteau gained the reputation as the most well-known underwater explorer in the world. He codeveloped the Aqua-Lung, an underwater breathing apparatus that supplied oxygen to divers, later modernized to today's scuba gear. He likewise invented a waterproof container for filming underwater, helped to start the first human undersea colonies, constructed jet-propelled submersibles for underwater observation, and designed a new wind-power system for boats.

Born: June 11, 1910; Saint-André-de-Cubzac, France
Died: June 25, 1997; Paris, France
Also known as: Jacques-Yves Cousteau (full name)
Primary field: Oceanography
Primary inventions: *Calypso* (ship); Aqua-Lung

Early Life

Jacques-Yves Cousteau (zhahk eev koo-STOH) was born in 1910 to Daniel and Elizabeth Duranthon Cousteau in a small town near Bordeaux, France. Cousteau's family traveled often in his youth, including overseas. During the summer of 1920, Cousteau and his brother were sent to camp at Harvey's Lake in Vermont while their father worked in New York City. One of the chores at the camp was to clean debris from the bottom of the lake near shore. This exercise not only helped improve Jacques's health but also gave him a lifelong love of underwater activity.

After being expelled from traditional high school, Cousteau was sent to a strict boarding school, where he graduated in 1929. In 1930, he gained entrance to the French Naval Academy at Brest. After graduation in 1933, he spent two years aboard a French naval cruiser. Returning to France in 1935, Cousteau decided to enroll in a naval aviation program in the hope of becoming a pilot. However, a 1936 car crash in which both of his arms were severely broken put an end to that dream. After months of recuperation, Cousteau was assigned to the navy's base at Toulon as a gunnery instructor. During the same year, he tested a pair of underwater goggles near the base. His utter fascination at what he saw changed his life, and he began to develop ideas for sustained exploration of underwater milieus.

Life's Work

During World War II, Cousteau served in the French Resistance against the occupying German army. In late 1942, he and French engineer Émile Gagnon invented the Aqua-Lung, a breathing apparatus that allowed divers to swim freely while being able to breath underwater. The device was valuable not only for underwater filming but also for inspecting and repairing ships and for removing enemy mines in the waters surrounding France. After the war, Cousteau showed a French admiral an underwater exploration film that had been made during the war. In 1946, the French navy placed Cousteau in charge of an assemblage, the Undersea Research Group, assigned to continue such investigation. From 1946 until Cousteau left the navy in 1949, he and his colleagues searched underwater caves, conducted physiological tests of the impact of deep diving, performed underwater archaeology by probing shipwrecks, and participated in the rescue of a bathyscaphe.

After leaving the navy, Cousteau sought to continue his undersea explorations. He acquired a former French minesweeping ship in 1950 and converted it for use by his diving team. The ship, named the *Calypso*, would be Cousteau's home away from home for much of the next forty years. In 1952, the Cousteau team discovered a sunken Roman cargo ship near Grand Congloué Island off the coast of France. The ship dated back to 230 B.C.E., making it the oldest ever uncovered up to that time. Subsequently, the *Calypso* and its crew studied marine life and environments in oceans (Atlantic, Pacific, and Indian), seas (Aegean and Red), and rivers (Amazon, Nile, Mississippi, and St. Lawrence). Cousteau recorded his findings on paper and film, which were later turned into books, documentaries, and television specials.

During the 1960's, Cousteau planned and implemented the Conshelf Project, which was designed to investigate the long-term effects of living under the ocean. The Cousteau team built three dome-shaped structures of various sizes as part of the project. Conshelf I, set up in the Mediterranean, housed two divers for a week in 1962. Conshelf II, built on the floor of the Red Sea, housed five divers for a month. Conshelf III, established off the coast of Nice, France, housed divers more than three hundred feet deep for a month.

Two other Cousteau inventions related directly to his explorations. In 1967, Cousteau launched two small submersibles created for underwater exploration. These vehicles, called Sea Fleas, permitted filming underwater and had mechanical arms for recovering objects. In 1980, Cousteau and two other Frenchmen designed a new engine system for ships that was partially based on wind power. Referred to as the Turbosail, the device furnished a renewable source of power while reducing reliance on oil-burning engines.

Cousteau used his influence to teach about the effects of pollution on the world's ecosystems. In doing so, he became an environmentalist and conservationist. For instance, in 1960 he led a protest against dumping radioactive waste in the sea. In 1973, he helped to establish the Cousteau Society for the Protection of Ocean Life. In 1990, Cousteau initiated a worldwide petition campaign to stop oil drilling and mining in Antarctica. Not only was the immediate campaign successful, but the world's nations also agreed to protect the area for the next half century. Because of his expertise and advocacy, Cousteau was invited to address the U.N. Conference on Environment and Development, which took place in Brazil in 1992.

Besides writing fifty books and producing two Academy Award-winning films, Cousteau was able to take advantage of the growing influence of television in order to educate and entertain a generation of underwater enthusiasts. As a result of a 1966 television special, Cousteau signed a contract with the American Broadcasting Company (ABC) in 1968 to produce a series, *The Undersea World of Jacques Cousteau*, which ran for eight seasons. In 1977, Cousteau produced a new series, *Cousteau Odyssey*, for the Public Broadcasting Service (PBS). In 1982, *The Cousteau Amazon* series premiered on Turner Broadcasting System. From 1985 through 1994, *Cousteau's Rediscovery of the World* was broadcast on American television. Overall, Cousteau and his team produced more than 120 television documentaries and garnered forty Emmy nominations.

Despite his success and notoriety, Cousteau encountered his share of heartache during his long career. During his team's deep-diving tests in the late 1940's, at least one close friend was killed as a result of carbon monoxide poisoning. In 1979, his youngest son, Philippe, was killed when his seaplane overturned and broke apart near Lisbon, Portugal. Cousteau's wife, Simone, died of cancer at age seventy-two in 1990. In January, 1996, the Cousteau team's beloved vessel, the *Calypso*, was rammed and sunk by a barge in Singapore. That same year, Cousteau prosecuted his son Jean-Michel over the use of the Cousteau name. Jacques Cousteau died in June, 1997, at eighty-seven.

Impact

During Cousteau's life, his work was attacked in certain quarters as nonscientific. That was somewhat ironic, given the alliance that the Cousteau team had with scientists who often came aboard the *Calypso*. Notwithstanding the latter criticism, Cousteau earned many national and international awards. In addition to several honorary degrees, he received a number of distinctions, among them the National Geographic Society Gold Medal, 1961; the Boston Museum of Science Bradford Prize, 1965; the Franklin Institute Potts Medal, 1970; the United Nations International Environmental Prize, 1977; the Lindbergh Award, 1982; the Bruno H. Schubert Foundation prize, 1983; the New York Zoological Society Gold Medal, 1985; the U.S. Presidential Medal of Freedom, 1985; the International Council of National Academy of Television Arts and Sciences Founder's Award, 1987; induction into the Television Hall of Fame, 1987; the National

Jacques Cousteau. (Library of Congress)

Geographic Society Centennial Award, 1988; induction into the French Academy, 1989; and the Third International Catalan Prize, 1991.

More than any scientist of his time, Cousteau exposed the effects of pollution on the world's waterways. The organization that he cofounded to preserve the environment, the Cousteau Society, has nearly 300,000 members and boasts branches in several nations. As of 2009, the Cousteau Society is busy turning the *Calypso* into a museum and raising funds for the construction of *Calypso II*. In addition to Cousteau's impact on the technical side of underwater exploration, his Aqua-Lung, as well as articles, books, and television series about his undersea exploration, increased public interest in recreational scuba diving.

Perhaps one measure of Cousteau's fame is how he is treated by popular culture. Countless authors and musicians have written and sung about Cousteau's exploits. For instance, American musician John Denver wrote the song "Calypso" as a tribute to the ship and its crew. The 1975 song reached number one on the *Billboard* charts.

—*Samuel B. Hoff*

THE *CALYPSO*

Previously used as a minesweeper during World War II, the *Calypso* was retooled for use by Jacques Cousteau and his crew pursuant to its purchase in 1950. The ship measured about 140 feet long and traveled at a maximum ten knots. It included an underwater observation chamber in the front of the ship, along with an engine room, a steering room, a radio room, a mess hall with a kitchen, and cabins for crew members to sleep in. The ship possessed sophisticated navigation devices, such as sonar and radar.

In addition to the diving and photography equipment, the *Calypso* had its own scientific laboratory. Crew members performed scientific experiments along with other duties and chores. The *Calypso* was essentially the main part of a fleet of equipment employed for ocean research. Other than the ship itself, the fleet encompassed a helicopter and several submersibles. In 1985, a new ship called the *Alcyone* joined *Calypso* on its voyages. The former ship was outfitted with the Turbosail engine system, which Cousteau designed with Professor Lucien Malavard and engineer Bertrand Charrier. The Turbosail system permitted ship operators to alternate between fuel oil and wind power as conditions warranted.

In 1996, the more-than-four-decades-old *Calypso* was accidentally holed and sunk by a barge in Singapore. For viewers of Cousteau's television series, "*Calypso*" had been synonymous with the name of its captain, who died the following year.

FURTHER READING

Cousteau, Jacques-Yves, and Frederic Dumas. *The Silent World*. Washington, D.C.: National Geographic Adventure Classics, 2004. This reprint of Cousteau's first book, published in 1953, offers a fascinating look into his early projects.

DuTemple, Lesley A. *Jacques Cousteau*. Minneapolis, Minn.: Lerner, 2000. This monograph is a companion to the A&E Television Network's *Biography* series program on Cousteau.

King, Roger. *Jacques Cousteau and the Undersea World*. Philadelphia: Chelsea House, 2001. One of several works on the undersea pioneer written during the decade of the 2000's.

Olmstead, Kathleen. *Jacques Cousteau: A Life Under the Sea*. New York: Sterling, 2008. Details the life and accomplishments of the French explorer. Written for a juvenile audience.

Zronik, John. *Jacques Cousteau: Conserving Underwater Worlds*. New York: Crabtree, 2007. This brief work appears in workbook form and contains an excellent description of the *Calypso*. Written for a juvenile audience.

See also: Harold E. Edgerton; Edwin Albert Link; Ruth Patrick.

Joshua Lionel Cowen

American toy train manufacturer

Cowen did not invent the toy train, electric or otherwise, but his Lionel electric toy trains set the standard in the toy train market during the twentieth century and are a leading collectible of the twenty-first century.

Born: August 25, 1877; New York, New York
Died: September 8, 1965; Palm Beach, Florida
Primary field: Manufacturing
Primary invention: Lionel electric toy trains

Early Life

Joshua Lionel Cowen was born Joshua Lionel Cohen, but no biographer knows with certainty why he changed his name in 1910. Some have speculated that it was to avoid the widespread anti-Semitism in the American toy-making industry at that time, although Cowen never attempted to conceal his Jewish heritage. He was the eighth of nine children of Hyman Nathan and Rebecca Kantrowitz Cohen, who had immigrated to the United States shortly after the American Civil War. Cowen's father manufactured cloth caps, employing several workers, and later expanded into real estate and jewelry. The family was comfortable but not wealthy.

Mechanical devices fascinated Cowen, who built his first toy train at the age of seven when he attached a small steam engine to a wooden locomotive he had built himself. Unfortunately, the engine exploded and damaged the wallpaper in his family's kitchen. Cowen attended Elementary School Number One in lower Manhattan and the Peter Cooper Institute for high school, where he studied technical subjects. He entered the City College of New York in 1893 but quickly dropped out. He then enrolled at Columbia University but left after one semester.

Cowen got his first job at the age of fourteen working in a trade magazine office and worked at dry-cell battery manufacturer Henner and Anderson from 1896 to 1897. Then he assembled battery-powered lamps for the Acme Electric Lamp Company.

Cowen met Cecelia Liberman in 1902 and married her in 1904. They had two children, Lawrence and Isabel. Cecelia died in 1946, and Cowen married Lillian Appel Herman three years later.

Life's Work

Cowen filed his first patent in 1899 for an ignition device for photographer's flash powder. The igniter used dry-cell batteries to heat a wire fuse. The U.S. Navy contracted with him to build twenty-four thousand of the devices to use as detonators for mines. Cowen filed his second patent in 1900 for an electric explosive fuse that consisted of a cardboard tube packed with a flammable chemical through which wires passed to provide the heat for ignition.

Cowen and a partner formed the Lionel Manufac-

Joshua Lionel Cowen is honored with a display at the Lionel headquarters in Chesterfield Township, Michigan. Cowen created his first electric toy train, the Electric Express, in 1901. (AP/Wide World Photos)

LIONEL'S ELECTRIC TOY TRAINS

The first electric toy trains were manufactured by the Carlisle and Finch Company in 1893. They ran on metal strips and were powered by two wet-cell batteries. Joshua Lionel Cowen's first train, the Electric Express, ran on four dry-cell batteries. By 1906, Cowen had developed a transformer that connected the tracks to wall outlets and reduced the outlet's 110 volts to 20, eliminating the need for batteries. Originally, one track carried the positive charge, and the other the negative. Another of Cowen's innovations was the three-track system in which the center track was positive and the two outside ones were negative. This system was less susceptible to short circuits. The tracks of Cowen's earliest trains had a gauge of $2\frac{7}{8}$ inches, but for many years the less expensive Lionel trains used a $1\frac{1}{4}$-inch gauge, called the "O" gauge, and the more expensive ones a $2\frac{1}{8}$-inch gauge, called the "standard" gauge.

Lionel's leading standard-gauge train for many years was the Pullman Deluxe. The base system was a No. 42 engine and three passenger cars. Introduced in 1912, it originally cost $62.50. For another $12.50, the buyer could substitute engine No. 54, which was finished in brass and nickel. In 1921, a second motor was added to the No. 42 so that it could pull more cars. By 1929, the Transcontinental Limited stretched nine feet and cost $110, more than a used car in good condition. However, freight trains were more popular overall, because the purchaser could add milk, cattle, crane, flat, oil, and other cars, and each one came with a caboose. Finally, Lionel sold accessories, such as bridges, tunnels, street lamps, conveyors, culverts, newsstands, crossing gates, houses, water towers, oil derricks, gantry cranes, barrel loaders, ice depots, freight sheds, floodlight towers, signal towers, train depots, fueling stations, artificial grass, artificial coal, coal elevators, forklifts, sawmills, and miniature people.

For the largest layouts, the No. 840 Power Station was available. Besides looking like a power station, it contained two transformers and six electrical switches. Among Lionel's later innovations were a "chugger" sound effect in 1933, a whistle in 1935, automatic couplers in 1945, smoking trains in 1946, and magnetic traction in 1950.

turing Company in 1900 with the intention of selling small electric devices. In 1901, Cowen invented a battery-powered portable electric fan. Unfortunately, it circulated air poorly. However, Cowen used the fan's motor to power his first electric train, the Electric Express. Essentially a cigar box on wheels, it was sold not as a toy but rather as a department store window advertisement. To everyone's surprise, the store's customers were more interested in the train than what it was advertising, so the store ordered more for resale. Cowen's second train, the City Hall Park, appeared in 1902, the same year as the first Lionel catalog. The City Hall Park was the first switch to allow figure-eight track configurations and the first accessory, a two-foot-long suspension bridge. By 1906, he was marketing the trains exclusively as toys. Annual sales grew from $22,000 in 1907 to $839,000 in 1921. In 1918, the Lionel Corporation was formed with Cowen at the head, but from then on he spent most of his time on marketing rather than inventing.

During World War I, Lionel manufactured compasses and other navigational equipment, but he returned to making toys after Germany surrendered. In 1929, Cowen bought control of Ives, one of his leading competitors, and intended to take early retirement. However, the Great Depression forced a change of plans. First, the stock market crash reduced the funds available for his retirement. Second, Lionel's sales declined for the first time, from $2.2 million in 1929 to $1.9 million in 1930, and in 1931 Lionel lost money for the first time. By 1934, Lionel had to go into receivership, although Cowen remained as head of the corporation. Finally, Cowen was a member of the board of directors of the Bank of the United States, which failed in 1930, and New York's state superintendent of banks required him to pay $850,000 out of his own money to make restitution to account holders.

Lionel returned to profitability in 1934 with two products. First, it licensed Mickey and Minnie Mouse from Walt Disney for a windup handcar. Lionel sold 253,000 of the one-dollar toys by Christmas and took orders for an additional 100,000 that were delivered in 1935. The other product was the Union Pacific M-10000 train, which retailed for $19.50 and became the best-selling Lionel train up to that time. Lionel came out of receivership in 1935 and went public in 1937.

Lionel manufactured compasses, navigational instruments, and percussion primers during World War II. Although the corporation manufactured no toy trains from 1942 to 1945, sales rose to $7.2 million in 1943 from military contracts alone. After the war, Cowen passed responsibility for day-to-day operations to his son, Lawrence, but stayed on as chairman of the board. In 1946, sales reached $10 million a year; they peaked at $32.9 million in 1953, when Lionel was the largest toy manufacturer in the world. Two-thirds of the toy trains sold in the United States and 62 percent of those in foreign countries were Lionel trains. However, annual sales dropped to $14.4 million by 1958, because the toy market changed. Most American households now owned a television, and airplanes and cars had overtaken trains as the most popular toys for boys. While Lionel manufactured both kinds of toys, it was not a leader in either category.

Lionel attempted to diversify, but it consistently guessed wrong in choosing new products, including an electric cattle guard, a toy chemistry set, a toy construction set, fishing reels, and a 3-D camera. The last product lost hundreds of thousands of dollars, because the 3-D camera market turned out to be a fad, and the fishing reels, while initially profitable, eventually lost market share to inexpensive Japanese imports. Under pressure from stockholders, Cowen resigned as chairman of Lionel in 1958 and sold his Lionel shares in 1959.

Impact

The U.S. Postal Service included the 1929 Lionel catalog cover in its 1998 Celebrate the Century series of stamps. In 1999, the A&E cable channel produced a show about the top ten toys of the twentieth century in which it ranked Lionel toy trains as number four, behind the yo-yo, crayons, and Barbie dolls.

Cowen's marketing had the negative impact of reinforcing sexual stereotypes, because he marketed trains exclusively to boys. One of the few toys for girls that Lionel ever manufactured was an operational electric range so that girls could learn to become housewives. In 1957, Lionel finally attempted to market a train to girls, called the Lady Lionel, but its pastel colors, including a pink locomotive, did not appeal to girls any more than it did to boys and contributed to Cowen's departure. So few sets were sold that they are especially valuable in the twenty-first century as collectibles.

Lionel trains are still being manufactured in the twenty-first century, but it is a completely different market. Toy trains, which can cost more than $1,000, are mostly owned by adult hobbyists rather than preadolescent boys. The Train Collectors Association, founded in 1954, boasts of a membership of more than thirty thousand. *Classic Toy Trains*, the leading magazine of the hobby, has a circulation of seventy thousand and found from a year 2000 survey of subscribers that their average age was fifty-four. Richard Kughn, who owned Lionel from 1986 to 1996, was a typical hobbyist in that he remembered receiving a Lionel train for Christmas when he was nine years old in 1938. In other words, the twenty-first century market for toy trains is a niche, rather than a mass, market.

—Thomas R. Feller

Further Reading

Carp, Roger. *The Art of Lionel Trains: Toy Trains and American Dreams*. Waukesha, Wis.: Kalmbach, 2003. An illustrated history of Lionel catalogs and print advertising that occasionally points out the sexual stereotyping in Cowen's marketing philosophy.

Hollander, Ron. *All Aboard! The Story of Joshua Lionel Cowen and His Lionel Train Company*. 1981. Rev. ed. New York: Workman, 2000. Illustrated biography of Cowen and a history of the Lionel Corporation. Includes many sidebars, photographs of Lionel trains, information on Cowen's competitors, and commentary on the state of the toy and model train market as of 2000.

Kelly, Jim. "MR News: One Hundred Years of Lionel Trains." *Model Railroader* 67, no. 1 (January, 2000): 56. An appreciation of Cowen on the one hundredth anniversary of the founding of the Lionel Corporation.

McKerrel, Mac. "Keeping Track of Santa." *The Business Journal* 20, no. 50 (December 8, 2000): 66. A middle-aged man recollects receiving a Lionel train for Christmas when he sees a photograph of that particular model.

Sobey, Ed, and Woody Sobey. *The Way Toys Work: The Science Behind the Magic 8 Ball, Etch a Sketch, Boomerang, and More*. Chicago: Chicago Review Press, 2008. One of the toys described and analyzed is the electric toy train.

Souter, Gerry, and Janet Souter. *Lionel: America's Favorite Toy Trains*. Osceola, Wis.: MBI Publishing, 2000. Illustrated history of Lionel trains and their competitors up to 2000. Includes many photographs and sidebars and much biographical information on Cowen.

Watson, Bruce. *The Man Who Changed How Boys and Toys Were Made: The Life and Times of A. C. Gilbert*. New York: Penguin Books, 2002. Biography of the inventor of the Erector Set and one of Cowen's top competitors.

See also: Edwin Binney; Beulah Louise Henry.

SEYMOUR CRAY

American computer designer and electrical engineer

Known as the "father of supercomputing," Cray created the world's fastest computers in the 1960's and early 1970's. His machines were made for a small group of scientific users but became prototypes for advances in computing that eventually became mainstream.

Born: September 28, 1925; Chippewa Falls, Wisconsin
Died: October 5, 1996; Colorado Springs, Colorado
Also known as: Seymour Roger Cray (full name)
Primary fields: Computer science; electronics and electrical engineering
Primary invention: 6600 computer

EARLY LIFE

Seymour Roger Cray was the son of Seymour and Lillian Cray. The elder Seymour was a civil engineer who worked for the town of Chippewa Falls, Wisconsin. The younger Seymour showed an interest in science and technology at a very early age. He ran wires though the family home so that he and his younger sister Carol could communicate with Morse code. He was also interested in photography, and he was allowed to experiment with electronics and chemistry at home. In high school, he excelled in science. After high school, he entered the Army and worked with electronics and radio equipment in Europe and the Philippines during World War II.

After the war, he attended the University of Wisconsin and then the University of Minnesota, where he earned a bachelor's degree in electrical engineering in 1950 and a master's degree in applied mathematics in 1951. During his college years, he worked as an electronics repairman. He developed a unique combination of skills, and his deep familiarity and practical experience with electronics, when augmented with advanced studies in mathematics, gave him an ideal background for what would become his life's work: the design of logic circuits and other hardware for the world's most powerful computers. Fortunately for Cray, he soon found himself in a perfect environment for learning almost everything that had been accomplished up to that time in terms of computer engineering. One of his teachers at the university recommended that he apply at an engineering firm that was located in a nearby factory that had been used to build wooden gliders for the invasion of Normandy.

LIFE'S WORK

The firm was Engineering Research Associates (ERA), founded by William Norris and other cryptographers who had served in the U.S. Navy. They developed mechanical devices to break the Germans' Enigma code, thus allowing the Navy to find and destroy Nazi U-boats. In their postwar facility at St. Paul, Minnesota, they continued their work as civilians, but their primary customer was the Navy, and the nature of their work was kept secret from the general public. When Cray joined ERA in 1950, they had recently created a revolutionary new technology, the first computer-memory storage system, consisting of pieces of magnetic tape glued to a large rotating metal drum. Cray quickly immersed himself in their work, and along with other newly hired engineers, he was given classes in Boolean algebra and other relevant topics. He soon distinguished himself as an outstanding new talent and rose quickly within ERA, where he helped to design one of the first scientific computers, the ERA 1103, and remained with this group though various corporate changes, including their work for Sperry Rand's UNIVAC Division.

In 1958, Cray joined William Norris, who had left Sperry Rand to become the chief executive officer of Control Data Corporation (CDC), a new company that carried on the development of scientific computers. He began working on new designs, with transistors replacing vacuum tubes, resulting in the CDC 1604 (1960), the most powerful computer in the world at the time. Most of these machines, which cost millions of dollars to produce, were sold to government agencies and scientific research labs such as the Lawrence Livermore National Laboratory in California. However, the commercial success of these products became increasingly distracting for Cray, who required long stretches of uninterrupted time to concentrate on his work. Since Cray was the director of engineering, his request to have his own facility in a more secluded environment was granted by Norris. Chippewa Falls, Wisconsin, Cray's own hometown, became the new location, enabling him to live next door to his lab and to set his own hours. Cray continued to top his own world records for processing speed with each new product. The CDC 6600 computer, introduced in 1964, used revolutionary new designs in processor architecture, peripherals, and cooling. It was utilized for modeling nuclear reactions and other demanding tasks. His next computer, the CDC 7600, was over five times faster.

The 6600 Computer

Supervised by Seymour Cray, with system design by James E. Thornton, the CDC 6600 was the second major product to come from Cray's work for the Control Data Corporation (CDC). Building on the success of the CDC 1604, Cray continued using transistors for logic gates but switched from germanium to silicon, to overcome speed limitations. Another speed-boosting innovation was Cray's use of multiple processors: The 6600's central processor was freed from input and output tasks, which were handled by external processors. Its 60-bit word length could accommodate very large pieces of data. The central processor itself comprised ten parallel units that were each tuned for specific types of operations and that could engage in simplified components of a complex problem. The central processor was housed in an aluminum frame shaped like a plus sign when viewed from above, and there was space in the center for the thousands of wires, which were cut exactly to their minimum possible lengths in order to reduce latency.

The main chassis of the machine was about seven feet tall, with each of its four arms extending out six feet from the center. Instead of switches and lights, operators could use the machine with a keyboard and a pair of CRT monitors, which provided status displays. These peripherals connected to another external processor, which translated the data back and forth between the central processor and the communication interfaces. Another innovative aspect of the machine was its cooling system. Instead of fans, the machine was cooled by Freon gas circulating through coils, somewhat like a household refrigerator. A complete 6600 system with peripherals cost $6 million.

First introduced in 1964, the 6600 was about ten times faster than anything else available at the time. The machine was regarded by many as the first supercomputer. Optimized for the rapid floating-point processing required in scientific applications, the 6600 could reach three million instructions per second (MIPS). The supercomputer stimulated the development of operating system and compiler software so that customers, primarily government agencies, could harness the computer's power for practical use. Cray, already eager to make the 6600 obsolete by developing an even faster computer, was more interested in the speed and power of the processors, and other team members worked on the software.

The development of peripherals also was stimulated by the 6600. In addition to the monitor and keyboard interfaces, CDC developed a disk drive for more rapid storage and retrieval of data, replacing the magnetic drums used in previous computers. These new kinds of peripherals eventually became standard in computer systems. The parallel processing architecture of the 6600, in which computations were divided into simpler tasks for greater speed in execution, influenced the development of reduced instruction set computing (RISC) processors.

It used an instruction pipeline, so that incoming data could enter the processor while a previous instruction was still being executed. From approximately 1969 to 1975, this was the fastest computer, although it was not as profitable for CDC as its predecessor.

In 1972, Cray left CDC with several other employees and started his own company, Cray Research, on the same property in Chippewa Falls. He introduced the Cray-1, which used another of his innovations, vector processing, which increased speed by working with long arrays (lists) of numbers at once. Los Alamos National Laboratory was given the first preview edition of a Cray-1 in 1976, and the National Center for Atmospheric Research purchased one for more than $8 million. More than one hundred Cray-1 computers were sold. In 1980, Cray resigned from Cray Research and moved to Colorado Springs, Colorado. He eventually formed another company, Cray Computer Corporation, and introduced the Cray-3, which used semiconductors made of gallium arsinide. Although innovative, this product was not commercially successful, and Cray started another company, SRC Computers. Cray and his staff began work on a new computer using the massively parallel architecture that was proving fruitful for other researchers, but he was in a car accident on September 22, 1996, and died of his injuries two weeks later.

Impact

While the term "supercomputer" was redefined by each successive product that his companies released, Cray made many specific contributions in the course of his lifelong pursuit of processing speed and efficiency. Among these contributions are the concept of multithreading (introduced with the CDC 6600's ten independent processor states), the use of vectors as an architecture component, the simplification of processing instructions (a forerunner of reduced instruction set computing, or RISC, architecture), miniaturization of essential hardware (primarily in the transition from vacuum tubes to transistors and printed circuits), and cooling systems (with M. Dean Roush at CDC).

Along with their insights and creativity as engineers, Cray and his colleagues influenced the culture of research and development in computing. With relatively small teams of dedicated and talented people, and relatively meager resources, Cray competed successfully against much larger companies. He became almost legendary by rejecting corporate formalities, bureaucratic time consumption, and petty politics in favor of concentration, focus, and productivity.

Cray's supercomputers gave American scientists the ability to simulate nuclear explosions, helping to provide deterrence during the Cold War years while avoiding the physical and geopolitical dangers of actual detonations. The supercomputers contributed to rapid growth and development in computer hardware and software, leading in turn to one of the most radical transformations in human culture at the turn of the century.

—*John E. Myers*

Further Reading

Billings, Charlene W., and Sean M. Grady. *Supercomputers: Charting the Future of Cybernetics*. New York: Facts On File, 2004. Historical approach accessible to younger and/or general readers. Includes an entire chapter on Seymour Cray's work as well as precursors, and possible future trends. Glossary, bibliography, Web sites, index.

Fritz, Sandy, et al. *Understanding Supercomputing: From the Editors of "Scientific American."* New York: Warner Books, 2002. Futuristic exploration of trends in hardware, with mention of Seymour Cray's use of gallium arsinide for the Cray-3. Illustrated, with index.

Lundstrom, David E. *A Few Good Men from Univac*. Cambridge, Mass.: MIT Press, 1988. Personal account of Lundstrom's experiences with the Control Data Corporation and Seymour Cray. Photos, drawings, and reproductions.

Murray, Charles J. *The Supermen: The Story of Seymour Cray and the Technical Wizards Behind the Supercomputer*. New York: John Wiley & Sons, 1997. Definitive, not overly technical narrative describes the main inventors, the evolution of their creative work environment, constantly shifting business arrangements, corporate sponsors, and high-powered customers. Photos, notes, index.

Price, Robert M. *The Eye for Innovation: Recognizing Possibilities and Managing the Creative Enterprise*. New Haven, Conn.: Yale University Press, 2005. History of the Control Data Corporation written by its former chief executive officer, with an emphasis on how the CDC management style enabled Seymour Cray and other figures to work together, competing successfully against much larger companies such as International Business Machines (IBM). Bibliographical references, index.

Thornton, James E. *Design of a Computer: The Control Data 6600*. Glenview, Ill.: Scott, Foresman, 1970. Detailed description of one of the earliest supercomputer's system architecture. Foreword by Seymour Cray.

See also: John Vincent Atanasoff; Walter H. Brattain; Jack St. Clair Kilby; Robert Norton Noyce; William Shockley.

Bartolomeo Cristofori

Italian engineer

A musical-instrument maker famous for his ingenuity, Cristofori set out to design a new instrument by improving the sound and mechanism of the harpsichord. He is credited with having invented the piano in Florence around 1700.

Born: May 4, 1655; Padua, Republic of Venice (now in Italy)
Died: January 27, 1732; Florence (now in Italy)
Also known as: Bartolomeo di Francesco Cristofori (full name); Bartolomeo Christofani; Bartolomeo Cristofali
Primary field: Music
Primary invention: Piano

Early Life

Bartolomeo Cristofori (bahr-toh-loh-MEH-oh krihs-TOH-foh-ree) was born to Francesco Cristofori and Laura Papafava in Padua in the Republic of Venice in 1655. He was christened in the parish of San Luca two days later, and his godparents were Camillo Chinoni and Pani Lina, maid to Lady Laura Papafava. Cristofori remained quite close to his mother's family, as is confirmed by a reference to a Roberto Papafava in Cristofori's second will. The name also occurs in one of Cristofori's letters sent from Florence in May, 1693.

Almost nothing is known of Cristofori's family life and his early years in Padua except that he had a younger brother, Pietro Filippo, whose christening record dating to May, 1657, proves that the family surname was Cristofori, and not Christofani or Cristofali, as Cristofori has at times been referred to. Even though there is no record of where his workshop was located, in his hometown Cristofori must have acquired considerable notoriety as an instrument maker. Indeed, while traveling to Venice to attend the carnival in 1688, Prince Ferdinando de' Medici, a humanist, patron, and lover of music, stopped at Padua and decided to recruit Cristofori, who agreed to the appointment at a salary of twelve scudi per month. A young man of thirty-three, Cristofori moved to the court of Ferdinando in Florence in May of that year and lodged and worked as harpsichord maker for the prince in the Galleria dei Lavori of the Uffizi.

A grand piano made by the Italian harpsichord maker Bartolomeo Cristofori in 1720. (The Granger Collection, New York)

Life's Work

Cristofori's activity as harpsichord maker at the court is well recorded, partly thanks to the many bills Cristofori submitted to his employer. It is known that on August 15, 1690, he was paid 1,036 lire for an oval spinet (a harpsichord with the longest strings in the middle of the case). This and other instruments built by Cristofori in the 1690's (for example, an upright harpsichord currently held in the museum of the Luigi Cherubini conservatory in Florence) are all documented in an inventory, dated to 1700, and show Cristofori's versatility as instrument maker.

The above-mentioned inventory also alludes to "a large *Arpicembalo* [harp-harpsichord] by Bartolomeo Cristofori, of new invention, that produces soft and loud." This is the first reference to the piano, on which Cristofori had been working since 1698. The limitations of Cristofori's piano were, however, all too obvious. Rather expensive to make, the instrument had unsophisticated hammer heads, and its range was a mere four octaves. All this meant that news of its existence did not spread rapidly, and only in 1711 did Francesco Scipione Maffei report on the new invention, which the Italian scholar had been able to examine two years earlier. In an article published in the *Giornale de'letterati d'Italia* of Venice, Maffei provided a thorough description of the new instrument illustrated with a diagram of the mechanism. Though he acknowledged that the sound of the piano was felt to be too soft and dull, Maffei recognized the importance of Cristofori's new instrument. He further reported that, by 1711, Cristofori had already built three pianos.

Cristofori was then at the peak of his career when his patron Ferdinando died on October 30, 1713. There is evidence that Cristofori continued to work for the prince's father, Cosimo III, and not merely as custodian of Cosimo's musical collection—as it is very often wrongly believed—but as instrument maker, or *strumentaio*. Proof of Cristofori's continuing activity after Prince Ferdinando's death is given by an inventory of the instruments owned by the Florentine court, dated 1732, which shows the steps taken by Cristofori to enlarge the musical collection of the Medici. The three surviving pianos built by Cristofori in 1720, 1722, and 1726—all signed by "Bartolomeo Cristofori of Padua, inventor," as a Latin inscription proudly proclaims—show that he endeavored to improve the quality of his pianos and confirm that Cristofori was active until practically the end of his life. In his last years, Cristofori owned houses in Florence, first in San Remigio and subsequently in San Iacopo tra' Fossi, both locations not far from the Uffizi. The only known portrait of Cristofori also dates from his Florentine period. Purchased by G. Schünemann for a Berlin museum in 1934 but destroyed during the course of World War II, it was painted in 1726 and portrays the inventor standing next to a piano against the backdrop of the city of Florence. Apart from the above-mentioned pianos, a total of six surviving instruments (oval spinets, harpsichords, and a double bass) are attributed to Cristofori. They are all held in museums across Europe and the United States.

Toward the end of his life, Cristofori wrote two wills. In the first, dated January 24, 1728, he bequeathed all his possessions to one of his most conspicuous pupils, Giovanni Ferrini, famous for making a harpsichord once owned by Elisabetta Farnese, queen of Spain. A second will superseding the first followed on March 23, 1729. In it, Cristofori bequeathed his possessions to

The Piano

At times classified as both a percussion instrument and a string instrument, the piano is played by means of a keyboard instrument that produces sound by striking strings with felt hammers. The hammers immediately rebound, allowing the strings to continue vibrating at their resonant frequency. These vibrations are transmitted through a bridge to a soundboard that amplifies them. Modern pianos come in two basic configurations: the grand piano and the upright piano. Grand pianos have the frame and strings placed horizontally, with the strings extending away from the keyboard.

Despite its relatively recent invention at the beginning of the eighteenth century, the piano has had a rather eventful history since Bartolomeo Cristofori's days. The new instrument remained practically unknown until Francesco Scipione Maffei's encomiastic article inspired the next generation of piano builders, who rapidly appropriated Cristofori's invention. Except for Gottfried Silbermann's prototype, in which the instrument was equipped with a forerunner of the modern damper pedal, all designs were, however, virtually direct copies of Cristofori's original piano. Between 1790 and 1860, the piano underwent considerable changes that led to the modern form of the instrument. It became more robust, its sound acquired more power, and its tonal range reached the seven or more octaves found on modern pianos. Other technical innovations included the use of a strong iron frame against the force of string tension, as well as the use of felt hammer coverings instead of layered leather hammers.

Throughout the nineteenth century, the piano repertoire expanded considerably, and Cristofori's invention became one of the most familiar musical instruments of the time. Its versatility was explored by renowned piano composers such as Ludwig van Beethoven, Frédéric Chopin, and Franz Liszt, whose music was to some extent also determined by continuing technical innovations on the instrument. As an example, the double escapement action was invented in 1821. This device, which allows a note to be repeated even if the key has not reached its maximum vertical position, facilitates rapid playing. Modern upright and grand pianos attained their present forms by the end of the nineteenth century. Improvements and lower costs made the piano aptly suited not only for public concerts but also for domestic use and solo performance.

Anna and Margherita del Mela—sisters of Domenico del Mela, builder of the first upright piano—who had assisted him during his illnesses, and to his niece Laura, daughter of Elisabetta Cristofori. Cristofori died in Florence on January 27, 1732, and was buried in the cemetery of Santa Croce. On the inventor's death record in the church of San Iacopo tra' Fossi (demolished in 1847), the date of his death reads instead "1731" because the document follows the Florentine calendar in which the year began on March 25, thus causing an apparent one-year discrepancy for some dates. Among Cristofori's Italian pupils, aside from Ferrini, were Gerolamo da Firenze and Gherardo da Padova. Neither was, however, able to match the skills of his master. More talented were instead the German C. G. Schröter and Gottfried Silbermann.

Impact

Irrespective of whether Cristofori was fully aware of earlier attempts to make keyboard instruments with struck strings, he was the first person to design the modern piano as it is now known. According to his contemporary witnesses, the new instrument, made of cypress wood, would improve the quality of the harpsichord, "which does not wholly convey human feelings." Building on his expertise as harpsichord maker, Cristofori succeeded in designing a piano in which the hammers strike the strings but do not remain in contact with them because this would dampen their vibrations. Although Cristofori's piano was made with thin strings, it was louder and more powerful than the harpsichord. Cristofori continued to improve the quality of his pianos until the end of his life.

In spite of his major achievement, Cristofori's reputation went into eclipse shortly after his death. Paradoxically, Maffei's journal article of 1711 contributed to Cristofori's obscurity. Translated into Latin and published in Joachim Adlung's *Musica mechanica organoedi* (1767; music for organ), Maffei's piece inspired the German Gottfried Silbermann to build a piano that overshadowed Cristofori's work. For over one hundred years, Silbermann was credited with the invention of the piano until scholars working at the turn of the twentieth century (most notably Leo Puliti and A. Kraus) finally corrected this error.

—*Alejandro Coroleu*

Further Reading

Dolge, Alfred. *Pianos and Their Makers: A Comprehensive History of the Development of the Piano*. New York: Dover, 1972. Originally published in 1911, this is one of the first attempts among English-speaking scholars to restore Cristofori's role in the history of piano making.

Good, Edward. "What Did Cristofori Call His Invention?" *Early Music* 33, no. 1 (2005): 95-97. A short discussion on the meaning of the word *Arpicembalo* (harp-harpsichord), as Cristofori's new invention was referred to in the inventory of instruments made by him prior to 1700.

Parakilas, James, ed. *Piano Roles: Three Hundred Years of Life with the Piano*. New Haven, Conn.: Yale University Press, 1999. A beautifully illustrated collection of essays that pays equal attention to historical, artistic, and technological issues related to the piano. Appropriately, it takes Cristofori as its starting point and analyzes the evolution of piano making and performing in the last three centuries. Bibliography, index.

Pollens, Stewart. *The Early Pianoforte*. New York: Cambridge University Press, 1995. A scholarly survey on the history of the piano back to 1440, it devotes several chapters to the work of Cristofori. It includes thorough research on the Italian and Latin sources to Cristofori's life, which are meticulously translated into English. Illustrations, bibliography, index.

Rimbault, Edward Francis. *The Pianoforte: Its Origin, Progress and Construction*. London: Robert Cocks, 1860. Although Rimbault's contribution has long been superseded, it is still of much interest. It constitutes a good example of scholarly work on the piano before the invention was formally attributed to Cristofori. Plates.

See also: Emile Berliner; Hugh Le Caine; Leonardo da Vinci; Robert Moog; Charles Wheatstone.

Sir William Crookes

English physicist

Crookes discovered the element thallium and greatly improved the technique used to produce a vacuum in the glass Crookes tube, the forerunner of the television tube. He used the Crookes tube to discover many of the properties of cathode rays, and these studies led directly to discoveries by others, including X rays and electrons.

Born: June 17, 1832; London, England
Died: April 4, 1919; London, England
Primary fields: Chemistry; physics
Primary inventions: Spinthariscope; vacuum tube

Early Life

William Crookes (krooks) was the oldest son of sixteen children born to Joseph Crookes and his second wife, Mary Scott. Joseph was a prosperous tailor who also did well in real estate investments. Crookes left school at the age of fifteen and entered the Royal College of Chemistry in London. There he became an assistant to the famous scientist August Wilhelm von Hofmann. Working with Hofmann, Crookes became a meticulous and accomplished experimentalist. Hofmann introduced him to several well-known scientists, including Michael Faraday, who seems to have been Crookes's ideal. They were much alike; both Faraday and Crookes were brilliant lecturers and experimentalists, but both had to depend on others for advanced mathematics.

In 1854, friends aided Crookes's appointment as superintendent of the Meteorological Department at Radcliffe College, England, and in 1855 he taught chemistry at the College of Science at Chester. He moved into a fine house in London in 1856 (aided by a handsome inheritance from his father). He had a laboratory built into his home and worked as a chemical consultant, devising useful processes such as using sodium amalgamation for gold extraction, utilizing sewage and animal refuse, developing a chemical water-analysis scheme, promoting the use of carbolic acid in halting a cattle plague, and designing electric light bulbs. None of his commercial processes was more than modestly successful, but his house was the first in England to have electric lights. Also in 1856, he married Ellen Humphry of Darlington. They eventually had ten children, seven of whom survived early childhood; one of the survivors died at age thirteen.

Life's Work

In addition to his other ventures, Crookes edited several photographic and scientific journals. The most important of these was the *Chemical News*, which he founded in 1859 and for which he served as editor and proprietor until his death. He kept abreast of the latest advances in chemistry by publishing them in the magazine. Spectroscopy was invented in 1860, and it immediately drew Crookes's attention. It involved heating a material to incandescence and examining the light it emitted using a slit, lenses, and a prism. Light from the glowing sample passed through the slit, then the lenses focused that light onto the prism, which separated the light into rainbow patterns of variously colored slit images. These patterns of bright lines separated by dark spaces were different for different elements and therefore could be used to identify the elements present. This is the essence of spectroscopy.

Sir William Crookes in 1900. (Library of Congress)

Crookes had previously worked

with selenium ores, so in 1861 he explored them spectroscopically. He soon noticed a bright green line that belonged to no known element. He named the new element "thallium," from the Greek *thallos*, "green twig." Although Crookes was able to refine only a tiny bit of thallium, he is credited with having discovered this element. He wanted to establish a very accurate weight for thallium, so he began to weigh small amounts in a vacuum. In the process, Crookes developed a method for obtaining a pressure one million times less than atmospheric pressure.

While weighing masses in a vacuum, Crookes found that some objects seemed to weigh slightly more warm than cold. Since these objects were in a vacuum, buoyancy effects could not account for this. He thought that light falling on an object might exert a very small force on it, or perhaps the infrared waves radiated by an object at room temperature might affect its weight. Crookes set about exploring this idea. He placed a small windmill with four sails, or vanes, inside a glass sphere and evacuated the air. With a needle for a pivot, the windmill turned with very little friction. One side of each vane was darkened with soot, while the other side remained a light color. He had expected that light falling on and being reflected from the bright side of the vanes would make them move away from the light, but they did not. Instead, the dark sides rotated away from the light. Crookes called his device a radiometer.

The radiometer provoked much discussion then, and it remains a popular scientific toy today. It can often be seen in the windows of novelty shops with its windmill spinning merrily in the sunlight. It turns out that the pressure of light is far too small to cause it to spin. Instead, residual air molecules clinging to the vanes are heated by the energy absorbed by the dark side of the vanes until they have enough energy to break free. As they break free, they give a minute kick to the vane, causing the dark side to rotate away from the light. Even lacking a full understanding of how it worked, Crookes used the radiometer to confirm a prediction by James Clerk Maxwell that the viscosity (resistance to flow) of a gas is independent of pressure except at very low pressures.

The next subject to capture Crookes's attention was the cathode rays in a Crookes tube. Crookes did not invent the tube, but his experiments with it were so remarkable that his name became forever associated with it. A Crookes tube is a glass tube with a volume of about a liter. Electrodes are placed in both ends, which are sealed. The air is sucked out, and a high voltage is applied to the electrodes. Cathode rays then stream from the negative electrode (called the cathode). Crookes showed that these cathode rays are a stream of particles because an object casts a crisp shadow when placed partially in the beam's path. (Electromagnetic waves would have bent somewhat into the shadow region.) Crookes found that they are negatively charged particles because they are deflected with a magnet. He speculated that the particles were negative gas ions.

Crookes was also involved in the study of radioactiv-

The Spinthariscope

In 1903, William Crookes observed the fluorescence of a zinc sulfide screen as alpha particles from radium struck it. The three kinds of radiation known at the time to be emitted by radioactive elements such as radium had been named alpha, beta, and gamma (the first three letters of the Greek alphabet). Although not known until five years later, alpha particles are helium-4 nuclei (two protons bound together with two neutrons). Each alpha particle striking a zinc sulfide molecule produced a flash of light, a scintillation. When Crookes examined the screen under a microscope, he could see the individual scintillations. This was the first radiation detector that could detect individual events. Photographic film, for example, recorded only the combined effects of billions of billions of events.

Crookes took a small brass tube and placed a zinc sulfide screen at one end and a lens at the other end. A speck of radium on a needle was positioned about one millimeter above the screen. Its distance from the screen could be adjusted with a thumbscrew. With the source far from the screen, individual scintillations could be seen by looking at the screen through the lens. If the radium was brought close to the screen, the screen became a turbulent, luminous sea. Crookes named this invention a "spinthariscope," from the Greek word *spintharis*, "spark."

The spinthariscope became a toy of the well-to-do. It was a great hit at parties, and everyone had to have one. Later, Ernest Rutherford and his assistants used a spinthariscope-like device to measure the charge on an alpha particle and to show that most of the mass of an atom is concentrated in a central nucleus. Rutherford fired alpha particles at a thin gold foil. Carefully counting scintillations showed how many alpha particles were scattered at various angles. These data were also used to estimate the size of the nucleus.

ity. He showed that the gas emitted by uranium during its decay was helium 4. He also found that elements more radioactive than uranium could be extracted from uranium. Over time, the residual uranium regained its radioactivity, while the extracted elements became less radioactive. These experiments laid the groundwork for the discovery of decay chains. For example, it was later learned that uranium decays to thorium, which decays to radium, which decays to radon, and so forth, on down to lead. Consistent with Crookes's findings, radium and radon are more radioactive than uranium and therefore decay more quickly.

Crookes's brother Philip died in 1869, a time when Spiritualism flourished in England. Spiritualism teaches that the spirits of those who have died can be contacted by individuals called mediums—intermediaries between the living and the dead. Crookes wanted to believe, but he exposed some mediums as frauds. He eventually was persuaded that there were some authentic mediums: Daniel Dunglass Home and Eva Fay from America, and a fifteen-year-old English girl, Florence Cook, who supposedly produced a spirit named Katie King. Early in his studies of the radiometer, Crookes found the motion of the vanes so remarkable that he wondered if some new force were involved, perhaps a psychic force. If so, the radiometer might be used to detect true psychic power. (This test was unsuccessful.) His investigation of Spiritualism continued from 1870 to 1874. After his active investigations ceased, he continued to maintain that some mediums had real power to contact departed spirits. He died in London in 1919.

Impact

Crookes was one of the preeminent scientists of his day, and therefore one of the most influential. His discovery of thallium established his reputation, and on that basis he was elected a fellow of the Royal Society in 1863. The Royal Society of London was the most prestigious scientific society in England, and he later served as its president. At various times, he was also the president of the Chemical Society, the Institution of Electrical Engineers, the British Association, and the Society of Chemical Industry. He was a member of twenty other scientific societies. He was knighted in 1897, and in 1910 he received the Order of Merit. Altogether, he was awarded fourteen medals and citations.

Crookes developed a vacuum system that could reduce pressure to one-millionth of an atmosphere. This method would later be used by Thomas Alva Edison in the production of electric light bulbs. Crookes had speculated that the particles of cathode rays were negative gas ions, but in 1897 Joseph John Thomson identified these particles as electrons—the first subatomic particles discovered. It is likely that had he been looking for them, Crookes would have discovered X rays. Occasionally, when he operated a Crookes tube, he had lightproof film packets nearby. After using the film packets, he developed the film and found it foggy. Although he complained to his film supplier, it is likely that the film was fogged by X rays from his Crookes tube.

During his last years, Crookes remained active in various science organizations and served as a government consultant. For example, at government request he designed goggles that would protect workers from harmful rays (probably ultraviolet) emitted by molten glass. He wrote numerous scientific articles and books on chemical analysis, dyeing, diamonds, and manufacturing sugar from sugar beets.

—*Charles W. Rogers*

Further Reading

Boorse, Henry A., Lloyd Motz, and Jefferson Hane Weaver. "Cathode Rays: 'A Fourth State of Matter'—William Crookes (1832-1919)." In *The Atomic Scientists: A Biographical History*. New York: John Wiley & Sons, 1989. Crookes found the behavior of low-pressure gas to be so bizarre that he called it the "fourth state of matter." The book discusses some of Crookes's work along with biographical information.

Brock, William H. "The Radiometer and Its Lessons: William Carpenter Versus William Crookes." In *Science and Beliefs: From Natural Philosophy to Natural Science, 1700-1900*, edited by David M. Knight and Matthew D. Eddy. Burlington, Vt.: Ashgate, 2005. Discusses the multiyear debate between Crookes and the physiologist William Benjamin Carpenter, who praised Crookes's scientific investigations of the radiometer but deplored his unscientific investigations of the Spiritualist mediums Daniel Dunglass Home and Eva Fay.

________. *William Crookes (1832-1919) and the Commercialization of Science*. Burlington, Vt.: Ashgate, 2008. A comprehensive biography of Crookes discussing his scientific and editing work, chemical solutions to agricultural problems, other business ventures such as gold mining and electric lighting, and investigations into Spiritualism.

Gribbin, John. "Inner Space." In *The Scientists: A History of Science Told Through the Lives of Its Greatest Inventors*. New York: Random House, 2004. Discusses the Crookes tube, Crookes's studies of cathode rays, his conclusion that they are particles, and his proof that they travel much slower than light. The rest of the chapter provides context.

See also: Robert Wilhelm Bunsen; Sir James Dewar; Thomas Alva Edison; Michael Faraday; Joseph von Fraunhofer; Wilhelm Conrad Röntgen.

Caresse Crosby

American garment maker

Crosby designed, developed, patented, produced, and marketed a modern brassiere in 1914 upon which American designers and manufacturers modeled the expansion of the brassiere industry in the United States.

Born: April 20, 1892; New York, New York
Died: January 24, 1970; Rome, Italy
Also known as: Mary Phelps Jacob (birth name); Polly Jacob Peabody
Primary field: Household products
Primary invention: Backless brassiere

Early Life

Called Polly by her family at her insistence, Caresse Crosby was born Mary Phelps Jacob, the oldest of three children of Mary Phelps and William Jacob, an upper-class family with impeccable pedigrees on maternal and paternal sides. Her brothers were Len and Buddy. She grew up in an elegant brownstone on West Fifty-ninth Street in New York City. Her family was aristocratic, employing servants and governesses who attended to the needs of each of the children. In 1897, the family moved to New Rochelle, New York. Polly played dress up in her mother's clothes and fantasized in her treehouse.

Crosby received no formal schooling, though soon she was sent to live with her cousin Ben Barnum, who enjoyed the attention of a private tutor. She learned to read under the tutelage of her British teacher, Blanche Kimber. She read, wrote, drew, produced a gazette with her cousin, danced, rode horses, and visited nearby families. Charles Dana Gibson, originator of the "Gibson Girl" icon, photographed her several times. In the meantime, her family returned to Manhattan, where she eventually rejoined them in 1903 after Ben was sent off to boarding school. Crosby attended Miss Chapin's School from 1903 to 1906. By the time she was fourteen years old, she met her first husband, Richard Rogers Peabody, who later proposed to her, hoping that she might wait for him until his Harvard graduation some years ahead. At the age of fifteen, Crosby attended boarding school at Rosemary Hall in Greenwich, Connecticut, a sister school to Choate, while her father moved to Texas to cure his asthma. He died over the Christmas holiday.

Life's Work

In the spring of 1914, Crosby experienced the distinction of having been the only American debutante to be presented to King George V at court in Windsor, England. After returning to the United States, she settled again with the Barnums on East Forty-fifth Street in an experimental communal home called the Home Club. Crosby and the other young women in residence each wore a whalebone corset and corset cover underneath their clothing, which was de rigueur for the time to provide appropriate foundation and support for fashionable styles as well as to conform to standards of the female form. That November, her great discomfort with, and hatred of, the binding corset cover compelled her to discard it and design a backless brassiere, which would become the first modern bra.

Crosby intended for women to wear her corselette with backless and sheer gowns, as well as those revealing a great deal of décolleté. Her bra was secured over the bust by tapes that crossed at the waist and tied there at the front—quite an improvement from her hastily constructed prototype. The bra was a "one-size-fits-all" undergarment that was adjusted by changing the length of the ties at the end of each tape until the wearer found the fit acceptable. Crosby chose elastic for its straps to prevent the kind of binding she found uncomfortable in the original corset cover. She found her invention appropriate to wear while playing sports, especially tennis.

Upon her return to the United States after a trip to Europe that fall, Crosby was granted a patent for her backless brassiere on November 3, 1914, under the name M. P. Jacob. She fully credited herself for invention of the brassiere and attributed her creativity to an ancestor on her mother's side, Robert Fulton, who made improvements in steam navigation and ultimately invented the first commercially viable steamboat.

Crosby married Peabody in 1915 and had two children with him. Over the next five years, she was consumed with postpartum depression, isolation, and familial obligations. When her husband enlisted in World War I, she joined the American Red Cross and worked as a switchboard operator. Crosby wearied of dealing with her husband's posttraumatic stress disorder that led to his alcoholism. His inability to settle into domestic life resulted in his eventual commitment to a sanitarium. In 1920, Crosby filed legal paperwork with the Commonwealth of Massachusetts indicating that she was a married woman conducting business, the Fashion Form Brassiere Company, separately from her husband.

By 1921, Crosby had broached the subject of separation or divorce from her husband. She sought to earn money to support herself and her children by selling her brassiere. Her company's small factory was based on Washington Street in Boston. Besides providing space for the two employees who cut fabric and sewed the pieces together, thus fashioning brassieres that were successfully marketed to several department stores, she used the business as a setting for assignations with her lover Harry Crosby. Sales of her product were dismal, however. She shut down the factory and left Boston for New York City.

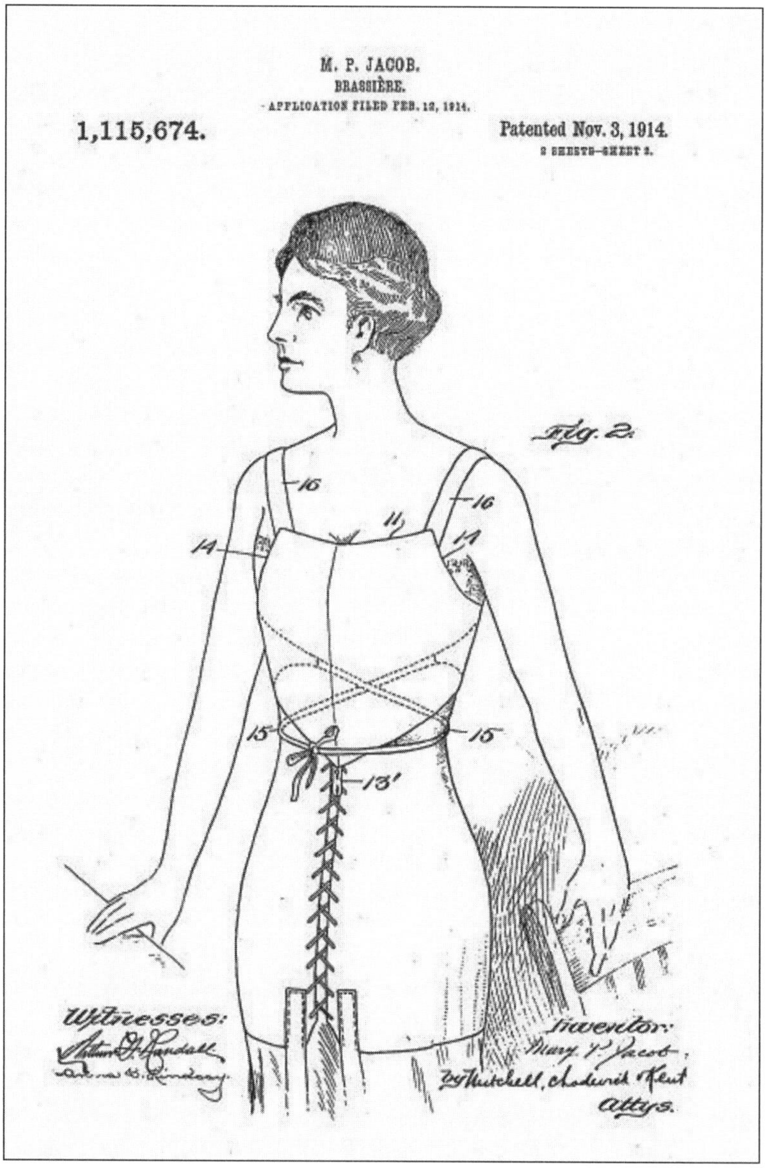

After selling her patent to Warner Brothers Corset Company and moving to New York, Crosby tried her hand at acting, taking the stage name Valerie Marno. Her daughter Polleen's illness drew Crosby home before she realized any great success in that profession. With her divorce from Peabody final in February, 1922, she spent much of the rest of the year in Paris with Harry Crosby. On September 9, 1922, the couple married. They brought her children with them in their return to Paris, where she began a new life and career as a wealthy expatriate traveling in fashionable and intellectual Parisian circles. In 1927, the couple founded Black Sun Press. The Crosbys published the writings of D. H. Lawrence, James Joyce, Kay Boyle, Ernest Hemingway, Hart Crane, T. S. Eliot, and Ezra Pound, along with other writers. Harry Crosby killed himself in 1929, and though Caresse remained in Paris until 1936, she eventually returned to the United Sates, where she continued working with artists and writers as well as channeling her efforts into politics. In 1949, she founded Women of the World Against War, which evolved into Women Against War and Citizens of the World in 1950.

Caresse Crosby's backless brassiere, from the original patent application of 1914. (U.S. Patent and Trademark Office)

Impact

Crosby's desire to dance and socialize in comfort resulted in a product that allowed women to perform their daily activities in comfort without negatively affecting their well-being. The backless brassiere's light weight and unobtrusiveness offered unrestricted movement and air circulation during stifling temperatures. While her bra was not the first of its kind, its design was popular, comfortable, and easy to manufacture. When the United States entered World War I in 1917, the U.S. government requested that women stop buying corsets in order to conserve metal for military purposes. Unfortunately, she sold her patent to Warner Brothers Corset Company, which profited greatly from her invention, making more than $15 million over the next thirty years.

Upon her death in 1970, her extensive literary endeavors were eclipsed by her simple invention at the age of twenty-two. As the inventor of the first modern bra, Crosby created a foundation from which other designers and inventors could build.

—*Rebecca Tolley-Stokes*

The Backless Brassiere

Caresse Crosby designed the first modern bra using two pocket handkerchiefs, ribbons, a needle, and thread. She pinned the handkerchiefs together on the bias as a friend sewed the ribbons to the points below Crosby's breastbone. Crosby then knotted the handkerchiefs' ends around her waist while her friend pulled the ribbons taut and attached them to the knots at Crosby's waist. Besides providing comfortable support, Crosby's brassiere flattened full bosoms as much as possible, which conformed to the style of the time—the virginal appearance. The simplicity of her bra was appealing because it lacked buttons, bones, and hooks that pressed painfully into women's flesh, thus marking and causing the skin to redden and swell. Other young women were impressed by her ingenuity and asked Crosby to construct similar garments for them. Wearing comfortable clothing and undergarments was important to this group of young women, as their main social outlet was attending balls. Some sources credit Crosby's invention to the year 1913 (instead of 1914), but this may be due to her faulty sense of chronology.

The popularity of Crosby's invention surpassed her immediate social circle. After Crosby received a letter from a stranger asking to buy her brassiere for a dollar, she turned her eye toward the possibilities of entrepreneurship and took steps to protect her idea. A Harvard law clerk, Mr. Jones, employed by Mitchell Chadwick & Kent, assisted Crosby's patent application for a corselette, essentially a corset cover that served as an undergarment but which lacked whalebone support and construction. Jones's excitement about the product was evidenced by a series of schematic brassiere drawings that he produced for her the next day. Originally, Jones asked Crosby for $50 to file the patent, but she could not afford the fee. They agreed that she would pay $5 up front and an additional sum once the patent was obtained. Jones filed the application on February 12, 1914.

Crosby borrowed $100 from a friend and rented a room in the sweatshop district of Boston. She rented two sewing machines and employed two Italian girls to sew brassieres according to her design. They produced several hundred backless brassieres, which Crosby took great care in packaging and marketing. She made personal calls to three department stores that each bought one dozen bras. Unfortunately, the bras did not sell. Crosby failed to pursue additional marketing opportunities because she was occupied by her wedding plans. She sold her patent years later for $1,500, a large sum at that time, through Johnny Field, a contact she had at the Warner Brothers Corset Company in Bridgeport, Connecticut.

Further Reading

Carson, Anne Conover. *Caresse Crosby: From Black Sun to Roccasinibalda*. Santa Barbara, Calif.: Capra Press, 1989. Details the subject's life after her husband's death in 1929, including her poetry, political activism, and operation of an art gallery.

Crosby, Caresse. *The Passionate Years*. New York: Dial Press, 1953. An autobiography in which Crosby recalls her childhood, marriages, work as a publisher, and relationships with notable artists as well as minor figures in expatriate circles.

Hamalian, Linda. *The Cramoisy Queen: The Life of Caresse Crosby*. Carbondale: Southern Illinois University Press, 2005. Focusing on the literary and social contexts of Crosby's life, this biography considers the subject's personal and professional struggles as a publisher and promoter of modern writers and artists.

Wolff, Geoffrey. *Black Sun: The Brief Transit and Violent Eclipse of Harry Crosby*. New York: Random House, 1976. Biography of Caresse Crosby's second husband and their lives at the center of the Paris expatriate community in the 1920's as founders of the Black Sun Press.

See also: Levi Strauss.

CTESIBIUS OF ALEXANDRIA

Greek engineer

Ctesibius is generally considered the "father of pneumatics" because of his experiments, devices, and writings on the elasticity of air. He is best known for inventing the force pump and water organ and for refining the water clock.

Born: c. 290 B.C.E.; Alexandria, Egypt
Died: Probably after 250 B.C.E.; Alexandria, Egypt
Also known as: Ktesibios
Primary fields: Civil engineering; mathematics; physics
Primary inventions: Force pump; water organ; precise water clock

EARLY LIFE

Ctesibius (teh-SIH-bee-uhs) was born in Alexandria, Egypt, around 290 B.C.E. Little is known about his early life. He was the son of a barber and may himself have been a barber before pursuing his career as an inventor.

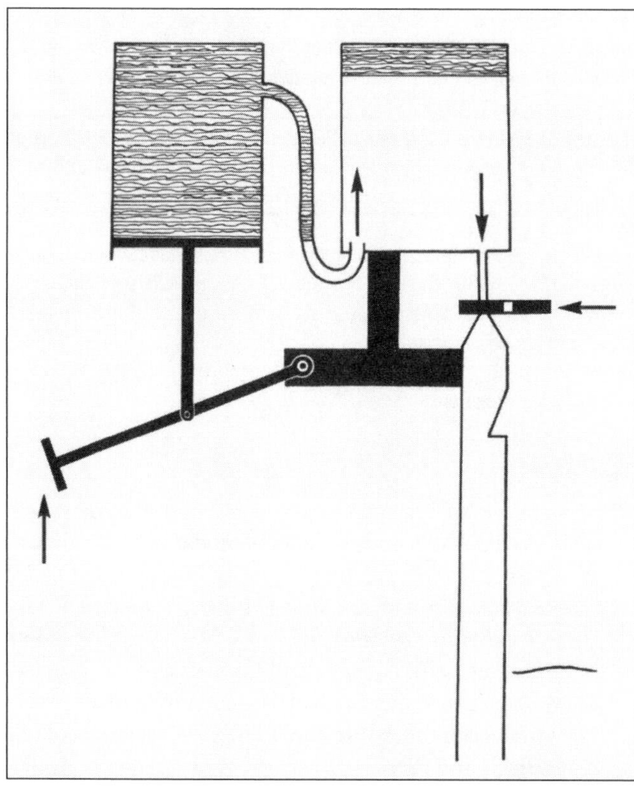

A diagram of the mechanism of Ctesibius's water organ. (The Granger Collection, New York)

He demonstrated his ingenuity and cleverness at an early age through the invention of practical devices for his father's barbershop. In one such device, Ctesibius designed a retractable mirror operated by a series of pulleys set into wooden channels. As the mirror was raised or lowered, the pulleys would move the air in the channels, causing an audible sound. The young inventor's observations of how air was affected by the counterweights in the channels led Ctesibius to pursue further research into hydraulics and hydraulic machines.

LIFE'S WORK

How and when Ctesibius left his trade as a barber and devoted himself to the study of pneumatics and hydraulics is unclear. Regardless, it was at the Mouseion of Alexandria, which included the famed library, that Ctesibius was most likely able to conduct his experiments on air and water and to write his treatises, which survive only in fragments quoted by other ancient authors. It was probably during his tenure at the Mouseion that Ctesibius made his lasting contributions to physics and engineering, but with the initial intention of devising practical applications for his pneumatic devices.

By far Ctesibius's most enduring achievement was the force pump. The device consisted of an inverted-T pipe with cylinders attached at both arms of the T. Each cylinder contained a plunger and a valve, and the T-joint contained two additional valves. As pressure was applied to one plunger, water was forced into the joint of the T-pipe, and pressure released from the second plunger, raising it up. This action created a corresponding reaction in the valves: The intake valve in the relaxed cylinder opened to allow more water to enter; its corresponding valve in the T-joint closed, preventing water from backing up; and simultaneously, the intake valve in the stressed cylinder closed, and its corresponding valve in the T-joint opened, forcing the water into the joint and out a single discharge pipe.

Surviving examples of force pumps and descriptions in literary sources provide ample evidence for reconstructing Ctesibius's device. These sources further suggest that Ctesibius is to be credited with the invention of the cylinder, plunger, and valve. It is a great irony that Ctesibius's force pump, which the Romans would later employ effectively in fire extinguishers, offered no remedy for saving the Library of Alexandria from consummation.

Many of Ctesibius's treatises and inventions were refinements of his work on the force pump. He applied his knowledge of the elasticity of air to devising a water organ. He also discussed his ideas on the science of air in his book *On Pneumatics*, which survives only in fragments from various ancient sources. One of the best sources for excerpts of Ctesibius's treaty on pneumatics is Hero (or Heron) of Alexandria, who copied extensively from his mentor and may have been his pupil at the Mouseion of Alexandria. Other works by Ctesibius have been cited by ancient authors, but those original texts remain mostly unknown. Included among these are an account of Ctesibius's life work and treatises on mechanics and military devices.

The water clock of Ctesibius was not strictly a new invention but rather a marked improvement of a long-standing device. The simple water clock had a long tradition going back to the second millennium B.C.E. Early Greek water clocks measured a set unit of time without recording intermediate periods, much like an egg timer. Ctesibius was the first person to substantially improve the simple design. His innovations were threefold. First, he added a supply tank that allowed a constant inflow of water to the reservoir tank set at a lower position. Second, in the reservoir tank, he placed a float with a grooved vertical bar (a rack) on which was mounted a figure with a pointing device. This was used in conjunction with a vertical scale aligned with the pointer. Third, he regulated the rate at which the pointer marked hours by means of a separate wheel with teeth (a pinion). As the float moved up with the level of the water, the teeth of the rack engaged those of the pinion, controlling and standardizing the motion of the pointer. A deficiency in his design—and one that Ctesibius himself recognized—was the water clock's inability to compensate for seasonal hours. He tried to remedy this by varying the time scale with curved lines along a cylinder. The cylinder would then be rotated to the appropriate scale according to the current date. Ctesibius's original device does not survive, but the Roman architect Vitruvius describes it in his treatise *De architectura* (c. 20 B.C.E.; *On Architecture*, 1711). This represents the first reference to the use of gear wheels, especially a rack-and-pinion drive.

Ctesibius was able to apply his new knowledge of pneumatics and hydraulics toward other practical and sometimes whimsical inventions. He equally applied his pneumatic technology to improve devices for war (catapults that employed torsion springs and a version of the siege tower), service (hydraulic lift), entertainment (mechanical birds that sang using variations of air pressure, and automata for entertainment at parties), and belief (automata for providing magical signs from the gods for the masses at temple rituals).

THE HYDRAULIS

The hydraulis, or water organ, was the first keyboard instrument and was the natural outgrowth of Ctesibius's force pump. It represented a mechanization of a simple musical instrument, the panpipes, which was popular among ancient Greek musicians. More than a mechanized version of a simple wind instrument, however, the hydraulis opened the door to new types of musical instruments, genres of sound, and modes of performance.

The hydraulis displays a developed understanding of the technology of the force pump and pneumatics. While its practical uses were few, the hydraulis exemplified Ctesibius's proclivity, seen at an early age, to transform theoretical ideas and experimental mechanics into functional devices. The instrument consisted of a pair of levers that operated two cylinders. The cylinders forced air into an inverted funnel set in a chamber partially filled with water. From the top of the funnel (that is, the narrow opening), air was circulated through the pipes of the organ via channels. A series of valves connected to the keyboard regulated which channels were open and for how long. The varying size of the channels and organ pipes further dictated the quality of the sound generated. In essence, the force applied to the levers was transferred through the water in the inverted funnel and to the air inside the channels. The added energy increased the air pressure, which was released when the keys were played and a sound generated.

Although its initial value as an instrument was not highly appreciated, by the first century C.E. it became a popular instrument of entertainment. Representations of the hydraulis have survived in the form of Roman baked-clay models, in mosaics, and in relief sculpture. Parts of two water organs have been found near Acquincum (modern Budapest, Hungary) and Dion, Greece.

IMPACT

Ctesibius was truly the first to marry the philosophical inquisitiveness of Greek philosophers studying the nature of water and air with more technological applications in order to conceive and to create practical devices.

Numerous devices, both ancient and modern, are essentially permutations of his force pump or water organ. Among the most commonly recognizable of these later inventions are the pipe organ, cuckoo clock, and fire extinguisher. Along with Archimedes, Ctesibius is one of the few inventors to have a device bearing his name, *mechina ctesibica* (force pump).

Ctesibius's writings were no less important. Because no complete text of his treatises survives, the notoriety of Ctesibius must be recognized in the extent to which he was quoted in antiquity. The leading minds of the Greco-Roman world repeatedly mention, paraphrase, or quote his work on pneumatics.

The patrons of the Mouseion of Alexandria, and thus Ctesibius, were the Ptolemaic kings of Egypt. Their patronage prompted mechanical developments of practical, whimsical, and, especially, strategic devices and technologies. From what remains of his writings, one may infer that Ctesibius worked to advance practical mechanics in order to improve weapons and artillery, a strategy he thought was better for preserving peace than simply philosophy or sophistry. Ctesibius was a doer, not just a thinker. Even today, individuals who make notable contributions to the theoretical and practical application of systems, control, and automation are awarded the Ktesibios Award by the Mediterranean Control Association.

—*Víctor M. Martínez*

FURTHER READING

Drachmann, A. G. *Ktesibios, Philon, and Heron: A Study in Ancient Pneumatics*. Copenhagen: Ejnar Munksgaard, 1948. The discussion of Ctesibius and his works is part of a larger study on ancient pneumatics. It includes a reliable discussion of Ctesibius's three major devices—the force pump, water organ, and water clock. Illustrations, bibliography, index.

Irby-Massie, Georgia L., and Paul T. Keyser. *Greek Science of the Hellenistic Era: A Sourcebook*. New York: Routledge, 2002. Offers accessible translations of some of the ancient literary sources that mention Ctesibius or his inventions. Translations are included within the broader context of Greek science and thought. Bibliography, index.

Lewis, Michael. "The Hellenistic Period." In *Handbook of Ancient Water Technology*, edited by Örjan Wikander. Technology and Change in History 2. Boston: Brill, 2000. Chapter focuses on the political and social background in which Hellenistic thinkers and inventors such as Ctesibius flourished and advances in hydraulics and pneumatics occurred. Emphasis is placed on how practical needs influenced hydraulic developments. Illustrations, bibliography, index.

_______. "Theoretical Hydraulics, Automata, and Water Clocks." In *Handbook of Ancient Water Technology*, edited by Örjan Wikander. Technology and Change in History 2. Boston: Brill, 2000. Chapter discusses the development of hydraulic technology and its applications in antiquity. Attention is given to the contributions of Ctesibius to the practical application of hydraulic theories and experiments. Illustrations, bibliography, index.

Oleson, John Peter. *Greek and Roman Mechanical Water-Lifting Devices: The History of a Technology*. Phoenix Supplement 16. Buffalo: University of Toronto Press, 1984. Detailed scholarly source that discusses Ctesibius's contribution (force pump) to the broader field of pneumatics. Text analyzes the ancient literary sources (with commentary and translations) and gives a historical analysis of Ctesibius's contribution to the development of the pneumatics. Translations, illustrations, bibliography, index.

See also: Archimedes.

Nicolas-Joseph Cugnot

French engineer

Cugnot invented a vehicle powered by steam called the fardier à vapeur, *or steam dray. This three-wheeled carriage was said to be able to pull up to four tons at a speed of four kilometers per hour.*

Born: February 26, 1725; Void, France
Died: October 2, 1804; Paris, France
Primary fields: Automotive technology; military technology and weaponry
Primary invention: Steam dray (*fardier à vapeur*)

Early Life

Nicolas-Joseph Cugnot (koon-yoh) was born on February 26, 1725, in Void, a small village in eastern France. The child of farmers, Cugnot attended school in Void and later in nearby Toul, where he showed great talent in mathematics and physics. This skill led him to enroll, when he was sixteen, in L'Ecole Royale du Génie de Mézières, a school of military engineering located about one hundred miles west of Toul.

After graduating, Cugnot entered the French army as an officer in the artillery corps. Sent to Vienna when the duke of Lorraine was crowned Emperor Francis I of Austria, Cugnot benefited greatly from his introduction to the German-speaking world. While on post, Cugnot read German engineer Jakob Leupold's *Theatrum Machinarum* (1724), which described all the steam machines invented up to that time. Introduced to the mechanical structure of steam engines, Cugnot was intrigued by the potential of such a novel source of power. He was later sent to Brussels, where he was assigned to fortification design. Wrestling with the mechanical problems involved in constructing artillery defenses and maximizing the effective use of cannon through flexible emplacement, Cugnot began to consider the possibility of using steam power to quickly move immensely heavy weapons to new locations.

Life's Work

In 1763, at the age of thirty-eight, Cugnot was discharged from the army. Awarded a 600-franc pension in recognition of his invention of a new cavalry musket, he was secure from penury but certainly not wealthy. Taking advantage of his financial security, Cugnot immediately moved to Paris, where in 1766 he published a book titled *Éléments de l'art militaire ancien et moderne*. In 1767, he began work on the design of a military vehicle powered by a steam machine. Needing more funds to build his invention than his pension could supply, he contacted General Gribeauval, his superior officer in Vienna and now inspector general of the French army in Paris. Impressed with Cugnot's design and plans, Gribeauval ordered him to build a small prototype of his machine. Gribeauval successfully guided Cugnot's project through the mazes of royal bureaucracy, gaining the support of the Marquis de Monteynard, the minister of war, and the financial support of King Louis XV.

Cugnot's first working prototype, which took almost

The Steam Dray

The improved version of the steam dray that Nicolas-Joseph Cugnot presented officially to King Louis XV and his court on April 22, 1770, was able to move at a speed of about 4 kilometers per hour (2.5 miles per hour), although this was less than the speed requested by General Gribeauval. The *fardier à vapeur* had three heavy wooden wheels reinforced with metal: one in the front, which was used for steering, and two in the back to support the load. The two-cylinder steam engine and copper boiler were positioned at the front of the machine. Behind the narrow driver's seat was a platform for transporting equipment. This platform, made of wood reinforced by metal, supported the weight of the load. The steam engine was held on the platform by two arms made of iron. When the platform was not loaded, this vehicle was unstable because of the uneven distribution of the weight. The instability of Cugnot's *fardier* made it difficult to maneuver.

When the *fardier* was demonstrated to the king, the smoking behemoth performed with some success. Still, the problems of maintaining steam had not been satisfactorily resolved. The *fardier* still needed to stop every ten to twelve minutes to build up enough steam pressure to continue to drive a little further. Worse, it lacked any efficient way to replenish the boiler's supply of water, requiring a difficult and time-consuming process for resupply. Fuel could be loaded in the boiler only when the *fardier* was stopped. The boiler did not close perfectly, and steam escaped, making it difficult to maintain a high enough pressure inside the boiler. Safety was another concern, as the machine lacked both a safety valve and a pressure gauge. Nevertheless, Cugnot's efforts were impressive for his time.

three years to develop, made its debut before Gribeauval and other high-ranking French officers in Paris on October 23, 1769. Called a *fardier à vapeur* by its inventor (and a "locomotive" by the English press that reported it), the machine was not a complete success. Though it moved a short distance under its own power, it needed to stop frequently to allow more steam pressure to build up inside the boiler. It would take between twelve and fifteen minutes for the pressure to reach the desired level and allow the prototype to move again. Nevertheless, the concept proved to be workable, so the king and the army asked Cugnot to build a full-size *fardier* capable of carrying a load of about four tons.

In January, 1770, Gribeauval sent an order to the Arsenal in Strasbourg in eastern France to immediately build two 14-inch pumps and pistons in accordance with Cugnot's plans. These important parts were to be delivered to the Arsenal in Paris, where in the following months Cugnot continued his second *fardier* development. The construction was completed in early April, 1770. On April 22, 1770, the *fardier*, now called a "steam dray" in English, was presented officially to King Louis XV and his court.

Cugnot was awarded a large sum of money to continue development, building a second model powered by a different and improved two-cylinder steam engine. By mid-November, 1770, the new machine was ready for trial and performed admirably, pulling a 2.5-ton payload from the military arsenal in the suburbs of Paris to Vincennes at the respectable rate of 2 kilometers per hour (1.2 miles per hour). In fact, during a later trial, the machine malfunctioned, hit a wall, and was damaged (producing the first automobile accident in recorded history). Even with its limitations, however, the *fardier* showed considerable promise. The development of more reliable and efficient steam engines would resolve many of its

Nicolas-Joseph Cugnot's 1770 three-wheeled steam carriage. (The Granger Collection, New York)

most pressing problems. Cugnot's *fardier* had to be repaired after its accident and was ready for a new trial on July 2, 1771. This new attempt took place either in a park in Meudon or on the road between Paris and Vincennes (accounts vary). New trials were scheduled for the later part of the summer of 1771, but Cugnot's supporters, such as the duke of Choiseul, who had been sent into exile, fell from power and were replaced by conservatives who failed to see the potential of steam power, which could be applied to military or civilian usage.

Cugnot's invention was abandoned, his funding stopped, and his steam machine barely avoided destruction twice during the French Revolution. Napoleon Bonaparte was apparently interested in renewing development, but Cugnot's advancing age and Bonaparte's campaign in Egypt were obstacles that could not be overcome. Though Bonaparte granted Cugnot a pension of one thousand francs per year, the project was never completed and Cugnot in his later years complemented his pension by teaching military engineering at the Arsenal in Paris. Although Cugnot had modest means, he lived above the poverty level on Tournon Street in Paris, where he died on October 2, 1804, at the age of seventy-nine.

Impact

Cugnot was among the first engineers to recognize the great potential of self-powered vehicles. While the size and weight of steam engines made them impractical for personal use, their application to military transport seemed a realistic goal. Hampered mainly by the technical limitations of steam technology at the time, Cugnot was a pragmatic engineer who persevered in developing his *fardier* into a workable machine. Ultimately, Cugnot's project was ended by superiors who lacked his vision. His mechanical accomplishment stands as the pioneering work that foreshadowed the great revolutions in power and transportation of the nineteenth century. The opinions of French scientists at the end of the eighteenth century regarding Cugnot's steam machine are well described by Marquis de Saint-Auban, who on March 12, 1779, wrote a letter to the members of the Royal Society of Arts and Sciences of Metz stating that Cugnot's steam dray was supposed to replace horse-drawn carriages and that his machine was as ingenious as it was useless. Saint-Auban described its flaws in a disparaging way. Not only was it clear that the military withdrew their support for Cugnot's invention but even French scientists failed to see its relevance in improving transportation.

Cugnot's dream became an everyday reality in the locomotives that ran on the world's railways, the great steam tractors that transformed agriculture, and, as the twentieth century dawned, the steam-powered automobiles that competed (in many ways successfully) with the internal combustion engine. His second *fardier* has survived and is presently on display at the Conservatoire National des Arts et Métiers in Paris.

—*Denyse Lemaire and David Kasserman*

Further Reading

Burness, Ted. *Ultimate Auto Album: An Illustrated History of the Automobile.* Iola, Wis.: Krause, 2001. Traces more than two hundred years of automobile history. A wonderfully illustrated book.

Crump, Thomas. *A Brief History of the Age of Steam: The Power That Drove the Industrial Revolution.* New York: Carroll & Graf, 2007. Begins with the invention, by Thomas Newcomen, of the first steam machine in England in 1710 and explains how steam changed the world by introducing the Industrial Revolution.

Eckermann, Erik. *World History of the Automobile.* Translated by Peter L. Albrecht. Warrendale, Pa.: Society of Automotive Engineers, 2001. Offers an extensive history of the development of the automobile throughout the world. Abundantly illustrated.

Sutcliffe, Andrea. *Steam: The Untold Story of America's First Great Invention.* New York: Palgrave Macmillan, 2004. Traces the development of steam power and its effects on American society.

See also: Carl Benz; Gottlieb Daimler; Rudolf Diesel; John Boyd Dunlop; Henry Ford; Charles F. Kettering; Étienne Lenoir; Hiram Percy Maxim; André and Édouard Michelin; William Murdock; Thomas Newcomen; Ransom Eli Olds; Stanford Ovshinsky; Charles Parsons; Sylvester Roper; Thomas Savery; Ignaz Schwinn; Richard Trevithick; Felix Wankel; James Watt; Alexander Winton.

GLENN H. CURTISS

American manufacturer of airplanes

An important inventor of the era when the internal combustion engine came of age, Curtiss made major breakthroughs in both the aeronautical and automobile industries, helping to usher in the modern world.

Born: May 21, 1878; Hammondsport, New York
Died: July 23, 1930; Buffalo, New York
Also known as: Glenn Hammond Curtiss (full name)
Primary fields: Aeronautics and aerospace technology; automotive technology; military technology and weaponry
Primary inventions: JN-4 (airplane); internal combustion engines

EARLY LIFE

Glenn Hammond Curtiss was a prime example of how brilliance is not necessarily defined by education. Born in rural New York, Curtiss received only a rudimentary education. Less interested in classroom studies than in tinkering with mechanical devices, he left school after only seven years of formal education to find a job that suited his mechanical proclivities. Curtiss found such a job at the Eastman Dry Plate and Film Company, which later became the Eastman Kodak Company, the prominent camera producer. He became a valuable employee, inventing several devices that the company included on its assembly line. Curtiss developed a stencil machine, a lens grinder, and an improved chemical mixer. He also began to tinker with cameras, designing several improved models, although he dropped the project rather than compete with his employer.

Bicycling was a major craze in the late nineteenth century, and Curtiss looked for ways to profit from the fad. He started as a bicycle messenger for a telegraph company, raced bicycles of his own design in local races, and opened his own bicycle shop in his hometown. When the first internal combustion engines appeared in the 1890's, Curtiss was one of the first to see an application for them. He began to attach engines to his bicycles, becoming one of the first motorcycle manufacturers in the United States. The internal combustion engines were crude and unreliable, however, so Curtiss started designing his own, with remarkable results. In 1903, he set the world speed record for a motorcycle, averaging an amazing 64 miles per hour. Only four years later, he more than doubled that speed in setting a new record, 136 miles per hour. The engine for the second test produced forty horsepower, one of the most powerful internal combustion engines of its day.

LIFE'S WORK

Curtiss's life and career changed in 1906, when he became interested in airplanes. Wilbur and Orville Wright were very interested in Curtiss's engines because they were light, powerful, and reliable. Curtiss began to investigate the potential of airplanes, ultimately accepting an invitation from Alexander Graham Bell, the inventor of the telephone, to join an organization he was creating. The Aerial Experiment Association (AEA) brought together a number of American and Canadian inventors to develop aircraft technology in competition with the Wright brothers. While the Wrights worked in private, the AEA operated in public with an official government observer present to document its achievements. This would cause major problems later. The AEA claimed many "official" firsts in the field of aeronautics by demonstrating them in public, but most of its "firsts" had already been accomplished by the Wright brothers, who began to challenge the validity of the AEA's accomplishments.

A JN-4 (Jenny) on a training flight in 1918. (U.S. Army Signal Corps/George Johnson, Aviation Section)

The clash between the Wrights and Curtiss and the AEA started in Europe in 1909. Curtiss flew an aircraft designed by himself and the AEA in the Grande Semaine d'Aviation, the first flying meet ever held, at Rheims, France. The Wright brothers sued Curtiss and the AEA for violating their aircraft patents, particularly the patent on the aileron, a flexible panel on the wing that helps to maneuver the airplane. Curtiss ignored the lawsuit and won the race, earning as a reward a trophy and the right to become the second licensed pilot in Europe (the French aviation pioneer Louis Blériot was the first). The fame Curtiss earned in this race also earned him the honor of receiving the very first pilot's license in the United States, even ahead of the Wright brothers. This first aircraft race was hardly a speedy one. Curtiss averaged 47 miles per hour, much slower than his motorcycles. Nevertheless, Curtiss saw the future of aviation and decided to abandon his motorcycle venture to concentrate on aviation.

Back in the United States, Curtiss continued to win airplane races, and his aircraft designs (the AEA disbanded in 1909) began to attract the attention of the U.S. military, which was intrigued at the potential of the new flying machines. The Wright brothers were pitching their machines to the U.S. Army, so Curtiss concentrated on sales to the U.S. Navy. He moved to San Diego, California, location of one of the Navy's biggest bases, and began to work with the Navy to produce an aircraft to the Navy's particular needs and specifications. Curtiss's fourth design, the Model D, went into limited production as a training aircraft, and Curtiss, as one of the few licensed pilots in the world, trained the first naval aviators. In a foreshadowing of the great aircraft carriers in the Navy's future, Eugene Ely flew a modified Model D off the USS *Birmingham* and two months later, in 1911, landed the plane on the armored cruiser USS *Pennsylvania*.

Designing airplanes for the Navy gave Curtiss an advantage in selling airplanes to various customers. Airfields and airports did not exist in the early twentieth century because the airplane was a new device, and this limited the sales of airplanes. Curtiss, on the other hand, sold airplanes to the Navy, which needed to operate on the world's oceans, so Curtiss's planes were equipped with floats that allowed them to land on water. Curtiss's new design in 1911, the A-1 Seaplane, sold well. The U.S., British, Japanese, German, and Russian navies all purchased planes from Curtiss or bought the rights to produce them under license. The aircraft was such an innovative design that Curtiss became the first recipient of the Collier Trophy, an annual award given out since 1911 for the greatest achievement in aviation. The sale of the A-1 provided enough money for Curtiss to open two new companies. The Curtiss Aeroplane Company produced aircraft designs, while the Curtiss Motor Company designed engines for use on aircraft produced by other companies. Curtiss's financial success, however, only led to more legal wrangling with the Wright brothers, who continued to file lawsuits claiming that Curtiss was

The JN-4 Jenny

The basic JN-4 had a wingspan of 43 feet, 8 inches, and a length of 27 feet, 4 inches. Derived from the earlier, underpowered JN-3, the JN-4 Jenny featured more advanced control surfaces that made it ideal as a training and observations aircraft. Compared to the JN-3, the Jenny had ailerons on both sides of both wings and a bigger rudder. The earlier aircraft experienced handling problems, and the new control surfaces, along with a larger upper wing (total wing area of 352 square feet), improved maneuverability and made the aircraft more forgiving to trainee pilots who made errors while in flight. The forgiving characteristics of the aircraft also endeared it to many new pilots after World War I; the plane was ideal for the casual pilot who did not need a high-performance aircraft.

Like all aircraft of the era, the Jenny had a wooden frame covered with fabric, a light and simple construction that required little advanced skill to repair. The JN-4 had tandem cockpits with full controls in each seat, meaning that either the front or rear pilot could fly the aircraft. This was especially useful when used as a training aircraft, as the backseat instructor could take control of the plane from the front seat student if necessary. The original OX-5 engine was also very simple. Whereas European aircraft designers opted for complex rotary engines, Glenn H. Curtiss's own OX-5 was an inline design not all that different from a standard automobile engine. This meant that an average pilot/mechanic could repair the engine himself. The OX-5 generated 90 horsepower, enough to lift the 2,000-pound aircraft to a maximum altitude of 6,500 feet and a top speed of 75 miles per hour. The engine power was especially useful to the naval models that had to lift the bulky floats attached to the plane as well. Later models of the JN-4 featured upgrades and changes that reflected early experience with the design and changes requested by wartime users. The final version, the JN-4H model, featured a 150-horsepower engine produced by Wright and was the only armed version. It carried machine guns and small practice bombs as an advanced weapons trainer.

violating their patents on aircraft control surfaces. The lawsuits dragged on for years until finally, in 1913, the courts ruled in the Wrights' favor, and Curtiss had to design new aircraft without the Wrights' patented aileron.

The Wrights' success in the lawsuit was short-lived, however. Wilbur died in 1912, and Orville, weary of the constant battles over their patents, sold the Wright Company to a group of investors. Confident that the Wright Company, which was getting out of the aircraft design business to concentrate on aircraft engine productions, would not continue to sue, Wright returned to designing airplanes. Curtiss designed the H-4, a series of very large "flying boats." He sold this design to the U.S. Navy and a modified design to the British navy. When World War I broke out, the U.S. government temporarily merged all of the aircraft companies into the Manufacturers' Aircraft Association (MAA), forcing the aircraft companies to work together. The government also suspended patent protections, forcing members of the MAA to share their technology and design expertise. Curtiss took advantage of the arrangement, and he produced the greatest share of American aircraft during the war. He produced a new training aircraft, the JN-4, called the Jenny, for the U.S. Army and a modified floatplane version, the N-9, for the Navy. Altogether, Curtiss produced more than sixty-eight hundred JN-4 and N-9 aircraft before production ceased in 1922.

World War I was a great benefit to Curtiss's companies, but peacetime was not as lucrative. Curtiss Aeroplane survived thanks to two new areas of production. Curtiss's background in large flying boats paid off when increasingly larger flying boats became the preferred mode of long-distance travel in the 1920's and 1930's. Curtiss's expertise in seaplanes also benefited the company when competing for the Schneider Trophy, a prestigious award granted to the winner of an annual seaplane race. Curtiss won two Schneider Trophies, in 1923 and 1925, cementing his reputation as the country's greatest aircraft manufacturer. The Curtiss Company eventually triumphed over its old adversary when, in 1929, Curtiss acquired the Wright Company, forming a new entity, the Curtiss-Wright Company, that dominated aircraft design and aircraft engine production in the 1930's.

Impact

Curtiss and his company produced some of the great mechanical achievements of the twentieth century. His early work on internal combustion engines helped to drive the birth of the motorcycle industry and, by extension, feed America's enthusiasm for speed. By challenging the Wright brothers' lock on aircraft design, he freed American aircraft designers to create the most innovative and advanced aircraft in the world. Curtiss was one of the founders of civilian air travel, and his JN-4 design survived long after the war that prompted its creation. His aircraft introduced a large number of Americans to flying for the first time, and his famous racing planes capitalized on the growing enthusiasm for flight. Besides his World War I and civilian work, his company later produced some of the most important aircraft of World War II, such as the P-40 fighter, SB2C dive bomber, and C-46 transport. His demonstration that aircraft could play a role in naval warfare, however, had the biggest impact among his military projects. His floatplanes and airplanes, whether flying off a cruiser deck or on their own floats, showed that airpower and naval power could function together, foreshadowing the great aircraft carrier battles of World War II and beyond.

—Steven J. Ramold

Further Reading

House, Kirk W. *Hell-Rider to King of the Air: Glenn Curtiss's Life of Innovation.* Warrendale, Pa.: SAE International, 2003. Curtiss is rightfully known for his aviation achievements, but he was a prolific inventor before his entry into aircraft design. House's book details Curtiss's earlier life and inventions, particularly his achievements in motorcycle design and racing.

Roseberry, Cecil R. *Glenn Curtiss: Pioneer of Flight.* Syracuse, N.Y.: Syracuse University Press, 1991. This volume is a basic history of Curtiss's aviation achievements, with a secondary discussion of his legal fights with the Wright brothers. While not the most stirring biography of Curtiss, this book does provide a clear, straightforward account of Curtiss's life and accomplishments.

Shulman, Seth. *Unlocking the Sky: Glenn Hammond Curtiss and the Race to Invent the Airplane.* New York: HarperCollins, 2002. The author vividly describes the legal wrangling between the Wright brothers, who laid claim to all technology related to powered flight, and Curtiss, who represented all of the other aircraft pioneers who felt the Wrights were claiming innovations developed by others. A very readable account, the book ends with Curtiss's eventual triumph over the Wrights when he acquired their aircraft company.

See also: George Cayley; Edwin Albert Link; Nikolaus August Otto; Sylvester Roper; Elmer Ambrose Sperry; Wilbur and Orville Wright.

Louis Jacques Daguerre

French physicist

Improving on the discoveries of Nicéphore Niépce and others, Daguerre perfected a photographic process that made possible the first permanent images produced by cameras.

Born: November 18, 1787; Cormeilles, near Paris, France
Died: July 10, 1851; Bry-sur-Marne, near Paris, France
Also known as: Louis-Jacques-Mandé Daguerre (full name)
Primary field: Photography
Primary invention: Daguerreotype

Early Life

Louis-Jacques-Mandé Daguerre (lwee zhahk mahn-day dah-gaihr) was the son of Louis Jacques Daguerre, an employee of the local magistrate's court in Cormeilles, and Anne Antoinette Hauterre. Shortly after the birth of a daughter, Marie Antoinette, in 1791, the family moved to Orléans, where the elder Louis worked as a clerk at the royal estates. Young Louis and his sister received little formal education; however, Louis demonstrated such a remarkable gift for drawing and sketching that he was soon apprenticed to an architect under whom he trained for three years as a draftsman.

Although Daguerre learned valuable rules of perspective and accuracy during his apprenticeship, he was determined to study art in Paris. He enjoyed drawing much more than architectural design, but his father opposed art as a career choice. In a compromise measure, Daguerre was apprenticed to a well-known Parisian stage designer, Ignace Eugéne Marie Degotti, in 1804. Working in Degotti's studio, Daguerre learned quickly and was given a major role designing several important productions.

Daguerre's irrepressible personality made him many friends in the artistic community. He enlivened parties where singing, dancing, and acrobatics were popular, sometimes even making dramatic entrances walking on his hands. He also performed in choreographed scenes in the Paris Opéra and executed tightrope acrobatics with great skill. Throughout his life, Daguerre benefited from an abundance of energy and endurance.

Life's Work

In 1807, Daguerre became an assistant to Pierre Prévost, a panorama painter, and in 1810 married Louise Georgina Smith, sister of a painter who later became Daguerre's colleague. The popularity of panoramas, immense paintings exhibited in circular buildings, had made Prévost famous. He and another businessman collaborated to build an exhibition in which the display measured more than 100 feet in diameter and featured a painting more than 350 feet in length and 52 feet in height. Daguerre's earlier training as a draftsman contributed to the accuracy of these paintings, which frequently depicted patriotic scenes. He remained in Prévost's employ until 1816, when he returned to stage design under contract to the small but well-established Théâtre de l'Ambigu-Comique. A new genre known as melodrama attracted enthusiastic audiences that Daguerre impressed with extravagant visual illusions. He created stage designs for thirteen shows in the years 1816-1822, utilizing spectacular visual effects and increasing his reputation as an innovator in the theatrical world. It was during these years that he began experimenting with a range of lighting effects using gas lamps.

As early as 1822, Daguerre worked to develop a new form of public entertainment, the diorama. In the earlier "diaphanorama" created by Franz Niklaus König, transparent paintings exhibited in darkened rooms were illuminated by specialized lighting and reflection. Daguerre improved the diaphanorama so much that he was able to patent the diorama as a new invention. His earlier panorama displays only portrayed subjects from one perspective during a fixed time, but the diorama treated awestruck viewers to gradations of light that seemed to flow over and sometimes even through paintings. In ten or fifteen minutes, the illusion revealed landscapes or chapel scenes passing from day to night. Natural disasters such as erupting volcanoes and tumbling landslides were also portrayed.

In connection with his work in lighting and design, Daguerre hoped to discover a mechanical means by which natural scenes and perhaps even portraits of people could be preserved. Although Daguerre had used a camera obscura—a device that focused sunlight through a lens to cast an image—in order to improve the realism of his paintings, the images always vanished when the light failed. Other inventors were also interested in developing a way to record images created by sunlight.

As early as 1816, Nicéphore Niépce had begun experimenting with a variety of materials, including paper treated with various light-sensitive chemicals. In 1826, he succeeded in producing an image on a pewter plate coated with bitumen, a process he named "heliography," or sun-drawing. Hearing of Niépce's work, Daguerre contacted the inventor to suggest an alliance, but Niépce hoped to patent his work in England. When this plan failed, he agreed to a partnership with Daguerre, who had been experimenting on his own with lenses and varying chemical treatments to metal plates. As the two men corresponded, Niépce revealed his findings to Daguerre, who struggled to improve upon them.

It was not until after Niépce's death that Daguerre discovered, in 1837, substantially improved methods of recording images. He managed to decrease exposure times from seven or more hours to minutes and to devise a treatment that kept the images from fading when exposed to light. Daguerre announced his success but kept his methods secret, since he believed that the process could easily be copied and would bring him no profit if he simply patented it. He claimed to be the true inventor of the new process and attempted to sell subscriptions, planning to grant Niépce little credit for his research and his heir Isadore Niépce a reduced percentage of any earnings. Although businessmen and members of the art industry were very interested, few were willing to invest, and the project stalled.

In an unusual move, the French government granted the partners Daguerre and Isadore Niépce sizable lifetime annuities in exchange for all rights to the entire photographic procedure. Daguerre received a larger grant than Niépce for revealing the secrets of his diorama design and for his promise to disclose any future enhancements to the photographic process that he might discover. The "daguerreotype" was made public as a gift from the French people to the world, and Daguerre was

"View of the Boulevard du Temple" daguerreotype, Paris, 1838/1839. Although the photograph accurately portrays the street, trees, and buildings, only one person on the busy boulevard was recorded—a man who stood still as his shoes were polished (bottom left corner). Exposure time for a daguerreotype was so long that carriages and pedestrian activity moved too fast to be registered on the light-sensitive copper plate.

The Daguerreotype

Photography as a practical process began when Jacques Daguerre discovered a way to fix, or make permanent, the images cast on silver-coated copper plates treated with light-sensitive iodide. The metallic plates were exposed as the light traveled through a camera lens, changing the chemical composition of the plates. These were then treated with a mercury vapor, a process that converted the emergent image from a negative to a detailed, positive picture.

The last step in the process made the images permanent. Once the exposed plates had been rinsed in a hot saltwater solution that dissolved the silver iodide that had not been affected by light, the images were fixed and did not fade when exposed to light. Variations of the developing process continued to be an integral part of film-based photography.

As advantageous as this process appeared, there were important limitations. The lengthy exposure time required for success was the greatest drawback to the earliest daguerreotypes, initially making attractive portraits impossible. Each picture required a repetition of the entire process on new plates, and the equipment was frequently judged too cumbersome for practical fieldwork. Also, the fragile images damaged easily and could be seen only when viewed from an angle, due to the glare produced by the silver coating on the plates.

Freed from patent restraints by the public announcement of Daguerre's process, entrepreneurial camera designers rapidly improved the lenses and other mechanical features of cameras. For example, a mirror prism placed in front of the lens corrected the reversed images produced by the original cameras. Another inventor created a camera that relied on concave mirrors to reflect images rather than passing light through a lens.

New lens combinations, widened apertures, and an improved chemical process further reduced long exposure times. Antoine Claudet discovered that treating the silver-coated copper plates with both iodide and chlorine greatly accelerated their sensitivity to light. Thus, it became possible to take portraits in the shade in only five to twelve seconds and in full sunshine in only one to four seconds.

Photo-etching methods of deriving prints from finished plates enabled printers to duplicate copies of the originals for publications, but this process was difficult and never became practicable. However, daguerreotypes were used to increase accuracy and to reduce the production time involved in creating lithographs and traditional engravings.

By 1847, French photographers had begun to favor a paper-based process developed by William Fox Talbot. An important new process introduced in 1851 by Frederick Scott Archer that utilized glass plates dipped in a solution containing collodion, or nitrocellulose, contributed to a marked decline in daguerreotype production. Nevertheless the striking, silvery images continued to be highly prized in the United States for many years. Recent interest in the daguerreotype has led to a renewed use of the process, primarily for aesthetic reasons.

appointed an officer of the Legion of Honor for his accomplishment.

Daguerre attempted to refine the daguerreotype process after publishing *Historique et description des procédés du daguerréotype et du diorama* (1839; *An Historical and Descriptive Account of the Various Processes of the Daguerreotype and the Diorama*), but he was unable to compete with a number of improvements that were rapidly devised by others. He left Paris in 1840 to live in the nearby village of Bry-sur-Marne, where he continued to experiment with photographic equipment and painting methods. In addition, he completed projects in design and the graphic arts as well as receiving admiring visitors from around the world. He died unexpectedly in 1851, apparently of heart failure.

Impact

The revelation of Daguerre's invention was hailed as a victory of science, one that opened a new world of instant representation. An eager public awaited the 1839 disclosure of the inventor's process, and by the end of the year enterprising individuals made and displayed daguerreotypes in Britain, the United States, and other countries. The daguerreotype galvanized members of the art world and the public as inventors, lens grinders, lithographers, and chemists sought to make full use of the amazing potential offered by the process.

Photographers began recording landmarks, architectural works, and natural objects in regions as diverse as Switzerland, Egypt, and the United States. Daguerreotypes were prized because they recorded realistic images. Publishers often preferred these truthful representations to romanticized paintings that exaggerated space and size for emotional effects. Printmakers, painters, and fledgling photographers joined to produce an enriched visual culture affecting much of the Western world.

Photography grew rapidly in France, attracting many

practitioners. A thousand-piece daguerreotype collection was displayed at an 1844 exposition, and in 1847 as many as two thousand cameras were sold in Paris. In the past, only wealthy art patrons and members of the royalty had been able to afford hand-painted portraits, but with the daguerreotype's increasing availability, many more people could enjoy permanent mirrorlike self-images.

Daguerre's collection of daguerreotypes and the records of his experiments burned when his laboratory, situated in his diorama building, went up in flames in 1839. However, his place in history as a successful painter, physicist, and chemist remains. For example, his name was included in a list of seventy-two world-class French scientists engraved on the Eiffel Tower. Also, although some have considered his scientific methods haphazard and his ambitions overriding, Daguerre was largely successful in convincing the public that he was the discoverer of photography. In more recent academic studies, many historians credit Niépce's earliest heliograph as the true original.

—*Margaret A. Koger*

Further Reading

Bann, Stephen. *Parallel Lines: Printmakers, Painters, and Photographers in Nineteenth-Century France.* New Haven, Conn.: Yale University Press, 2001. Scholarly description of the art history of the era. Reveals the ways photographic technology resulted in an expansion of traditional techniques in printmaking and painting, enriching the culture as a whole.

Barger, Susan M., and William White. *The Daguerreotype: Nineteenth-Century Technology and Modern Science.* Washington, D.C.: Smithsonian Institution Press, 1991. Traces the origin and development of the daguerreotype and discusses curatorial issues, restorations, and recent research findings on the chemistry of the process. A detailed technical study with illustrations.

Daguerre, Louis-Jacques-Mandé. *An Historical and Descriptive Account of the Various Processes of the Daguerreotype and the Diorama.* New York: Winter House, 1971. Daguerre's instruction manual, Niépce's description of heliography, documents relating to the annuity grant, and excerpts of selected correspondence from Niépce to Daguerre. Includes a range of subjects portrayed in over thirty reproductions of daguerreotypes.

Davis, Keith F., Jane Lee Aspinwall, and Marc F. Wilson. *The Origins of American Photography: From Daguerreotype to Dry Plate, 1839-1885.* Kansas City, Mo.: Hall Family Foundation, 2007. Written in association with the Nelson-Atkins Museum of Art. An expansive history of the pioneers of the daguerreotype and photography in general in the United States. Covers improvements in equipment design as well as advances in portraiture, news reporting, and landscape photography.

Gernsheim, Helmut, and Alison Gernsheim. *L. J. M. Daguerre: The History of the Diorama and the Daguerreotype.* New York: Dover, 1968. A detailed examination of the inventor's diorama, the development of the daguerreotype, and its subsequent influence in France, the United States, and Britain. Also contains invaluable biographical detail illustrating the extravagant character and colorful career of Daguerre in the context of his era.

See also: Léon Foucault; Samuel F. B. Morse; Nicéphore Niépce.

Gottlieb Daimler

German mechanical engineer

Daimler was a leader in the early automotive industry and a pioneer of the internal combustion engine, the motorcycle, the four-wheel gasoline-driven automobile, and the world-famous Mercedes-Benz car.

Born: March 17, 1834; Schorndorf, Württemberg (now in Germany)
Died: March 6, 1900; Cannstatt, Germany
Also known as: Gottlieb Wilhelm Daimler (full name)
Primary fields: Automotive technology; mechanical engineering
Primary inventions: Daimler's motorcycle; gas engine

Early Life

Gottlieb Wilhelm Daimler (GOT-leeb VIHL-hehlm DIM-lur) was born on March 17, 1834, in the town of Schorndorf, Württemberg (now in Germany), the son of a baker named Johannes Daümler and his wife, Frederika. At the age of thirteen, he completed his six-year primary studies in Lateinschule, a prestigious grammar school. He showed an aptitude for mathematics, especially geometry, and attended drawing classes on Sundays.

Daimler's first job was as a gunsmith's apprentice. He completed his apprenticeship by making a double-barreled gun. For a period, he worked in France to gain practical experience in mechanical engineering. From 1853 to 1857, he worked at a Strassburg steam engine factory. He then attended the Stuttgart Polytechnic School, taking up mechanical engineering and completing his training in 1859. While most engineering students tried to exploit the power of steam engines, Daimler gained experience by working in various German engineering firms.

A model poses with the world's first gas-powered motorcycle, built in 1885 by Gottlieb Daimler. (AP/Wide World Photos)

Two years later, recognizing the need for a small, low-power engine capable of economical, intermittent operation, Daimler left to tour France and England, where he undertook various technical jobs. In Paris, he saw Étienne Lenoir's new gas engine. He also visited the 1862 London World Fair, where he observed the latest European engineering advances. For a while, he worked as a draftsman in Geislingen, devising systems and tools to mechanize an old factory.

At the end of 1863, he became the workshop inspector at Bruderhaus Maschinen-Fabrik in Reutlingen, where he met Wilhelm Maybach (his future business partner and lifelong friend) in 1865. He married Emma Kurtz on November 9, 1867; they had five children. He left Reutlingen in 1869 and joined a mechanical engineering company in Karlsruhe, where Carl Benz had worked earlier.

Life's Work

In 1872, Daimler became technical director at the world's largest manufacturer of stationary engines of the time, Gasmotorenfabrik Deutz, Nikolaus August Otto's company. Daimler hired fellow inventor Maybach. In 1876, Otto invented the four-stroke engine, known as the Otto cycle, which was to replace the steam engines predominant at that time. It was patented in 1877 but was soon challenged by Carl Benz. In Mannheim, unknown to the other three inventors, Benz was creating a reliable two-stroke gas engine based on the same principle. He completed his engine on New Year's Eve, 1878, and received a patent in 1879. In 1882, serious personal differences between Daimler and Otto resulted in Daimler's being fired. Maybach later resigned.

That year, Daimler and Maybach moved back to Stuttgart and purchased a cottage in Cannstatt, where they started their own engine-building shop in 1885. Among many developments, they patented one of the first successful high-speed internal combustion engines. They used their fuel-injected engines to develop the first gas-engine motorcycle, and they created a carburetor, which mixes gasoline with air for the engine. They also assembled a larger version of their engine, which they called the *Standuhr* (grandfather clock) for its resemblance to an old pendulum clock.

Unknown to Maybach and Daimler, Benz had built the first automobile and was granted a patent for his motorized tricycle in 1886. That year, Daimler and Maybach installed a larger version of the grandfather clock engine into a stagecoach, which became the first four-wheel automobile to reach 16 kilometers per hour (10 miles per hour).

Daimler and Maybach also used their engine in other types of transport and even in Daimler's balloon, usually regarded as the first airship, where it replaced a hand-operated engine designed by Friedrich Hermann Wolfert of Leipzig. With the new engine, Daimler successfully flew over Seelberg on August 10, 1888.

Daimler and Maybach sold their first foreign licenses for engines in 1887, with Maybach representating the company at the Paris World's Fair. Engine sales increased. Daimler bought another property at Seelberg in Cannstatt. In 1889, their efforts led to their first automobile, a two-stroke-engine, four-wheeled vehicle. It was licensed to be built in France; they presented it to the public in Paris in October, 1889. It was also in this year that Daimler's first wife, Emma, died.

In 1890, Daimler and Maybach founded Daimler Motoren-Gesselschaft (DMG) in order to build their high-speed engines. As they struggled financially, two financiers and munition makers, Max von Duttenhofer and William Lorenz, along with the influential banker Kilian von Steiner, agreed to inject some capital, converting the company into a public corporation on November 28, 1890. DMG expanded. The newcomers did not believe in automobile production and ordered the creation of additional building capacity for stationary engines. They also considered merging DMG with Otto's company. Maybach was denied a seat on the board, and he left the company on February 11, 1891.

In 1892, DMG sold its first automobile. Age fifty-eight and ill with heart disease, Daimler traveled to Florence, Italy, on his doctor's orders. There he met Lina Hartmann, a widow twenty-two years his junior and the owner of the hotel where he was staying. They married on July 8, 1893. On his return, Daimler experienced difficulty with other stockholders, and he resigned that year—a move that would prove short-lived.

Maybach, Daimler, and his son Paul had designed a third engine, the *Phoenix*, which DMG manufactured. The *Phoenix* became famous around the world, winning the first car race in history—from Paris to Rouen in 1894. In order to stabilize DMG, British industrialist Frederick Simms negotiated for Daimler's return to DMG, securing the right to license the *Phoenix* engine and use Daimler's name in the engine's branding. In 1895, the year DMG assembled its thousandth engine, Maybach also returned as chief engineer. In 1899, DMG produced the first Mercedes automobile—considered the first modern gasoline-powered car. (The car was named after the

Daimler's Motorcycle

Gottlieb Daimler is credited with inventing the first gas-powered motorcycle. Motorcycle sport is popular in many countries, especially with the young. A motorcycle is a single-track, two-wheeled motor vehicle powered by an engine. It evolved from the "safety" bicycle, which offered advantages in stability, braking, and ease of mounting. Safety bicycles became popular in the late 1880's. They had two wheels of identical size and a chain-driven rear wheel. In 1885, they were simply called bicycles.

That year, Daimler produced his first vehicle, a motorcycle. He attached the gasoline engine to a wooden bicycle, replacing the pedals. His motorcycle was powered by a single-cylinder Otto-cycle engine mounted vertically in the center of the machine. It had one wheel in front, one rear wheel, and a spring-loaded outrigger wheel on each side for added stability. Its chassis mostly consisted of wood; the wheels had wooden spokes and iron rims.

These designs were called "boneshakers" because of the jarring ride they delivered. Daimler's motorcycle may have also included a spray-type carburetor, then under development by himself with his longtime business partner, Wilhelm Maybach, for use in the Daimler automobile that appeared in 1889.

After Dailmer's motorcycle was introduced, other designers followed, including Alex Millet in 1892, Hildebrand & Wolfmüller in 1894, and DeDion-Buton in 1895. By the time Michio Suzuki was designing his first loom, other European companies such as Peugeot, Norton, and Husqvarna were producing motorcycles, as well as Indian and Harley-Davidson in the United States.

Daimler is generally credited as the "father of the motorcycle." However, in 1867 Sylvester Roper in the United States built a primitive motorcycle, a steam-powered bike. Although it did not catch on, it anticipated modern motorbike features, including the twisting-handgrip throttle control. It was powered by a charcoal-fired two-cylinder engine, whose connecting rods directly drove a crank on the rear wheel. This machine predates the invention of the safety bicycle.

What gives credibility to Daimler's claim of having developed the first "true" motorcycle is the fact that his motorcycle was propelled by a gas engine, while Roper's two-cylinder engine was powered by steam. Daimler is rightly considered a pioneer of the motorcycle and automobile industry.

daughter of Emil Jellinek, a businessman who raced Daimler's cars.)

Daimler finally succumbed to the pressures of his forty-year career and heart disease, dying in 1900. In 1907, Maybach resigned permanently from DMG. In 1924, DMG's management signed a long-term agreement with Benz and Cie. Two years later, the two companies merged to become Daimler-Benz AG.

Impact

Daimler was a pioneer in automotive history whose efforts immensely impacted the car industry and the creation of the modern automobile. Indeed, Daimler's impact was second only to that of Carl Benz. Independently, Benz and Daimler created vehicles that are now recognized as the ancestors of modern gasoline-powered vehicles. Although they used different approaches—Benz, the spark ignition, and Daimler, the high-speed motor—both paved the way to the future development of the automobile.

Daimler's contributions extend beyond the modern motorcar, however: Before his major breakthrough, he produced the first gas-engine motorcycle and the first four-wheeled, gas-driven car within a year's span. His development of the carburetor launched the age of gasoline-powered automobiles. When he constructed the improved two-stroke, four-cylinder engine in 1889, the stage was set for the modern automobile—which he produced ten years later with the first Mercedes.

Since that time, gas-powered automobiles have had both positive and negative effects: They led to the decline of the railroads and eventually increased greenhouse gas emissions, which many believe are largely responsible for global warming. The automobile also caused both demographic and social upheavals, as more people moved from urban to outlying suburban areas and as teenagers and young adults enhanced their independence from parents and family life. At the same time, today's economy, social flexibility, and productivity are hard to imagine without the automobile.

Another of Daimler's major legacies is his foundation of what became Daimler-Benz AG, which produced the famous Mercedes-Benz automobiles, still considered a gold standard for passenger cars. Many of the innovations Daimler developed are still used in modern vehicles. Thanks to his pioneering inventions and his major role in the automobile revolution, people around the world have enjoyed freedom of movement and increased standards of living.

—*Tel Asiado*

Further Reading

Adler, Dennis. *Mercedes-Benz: 110 Years of Excellence*. Osceola, Wis.: Motorbooks International, 1995. Enthusiast's series of a full-color gallery of Mercedes-Benz models spanning over a century. Model history and evolution, specifications, technical notes, and index.

Georgano, G. N., ed. *The Complete Encyclopaedia of Motorcars, 1885 to Present*. 2d ed. London: Ebury Press, 1973. Features the history of the automobile into the 1960's. Photographs, index.

Stein, Ralph. *The Automobile Book*. London: Paul Hamlyn, 1962. Discusses engineers such as Étienne Lenoir, Gottlieb Daimler, Siegfried Marcus, and Carl Benz. Photographs.

Twist, Clint. *The Power Generators*. London: Wayland, 1991. Shows how fuels are used to make power and how power generation has developed over time. Written for a juvenile audience. Glossary, index.

See also: Carl Benz; Nicolas-Joseph Cugnot; Rudolf Diesel; John Boyd Dunlop; Henry Ford; Charles F. Kettering; Étienne Lenoir; Hiram Percy Maxim; André and Édouard Michelin; Ransom Eli Olds; Nikolaus August Otto; Stanford Ovshinsky; Sylvester Roper; Ignaz Schwinn; Felix Wankel; Alexander Winton.

Nils Gustaf Dalén

Swedish physicist and engineer

Dalén invented the sun valve, a device that made it possible for lighthouses to function unattended for a maximum period of one year. He also invented a flashing apparatus, the Dalén mixer, and an automatic mantle changer, as well as Agamassan, all of which helped to improve the lighthouse system.

Born: November 30, 1869; Stenstorp, Sweden
Died: December 9, 1937; Lidingö, Sweden
Primary fields: Mechanical engineering; physics
Primary inventions: Sun valve; AGA lighthouse system

Early Life

Nils Gustaf Dalén (neels goo-STAHF dah-LAYN) was the third child born to farmers in Stenstorp, Sweden. Since Dalén was not a particularly studious boy, his parents felt that he was the best suited of their children to manage the farm. Because he planned to be a farmer, once Dalén had finished his secondary schooling he enrolled at a school of agriculture with the intention of studying dairy farming. However, Dalén had already started inventing machines while he was living on the family farm. His first invention was a threshing machine, which he powered with an old spinning wheel. His next invention was a mechanism for measuring the butterfat content of milk. This invention brought him to the attention of Gustaf de Laval, founder of the company AB Separator, located in Stockholm. Impressed by Dalén's exceptional talent in mechanics, de Laval recommended that he pursue a technical education. Dalén took de Laval's advice and abandoned his study of dairy farming.

He attended the Chalmers Institute at Gothenburg from 1892 to 1896, graduating with a degree in engineering. Still interested in dairy farming, Dalén invented a pasteurization machine as well as a milking device. He spent a year in Switzerland, where he studied with Professor Aurel Stodola at the Eidgenössisches Polytechnikum. When he returned to Sweden, Dalén did research at Gothenburg and worked for AB de Lavals Angturbin as a turbine designer. He constructed a hot-air turbine with related compressors and air pumps. The turbine project was not successful, however, and Dalén turned his attention toward another area in which de Laval was involved—the industrial use of the gas acetylene. With Henrik von Celsing, whom he had met at Chalmers, he founded the firm Dalén and Celsing.

Life's Work

The year 1901 was significant for Dalén both personally and professionally. He married Elma Persson and accepted a position as technical chief of the Swedish Carbide and Acetylene Company. In 1904, he began working for the Gas Accumulator Company, and he became the company's chief engineer two years later. In 1909, the company was reorganized and named the Swedish Gas Accumulator Company (Svenska Aktiebolaget Gasaccumulator, or AGA), and Dalén became managing director of the firm.

In 1901, Dalén's company bought the patent rights to the French invention of dissolved acetylene. In 1905, John Höjer, chief engineer for the Board of Pilotage, Lighthouses, and Buoys, brought to the attention of Dalén the large market potential of acetylene, which could be used as fuel in lighthouse beacons, and mentioned the need for economical automatic flashing beacons. Dalén began researching and working on an automatic flashing beacon and produced a flashing apparatus, the AGA flasher, that not only improved lighthouse beacons but also was used in railroad signals. The first railway signal using this flashing apparatus went into operation in 1908. Dalén continued his research on lighthouse beacons and invented the sun valve, or Solventil, in 1907. The device made it possible for lighthouses to function unattended for a maximum period of one year. The sun valve caused a beacon to light at dusk and to extinguish at dawn automatically, thereby conserving fuel. In 1912, he received the Nobel Prize in Physics for this invention.

In his work with lighthouse beacons, Dalén also invented two devices for use with incandescent mantles. One was a mixer that maintained a constant, correct balance of gas and air. The other was a device that made possible the removal of broken mantles and their replacement with new ones.

Dalén also worked on ways to reduce the risks involved in the storage and use of acetylene, a dangerously flammable compound. He filled the casing of the cylinders used in the transport and storage of acetylene dissolved in acetone with Agamassan, or Aga, a porous mixture that absorbs acetylene. Unlike Dalén's mixture, other materials that had been used for filling the casings lacked elasticity, crumbled, and permitted the formation of explosive pockets of the acetylene.

In 1912, while Dalén was testing safety devices used on cylinders of acetylene, he was seriously injured and blinded by a sudden explosion. While he made a good recovery from his other injuries, he remained blind. Despite this handicap, Dalén continued his research. In the following years, he received a number of honors and awards. In 1913, he was chosen for membership in the Royal Swedish Academy. He was also awarded the Morehead Medal by the International Acetylene Association. In 1918, he received an honorary doctorate from Lund University. He was elected to the Academy of Science and Engineering in 1919.

As well as receiving awards and honors, Dalén continued to be valued as a working inventor and engineer. He received the contract for lighting the Panama Canal. Sometime later, he became interested in yet another field of research, thermal technics. His research in this area led him to develop the AGA cooker in 1922. The AGA cooker was a stove requiring only eight pounds of coal to maintain cooking heat for twenty-four hours. The stove was very successful and used throughout the world.

Dalén's son Gunnar eventually succeeded his father in the position of director of Swedish Gas Accumulator. Nils Gustaf Dalén died at his villa in Lidingö, Sweden, on December 9, 1937, at the age of sixty-eight.

Impact

Dalén was interested in advancing technology in a wide range of fields. His first inventions were related to farming and included a device for measuring the butterfat content of milk. In the late 1900's, he was involved in the development of a gas turbine combustion engine for use in airplanes. During World War I, he was part owner of an airplane factory that produced approximately one hundred planes. However, Dalén's major impact on research and technology resulted from his work with AGA. His inventions that were the core components of the AGA lighthouse system greatly improved the function of lighthouse beacons. These inventions also enabled lighthouses to function automatically and reduced the cost of their operation. Consequently, the number of lighthouses increased and resulted in greater safety at sea. His AGA flasher system also enhanced safety in railway transportation, as it was used in railroad signals. The safe transportation and storage of the explosive gas acetylene resulted from his work with creating a cylinder to safely contain the gas.

—*Shawncey Webb*

The AGA Lighthouse System

From 1905 to 1916, Nils Gustaf Dalén developed the AGA lighthouse system. The system required the invention of the following essential components: the AGA flasher with sun valve, the Dalén mixer, and the automatic mantle changer. The term "Dalén light" is used to refer to both the entire beacon system and to the various individual parts.

Dalén had to work in two areas of research to invent a marketable system. First, an automated system had to be able to maintain a fully functioning beacon for an extended period of time. Second, he had to reduce the cost of fueling the system with acetylene, which was preferred for its brightness, and at the same time make the use of the highly explosive gas safe.

Dalén first addressed the problem of the cost associated with a constantly burning light. He developed an intermittent light regulator, the AGA flasher, which reduced the gas consumption by 90 percent. Continuing his research, he invented the sun valve, also known as the solar valve, or Solventil, which used the natural daylight and its absence at night to turn the beacon light on and off. The valve used an arrangement of four metal rods, with a center rod surrounded by three parallel rods. The center rod was blackened and absorbed light; the three surrounding rods were gilt and reflected light. In darkness, all of the rods were of equal temperature and length. When dawn came, the blackened rod absorbed light, thus acquiring a slightly higher temperature and a slightly longer length than the other rods. This triggered a mechanism that cut off the gas supply and extinguished the light. At dusk, the process reversed, causing the gas valve to open, permitting a pilot flame to light the beacon. The combination of the sun valve and the AGA flasher proved extremely economical; it used 94 percent less gas than the continuously burning beacon.

Next, Dalén considered the problem posed by the explosive nature of acetylene. He developed Agamassan, or Aga, a porous mixture of charcoal, cement, asbestos, and water that he placed in the casing of the cylinders containing the acetylene, making its storage safe. Dalén next addressed the need for large lighthouse beacons at sea to have the greatest intensity of light possible in combination with full automation. To obtain the needed light intensity, he used incandescent mantles that required a mixture of acetylene and air at the ratio of one part acetylene to ten parts air, a highly explosive mixture. He invented the Dalén mixer to mix the gas and air at this ratio without danger of explosion. He also invented an automatic mantle changing system. Equipped with a magazine of twenty-four mantles, the changer made a beacon function automatically for a full year without any maintenance. The AGA lighthouse system was the main system used in lighthouses from its first stages of development in 1906 through the 1960's.

Further Reading

Almqvist, Ebbe. *History of Industrial Gases*. New York: Kluwer Academic/Plenum, 2003. An excellent source for understanding the use of acetylene in industry and for the history of the development of the industrial gas business. Contains extensive coverage of both Dalén's role and that of AGA in the acetylene industry.

Dardo, Mauro. *Nobel Laureates and Twentieth Century Physics*. New York: Cambridge University Press, 2004. Discusses briefly Dalén's winning the Nobel Prize in Physics in 1912 and the unusual circumstances surrounding his selection.

James, Tim. *AGA: The Story of a Kitchen Classic*. Bath, England: Absolute Press, 2002. Discusses the success and popularity of Dalén's stove, which used only eight pounds of coal to provide twenty-four hours of cooking.

Schobert, Harold. *Energy and Society: An Introduction*. New York: Taylor & Francis, 2002. Chapter 23 discusses Dalén's interest in airplane engines and his attempts to produce a gas turbine engine.

See also: Georges Claude; Martha J. Coston; Fritz Haber; Louis Pasteur.

Raymond Damadian

American physicist

Damadian was the first scientist and physician to apply nuclear magnetic resonance technology to diagnostic medicine. His achievements in the field of magnetic resonance imaging are among the most critical advances in medical technology in recent memory.

Born: March 16, 1936; Melville, New York
Also known as: Raymond Vahan Damadian (full name)
Primary field: Medicine and medical technology
Primary invention: Magnetic resonance imaging (MRI) machine

Early Life

Raymond Vahan Damadian was born in 1936 in Melville, New York, to Vahan and Odette Damadian. The family moved to the Forest Hills section of Queens, where Damadian grew up. As a young man, Damadian studied violin at the Juilliard School of Music and was an avid tennis player. He attended Forest Hills High School, which had an excellent reputation for science and mathematics. In 1952, he won a Ford Foundation scholarship to attend the University of Wisconsin in Madison. There he gave up the violin and competition in Junior Davis Cup-level tennis to major in mathematics and minor in chemistry. By the time he earned his bachelor of science degree in 1956, he had completed all the requirements for medical school. In that same year, he became one of four non-Jewish students accepted to the new Albert Einstein College of Medicine, part of Yeshiva University in New York.

By Damadian's own admission, he was not good at memorizing facts, but he was intrigued by the puzzle-solving aspect of diagnosing disease. Motivated by memories of the death of his grandmother from breast cancer when he was only ten years old, Damadian focused on internal medicine. He soon decided to pursue research rather than clinical work, believing that he could do the most good for the most people by finding better ways of diagnosing diseases rather than by treating them.

Damadian earned his medical degree in 1960 and married one week later. An internship and residency followed at Downstate Medical Center, Brooklyn (now the State University of New York Health Science Center at Brooklyn). During this time, he began to focus on kidney function and in 1962 would begin a postdoctoral fellowship in nephrology at the Renal Division of the Department of Internal Medicine at Washington University School of Medicine in St. Louis, Missouri. This work would eventually lead him to diagnostic magnetic resonance imaging (MRI).

Life's Work

Damadian began research on membrane sodium pumps. In 1963, he moved to Harvard Medical School's Biophysics Laboratory, where he audited a quantum physics course taught by Edward Purcell that introduced him to nuclear magnetic resonance (NMR) spectroscopy. Before things could go any further, however, Damadian was called to active duty for the Vietnam War. In 1965, as a U.S. Air Force captain, he was sent to the USAF School of Aerospace Medicine, Aerospace Medical Division, at Brooks Air Force Base in San Antonio, Texas. He remained in Texas until his service ended in 1967 and then returned to Downstate's De-

Indomitable

In 1972, Raymond Damadian filed the pioneer patent for magnetic resonance imaging (MRI) technology, titled "Apparatus and Method for Detecting Cancer in Tissue." *Indomitable*, as the apparatus came to be called, consisted of a chamber surrounded by the first human-sized superconducting magnets (later machines would employ permanent magnets or iron-frame electromagnets). MRI technology is based on nuclear magnetic resonance (NMR) technology. In both, when hydrogen nuclei (usually water molecules) are exposed to a strong magnetic field, the nuclei align within the field. The material being scanned is then pulsed with a short radio wave that pushes some of the nuclei out of alignment. The time it takes the nuclei to return to the aligned state is called a relaxation time. Relaxation signals vary in different tissues depending on the composition of nuclei within them. MRI scanners use pulse sequences to produce two scans: T_1 and T_2. Damadian discovered that by moving the magnet back and forth over a surface, it is possible to focus the relaxation signals and locate objects spatially against background information. This technique he called field-focusing nuclear magnetic resonance (FONAR). By using powerful magnets, it was possible to penetrate the human body noninvasively to detect relaxation times from embedded tissues. T_1 and T_2 are used as a diagnostic pair: T_1 provides anatomical details, and T_2 is used for the detection of pathologies. Typically, lesions show up brightly in T_2. By referencing T_2 values to T_1, the lesions can be located and evaluated as to size and invasiveness. Because relaxations are based on inherent cellular chemistry—the response of atoms to a magnetic field and radio pulse—no contrasting agents are required to detect differences in composition.

As nuclei relax, they in turn emit their own radio signals. An MR scanner uses the radio signals emitted from cells to map the body. Relaxation times and density differences account for the contrast and anatomical detail that are unique to MRI and that allow the mapping of soft tissues. This discovery, coupled with the ability to capture the signals emitted, was part of the 1972 patent. Emitted signals can be converted to pixels captured on a screen; the stronger the emission, the brighter the pixel signal and the greater the nuclei component of the tissue. Because every normal tissue has a certain background density associated with it, it becomes relatively easy to detect lesions or defects based on intensity variations from the expected pattern.

Since *Indomitable*, MRI machines have become smaller, cheaper, and more sophisticated, allowing them to be purchased by more medical facilities and increasing their role in diagnostic medicine. Continued refinements in imaging technology only further increase their worth to the medical field. *Indomitable* is now on display at the National Museum of American History at the Smithsonian Institution as a tribute not only to the man who invented it but also to the thousands of patients who have benefited from Damadian's indomitable spirit.

partment of Internal Medicine, Biophysical Laboratory, where he would remain on the faculty for the next eleven years.

Damadian's research indicated that ion imbalances existed in cancer cells, making them chemically different from normal cells. Since this was true, there should be some way to detect the imbalances using chemical analysis. Levels of potassium ions and sodium ions were critical, and from his work he came up with a new theory for how ions are exchanged in living cells. In 1969, he linked his research to NMR spectroscopy, using the technique to successfully map potassium levels inside tissues for the first time. Clear differences were observed between potassium levels in normal tissues and in tumors. Abnormal ion compositions inside cancerous cells resulted in changes to viscosity that could be seen by NMR. Decreased viscosity was found to prolong NMR relaxation times, and these changes were associated with tumor tissue.

In 1970, Damadian further tested the link, comparing NMR relaxation rates between rat normal tissue and rat tumor tissue; tumor tissues showed substantially prolonged rates compared to normal tissues. Relaxation times were elevated regardless of tumor type, and it was further demonstrated that normal tissues showed wide variation in NMR relaxations, which is why they could be imaged so well. This work was published in the journal *Science* in 1971, and it was here that Damadian first proposed the idea for making an NMR scanner that could noninvasively detect cancers in humans.

In 1972, Damadian patented the plans for the first whole-body MR scanner, a machine he constructed with the help of two graduate students, Lawrence Minkoff and Michael Goldsmith. Work began in 1976, and the machine was named *Indomitable* to reflect the struggles overcome during its generation. In 1977, the first-ever whole-body scan of a human was produced. The scan was of Minkoff, the only member of the team small enough to fit inside the machine.

Imaging developments for NMR techniques spanned

the 1970's, and refinements to imaging technology continue to this day. Initial imaging was geared to enhancing chemical NMR, but with Damadian's work, imaging became important for picture generation. Richard Ernst developed two-dimensional Fourier MR imaging early in the decade. Paul Lauterbur used magnetic field gradients to make two-dimensional images, and in 1974 Sir Peter Mansfield devised a faster pulse-sequence method for producing images. In 1980, Ernst's work was combined with phase encoding to produce the spin-warp imaging that would dominate the technology.

For all his work in the field, Damadian is considered the father of diagnostic NMR. He holds the pioneer patent for MR scanning, was the first to achieve a whole-body scan of a human, and was the first to produce a commercial MR scanner. Damadian holds more than forty-five patents and in 1978 founded the FONAR Corporation to manufacture MR scanners for commercial sale. Damadian remains active in research on MRI, and FONAR continues to be a leading manufacturer of machines throughout the world.

Damadian has won numerous awards over the years, including the Lawrence Sperry Award (1984), the National Engineers' Special Recognition Award (1985), the National Medal of Technology (1988), the Lemelson-MIT Lifetime Achievement Award (2001), the Benjamin Franklin Medal and Bower Award (2004), the National Inventor of the Year Award (2007), and the Caring Award, presented by the Leslie Munzer Neurological Institute of Long Island (2008). In 1989, he was inducted into the National Inventors Hall of Fame. In 2003, controversy arose when that year's Nobel Prize in Physiology or Medicine was awarded to Paul Lauterbur and Sir Peter Mansfield for their work on the development of MRI techniques. Conspicuously absent to many in the field was Raymond Damadian, the man responsible for the underlying science of MRI.

Impact

The impact of Damadian's work cannot be overstated. Magnetic resonance images provide incredible levels of detail far beyond standard X rays, allowing detection of diseases with noninvasive diagnostics. The signal advantage of MRI is that it allows visualization of the soft tissues where a majority of diseases occur; such tissues cannot be visualized with standard X-ray techniques. Further, noninvasive diagnostic techniques are crucial to early detection of disease, as they encourage more individuals to receive testing and early treatment. MRI has been adapted to the diagnosis of various cancers, multiple sclerosis, neurological disorders, cardiac and pulmonary disease, and other soft-tissue diseases.

The FONAR Corporation produced its first commercial scanner in 1980, introducing it to the American Roentgen Ray Society and Radiological Society of North America. In 1981, the first commercial scanners shipped. While *Indomitable* used superconducting magnets, the first commercial scanners used permanent magnets and then later the first iron-frame electromagnets. Scanners have become more technologically sophisticated, physically smaller, and more cost-effective, making them more widely available to hospitals and stand-alone imaging centers. In 1984, FONAR produced the first oblique MRI and in 1985 the first multiangle oblique MRI, both of which increased accessibility to more areas of the body. Damadian's more recent inventions include a full-sized MRI operating room that allows surgeons precise localization information during surgery, and the Stand-Up MRI, which allows physicians to see problems associated with weight-bearing dysfunction, such as pain associated with the spine. The new machine allows imaging to occur through several positions to pinpoint problems.

—*Elizabeth A. Machunis-Masuoka*

Further Reading

Damadian, Raymond. "America's Forgotten Asset." *Saturday Evening Post* (May/June, 1994): 58-59, 102-103. As a holder of the pioneer patent for MRI, and having fought patent infringement of his work, Damadian is an ardent supporter of patent protections as a way of stimulating and safeguarding the spirit of invention. This article outlines his argument in favor of patent protections.

_______. "Tumor Detection by Nuclear Magnetic Resonance." *Science* 171 (March 19, 1971): 1151-1153. The first scientific paper published demonstrating that NMR could be used to conclusively differentiate between normal and malignant tissues. Within this paper is the first proposal for adapting the technique to noninvasive diagnostics in humans.

Dreizen, Paul. "The Nobel Prize for MRI: A Wonderful Discovery and a Sad Controversy." *The Lancet* 363 (January 3, 2004): 78. Outlines the sequence of events for the development of early MRI technologies and supports the call for recognition of Damadian for his primary role.

Mattson, James, and Merrill Simon. *The Pioneers of NMR and Magnetic Resonance in Medicine: The Story of MRI.* Jericho, N.Y.: Dean Books, 1996. Excellent book that provides biographies of the major contributors to the field of NMR in medicine. Chapter 8 is dedicated to Damadian. Original manuscripts and sources are provided.

Pincock, Stephen. "U.S. and U.K. Researchers Share Nobel Prize." *The Lancet* 362 (October 11, 2003): 1203. Briefly summarizes the work of Paul Lauterbur and Sir Peter Mansfield in the field of MRI as justification for their receipt of the 2003 Nobel Prize in Physiology or Medicine.

See also: Godfrey Newbold Hounsfield; Wilhelm Conrad Röntgen.

Abraham Darby

English ironmaster

Darby is best known for his method of using coke instead of charcoal for smelting iron ore, opening up the possibility of greatly enhanced production of cast iron that in turn made possible the construction of modern machinery.

Born: c. 1678; Wren's Nest, near Dudley, Worcestershire, England
Died: May 8, 1717; Coalbrookdale, Shropshire, England
Primary field: Manufacturing
Primary invention: Iron ore smelting with coke

Early Life

Abraham Darby was the only son of John Darby, a farmer and a producer of nails, who introduced his son to the manufacture of iron products. At that time, nails were generally made from bulk iron by individuals working as craftsmen. By the seventeenth century, nails had proved essential for the construction industry in England. Though builders crafted the houses most often from local wood supplies, they purchased the nails from craftsmen such as John Darby.

The Darby family was Quaker, at a time when Quakers were often ostracized by their non-Quaker neighbors. As a result, Quakers generally did business only within their religious community and maintained a low profile. They were, however, dedicated businesspeople, and those who were merchants sold the products made by their fellow Quakers to society in general. Members of the Darby family were pillars of the local Friends community, and they passed on their allegiance to their descendants.

Life's Work

As a young teenager, Abraham Darby was apprenticed to Jonathan Freeth, a fellow Quaker and malt mill maker in Birmingham. In 1699, having just finished his apprenticeship, Darby moved to Bristol, where he set up business as a malt mill maker, probably on Cheese Lane. The manufacture of malt mills quickly lost its allure, however, and in 1702 Darby entered into a partnership with three other Quakers making small items of brass used in the manufacture of large tools or machines. The four men founded the Bristol Brass Wire Company, and Darby became the resident manager. In 1704, Darby traveled to the Netherlands, at that time the source of most brass items used in England, to study production methods. Upon returning, he brought several Dutch workmen with him to help develop the company. Darby quickly switched his efforts to casting iron pots. In 1707, he took out a patent (number 380) on a method of casting bellied iron pots, for which there was a huge demand in eighteenth century England. The patent was challenged in court, but Darby won, creating for himself a kind of monopoly.

Darby had been considering moving his business out of Bristol. He formed several new partnerships and in 1708 moved his operations to Coalbrookdale, in Shropshire, where he established both a copper smelter and a brass manufacturing firm and set about mining copper in the area. However, he decided that the future lay in iron, not copper or brass, and these works were wound up in 1713.

Making use of a damaged iron blast furnace at Coalbrookdale, Darby devoted himself to the production of cast-iron pots. He experimented with the production of iron from local iron ore, which turned out to be better suited to the production of cast-iron products than other iron deposits elsewhere in England. Darby poured the liquid iron directly from the blast furnace into molds in the shape of the bellied pots.

As was the practice at the time, the blast furnace was run continuously until the fuel gave out. A sufficient amount of wood was necessary to sustain a months-long run of the furnace, and the wood had to be converted to charcoal. The charcoal was typically transported in panniers carried by donkeys to the vicinity of the furnace, but

Iron Manufacture

Iron ore, from which metallic iron can be extracted, is interlaced with other minerals, namely sulfur and phosphorus. Separating out the pure iron involves intermixing the iron ore with the carbonized fuel, either charcoal manufactured from wood or coke produced from coal. If the temperature is raised to 1,400° Celsius, the pure iron can be separated from its impurities. This high temperature was first achieved in the Middle Ages by the addition of a blast of air (hence, the term "blast furnace") during the process. Furnaces needed to be located near a stream so that a waterwheel could provide power for the blast, and in proximity to deposits of ore and sources of fuel, because the cost of transporting these items any distance was prohibitive. The iron that emerged from the blast furnace could be poured into molds so that it formed "pigs," or ingots.

Pig iron's high carbon content makes it very brittle. For most uses, it has to be further processed after reheating it in a forge to remove impurities. Prior to Abraham Darby's innovation using coke-fueled blast furnaces for smelting iron, few iron products were made directly from cast iron; practically all iron products were made from reworked pigs in which the excess carbon had been removed by reheating and then pounding the pig iron until most of the carbon had been removed. Darby found that cast iron could be used to make cooking pots, which were universally used in eighteenth century England and whose brittleness was not a problem. By setting up a business to produce three-legged cast-iron cooking pots, Darby created for himself a market niche that he and his firm heavily exploited.

Under Darby's son and successor, Abraham Darby II, the business was greatly expanded to produce parts for agricultural plows, steam engines, and cannon, not to mention iron bridges. (Abraham Darby III built the Iron Bridge across the Severn River near his works at Coalbrookdale.) The Darbys were the instigators of industrial iron manufacture in England. The processes they pioneered were later introduced elsewhere in the world and laid the basis for the Industrial Revolution.

lengthy transport tended to break down the charcoal. Thus, blast furnaces were usually located in close proximity to forests. Converting the timber into charcoal was both labor- and capital-intensive, as was transporting the charcoal. By using coke (a derivative of coal) instead of charcoaled wood, Darby was able to produce more than four hundred tons of pig iron in a single season. The average blast furnace, on the other hand, was lucky to produce one hundred tons before its supply of fuel was exhausted.

Unfortunately, Darby became ill at a young age, before he was able to establish his ironworks on a firm footing, and he died on May 8, 1717, at the age of thirty-nine. Fortunately, he had partners in the firm who were able to carry on the business until his son, Abraham Darby II, was old enough to take over the firm. The partners worked in close collaboration with his widow, Mary Sergeant.

Impact

Darby's method of using coke instead of charcoal for iron smelting laid the foundation for the iron industry and helped launch the Industrial Revolution. This innovation was certainly influenced by material factors. In early eighteenth century England, the shortage of timber created the impetus to find a cheaper alternative to wood-derived charcoal as a fuel for blast furnaces. However, it was not until the late eighteenth century that the production of iron using coke fuel became widespread.

Using his smelting method to produce widely popular bellied iron pots, Darby created a financially secure business that lasted throughout the century. As an innovative industrialist who created a family firm that continued to dominate the iron industry, Darby became a model for the future leaders of British industry. Once the success of Darby's method became known, many other inventors developed processes that built upon Darby's innovation, so that by the nineteenth century the British iron industry led the world.

—*Nancy M. Gordon*

Further Reading

Gordon, Robert B. *American Iron, 1607-1900*. Baltimore: The Johns Hopkins University Press, 1996. Although the book is devoted to the development of the iron industry in America, the opening chapters contain some useful descriptions of early iron-smelting processes in Great Britain.

Hyde, Charles K. *Technological Change and the British Iron Industry, 1700-1870*. Princeton, N.J.: Princeton University Press, 1977. Argues that cost factors were the major drive behind the shift from charcoal to coal for smelting and that these factors did not favor coal until at least 1750. Provides statistics.

Raistrick, Arthur. *Quakers in Science and Industry*. New York: Kelley, 1968. Contains a chapter devoted to "The Ironmasters," showing the major role played by Quakers, and notably the Darby family, in the development of the iron industry. Also contains an extensive account of the technology of eighteenth century iron manufacturing.

Schubert, H. R. "Extraction and Production of Metals: Iron and Steel." In *A History of Technology*, edited by Charles Singer et al. Volume 4. Oxford, England: Clarendon Press, 1958. This standard work on technological development includes some useful drawings of early metal-processing equipment.

See also: Friedrich Bergius; Sir Henry Bessemer; William Murdock; Thomas Newcomen; Robert Stirling.

Sir Humphry Davy

British chemist

Davy was one of the first men to make a living from the practice of science, as a lecturer and experimenter. He became a shining exemplar of both pure and applied science, by virtue of his discoveries and his adaptations of theory to practice in such devices as the miner's safety lamp.

Born: December 17, 1778; Penzance, Cornwall, England
Died: May 29, 1829; Geneva, Switzerland
Primary fields: Chemistry; physics
Primary invention: Safety lamp

Early Life

Humphry Davy was the eldest of five children of woodcarver Robert Davy and his wife, Grace, née Millett. The Davy family had been prosperous in previous generations, but the only property Robert Davy inherited was a small farm overlooking St. Michael's Mount. His fortunes grew gradually worse; when he died in December, 1794, he left his widow with massive debts. When Humphry was nine, the rest of the family moved to Varfell, and Humphry was taken in by his godfather, John Tonkin, an apothecary-surgeon. Tonkin briefly sent him to school in Truro but then decided he could do a better job of educating the boy himself.

Following his father's death, Humphry's mother opened a milliner's shop in Penzance, which eventually enabled her to pay off Robert's debts; in the meantime, Humphry promised to provide for his siblings as best he could. In February, 1795, he was apprenticed to John Bingham Borlase, an apothecary-surgeon in Penzance, and zealously embarked upon an assiduous course of self-education in science. He was taught to read French by a refugee priest—an accomplishment that enabled him to read Antoine Lavoisier's *Traité élémentaire de chimie* (1789; elementary treatise on chemistry) in 1797; he was much enthused by Lavoisier's account of the newly discovered chemistry of oxygen.

In 1798, Davy caught the attention of a local member of Parliament, Davies Giddy, who subsequently changed his surname to Gilbert and became an important pro-

An 1830 engraving of Sir Humphry Davy. (Library of Congress)

moter of science and technology in Cornwall. Giddy gave Davy the run of his own library and a laboratory set up by his physician, then introduced him to Thomas Beddoes, an unorthodox physician who proposed to establish a "pneumatic institute" in Clifton, near Bristol, backed by two prominent members of Erasmus Darwin's Lunar Society, Josiah Wedgwood and James Watt. Beddoes thought that diseases were caused by airborne "miasmas" and intended to experiment with the therapeutic use of "factitious airs" recently discovered by Joseph Priestley, who had discovered oxygen independently of Lavoisier. Although Tonkin was horrified, Davy quit his supposedly safe profession on October 2, 1798, in order to work as Beddoes's assistant.

Beddoes rewarded Davy's boldness by publishing the latter's speculative essay on heat and light, which opposed Lavoisier's hypothesis that heat was an element, preferring to regard it as molecular motion, but argued wrongly that light might be an element capable of entering into molecular combinations. Beddoes had strong literary connections; his sister-in-law was the novelist Maria Edgeworth, and his son, Thomas Lovell Beddoes, later became a significant Romantic poet. Davy also wrote verse and had several poems accepted by Robert Southey for his *Annual Anthology* of 1799, including "The Sons of Genius," in which Davy expressed his hope "to scan the laws of nature, to explore/ The tranquil region of mild Philosophy/ Or on Newtonian swings to soar/ Through the bright regions of the starry sky." Davy also made the acquaintance of Samuel Taylor Coleridge and William Wordsworth, who employed him to see the second edition of *Lyrical Ballads* (1798) through the press and with whom he remained on friendly terms thereafter.

LIFE'S WORK

The research that Davy undertook while assisting Beddoes bore its first fruit when he discovered the exhilarating and narcotic effects of nitrous oxide, which became known as "laughing gas." His first report on his work, *Researches, Chemical and Philosophical* (1799), came to the attention of Count von Rumford (Benjamin Thompson) of the Royal Institution, who offered Davy an appointment as a lecturer. The Royal Institution had recently begun a program of public lectures for artisans and the gentry, and Davy was an immediate success with the latter crowd. He soon won a reputation for extraordinary eloquence and began attracting a celebrity audience, thus initiating the British tradition of the popularization of science.

Rumford's primary research objective at the time—spurred on by the president of the Royal Society, botanist Joseph Banks—was to apply chemistry to the problem of increasing crop yields, in order to make Britain less vulnerable to famine and food shortages caused by naval blockades. Davy became heavily involved in this work, although his first individual project was an investigation of the chemistry of tanning, from which he concluded that tanners had already established a best practice by long trial and error, for which chemistry merely needed to provide a scientific rationale. Banks was so pleased with Davy's work that he became his next patron; Davy was elected a fellow of the Royal Society in 1803 and was appointed as one of its two secretaries in 1807. By then, he was financially independent, one of the first men ever to make a living from scientific practice—a development that prompted William Whewell to coin the term "scientist" to label the emergent profession.

Davy followed up his early intuition about heat by deciding that electricity too must be a force and not a substance, and he became fascinated with its chemical effects. He discovered that electrical batteries could dissociate chemical compounds in solution—a trick that proved extremely fertile in terms of new discoveries. He was able to ascertain that many common substances were formed by the combination of oxygen with metals; by using electricity to dissociate these compounds, he discovered potassium, sodium, barium, strontium, calcium, and magnesium in rapid succession. He also isolated chlorine from muriatic acid and probably tried to repeat his old experiments at Beddoes's pneumatic institute by breathing it in to investigate its possible therapeutic value. His health had already begun to deteriorate, after an attack of "gaol fever" (typhus) suffered in 1908 when he was asked to advise on the ventilation of Newgate Prison, and it continued to get worse thereafter.

Davy was knighted on April 8, 1812, and married a wealthy widow, Jane Apreece, née Kerr (1780-1855) three days later. His research further imperiled his health when he began experimenting with the explosive nitrogen trichloride; an accident that disabled his hand forced him to engage an amanuensis. The assistant he chose, Michael Faraday, became his servant, traveling with him in the capacity of valet on trips to the Continent, which Davy took with increasing frequency. While returning from one such trip via Scotland in 1815, Davy received a letter from the Reverend Robert Gray of Bishop's Wearmouth (now Sunderland) imploring him, as England's leading scientist, to investigate explosions in mines with a view to preventing them. Davy broke his homeward journey in northeastern England to collect specimens of the gas known as "firedamp," whose chemical makeup he quickly ascertained—it proved to be methane—and whose investigation in the laboratory enabled him to design a "safety lamp" that would prevent it from exploding.

The safety lamp—one of the first great triumphs of "applied science"—completed Davy's fame, all the more so because he refused to patent it, making a gift of the discovery to anyone who might benefit from it. He published a book celebrating the discovery in 1818 and was made a baronet (that is, his knighthood became hereditary—a rather futile gesture, since he was childless) in the same year. In 1820, he succeeded Joseph Banks as president of the Royal Society and celebrated by presenting his researches in electromagnetism to the society in the course of the next two years. He was becoming increasingly irascible, perhaps in consequence of his perpetual ill health, and stubbornly defended his own ideas against those of younger men. He waxed indignant when George Stephenson claimed to have invented a safety lamp before him, but his most serious rift was with his protégé Michael Faraday, whom he had gradually promoted to colleague and collaborator, and for whom he had arranged publication of his early work. When Faraday allowed his own name to be put forward in 1921 for a fellowship of the Royal Society without consulting Davy—presumably for fear of an angry reaction—Davy became infuriated; Faraday went on to revolutionize the science of electricity.

In the hope of overcoming his increasingly troublesome breathing difficulties, Davy undertook further trips to the Continent. After suffering a stroke in December, 1826, he abandoned his scientific work but obtained an unexpected late best seller with a book on his lifelong hobby of fly-fishing, *Salmonia* (1828). While taking a final continental tour in the company of a young medical student, James Tobin, he embarked on a curious valetudinarian study, in the form of a series of philosophical dialogues focused on a cosmic vision, by means of which he attempted to fulfill the final part of the prospectus set out in "The Sons of Genius." He did not complete it, dying in Geneva in 1829, but the extant text was published posthumously as *Consolations in Travel* (1830).

The Safety Lamp

Sir Humphry Davy's careful analysis of "firedamp" not only proved that it was methane but also established the relatively high temperature at which a mixture of methane and oxygen became explosive. It was this measurement that suggested a means of preventing such explosions. He designed a lamp in which gases were fed to and exported from the flame through coiled tubes, which allowed them to cool in transit. This ensured that the lamp could not export enough heat to its surroundings to ignite ambient firedamp. As a further precaution, Davy enclosed the flame within a cylinder of wire gauze, which also helped to dissipate the heat of combustion.

Davy's lamp not only provided miners with safe lighting but also functioned as a firedamp detector; changes in the quality of the flame gave them notice of the gas's presence, enabling them to guard against the asphyxiating effects of the gas as well as its explosive potential, thus saving even more lives. An important item of spin-off from the research program was Davy's discovery that methane and air could combine without an explosion in the presence of a coil of platinum wire—the first example of such a catalytic process to be discovered and a significant example of research in applied science feeding back a significant discovery in "pure science."

Impact

Davy was enormously influential in formulating the public attitude to science in the early nineteenth century. He was by no means an uncontroversial figure; along with Joseph Priestley, another scientist closely acquainted with the leading Romantic poets, he was routinely pilloried by the Tory press as a practitioner of "Jacobin science," supposedly affiliated with dangerous revolutionary ideas imported from France. The fact that he became a celebrity and a role model, however, was a godsend to the advancement of British science; he really was a scientific revolutionary, in the best sense of the term.

Davy's discovery of so many new chemical elements resulted from the fact that he was fortunate enough to be in the right place at the right time, but his work in applied science, forging valuable alliances between chemistry, agriculture, and craftsmanship, was much more personal in nature. His brilliance as a popular lecturer was also unique. Although he spoiled his image somewhat by turning on Faraday, he did have some justification for his sentiments in that regard. Some of his guesses proved much better than others, but his enthusiasm to formulate and test bold hypotheses, and his unrelenting intellectual curiosity—still very evident in *Consolations in Travel*—ensured that he became the very model of a questing scientist.

—Brian Stableford

Further Reading

Davy, Humphry. *The Collected Works of Humphry Davy.* 9 vols. London: Ganesha Publishing, 2001. A new edition of the definitive collection of Davy's writings, from *Researches, Chemical and Philosophical* onward; this edition adds new portraits and illustrations and an introduction by David Knight.

Fullmer, June Z. *Young Humphry Davy: The Making of an Experimental Chemist.* Philadelphia: American Philosophical Society, 2000. A detailed account of the early phases of Davy's career, in Penzance, Clifton, and London, focusing on the exceptional creativity of his thinking with respect to the theories of the day.

Knight, David. *Humphry Davy: Science and Power.* Cambridge, England: Cambridge University Press, 1998. A comprehensive biography, whose main contextual focus is on the development of scientific institutions in the early part of the nineteenth century, as exemplified by Davy's career.

Thorpe, T. E. *Humphry Davy: Poet and Philosopher.* Eastbourne, England: Gardners Books, 2007. A succinct account of Davy's life and thought, neatly tailored for the instruction of general readers. Pays more attention than the strictly scientific biographies to his personal life and includes a sympathetic appreciation of his literary work.

See also: Charles Babbage; Michael Faraday; Joseph-Louis Gay-Lussac; Joseph Priestley; George Stephenson; Richard Trevithick; Alessandro Volta.

Mark Dean

American computer scientist

Dean envisioned and built hardware that contributed to the successful manufacture and public acceptance of early personal computers. As an engineer and executive, he advanced information technology to perform diverse functions and process and store vast amounts of data.

Born: March 2, 1957; Jefferson City, Tennessee
Also known as: Mark Edward Dean (full name)
Primary fields: Computer science; electronics and electrical engineering
Primary invention: Microcomputer ISA bus

Early Life

Mark Edward Dean was born to James and Barbara (Peck) Dean in Jefferson City, Tennessee. His father supervised dams for the Tennessee Valley Authority, and his mother taught in local schools and was a social worker. Dean first attended the segregated Nelson Mary School, where his maternal grandfather, Eugene Peck, served as principal. A mathematically talented child, Dean benefited from advanced lessons in geometry and trigonometry at that school. By third grade, Dean was studying at the integrated Jefferson Elementary.

Dean assisted his father with technical projects at home and saw turbines, generators, and computers that controlled processes at the dams where his father worked. He read *Popular Electronics* and built electronics kits, including a computer. In eighth grade, Dean realized that he wanted to pursue a career in electrical engineering, specifically designing computers for International Business Machines (IBM). Dean lettered in sports at Jefferson High School, where he studied advanced mathematics and earned outstanding grades. He restored automobiles, a hobby he continued to practice as an adult. Dean's family advised him and his younger sister Ophelia, who later became an engineer, to disregard people who discriminated against them. Dean pursued his goals despite obstacles, recognizing that his unique talents were often more valuable to people than their racial prejudices.

After he graduated from high school in 1975, Dean enrolled in the University of Tennessee, southwest of his hometown. Receiving a Minority Engineering Program scholarship, he majored in electrical engineering. He alternated attending school and working for Alcoa Aluminum as part of the university's cooperative program, which was mandatory for minority scholarship recipients. Dean graduated with honors in 1979 with a bachelor's degree in electrical engineering. One of his professors encouraged IBM to hire the young man for a research position at its office in Boca Raton, Florida, where engineers focused on personal computer (PC) innovations. Dean's collegiate experiences shaped his attitude in such a way that, during his career, he provided employment opportunities for minority and female computer scientists and engineers.

Life's Work

Dean thrived in IBM's professional environment. His colleagues, including Dennis Moeller, encouraged Dean's imaginative approaches to developing IBM's first PCs and expanding their capabilities, starting with the XT (released in 1983). That work resulted in Dean's designing hardware for the AT (1984). He enrolled in night classes at Florida Atlantic University to acquire more technical expertise by pursuing a master of science degree in engineering. Advised by Dr. Alan B. Marcovitz in the Electrical Engineering Department, Dean graduated in 1982. His thesis, "Using a Synchronous System Architecture to Build a Low Cost Graphics Terminal," described how to use cathode-ray tubes to produce and show images.

For IBM, Dean and Moeller created the Industry Standard Architecture (ISA) bus for PCs, their most historically significant invention, which received U.S. Patent number 4,528,626 in 1985. Dean also invented the Color Graphics Adapter (CGA) and a monochrome adapter to enhance PC monitor displays of text and images in black, white, and color. He designed components for the IBM PS/2 Models 70 and 80 and acquired patents assigned to IBM. On March 13, 1988, Dean married Paula Jayne Bacon in Palm Beach County, Florida.

After working ten years in Florida, Dean decided to earn a Ph.D. in electrical engineering to build his IBM career as an administrator and to secure credentials to teach at the university level should the opportunity arise. IBM financed Dean's doctoral work at Stanford University in Palo Alto, California, which he began in 1989. Working with advisers Drs. Mark Horowitz and David L. Dill, Dean wrote a dissertation discussing a computer architecture he designed, titled "STRiP: A Self-timed RISC Processor," to receive his Ph.D. in June, 1992.

Dean next served as advanced systems development director at IBM's Austin, Texas, research laboratory. His work involved designing systems for PowerPC processors and RS/6000 workstation technology. He continued advancing professionally within IBM. In 1995, he

Microcomputer ISA Bus

Mark Dean considered existing computer bus technology when he designed improved bus architecture for IBM personal computers (PCs) with colleague Dennis Moeller in the early 1980's. Prior to their bus invention, most microcomputers contained a bus with 8 bits, referring to the basic memory unit in a binary number system. Dean wanted to create a 16-bit bus with greater memory capacity. He consulted several patents issued in the late 1970's for relevant inventions, such as "Peripheral Processing System" (number 4,047,158), "Data Transfer Control Apparatus and Method" (number 4,112,490), and "Direct Memory Access Expander Unit for Use with a Microprocessor" (number 4,180,855), developed by engineers for rival computer manufacturers, including Intel Corporation and GTE Automatic Electric Laboratories, Inc.

While working on IBM's PC AT, Dean and Moeller developed what they referred to as the IBM bus. Dean described this invention as a computer containing a central processing unit (CPU), memory, a direct memory access controller (DMA), and a bus interface for peripheral devices to transmit information to the CPU and other peripheral devices as needed. The IBM bus enabled a user to attach simultaneously several external peripheral devices such as monitors, printers, mouse, disk drives, modem, and keyboards to a computer in order for the peripherals to interact with the computer's CPU to perform desired tasks. Dean and Moeller filed this invention's patent application using the formal title, "Microcomputer System with Bus Control Means for Peripheral Processing Devices," in March, 1984. Approved in July, 1985, as U.S. Patent number 4,528,626, that invention's rights were assigned to IBM.

Known commercially as the Industry Standard Architecture (ISA) systems bus, Dean's invention became a basic architectural component in IBM and similar PCs when the PC AT was distributed in the 1980's and other computer manufacturers were permitted to duplicate the ISA's design without compensating Dean, Moeller, or IBM. Because it broadened computing possibilities, Dean's bus contributed to increased consumer demand for PCs and expanded industrial manufacturing of computers and peripheral accessories. Bus applications expanded to support more peripherals such as flash drives and joysticks and to connect computer networks.

By 1986, other inventors had begun referencing Dean's initial bus patent in their patents for bus appropriations. Dean's ISA bus continued to influence inventors' computer architecture concepts through the early twenty-first century. Dean improved his original bus design and utilized bus technology to advance computer technology, receiving additional patents for those inventions, including "System Bus Preempt for 80386 When Running in an 80386/82385 Microcomputer System with Arbitration" (number 5,129,090) in 1988, to stop bus operations when signaled, and "Bus Interface Logic System" (number 5,768,550) in 1995, to coordinate data transmitted by two processors involving several bus transactions.

achieved the status of IBM fellow, which recognized his technical leadership in the corporation. He was the first African American selected for that prestigious title. Promoted to director of the Austin research laboratory in 1997, Dean announced the next year that his engineering team had created a one-gigahertz microprocessor. Dean promoted design plans for a versatile electronic tablet capable of diverse communication and entertainment tasks, but IBM did not develop that idea.

In 2000, Dean accepted the position of systems research vice president for IBM's Thomas J. Watson Research Center in Yorktown Heights, New York. He guided engineers designing architecture of the swift Blue Gene supercomputers for complex biotechnology computations. This work appropriated aspects of cellular microprocessor research Dean had directed in Texas. In 2002, he became storage technology vice president for IBM's Systems and Technology Group in Tucson, Arizona. He contributed to such patented inventions as a magnetic thread data storage device (number 7,206,163). Dean and his wife divorced on June 6, 2002.

Dean's next promotion resulted in his moving to Silicon Valley in 2004 when he became an Almaden Research Center executive in San Jose, California. He led researchers seeking alternatives to hard drives and searching for strategies to fulfill evolving computing needs. During 2007, Dean went to Africa as an IBM Global Innovation Outlook representative to discuss digital technological demands of individuals, companies, and governments. He wrote an article, "Mobile Phone, not PC, Bridges Digital Gap," printed in the *San Jose Mercury News* on February 10, 2008, which stated that wireless technology with diverse capabilities and resources will replace PCs for global populations to have affordable access to digitized information.

By 2008, Dean was serving as vice president of technical strategy and global operations for IBM Research. Interested in medical applications, he contributed his systems experience while overseeing research including computer simulations of such physiological processes as protein folding and a project with scientists from IBM and Stanford University's Center for Probing the Nanoscale enhancing magnetic resonance imaging (MRI) resolution performance to achieve 100 million times more precision than existing MRI technology.

Dean published articles in *IBM Journal of Research and Development* and numerous conference proceedings. He belongs to the IBM Academy of Technology and serves as a board member for the Computer History Museum. A National Society of Black Engineers volunteer, Dean speaks at high schools and colleges about his inventing experiences and African American engineers' technological accomplishments. He and his second wife, Denise, a former IBM executive, reside in Morgan Hill, California. Dean envisions infinite possibilities for technological achievements and continues inventing at IBM and mentoring colleagues, intending to extend his patent tally beyond the approximate forty he had acquired by the early twenty-first century.

Impact

Dean designed computers that were the catalyst for the information technology revolution in the late twentieth century. His innovations, specifically graphic display adapters and the ISA bus, improved PC performance and expanded acceptance and use of computers. Within the two decades after PC technology was introduced in the 1980's, computers no longer were confined to laboratories. PCs became standard tools in many businesses and homes, particularly because of features Dean made possible. Widespread use of PCs created employment opportunities in computer design and programming to develop improved systems and software for practical needs and entertainment. Dean's inventions helped generate billions of dollars from sales and salaries to expand and strengthen economies.

Dean's technical skills inspired other computer designers who appropriated his ISA bus design, which was available in the public domain, and built clones of IBM PCs. The computer industry expanded to produce hardware, especially desktops, and such peripherals as scanners, printers, and speakers. Faster microprocessors Dean developed also became broadly incorporated. Dean's inventions for early PCs remained fundamental to twenty-first century computer designs, with approximately ninety percent of modern PCs containing those components. Variations of the ISA concept he invented continued to be incorporated in computers despite alternatives such as the Peripheral Component Interconnect (PCI) bus.

Dean received numerous honors, such as the 1988 *PC Magazine* World Class Award, recognizing his contributions. In 1997, he became the third African American to be inducted into the National Inventors Hall of Fame, and he was presented with the Black Engineer of the Year President's Award and Ronald H. Brown American Innovators Award. Two years later, the National Society of Black Engineers gave Dean its Distinguished Engineer Award. Dean was Black Engineer of the Year in 2000. The next year, the National Academy of Engineering elected Dean for membership. Dean was selected as an Institute of Electrical and Electronics Engineers fellow in 2002. IBM rewarded Dean's contributions with multiple Invention Achievement Awards and Corporate Awards. In 2006, Dean accepted the National Institute of Science's Outstanding Scientist Award. Stanford University named Dean to its Multicultural Alumni Hall of Fame in 2007.

—*Elizabeth D. Schafer*

Further Reading

Barber, John T. *The Black Digital Elite: African American Leaders of the Information Revolution*. Westport, Conn.: Praeger, 2006. Chapter 3 features Dean, providing a biographical sketch and facts regarding his engineering accomplishments. Highlights Dean's attitudes concerning race and information technology and his suggestions for achieving success.

Governar, Alan. *Untold Glory: African Americans in Pursuit of Freedom, Opportunity, and Achievement*. New York: Harlem Moon/Broadway Books, 2007. In a March 7, 2005, interview, Dean discusses his educational and professional experiences and how he became interested in engineering. Presents details unavailable in other sources and two photographs.

Poletti, Therese. "IBM Research Chief a Tinkerer and Thinker." *San Jose Mercury News*, March 20, 2005, p. 1F. Examines Dean's work and aspirations at Almaden Research Center. Includes quotations and insights from colleagues and relatives. A Q&A section with Dean and two photographs supplement the article.

Reilly, Edwin D. *Milestones in Computer Science and Information Technology*. Westport, Conn.: Greenwood Press, 2003. Notes technical aspects of early bus technology in microcomputers and how the ISA bus Dean designed differed. Explains why Dean's invention became the preferred bus architecture.

Taborn, Tyrone D. "Separating Race from Technology: Finding Tomorrow's IT Progress in the Past." In *Learning Race and Ethnicity: Youth and Digital Media*, edited by Anna Everett. Cambridge, Mass.: MIT Press, 2008. Emphasizes Dean's significance as an African American technological role model who can inspire minority youth to seek digital competence and goals.

See also: Bill Gates; Ted Hoff; Steve Jobs; Steve Wozniak.

John Deere

American manufacturer

Deere developed a revolutionary steel plow that facilitated agriculture on the Great Plains in the United States, and he oversaw the growth of a company that eventually became a world leader in producing farm machinery.

Born: February 7, 1804; Rutland, Vermont
Died: May 17, 1886; Moline, Illinois
Primary fields: Agriculture; manufacturing
Primary invention: Steel plow

Early Life

John Deere, the fifth child of William and Sarah Deere, was born in 1804 in the farming hamlet of Rutland, Vermont, where his father worked as a merchant and tailor. William left the family in 1808 for a business trip to England and was never heard from again. Raised by his mother and older brothers, Deere apprenticed as a blacksmith at age fifteen and went to work as a journeyman four years later. Sometime during his apprenticeship, he began courting Demarius Lamb; they married in 1827. For more than a decade, Deere struggled to make his living as a blacksmith, sometimes hiring out to local shops, on other occasions attempting to run his own business. The glut of blacksmiths in the region, however, made it difficult for him to obtain sufficient work to pay off his debts, and fire damaged his shop on more than one occasion. Frustrated and unable to settle his financial obligations, in 1836 Deere sold his business and headed west. His pregnant wife and three young children remained behind, joining him a year later after he had established himself in the town of Grand Detour, Illinois. The tiny settlement on the Rock River needed a blacksmith, and there Deere began what would become a series of business ventures that would transform him from a simple tradesman into the head of a thriving farm implements manufacturing enterprise.

Life's Work

From the day he opened his shop in Grand Detour, Deere had all the work he could handle. One of the common tasks required of blacksmiths in the region was that

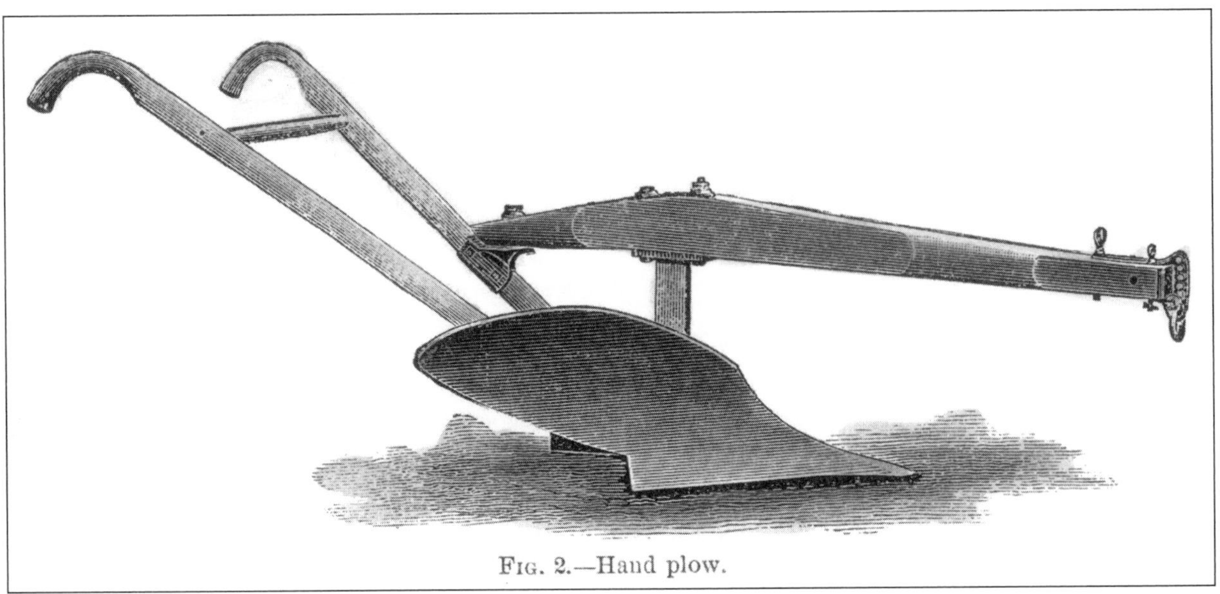

A wood engraving of John Deere's steel plow. (The Granger Collection, New York)

they manufacture and repair farm implements, including plows. In the 1830's, most of the cutting edges on both breaking plows (large instruments used to make first cuts in previously untilled soil) and cultivating plows (smaller ones used to prepare soil for planting) were then being made from wrought iron. Deere discovered that by creating blades from polished steel, he could provide farmers with a tool that would cut through the thick, clay prairie soil without becoming caked up, thus reducing time spent cleaning off the equipment. Deere began manufacturing steel plows in 1837, and for the next decade his skill in producing these implements, coupled with his zeal in promoting their use by farmers throughout the region, allowed him to increase his sales steadily. By 1846, he was turning out a thousand plows a year in his Grand Detour shop. In 1848, he decided to move his operations to Moline, seventy-five miles west on the banks of the Mississippi River. There he built a factory that took advantage of the latest innovations in manufacturing technology, allowing him to grow his business exponentially. Then and later he was aided by a workforce that consisted largely of immigrants who brought with them skills they had learned in Europe and a work ethic that helped the company meet the ever-increasing demand for a variety of plows and other farm machinery. Over the years, Deere developed exceptional loyalty among his workers, who appreciated his hands-on approach to business and his concern for their personal welfare.

Unfortunately, Deere's ability as a craftsman was not matched by a keen business sense. He tried on several occasions to establish partnerships, both in Grand Detour and Moline. At one time or another he was a principal in companies that bore names like L. Andrus and Company; Deere, Atkinson, and Company; Deere, Tate, and Gould; John Deere and Company; Deere and Company; and the Moline Plow Factory. Throughout his years as an active businessman, Deere struggled with credit problems—sometimes as the one in debt but just as often as the one to whom money was owed. He also had to deal with competition that frequently pirated his innovations (although on occasion he, too, was accused of stealing ideas from others), and he found himself involved in numerous lawsuits over patent and trademark rights. The most famous of these lawsuits involved a rival company set up by former associates of Deere who called their business the Moline Plow Company. That name was similar to the one Deere was then using to identify his product, "the Moline Plow." Customers were often confused by the similarity and sometimes sent business to the rival company. In a suit lasting more than four years, Deere finally won a judgment that gave him public credit for his work in developing his special line of plows. An appeals court judge reversed the decision, however, forcing Deere to abandon the generic name for his plow and identify it more closely with Deere and Company.

One of the most significant events in Deere's career occurred in 1858, when his son Charles, who had joined the firm in 1854, became general manager of his father's company. Trained in business and innately adept at management and strategic planning, the younger Deere moved quickly to reorganize operations to take advantage of the growing demand for farm implements not only in the region but throughout the country as well. John Deere's sons-in-law and a few key associates joined Charles in running daily operations. By the second half of the century, Deere's company was selling plows, cultivators, harrows, drills and planters, and even wagons and buggies. John Deere even experimented with development of a steam-driven plow to replace those dragged by animals; unfortunately, this primitive tractor was too far ahead of its time to be of practical value.

In the years after the Civil War, Deere withdrew from active management of the company that bore his name, spending more of his time working his own farm outside Moline and becoming more involved in civic and philanthropic affairs. Although he was designated as president of the newly formed corporation Deere and Company in 1868, he watched from the sidelines as Charles led the firm to a position of national prominence as one of America's leading manufacturing firms for farm equipment. In 1873, Deere and Company introduced a new trademark: the leaping deer. By 1875, company revenues exceeded $1 million, and it had established branch offices in places like Kansas City, St. Louis, Minneapolis, and Council Bluffs, Iowa, to help respond more quickly to the needs of the population in areas far removed from Moline.

Deere's wife died in February, 1865. A year later, he went back to Vermont to marry her sister Lusena, bringing her back to Moline to run his household. In April, 1873, Deere was elected for a one-year term as mayor of Moline, during which he found himself at the center of a battle to impose temperance ordinances throughout the city. He worked diligently to upgrade the city's infrastructure, especially street improvements and fire protection. Deere also found time to make frequent trips back to Vermont and out to the West Coast. In 1885, Deere's health began to fail, and despite trips to resort areas designed to aid in recovery, he continued to decline steadily. He died in May, 1886.

IMPACT

Deere's innovations in the design of plows and other agricultural equipment aided in the emergence of the Midwest as the breadbasket of America. Most immediately, his plow provided farmers a way to till more acreage without having to stop frequently to clean their equipment, which constantly accumulated clods of the sticky soil characteristic of the region. Additionally, Deere's

THE STEEL PLOW

The legend surrounding John Deere's "invention" of the steel plow has many elements of typical American folklore. Ostensibly, Deere took a piece of discarded steel blade from a commercial sawmill, chiseled off the teeth, and shaped the flat steel into a shining plowshare that would slide through thick, sticky prairie soil, creating long, straight furrows. Almost overnight, farmers discarded their old wrought iron plows for those manufactured from steel, thereby creating a revolution in American agriculture.

There are elements of truth in the story, but the actual creation of Deere's plow is somewhat more prosaic. Deere did, in fact, fashion his first plow from a piece of discarded steel. Knowing that midwestern farmers were having to stop frequently to clean off parts of their plows that were constantly being clogged by the heavy black humus they were trying to cultivate, Deere imagined that a plowshare (the cutting blade) and its attendant moldboard (the device that turned over the soil to create neat furrows for planting) might be more effective if made from a material that would resist such contamination. Already familiar with the properties of polished steel, Deere took advantage of the opportunity presented to him by reshaping the steel and fashioning the wooden handles and shafts himself. One of his principal innovations was to shape the moldboard into a parallelogram that permitted the farmer to turn the soil more easily as it was cut.

Properly speaking, however, Deere did not invent the steel plow; others had experimented with steel in constructing plows before Deere manufactured his instrument. His principal contribution was to create a plow that was effective in reducing the amount of clogging farmers experienced when plowing the rich prairie soil. Although the first plows Deere created have been lost, early versions still available suggest he often combined steel and wrought iron in his designs—probably depending on what materials he had available at the time. As he became more successful in his business, he was able to use more steel, which he obtained from mills in the eastern United States. An additional key to his success lay in the combination of inventiveness with a strong belief in the principle of constant improvement. Never fully satisfied with a product once he had begun to market it, Deere was continually consulting with farmers to learn how he might modify his plows to perform even better.

constant effort to improve the quality and functionality of his products led to the development of new and better machines that allowed farmers to cultivate and harvest larger tracts of land. Although not a shrewd businessman himself, Deere managed to surround himself with family and associates who understood how to organize and grow a company in what was sometimes a hostile business climate. Despite his personal limitations, Deere served as a model for those with whom he worked; his determination to succeed as a business owner in a highly competitive market led to the eventual growth of his company into one of the country's leading manufacturing enterprises.

—*Laurence W. Mazzeno*

FURTHER READING

Broehl, Wayne. *John Deere's Company: A History of Deere and Company and Its Times*. New York: Doubleday, 1984. Comprehensive account of the founding and growth of John Deere's business, from its inception to the 1980's. Contains numerous photographs, charts, and other pertinent business data.

Clark, Neil M. *John Deere: He Gave the World the Steel Plow*. Moline, Ill.: Desaulniers, 1937. Illustrated narrative dramatizing Deere's life and accomplishments as an inventor and businessman, commissioned by the Deere company to commemorate the one hundredth anniversary of the creation of the steel plow.

Dahlstrom, Neil, and Jeremy Dahlstrom. *The John Deere Story: A Biography of Plowmakers John and Charles Deere*. De Kalb, Ill.: Northern Illinois University Press, 2005. Well-researched and highly readable biography of the two men who transformed John Deere's idea for a useful, marketable plow into one of the world's great manufacturing companies.

Magee, David. *The John Deere Way: Performance That Endures*. Hoboken, N.J.: Wiley, 2005. Examines the business climate of John Deere's company at the turn of the twenty-first century, explaining how the values and vision of its founder have been preserved and strengthened by successors who transformed the original company into a highly successful worldwide enterprise.

See also: Thomas Jefferson; Cyrus Hall McCormick; Jethro Tull.

LEE DE FOREST

American radio engineer and scientist

De Forest's pioneering work in developing the technology for wireless reception paved the way for the development of radio, and his efforts to perfect the process for printing sound on film were instrumental in launching the era of "talking" motion pictures.

Born: August 26, 1873; Council Bluffs, Iowa
Died: June 30, 1961; Hollywood, California
Primary fields: Communications; electronics and electrical engineering
Primary inventions: Audion (triode vacuum tube); talking motion pictures

EARLY LIFE

Lee De Forest was born in Council Bluffs, Iowa, in 1873, the eldest child of a Congregationalist minister. When he was six years old, his father accepted the presidency of Talladega College in Alabama, an institution founded in 1865 to educate newly freed African Americans. Life in the Deep South was hard on a boy whose family was shunned by the white community, and De Forest spent much of his time on his own. At an early age, he showed an interest in science and engineering, and he was especially fascinated by the work of America's best known inventor, Thomas Alva Edison. When he was seventeen, his father, assuming his son would pursue studies to become a minister, sent him to a preparatory school in Boston to ready him for entrance to a university. In 1893, De Forest entered Yale, but instead of matriculating at Yale College, he enrolled at Yale's Sheffield Scientific School. While an undergraduate, he developed an interest in electricity and electrical engineering. After graduation in 1896, he stayed at Yale to pursue a doctorate. He chose as his dissertation topic a study of the action of short Hertzian waves (radio waves)—exceptionally good preparation for a young man intent on making a name for himself in the newly developing field of wireless technology.

After receiving his Ph.D., De Forest headed to Chicago and found a job with Western Electric, where he proved to be a mediocre employee but an inveterate tinkerer. The new field of wireless communications was just then achieving worldwide attention, as the Italian

Guglielmo Marconi had only recently demonstrated that it was possible to send and receive signals through the air over relatively long distances. De Forest was determined to make his mark in that arena. Though officials at Western Electric saw no future for the company in wireless communications, De Forest spent considerable time (much of it after-hours) developing a responder that might be used to receive sound waves sent from some distance away. Let go by Western Electric in 1900, he spent the next year working as a teacher and translator of scientific publications, devoting his spare time to perfecting the device he called a "Sponder." He considered his device ready for public testing in 1901. With two associates as partners, he set off to make his fortune in wireless telegraphy.

Lee De Forest holds his invention, the triode vacuum tube, or audion. (Getty Images)

Life's Work

In 1901 at the America's Cup yacht races, De Forest demonstrated to the world the practicability of his responder, transmitting results from the race course to New York as Marconi had done two years earlier. In that year, he organized his first corporation, the Wireless Telegraph Company of America, the first of what would eventually be more than two dozen firms set up to promote his inventions. Although most in the community of inventors and investors were still skeptical of the device's reliability, one man stepped forward to serve as a backer: Abraham White. In 1902, White became De Forest's principal champion, helping organize a number of business enterprises that, in reality, were little more than shell corporations designed to allow White and several unscrupulous investors to take advantage of the notoriety of the new communications medium and De Forest's business naïveté. De Forest was given a modest salary and set up in an office where the public could see him working on his inventions. His principal residence became New York City, where he lived for more than two decades. In 1904, his equipment was featured at the St. Louis World's Fair. All the while, White was making outrageous and sometimes blatantly false claims about the success of the company and De Forest's inventions, selling stock to gullible investors. Little of this income was invested in research; most went to further advertising gimmicks and into White's pockets. De Forest may not have been aware of the extent to which his partner was defrauding the public. The two had a falling out in 1906 when legal challenges were made to De Forest's rights to market some of his equipment. De Forest eventually lost his company and was once again nearly penniless. To make matters worse, in 1906 he entered into a disastrous marriage that lasted only a few months. He would marry and divorce twice more between 1907 and 1928.

By 1906, De Forest had begun experimenting with a new form of receiver based on the work of British inventor John Ambrose Fleming. Convinced that a two-electrode vacuum tube filled with gas could be used to detect and amplify radio waves, he modified one that Fleming had designed and filed for a patent, which was granted in 1906. Not fully satisfied with his device, he continued to tinker with it, eventually adding a third component to his tube, a gridiron-shaped piece of metal inserted between the original electrodes. This tiny piece of metal allowed him to control the flow of electrons in the tube and amplify sounds sent to a listening device. Patented in early 1908, the audion, as De Forest would call it, would be the invention that assured him a place among the world's most important inventors, as it was the device that would eventually allow reception and amplification of the human voice and other sounds—the basis for modern radio.

Curiously, De Forest did not realize the significance of his discovery. Working on wireless technology, he was satisfied that the device provided sufficient amplitude to allow listeners to pick up telegraphic signals sent through the air. Since 1902, De Forest had invested considerable energy and time marketing his wireless system to the U.S. Navy and later to the United Fruit Company. Both organizations saw the benefit of being able to communicate by wireless to ships at sea, and for a time De Forest was successful in raising capital and generating profits from his venture. Unfortunately, the Panic of 1907 had caused investors to look warily at wireless telegraphy, and over the years that skepticism turned into efforts to seek legal recourse against inventors and companies that had not delivered on promises of improved technology and handsome dividends.

In 1912, De Forest and several associates in his new company were sued for fraud. To raise capital, he tried to sell several of his patents to American Telephone and Telegraph Company (AT&T) for $500,000, but AT&T's representative eventually negotiated a deal to purchase them for a mere $50,000. The same story was repeated in numerous instances throughout De Forest's career, as one grand idea after another brought him only a fraction of the millions he thought he deserved for his hard work and ingenuity. Although De Forest was acquitted two years later, he was once again without sufficient financial support to continue as an independent entrepreneur. To make matters worse, his claim to have invented a device to amplify sound was challenged in 1914 by Edwin H. Armstrong, who had developed and patented a similar device two years earlier. The ensuing litigation was not settled until 1926, long after De Forest had lost interest in wireless telegraphy and turned his attention to a new topic, the possibility of producing motion pictures with sound.

Beginning in 1913, De Forest concentrated on perfecting a system for capturing sounds that could be attached in some way to motion-picture film. In his view, this would not only allow viewers to hear actors as they spoke their lines but also per-

The Audion

The development of the audion, or triode vacuum tube, has been called one of the most significant technological inventions of all time. While Lee De Forest is generally credited with this invention, his work actually was closely linked to the earlier invention of a diode tube by John Ambrose Fleming and the later creation of a feedback circuit by Edwin H. Armstrong—although De Forest claimed to have been solely responsible for adapting Fleming's diode and for indirectly creating the feedback circuit. Interested in improving receivers for wireless telegraphy, De Forest began experimenting with improvements on Fleming's diode almost immediately after Fleming received his U.S. patent in 1905. In just a little more than a year, De Forest applied for his own patent, claiming his device was notably different from Fleming's and a significant advance in receiving telegraph signals via sound waves sent from locations miles away from his receiver.

Technically, De Forest's audion worked on the principle of radio waves' ability to affect electrical current. The first audion was a diode tube quite similar to Fleming's. It consisted of a gas-filled glass cylinder containing a filament, an arrangement similar to an incandescent light bulb, into which a second metal plate was inserted. The positive terminal of a 22-volt battery was connected to the metal plate, and a pair of headphones added to the circuit; the negative terminal was connected to the lamp filament. Almost immediately after De Forest obtained his first patent for the audion in 1906, he began making modifications to his device. The most significant alternation consisted of the insertion of a thin metal wire, bent in the shape of a gridiron, between the filament and the plate. Doing so allowed him to regulate the flow of electrical current being generated by the action of the radio waves, permitting a continuous flow of electricity and making it possible to "tune" the receptor to achieve greater audibility. De Forest did not progress further with his invention at the time, satisfied that he could receive and detect telegraphic signals with sufficient accuracy to make the audion commercially successful as a receiver for wireless telegraphy. He did take steps to demonstrate how the audion could be used to transmit voice and music, "broadcasting" programs as early as 1907. Soon, a method for achieving sufficient amplification was available, attained by linking a number of audions in sequence. The original headphones were soon replaced by speakers, and the radio industry was born.

mit filming of events such as concerts and operatic performances, which could then be viewed in movie theaters by thousands who for reasons of money or location could not attend live performances. For nearly a decade, De Forest sought ways to imprint sound directly on film, and by 1922 he had managed to do so. In that year, he began demonstrating his new invention publicly. Calling his products "Phonofilms," De Forest recorded speeches, short dramas, symphonies, and operas (including a performance by renowned tenor Enrico Caruso). Unfortunately, he was not able to interest the major movie studios in his process, and since these controlled most movie houses in America, he was forced to show his Phonofilms in small independent theaters. Nevertheless, those who saw his productions marveled at this new phenomenon. It was not long before Hollywood took notice, although studio officials decided not to purchase De Forest's sound-on-film technology. Instead, they opted to develop their own systems, initially settling on one that used a disc for sound that accompanied the film. Once again, De Forest failed to profit substantially from his invention.

As with all his other business ventures, De Forest's Phonofilm Corporation failed to generate sufficient capital to remain solvent. His various radio companies eventually went bankrupt as well, and their assets were purchased by the Radio Corporation of America (RCA). By 1929, De Forest's financial situation appeared dire, and he determined he would no longer try to make a living in New York. In 1930, he moved to California to restart his career as an inventor for the movie industry. He married for a fourth time in 1930, and that union proved lasting.

The last years of De Forest's life brought mixed success. Beginning in 1930 with his election to a one-year term as president of the Institute of Radio Engineers, De Forest waged a campaign against what he considered the overcommercialization of radio during the 1920's. Believing the medium was best used for transmission of high-quality programming with limited commercials, he spoke and wrote against the trend toward excessive advertising and the inclusion of programming that catered to what he considered lower-class tastes (including jazz, which he excoriated on more than one occasion). He declared bankruptcy in 1936 but continued working on inventions and filing for patents on devices aimed at improving movie production and projection. He even developed some rudimentary devices that would eventually be used to launch the television industry. During World War II, he made himself available to the government, assisting the Navy by constructing a terrain altimeter that allowed pilots to determine their positions over the ocean with greater accuracy.

By the 1940's, the radio industry began to acknowledge De Forest's role in launching the medium. He received several tributes, and media began referring to him by the title he had long used to describe himself, the "father of radio." In 1959, he received an honorary Oscar from the Academy of Motion Picture Arts and Sciences for his pioneering work in the industry. All the while, however, he was struggling to make a living by selling some of his inventions and working at various radio schools. Although he was granted more than two hundred patents during his lifetime, none proved substantially remunerative. He never retired, instead continuing to go to his laboratory in Hollywood every day to investigate new ways to improve products and processes for the electronics industry. He died on June 30, 1961, believing (with some justification) that he had played a major role in ushering in the electronic age worldwide.

Impact

Determining the true extent of De Forest's contributions to technological advancement requires considerable skill in sorting out myth from fact. Throughout his life, De Forest made great claims for himself as the "father of radio" and insisted that he had done more than any other inventor to advance the development of this new medium. Not everyone agreed with him then or later, and many scientists and historians have downplayed his contributions by pointing out his deficiencies as a theorist. Nevertheless, there is no question that the audion he designed in 1905-1906 and improved in 1907 by adding a grid that permitted better reception and amplification of sound was a key component in allowing for the future development of radio. At the time, De Forest himself did not realize the significance of his invention, and it was not until Edwin H. Armstrong modified De Forest's original design to improve amplification that commercial radio became feasible. In a similar fashion, De Forest's work in perfecting a mechanism for producing talking movies by imprinting sound on film to allow for synchronous transmission of picture and sound was revolutionary. Unfortunately, the major studios refused to work with him or to adopt his technology, choosing instead to develop other methods for generating talking pictures. By the time the movie industry adopted his sound-on-film method years later, the "talkies" had become standard fare at movie houses across the United States.

What is clear, however, is that De Forest's pioneering

work in developing the audion made radio possible. Similarly, his efforts to market his Phonofilms during the mid-1920's spurred major movie studios into action to move from silent films to talking pictures, if only as a means of capitalizing on the public's curiosity with the films De Forest was presenting to limited audiences. There is also strong evidence to suggest that De Forest's work with the federal government, particularly the Navy, advanced the military's ability to communicate at sea and conduct air warfare more effectively. While claims advanced by some that he should be considered the "father of the electronic age" may be exaggerated, it is not too much to say that his work was vital to the emergence of new methods of communication that materially improved the lives of American citizens and radically changed lifestyles throughout the country.

—*Laurence W. Mazzeno*

FURTHER READING

Douglas, George H. *The Early Days of Radio Broadcasting*. Jefferson, N.C.: McFarland, 1987. History of the early days of commercial radio, focusing on the decade between 1920 and 1930. Includes a brief sketch of De Forest's career and contributions to the industry.

Douglas, Susan J. *Inventing American Broadcasting, 1899-1922*. Baltimore: The Johns Hopkins University Press, 1987. Detailed examination of early attempts to develop commercially viable wireless technology. Extensive analysis of De Forest's contributions to the industry, as both an inventor and entrepreneur.

Hijiya, James. *Lee De Forest and the Fatherhood of Radio*. Bethlehem, Pa.: Lehigh University Press, 1992. Biography focusing on De Forest's character. Searches for the sparks that motivated him as an inventor and entrepreneur.

Maclaurin, William Rupert. *Invention and Innovation in the Radio Industry*. New York: Arno Press, 1971. Discusses De Forest's career in the context of a larger survey of technological advancements in the radio industry. Explores the causes for these developments and examines the impact of the new medium on American society.

Riordan, Michael, and Lillian Hoddeson. *Crystal Fire: The Birth of the Information Age*. New York: W. W. Norton, 1997. Traces the growth of the electronics industry resulting from the development of the transistor, an advance on the audion. Explains the importance of De Forest's invention to spurring the growth of the radio industry and leading to advances in communications technology.

Schubert, Paul. *The Electric Word: The Rise of Radio*. New York: Arno Press, 1971. Reprint of a 1928 book detailing the emergence of the radio industry, tracing the development of wireless technology and placing De Forest's career in the context of worldwide efforts to commercialize this new method of communication.

Weightman, Gavin. *Signor Marconi's Magic Box*. Cambridge, Mass.: Da Capo Press, 2003. Describes De Forest's contributions to the development of radio and sketches his relationship with the inventor Guglielmo Marconi, with whom he had a brief rivalry.

Zouary, Maurice H. *De Forest: Father of the Electronic Revolution*. Rev. ed. Bloomington, Ind.: 1st Books Library, 2000. Highly dramatic retelling of De Forest's career, celebrating his achievements in ushering in the electronic revolution. Includes clippings of news stories and other documents that attest to his accomplishments.

See also: Edwin H. Armstrong; Walter H. Brattain; Karl Ferdinand Braun; Thomas Alva Edison; Reginald Aubrey Fessenden; Guglielmo Marconi.

Sir James Dewar

Scottish physicist and chemist

Dewar is probably best known for the Dewar flask, the vacuum flask or bottle used for storing hot or cold substances. He is also a coinventor of cordite, the smokeless gunpowder. Scientists know Dewar best for his research in low-temperature physics.

Born: September 20, 1842; Kincardine-on-Forth, Scotland
Died: March 27, 1923; London, England
Primary field: Chemistry
Primary invention: Dewar flask

Early Life

James Dewar was the youngest of six sons born to Thomas and Agnes Eadie Dewar. Thomas, owner of the principal inn of Kincardine, the Unicorn Inn, was well respected and was often called on to witness legal papers. Dewar lost his mother in 1852. During the winter of that year, he fell through the ice while skating and contracted rheumatic fever, which forced him to walk with crutches and to miss school for two years. During this time, he developed a love of literature and became friends with the village joiner, who taught him how to build violins. One violin that Dewar built in 1854 was played at his fiftieth wedding anniversary in 1921. (Dewar claimed that part of his skill as an experimenter was the result of the hand dexterity that he developed during this time.) Dewar attended the New Subscription School, where he was a top student before his illness, and continued to excel academically after his bout of rheumatic fever.

Upon his father's death in 1857, Dewar lived with a brother for a time before boarding with Dr. Lindsay, a brilliant teacher at the Dollar Institution, where Dewar flourished under the mentorship. In 1859, Dewar entered the University of Edinburgh, where he earned first-class honors in 1862. Dewar was taught chemistry by Lyon Playfair (later Lord Playfair), who became his doctoral adviser. Dewar's first scientific publication was read by Playfair in 1867 at the Royal Society of Edinburgh, in which Dewar was not yet a member (he would be inducted in 1869). After receiving his degree from Edinburgh, he became an assistant to the new chair of chemistry, Alexander Crum Brown. Crum Brown had developed a method to represent benzene more conveniently than the method used by German organic chemist August Kekulé. Dewar then developed a machine to print Crum Brown's new graphic notation. Playfair sent a copy of the instrument to Kekulé, who invited Dewar to his laboratory for a summer. In 1869, Dewar became a professor at the Royal (Dick) Veterinary College, where he was an effective, enthusiastic teacher. Dewar married Helen Rose Banks in 1871. Their marriage was a happy one.

Life's Work

Research was Dewar's primary interest. While at the veterinary college in Edinburgh, he introduced himself to John Gray McKendrick. They began a study of the physiological effects of light, discovering that a measurable electrical current is produced when light enters the eye. This effect was studied using eyes from several different animals.

In 1875, Dewar was appointed Jacksonian Professor

The Dewar Flask

The loss or gain of heat energy can occur by several methods. Among those methods are conduction, convection, and radiation. Sir James Dewar invented a container to stop—or at least drastically slow down—heat transfer. He used glass, which is a poor heat conductor. By placing one glass container inside another container, he was able to eliminate the conduction of heat. By creating a vacuum between the two glass containers, he eliminated convection of heat. The vacuum side of the glass containers was coated with silver, allowing the reflection of radiation and thus preventing heat transfer by radiation. Often the two containers were made from the same piece of glass with a small hole to pull a vacuum and to apply the silver coating. A durable container of wood or metal held the glass container. Either wood shims or a small spring held the glass away from the outer container, thus creating another conduction barrier. In modern versions of Dewar's flask, such as the Thermos bottle, plastic is often used for the outer shell.

The Dewar flask was invented to store cold materials. Without the ability to store liquid oxygen or nitrogen for a period of time, the cold liquid was useless for experimentation. Dewar's flasks could be used to store liquids such as oxygen for days and even weeks. However, Dewar did not patent his design, and as a result, the Thermos company was able to profit from Dewar's design with its famous Thermos bottle, which today is used for many types of portable, cold- and heat-preserving storage devices.

Sir James Dewar in 1911. (©Smithsonian Institution)

of Natural Experimental Philosophy at Cambridge University, where he collaborated with colleague George D. Liveing in a twenty-seven-year partnership that produced seventy-eight papers on spectroscopy. In 1877, Dewar became the Fullerian Professor of Chemistry at the Royal Institution in London. He kept both chairs, dividing his time between Cambridge and London. London had much better research facilities and was the place where his most noteworthy research was done. It was there that he began to work in the field of low-temperature physics. He had to devise the equipment necessary to study the characteristics of materials at low temperatures. It was at the Royal Institution that Michael Faraday had done the initial work on liquefaction of gases.

By the end of 1877, the equipment to produce liquid oxygen had been built in the Royal Institution's laboratory. Dewar even created an optical projector that allowed an audience to watch oxygen become a liquid. Soon he had produced a machine that would generate twenty liters of liquid oxygen per hour. This was easily a sufficient amount to use in experiments to determine properties of materials at low temperature. In one study, Dewar tested the electrical resistance of metals at very low temperatures, finding that the electrical resistance decreased as the temperature was lowered. It was concluded that if the temperature could be lowered to absolute zero, there would be no resistance. Dewar could never reach absolute zero but did achieve temperatures lower than anyone else had at the time. Another study found that seeds that were cooled to liquid nitrogen or liquid oxygen temperatures did not lose the ability to germinate. Dewar also determined the heat capacity of elements at the boiling point of hydrogen (–252° Celsius). He found that liquid oxygen and liquid ozone were attracted to the poles of a magnet.

Without the ability to store liquid oxygen or liquid nitrogen for a period of time, the cold liquid was useless for experimentation. Dewar designed vacuum flasks that could store such liquids for days and even weeks. He did not choose to patent the design, however, and the Thermos company eventually based its famous bottle on his design.

The use of supercooled charcoal as an absorbing agent is another outstanding invention. It allowed metals to be used to build Dewar flasks. Metals continually give off a small amount of gas, which ruins the vacuum needed to produce a good Dewar flask. Supercooled charcoal is an excellent absorber, allowing the retention of the necessary vacuum. In some situations, Dewar used supercooled charcoal to produce a vacuum. Some of his research with the absorbent qualities of charcoal led to its use in gas masks.

In 1888, as a member of the Explosives Commission with Sir Frederick Abel, Dewar invented cordite. Cordite is a smokeless powder that became the standard powder used in munitions. Dewar also invented a portable device to carry oxygen. This device was to be used to prevent altitude sickness in soldiers during airplane trips.

When World War I began, the resources and manpower to continue the low-temperature work were not available. Sir Dewar (knighted in 1904) began to study surface tension in soap bubbles. He continued this work until his death on March 27, 1923. In fact, he was at work late one evening just a few days before his death.

Impact

Nonscientists are perhaps most familiar with Dewar's invention from the Thermos bottle based on it. This and similar products have made it possible to carry hot and cold liquids to picnics or to work for lunch. Even ice chests to transport food are based on the concept of the Dewar flask.

Dewar's invention has allowed scientists to be able to conduct low-temperature studies. The modern scientist thinks nothing of having a "Dewar" of liquid nitrogen for use in research for a week or more. Sir James Dewar made this possible. Today many scientific instruments use liquid nitrogen to maintain a low operating temperature. This use of liquid nitrogen is possible because containers built on the concept of the Dewar flask can hold cold materials for days and weeks.

More than producing the tools for low-temperature studies, Dewar showed scientists how to conduct low-temperature studies. With John Ambrose Fleming, Dewar studied conduction, thermoelectricity, dielectric constants, and magnetic permeability of metals and alloys at low temperatures. With Sir William Crookes, he studied the emanations from radium. Following the work with Crookes, he worked with Pierre Curie on the gas given off by radium. Dewar opened up the whole new field of low temperature science through his inventions and his leadership.

An area of study related to the Dewar flask was the production of extreme vacuum. The better the vacuum inside the flask, the better the flask was at maintaining the temperature of the material inside. The use of supercooled charcoal as a gas-absorbing material made it possible to use a pump to enhance and maintain the vacuum inside the walls of the Dewar flask.

Finally, Dewar and Abel's invention of cordite made it possible to eliminate the smoke produced by gun cotton. Cordite is an explosive consisting of nitroglycerine and gun cotton in cords or threads. The resulting stable explosive was found to be superior to anything that the British military had previously possessed. The invention of cordite therefore improved the safety of soldiers and vastly improved the ability of commanders to communicate on the battlefield.

—*C. Alton Hassell*

Further Reading

Armstrong, Henry E. *James Dewar*. London: Ernest Benn, 1924. Dewar had asked that no book of his life be published. His friend Henry Armstong gave a Friday evening lecture to the members of the Royal Institution about Dewar which he then published. It is an informative, personal look at Sir James Dewar.

Crichton-Browne, Sir James. "Annual Report of the Board of Regents of the Smithsonian Institution." *Science Progress* (July, 1923): 547-553. Sir Crichton-Browne knew Dewar and presents a summary of his life, providing the insights of a contemporary.

Dewar, Lady, ed. *Collected Papers of Sir James Dewar*. Cambridge, England: Cambridge University Press, 1927. After Dewar's death, several friends and colleagues of Dewar aided Lady Dewar in producing a compilation the papers that Dewar published, except those published in the *Collected Papers on Spectroscopy* by G. D. Liveing and Sir J. Dewar (1915).

Young, H. *A Record of the Scientific Work of Sir James Dewar*. London: Chiswick Press, 1933. Focuses on the work of Dewar rather than his life. An intriguing look at the many different areas of science to which Dewar contributed.

See also: Sir William Crookes; Michael Faraday; Heike Kamerlingh Onnes; Hudson Maxim; Alfred Nobel.

Rudolf Diesel

German mechanical engineer

At the outset of his career, Diesel sought to develop a fuel-driven power source that could replace the unwieldy steam engine. The possibility of internal combustion technology was just emerging. As Diesel's experimentation with pressure-ignited engines evolved, the system that bears his name managed to rival, and even to surpass, fuel-efficiency levels in standard gasoline-powered engines.

Born: March 18, 1858; Paris, France
Died: September 29, 1913; presumed drowned at sea in the English Channel
Also known as: Rudolf Christian Karl Diesel (full name)
Primary fields: Automotive technology; mechanical engineering
Primary invention: Diesel engine

Early Life

Rudolf Christian Karl Diesel (DEE-zuhl) was born to Theodor and Elise Diesel (née Strobel) in Paris, France. Although both parents were from established German families (he from Augsburg, she originally from Nuremberg), they met in Paris but were married in 1855 in London. They had three children: Louise, born in 1856; Rudolf, in 1858; and Emma, in 1860. Rudolf's childhood and early adolescence were spent in Paris, where his father began a business manufacturing fine leather products. Business difficulties, as well as repercussions of the Franco-Prussian War of 1870, would eventually force the family to move back to Germany in 1877. In the interim, Rudolf was sent to Augsburg, where he studied first in a commercial school and then in the Augsburg industrial school. His experience in the latter school convinced him that he wanted to pursue a career in engineering.

In 1875, he graduated with excellent grades and went on to attend the Technische Hochschule in Munich, where he received enthusiastic support from a well-known professor, Karl Max von Bauernfeind. Another individual who influenced Diesel during his studies in Munich was Carl von Linde, whose lectures focused on the developing industrial use of steam engines. By 1881, Diesel had begun his career as an engineer in the newly founded Paris branch of the German Linde Refrigeration firm. His interest in using compressed-gas technology as a power source in engines was sparked during this time.

Life's Work

Between 1881 and 1889, Diesel filled a number of roles as an employee of Linde Refrigeration. Although some of his service, both in France and in Germany, involved work as a sales representative, Diesel's early engineering research was already focused on a main problem raised by his professors: surpassing the efficiency performance—in terms of both fuel consumption and compression levels reached—of the steam engine. Demands of the refrigeration industry already involved procedures for compressing gases and therefore the use of an external engine power source. The challenge was to devise a self-contained power source to provide mechanical energy. Diesel's first accomplishments, for example, were associated with experiments (ultimately unsuccessful) with an internal combustion engine using ammonia vapors.

In 1893, his work gained wider attention when he published a pamphlet titled *Theorie und Konstruktion eines rationellen Wärmemotors* (theory and construction of a rational heat engine). Two important engineering firms, the Krupp works and Heinrich Buz's Augsburg Engine Works, were the first to back his endeavors to design a high-compression engine that, according to Diesel's claims, could obtain more than 70 percent conversion of the heat energy supplied by burning fuel into mechanical power via pistons in an internal combustion cylindrical chamber.

After a few unsuccessful experiences (following rejection of his first request for a patent in 1892), Diesel's report on the product of his work at the 1897 meeting of the German Engineers' Association was followed by his first commercial contract for his engine: Adolphus Busch, the German American head of the well-known brewery, bought the rights to Diesel's U.S. and Canadian patents. The first two-cylinder, sixty-horsepower diesel engine (manufactured in Germany) was installed in the Anheuser-Busch Brewery in 1898. Headquarters of the Diesel Motor Company of America (with Adolphus Busch as president) were set up in the same year in New York City.

Within two years, the industrial prospects of Diesel's engines suddenly became internationally recognized when he won the Grand Prix at the Paris World Fair in 1900. During the 1890's, Diesel had applied his theory of constant-pressure combustion to ignite—that is, explode—fuel to create the expanding energy to drive the

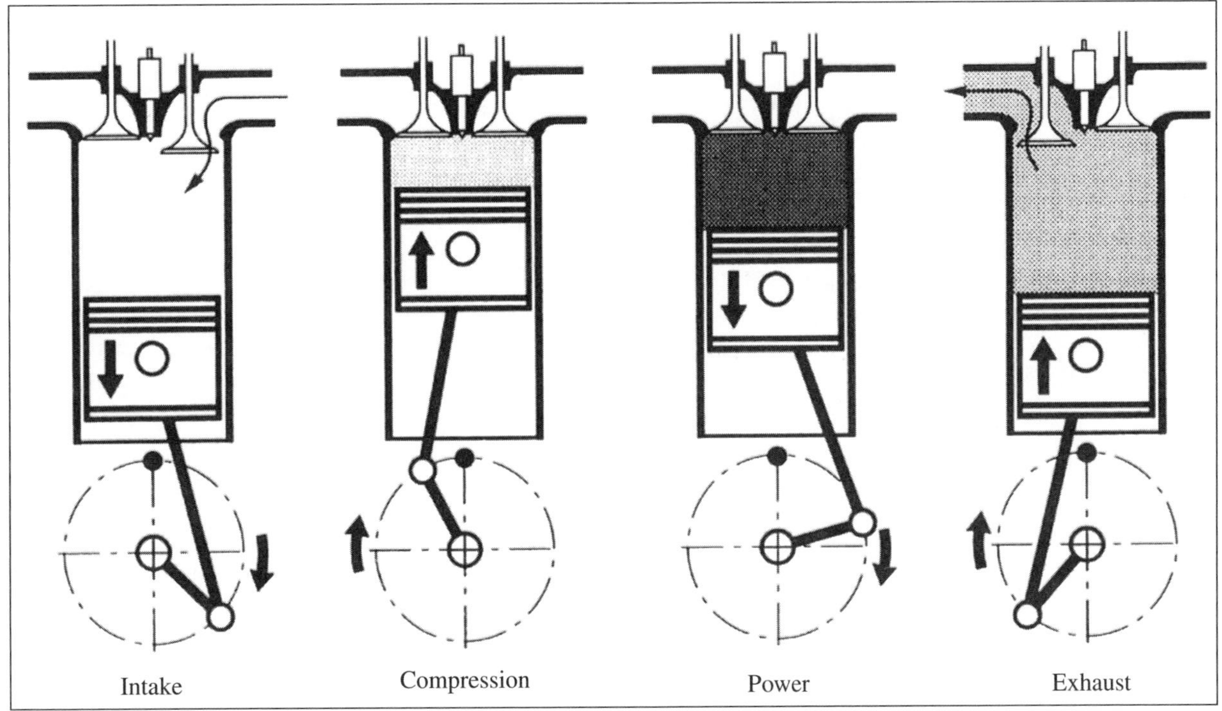

The four strokes of a diesel engine. (Robert Bosch Corporation)

cylinders of his experimental engine. His design used compression ignition instead of the spark-plug technology of the gasoline-powered engine.

As late as 1896, he had achieved only a 54 percent conversion of heat energy into mechanical power, and Krupp almost decided to drop involvement in further development plans. Over the next year, Diesel concentrated his efforts on key improvements: developing a fully unified combustion chamber for both cylinder heads and pistons, and introducing what he called a sieve vaporizer to improve the combustibility of fuel at the point of injection. His success was marked by a striking improvement in the conversion of heat energy into mechanical power, which went up to nearly 76 percent. Pressure ratings within the cylinders reached 34 atmospheres, or 500 pounds per square inch (psi). This surpassed the steam engine's net efficiency (a combination of indices) by a wide margin, although more work had to be done to achieve the mechanical efficiency of steam devices.

Step-by-step improvements brought not only a Grand Prix in Paris in 1900 but also an expansion in the number of patents that could be marketed by Krupp and the Augsburg Engine Works. At this stage, diesel engines were used mainly in heavy industrial applications; the models produced, therefore, were quite large and bulky.

Although the basic engineering principles of diesel engine (fuel combustion induced by high temperatures produced by high compression levels in cylinders) remained essentially the same as the years passed, major efforts went into finding an optimum fuel. Experimentation with fuel substances ranged from liquids derived from soft-coal extracts (used first in American-produced engines) to pure peanut oil, which Diesel's engine used at the Paris World Fair. Some early twentieth century engines used kerosene to start up, switching to pure alcohol for extended (and apparently more efficient) operation. This option was abandoned not only because of the higher cost of alcohol but also because such engines were particularly delicate when fitted with complex fuel injectors and air-density regulator devices. Until late twentieth century energy cost considerations encouraged researchers to return attention to fuels derived from vegetable sources (biodiesel fuels), most diesel engines, with the exception of the huge engines used in oceangoing ships (which used very thick, and safer, "bunker fuel"), were designed to run on very light fuel oils that resemble common kerosene.

One should note that Diesel's business ventures, which

Operating Features of the Diesel Engine

The major differences between a conventional gasoline-powered engine and a diesel engine lie in the critical process of ignition within the cylinders. In the system developed by Rudolf Diesel, a very high level of air compression is built up in the cylinder before atomized droplets of fuel are injected. High compression—about 40 bar, or some 600 pounds per square inch (psi), compared with about 200 psi in conventional gas engines—heats trapped air to temperatures high enough (about 1,000° Fahrenheit, or 538° Celsius) to ignite injected fuel without the need for an electrical spark.

Diesel's early engines used what are called air-blast injection nozzles. This involved a first-stage compression of fuel using an auxiliary gas engine, creating an atomized mixture at the time of injection. Later solid-injection engines would use a mechanical pump to compress fuel. This simplifies the injection process by using pressure-activated injectors that shoot a concentrated jet of fuel into the combustion chambers.

Diesel engines outperform standard engines in terms of both fuel efficiency and carbon monoxide output. Estimates of diesel fuel efficiency (which stems from the higher density of diesel fuel, which releases more energy per unit of volume than gasoline) suggest savings ranging from 20 to 40 percent compared to gasoline. This efficiency also extends to the critical realm of greenhouse gas emissions. Although diesel emits more greenhouse gases than gasoline, its higher miles-per-gallon efficiency results in less overall pollution.

A recurrent but relatively easily resolved problem associated with diesel engines typically occurs at the time of starting. Because the ignition process depends on achieving high temperature levels as quickly as possible inside each cylinder, it is sometimes necessary to prevent a drop in overall engine block temperature (especially in cold climates) from causing low temperatures in the cylinder walls, which could cause fuel to "gel," or solidify.

Diesel engines routinely require careful internal adjustments to avoid, or at least reduce, the emission of a blue-black smoke. This smoke is emitted usually for a short time while the engine is started because the optimum temperature inside the cylinders has not yet been reached. The phenomenon is more critical, however, if the engine is being "pushed" to higher revolutions per minute than it can accommodate. The smoke emitted in such cases represents lost fuel.

very soon made him a rich man, were founded with the announced intention to reform relations between industry owners and workers—relations that were becoming more and more strained as the industrial age progressed. Diesel made an effort to publicize his views on the subject (including a scheme for some degree of worker-ownership shares) in a book entitled *Solidarismus*, published in 1903, but no effective follow-up (or popular recognition of the book) seems to have occurred.

Impact

When Diesel died less in 1913, no one could have predicted that manufacturing and industrial developments in the twentieth century would create a demand for a wide variety of diesel engines, especially in the automotive and trucking industries. Modern diesel engines incorporate a number of improvements to the early models developed by Rudolf Diesel. For the layperson, the most obvious improvements involved increased compactness and efficiency in the fuel-injection stages, making possible the use of diesel engines in passenger cars, a trend that began slowly in the 1930's and expanded rapidly in the last quarter of the twentieth century. Although this phenomenon spread mainly in the sport utility and small to mid-range truck market in the United States, in Europe diesel-powered cars would eventually seriously rival gasoline-powered vehicles. The biggest area of performance by diesel engines is associated with heavy work vehicles.

The most obvious impact of diesel power occurred in heavy-duty transport: rail, buses, and powerful semitrailer trucks used in long-distance hauling. Diesel engines for these vehicles have the highest revolutions per minute (rpm) ranges—about 1,200 rpm, compared with 300-1,200 rpm for average vehicle engines. Huge diesel engines, called "cathedral engines," have been used to power large oceangoing ships.

—Byron Cannon

Further Reading

Kates, Edgar J. *Diesel and High Compression Gas Engines*. Chicago: American Technical Society, 1974. This author published a variety of layperson's guides to diesel engines over a thirty-year period, discussing their potential use in electrical plants and—at a critical time when the railway industry was in transition—for powering locomotives.

Nitske, Robert. *Rudolph Diesel*. 2d ed. Norman: University of Oklahoma Press, 1994. One of the standard but very complete biographies of Diesel in English.

Pahl, Greg. *Biodiesel: Growing a New Energy*. White River Junction, Vt.: Chelsea Green, 2005. A study of research seeking to improve energy-efficiency standards and reduce emissions from diesel engines by using fuel derived from plant oils. Foreword by Bill McKibben.

Thomas, Donald E. *Diesel: Technology and Society in Industrial Germany*. Tuscaloosa: University of Alabama Press, 1987. This biography completes that of Nitske, adding new accounts of personal relations affecting Diesel's work.

See also: Carl Benz; Nicolas-Joseph Cugnot; Gottlieb Daimler; John Boyd Dunlop; Henry Ford; Charles F. Kettering; Étienne Lenoir; Hiram Percy Maxim; André and Édouard Michelin; Ransom Eli Olds; Nikolaus August Otto; Stanford Ovshinsky; Sylvester Roper; Ignaz Schwinn; Felix Wankel; Alexander Winton.

Walt Disney

American animator, film producer, film director, businessman, and screenwriter

Disney wanted to entertain, not invent, but his expanding vision of entertainment required new technology. Disney began with simple, hands-on devices but ended as head of an innovative research facility designed to turn his visions into reality.

Born: December 5, 1901; Chicago, Illinois
Died: December 15, 1966; Burbank, California
Also known as: Walter Elias Disney (full name); Retlaw Yensid
Primary field: Entertainment
Primary invention: Audio-animatronics

Early Life

Walter Elias Disney (DIHZ-nee) was the youngest of four sons of Elias and Flora Call Disney, and had a younger sister. His father worked as a carpenter and contractor. In 1906, Elias moved the family from Chicago to a farm at Marceline, Missouri. For Walt, the farm and small town of five thousand people provided freedom and an idyllic vision of cohesive and caring community life that would influence many of his films and even the original Main Street of Disneyland. Although farming was backbreaking work for Elias and his two oldest sons, Walt was allowed to run free, learning a love for nature also evident in his films. He began drawing early and probably saw his first film in Marceline.

Elias was demanding and authoritarian. His two oldest sons fled, and, without them, Elias could not maintain the farm, which he sold in 1910. In 1911, the family moved to Kansas City, Missouri, where Walt's world was transformed, his freedom lost. Elias bought a paper route, paying some children to deliver the papers, but Walt and his brother Roy worked for free. At age nine, Walt rose before dawn, delivered papers, went to school, and delivered more papers after school, holding other jobs for spending money. This rigorous routine may have taught him his obsessive work habits, but it also created the desire for freedom and autonomy that made him resist later attempts to control his career or his studio. Walt was not a good student, but teachers encouraged his interest in drawing. When his family moved back to Chicago, Walt became a cartoonist for his high school paper and attended some art classes. Although underage, he dropped out of high school to join the Red Cross Ambulance Corps. After World War I, he returned to Kansas City.

Life's Work

Disney briefly worked for the Pesmen-Rubin Commercial Art Studio and the Kansas City Slide Company, while studying animation and unsuccessfully trying to establish his own studio. Bankrupt, he left for California, where he and his brother Roy formed Disney Brothers Studio (later Walt Disney Productions). There, Disney and Kansas City colleague Ub Iwerks (longtime Disney associate, animator, and inventor) produced short comedies for the studio's *Alice in Cartoonland* series. In 1927, Disney began a more popular series, *Oswald the Lucky Rabbit*, but he lost most of his animators and his rights to *Oswald* to his distributor. Angered but undefeated, Disney produced his first internationally successful figure, Mickey Mouse, in 1928.

By then, audiences craved sound. Music and sound effects had accompanied cartoons, but Disney wanted sound that seemed to come from action on the screen. He achieved this in *Steamboat Willie* (1928), with bar and exposure sheets that tied music to screen action. The Silly Symphonies followed. These began with *The Skeleton Dance* (1929) and included the first Technicolor cartoon, *Flowers and Trees* (1932), which won the first Academy Award to be given to an animated film. The virtually plotless symphonies were tone poems integrating sound and action.

The Three Little Pigs (1933) paved the way for a feature-length cartoon. Disney questioned whether audiences would accept animated figures that spoke and sang as if human. To achieve audience identification with characters and their emotions, Disney insisted on a new style of exaggerated realism, rooted in observation of muscles and flesh in real-life action. Animators took art classes and observed wildlife to achieve realistic studies of how bodies move and the effect of gravity on them in motion and at rest. Characters were treated as thinking, living beings. The pigs, distinguished by actions and emotions, not appearance, overwhelmingly demonstrated audience acceptance.

Disney also needed the illusion of depth. Other studios had attempted to produce multiplane cameras, but Disney's studio created the first workable version. It could shoot down through multiple, separately lighted levels of animation. The top levels were basic animation cels; below them were scenic details, and at the bottom was a plain sky or neutral background. As the camera moved, its movements carefully calculated by engineers, different scenic details came into focus. This camera and the new animation style are discussed at length by longtime Disney animators Frank Thomas and Ollie Johnston in *Disney Animation: The Illusion of Life* (1981); they provide both photographs and a diagram of the camera. The device proved effective in the Academy Award-winning *The Old Mill* (1937), a tone poem about an old mill and what happens there on a stormy night.

Walt Disney. (Library of Congress)

With these tools, Disney produced animated film's first full-length feature, *Snow White and the Seven Dwarfs* (1937). The Academy Award-winning eighty-minute film involved some six hundred employees and an estimated quarter million to two million drawings. Attempting to surpass this success, Disney created *Fantasia* (1940), a feature-length development of his tone poems. Philadelphia Orchestra conductor Leopold Stokowski and noted critic Deems Taylor worked with Disney and appeared in this performance of classical music illustrated by animated figures (including Mickey Mouse's appearance in Paul Dukas's "The Sorcerers' Apprentice"). To give the illusion of how music would sound in a concert hall, Disney's studio created Fantasound, an anticipation of later stereophonic developments in its use of multiple speakers and microphones. The sound system was too heavy and expensive for most theaters; Disney hoped for a three-dimensional widescreen production for limited release in better theaters. By this time, however, World War II, raging in Europe, had closed most overseas markets. Eager for immediate profits, RKO Pictures, the distributor, and bankers forced a shortened version into immediate general release; the uncut version was not made public until release of its sixtieth anniversary DVD. The profits from *Pinocchio* (1940) and *Bambi* (1942) were less than expected, and Disney began the worst decade of his adult life.

The 1940's were marked by labor problems, production of war-training films, and financial distress. After the war, Disney turned to television, returning his studio to renewed success; television, its development delayed by World War II, was only then becoming available to the general public. Other studio heads viewed television as a competitive menace, but Disney saw it as a vehicle for advertising his films and financing his new dream, a fantasy-themed amusement park. His television series, under different names, ran for twenty-nine seasons, while he simultaneously pioneered a series of live-action animal films, beginning with *Seal Island* (1948), and, with *Treasure Island* (1950), began live-action adventure films.

In 1952, to provide tools for what would become Disneyland, Disney established WED (his initials), a research and development unit that employed Imagineers—a mingling of animators, story people, set designers, artists, and others—to develop the inventions he would need. WED produced the audio-animatronic robotic figures that populated Disneyland and the 1964-1965 New York World's Fair. Disneyland opened on July 17, 1955, and attracted 3.6 million people its first year. At the time of his death, Disney was planning Florida's Disney World and envisioning the Experimental Prototype Community of Tomorrow (EPCOT), a futuristic city that was never built.

Audio-Animatronics

In 1949, while visiting New Orleans, Walt Disney bought a mechanical bird. Imagining the possibility of three-dimensional animation, he sent the bird to his machine shop to see how it worked. This was the start of audio-animatronics, the robotic devices that provided the illusion of reality at Disneyland and the 1964-1965 New York World's Fair. From the bird, he moved on to a dancing figure and then to a barbershop quartet. At the beginning, these were crude devices, capable of only simple, repetitive movements. They rested on cabinets containing large drums. As the drums turned, cams moved levers that in turn connected to the wires that moved the figures. A movie projector on the cabinet's floor moved the drum while providing a synchronized sound track. The first major application was in Disneyland's Enchanted Tiki Room, where birds, flowers, and tiki gods performed. A convincingly real robotic robin sang along with Julie Andrews in Disney's 1964 hit musical *Mary Poppins*.

By then, audio-animatronic figures had become popular features of the New York's World's Fair. Disney's Abraham Lincoln, created from an 1860 life mask, rose, gestured, and spoke; he was the most sophisticated such figure to date. Solenoid coils inside the head governed facial expressions, hydraulic and pneumatic valves controlled body motions, and Duraflex created a realistic skin. Frames of movement were recorded on reel-to-reel audio tapes, which, when played back, triggered mechanisms that caused the figure to move. Words, music, and special effects were synchronized. (Audio-animatronic figures were computerized after Disney's death.) Other audio-animatronic figures appeared in the Pepsi/UNICEF It's a Small World show and General Electric's Carousel of Progress. It's A Small World took boatloads of spectators through different regions of the world where children, modeled to look alike except for skin color, played and sang representative songs. The General Electric exhibit featured a stationary stage around which the seated audience moved. The audience saw four households set in the late 1800's, the 1920's, the 1940's, and the 1960's, each demonstrating how electricity has improved everyday life. The WEDway People Mover, Disney's proposed mode of mass transportation, transported spectators in automobiles through a series of scenes from prehistoric times with audio-animatronic dinosaurs to a space city of the future.

Audio-animatronics had already proved successful at Disneyland. The popularity of the World's Fair exhibits guaranteed the success of the Orlando, Florida, theme park, then being planned at the time of Disney's death.

Impact

Winner of more than thirty Oscar and Emmy awards and recipient, in 1964, of the nation's highest civilian honor, the Presidential Medal of Freedom, Disney possessed an unusual gift for storytelling and a rare understanding of the emotions and dreams of popular audiences, combined with an obsessive concern for detail, equally obsessive work habits, and a belief that hard work and imagination could solve all technical problems. Repeatedly, those who worked with him, while acknowledging that he could be difficult, marveled at his ability to spread his enthusiasm and to find people's previously unknown talents. Never content unless a new effort was superior to his last, Disney transformed an originally small studio into the world's best-known name in popular entertainment. From development of internationally recognized cartoon characters through films popular in repeated reissue, his drive was toward animation and later live or robotic action that was both realistic and emotionally appealing. This forced him to imagine the inventions needed to realize his dreams and create the research facilities to provide them. His animated cartoons, animated and live-action feature films, and first theme park, as well as the establishment of WED, also ensured that his vision would be continued after his death.

—*Betty Richardson*

Further Reading

Barrier, Michael. *The Animated Man: A Life of Walt Disney*. Berkeley: University of California Press, 2007. Barrier brings a formidable body of knowledge of animation history and a critical mind to this formally written biography, emphasizing Disney's work, not his personal life.

_______. *Hollywood Cartoons: American Animation in Its Golden Age*. New York: Oxford University Press, 1999. Historical study of major animation studios up to 1960, with coverage of Disney, early rivals, and later developments at Warner Bros., Metro-Goldwyn-Mayer (MGM), and United Productions of America (UPA).

Gabler, Neal. *Walt Disney: The Triumph of the American Imagination*. New York: Alfred A. Knopf, 2006. Detailed, well-researched, generally balanced biography that refutes many myths and rumors, although Gabler's psychological analysis of Disney does not adequately explain Disney's singular achievements. Extensive bibliography.

Maltin, Leonard. *Of Men and Magic: A History of American Animated Cartoons*. 1980. Rev. ed. New York: Penguin Books, 1987. Covers animation history from the beginning to the 1980's, with extensive coverage of Disney's studio. Filmography and list of Academy Award-winning short cartoons. Brief glossary of animation terms.

Thomas, Bob. *Walt Disney: An American Original*. 1976. New York: Hyperion, 1994. Customary starting place for Disney research. A readable, generally accurate biography by a well-known Hollywood biographer. Tone is admiring, rather than critical. Little detail about inventions.

Thomas, Frank, and Ollie Johnston. *Disney Animation: The Illusion of Life*. New York: Abbeville Press, 1981. An insightful look into the Disney animation process by longtime Disney animators.

Tumbusch, Tom. *Walt Disney: The American Dreamer*. Dayton, Ohio: Tomart, 2008. Relatively brief, clearly written study of Disney's career, with emphasis on how he achieved his goals. Color illustrations include some early merchandising wares and design for EPCOT. Bibliography.

Watts, Steven. *The Magic Kingdom: Walt Disney and the American Way of Life*. Boston: Houghton Mifflin, 1997. Detailed study of Disney's studio, inventions, and achievements in the context of social and political issues of his times. Bibliographic essay includes studies of some film productions and individual Disney characters.

See also: Nolan K. Bushnell; Joshua Lionel Cowen; William Redington Hewlett; Steve Jobs; Paul Winchell.

Carl Djerassi

Austrian American chemist

Djerassi synthesized norethisterone, the first and most widely used oral contraceptive. He has also contributed to the fields of steroids, antihistamines, alkaloids, antibiotics, anti-inflammatory agents, terpenoids, sponge sterols, and physicochemical techniques. He is a published poet, novelist, autobiographer, and playwright, and he originated the genre that he calls "science-in-fiction."

Born: October 29, 1923; Vienna, Austria
Primary field: Chemistry
Primary invention: Birth control pill

Early Life

Carl Djerassi (djeh-RAH-see) was born on October 29, 1923, the only child of Samuel Djerassi, a Bulgarian physician, and Alice Djerassi (née Friedmann), an Austrian dentist. Both his parents were Jewish but were not observant, and Carl has described himself as a "Jewish atheist." He attended the high school (*Realgymnasium*) that Sigmund Freud had attended. His parents divorced, and he spent most of his time with his mother in Vienna and summers in Sofia with his father. After the Anschluss (Nazi Germany's annexation of Austria) in 1938, his father remarried his mother so that she and Carl could procure Bulgarian passports and immigrate to the United States.

In December, 1939, mother and son reached New York City with little money. Carl attended two semesters at Newark Junior College. With the chutzpah characteristic of an immigrant unfamiliar with how to obtain a scholarship, Djerassi wrote to Eleanor Roosevelt, who forwarded his letter to a foundation that awarded him a scholarship for the spring, 1941, semester to Tarkio College in Missouri. He spent two semesters and a summer at Kenyon College in Gambier, Ohio, receiving his A.B. summa cum laude at age eighteen in 1942.

For a year, Djerassi became a junior chemist at CIBA Pharmaceutical Products in Summit, New Jersey, where he cosynthesized pyribenzamine (tripelennamine), one of the first antihistamines and a popular drug for allergy sufferers. In 1943, he obtained a fellowship at the University of Wisconsin, where he worked with steroid chemist Alfred Wilds. Djerassi converted testosterone, the male sex hormone, to estradiol, the female sex hormone, which had previously been extracted from large amounts of pregnant mare's urine. He received his Ph.D. degree in 1945 at age twenty-one. He returned to CIBA (1945-1949), resuming his research on antihistamines and steroids.

Impatient, independent, and unconventional, Djerassi at age twenty-five hoped to establish his reputation on research publications and then enter academia later in a more advanced position. Cortisone was considered a wonder drug for arthritis and inflammatory diseases but was incredibly expensive since it required a thirty-six-step synthesis from deoxycholic acid prepared from cattle bile. Djerassi entered the international race begun at several universities and pharmaceutical firms to prepare this rare hormone from more available sources.

Life's Work

In 1949, George Rosenkranz, scientific director of Laboratorios Syntex S.A. in Mexico City, offered Djerassi an associate directorship of research to try to synthesize cortisone from diosgenin, a steroid sapogenin readily extracted from the tubers of *Dioscorea*, an inedible Mexican yam. Djerassi had never heard of Syntex, and Mexico was not known for research, but he thought that he and the company had a common goal—to establish a scientific reputation.

In a tour de force of less than two years, Djerassi, Rosenkranz, and coworkers divided into two groups and won the race to synthesize cortisone. A few months later, they reported a second synthesis, from hecogenin, another sapogenin from the waste products of Mexican sisal, an *Agave* hemp plant. Their success was touted in leading magazines and put them on the "international steroid map."

In 1951, Syntex was the only firm that could synthesize progesterone, the female sex hormone, in large amounts from diosgenin obtained from Mexican yams. However, none of their syntheses ever contributed directly to treating a single arthritic patient. Within a few months, the Upjohn Company, employing a combined chemical-microbiological method, succeeded in converting the female sex hormone progesterone to cortisone in high yield and by the shortest synthesis, and Syntex became the major supplier of raw material for the synthesis of cortisone.

Because progesterone, which Syntex was then preparing in large amounts, was known to inhibit ovulation, thus preventing a pregnant woman from being fertilized again during pregnancy, it could be considered as nature's contraceptive. Djerassi's team synthesized 19-norprogesterone, which was found to be four to eight times as active as natural progesterone, which was the most effective progestational hormone. They succeeded in producing 19-nor-17 alpha ethynyltestosterone. They submitted it for biological evaluation, which showed it to be the most potent oral progestin then known. Because Syntex had no pharmaceutical outlets or biological laboratories, it chose Parke-Davis to market the drug under the trade name of Norlutin after receiving approval from the U.S. Food and Drug Administration in 1957. It is still one of the two most widely used oral contraceptives.

The international acclaim that Djerassi garnered for his steroid and contraceptive research brought him what he had long sought—an academic position. In 1952, he became a tenured associate professor at Wayne University (now Wayne State University) in Detroit, Michigan. He became full professor the following year. During his five years at Wayne, he initiated the research that he considered his most important contribution to chemistry, the application of physicochemical techniques to characterize and determine the structures of organic compounds, which have become standard methods.

Carl Djerassi poses with his wife, biographer Diane Wood Middlebrook, outside their home in July, 1991. (Time & Life Pictures/Getty Images)

THE PILL

Carl Djerassi was inducted into the Inventors Hall of Fame in 1978 for his discovery of oral contraceptives (U.S. Patent number 2,744,122; filed November 22, 1951). He considered his two years at Syntex (1949-1951) "among the most productive ones of my chemical career," since less than half a year after his synthesis of cortisone, he synthesized the first oral contraceptive.

In 1921, Ludwig Haberlandt, an Austrian endocrinologist, proposed that extracts of corpus luteum (Latin for "yellow body"), which produces progesterone, a steroid hormone involved in the female menstrual cycle and the embryogenesis in the body of humans and other species, could be useful for birth control. It was only weakly active when taken orally, so daily injections were needed. Paul Ehrlich established relationships between biological activity and chemical structure that enabled scientists to predict which drugs might be useful.

Using these principles as guidelines, Djerassi, George Rosenkranz, and their team sought to modify the progesterone molecule to form an orally active substance with its biochemical properties. On October 15, 1951, Luis Miramontes, their young undergraduate chemistry student, synthesized 19-nor-17 alpha ethynyltestosterone (generic norethisterone). Several weeks later, the team filed their patent application for this compound that became one of the first ovulation-inhibiting ingredients of oral contraceptives. Djerassi reported their results at the April, 1952, American Chemical Society meeting in Milwaukee, Wisconsin, and they published their article three years later in the *Journal of the American Chemical Society*. After clinical studies by Gregory Pincus and others, the U.S. Food and Drug Administration (FDA) approved the use of norethindrone, now one of the world's most widely used steroid contraceptives. According to Djerassi, if these drugs had been discovered two decades later, they would not have been approved because of more stringent FDA regulations.

In view of the pill's extensive use, considerable clinical research on possible side effects made it the most intensively studied drug in modern medicine. By the close of the 1960's, evidence of an increased risk for strokes, cardiovascular disease, and blood clots were ignored but were later exaggerated. The risks were reduced considerably by decreasing the amounts of the progestin and estrogen components, and the pill was found to reduce the risk of ovarian and endometrial cancers. For healthy young women, the benefits of the pill more than outweigh any risks, making it the most effective and probably the safest contraceptive.

An ardent feminist since his third marriage, Djerassi has described himself as the pill's mother and Gregory Pincus, who "fertilized" norethindrone, as the pill's father.

Djerassi returned to Syntex for a second three-year term as vice president for research. In 1959, he became professor of chemistry at Stanford University, and he became professor emeritus in 2002. He retained his ties to industry and served in important positions with Syntex, Zoecon, and other firms.

While in Mexico, Djerassi had become interested in natural products obtained from the giant cactus, which led him to determine the structures of hundreds of alkaloids, terpenoids, and other natural products. He also worked on artificial intelligence and on the biosynthesis and biological function of sterols and phospholipids in marine animals. He has served as a mentor to hundreds of graduate students and postdoctoral fellows.

In 1965, Djerassi and Dale and Pamela, the two children of his second marriage, which ended in divorce in 1976, bought some undeveloped land in the Santa Cruz Mountains, which he called SMIP, for "Syntex made it possible" (later, during the Vietnam War, for *sic manebimus in pace*, "thus we will remain in peace"). He purchased additional land; by 1972, he had twelve hundred acres, which he converted into a cattle ranch.

On July 5, 1978, Pamela, an artist suffering from depression, committed suicide. Djerassi called this "the greatest tragedy of my life." He decided "to create something living out of a death . . . patronage of the type that would have benefited Pami." He and his third wife, Diane Middlebrook, a biographer, poet, and Stanford professor, whom he had married in 1979, established a colony for women artists at the SMIP ranch. Expanded to include artists, composers, writers, choreographers, and poets of both sexes and administered by the nonprofit Djerassi Foundation, this resident artists program has supported some fifteen hundred artists.

In summer, 1985, Djerassi underwent an operation for cancer, which forced him to come to terms with his own mortality. He decided to embark on a third career (after his scientific careers in industry and academia) in creative writing. Under Diane's influence, he was transformed from a traditional "uptight" research scientist to a more emotionally open novelist, poet, and playwright, specializing in what he calls "science-in-fiction," as opposed to science fiction.

A winner of numerous awards, Djerassi is one of the few American scientists to receive both the National Medal of Science (for the first oral contraceptive, 1973) and the National Medal of Technology (for promoting new approaches to insect control, 1993).

Impact

Djerassi's name is virtually synonymous with "the pill," the first and most widely used oral contraceptive, based on the steroid norethisterone (or norethindrone), which he synthesized. This discovery and application changed the world by separating the act of sex from reproduction, ushered in the sexual revolution of the 1960's, and led to the further emancipation of women. In fact, history can be divided into the pre-pill and post-pill eras. In what has been characterized as a "golden age" in pharmaceuticals, the pill's biological consequences engendered profound changes in society and religious, political, economic, and cultural attitudes on the pill's acceptance and use.

An award-winning scientist, Djerassi carried out fundamental and significant studies on organic, physical, and steroid chemistry and spectroscopic methods for the characterization and identification of chemical compounds. Beginning in the late 1990's, he became a true Renaissance man by completing half a century of dual research careers in industry and academia and dedicating himself to a new, third career in creative writing along two lines, one fictional and one autobiographical. His short stories, novels, poetry, and plays have won critical acclaim, and he has championed the science-in-fiction genre.

—*George B. Kauffman*

Further Reading

Djerassi, Carl. *From the Lab into the World: A Pill for People, Pets, and Bugs*. Washington, D.C.: American Chemical Society, 1994. A collection of twenty-four published and unpublished essays over four decades reflecting his personal growth from a laboratory scientist to an articulate spokesman on scientific issues and the ways that laboratory developments affect people around the world.

_______. *The Pill, Pygmy Chimps, and Degas's Horse: The Autobiography of Carl Djerassi*. New York: Basic Books, 1992. An autobiography chronicling his personal and scientific life and art collecting.

_______. "Steroid Oral Contraceptives." *Science* 151 (March 4, 1966): 1055-1061. A review, replete with structural formulas, of the history and chemistry leading to oral steroid contraceptives.

_______. *Steroids Made It Possible*. Washington, D.C.: American Chemical Society, 1990. This copiously illustrated autobiography describes Djerassi's life and career from his birth to the date of publication and provides glimpses of his personal and family life and newfound commitment to creative writing.

_______. *This Man's Pill: Reflections on the Fiftieth Birthday of the Pill*. New York: Oxford University Press, 2001. A first-person memoir marking the half-century anniversary of the discovery of the first synthesis of a steroid oral contraceptive.

Kauffman, George, and Laurie M. Kauffman. "The Steroid King." *The World and I* 7, no. 7 (July, 1992): 311-319. This article, based on an interview with Djerassi and other sources, provides an overview of his dual research careers in academia and industry and his then new career in creative writing.

Marks, Lara V. *Sexual Chemistry: A History of the Contraceptive Pill*. New Haven, Conn.: Yale University Press, 2001. An account of the history of the pill and the effect of religious, political, economic, and cultural attitudes regarding its acceptance and use. The contributions of chemists are relatively neglected.

Rosenkranz, George. "The Early Days of Syntex." *Chemical Heritage* 23, no. 2 (Summer, 2005): 8, 10, 12-13.

Zaffaroni, Alejandro. "Life After Syntex." *Chemical Heritage* 23, no. 2 (Summer, 2005): 9, 11, 13. Two articles by chemists Rosenkranz of Syntex and Zaffaroni of ALZA, who played pivotal roles in the development of the steroids used in the oral contraceptive.

See also: Percy Lavon Julian; Max Tishler.

Herbert Henry Dow

American chemist

Dow's work in developing processes for extracting chemicals from brine and combining chemicals into compounds with commercial potential helped establish the chemical industry in America and led to the development of hundreds of products that improved Americans' lives and raised the country's standard of living.

Born: February 26, 1866; Belleville, Ontario, Canada
Died: October 15, 1930; Rochester, Minnesota
Primary field: Chemistry
Primary invention: Method for extracting bromine from brine

Early Life

Herbert Henry Dow was born on February 26, 1866, in Belleville, Ontario, Canada, where his father had recently moved from New England to oversee operations in a sewing machine factory. The job did not pan out, and the Dows moved back to New England until 1878, when they relocated to Cleveland, Ohio.

Dow graduated from high school in 1884 and enrolled in the new Case School of Applied Sciences (later to become a part of Case Western Reserve University). For his senior thesis, Dow decided to investigate a process for chemically extracting various elements from brine, saltwater residing in pools below ground throughout the Midwest and filled with trace elements of bromine, chlorine, calcium, and magnesium. Dow was particularly interested in capturing bromine, because bromide compounds were being used in the production of pharmaceuticals and photographic supplies. At the time, bromine was being obtained by first boiling the brine to allow the salt to crystallize, then mixing chemicals into the remaining solution to separate the bromine. Dow was convinced he could capture bromine directly from brine without evaporation, speeding up the process of extraction and eliminating the need to dispose of tons of salt, the commercial value of which fluctuated widely.

After graduating from Case in 1888, Dow moved to Canton, Ohio, where he set up a company to put his theories into practice. Although his initial effort failed to bring commercial success, he was convinced of the efficacy of his processes. In August, 1890, he moved to Midland, Michigan, site of the largest underground brine sea in the country. With financing from a group of Cleveland businessmen, he set up the Midland Chemical Company, building a small plant to extract bromine from brine and process it for commercial sales. Although he worked at the plant almost incessantly, he took time in 1892 to marry Grace Ball, a local schoolteacher, with whom he would have four children.

Life's Work

Dow's early efforts to combine his work as a researcher and businessman were not particularly successful. In 1892, he reorganized his company, obtaining financing from several new company directors who turned out to be less interested in experimentation than in making money from proven methodologies. Hence, Dow's decision to switch from manufacturing ferric bromide to potassium bromide pleased his directors when it led to increased profits for the company, but his insistence on spending time looking for other ways to use the brine solution when the company was doing well led to his dismissal as Midland Chemical's general manager. Dow returned to Ohio briefly to perfect a method for extracting chlorine from brine, but by 1896 he was back in Midland. New sources of financial support allowed him to build a new plant and organize the Dow Chemical Company in May of 1897. The firm had difficulties initially, but within three years Dow Chemical was so successful selling chlorine bleach that it absorbed Midland Chemical and became the country's principal supplier of a number of chemical products. Though his investors realized handsome dividends, Dow insisted that a portion of profits be invested in plant improvements and continuing research. In 1900, he instituted what was then a revolutionary practice: a profit-sharing plan for his employees to allow them to benefit from the company's continued growth.

In 1902, Dow fought off a challenge from British manufacturer United Alkali, the world's largest manufacturer of bleach, to drive him out of the bleach market. Buoyed by that success, Dow determined to begin exporting bromides to Europe. At the time, the worldwide market was controlled by a cartel of German companies that had already seen their U.S. sales adversely affected by Dow's emergence as a major supplier in America. In 1904, the German cartel informed Dow that he must cease efforts to export bromine or face economic repercussions.

Dow refused to cave to pressure, and for four years his company engaged in a price war with the German firms who dumped bromine on the American market, charging as little as 10.5 cents per pound—well below production costs. These companies maintained a much higher sales price in Europe in order to keep their operations solvent, so to compete with them Dow bought imported bromine at the discounted price, repackaged it, and sold it in Europe at the going rate there. Finally, in 1908, the German companies proposed a new arrangement whereby Dow would control the American market but not export to Germany; other parts of the world would be available for open competition. For the first time in history, an American firm had actually bested the German chemical giants, and when the Germans proposed a similar arrangement to Dow for sharing the chlorine market, he was able to turn down their offer, confident that he could compete by producing his products more cheaply while maintaining high quality. Surprisingly, in 1913, at a point when sales for chlorine bleach were at a peak, Dow announced that the company would move away from manufacturing that product—presumably because he saw that competitors would eventually be able to challenge Dow Chemical's undisputed prominence in that field.

Extracting Bromine from Brine

Work on his senior thesis at the Case School of Applied Sciences convinced Herbert Henry Dow that there were potentially vast profits to be made from extracting trace elements such as bromine from the brine that lay beneath the ground throughout the Midwest. He also realized that it would become increasingly more expensive to extract those elements using current technology, which required that the brine be boiled as a first step in the extraction process, because fuel for boiling was becoming scarce in the region. Dow reasoned that he could capture bromine through a process he called "blowing out." First, using chemicals such as calcium hydroxide, calcium chloride, and calcium hypochlorite to oxidize the cold brine, Dow dripped the brine solution over burlap sacks. He then passed a current of air across the sacks, blowing out bromine gas. He arranged to have this gas come into contact with scrap iron, causing a chemical reaction that produced ferric bromide, a substance with an established market for sales. Later, he would modify his mixture, adding potash to create potassium bromide, a product in even higher demand.

Although Dow conceived the theory for extracting bromine from cold brine while still an undergraduate, it took him several years after graduation to transform his ideas into a workable mechanism that could produce bromide compounds in sufficient quantity to allow him to run a profitable business manufacturing them. Nevertheless, once Dow had perfected his blowing-out process for treating the cold brine, he began experimenting with another method for extracting bromine: electrolysis. To supplement the blowing-out process, an electrical current was passed through the oxidized brine, speeding up the process of collection. Working diligently in his laboratory, Dow developed a mechanism for carrying out this theory as well. His major accomplishment, however, was to extrapolate his laboratory practices to machinery that allowed him to treat millions of gallons of brine solution and extract tons of bromide compounds, making it possible for his company to become commercially successful.

During World War I, as Germany's relations with the United States became increasingly more hostile, it became exceedingly more difficult to import products from that country. The problem turned out to be a boon for Dow, who discovered that he now had new markets for some of his products and additional markets for ones he had only recently begun to develop. One of the principal new lines Dow Chemical produced during the war was synthetic indigo dye, an item in high demand in the clothing industry. Dow was convinced that another derivative from brine, magnesium, had a future as part of an alloy replacing steel and even aluminum. Its light weight made it appear to be perfect for aircraft and automobiles, but Dow was unable to convince manufacturers to use magnesium alloys during the war. Only years later, during World War II, did magnesium alloys become a major component in aircraft construction. Dow managed to sell a small amount of magnesium to the government, as it was an important component in making flares. He also found himself serving as a major supplier of phenol, a component critical for manufacturing explosives. Shortly before the United States entered World War I in 1917, government representatives asked Dow to participate in manufacturing poison gases. Reluctantly, he provided space and personnel for research and development, and ultimately tear gas and mustard gas were produced at the Dow facility. Fortunately, none of these products were ever used by the United States on the battlefield.

By the end of the conflict, Dow Chemical was an undisputed leader in chemicals manufacturing, offering a wide diversity of products for a variety of industries both at home and abroad. Although Dow was forced to lay off much of his workforce immediately after the armistice was declared, the company soon returned to profitability, largely because Dow had continued his practice of product diversification. Over the next decade, the company began producing dozens of new products, including aspirin, which was sold to others who marketed the product under their own brand names. In 1922, Dow led efforts to gain some tariff protection for the American chemical industry, ensuring his company a level playing field with European competitors. Meanwhile, the men Dow had hired as his chief lieutenants during the company's first twenty years were spearheading sales, research, and production at the Midland headquarters and offices in other American cities, operating on the principle Herbert Dow had articulated during the company's infancy: Dow Chemical would make a product only if it could do so better and more economically than any competitor.

After the war, Dow turned his attention to the automotive industry. For some time, he concentrated on creating a new magnesium alloy for use in making automobile parts. The pistons he created showed promise in race cars, but fears that magnesium was highly flammable kept automobile companies from adopting Dow's parts on a wide scale. He did achieve great commercial success with a new fuel additive, tetraethyl lead, a product with high bromine content. This product prevented "knocking" in automobile engines, allowing them to run more smoothly. The exceptionally high demand for tetraethyl lead drove Dow Chemical to explore ways to extract bromine and other chemicals from seawater, a project that proved commercially successful in 1934. Unfortunately, Herbert Dow did not live to see this new advance. He died on October 15, 1930, from cirrhosis of the liver—but not before his peers in the industry awarded him the Perkin Medal for his achievements in industrial chemistry. At his death, the company he created was doing $15 million in annual sales and employing approximately two thousand people.

IMPACT

Dow's work to produce bromine and later chlorine in large quantities for commercial sale, and his concurrent effort to establish the business that would carry out his revolutionary ideas for the manufacture of products generated from chemical processes, led to the establishment of one of America's largest and most influential chemical products companies. Dow Chemical supplied products used for cleaning, for manufacture of pharmaceuticals, for agricultural products, and for military weaponry. Research at Dow Chemical led to the development of dozens of products that materially improved the living standard of American citizens. Dow's insistence that his company continually investigate new products or new uses for existing ones set a standard for others involved in manufacturing products made from chemicals. Dow's practice of involving faculty and students from the Case School in research and product testing set a precedent for university-industry partnerships that became a standard adopted across the nation during the twentieth century.

Nevertheless, even in Dow's time the company became involved in manufacturing chemical products that would have an adverse impact on the environment. To many in the United States, Dow Chemical's role in manufacturing napalm, a powder mixed with gasoline and used in a "scorched earth" bombing campaign during the Vietnam War, seemed a natural outgrowth of Dow's complicity in producing poison gases in 1917-1918. Increasingly, the company came to be seen as a greedy international firm intent on making money regardless of the impact its products had on the environment or individuals. These unfortunate judgments marred the otherwise remarkable record of a company founded by a man who believed in the power of chemistry to make life better for his fellow citizens.

—*Laurence W. Mazzeno*

FURTHER READING

Brandt, E. N. *Growth Company: Dow Chemical's First Century*. East Lansing: Michigan State University Press, 1997. Highlights Dow's contributions to the development of the chemical industry in the United States and traces the growth of the company he founded to its emergence as a major international corporation.

Campbell, Murray, and Harrison Hatton. *Herbert H. Dow, Pioneer in Creative Chemis*try. New York: Appleton-Century-Crofts, 1951. Brief biography of Dow written for a general audience that highlights his achievements and the personal qualities that made him an exceptional scientist and businessman. Traces his early struggles to perfect methods of extracting trace elements from brine and his battles to establish his company in the worldwide marketplace.

Chandler, Alfred D., Jr. *Shaping the Industrial Century: The Remarkable Story of the Evolution of the Modern Chemical and Pharmaceutical Industries*. Cambridge, Mass.: Harvard University Press, 2005. Contains a discussion of the Dow Chemical Company's rise to prominence within the context of a larger examination of the growth and development of two important American industries during the twentieth century.

Levenstein, Margaret. *Accounting for Growth: Informa-*

tion Systems and the Creation of the Large Corporation. Stanford, Calif.: Stanford University Press, 1998. Extended analysis of Dow Chemical as an example of a company employing increasingly sophisticated information management systems to control operations and growth. Contains a chapter outlining Herbert Dow's role in establishing the business, an appendix offering brief biographies of principal figures involved in the company during its early days, and a chronological record of compounds and products sold by Dow between 1891 and 1914.

Mayo, Anthony J., and Nitin Nohria. *In Their Time: The Greatest Business Leaders of the Twentieth Century*. Cambridge, Mass.: Harvard Business School Press, 2005. Discusses Dow's career in the context of a wider analysis of the lives and accomplishments of the most influential business leaders of the twentieth century.

Whitehead, Don. *The Dow Story: The History of the Dow Chemical Company*. New York: McGraw-Hill, 1968. Account of the founding and development of the multinational chemical company, focusing on Herbert Dow's life and his contributions to the growth of the chemical industry in the United States.

See also: Wallace Hume Carothers; Michael Faraday; Charles Martin Hall; Stephanie Kwolek; Roy J. Plunkett.

Charles Stark Draper

American aeronautical engineer

Draper is often referred to as the "father of inertial navigation." His work with gyroscopes led to the development of the guidance computer for NASA's Apollo program and improved gun sights for antiaircraft weapons.

Born: October 2, 1901; Windsor, Missouri
Died: July 25, 1987; Cambridge, Massachusetts
Primary fields: Aeronautics and aerospace technology; military technology and weaponry
Primary inventions: Inertial navigation systems; Mark 14 gun sight

Early Life

Charles Stark Draper was born to Arthur and Martha Draper in Windsor, Missouri. His father was a dentist and his mother was a schoolteacher. In 1917, Draper enrolled in the University of Missouri, where he planned to study medicine. In 1919, he transferred to Stanford University in California, graduating in 1922 with a bachelor's degree in psychology. He then attended Herald's Radio College in order to work as a ship radio operator. After finishing his training, Draper took a road trip cross-country with a friend who was attending Harvard. On their way to Boston, they drove through Cambridge. Draper was taken with the town, especially the Massachusetts Institute of Technology (MIT). That day, he enrolled in MIT's electrochemical program.

In 1926, Draper received his bachelor's degree in electrochemical engineering. He stayed at MIT, studying mathematics, physics, chemistry, and aeronautics. Draper was given a nondepartmental master of science degree in 1928. He became an aeronautic engineering research assistant at MIT the following year. He continued taking a wide range of courses while working on his Ph.D. and became renowned for having the most credits of any MIT graduate student without a doctorate. MIT eventually pressured Draper to complete his degree. He finally finished his doctorate in 1938. He married Ivy Willard later that year.

Life's Work

Draper became a professor at MIT in 1939. The college also put him in charge of its Instrumentation Laboratory, which now bears his name. His first project after taking over the MIT lab was to improve navigation by developing a new gyroscopic rate-of-turn indicator. The Sperry Gyroscope Company funded Draper's research. Simply put, a gyroscope is a spinning wheel device that aids stability. Small gyroscopes, which resemble complex toy tops, are sold at educational and toy stores. Gyroscopes measure angular velocity—the amount of angular displacement (the difference in angle of the radius of the wheel over a time interval) divided by the total elapsed time. Angular velocity is measured in radians per second. Gyroscopes measure angular velocity in an inertial reference frame, a set of coordinates in space that is not accelerating. By knowing the initial orientation within the reference frame, and calculating in the angular velocity, it is possible to always know the system's current orientation.

Draper was successful in creating more sensitive gyroscopic instruments, but they did not have practical applications until the beginning of World War II. Draper used his improved rate-of-turn indicator to develop the Mark 14 gun sight, which made antiaircraft fire from ships possible. The USS *South Dakota* was the first to use the device. In 1942, the ship successfully shot down thirty-two Japanese aircraft during the Battle of Santa Cruz. The Mark 14 gun sight was able to semiautomatically correct for wind, range, and ballistics using the ship's deck as the inertial reference frame. The gun sight became popular with Allied forces; more than eighty-five thousand of the devices were installed on American and British vessels. Draper also worked on a gun sight for airplanes. Later models gave American pilots an advantage during the Korean War.

During the years following the end of World War II, Draper began working on an inertial navigation system (INS), which is used to determine the current position of a ship or plane based on the initial location and acceleration. Draper and his colleagues at MIT worked with the Air Force Armament Lab on the guidance system. Draper's INS would be unaffected by enemy countermeasures or bad weather. He based his guidance system on the principles behind the Mark 14 gun sight, which used a gyroscope with only one direction of freedom; the gyroscope floated inside a viscous liquid. For the INS, Draper created a floating gyroscope accelerometer with three directions of freedom that measured position, velocity, and acceleration. His new accelerometer connected to an airplane's instruments measuring direction and altitude, forming an inertial guidance system.

There was much debate within the scientific community about whether an INS would actually work. The most vocal critic was American physicist George Gamow. To prove his system worked, Draper set up a test flight in 1953. However, since it was a military program, it was not made public until 1957. Draper, seven other MIT engineers, and an Air Force crew flew from Bedford, Massachusetts, to Los Angeles. During the twelve-hour flight, no one touched the plane's controls until they were ten miles from Los Angeles, to pre-

INERTIAL NAVIGATION SYSTEMS

In the years following World War II, the scientific debate over the plausibility of building an inertial navigation system (INS) increased. Charles Stark Draper and his supporters believed it was possible. Others, such as physicist George Gamow, disagreed. A member of the Air Force Scientific Advisory Board, Gamow felt that the military was wasting money working on an INS. He was convinced that the "problem of the vertical" could not be solved.

The problem of the vertical came from Albert Einstein's "black box" argument: An observer inside this box would not be able to tell the difference between gravity and linear acceleration. This argument presented problems for Draper and his colleagues working on creating an INS, or black-box navigation. The navigation system on an airplane would need to be able to identify the true vertical. For example, when navigating with two accelerometers, they are oriented "local vertical," meaning horizontally at right angles to the local direction of gravity. When the black box accelerates, a plum bob would not give a correct indication of true vertical. Another problem could arise if direction of travel was unknown. In that case, it would be impossible to know if the gyroscopes were even being held horizontally.

Mathematician Max Schuler believed that an INS was possible in theory and began working on the calculations dealing with the effect of a vessel's acceleration on the onboard gyrocompass. Schuler was trying to find a way to minimize that effect. His work, eventually published in 1923, was central to solving the problem of the vertical. On a ship traveling the surface of the earth, it is impossible to determine the vertical using a plum bob if the ship accelerates. Schuler's theoretical solution was to increase the length of string holding the plum bob weight so that it puts the mass at the center of the earth. In this case, the string would indicate the vertical, no matter how the ship moved or accelerated. An actual version could not be constructed, but Schuler argued that the effect could be achieved with a gyroscope system. The gyroscope could be set to the same oscillation period, eighty-four minutes, as the earth-radius pendulum.

Scientists working on the problem of the vertical and INS were confident that Schuler's idea would work. The easiest way was to construct an earth-radius pendulum using two accelerometers at right angles, stabilized by gyroscopes. Draper and his colleagues thought this was a viable solution to the problem of the vertical.

In the late 1940's, Draper finally put an end to the debate over black-box navigation. He and Gamow were both members of the Scientific Advisory Board; Draper set up a conference for those working on the INS to discuss the status of their research. Though Gamow was invited, he did not attend the meeting. His absence was perceived as admitting that he was wrong about the vertical problem. Within a few years, Draper had successfully created an inertial navigation system.

pare for landing. The plane had successfully adjusted its altitude and speed on its own as it flew across country.

Draper also worked on designing a system for U.S. Navy ships and submarines. Draper's Ships Inertial Navigation System (SINS) was not affected by the fact that over the course of months a ship's gyroscopes tend to need recalibrating. Navy leaders funded Draper's research, hoping to use it in nuclear submarines. They also asked him to develop a navigation system for ballistic missiles that would work in coordination with SINS. The systems were first installed in ships, planes, and submarines in 1956 and in ballistic missiles four years later.

In 1961, Draper and the other engineers at the instrumentation laboratory began working on guidance and control systems for the Apollo program of the National Aeronautics and Space Administration (NASA). Robert Seamans, deputy administrator of NASA, had taken the Weapons System Engineering course that Draper set up to educate civilian and military personnel about his INS. Seamans gave Draper the Apollo contract. It was Draper's invention that successfully guided astronauts Neil Armstrong, Buzz Aldrin, and Michael Collins to the Moon in 1969 and brought them back safely.

During the late 1960's, antiwar protests occurred often at MIT, mainly because of the lab's strong military ties. MIT faculty and administration debated the effects the military funding was having on the college. In 1973, the lab was moved off MIT's campus and renamed the Charles Stark Draper Laboratory.

Charles Draper died on July 25, 1987, in Cambridge. He and his wife had four children: James, Martha, Michael, and John. Draper was eighty-five.

Impact

Draper had a large impact on military and civilian life. The gun sight that he invented in the 1940's gave U.S. Navy ships an advantage against enemy aircraft. Draper's design also created a new field of research: aided tracking fire control. The Draper laboratory is among many groups working to improve the military's "Dismounted Soldier" project, developing ways to fire missiles, drop bombs, and deliver supplies without putting pilots and flight crews at risk. The military's Joint Precision Airdrop System (JPADS), which uses guided parachutes in resupply missions, was first used in combat in Afghanistan in 2006. The laboratory is also working on low-cost guidance systems for ballistic missiles. With these systems, the Navy would be able to fire long-range missiles in support of ground troops. The project has already increased the range and accuracy of two types of missiles used by the Navy.

Draper's inertial guidance system was being installed on commercial airplanes by 1970. Draper also played a key role in the Apollo missions to the Moon. Newer versions of his system have been built for the space shuttle and International Space Station (ISS). When the ISS had problems with its onboard Russian computers in 2007, guidance control was maintained by Draper's INS until the computers could be repaired. Future NASA missions, both manned and unmanned, will no doubt be equipped with versions of Draper's inertial navigation system.

—Jennifer L. Campbell

Further Reading

Hall, Eldon. *Journey to the Moon: The History of the Apollo Guidance Computer*. Reston, Va.: American Institute of Aeronautics and Astronautics, 1996. A history of the creation of the guidance computer used during the Apollo missions. The author shows how the Apollo program helped advance the semiconductor industry and the electronics revolution. Suitable for anyone interested in the history of computers or space exploration.

Johnson, Steven. *The Secret of Apollo: Systems Management in American and European Space Programs*. Baltimore: The Johns Hopkins University Press, 2006. A valuable resource for anyone interested in the space program, its business and management operations, or Cold War history.

Mackenzie, Donald. *Inventing Accuracy: A Historical Sociology of Nuclear Missile Guidance*. Cambridge, Mass.: MIT Press, 1990. Based on archival documents and interviews with those working in the field. The author discusses the relevant technology and explains it in a nonmathematical way. Focuses on social and historical contexts.

See also: Harold E. Edgerton; Albert Einstein; Léon Foucault; Elmer Ambrose Sperry.

CHARLES RICHARD DREW

American physician and medical researcher

Drew developed a system of collecting and storing blood plasma in what is known as a blood bank, which was utilized for Allied fighting men in World War II. Whereas previously blood could be preserved for only about seven days, Drew's method made it possible to store the plasma for much longer periods of time.

Born: June 3, 1904; Washington, D.C.
Died: April 1, 1950; near Burlington, North Carolina
Primary field: Medicine and medical technology
Primary invention: Blood bank

EARLY LIFE

Charles Richard Drew was the first of five children born to Richard (a carpet layer) and Nora (a teacher) Drew. He was an exceptional student and athlete, earning four varsity letters in high school. Voted best overall athlete in both his junior and senior years, he graduated from Dunbar High School in 1922 with honors and a partial athletic scholarship to play football at Amherst College. As the scholarship paid only some of his expenses, he took a part-time job as a waiter. Between his athletic activities and his job, his grades suffered during his first two years of college but improved by his junior year. His athletic career continued to be outstanding. He was an all-American halfback and captain of the track team.

Upon graduation in 1926, Drew took a position at Morgan State University in Baltimore, Maryland. He wanted to become a doctor but was unable to pay for medical school at the time. He worked at Morgan, saved his money, and after two years resigned to enroll in the McGill University Medical School in Montreal, Canada. In 1933, he was awarded a medical degree and a master of surgery degree from McGill, where he had won first prize in physiological anatomy and two fellowships in medicine. From 1933 to 1935, he interned at the Royal Victoria Hospital and completed his residency at Montreal General Hospital. He returned to the United States to teach pathology at Howard University College of Medicine in Washington, D.C. In 1939, he married Minnie Lenore Robbins, with whom he had four children.

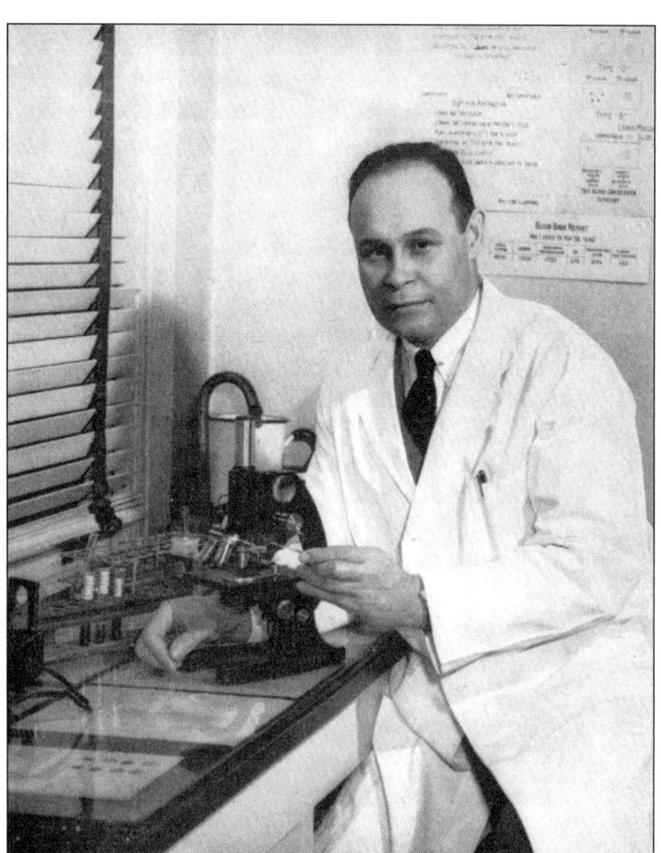

Charles Richard Drew. (Associated Publishers)

LIFE'S WORK

Drew's life work began in earnest after he earned his doctorate from Columbia University in 1940. He was a General Education Board fellow in surgery at Columbia from 1938 to 1940 and a resident in surgery at Presbyterian Hospital. His research on blood plasma and transfusions discussed methods for separating red blood cells from plasma to preserve them for later reconstitution and use. Conventional blood-preservation methods at the time focused on whole blood, which could be stored for only about seven days. Drew found that plasma could be stored much longer. In his two-hundred-page doctoral dissertation titled "Banked Blood: A Study in Blood Preservation," he showed that blood could be preserved longer if the red blood cells were separated from the plasma and frozen separately. When a blood transfusion was needed, the separated elements could be reconstituted.

World War II was under way in Europe, and doctors needed blood supplies for wounded soldiers and civilians. Aware of Drew's findings, one of Drew's former teachers, then living in England, requested that he send ten thousand glass containers of dried plasma to England to be used in transfusions. This required an all-out effort to collect blood at New York hospitals for export to England. Because the United States might also soon be drawn into the war and need a large blood supply, Drew devised a new mass-production technique to separate the blood components and stockpile them.

British scientists were using modified cream separators to separate plasma from red blood cells, a system far more productive than spinning off the red cells using test tubes and centrifuges or simply allowing the cells to separate and settle apart from the plasma over a period of several days. Drew ordered two of the modified cream separators from England and, with his associates, constructed similar machines to mass-produce clear plasma from the whole blood being collected by the American Red Cross and the National Research Council. This new system produced the volume of plasma likely to be needed when America went to war.

With war imminent, the American Red Cross named Drew director of its blood bank, and he was made assistant director of the National Research Council to manage blood collection for the American armed services in early 1941. Throughout the war, Drew's collection and preservation process was used; mobile blood banks were used at the front lines to treat wounded soldiers and stabilize them sufficiently to get them to hospitals.

THE BLOOD BANK

While Charles Richard Drew was a student at McGill University, he worked with visiting British professor Dr. John Beattie on his research in blood transfusions. It was understood that to avoid negative reactions in a blood transfusion, the donor and recipient blood types (A, B, AB, and O) have to match. Otherwise, the patient's immune system will attack the donated blood cells. At that time, whole blood was usually transfused, and therein was another problem: Whole blood was impossible to preserve for long periods of time, so a method was needed to preserve blood for transfusions so it would be available whenever needed.

Drew found that the red blood cells had a rapid deterioration rate. They are the blood components that carry hemoglobin, which combines with oxygen from the lungs and distributes the oxygen throughout the body. With the red blood cells removed, the liquid portion of blood, the plasma, could be stored practically indefinitely. Plasma, with no red blood cells (which contain the substance that determines blood type), could be used in transfusions without having to match donor and recipient blood types. This was particularly valuable in emergency cases. Drew transformed the test tube method of separating red cells from plasma into a mass-production technique.

Although blood plasma is not a substitute for whole blood in certain kinds of transfusions, it remains in the circulation for a much longer period than the previously used saline or glucose solutions, and it helps prevent or cure shock. In cases of burns, shock (without blood loss), or some cases of anemia in which the main concern is increasing the volume of circulating blood, plasma has been found to be highly valuable.

Using a dehydration process, Drew dried plasma for preservation and convenient transportation. To prepare it for transfusion, the plasma was simply reconstituted with distilled water just before it was to be used. In its reconstituted form, it stays fresh for about four hours. Plasma was found to be viable even a year after storage.

Drew's process of collecting, preserving, and using plasma was invaluable during the years of World War II. Because the demand for plasma was extremely high during the war years, Drew also pioneered the use of trucks equipped with refrigerators ("bloodmobiles") to carry the plasma to those who needed transfusions. Thanks to his work, hundreds of thousands of lives have been saved with blood plasma and its ability to stabilize injured people, regardless of blood type.

One negative development occurred when the military ordered that all collected blood be separated by the race of the donor. Drew and other scientists and medical professionals tried unsuccessfully to convince the military that there was no difference between the blood of black and white people. They argued that men could die unnecessarily while waiting to receive the "right" blood, but they could not persuade the military to change the policy, which remained in force through the war.

In May, 1941, when Drew resigned as director of the American Red Cross, it was rumored that he left in protest over the segregated blood issue. Years later, however, his widow denied this rumor, saying that he returned to Howard University because he missed working as a teacher and surgeon. That same year, he was made head of Howard University's surgery department and chief surgeon at Freedman's Hospital. By 1944, he had become chief of staff at the hospital, a position he held until 1948.

Drew received numerous awards and prestigious appointments for his exemplary career. Among them were honorary degrees from Virginia State College in 1945 and from his alma mater, Amherst College, in 1947. He held membership on the American Board of Surgery, the first African American to do so. In 1944, he was awarded the Spingarn Medal by the National Association for the Advancement of Colored People (NAACP) for his outstanding achievements.

On April 1, 1950, while driving through North Carolina with a small group of students and colleagues to the annual meeting of the John A. Andrews Clinical Association in Tuskeegee, Alabama, Drew fell asleep at the wheel, and the car struck a soft shoulder and overturned. His injuries were the most serious: a closed head wound, a chest crushed by the steering wheel, and severe injuries to his arms and legs. He was taken to Alamance County General Hospital in nearby Burlington, where, according to urban legend, he was refused treatment because of his race. In fact, he received immediate care but was too badly injured to survive.

Impact

Drew was a pioneer in blood collection and plasma processing. His experimentation turned biological research into mass-production methods that resulted in a new way to produce large quantities of transfusible blood. His work saved the lives of thousands of World War II servicemen and servicewomen and created a system of blood transfusion that saved lives in other wars and calamities. He devised a quantitative procedure for separating blood cells from plasma and preserving the components for longer periods of time than had previously been possible. His blood bank was a revolutionary advancement in modern medical practice, and the American Red Cross blood program today is a direct result of his groundbreaking work in mass-producing human plasma.

—*Jane L. Ball*

Further Reading

Haber, Louis. *Black Pioneers of Science and Invention.* New York: Harcourt, Brace & World, 1970. Includes fourteen chapters on African American innovators, inventors, and scientists. The final chapter is devoted to Drew.

Hudson, Wade. *Book of Black Heroes: Scientists, Healers, and Inventors.* East Orange, N.J.: Just Us Books, 2003. Includes a short biographical sketch of Drew written for a juvenile audience.

Love, Spencie. *One Blood: The Death and Resurrection of Charles R. Drew.* Chapel Hill: University of North Carolina Press, 1997. An extensively researched, insightful discussion of how rumors and opinions affect history, with focus on how Drew died, medical care and race relations in America at the time of his death, and some of the myths surrounding his death.

Schraff, Anne E. *Dr. Charles Drew: Blood Bank Innovator.* Berkeley Heights, N.J.: Enslow, 2003. Biography of Drew written for a juvenile audience.

Trice, Linda. *Charles Drew: Pioneer of Blood Plasma.* New York: McGraw-Hill, 2000. Discusses Drew's life and work as inventor of large-scale production of human plasma. Young adult reading level.

See also: Helen M. Free; Willem Johan Kolff; Rosalyn Yalow.

Richard G. Drew

American engineer

Drew, an engineer at the Minnesota Mining and Manufacturing Company (3M), invented transparent adhesive tape in 1930. His work evolved into a line of pressure-sensitive tape products numbering over nine hundred and generating $24.5 billion in sales by 2007.

Born: June 22, 1899; St. Paul, Minnesota
Died: December 14, 1980; Santa Barbara, California
Also known as: Richard Gurley Drew (full name)
Primary field: Household products
Primary inventions: Scotch tape; masking tape

Early Life

Richard Gurley Drew was born on June 22, 1899, in St. Paul, Minnesota. After high school, Drew attended the University of Minnesota to study engineering. For three semesters, he studied engineering during the day and paid his college expenses by playing banjo in various Twin City dance orchestras at night.

Drew found this schedule grueling, however, and quit the university. He continued to play the banjo and spent his afternoons on a correspondence course in machine design. He was twenty-two years old and had not yet found his career path, but that would change when Minnesota Mining and Manufacturing Company (3M) decided to increase the size of its research laboratory in 1921.

William Vievering, 3M's first quality-assurance expert, ran a blind advertisement in a St. Paul newspaper looking for an assistant in the research lab. Drew was ready for a change and wrote back, "I realize that my services would not be worth much until a certain amount of practical experience is gained, and I would be glad to start with any salary you see fit to give." He got a job as a lab technician and worked for his entire career at the company.

Life's Work

Drew's life work was with 3M. From 1921 until he retired in 1962, he continued to work on new products, earning thirty U.S. patents as a result of his inventive efforts. His first major invention was an improved masking tape for auto body workers, patented in 1925. The tape made possible the two-tone paint schemes popular at the time because it stayed on the car through the paint process but came off after the paint dried without removing any of the paint when the tape was peeled away.

In 1930, Drew invented the product that revolutionized the tape industry. It was the first waterproof, see-through, pressure-sensitive tape that also acted as a barrier to moisture. The product was such a resounding success that even though the Great Depression was soon upon the country, 3M continued to thrive and did not have to lay off workers. Called Scotch tape, the product got its name when an auto painter became frustrated with Drew's sample masking tape (with adhesive only on the outer edges, not the middle), which fell off the car. He exclaimed to Drew, "Take this tape back to those Scotch bosses of yours and tell them to put more adhesive on it!" In his pejorative statement, "Scotch" meant "cheap." The pressure-sensitive tape that Drew later developed was highly successful because it had many uses around the house, from repairing torn pages in books to fixing broken toys and ripped curtains.

Propelled in large part by Drew's approach to inventing, the company culture of 3M was changed in the 1930's. Drew and two other men who were hired at the same time in 1921, Richard Carlton and Francis Okie, formed what could be called a "dream team" at 3M. They

Scotch Tape

When Richard G. Drew first began work at the Minnesota Mining and Manufacturing Company (3M) in the early 1920's, the company's major product was sandpaper. As part of product testing 3M's Wetordry sandpaper, Drew visited a local body shop, which needed sandpaper to prepare metal surfaces prior to painting.

Drew noticed the problems that the painters were having with the popular two-tone paint jobs. They were using a gummed tape to make the sharp edge between the colors, and when they removed the tape, some of the paint came with it. Drew was inspired to develop a tape that would meet the demands of the auto body industry.

3M already had some of the technology in place to produce a masking tape that would do the job because the sandpaper it manufactured required an adhesive compound to attach the "sand" to the "paper." Drew designed a sample masking tape and took it to the auto body painters for testing. To make the two-inch-wide tape more affordable, he applied adhesive only to the edges. When a car painter used the test tape, it fell off and, as the story goes, the painter told Drew to return the tape to his "Scotch bosses." The name "Scotch" was memorialized when Drew later designed the first line of successful transparent adhesive tape that he called Scotch tape. Today, even the tape dispensers are clad in plaid (suggesting a kilt).

The first tape that Drew invented was the result of two years' effort experimenting with vegetable oils, various resins, linseed, and glue glycerin. The final version was made in 1925 from cabinetmaker's glue; the tape was kept sticky with glycerin and used crepe paper for backing. This new Scotch Brand Masking Tape stuck to the car body but came off without pulling the paint with it.

Drew's invention set the stage for further development of a wide variety of tapes, all under the Scotch trademark. The one most widely known to the public was invented in 1930 under the name Scotch Brand Cellulose Tape. The name was later changed to the now famous Scotch Brand Transparent Tape.

The impetus for the transparent tape came in 1929, when the Flaxlinum Company, a St. Paul insulation firm, was contracted to insulate railroad refrigeration cars. The company needed a moisture-proof tape with which to wrap the insulation bats. The Scotch Brand Masking Tape did not work, however. By the time Drew and his assistants solved the problem a year later, the Flaxlinum Company was no longer interested, but there were many other potential customers such as bakers, meatpackers, and grocers. Pressure-sensitive tape soon became a ubiquitous feature of the manufacturing world.

were the early architects of innovation, independent thinkers who liked to tinker with ideas.

Over the years, Drew served as a mentor to many young engineers and inventors at the company. One of those was Paul Hansen, who worked as technical director at 3M. Hansen stated that working with Drew taught him many timeless lessons, which included these maxims: Anything worth doing is worth doing before it is perfected. Be a jack of all trades but a master of one. Put things in a nutshell. Be able to look at the broad picture and see the simple definition of the problem or task. It is easier to ask forgiveness than permission. Follow your instincts; your instincts are actually your total experience in practice. Don't keep blinders on all the time. It is good to have goals, but look around for opportunities at the same time. Most people are not stubborn enough; too many people give up at the first sign of failure. The reward for persistence is internal. People are generally recognized for the products of the work. The satisfaction also has to come from the effort that goes into making the success a reality.

In 1943, Drew established and became director of the Products Fabrication Laboratory (later the 3M Corporate Research Laboratory). Over the next twenty years, the lab worked on products ranging from improved reflective sheeting for traffic signs to breathable surgical tapes. The lab also performed experiments that led to the development of the Post-it note forty years later.

In 1978, Drew was inducted into the Minnesota Inventors Hall of Fame, and in 2007 his influence and achievements were again recognized as the National Inventors Hall of Fame inducted him as a member. Drew died at the age of eighty-one in 1980. His ever-handy products continue to live on.

IMPACT

Drew's place in history was firmly established by his invention of transparent adhesive tape. (More than 4.1 million miles of Scotch tape are sold every year, enough to circle Earth 165 times.) Still, Drew's greatest impact arguably could be the role he played in changing corporate culture as it relates to the inventive spirit.

One of Drew's first assignments with 3M was to improve the company's line of sandpaper. It was during this time that Drew became interested in making a tape that would mask off parts of a car so that different colors of paints could be applied. It was a frustrating process trying to get the right combination of materials for the tape, especially for its backing. After some time, William L. McKnight, president of 3M, told Drew to quit his personal project and return to the sandpaper project.

Drew, however, continued to work on the tape project, even going so far as writing multiple purchase orders for $99. (Everything over $100 had to be approved by management.) Drew eventually achieved success despite management's directives, and McKnight realized that the creative spirit should be encouraged, leading to what today is known in business as "bootlegging," or the 15 percent rule. Under this policy, employees are encouraged to use 15 percent of their working hours on projects of their own choosing. This policy helped 3M grow into one of the most innovative and successful companies in the world, and many other corporations followed suit, establishing similar work atmospheres for research and development.

—*Tom A. Hull*

FURTHER READING

Raber, Linda R. "Scotch Tape: An Innovation That Stuck." *Chemical and Engineering News* 85, no. 43 (October 22, 2007): 64. A short but valuable summary of the importance of Scotch tape and its designation in 2007 as an American Chemical Society National Historic Chemical Landmark. Drew's persistence is highlighted by Raber's citing the two years of experiments he conducted to solve the problems associated with his new adhesive tape.

3M Company. *A Century of Innovation: The 3M Story.* St. Paul, Minn.: Author, 2002. A comprehensive history of the company that is rich in details about Drew's contributions. Places Drew's work in the context of 3M's goals and how they were modified over the years for the company to thrive in a competitive world market.

Yoder, Robert M. "Stick-Up Man." *Saturday Evening Post* 221, no. 24 (December 11, 1948): 45-101. An excellent introduction to Drew that explains how he first got his job at 3M and how his inventions have affected society.

See also: Patsy O'Connell Sherman; Lewis Waterman.

John Boyd Dunlop

Scottish veterinarian

Dunlop developed many aspects of the pneumatic tire at exactly the right historical moment: Cycling was in its infancy, and the age of the motorcar was just around the corner. His inventions ensured the success, safety, and popularity of bicycles, automobiles, and other vehicles.

Born: February 5, 1840; Dreghorn, Ayrshire, Scotland
Died: October 23, 1921; Dublin, Ireland
Primary field: Automotive technology
Primary invention: Pneumatic rubber tire

Early Life

John Boyd Dunlop (DUHN-lop) was born into a farming family on February 5, 1840, in Dreghorn, Ayrshire, Scotland, the son of John Dunlop, a tenant farmer, and his wife, Agnes (née Boyd). As a young boy, he attended the local parish school and so excelled that even at an early age the schoolmaster had him teach arithmetic to the younger pupils. At some point, however, he was told that he was born two months earlier than expected. This apparently trivial point appears to have seriously disturbed Dunlop: He believed that it must have affected his health, and for much of his life he tended to avoid travel and other exertions. Indeed, he was considered somewhat too fragile as a boy to work on the farm and had to complete his schooling in Edinburgh. Having spent much of his childhood on the family farm, he developed a love of animals that undoubtedly influenced his decision to pursue a career in veterinary medicine.

He attended the Royal (Dick) Veterinary College in Edinburgh (now part of the University of Edinburgh) and was an excellent student, completing his studies in April, 1859, at the age of nineteen. After earning his diploma, along with an honorary fellowship of the Royal Veterinary Society of Edinburgh, he worked as a veterinarian in the city for several years before moving to northern Ireland in 1867 and establishing a very successful practice in Belfast. He married Margaret Stevenson, a farmer's daughter, in 1871, with whom he had a son, John (Johnnie), and a daughter, Jean.

Life's Work

Dunlop became well known in Belfast as a kind man and an excellent vet, a reputation that contributed to the success and growth of his practice. Within twenty years, his was one of the largest practices in Ireland, so large that he had to employ twelve men just to shoe horses. (Veterinarians at this time were essentially horse doctors and were almost indispensable, as horses were in such widespread use for personal and commercial transportation.) Dunlop had to cover a large area in his work and would have endured many uncomfortable rides, which, for a man of a delicate constitution, would have made him only too well aware of the bumpy nature of the city's streets.

His concern for the welfare of animals led him to attempt to ease the discomfort of horses that had to strain to haul heavy loads. The family doctor, Sir John Fagan, who was also a client of the veterinary practice, mentioned that he often attempted to improve his patients' comfort by having them lie on air-filled cushions, an idea that Dunlop attempted to apply to horse collars. Fagan

In 1887, John Boyd Dunlop rebuilt the tires of a tricycle for his son, Johnnie (pictured). The following year, Dunlop received a patent for his pneumatic tires, and the modern tire industry was soon established. (Roger Viollet/Getty Images)

also suggested that ten-year-old Johnnie take up cycling as exercise.

The pedal bicycle had itself been invented only a few decades earlier by Kirkpatrick MacMillan in 1839, but its wheels were bare metal, giving no comfort over the jolts and vibrations of the roadways. Solid rubber tires were introduced after Charles Goodyear's improvement of the vulcanization process (patented in 1844) that made rubber sufficiently durable for such use, but they gave only moderately better comfort. The bicycle itself underwent many developments, culminating in the invention of the "safety cycle" by John Kemp Starley in 1885. One of the most significant and fundamental changes to the bicycle, and one that would revolutionize its use, was made by Dunlop just three years later.

Johnnie complained of the jarring he experienced in riding over the bumps of Belfast's cobbled streets, prompting his father to set himself to make cycling more enjoyable for his son. He realized that air would cushion the ride of a cyclist, just as it cushioned his horses' collars and Fagan's patients: He made the crucial mental leap to see that a hollow tube filled with air, attached to the rim of each wheel, would provide the means to achieve this. Dunlop's first experiments used a solid wooden wheel, to which he attached the inflated rubber tube inside a rubberized canvas cover nailed to the wheel. By comparing the bouncing and rolling properties of this wheel with one shod in solid tires, he not surprisingly found that the cushioned tires performed better. Next, Dunlop applied his principle to the rear wheels of his son's tricycle. He improved the construction of the covered air tubes, attached them around wooden wheel rims, and even included a primitive valve for inflation of the tire. A trial of the modified tricycle in February, 1888, conducted secretly at night, immediately established its improved comfort and speed. These successes led Dunlop to demonstrate his technology to local businessmen, and he applied for a patent for his pneumatic tires in July, 1888.

Many more tests were made, culminating in Dunlop designing and purchasing tires from a Scottish company that were fitted to locally built cycles. These were put on sale, complete with pneumatic tires. A local racing cyclist, William Hume, also ordered a machine equipped with the new tires, and when in May, 1889, Hume defeated many superior riders who raced with solid rubber tires, the future of the pneumatic tire seemed secured. Later that year, Dunlop went into business with the entrepreneur William Harvey Du Cros, whose sons had been among the riders Hume de-

Pneumatic Tires

The tires of any automobile, bicycle, or other wheeled vehicle are generally the only part of that vehicle that is in constant contact with the surface of the roadway. As such, they are a crucial part of the vehicle's design, being integral to any consideration of its potential speed and maneuverability, the comfort of its ride, and its safety. The pneumatic tire is beneficial in all these aspects when compared with solid tires—and certainly when compared with bare wheel rims.

Modern pneumatic tires follow a design that is not much different from John Boyd Dunlop's. They consist of a continuous air-filled rubber cushion that forms a ring around the rim of a wheel. This is surrounded by outer protective layers that help maintain the integrity of the crucial inner tube. Rubber and rubberized fabric are still the basic components, and steel wire is still used to hold the tire to the rim. Chemicals are added to the rubber to improve its resistance to wear, heat, and aging. Dunlop's original tires were made from natural rubber, which is slightly air-permeable and hence suffered from very slow deflation, just like a balloon. The inner tubes of modern tires use synthetic butyl rubber, which is much more impermeable.

Robert William Thomson's invention of the pneumatic tire in 1846 was far ahead of its time. His design was rather elaborate, and, although it worked well, was too costly and impractical. Nevertheless, his experiments with horse-drawn wagons did establish significant improvements in traction on a variety of surfaces. Had there been sufficient demand for his innovation, history would have remembered and celebrated Thomson, and not Dunlop, as the true inventor of the pneumatic tire.

Dunlop, on the other hand, was also lucky. In 1888, he independently "reinvented" the pneumatic tire at a crucial point in the history and development of transportation. Cycling was just beginning to take off, and the internal combustion engine was soon to be invented, giving birth to the motorcar. Equally important was the fact that the rubber industry and rubber technology were well established in Dunlop's time. The pneumatic tire took cycling from the realm of racing, where only the most determined sportsmen would tolerate such excessive vibrations, and turned it into a highly popular pastime that could be enjoyed by all. Moreover, in practical terms, the motorcar would have been impossible without pneumatic tires. All of these factors contributed to the demand for, and success of, Dunlop's pneumatic tires.

feated, and the two men launched the Pneumatic Tyre and Booth's Cycle Agency.

After retiring from practice in 1892, Dunlop remained active in the tire business. Du Cros, meanwhile, helped steer the company through many troubles, the principal of which was the revelation that Dunlop's patent was invalid: His fellow Scot, Robert William Thomson, had already patented the pneumatic tire in 1846. However, Dunlop and the firm held auxiliary patents, notably for the non-return valve, wheel rims, and methods of attaching the tire to the rim. The company survived much turmoil and litigation and would ultimately become the Dunlop Rubber Company, an international group that by 1954 comprised over 130 companies manufacturing a broad range of rubber goods, sports and cycling equipment, and, of course, tires.

Dunlop lived quietly in Ballsbridge, near Dublin, in his retirement. Despite his tendency to hypochondria, he enjoyed good health all his life and lived until the age of eighty-one. He had no serious illness until late 1921 when, suddenly and unexpectedly, he died following a slight chill on October 23. Dunlop had worked on a history of the pneumatic tire over the last few years of his life; the book was published posthumously by his daughter, Jean McClintock.

Impact

Dunlop's "reinvention" of the pneumatic tire revolutionized virtually all of land transportation. It is hard to think of riding in any road vehicle without the cushioning that tires provide. It is truly remarkable to realize that all of Dunlop's original experiments, and the technological advances that they brought, were achieved by a man who was neither a cyclist nor an engineer, but a vet, working only with his own hands and with the relatively simple tools and materials available to him at home and at his business.

Despite having no valid patent, Dunlop managed to bring his tires to the world, and they are now as ubiquitous as the bicycle and the automobile: Modern life is almost unimaginable without them. He made little profit from his invention, yet his name is remembered through the quirk of fate that he was—historically—in the right place at the right time. Nevertheless, his unique circumstances and his critical realization of the potential applications of pneumatics justify his place in history.

Dunlop's tires changed the world in many other unexpected ways as well. Ironically, they had a significant effect upon the veterinary profession. When the popularity of cycling and the automobile rocketed, with a corresponding drop in horse riding, "horse doctors" were forced to expand their horizons. They began treating pets and other types of animals, becoming much more like the veterinarians that are familiar today.

—Thomas D. McGrath

Further Reading

Du Cros, Sir Arthur. *Wheels of Fortune: A Salute to Pioneers*. London: Chapman & Hall, 1938. Detailed account of the business partnership between Dunlop and Du Cros, of the development of the pneumatic tire, and of the early fortunes of the Dunlop Rubber Company, as told by Du Cros's son. The narrative is filled with many personal and historical particulars. Appendixes, index.

Haney, Paul. *The Racing and High Performance Tire*. Warrendale, Pa.: Society of Automotive Engineers, 2003. A somewhat technical, but highly informative, description of pneumatic tires and of how and why their construction and behavior relates to vehicle safety and performance. Tables, index, list of Internet resources.

Herlihy, David V. *Bicycle: The History*. New Haven, Conn.: Yale University Press, 2004. Extensively researched and illustrated history of the bicycle that also looks individually at the history and development of many of its components, including the tires. Bibliographic notes, index.

McMillan, James. *The Dunlop Story: The Life, Death and Re-birth of a Multi-National*. London: Weidenfeld and Nicolson, 1989. A retelling of the story of this company, from Dunlop's initial experiments, to his partnership with Du Cros, and into the middle of the twentieth century. Many of the company's innovations in tire and rubber technology are highlighted. Bibliographic notes, index.

Tompkins, Eric. *The History of the Pneumatic Tyre*. Suffolk, England: Eastland Press, 1981. A detailed account of the development of the pneumatic tire up to recent times, written by a retired former employee of the Dunlop company. Indexes.

See also: Carl Benz; Nicolas-Joseph Cugnot; Gottlieb Daimler; Rudolf Diesel; Henry Ford; Charles Goodyear; Charles F. Kettering; Étienne Lenoir; Hiram Percy Maxim; André and Édouard Michelin; Ransom Eli Olds; Nikolaus August Otto; Stanford Ovshinsky; Sylvester Roper; Ignaz Schwinn; Felix Wankel; Alexander Winton.

George Eastman

American businessman

Eastman invented roll film, making it possible for photographs to be taken more speedily without using breakable glass plates and hazardous chemicals. His invention allowed ordinary people to indulge in photography and opened the way for the rise of the motion-picture industry.

Born: July 12, 1854; Waterville, New York
Died: March 14, 1932; Rochester, New York
Primary field: Photography
Primary inventions: Roll film; Kodak camera

Early Life

George Eastman was born to George Washington Eastman and Maria Kilbourn. He had three older siblings, one of whom died in infancy. In 1865, his family moved to Rochester, New York, after his father established the Eastman Commercial College there. His father died in 1867, the college failed, and an older sister died in 1870. At the age of fourteen, Eastman quit high school to support his mother and sister as a messenger boy for an insurance company, earning three dollars per week. He eventually went to a different insurance company, where he made five dollars per week and was soon in charge of filing and writing policies. He was ambitious and bright, studying accounting at night, hoping to get a better-paying job. By 1874, he was working at a bank and earning fifteen dollars per week.

George Eastman. (©Smithsonian Institution)

At age twenty-four, he developed an interest in photography when he planned a vacation trip to Santo Domingo and it was suggested that he make a photographic record of his trip. He was irked to find how complicated that would be: The paraphernalia required to take photographs was very complicated. He needed not only a huge camera that required a heavy tripod to support it but also chemicals, tanks, a jug of water, glass plates, and a tent in which to make and apply the emulsions for the glass plates and in which to develop the exposed plates before they dried. In addition, he had to take lessons, at a cost of five dollars, to learn how to use all the gear for the picture taking. He did not go to Santo Domingo, but he continued to be fascinated with photography. Even as he continued working in the bank, he began what would become his life's work—finding new and simpler ways to make photographs.

Life's Work

About 1878, Eastman was inspired to find a way to eliminate much of the gear needed to take photographs. He probed journals dealing with photography and learned of a British emulsion process that kept the treated glass plates sensitive enough to take pictures even after the emulsion dried. He experimented with gelatin emulsions of his own design based on British formulas, working at night in his mother's kitchen after he had put in a day's work at the bank. It took him three years, but he finally produced a formula that worked. By 1880, he developed and patented a machine that would prepare the plates in greater numbers than previously possible. He decided to start his own company, the Eastman Dry Plate and Film Company, to make dry plates to sell to photographers.

On a leased third floor of a building in Rochester, he started making his dry plates. As the business grew, he saw the need for a product that would serve both professional photographers and amateurs. To make photography more convenient and accessible, Eastman worked to find a component to produce the photographic images that was lighter and more flexible than the bulky and breakable glass plates. After some experimentation, he found that an emulsion-coated paper on a roll could be used in cameras instead of glass plates. The paper roll film was successful even though the quality of the pictures taken with the film was not very satisfactory because the grain of the paper showed on the developed pictures. Eastman continued to experiment, using layers of gelatins that ultimately allowed the photographic image to be recorded on one of the gelatin layers instead of on the paper. This gelatinous flexible film eventually evolved into the familiar roll film.

Shortly thereafter, Eastman, along with associate William Hall Walker, designed and began the manufacture of a smaller, lighter-weight camera that could use the roll film. The result was the first Kodak camera, initially called the "roll holder breast camera." People who bought and used the camera got their pictures developed and printed by sending the entire camera back to the Eastman Company along with a $10 processing fee; they received back their printed pictures and their camera reloaded with a new 100-exposure roll of film, ready to use again.

By 1900, Eastman was interested in further increasing the burgeoning interest in photography. To make it a hobby for the masses, he introduced a camera costing one dollar, the Brownie, which he ostensibly intended for children. His earlier camera cost around $15 and was therefore out of the reach of many ordinary people. By 1901, the Brownie's price had dropped to 25 cents. Owners no longer had to send the camera to the manufacturer for processing; they bought and loaded the film, took the pictures, and needed to send only the film to the company for development and printing.

The Brownie was a fixed-focus lens box camera made of wood or metal (after 1930, plastic). Eastman's company also manufactured a folding camera that was compact and portable. Unlike other such cameras marketed around the country at the same time, the Brownie was both efficient and inexpensive; it was even capable of producing the popular postcard-size pictures.

Eastman's company became one of the most lucrative in the country. He stepped down from day-to-day management of the business by 1925 and became chairman of the board. He shifted his sights to philanthropy, becoming one of the most generous philanthropists of his

Roll Film

George Eastman's primary goal was to simplify the photographic process and reduce the amount of gear, time, and effort needed to take a picture. When he first set this goal, photographers had to go through a complicated process. A glass plate had to be coated with a liquid emulsion just moments before the picture was to be taken. Then, once the exposure was made, the picture had to be developed immediately. This required having a mobile darkroom to accommodate all the chemicals and paraphernalia right on the site where the pictures were to be taken.

Eastman, along with collaborators, first developed a dry, pre-coated plate that could be used in much the same way as the wet one, but with the convenience of being already prepared for exposure for the picture taking. However, in order to use a small camera that would not need a tripod, he worked to produce a dry, transparent, flexible film and a small camera to use it. The film he developed took pictures in black and white. He used paper as a light and flexible support for the needed emulsion. He coated the paper with layers of a soluble gelatin followed by layers of insoluble, light-sensitive gelatin.

The layers of gelatin had different roles to play in the making of a photograph. Some filtered light or controlled the chemical reactions that took place. Others, that made the actual image, contained silver-halide crystals, which underwent a photochemical reaction when exposed to light through the camera lens and thus captured the photographic image. Once the film was exposed, it was developed using chemicals that broke down the crystals into silver, enhancing the image. Another chemical was then used to halt the light sensitivity of the film and to set the negative image so that a picture could be printed.

This new flexible film, mounted on a spool, needed a new kind of camera, and Eastman invented the Kodak camera. A rectangular box with a fixed-focus lens, his camera could hold the spool of film and a take-up spool that allowed as many as one hundred exposures to be made without the need to unload or reload the camera.

These two inventions took photography out of the exclusive purview of professional photographers and introduced it to the masses as a way to record and save precious memories. They also opened up a new and lucrative business that made millionaires of Eastman and his associates. A direct by-product of Eastman's work was the development of the motion-picture industry, which owes much to Eastman's invention of transparent roll film.

time, an era that included such philanthropic giants as Andrew Carnegie and John D. Rockefeller. He donated more than $75 million over the years to various causes, including wage dividend benefits (profit-sharing) as incentives for his employees at the Eastman Kodak Company, setting up dental clinics in Rochester, and supporting the city's theater and symphony orchestra. Other recipients of his largesse were the University of Rochester, which he endowed with funds for a school of music and a school of dentistry; the Massachusetts Institute of Technology, which was given buildings; and Tuskegee and Hampton Institutes, which received some of the $30 million he earmarked just for educational institutions.

By 1930, Eastman had begun to experience poor health. He suffered from a degenerative spinal disorder, which may have been spinal stenosis (resulting from calcification in the vertebrae). His beloved mother had suffered the same kind of disease and was confined to a wheelchair during the final two years of her life. Having always been a very active person who traveled, often to Europe, and was involved in business and civic affairs, Eastman became increasingly depressed as he foresaw his coming incapacitation. Never married, though long involved in a platonic relationship with the wife of a business associate, he never really got over the loss of his mother when she died in 1907. He remembered how painful her last two years were and did not want the same end for himself. On March 14, 1932, he put his affairs in order and wrote a final note that read, "My work is done. Why wait?" and committed suicide with a pistol.

Impact

Eastman's inventions changed American photography, making photography something the masses could enjoy, where before only a few professionals could deal with its complexities. His roll film eliminated the fragile, cumbersome glass plates needed to catch the images in the bulky cameras of the time. Instead of relying on the slow, complicated process that produced one picture at a time using several procedures, Eastman's roll film sped up the process and allowed numerous images to be captured in fairly rapid succession. After roll film, he produced a camera to use the film, one that was smaller than its predecessors, easier to use, and certainly cheaper to buy. He said in his Kodak advertisements, "You press the button, we do the rest."

The Eastman Kodak Company made photography an easier business for professional photographers as well as an affordable, fun hobby for amateurs, and Eastman's work made him a millionaire. The wealth that he acquired because of his inventions was shared with others. He became involved in many philanthropic endeavors. Even before he became a millionaire, he began sharing his fortune with the employees of his company: He was one of the earliest businessmen to set up pension plans and insurance plans for workers. Once his fortune was made, he shared it in several different areas, particularly to the advantage of his hometown of Rochester, and to educational and medical institutions all over the country.

—*Jane L. Ball*

Further Reading

Ackerman, Carl W. *George Eastman: Founder of Kodak and the Photography Business.* Washington, D.C.: BeardBooks, 1930. A biography that gives an intimate view of Eastman's life, based on free access to Eastman's files and correspondence. Discusses events of the era affecting Eastman.

Brayer, Elizabeth. *George Eastman: A Biography.* Rochester, N.Y.: University of Rochester Press, 2006. A scholarly biography that shows the many facets of Eastman: cold, modest, generous. Discusses his business endeavors and personal life, including those private affairs that are either admirable or dubious, and insights into the patent infringement lawsuits he dealt with. Several rare photographs.

Tedlow, Richard S. *Giants of Enterprise: Seven Business Innovators and the Empires They Built.* New York: HarperBusiness, 2001. The histories of seven business leaders, with chapters devoted to each. Eastman's chapter (about thirty pages long) tells how he accomplished his business success.

West, Nancy M. *Kodak and the Lens of Nostalgia.* Charlottesville: University of Virginia Press, 2000. Concerned mostly with the advertising strategies of the Kodak Company and how important they were to the company's success, as well as how they helped lure the American consumer to the hobby of photography. Many ads are reproduced; some of Eastman's inventions, the Brownie camera especially, are discussed.

See also: Harold E. Edgerton; Thomas Alva Edison; Auguste and Louis Lumiére.

John Presper Eckert

American electrical engineer

Eckert helped design and build the ENIAC, the world's first fully electronic, general-purpose computer. He also founded the first commercial computer company, the Eckert-Mauchly Computer Corporation, which designed the first commercial computer in the United States, the UNIVAC.

Born: April 9, 1919; Philadelphia, Pennsylvania
Died: June 3, 1995; Bryn Mawr, Pennsylvania
Also known as: John Adam Presper Eckert, Jr. (full name)
Primary fields: Computer science; electronics and electrical engineering
Primary inventions: Electronic Numerical Integrator and Computer (ENIAC); Binary Automatic Computer (BINAC)

Early Life

John Adam Presper "Pres" Eckert, Jr., was born in Philadelphia in 1919. The Eckert family was part of the economic and social elite. His father, John Eckert, Sr., was a wealthy real estate developer who arranged for a chauffeur to take his son to elementary school (William Penn Charter School). Pres liked to design and build things, especially electronics. He built a crystal radio set at age eight. At the age of twelve, he won first prize in a local science fair with a remote-controlled boat that floated in a large basin of water. It was steered with electromagnets under the basin. At age fifteen, he designed, and set off on the school stage, a remote-controlled bomb with a push-button box in the audience. He also designed a sound system for a nearby cemetery to mask the sound of the crematoriums so that mourners would not be disturbed. In high school, Eckert belonged to the downtown Engineer's Club of Philadelphia. He also spent afternoons in the laboratory of television inventor Philo T. Farnsworth, who lived in nearby Chestnut Hill.

Eckert enrolled in the University of Pennsylvania's Wharton School of Business. While his parents encouraged him to major in business, he soon transferred to the university's Moore School of Electrical Engineering and graduated in 1941. He then began graduate work at the Moore School and was offered a position. He applied for his first patent in 1940 (awarded in 1942) for what was essentially a motion-picture sound system.

Life's Work

By the time of Eckert's graduation, the Moore School had become a major source of technical and computational assistance for the U.S. Army Ordnance Department Ballistics Research Laboratory. The focus for the laboratory was the production of very complex ballistics firing tables, which provided trajectories for weapons. The first major joint project in the 1930's had been to build a differential analyzer (an electromechanical computer similar to one built by Vannevar Bush at Massachusetts Institute of Technology) to calculate ballistic trajectories.

At the Moore School, Eckert focused his research on radar (timing devices that measured the distance to targets). His work on radar involved the development of high-speed electronic circuits and a mercury delay line, both of which he used in later computer construction. He also made improvements to the speed and the precision of the school's differential analyzer.

Eckert took a position in 1941 as lab assistant for a summer school course on electronics offered by the U.S. Department of War through the Moore School. It was a ten-week crash course for people holding degrees in related fields to build a pool of expertise for war research. During the course, Eckert met Dr. John William Mauchly, chairman of the Physics Department at Ursinus College. Mauchly was enrolled in the course and took a teaching position at the Moore School that fall.

Mauchly came to the Moore School with ideas on the development of a computer. Initially, no one at the Moore School was very interested. By 1943, the Ballistics Research Laboratory had fallen behind in calculating ballistics tables because of the high demand during World War II. The Army asked the Moore School to build a machine to assist them. Eckert became the project's chief engineer and oversaw the design of individual circuits.

Construction of the Electronic Numerical Integrator and Computer (ENIAC) began in 1944. Although it was still considered in a test phase, the machine was used in the spring of 1945 to do calculations for ballistics projects and for the atomic bomb project at Los Alamos National Laboratory. In 1946, the ENIAC was disassembled and moved to the ballistics laboratory in Maryland. It became the first large-scale, electronic, digital computer in daily use.

While working on the ENIAC, Eckert and Mauchly

developed the stored-program concept, which they incorporated into the design of their next computer, the Electronic Discrete Variable Automatic Computer (EDVAC). This concept involved storing data and programs together in memory so that the computer could be programmed without changing the electronics or rearranging plug boards. However, Eckert and Mauchly left the Moore School before the EDVAC was built.

Eckert wanted to pursue the commercial side of computers and partnered with Mauchly to found the Electronic Control Company. They received an order from the National Bureau of Standards (later the National Institute of Standards and Technology) to build the Universal Automatic Computer (UNIVAC) for the Census Bureau. While sorting out financing details on the UNIVAC, they built the Binary Automatic Computer (BINAC) for the Northrop Aircraft Company from 1947 to 1949. It was the first operational, electronic, stored-program computer in the United States. It was also the first machine that stored data on magnetic tape.

Eckert and Mauchly used their work on the BINAC to refine their plans for the UNIVAC. They also used the BINAC to demonstrate to potential customers and received orders for UNIVAC machines in advance of any construction on the first one for the Census Bureau. However, it was almost impossible to estimate production costs, and they ran into financial difficulties. In 1950, Eckert and Mauchly were forced to sell the company (which had become the Eckert-Mauchly Computer Corporation) to Remington Rand in order to avoid going bankrupt.

The first UNIVAC was delivered to the Census Bureau in 1951. It became only the second electronic computer produced for a commercial customer. The production of forty-five additional UNIVACs set up Remington Rand as the world's first large-scale computer company. The UNIVAC also showed the public just what a computer could do when it correctly predicted the winner of the 1952 U.S. presidential election based on samples of early returns—a surprising landslide victory for Dwight D. Eisenhower.

Eckert remained with Remington Rand and stayed with the company when it became Sperry Rand and finally Unisys. In 1989, he retired but continued to act as a consultant for

ENIAC

The Electronic Numerical Integrator and Computer, or ENIAC, was the most complex electronic equipment of any kind at the time it was built. It was programmable and used conditional (if-then) branching logic. Though the ENIAC was programmable, reprogramming the machine could take days. To give the computer new instructions, the operator had to change external wiring manually, similar to how a telephone operator used to rearrange plugs on a switchboard.

The ENIAC had been designed to calculate trajectories for weapons for the U.S. Army. Before the ENIAC, it took a person twenty hours to perform a trajectory calculation. The differential analyzer used at the Moore School before the ENIAC took thirty minutes. The ENIAC did the calculation in thirty seconds. The machine could execute up to five thousand additions per second.

The ENIAC took up eighteen hundred square feet with eighteen thousand vacuum tubes. It weighed thirty tons and consumed 174 kilowatts of power. The machine was made up of individual units arranged in a horseshoe shape along the outside walls of a large room. The units were accumulators, multipliers, a unit for division and square roots, a unit of three function tables to store values for use by the machine, a card reader for input, a card punch for output, and a programming unit.

The ENIAC stored decimal digits with a "ring counter" designed by John Presper Eckert that used ten "flip-flops" (0-9). A flip-flop consisted of a pair of vacuum tubes connected so that only one conducted electricity at a given time. The flip-flop was in a 1 (on) state when it was conducting and in a 0 (off) state when another was conducting. At a given time, only one flip-flop in the ring could be on. To add the number 2 to the number 3 already in the ring counter, the machine sent two pulses into the ring counter. This turned on the fifth flip-flop in the ring. Then, if six pulses were added, the "on" would travel all the way around the ring and produce a carry pulse that caused the next highest ring to advance one place as well as turn on the first flip-flop in this ring.

The ENIAC was much more reliable than early critics had predicted. Because of the known unreliability of vacuum tubes, Eckert chose to focus on careful circuit design for reliability. He employed a "worst case" design strategy. For example, if a resistor needed to be able to withstand at least 0.25 watt, he used resistors with ratings of 0.5 or above. He also used tubes that drew far less current than what they were rated for, and they lasted longer. Eckert used only a few basic types of circuits and made them easily accessible for servicing. He also designed vacuum tubes with an average lifetime of 2,500 hours once they reached a final operating temperature. However, they had a high failure rate during warm-up, so the ENIAC engineers did not turn off the machine. It was shut down on October 2, 1955.

the company. Between 1948 and 1966, Eckert took out patents on eighty-five inventions, almost all electronic in nature. He died of leukemia in Bryn Mawr, Pennsylvania, in 1995.

Impact

Pres Eckert, with John William Mauchly, invented the first general-purpose, electronic, digital computer. They also presented the first course in computing topics, founded the first commercial computer company, and designed the first commercial computer in the United States, which used the mercury delay-line memory developed by Eckert.

The ENIAC was the first electronic machine to solve complex numerical problems and had flexible enough programming that it could solve a variety of problems. It consistently and reliably solved numerical problems beyond human capacity and insoluble by any other means.

While World War II sparked the need for large numerical calculations and thus the need for computers, it was the perseverance and vision of Eckert and Mauchly that moved the computer out of university and government laboratories and into the commercial world. Although their attempts at commercialization were less than successful, Eckert and Mauchly built a foundation on which a viable computer industry developed in the United States. For many years, Remington Rand's product line was based on Eckert and Mauchly's basic designs.

—Linda Eikmeier Endersby

Further Reading

Hally, Mike. *Electronic Brains: Stories from the Dawn of the Computer Age*. Washington, D.C.: J. Henry Press, 2005. The first chapter presents a readable, person-driven account of Eckert's work. Appendixes include information on the technical elements for nontechnical readers. Illustrations, bibliography, index.

McCartney, Scott. *ENIAC: The Triumphs and Tragedies of the World's First Computer*. New York: Walker, 1999. Focuses on the human side of the development of the ENIAC. Provides interesting stories based on personal correspondence between Eckert and Mauchly. Illustrations, notes, bibliography, index.

Norberg, Arthur L. *Computers and Commerce: A Study of Technology and Management at Eckert-Mauchly Computer Company, Engineering Research Associates, and Remington Rand, 1946-1957*. Cambridge, Mass.: MIT Press, 2005. Provides a good, detailed analysis of Eckert's commercial ventures. Also provides information on ventures from other companies of the time. Illustrations, index, sources.

Stern, Nancy. *From ENIAC to UNIVAC: An Appraisal of the Eckert-Mauchly Computers*. Bedford, Mass.: Digital Press, 1981. Provides an account of all four machines built by Eckert and Mauchly and focuses on their entrepreneurship. Examines each machine in detail as well as controversies surrounding who invented the computer. Illustrations, bibliography, notes, appendixes, index.

Swedin, Eric G., and David L. Ferro. *Computers: The Life Story of a Technology*. Westport, Conn.: Greenwood Press, 2005. Very readable accounts of various people involved in the development of the computer. Contains small sections on the ENIAC, EDVAC, and UNIVAC but little personal information on Eckert. Illustrations, index, bibliography.

Williams, Michael R. *A History of Computing Technology*. 2d ed. Los Alamitos, Calif.: IEEE Computer Society Press, 1997. Chapter on the ENIAC including very detailed descriptions of the technical components. Minor personal details on Eckert. Illustration, end notes, further reading, appendixes (time tables), index.

See also: John Vincent Atanasoff; John Bardeen; John William Mauchly; George Stibitz.

HAROLD E. EDGERTON

American electrical engineer

Edgerton was an electrical engineer who pioneered the development of high-speed photography, employing and perfecting the electronic flash. He used the electronic flash to study motions as diverse as the splash of a milk drop and the flapping of the wings of a bat.

Born: April 6, 1903; Fremont, Nebraska
Died: January 4, 1990; Cambridge, Massachusetts
Also known as: Harold Eugene Edgerton (full name); Doc Edgerton
Primary field: Electronics and electrical engineering
Primary inventions: Electronic flash strobe light; high-speed photography

EARLY LIFE

Harold Eugene Edgerton was born on April 6, 1903, in Fremont, Nebraska, the eldest of three children to Frank Eugene Edgerton and Mary Nettie (Coe). His father was the high school principal and coached the football team. Edgerton's family moved several times. First, they moved to Washington, D.C., where his father served as a correspondent for the Lincoln, Nebraska, newspaper; then they moved to Lincoln, and finally to Aurora, Nebraska, where Edgerton attended high school. During that period, his uncle, Ralph Edgerton, a studio photographer, taught Edgerton the basics of photography. Edgerton bought his first camera when he was fourteen years old and set up a darkroom in his house so he could develop and process his own images.

As a child, Edgerton enjoyed taking apart mechanical devices to figure out how they worked and fixing those that were broken. While in high school, he worked for the Nebraska Power and Light Company. Although he was hired to perform janitorial and maintenance tasks in the office, many of the men who repaired the power lines were called into military service during World War I, and Edgerton was assigned to repair power lines. He described this job as challenging, because he had to solve different kinds of problems each day.

Edgerton decided to pursue a career in electrical engineering and entered the University of Nebraska, Lincoln, in 1921. He was awarded a bachelor of science degree in electrical engineering in 1925 and spent the next year working at General Electric in Schenectady, New York. In 1926, Edgerton began graduate studies in electrical engineering at the Massachusetts Institute of Technology (MIT), in Cambridge, Massachusetts.

LIFE'S WORK

Edgerton received his master's degree in electrical engineering from MIT in 1927. He was appointed an instructor in electrical engineering at the university, beginning a more than fifty-year association with the research institute. He also continued to work toward his Ph.D., investigating the effects of sudden changes, such as the power surge caused by a lightning strike on a power line, on the rotation of large electric motors. However, the motor rotated too fast for his eye to see the effects. Edgerton noticed that the device he was using to send power surges to the motor produced a flash of light accompanying each power surge. He realized that if he synchronized these light flashes with the rotation rate of the motor, its parts appeared to stand still.

In 1929, Edgerton asked Kenneth Beardsley, one of his graduate students, to use a pulsing mercury-arc lamp to examine motor rotation and to try to record the results photographically. Edgerton recognized that each light flash would expose an image, recording the motor's position in a photograph. By 1930, Edgerton was using a mercury arc that emitted sixty flashes per second, each having a duration of only $^{1}/_{100,000}$ second, to study the behavior of a motor as it began to rotate.

Edgerton and Beardsley were not the first people to combine a light flash with photography. The first flash photograph, made using a spark to expose the image, was made in 1851 by William Fox Talbot, shortly after photography was invented. At the time, photographs required very long exposures, so only stationary objects were suitable subjects. Talbot said that combining electric sparks with photography had the potential for obtaining photographs of moving objects. However, the spark photography technique was treated simply as a curiosity until Edgerton developed it as a serious research tool and a new art form.

Edgerton was awarded a doctor of science degree in electrical engineering in 1931, and his stroboscope was described in the May, 1931, issue of the research journal *Electrical Engineering*. Edgerton saw the value of his device as a tachometer, an instrument used to measure rotation rates, and submitted a patent application in 1933. In 1934, he contracted with the General Radio Company to produce his suitcase-size mercury-arc stroboscope, the Strobotach.

In 1928, Edgerton married Esther May Garrett, whom he first met when her family moved to Aurora, Nebraska, in 1915. They had three children, Mary, William, and Robert. During the summer of 1934, Edgerton and his family drove back to Nebraska for a visit. Edgerton stopped at factories on the route, trying to interest them in his Strobotach.

As word spread of his success in photographing rapidly moving objects, people visited Edgerton's laboratory seeking assistance on their own projects—initially, other faculty members who had research that might benefit from Edgerton's electronic flash. Edgerton credited MIT professor Charles Stark Draper with suggesting that he explore other uses for the strobe light. Draper told Edgerton, "The whole world is moving," inspiring Edgerton to take photographs of everyday objects and events. His first such photograph was a high-speed picture of water running from a faucet, highlighting the complexity of the motion. From then on, as Edgerton said, "it was just looking at one problem after another."

Edgerton and Kenneth Germeshausen, his research assistant, were both amateur photographers, so they began making still and motion pictures of all kinds of objects in rapid motion. These photographs showed everyday events in a way never before been seen. One photograph, taken in 1934, showing a football being placekicked, recorded the distortion of the football as the kicker's foot penetrated nearly halfway into the ball.

Three of Edgerton's photographs were included in the Royal Photographic Society's annual exhibition in London in 1933, the first time his photography was exhibited. Edgerton's most famous image is "Coronet," which shows in fine detail the symmetry of the splash made by a drop of milk striking a flat surface. That photograph was featured in the first-ever exhibit of photography at the Museum of Modern Art in New York City in 1937. Edgerton went on to photograph athletes in action; hummingbirds in flight; and bullets bursting balloons, cutting through playing cards, and penetrating a light bulb. Many of Edgerton's photographs were used as illustrations for articles in *National Geographic* and in *Life* magazines. In 1940, Edgerton was invited to Hollywood by MGM Studios to describe how his stop-action photography could be used in movies. This resulted in a short film, titled *Quicker than a Wink!* and starring Edgerton, which won an Academy Award.

Edgerton had formed a business partnership with Germeshausen in 1931. Together they improved on his original device. They wanted a brighter flash with an even shorter duration than the mercury arc could deliver. This effort resulted in the development of the xenon flashtube as a replacement for the mercury-arc source used in the original device.

Edgerton's electronic flash opened new avenues for the scientific study of the dynamics of fluids, air currents, and engines. During World War II, the U.S. Army sought Edgerton's help in developing an extremely bright flash for night aerial photography. The system Edgerton developed was used to monitor the night movement of enemy troops during the Battle of Monte Cassino in Italy and in the weeks before the Allied invasion of Normandy.

After World War II, Edgerton founded a company with Germeshausen and another of his research assistants, Herbert Grier. The company, now EG&G, received a contract from the Atomic Energy Commission

THE ELECTRONIC FLASH

The electronic flash is a device that produces a short, intense burst of light. The light pulse from an electronic flash can be used to "stop the motion" of a fast-moving object. The stroboscopic light is an electronic flash that produces a sequence of light pulses. The stroboscopic light can show a sequence of events, such as an insect flapping its wings, allowing the details of the motion to be studied.

Harold E. Edgerton's original electronic flash used a mercury-arc lamp. A large electric current passing through the mercury gas emitted a flash of light. However, the design quickly evolved as he sought to achieve a brighter flash of shorter duration, the modern electronic flash. This design consists of a gas discharge tube, a sealed cylindrical glass tube filled with inert gases. Electrical contacts at both ends of the tube are connected to a capacitor, a device that can store a large amount of electric charge. A battery or other electric power source is used to charge the capacitor. A high voltage is applied to the electrical contacts, ionizing the gas in the tube. These ions form a conductive path, and the capacitor releases its energy as an electric current through the tube, like a miniature lightning bolt. The flash ceases when the capacitor has used all of its stored energy. This discharge is very rapid, sometimes faster than one-millionth of a second. Once the current ceases to flow, the ions recombine with electrons that have been stripped off by the initial high voltage, and the flash is ready for use again. The choice of gas determines the color of the flash. Argon produces a bluish light, krypton reddish-green, and xenon a white flash resembling sunlight, making xenon ideal for photography.

to design timing and firing systems for atomic bomb testing. EG&G also developed a high-speed shutter for a camera that was used to photograph the explosion of atomic bombs, showing the structure of the intense fireball that developed as the atomic explosion propagated down the wires of the tower on which it was detonated.

In 1952, Edgerton developed an underwater camera for an expedition led by the underwater explorer Jacques Cousteau. Edgerton and Cousteau photographed the Romanche Trench, a deep trench in the Atlantic Ocean. Cousteau's crew nicknamed Edgerton "Papa Flash." On later expeditions with Cousteau, Edgerton participated in the location of the wreckage of the *Britannic*, a sister ship of the *Titanic* that was sunk by a German mine during World War I, as well as ancient wrecks. Edgerton faced the problem of determining the position of a camera when it was deep underwater. To solve this problem, he developed a special sonar, an underwater radar that sends out sound waves and detects their reflections. This led to Edgerton's pioneering work on side-scan sonar, which can profile the shapes of objects on the bottom of the sea.

Edgerton retired from MIT in 1968, when he reached the mandatory retirement age of sixty-five. However, he continued to teach and work in his research laboratory, called "Strobe Alley," for another two decades. In 1973, he recorded changes in the light and color of the solar eclipse in Akjoujt, Mauritania. That same year, he assisted a group using side-scan sonar to locate the wreck of the *Monitor*, the U.S. Navy's Civil War armored gunboat. Edgerton also participated in the search for the Loch Ness Monster in Scotland, using both special underwater cameras and sonar. As late as 1989, he was working on the design of a camera to be placed at the bottom of Loch Ness. Edgerton died of a heart attack in 1990.

Impact

Edgerton's work influenced science and engineering, artistic photography, and the public's perception of the world around them. The War Department awarded Edgerton the Medal of Freedom for this work during World War II. The strobe light that he developed has been incorporated into most cameras, from inexpensive models to sophisticated professional designs. His underwater cameras and side-scan sonar revolutionized undersea exploration. In 1988, the National Geographic Society awarded Edgerton its Centennial Award, naming him one of fifteen people worldwide who made major contributions to the knowledge of the earth, its inhabitants, and the natural environment during the first one hundred years of the society's existence. MIT preserved his Strobe Alley laboratory as a place for students and researchers to continue to explore applications of high-speed photography.

—*George J. Flynn*

Further Reading

Bruce, Roger R., ed. *Seeing the Unseen: Dr. Harold E. Edgerton and the Wonders of Strobe Alley*. Cambridge, Mass.: MIT Press, 1994. A well-illustrated, eighty-nine-page account of Edgerton's life, including information on his scientific and engineering achievements and his long career as an educator.

Ray, Sidney F., ed. *High-Speed Photography and Photonics*. Boston: Focal Press, 1997. A large collection of articles tracing the history of high-speed photography and describing its applications in commercial, industrial, and military settings.

Vandiver, J. Kim, and Pagan Kennedy. *Harold Eugene Edgerton, 1903-1990*. Biographical Memoirs 86. Washington, D.C.: National Academies Press, 2005. A twenty-three-page account of Edgerton's life and his exploits using high-speed photography. Written by one of Edgerton's former teaching assistants.

Zwingle, Erla. "Doc Edgerton: The Man Who Made Time Stand Still." *National Geographic* 172, no. 4 (October, 1987): 464-483. An excellent account of Harold Edgerton's life, his development of the strobe light, and the diversity of projects he undertook. Well illustrated with many of Edgerton's most famous photographs.

See also: George Eastman; Auguste and Louis Lumiére.

Thomas Alva Edison

American technologist, scientist, and businessman

Edison is mainly known as the inventor of the phonograph and the light bulb. During his lifetime, he obtained more than one thousand U.S. patents. His other inventions include a motion-picture camera, a stock ticker, an electric pen, and numerous types of telegraphs, telephones, and electrical equipment. He also developed complete power systems, business organizations, commercialization strategies, and the modern research laboratory.

Born: February 11, 1847; Milan, Ohio
Died: October 18, 1931; West Orange, New Jersey
Primary fields: Entertainment; manufacturing
Primary inventions: Light bulb; phonograph; kinetoscope

Early Life

Thomas Alva Edison was born to Samuel and Nancy Elliott Edison in the small town of Milan, Ohio, in 1847. In 1854, the family moved to Port Huron, Michigan. Like Milan, Port Huron was small but served as a local center for commerce and industry. From an early age, Edison absorbed the local culture of artisans and workshops and read extensively in his father's library. He also inherited an entrepreneurial spirit from his father. He attended school for only three months in his youth and was then educated at home by his mother.

From an early age, Edison, called "Al" in his youth, loved to experiment and investigate. He set up a laboratory in his parents' basement. In 1859, he took a job selling candy, magazines, and newspapers on the Grand Trunk Railroad running between Port Huron and Detroit. He spent his layover time in Detroit reading at the Detroit Public Library and performed chemistry experiments in the baggage car. One mishap in his chemical "laboratory" nearly burned the car. In his later writings, Edison states that it was during this time that he first noticed his hearing problem. As an adult, he became almost completely deaf.

In April, 1862, Edison demonstrated an entrepreneurial instinct that would serve him well later. News of the Civil War had increased his newspaper sales. On the day of the Battle of Shiloh, he saw the bulletin boards at the Detroit station surrounded by large crowds reading the announcements that 60,000 soldiers were killed and wounded. He decided that, if the same excitement were present at the small towns on the railroad, sales of papers would increase. He had the telegraph operator at Detroit telegraph the news on the battle to each station on the route to Port Huron. With the approval of the editor of the paper, Edison took along one thousand papers rather than the usual hundred. At one station where he normally stopped, he sold thirty-five papers. Edison raised the price of the newspaper at each station because there were crowds awaiting news. The papers he usually sold for five cents had gone up to twenty-five cents by the time he reached Port Huron. He made a great deal of money and began learning telegraphy the next day.

After Edison rescued the son of a telegraph operator from the path of a freight car in 1862, the operator rewarded him by giving him telegraph lessons. Edison first took a part-time job as a telegrapher in Port Huron. He eventually became an itinerant telegrapher and quickly became known as an expert receiver. He worked in several midwestern cities and continued his reading in tech-

Thomas Alva Edison. (Library of Congress)

nical and scientific literature. He spent much of his time thinking about how to improve telegraphy, which was a crude communication system at that time. To send a message from Boston to St. Louis required a chain of six operators.

In 1868, Edison moved to Boston and took a job with Western Union. He found financial backers in the telegraph community and worked on improving the telegraph. He obtained his first two patents—a vote recorder, which the state legislature would not buy, and a printing telegraph for stock quotations. The stock ticker proved more successful, and Edison left his job and devoted himself full-time to inventing.

Life's Work

Edison's professional career as an inventor took off when he visited New York City in 1869 to test an improved telegraph. After meeting Franklin Pope, a prominent telegraph engineer, Edison moved to New York. Pope and Edison set up a series of businesses to invent and promote printing telegraphs, which played a key role in the distribution of financial information. Edison sold a printing telegraph, or stock ticker, to Western Union. The profits allowed him to set up a large laboratory in Newark, New Jersey.

Between 1870 and 1876, Edison worked on telegraph improvements such as an automatic telegraph system, which did not require an operator to take down the message. He also developed a quadruplex telegraph, which would allow two messages to be sent in one direction and another two in the opposite direction over a single wire. This increased the capacity of a wire fourfold. He invented an electric pen, which made an exact copy of something that a person wrote. Both the quadruplex telegraph and the electric pen brought substantial profits, with which Edison expanded his laboratory and business.

In 1871, Edison married Mary Stilwell. Between 1873 and 1878, they had three children: Marion, Thomas, and William. However, Edison's work remained the most important aspect of his life. His work habits included long hours away from his family. He often worked late, took short naps rather than sleeping through the night, and ate around midnight.

In 1876, Edison took his family and his work to Menlo Park, New Jersey. There he built a new home and a laboratory solely for conducting experiments. This became an unparalleled facility for invention. Edison enjoyed the mental work, the creative part of the process of invention. He would have an idea, draw up a rough sketch, and discuss it with his assistants. They would examine the sketch and work with it until they could turn it into a workable machine.

The "invention factory" set up at Menlo Park produced the phonograph, the light bulb, a power distribution system that would bring electricity into homes, and a greatly improved telephone. Western Union, for which Edison continued to do work on improving the telegraph, was concerned about the competition from the telephone and asked Edison to work on an improvement. He improved the quality of the sound and made the telephone much easier to use by providing a separate mouthpiece and earpiece. He also developed a transmitter that would carry over longer distances and that was used for nearly a century. The telephone improvements netted Edison's company over a quarter of a million dollars.

An unexpected outcome of the telephone re-

A replica of Thomas Alva Edison's light bulb from 1879. It used a carbonized-thread filament that burned for forty hours. (The Granger Collection, New York)

THE LIGHT BULB AND ITS POWER SYSTEM

Thomas Alva Edison invented an electric light and an electric distribution system to power it. This invention began with a search for a lamp to replace gas lighting, which could be dangerous with the open flame. Another alternative, arc lighting, had proven more successful for outdoor lighting than for indoor, where it could give off dangerous sparks and provided too intense a light for small spaces. Others had tried unsuccessfully to develop an incandescent light bulb. However, Edison's "invention factory" system at Menlo Park, New Jersey, proved equal to the task.

The first problem with inventing a practical incandescent bulb was the filament. Most materials burned up too fast and could not give long, steady light. Edison and his team tried thousands of materials for more than a year. They began in September, 1878, with platinum wire filaments, which had a high melting point. To deal with this problem, they enclosed the filament in a vacuum bulb. However, a platinum filament would make the bulbs too expensive for wide use and require large and expensive copper-wire conductors in the power distribution system because of platinum's low resistance to the electric current. Edison realized that a system of incandescent lighting required high-resistance lamps in order to reduce the size and cost of copper conductors. With a good vacuum bulb, Edison turned to carbon for filaments. The successful choice of filament came by accident when Edison abstractedly rolled a piece of compressed lampblack between his fingers until it became a slender thread. Seeing this, he tried it as a filament. With a few further experiments, he found the right composition of materials. On October 21-22, 1879, Edison and his team tested the first successful incandescent lamp in a vacuum with a piece of carbonized thread as filament. Soon they began demonstrating it, but they continued to work on improving the filament. Within a year, Edison's company began producing commercial bulbs with a filament of carbonized Japanese bamboo.

Meanwhile, Edison focused more on inventing the electrical distribution system to power the bulb. His light bulb would only succeed commercially if numerous homes and offices had access to electricity to use the new light source. Edison modeled his distribution system on that of gas lighting, which included central stations, underground conductors, meters, and lamp fixtures. He also designed almost everything in the system, including a new electrical generator, new screw sockets to hold the bulb in the fixtures, and fuses to prevent electrical overloads.

The first permanent central station opened in Manhattan in 1882. It served Wall Street and many of the major newspapers. Edison invented a new lamp and electric distribution system that would change the world. However, eventually his system shifted from direct current, which Edison strongly defended, to alternating current. Edison's direct-current system worked efficiently in densely populated cities. However, alternating current could travel longer distances. By 1891, Edison had left behind the industry that he had helped found. His company merged into General Electric.

search was the invention of the phonograph in 1877. The telephone was originally envisioned as a way for telegraph companies to transmit messages between operators. However, speech was too fast to be written down. Edison devised a way to record the vibrations in the receiving instrument and play them back slower to record the words. This led Edison and his staff to realize that they could record sound, and the invention of the phonograph followed. The phonograph recorded and played back both words and music. While the phonograph made Edison an overnight celebrity (he was billed in the press as the "Wizard of Menlo Park"), he was unable to turn his early exhibition machine into a commercial product.

Edison brought together everything he had learned about invention and business in the development of the light bulb and the electric light and power system, beginning with a search for a lamp to replace gas lighting. Edison pulled together financial backing, numerous researchers, an expanded laboratory and shop facilities, factories, and marketing. The search for a filament took an enormous amount of time and resources. However, the demonstration of the first working light bulb in 1879 was only the beginning. Most homes did not have access to the electricity necessary to use the light bulb. Edison's laboratory then developed an electric power distribution system and opened the first electric power plant in New York in 1882. By the end of the nineteenth century, there would be over five hundred Edison plants in the United States and at least fifty in other countries.

In 1884, Edison's wife died after a long period of illness. Although work had always taken first place with Edison, he was devastated by her death. Within a year, he moved the family away from Menlo Park. In 1886, he married Mina Miller and moved his family and business to West Orange, New Jersey. There he created a laboratory that would set the example for research and development laboratories in the twentieth century.

With the invention of the kinetoscope in the late 1880's, Edison founded the American motion-picture industry. Edison and one of his trusted assistants, W. K. L. Dickson, began experimenting with celluloid film and found a way to do for images what they had done for sound. They recorded a series of images, each showing a tiny move forward. When viewed in rapid succession, the images gave the impression of movement. They developed a camera and the "peep-show" kinetoscope for viewing the films.

Although Edison's work as a businessman decreased over time, his inventive work continued for decades. Inventions included an improved phonograph, dictating machines, an improved storage battery, and a method for ore separation. Inventions such as the improved battery provided financial stability to Edison's laboratory and companies. Others, such as his magnetic ore separator, failed. Nevertheless, Edison persevered. He eventually became the nation's "inventor-philosopher," with reporters seeking his opinion on everything from diet to the existence of God.

He died at his home, Glenmont, in West Orange, New Jersey, on October 18, 1931. President Herbert Hoover asked the nation to dim its lights in his honor.

Impact

Edison changed the lives of Americans by bringing sound and light into their homes and businesses. While he became nationally and internationally famous upon his invention of the phonograph, some of his later inventions had a greater impact. The power distribution system that Edison developed to supply electrical power to his light bulb changed American homes forever. It not only provided light but also made possible the invention and use of numerous small household devices. Edison's inventions affected and sometimes created industries, including motion pictures, music, and electric power.

Edison's greatest contribution may have been the "invention of the method of invention," as Alfred North Whitehead called the greatest invention of the nineteenth century. Having begun his professional life as an independent inventor, Edison ended with perhaps the first modern research and development laboratory and team. His vision included what the twentieth century would term "innovation"—invention, research, development, and commercialization.

—*Linda Eikmeier Endersby*

Further Reading

Baldwin, Neil. *Edison, Inventing the Century*. New York: Hyperion, 1995. Engaging biography with information on Edison's inventions (no technical knowledge necessary). Includes information on Edison's prowess in business, promotion, and commercialization. Illustrations, bibliography, index.

Essig, Mark R. *Edison and the Electric Chair: A Story of Light and Death*. New York: Walker & Company, 2003. Focuses on Edison's argument in favor of his direct current (DC) rather than alternating current (AC). Recounts details of Edison's condemnation of AC through his promotion of its use in the first electric chair, which showed that AC was too dangerous for common use. Illustrations, index.

Israel, Paul. *Edison: A Life of Invention*. New York: John Wiley & Sons, 1998. Scholarly work that provides technical detail on Edison's inventive work in the nineteenth century and some biographical details. Relies heavily on documents annotated and published by the Edison Papers Project in New Jersey. Illustrations, bibliography, index.

Jonnes, Jill. *Empires of Light: Edison, Tesla, Westinghouse, and the Race to Electrify the World*. New York: Random House, 2003. Focuses on Edison's defense of his direct current against George Westinghouse's alternating current, which Nikola Tesla supported and for which he invented. Provides good information on the marketing, promotion, and commercialization after an invention. Illustrations, bibliography, index.

Melosi, Martin V. *Thomas A. Edison and the Modernization of America*. New York: Longman, 2008. Scholarly work detailing Edison's life and work. Focuses on the business side of invention and Edison's creation of systems of research, invention, and commercialization. Illustrations, bibliography, index.

Stross, Randall E. *The Wizard of Menlo Park: How Thomas Alva Edison invented the Modern World*. New York: Crown, 2007. Engaging account of Edison's life that focuses on Edison's invention of celebrity rather than on his technical inventions. Highlights Edison's self-conscious use of the rising popular press and what Stross calls Edison's launch of the first successful branding campaign. Illustrations, note on sources, index.

See also: Edward Goodrich Acheson; Ernst Alexanderson; Alexander Graham Bell; Emile Berliner; Karl Ferdinand Braun; William David Coolidge; Reginald

Aubrey Fessenden; Peter Carl Goldmark; Elisha Gray; H. Tracy Hall; David Edward Hughes; Miller Reese Hutchison; Eldridge R. Johnson; Lewis Howard Latimer; Auguste and Louis Lumière; William Murdock; Christopher Latham Sholes; Frank J. Sprague; Joseph Wilson Swan; Nikola Tesla; Elihu Thomson; Mark Twain; George Westinghouse; Granville T. Woods.

Albert Einstein

German American theoretical physicist

Einstein's special and general theories of relativity forever changed the scientific conceptions of space, time, mass, energy, and gravity. Those theories, along with quantum theory, constitute the foundation of all modern physics.

Born: March 14, 1879; Ulm, Württemberg, Germany
Died: April 18, 1955; Princeton, New Jersey
Primary field: Physics
Primary invention: Special and general theories of relativity

Early Life

Albert Einstein (IN-stin) was born to Hermann and Pauline Koch Einstein in their home at Bahnhofstrasse 135, Ulm, Germany, in 1879. Early fears for his mental development, primarily due to a skull unusual in size and shape along with a significant delay in learning to speak, eventually dissipated as he grew and matured normally. His elementary and high school performances were unremarkable. In a series of autobiographical sketches written late in life, he mentioned two "miracles" that established his lifelong interest in physics and mathematics. At the age of four or five, his father showed him a compass that excited him greatly and inspired deep curiosity about the inner workings of the physical world. At twelve, he received a book on Euclidean geometry. Impressed by the clarity and certainty of mathematical proofs, he quickly mastered the subject and then proceeded to teach himself differential and integral calculus.

Einstein's family moved to Milan, Italy, in June of 1894, leaving Albert behind to finish school. The following spring, Einstein left Germany to escape conscription into the army. He spent the summer of 1895 with his family in Italy, attempting to enroll in the Federal Institute of Technology in Zurich, Switzerland. He failed the entrance examination and was advised to obtain a Swiss high school diploma that would allow him to enroll in the institute. He chose a school in Aarau, obtaining a diploma and registering at the institute in October, 1896.

At the institute, Einstein was an indifferent if not difficult student. He skipped class often, preferring to teach himself from available books. He kept up with material covered in class by borrowing his fellow classmates' notes. He graduated without any apparent distinction in August, 1900, and found that no one wanted to hire him.

Einstein married Mileva Marić, a fellow student at the institute, on January 6, 1903. A daughter born to the two before marriage was given up for adoption; her subsequent life is unknown. Mileva delivered a son, Hans Albert, on May 14, 1904, and a second son, Eduard, on July 28, 1910.

After graduation, Einstein held a series of temporary jobs. On June 16, 1902, he obtained a permanent position with the Swiss Patent Office that he retained until accept-

Albert Einstein. (Library of Congress)

ing a university professorship in October, 1909. His duties at the patent office were light and left with him a great deal of time to think about physics.

Life's Work

In 1905, called Einstein's "miracle year," the twenty-six-year-old amateur physicist published a series of groundbreaking papers in the prominent science journal *Annalen der Physik*. His first paper explained the photoelectric effect using Max Planck's quantum theory of radiation. This paper formed the basis for much of quantum mechanics. His second paper dealt with Brownian motion, the random motion of microscopic particles suspended in a fluid such as water. Einstein explained it as the result of uneven pushes delivered by random collisions with molecules. His paper provided evidence for the existence of atoms.

His third paper addressed special relativity, treating the constancy of the speed of light as a fundamental scientific principle for the first time. This paper demonstrated that moving clocks will appear to run slow relative to clocks at rest (time dilatation) and that moving objects will appear shortened in the direction of their motion (Lorentz-Fitzgerald contraction). The special theory of relativity eliminated the need for a mechanical substance to support light waves (the "ether"). It also abolished the notions of absolute space and time: Motion can only be described relative to other objects; all observers do not perceive time in the same universal way.

A 1906 paper on the specific heat of solids was the first application of the new quantum theory to the solid state of matter. In one year, Einstein had invented an entirely new branch of physics (relativity) and made signif-

Special and General Theories of Relativity

During the late 1800's, many physicists recognized that James Clerk Maxwell's equations for electromagnetism were incompatible with the concepts of space and time underlying Sir Isaac Newton's three laws of motion. Attempts to explain electromagnetic waves (light and the newly discovered radio waves) as vibrations in an elastic substance called the "ether" predicted properties for light that could not be found experimentally.

Albert Einstein recognized that a key property of Maxwell's equations predicted that the speed of light must be constant for all observers under all circumstances. Einstein accepted this implied property of light as a postulate and followed this assumption to its inevitable conclusions. By applying this postulate to a simple clock based on the travel time of light pulses, he showed that time as measured by this clock (and by implication, all clocks) in motion must appear to an observer at rest to run slow. By careful consideration of how clocks are synchronized and how distances are measured, Einstein deduced that moving objects must appear to an observer at rest to shrink along the direction of motion. All of these effects were captured in a set of transformation equations that allowed lengths and times for a moving observer to be calculated from the corresponding lengths and times as seen by a stationary observer, and vice versa. These equations had already been worked out by Hendrik Lorentz in his theory of the electron, but Einstein's independent derivation from the constancy of the speed of light was a powerful argument for the validity of special relativity.

In a later paper, Einstein examined how the emission of light (a form of energy) from a body at rest would look to a moving observer whose standards of time and length would be affected by the motion. Einstein deduced that the energy of the light would have to come from a reduction in the mass of the body. The amount of energy released would be equal to the lost mass multiplied by the square of the speed of light (the famous $E = mc^2$ formula). This equivalence of mass and energy had been worked out for special cases as early as 1880. Einstein showed it to be a general property, true for all of physics.

It quickly became clear that gravity was a problem in special relativity. Einstein realized that on a small enough scale that gravity is indistinguishable from acceleration: An observer locked inside an elevator cannot determine whether the elevator is accelerating upward or is stationary in a constant gravitational field. Unifying this principle with special relativity occupied Einstein for the next ten years. Hermann Minkowski's insight of uniting time with three-dimensional space to make four-dimensional space-time proved crucial. At first, Einstein dismissed the space-time approach as useless theorizing, but it proved to be essential to his quest for a relativistic theory of gravity.

This work culminated in the general theory of relativity. General relativity treats space-time as a non-Euclidean geometry ("curved space"). Familiar Euclidean space is "flat," with no curvature: Unaccelerated objects move on straight lines. What appears in ordinary three-dimensional space to be a gravitational acceleration is actually motion along an unaccelerated but curved path in the non-Euclidean four-dimensional space-time.

icant pioneering discoveries in two other fields (statistical physics and quantum theory).

Einstein turned to the nature of gravity and its compatibility with special relativity in 1907, when he discovered the principle of equivalence, one of the cornerstones of the general theory of relativity. The concept states that uniform accelerations are almost indistinguishable from gravity. It took Einstein almost ten years to develop the mathematics that properly describe the equivalence principle. The general theory of relativity reached its final form in 1915 and was published in early 1916. General relativity regards gravity as a curvature of space and time, united in a four-dimensional space-time.

No theory this radical will get any respect from other scientists unless it makes some testable predictions. Einstein applied this new theory to the motion of the planets and for the first time explained an anomalous advance in the perihelion (the point of a planet's closest approach to the Sun) of the planet Mercury. Applying it to his favorite subject, light, Einstein showed that general relativity predicts that light should follow a curved path when passing near a strong gravitational source and that light should lose energy and increase in wavelength when climbing out of a gravitational field. This last effect is referred to as a "redshift" because light in the visible spectrum becomes redder as the wavelength becomes longer. It also implies that clocks at high altitudes will run slightly faster than clocks at low altitudes, an effect known as gravitational time dilatation.

The anomalous precession of Mercury had long been known to astronomers, and Einstein used it as a test of general relativity while developing the theory. Observation of a total solar eclipse in 1919 detected a gravitational deflection of starlight as it passed near the Sun, confirming Einstein's prediction, and spectral analysis of starlight from the white dwarf companion of Sirius confirmed the gravitational redshift of light. Modern experiments with atomic clocks have detected and measured gravitational time dilatation.

Announcement of the 1919 eclipse results brought Einstein worldwide fame. He was awarded the 1921 Nobel Prize in Physics for his work on the photoelectric effect and other contributions to physics; special and general relativity were both still considered too controversial to acknowledge. He and Mileva had moved to Berlin in 1914 and separated shortly thereafter, with the divorce finalized on February 4, 1919. Einstein married his divorced cousin, Elsa Lowenthal, on June 6, 1919. They remained together until her death on December 20, 1936.

Rising anti-Semitism in Germany began to impact Einstein's life and work from 1920 on. When the Nazis came to power in 1930, Einstein, his wife, and several family members and close friends emigrated to the United States after a short stay in Belgium. Einstein spent the rest of his life at the Institute for Advanced Study in Princeton, New Jersey, dying of an abdominal aneurysm at 1:15 A.M. on April 18, 1955.

Impact

Einstein's special theory of relativity was consistent with the work of many theoreticians working on the paradoxes of electromagnetism. It elegantly tied many of their partial results into a coherent theory and was readily accepted by them. As years passed, more and more researchers extended the theory and began using it to explain anomalous experimental results. In particular, the relativistic equivalence of mass and energy, formulated by Einstein in one of his 1905 papers, explains the enormous amounts of energy released in radioactive decay, nuclear fission, and nuclear fusion. Special relativity in quantum mechanics explains the fine structure of atomic spectra and the existence of antimatter. (Carl Anderson discovered the positron, the first antiparticle, in 1932.)

In 1916, Karl Schwarzschild used general relativity to predict the existence of black holes. Edwin Hubble discovered the expansion of the universe in 1924, a phenomenon best explained by general relativity. In 1930, J. Robert Oppenheimer used general relativity to predict the existence of neutron stars, discovered in the form of pulsars in 1965. The Hubble Space Telescope continues to discover "Einstein lenses" formed by the gravitational effect of galaxies on light from more distant objects. The images formed from these galactic lenses are all the information available on some of the most distant objects in the cosmos.

Atomic clocks have become so accurate that relativistic time effects, both special and general, are easily measured. The U.S. Global Positioning System (GPS) and the Russian Global Navigation Satellite System (GLONASS) must both correct for the effects of special and general relativity in order to provide users with accurate position data.

—Billy R. Smith, Jr.

Further Reading

Gamow, George. *Gravity*. 1962. Reprint. Mineola, N.Y.: Dover, 2002. An older book but one deservedly still in print. The author was a distinguished physicist, and his books are a delight to read. Covers the study of gravity from Galileo through Isaac Newton to Einstein, providing the background indispensable to a proper understanding of general relativity. The best introduction to gravity to be found.

Gardner, Martin. *Relativity Simply Explained.* Mineola, N.Y.: Dover, 1997. No one is better at explaining complicated mathematical ideas than Gardner. This book concentrates on special relativity, which makes it useful preparation for understanding Gamow's or Kaku's book. Copiously illustrated.

Isaacson, Walter. *Einstein: His Life and Universe.* New York: Simon & Schuster, 2007. Focuses on Einstein the public and private person rather than Einstein the scientist. The descriptions of his scientific and technical work are correct but take second place to the events in his personal life. Forthrightly faces Einstein's flaws as well as his virtues. Illustrations, notes, index.

Kaku, Michio. *Einstein's Cosmos: How Albert Einstein's Vision Transformed Our Understanding of Space and Time.* New York: W. W. Norton, 2004. Covers the important points of Einstein's work and life at a level that does not require significant mathematical or scientific training. Notes and bibliography, but no index.

See also: John Bardeen; Walther Bothe; Raymond Damadian; Charles Stark Draper; Michael Faraday; Enrico Fermi; Dennis Gabor; Galileo; Leopold Godowsky, Jr.; Gordon Gould; Heinrich Hertz; Ali Javan; Gottfried Wilhelm Leibniz; Hudson Maxim; Naomi L. Nakao; Sir Isaac Newton; Hans Joachim Pabst von Ohain; J. Robert Oppenheimer; Stanford Ovshinsky; Wilhelm Conrad Röntgen; Charles Proteus Steinmetz; Theodor Svedberg; Leo Szilard; Charles Hard Townes; Ernest Thomas Sinton Walton.

Willem Einthoven

Dutch physiologist and physician

Einthoven developed the string galvanometer to measure the electrical currents in the human heart. His invention evolved into the modern-day electrocardiogram.

Born: May 21, 1860; Semarang, Java, Dutch East Indies (now Indonesia)
Died: September 28, 1927; Leiden, the Netherlands
Primary field: Medicine and medical technology
Primary invention: String galvanometer (electrocardiogram)

Early Life

Willem Einthoven (INT-hoh-vehn) was born in Semarang on the island of Java in the Dutch East Indies to Jacob Einthoven and Louise M. M. C. de Vogel. His mother was the daughter of the East Indies director of finance. Einthoven's father was originally from Groningen in the Netherlands and was stationed in the East Indies as a military surgeon. When Willem was ten, his father passed away, leaving a wife and six children. His mother moved the family back to the Netherlands and settled in Utrecht.

Einthoven was a very good student and entered the University of Utrecht in 1879. As a university student, he was physically active. He was the president of the Utrecht Gymnastics and Fencing Union and a founder of the student rowing club. While studying under the anatomist Willem Koster, and after sustaining a broken wrist while playing sports, Einthoven spent his recovery time thinking about the movements and functions of the arm joints. This resulted in his first published paper on the elbow joint in 1882. Einthoven's second study was his doctoral thesis. Under the guidance of his mentor, the great physiologist F. C. Donders, Einthoven became interested in electrophysiology. His research was conducted on the electrophysiology of the eye and he graduated cum laude with a medical degree in 1885. Although he is not remembered for his eye research, it was responsible for earning him his first academic appointment as professor of physiology at the University of Leiden in 1886. He was only twenty-five years old.

Life's Work

As a young professor, Einthoven continued his research in electrophysiology, now focusing on the respiratory system. Into the early 1890's, he studied asthma and the nervous control of the bronchial muscles. He published several studies in this area before beginning his most famous work, the electrophysiology of the heart.

Einthoven's work on the heart was considerably influenced by his friend Augustus Waller. Waller published his research on the electrical changes of the heartbeat using a Lippman capillary electrometer in 1887.

This technique recorded the electrical activity of the heart by placing small tubes filled with mercury and sulfuric acid on the patient's chest. The mercury would expand and contract as the electrical current of the heart passed by the tubes. These movements were projected onto photographic paper to produce a cardiogram. This process was very tedious, and slight movements of the patient caused the mercury to move and make the tracings difficult to read. Even when good tracings were obtained, it took six or more hours to convert the data into a curve or cardiogram. These challenges, combined with the failure to find clinical applications, led Waller to abandon this research. However, Einthoven was more persistent.

In the early 1890's, Einthoven began using Waller's techniques in his laboratory, which was located in an old wooden building on a cobblestone street. Einthoven was further challenged by teams of horses passing by the building, causing vibrations of his capillary tubes placed on the patients' chests. One day, he became so irritated that he pulled up the floorboards, dug a deep hole, and lined the walls with rocks in an effort to minimize the movement. When this was unsuccessful, he also abandoned the Lippman capillary electrometer, but not the interest in the electrical activity in the heart.

Einthoven decided he needed a new instrument and began work with a d'Arsonval galvanometer. This instrument had a coil of wire suspended between the poles of a horseshoe magnet, but it was not sensitive enough to record the low-voltage activity of the heart. He replaced the wire with a string made of silver-coated quartz. The movements of the string were transmitted through a microscope and projected onto photographic film. His new instrument was called the string galvanometer, and its applications were published in 1901.

Einthoven set out to show the clinical significance of his string galvanometer. He began to test individuals with known heart problems to see how the tracings differed. Since the hospital was over a mile from his laboratory, Einthoven had the two buildings connected by a telephone wire. This allowed patients in the hospital to be tested and the tracings made in his lab. In 1906, he published one of his most important works, which showed the different tracings for heart ailments that included premature contractions of the heart, several different types of blocks in the conduction system, and enlargements of the chambers. He also studied the effects of specific cardiac drugs on the electrical events in the heart. In 1913, he published the improvements in the string galvanometer and a technique for determining the axis of the heart.

Willem Einthoven. (©The Nobel Foundation)

Einthoven corresponded with many researchers of his time, but one noteworthy physician was Sir Thomas Lewis. Lewis used Einthoven's electrocardiogram to identify other heart abnormalities, including atrial fibrillation—when the upper chambers of the heart become overexcited. Lewis's most significant contribution came during World War I, when he used the electrocardiogram to test the hearts of soldiers during exercise. He was able to identify heart problems that could not be diagnosed during rest. Einthoven credited Lewis with increasing general interest in his electrocardiogram.

In 1924, Einthoven visited the United States to demonstrate his instrument to researchers and physicians at several institutions, including Harvard and Johns Hopkins universities. While visiting, he learned that he was awarded the Nobel Prize in Physiology or Medicine. Since he was so far from Stockholm, he was unable to receive his award that year and officially accepted it in 1925. After receiving the Nobel Prize, Einthoven continued his work on the electrocardiogram and studied general electrophysiology of other systems in the body.

Einthoven passed away in Leiden in 1927 at the age of sixty-seven.

The Electrocardiogram

Willem Einthoven developed the first instrument that could consistently measure the electrical activity of the heart with precision. Initially, he used the electrometer developed by Augustus Waller. The output of this instrument formed curved lines (waves) that had points labeled A, B, C, D, E. The electrometer, however, was very difficult to use; therefore, Einthoven began to develop the electrocardiogram in order to measure the electrical activity of the heart more easily. This instrument also produced waves, and Einthoven named them P, Q, R, S, T. He did this because the points on curved lines in geometry are labeled beginning with the letter *P*. To this day, the labels Einthoven developed are used to identify the waves of the electrocardiogram.

The P wave reflects stimulation of the atria (upper chambers of the heart). The QRS complex reflects stimulation of the ventricles (lower chambers). The QRS complex is much larger than the P wave because the ventricles are bigger and have more muscle mass than the atria. During ventricular recovery, the T wave forms. The atria also must recover, but this happens at the same time that the ventricles are stimulated, so no wave is seen. If there is a problem with the atria, the P wave will look abnormal; if there is a problem with the ventricles, the QRS complex will look abnormal. The type of changes in the waves tells the clinician what is wrong, if anything, with the heart.

The electrocardiogram changed the way heart problems were diagnosed. It is easy to perform the test, and it is noninvasive. Since Einthoven's time, many other instruments and procedures have been developed for the heart, such as the echocardiogram and cardiac catheters, but the electrocardiogram is ubiquitous in hospitals because it is quick, simple, inexpensive, and noninvasive. If a patient comes to the hospital with chest pains, one of the first procedures performed is an ECG.

Impact

Although Einthoven was a research physiologist, he was also an engineer. In order to study the electrophysiology of the heart, he had to develop and refine the equipment needed to do his research. As he perfected the string galvanometer and published his work in the early 1900's, he generated much interest in his invention. By 1910, his instrument became known as the electrocardiogram and was being used in other countries, including the United States. A new laboratory at Johns Hopkins University was the first in the United States to install the electrocardiogram to study heart disease.

In the 1920's, the electrocardiogram used four electrodes that were placed on the arms and legs. Three electrodes were used to form three leads. The right leg electrode was used as a ground to minimize electrical interference. Einthoven's original invention was improved after his death in the 1930's. Researchers at the University of Michigan led by Frank N. Wilson combined the three electrodes in a different way to form three additional leads. Six new electrodes were eventually added to increase the total leads to twelve. These modifications made the electrocardiogram a much better diagnostic tool for the heart. Computer advances have made the electrocardiogram, also known as ECG or EKG, smaller and easier to use. Einthoven's ECG is now found in virtually all hospitals and clinics and is one of the major procedures used to diagnose ailments of the heart.

—*Bradley R. A. Wilson*

Further Reading

Bankston, John. *Willem Einthoven and the Story of Electrocardiography*. Hockessin, Del.: Mitchell Lane, 2004. An easy-to-read biography directed at preadolescents that tells the story of how Einthoven developed the electrocardiogram. The book begins with a discussion of the electrical events within the human body and ends with Einthoven's development of the electrocardiogram. Index.

Barold, S. Serge. "Willem Einthoven and the Birth of Clinical Electrocardiography a Hundred Years Ago." *Cardiac Electrophysiology Review* 7, no. 1 (2003): 99-104. Commemorating the hundredth anniversary of Einthoven's invention, this article summarizes his development of the electrocardiogram. It is a technical publication requiring knowledge of some scientific terminology. References.

Ershler, Irving. "Willem Einthoven: The Man." *Archives of Internal Medicine* 148 (February, 1988): 453-455. This article was written by the friend of George E. Fahr, who worked directly with Einthoven for several years beginning in 1909. Fahr's stories of Einthoven are the basis for this article. References.

Grob, Bart. "Willem Einthoven and the Development of the String Galvanometer: How an Instrument Escaped the Laboratory." *History and Technology* 22, no. 4 (2006): 369-390. Discusses how Einthoven successfully developed the electrocardiogram into a meaningful instrument. References.

Snellen, H. A. *Willem Einthoven (1860-1927), Father of Electrocardiography: Life and Work, Ancestors and Contemporaries*. Dordrecht, Netherlands: Kluwer Academic, 1995. First biography on Einthoven written in English. Based on Einthoven's publications and letters as well as those of his colleagues. It covers his work, his personality, and his relationship with his contemporaries. References, index.

See also: Wilson Greatbatch; Ida H. Hyde; Robert Jarvik; Gabriel Lippmann.

Gertrude Belle Elion

American biochemist and pharmacologist

Elion invented a revolutionary drug research methodology that focused on how normal and abnormal cells reproduce. This enabled her to develop target-specific drugs that killed or suppressed abnormal cells or pathogens without damaging normal cells.

Born: January 23, 1918; New York, New York
Died: February 21, 1999; Chapel Hill, North Carolina
Primary fields: Chemistry; medicine and medical technology
Primary inventions: Purinethol; azathioprine

Early Life

Gertrude Belle Elion (EHL-ee-on) was born into a religious and scholarly family in New York City in 1918. Her father, Robert Elion, had emigrated from Lithuania when he was twelve. Descended from a long line of rabbis, he became a dentist. Elion's mother, Bertha Cohen, was fourteen when she emigrated from Russia, and her family included biblical scholars. Elion and her younger brother Herbert had a happy childhood and received a sound education in the public schools. An outstanding student who had an insatiable desire for knowledge in all subjects, Elion especially enjoyed science books. She admired inventors, such as Louis Pasteur and Marie Curie.

A turning point in Elion's life occurred when she was fifteen years old and her beloved grandfather died a slow, agonizing death from cancer. Elion vowed to find a cure for the disease. In 1933, she became a chemistry major at Hunter College, the women's branch of the City College of New York. Fortunately, Hunter College was free and Elion had high grades. Otherwise, she would not have been able to attend college, since her family had become bankrupt during the stock market crash of 1929.

In 1937, Elion graduated with highest honors. A doctorate was required to become a chemical researcher, so Elion applied for scholarships or assistantships to graduate schools. Her applications were rejected, and jobs in research labs were scarce. She applied for a laboratory position for which she was qualified, but the interviewer thought a woman would be too distracting. At this point, Elion finally realized that there was gender discrimination in the sciences.

Eventually, she found work as a lab assistant, without pay at first. By 1939, she had some savings and was able

Gertrude Belle Elion, cowinner of the 1988 Nobel Prize in Physiology or Medicine. Her research led to the development of drugs effective against cancer, AIDS, and organ transplant rejection. (©The Nobel Foundation)

to start graduate school at New York University, where she was the only female in the chemistry class. She earned a master of science degree in chemistry in 1941.

Life's Work

Meanwhile, another tragedy occurred. In 1941, her fiancé, Leonard Canter, died of acute bacterial endocarditis, an infection of the inner lining of the heart. Penicillin, which would have saved his life, was not used as a drug until years later. She never married, and this personal loss further intensified her lifelong desire to cure diseases.

After World War II began, men were called to support the war effort, and more jobs became available to women. There was a shortage of industrial chemists, so Elion was able to find work as a quality-control chemist for the Quaker Maid Company in 1942. She learned about instrumentation, but the work was repetitive: She checked the acidity of pickles, the color of mayonnaise, and the mold levels of fruit. After a year and a half, she found a research job synthesizing sulfonamides at Johnson and Johnson, but the laboratory closed after six months.

In 1944, Dr. George Hitchings hired Elion to be his research assistant at Burroughs Wellcome (now GlaxoSmithKline), a pharmaceutical company in Tuckahoe, New York. From the beginning, Hitchings was impressed with Elion, and she was fascinated by his research in nucleic acid biochemistry. Thus began one of the most productive and famous collaborations in history. Hitchings encouraged her to follow her instincts, work independently, and publish papers. Although he guided Elion and reviewed her papers, he listed her name first on papers she wrote. She would continue that tradition with her own assistants in the future. Over the course of her career, she published more than 225 papers. Hitchings and Elion worked together for more than four decades and revolutionized medicine and pharmacology. Their research involved immunology, microbiology, and virology, as well as organic chemistry.

The traditional method for developing new drugs was a trial-and-error process in which new compounds were tried out on a target, usually a mouse. Hitchings and Elion used a new rational scientific approach requiring less time and speculation. They focused on how cells reproduce at various stages and studied the differences between the biochemistry of normal human cells and those of bacteria, tumors, and other pathogens (disease-causing agents).

In 1944, biochemist Oswald Avery discovered that deooxyribonucleic acid (DNA) was the carrier of genetic information (genes and chro-

Purinethol

Gertrude Belle Elion changed the way drugs are discovered with the new methodology that she and Hitchings created. They compared normal and abnormal cell metabolism and reproduction and then created antimetabolites to interfere with the life cycle of abnormal cells without harming normal cells. Elion focused on the purine bases (adenine and guanine), which are two of the four bases that are part of the larger nucleic acid (DNA) molecule, which carries genetic information.

Using this methodology in 1950, Elion synthesized a cancer drug, diaminopurine, which interfered with the metabolism of leukemia cells (abnormal white blood cells). It produced a complete remission in an acutely ill leukemia patient who had a relapse after two years and died. Saddened, Elion then made and tested over one hundred compounds. Finally, she substituted a sulfur atom for the oxygen atom on a purine molecule and made 6-mercaptopurine (6-MP), the first effective leukemia drug.

Elion's 6-MP (marketed as Purinethol in the United States) was the first childhood leukemia drug capable of causing a complete, though temporary, remission. Before the development of this drug, 50 percent of all children with acute leukemia died within three to four months. Eventually, a combination of 6-MP with other drugs could effectively cure childhood leukemia. By the early 1990's, the 6-MP therapy could cure 80 percent of patients with acute lymphoblastic leukemia.

6-MP also suppressed the immune system, which had implications for organ transplant surgery. In 1959, Robert Schwartz tested 6-MP on rabbits injected with a foreign compound, and the drug prevented their immune systems from producing antibodies. Then, the British surgeon Roy Calne used 6-MP on dogs receiving kidney transplants; the dogs given the drug outlived the dogs who did not receive 6-MP.

Elion remembered that she had synthesized azathioprine (Imuran), a complex version of 6-MP, and that this related compound did not affect cancer cells but was a better immunosuppressant than 6-MP. Calne then used Imuran for a successful organ transplant on a collie named Lollipop. Using the same drug, Dr. Joseph Murray performed the first successful kidney transplant between unrelated people in 1962. In the 1960's, Elion also developed allopurinol (Zyloprim), another compound related to 6-MP. This drug was effective for treating gout and many diseases occurring in South America.

mosomes). However, it was not until 1953 that James Watson and Francis Crick discovered the double helix structure of DNA. Thus, not much was known about nucleic acids at that time, but Hitchings and Elion understood that DNA was the essence of life and that all cells required nucleic acids to reproduce. Nucleic acids carry the information each living thing inherits from its parents. That information tells the cell how to carry out its activities and is coded in small molecules called bases.

Elion and Hitchings realized that if they slightly changed the natural bases, or DNA building blocks, in a cell so that the altered bases could not be used to make new nucleic acids, then these new bases would act as antimetabolites, chemicals that prevent cell metabolism. Mistaking these antimetabolites for natural bases and incorporating them, viruses, cancer cells, and pathogens would be poisoned and unable to reproduce or carry out their own chemical activities, thus stopping the spread of disease without harming normal cells. Elion and Hitchings called these false bases "rubber donuts" because they looked real but did not work.

In 1950, at the age of thirty-two, Elion synthesized two cancer drugs, diaminopurine and thioguanine, by using these methods. She also developed 6-mercaptopurine (Purinethol), the first effective treatment for childhood leukemia. Through the years, she invented many other life-saving drugs: azathioprine (Imuran), the first immunosuppressive agent used for organ transplants; allopurinol (Zyloprim) for gout; pyrimethamine (Daraprim) for malaria; trimethoprim (Septra) for meningitis, septicemia, and bacterial infections of the urinary and respiratory tracts; and acyclovir (Zovirax) for viral herpes.

Elion retired in 1983 but remained active in education and scientific organizations. Along with Hitchings and Sir James Black, she received the 1988 Nobel Prize in Physiology or Medicine. In 1991, she received the National Medal of Science and also became the first woman to be included in the National Inventors Hall of Fame. Although she never had time to finish her doctorate, George Washington University, Brown University, the University of Michigan, and other schools awarded her honorary doctorates. Elion died at the age of eighty-one on February 21, 1999.

Impact

The new drug-making methodology developed by Elion and Hitchings led to new drugs no one had ever thought possible. The holder of forty-five patents, Elion invented or helped develop the first effective drugs for an extraordinary range of diseases. When she discovered a compound, she explored all its implications and used it to find more information and to discover compounds against other diseases. Her innovative approach profoundly affected the whole field of drug development and became the standard in pharmaceutical research.

Elion's immunosuppressive drug, azathioprine, which could be used to prevent a patient's immune system from rejecting a transplanted organ as a foreign invader, made organ transplant surgery possible. Transplant operations have since become routine. By 1990, over 200,000 kidney transplants had been performed worldwide. In 2006, there were over 17,000 kidney transplants in the United States and an overall total of over 28,000 transplants, including pancreas, liver, intestine, kidney-pancreas, heart, heart-lung, and lung. By May, 2008, there were 99,258 people on the waiting list for an organ.

Elion's antiretroviral drug led to her research laboratory's development of azidothymidine (AZT), the first drug treatment for acquired immunodeficiency syndrome (AIDS), in 1984. Until 1991, AZT was the only drug approved for the treatment of AIDS. Her developments in cancer drugs have had a lasting impact on cancer research. She laid the foundation for the discovery of future cancer treatments, such as nelarabine (Arranon), a cancer drug licensed in the United States in 2005 to treat certain rare forms of leukemia and lymphoma when patients have exhausted standard options. The multitude of drugs invented by Elion continue to save countless lives every day throughout the world, and her humanistic spirit inspired future generations of scientists.

—*Alice Myers*

Further Reading

Ambrose, Susan A., et al. *Journeys of Women in Science and Engineering: No Universal Constants*. Philadelphia: Temple University Press, 1997. Based on interviews and written in the first person, this extensive collection of stories tells how eighty-eight women found their life's work and the challenges they faced. Includes a case study of Elion. Illustrated, with bibliography and index.

Brokaw, Tom. *The Greatest Generation*. New York: Random House, 1998. Celebrated broadcast journalist Tom Brokaw explores the concept of "hero" in biographies of both ordinary and famous Americans of the Great Depression and the World War II eras. Illustrated. Index.

Hutchison, Kay Bailey. *Leading Ladies: American Trailblazers*. New York: Harper, 2007. Celebrates the accomplishments and struggles of American women in traditionally male-dominated fields. A chapter on winners of the Nobel Prize in science includes a biographical portrait of Elion. Illustrated, with bibliography and index.

McGrayne, Sharon Bertsch. *Nobel Prize Women in Science: Their Lives, Struggles, and Momentous Discoveries*. Secaucus, N.J.: Carol, 1993. Very readable and well-researched biographies of fourteen female scientists who overcame gender discrimination as both students and researchers to accomplish groundbreaking scientific work. Illustrated. Notes and index.

Sherman, Irwin. *Twelve Diseases That Changed Our World*. Washington, D.C.: ASM Press, 2007. This historical examination of twelve diseases includes a chapter on AIDS that discusses Elion's antiviral work. Bibliography and index.

Yount, Lisa. *Contemporary Women Scientists*. New York: Facts On File, 1994. Elion is one of ten women profiled in this sensitive study of the obstacles facing female scientists. Illustrated, with bibliography and index.

See also: Robert Charles Gallo; Percy Lavon Julian.

Philip Emeagwali

Nigerian American computer scientist

Hailed as one of the fathers of the Internet, Emeagwali introduced a method to track oil flow underground using a supercomputer. His groundbreaking experiment benefited the oil industry and demonstrated the possibilities of computer networking.

Born: August 23, 1954; Akure, Nigeria
Also known as: Philip Chukwurah Emeagwali (full name)
Primary fields: Computer science; mathematics
Primary invention: Method for simulating oil reservoirs

Early Life

Philip Chukwurah Emeagwali (eh-MAY-ah-gwah-lee) was born August 23, 1954, in Akure in southwestern Nigeria. He was the first of nine children born to sixteen-year-old Agatha Emeagwali, a homemaker, and thirty-three-year-old James Emeagwali, a nurse's aide. As the oldest child of the poor family, Philip had numerous duties that required him to rise at 4:00 A.M. to help out. When Philip was nine years old, James, recognizing his son's special talent in mathematics, reduced his chores, allowing him more time to study mathematics. James frequently gave Philip one hundred math problems to complete in his head in an hour—an average of thirty-six seconds per problem—to improve his mathematical skills.

At age ten, Emeagwali took his high school entrance exam, receiving a perfect score in the mathematics section, and was promptly disqualified for fraud because authorities considered his accomplishment impossible. At the all-boys Catholic high school, Emeagwali, nicknamed "Calculus," studied languages, literature, geography, biology, and mathematics. After a little over a year there, the Igbo tribe to which the Emeagwali family belonged became embroiled in ethnic conflicts that killed one million people. The surviving tribal members lived in refugee camps in eastern Nigeria until the war ended. Emeagwali dropped out of school for three years but continued studying mathematics, physics, and chemistry at the public library. At seventeen, he passed a high school equivalency examination through the University of London.

Life's Work

At nineteen, Emeagwali accepted a scholarship to Oregon State University to study mathematics. In a computer science course at Oregon, Emeagwali, given the job of programming computers, first conceived the theory that global weather prediction could be accomplished through harnessing thousands of small computers in a global network he called a "Hyperball international network of computers." His theory challenged traditional wisdom that held that no number of smaller processors could outperform a supercomputer. He was denied grants to pursue his theory and could find no research laboratory interested in it. He continued to work on his theory privately for fifteen years, immersing himself in physics, mathematics, and computing.

Awarded his bachelor's degree in 1977, Emeagwali went on to attend George Washington University, receiving a master's degree in civil engineering in 1981. He then attended the University of Maryland, receiving a master's degree in applied mathematics in 1986. That year, he was also awarded a post-master's degree in ocean, coastal, and marine engineering from George Washington University. After working for a time as a civil engineer in Maryland and Wyoming, Emeagwali entered the doctoral program of civil engineering at the University of Michigan to study scientific computing.

At Michigan, Emeagwali was part of a group reviewing the major problems that confronted science and engineering. Using a supercomputer to simulate oil reservoirs particularly interested Emeagwali, as he was from an oil-rich nation that could benefit greatly from advanced knowledge in that subject. At that time, extraction of oil relied on drilling through rock into an oil pocket, a process so inexact that it yielded at best only a small percentage of the oil. Moreover, the procedure could be completed only by using supercomputers (which could cost upwards of $30 million each) to simulate the oil reservoirs and chart an oil flow that could still become inaccessible.

Emeagwali applied his weather prediction theory to the petroleum reservoir problem and set about trying to solve one of the most difficult problems in the computing field by using his own technology. He was granted permission to use a supercomputer by the U.S. government, but it was withdrawn when the manager discovered that he was black. Emeagwali learned of the Connection Machine (comprising 65,536 microprocessors), built by a company called Thinking Machines for use with artificial intelligence, and was granted use of one at Los Alamos National Laboratory in New Mexico. Accessing the computer remotely from Ann Arbor, Michigan, he ran his program and was amazed when the microprocessors completed their tasks at record-breaking speed, computing the amount of oil in the simulated reservoir and tracking an oil flow underground. Various oil companies purchased supercomputers similar to the one he had used, and many sought his expertise in implementing them.

Simulating Oil Reservoirs

While wrestling with the problem of accessing underground oil for the petroleum industry, Philip Emeagwali determined to use a supercomputer equipped with thousands of microprocessors rather than use the extremely expensive vector supercomputer, whose calculations were performed from a long list of numbers and whose ability to communicate was limited. Emeagwali programmed a Connection Machine that was equipped with 65,536 microprocessors. The processors were arranged as more than four thousand computational nodes, each with a cluster of sixteen processors and eight information channels emanating from each processor.

Never relying on mathematics and computer science alone, Emeagwali included physics in his calculations, specifically the second law of motion formulated by English mathematician and physicist Sir Isaac Newton. Emeagwali rightfully assumed that Newton's law concerning force, mass, and acceleration applied to the fluids below the Earth's surface. He reformulated Newton's law into mathematical equations codifying the laws of motion to simulate oil reservoirs. His calculations also considered inertia, previously unaccounted for in the equations developed by other scientists and mathematicians. Using advanced calculus, Emeagwali constructed nine equations and nine corresponding algorithms (precise statements that allow the computer to solve the equations). The eighteen differential equations (reformulated as 24 million algebraic equations) were founded upon the four primary forces in oil fields—pressure, gravitation, acceleration (or inertia), and viscosity. In programming his computer, Emeagwali divided a huge imaginary oil field into 65,536 smaller oil fields, and he distributed the equations equally among the 65,536 microprocessors. The supercomputer performed 3.1 billion calculations per second, a record set in 1989.

In the petroleum industry, Emeagwali's oil reservoir simulation is regarded as an outstanding contribution to oil field science. Reservoir modeling provides the industry with the necessary knowledge to recover oil efficiently. The equations provide geologists with the knowledge of favorable conditions for the injection of water to increase the production of oil, and the inclusion of inertia in the equations gives an accurate reflection of the amount of available oil. Emeagwali's unconventional method of computing and reservoir simulation aids engineers in recovering the maximum amount of oil in a reservoir and has saved the petroleum industry millions of dollars per oil field.

Emeagwali submitted his doctoral thesis on his supercomputer experiment. However, it was not accepted, and his degree was not awarded. He challenged the decision by suing the university, alleging racial discrimination, but his lawsuit was dismissed. He returned to his research on weather prediction, using the supercomputer to predict weather, and to his Hyperball network. Following his success with the Connection Machine, he conceived of his network as a "World Wide Brain" that would take the World Wide Web to the next level.

Emeagwali married the former Dale Brown, a molecular biologist, and they settled in Washington, D.C., with their son. Both became active spokespersons for the accomplishments of nonwhites in science. In 1989, Emeagwali was awarded the Gordon Bell Prize, considered the Nobel Prize for computing, given to an individual or a group who has made significant achievements in using supercomputers to solve scientific and engineering problems. Achieving international fame, he received numerous awards, including the Distinguished Scientist Award from the National Society of Black Engineers (1991); Computer Scientist of the Year, given by the National Technical Association (1993); and Eminent Engineer, Tau Beta Pi National Engineering Honor Society (1994). He was praised by President Bill Clinton as "one of the great minds of the information age," and has been ranked as one of history's eminent black achievers. In Nigeria, he is a national hero.

Impact

Emeagwali's most significant achievement was his contribution to computer knowledge. He never intended to work on computers themselves, but was concerned only with the power of the knowledge that drove them. At Oregon State University, he disliked computers, feeling more comfortable with performing calculations in his head, but he soon realized their enormous capabilities and began to theorize a future for them that was deemed all but impossible by others. His accomplishment with the Connection Machine not only benefited the petroleum industry but also demonstrated the possibility of a high-speed, relatively low-cost method of global communication. His microprocessor technology was utilized by Apple in its Power Mac G4 series.

Emeagwali understood that one problem with computers was their inability to "talk to each other." In an age of specialization, he examined issues from a multidisciplinary approach, applying the laws of physics, mathematics, and computers to advance beyond the 1970's idea of the Internet as a network of thousands of interconnected computers to an Internet composed of millions of computers communicating with one another. He understood that computers had the capability to simulate planetary motion to reveal both past and future events, as well as the capability to solve mathematical equations to simulate both the big bang theory of the origin of the universe and nuclear explosions. Hailed by the Cable News Network (CNN) as the "father of the Internet," Emeagwali has advanced technology significantly by expanding the boundaries of computing.

—*Mary Hurd*

Further Reading

Endeley, Catherine. "From the Motherland: Eight Africans and Their Contributions to the World." *Ebony*, April 1, 2008. Brief article describing Emeagwali as one of eight Africans making huge contributions in various fields. Discusses Emeagwali's supercomputer experiment and his position as a staunch spokesman for Africans abroad.

Henderson, Susan K. *African-American Inventors III: Patricia Bath, Philip Emeagwali, Henry Sampson, Valerie Thomas, Peter Tolliver*. Mankato, Minn.: Capstone Press, 1998. Written for middle-school students, this set of short biographies contains photographs, illustrations of the inventions, and copious references.

Moschovitis, Christos J., ed. *History of the Internet: A Chronology—1843 to the Present*. Santa Barbara, Calif.: ABC-CLIO, 1999. Well-researched history of computing beginning with transistors. Contains biographies of famous computing figures, time lines, photographs, and bibliographies.

White, Ron. *How Computers Work*. 6th ed. Indianapolis, Ind.: Que, 2007. Best-selling definitive guide to technology. Includes detailed information along with colorful illustrations of computers, scanners, cell phones, and optical disc technology. For readers of all levels.

See also: Tim Berners-Lee; Bob Kahn; Sir Isaac Newton; Alan Mathison Turing.

REFERENCE
SETON HALL UNIVERSITY
University Libraries So. Orange NJ 07079-2671